Global Mobile Commerce:
Strategies, Implementation, and Case Studies

Wayne W. Huang
Ohio University, USA

Yingluo Wang
Jiao Tong University, China

John Day
Ohio University, USA

INFORMATION SCIENCE REFERENCE

Hershey · New York

Acquisitions Editor:	Kristin Klinger
Development Editor:	Kristin Roth
Senior Managing Editor:	Jennifer Neidig
Managing Editor:	Sara Reed
Copy Editor:	Holly Powell
Typesetter:	Michael Brehm
Cover Design:	Lisa Tosheff
Printed at:	Yurchak Printing Inc.

Published in the United States of America by
Information Science Reference (an imprint of IGI Global)
701 E. Chocolate Avenue, Suite 200
Hershey PA 17033
Tel: 717-533-8845
Fax: 717-533-8661
E-mail: cust@igi-pub.com
Web site: http://www.igi-global.com/reference

and in the United Kingdom by
Information Science Reference (an imprint of IGI Global)
3 Henrietta Street
Covent Garden
London WC2E 8LU
Tel: 44 20 7240 0856
Fax: 44 20 7379 0609
Web site: http://www.eurospanonline.com

Library of Congress Cataloging-in-Publication Data

Global mobile commerce : strategies, implementation and case studies / Wayne W. Huang, Yingluo Wang & John Day, editors.

p. cm.

Summary: "This book provides a complete set of in-depth research investigations on global m-commerce strategies and technological standards, as well as case studies on the subject that elucidate the research through real-world examples. It will prove to be a valuable reference to drive the current and future activities of academic researchers and practitioners alike"--Provided by publisher.

Includes bibliographical references and index.

ISBN-13: 978-1-59904-558-0 (hardcover)

ISBN-13: 978-1-59904-560-3 (ebook)

1. Mobile commerce. 2. Telecommunication systems. I. Huang, Wayne, 1964- II. Wang, Yingluo. III. Day, John.

HF5548.34.G56 2008

658.8'72--dc22

2007016854

British Cataloguing in Publication Data
A Cataloguing in Publication record for this book is available from the British Library.

Table of Contents

Section I
Emerging M-Commerce Issues and Technologies

Section II
Issues in Europe

Section III
Issues in Asia Pacific

Section IV
Issues in the Americas

Table of Contents

Section I
Emerging M-Commerce Issues and Technologies

This section provides a discussion of general concepts, issues, and technologies that apply to the area of m-commerce. These chapters will address important concepts and future trends that provide a context for understanding m-commerce. In addition issues such as security and important technologies are discussed.

Chapter I
From Mobility to True Nomadicity and Ubiquity: Discussing Fluidity, Metaspaces,
Micromobility, and Multiple Profiling / *Erkki Patokorpi and Franck Tétard*....................................... 1

This chapter describes a new world of digital nomadicity, transgressing the confines of a more static type of mobile communication and collaboration. Building on the ideas of digital nomadicity, fluidity, and interactivity, the authors propose the concepts of metaspace, transient hierarchies, and multiple-profiling to round up a vision of truly nomadic and ubiquitous computing environments. Along with geographical and technological barriers or boundaries, the barriers created by local and parochial techno-social systems have to be taken into consideration in order to make us truly nomadic. A key question in the near future is how the user of advanced mobile technology could be empowered to have more control over the multiple spaces he or she inhabits and the numerous boundary crossings that he or she is forced to perform.

As m-commerce continues to grow, it is critical to examine future opportunities, trends, questions, and related concerns. The increasing adoption of short range technologies like Bluetooth, as well as long range technologies like WiMax, are increasingly aiding m-commerce. These technologies have increased the number of applications for mobile users, and strengthened the future of m-commerce. M-commerce requires careful e-commerce adaptation to include mobile access for enhanced services and business communications that are not only anytime, but also anywhere. This chapter presents the importance of, the components and technologies involved with, the future market forecast and key future trends and issues for m-commerce.

Chapter III

M-commerce allows customers to buy goods from anywhere and anytime using Internet and mobile environments. The success of m-payments using mobile phones primarily depends on the privacy and security of the underlying systems. The success also depends on the trust among the key players. This chapter surveys basic architectures of m-payment systems and compares their features in the security perspective including methods for authentication, replay detection, double spending prevention, proof of receipt, message confidentiality, user privacy, non-repudiation, unforgeability, preventing overspending, anonymity, untraceability, unlinkability, fairness, refundability, dispute resolution, and divisibility. Also several other success factors critical to m-payments services are explored.

Chapter IV

In this chapter an overview of a general, policy-based security architecture for securing the confidentiality, authenticity, and integrity of enterprise m-commerce data is presented. The security architecture is designed for operation in mobile environments where it provides authentication and data confidentiality and integrity security services to m-commerce systems based on a flexible and fine-grained encryption scheme customized by a scalable and extensible security policy. This chapter provides an overview of the design and components of this architecture and mentions some protocol implementations built according to the specifications of this architecture.

Organizations have to make the movement of raw materials, goods, and services across geographic boundaries as efficient and effective as possible. In order to enable organizations to immediately react to specific events, disruptions, and exceptions, logistics has to become mobile itself. M-logistics may therefore be seen as an enabler for efficient and effective m-commerce. Little research has been done to examine the potential barriers to the implementation of global m-logistics in different continents. This chapter explores and examines the current status of m-logistics in North America, Europe, and Asia (mainly China, South Korea, and Japan). The chapter focuses on global m-logistics as an essential function and key factor in efficient and effective global m-commerce.

Section II
Issues in Europe

This section provides a discussion of the m-commerce issues and technologies within the context and environment of the European continent. These chapters will continue to address important concepts and future trends while providing insight into the unique issues that face users and companies in this area of the world.

This chapter analyzes how companies define their customer value proposition and how the selection of successful mobile customer services is done in alignment with this strategic positioning. A set of five different strategic goals (price leadership, product quality leadership, customer intimacy leadership, accessibility leadership, and innovation leadership) are derived and this classification is applied to case studies of companies in countries including Switzerland, the United Kingdom, Germany, and The Netherlands.

Mobile services have evolved into an important business area and many companies in varying industries are offering different mobile services. This chapter develops a conceptual classification for mobile services that illustrates the characteristics of mobile services and gives indications how to describe mobile business opportunities and categorize services from a customer-centric perspective. The classification scheme, grounded in previous research, is based on the type of consumption, the context, the social setting, and the customer relationship with the service provider. The explorative classification is illustrated with two case studies of existing mobile services in the European market.

Many mobile operators, in pursuit of high returns on investment, upgraded their network infrastructures. They expected that this would stimulate high demand for advanced mobile services similar to those used on the Internet. However, these hopes have not been materialized in the Western world yet. It seems that mobile users are not interested or willing to massively adopt and extensively use the mobile data services (MDS) offered.
In this chapter, user perceptions and experiences from MDS are investigated in Denmark and Greece. Useful insights are provided to both researchers in the mobile domain, by underlining the importance of socioeconomic context in the use of MDS, as well as the key players in mobile market arena, by informing their marketing campaigns and corporate strategies.

Chapter IX

This chapter provides a detailed and systematic analysis of the issues for bringing mobile broadcasting to market, and of the solutions found in five major pilots throughout Europe.
One of the most anticipated applications in Europe's m-commerce landscape is mobile TV. It is widely argued that mobile digital television has the potential of becoming one of the next high-growth consumer technologies, provided it is able to master its inherent complexities in terms of the various stakeholders required to cooperate. In the European mobile market, digital TV on a mobile device is not a novelty. This chapter explores a number of standards and technologies related to the offering of high quality broadcasts over mobile devices.

In comparison to the large amount of money the European telecommunication industry has invested in the Universal Mobile Telecommunications System (UMTS) and third generation (3G) mobile infrastructure, there still is a very slow adoption of mobile applications in different domains. This is a result of a lack of methods to demonstrate and measure the value-creation potential of mobile business applications, and a lack of potential best practices and use cases in different domains. This chapter presents the results of a study examining a hospital's processes of drug supply in the pharmacy of the hospital as well as the meal supply in the kitchen. The economic potential that could be gained by implementing mobile terminals for the supply of drugs and meals is measured. The general conditions for the use of mobile devices in hospitals was considered, as well as the applicability of different kinds of mobile devices. Another question to be answered was where and how mobile terminals could be integrated in existing business processes. The analysis of advantages and risks that could occur during the roll-out of the mobile system was targeted as well.

Telematic services in the automotive sector have been rather unsuccessful in Germany over the past years. The three main reasons for discontinuing mobile services are usually mentioned: (1) the costs for data transfer were too high, (2) the services offered did not fit adequately to the users' needs, and (3) telematic services were too focused on technology and had hardly any economic aspects considered, making it almost impossible to deliver viable and sustainable services. Recent availability of new digital transmission channels such as UMTS or digital radio broadcast (DAB) and the declining prices especially for cellular radio almost eliminated the problem of transmission cost, leaving only two problems to solve. This chapter explores the question of how innovative mobile automotive services be systematically developed and structured and which steps have to be taken for deploying mobile services successfully.

Chapter XII

Marketing instruments using mobile devices (m-marketing) allow innovative forms of customer relationships and interaction. There is little knowledge about how consumers react to advertising via mobile devices. This chapter analyzes the extent to which consumers differ in their perceptions of advertising via mobile devices across different cultures. In order to achieve comparable results, the study focuses on push marketing activities in the form of text advertising messages sent to consumers in Japan and Austria. Results show that Japanese students regard m-advertising as more entertaining than Austrian students do. This finding might be consistent with the Japanese strong orientation on emotions and entertainment, which might explain their better attitude toward m-advertising. On the other hand, as cultural research has shown Japanese are more liberal concerning privacy, their relatively negative perception of irritation might show a weaker influence on advertising value and attitude toward m-advertising than among the Austrians.

Section III
Issues in Asia Pacific

This section provides a discussion of the m-commerce issues and technologies within the context and environment of the Asia-Pacific continent. These chapters will continue to address important concepts and future trends while providing insight into the unique issues that face users and companies in this area of the world.

This chapter presents an overview of wireless mobile technologies and its applications, with a focus on digital multimedia broadcasting (DMB) technology. Empirical findings are presented along with actual DMB subscriber usage results. The chapter attempts to provide stimulating answers by investigating the following questions: (1) Do users perceive easy access to DMB applications as a satisfactory service offered by DMB service providers? (2) Do users perceive high-quality DMB program contents as a satisfactory service offered by the DMB service providers? (3) Are there differences between different age groups in terms of their perception of DMB phone prices, phone usage time, program contents, and services?

The hospitality industry, more specifically restaurants, has recently started to exploit the benefits of mobile technologies. This chapter explores the perceived benefits of using PDAs in a restaurant in a business-to-employee (B2E) context. The findings indicated that the most common perceptions are increased efficiency; speedier service; better usability and ease of use; enhanced reputation/image; and increased accuracy. Most of the negative perceptions were related to the technical shortcomings of the technology such as unreliable transmission of data, system crashes, short battery life, and limited durability of the devices. The chapter concludes with recommendations for future practice and research.

Chapter XV

As the growth of the mobile market decreases and the market competition increases, mobile carriers have been trying to find new business models to retain their profits and expand their business boundaries. Development of value-added services provides a growth opportunity to mobile carriers. This chapter discusses the motivation of mobile value-added service in terms of value chain and mobile adoption. Value-added services presented in Korea are introduced: short messaging service, personalized call-ring service, mobile music service, mobile video service, mobile payment, and mobile games. The major characteristics of those value-added services are discussed within the context of "4Cs": customization, content-focused, connectedness, and contemporary. This chapter also discusses DMB as a new expecting value-added service and the impacts of value-added services on mobile market.

Chapter XVI

A growth curve of the mobile commerce (m-commerce) market would be like that of the mobile voice market or broadband Internet service in the past in Korea, and then m-commerce will bring the mobile operators the second revenue. Even though, the subscribers of m-commerce are continues ascent in external appearance, in effect it is have an important problem to though revenue. In this research, after defining the m-commerce market, we will discover trends based on technological, social, and politic changes and the development scenarios of the m-commerce market. We review the technological, social, and policy changes that have occurred in Korea in order to present the mega trends that could affect the m-commerce market most significantly, by finding out the inner and outer arena trends of the m-commerce market. And then, we show four scenarios: (1) gloomy market scenario, (2) dream market scenario, (3) market collapse scenario, and (4) rainbow compromise scenario. We expect that an analysis of the trend that could create an m-commerce market in Korea and a study of the development scenarios will provide some foresight to communication service providers in Korea and overseas countries in order to cope with the future m-commerce market.

Chapter XVII

The chapter addresses the mobile service pricing and affordability issues in China. The goal is to assist fast diffusion and sustainable development of mobile communication services in China through pricing mechanisms. Although the industry has been on a fast track since the early 1990s, a large number of people still lack basic services; most of them are from rural areas where the tariffs of mobile services are prohibitively high compared to their incomes. Furthermore, people in the urban areas, especially in south-eastern provinces of China, are demanding a wider scope of personalized value-added services. Community-based individual tariffs and a business model which suits the community culture rooted in Chinese tradition is described.

Section IV
Issues in the Americas

This section provides a discussion of the m-commerce issues and technologies within the context and environment of the American continent. These chapters will continue to address important concepts and future trends while providing insight into the unique issues that face users and companies in this area of the world.

This chapter investigates the current trends of m-commerce in the retail industry in an effort to establish a greater understanding and awareness of the technology, problems, business models, applications, and critical success factors (CSFs) it provides to consumer subscribers and business users. The retail segment is expected to stimulate the future growth of m-commerce with the potential to purchase goods and services, exchange financial transactions, and establish home delivery in a matter of minutes with the touch of a button and no geographical limitations. This unique business opportunity, with all of its accomplishments, potential, and uncertainties is the central focus of this discussion. The chapter concentrates on questions such as: Is m-commerce widely adopted in other countries? What kinds of technology are enabling this spread of m-commerce in the retail industry? How do the CSFs for m-commerce affect the retail business? What are some different types of m-commerce applications? What does the future hold for m-commerce in the retail industry and beyond?

Chapter XIX

This chapter investigates the user interface perception and resources for mobile technology (MT) support in health care service activities. MT is an emerging and enabling technology in health care, although there is little evidence from the perspective of health representatives on the effect of having a suitable MT system infrastructure for each service. Moreover, the implementation of new technology competes with funding available for health institutions resources and introducing all of them is prohibitive. A case study using a multi-criteria approach was investigated involving three categories of hospitals in Chile, and empirical data was collected comprising diverse health sector representatives. The main contribution is the proposed research decision-making model using the analytic hierarchy process (AHP) to evaluate and compare information and communications systems such as fixed, wireless, or computer-assisted provisions for health-related activities and the identification of the high-priority dimensions in the health care service. The study revealed that mainly private hospitals have access to advanced network and Internet access; hence the technical basis for developing new applications.

Chapter XX

Wi-Fi technology can keep everyone connected all the time and is changing the way people work, play, and communicate. People around the world are using Wi-Fi technology to work, study, play, travel, shop, and bank. Wi-Fi technology is also quickly gaining a foothold on many institutions as a means to achieve mobility and anywhere, anytime access. Wi-Fi technology opens a new dimension of computer networking in higher education. Wi-Fi technology is affecting not only the classroom environment and technology access, but also the actual activities of learning and teaching. This chapter provides the general picture of Wi-Fi technology implementation in the global setting and in higher education in the United States and then examines the following aspects of Wi-Fi technology: Wi-Fi standards, Wi-Fi security, the adoption of Wi-Fi, Wi-Fi to support teaching and learning, challenges of Wi-Fi implementation, and future trends and directions.

Foreword

Commerce has always been connected with networks. For thousands of years, transportation networks determined where commerce happened. Traders congregated where they could ford rivers, paddle or sail their boats into protected waters, or where paths crossed. Transportation networks are required to exchange goods, but business always has an information component, and information is almost always exchanged before goods change hands. Postal systems, which are over 2,500 years old, enabled traders to exchange information prior to a transaction. However, a postal system, a cousin of transportation networks, is controlled by the same geography.

When electronic networks emerged, starting with the telegraph in 1833, traders could begin to interact from a distance with speeds far exceeding those of a postal system, and the first shackles of the tyranny of distance were rattled and loosened. We are now seeing the results of nearly two centuries of extension and reinvention of the original telegraph. The Internet gave us the first glimpse of the potential of massive public electronic networks to transform commerce. In the last decades, many industries have been transformed, new businesses emerged, and consumers' habits have been changed on many dimensions. The Internet, however, has its limitations. The typical Internet connection, a computer, is rather large, even when a laptop and its geographic location are imprecise. Furthermore, several people might share the same computer, and even the same account. In terms of the four fundamental information drives, namely ubiquity, uniqueness, universality, and unison (Junglas & Watson, 2006), the Internet is quite constrained. In particular, it lacks ubiquity because customers need to find an access point, fixed or wireless, to conduct commerce. It lacks uniqueness because a computer is not linked to a particular person.

M-commerce, based on the mobile phone network, loosens the shackles of commerce a stage further because consumers now carry their access points with them, and almost always can connect to the network (air and sea being an exception). Phones are rarely shared and thus owners are identified. In particular, GSM has a subscriber identity module (SIM) card to enable owners to easily transfer their identities between phones. Furthermore, current technology enables the location of many mobile phones to be identified within a few meters. Consequently, a business can know who the customer is and where they are. In terms of the information drivers, m-commerce is a step up from e-commerce because it offers higher levels of ubiquity and uniqueness. The next generation of commerce, u-commerce (Watson, Pitt, Berthon, & Zinkhan, 2002), will escape the confines of a particular network and ubiquity will be further enhanced, along with the other information drives.

As you read this book, with its extensive and deep examination of m-commerce, try to keep in mind the greater picture and overall path of commerce. Look back, by asking yourself what opportunities are created by m-commerce that did not exist with e-commerce, which in turn created ventures not feasible with geographic networks. Look forward by asking yourself what opportunities will be created by the transition from m-commerce to u-commerce. I hope this forward looking foreword will help you see the future more vividly and thus enable you to understand more clearly the current and next stages of commerce.

Richard T. Watson
University of Georgia

REFERENCES

Junglas, I. A., & Watson, R. T. (2006). The U-constructs: Four information drives. *Communications of AIS, 17,* 569-592.

Watson, R. T., Pitt, L. F., Berthon, P., & Zinkhan, G. M. (2002). U-commerce: Expanding the universe of marketing. *Journal of the Academy of Marketing Science, 30*(4), 329-343.

Preface

M-commerce uses the potential of wireless technologies to expand the reach of e-commerce applications to any time and any place. Mobile applications can be used to support transactions with customers and suppliers and to conduct e-business within and across organizational boundaries and are becoming an integral part of an organization's strategy.

M-commerce has great potential to promote global trading and commerce across geographic boundaries. Currently, however, this great potential has been limited by different perspectives of m-commerce strategies and implementations in different regions of the world, as well as adoption of different mobile communication standards and unbalanced development of m-commerce in different regions.

While mobile technology itself aims to get rid of geographic limitations and boundaries and promote global m-commerce, differences in existing m-commerce strategies/perspectives, mobile communication standards (especially in third generation [3G] and fourth [4G] mobile communication standards), and business models, have been confusing to m-commerce service providers and investors as to how to understand those different m-commerce perspectives/strategies and mobile communication standards. In order to successfully implement global m-commerce development strategies, these issues must be addressed. This book attempts to take a first step towards bridging that gap to explore and examine those important issues from the different perspectives of the three continents: Europe, North America, and Asia.

SECTION I: EMERGING M-COMMERCE ISSUES AND TECHNOLOGIES

This section provides a discussion of general concepts, issues, and technologies that apply to the area of m-commerce. These chapters will address important concepts and future trends that provide a context for understanding m-commerce. In addition, issues such as security and important technologies are discussed.

Chapter I: From Mobility to True Nomadicity and Ubiquity: Discussing Fluidity, Metaspaces, Micromobility, and Multiple-Profiling

This chapter describes a new world of digital nomadicity, transgressing the confines of a more static type of mobile communication and collaboration. Building on the ideas of digital nomadicity, fluidity, and interactivity, the authors propose the concepts of metaspace, transient hierarchies and multiple-profiling to round up a vision of truly nomadic and ubiquitous computing environments. Along with geographical and technological barriers or boundaries, the barriers created by local and parochial techno-social systems have to be taken into consideration in order to make us truly nomadic. A key question in the near future is how the user of advanced mobile technology could be empowered to have more control over the multiple spaces he or she inhabits and the numerous boundary crossings that he or she is forced to perform.

Chapter II: The Future of M-Commerce: The Role of Bluetooth and WiMax

As m-commerce continues to grow, it is critical to examine future opportunities, trends, questions, and related concerns. The increasing adoption of short range technologies like Bluetooth, as well as long range technologies like WiMax, are increasingly aiding m-commerce. These technologies have increased the number of applications for mobile users and strengthened the future of m-commerce. M-commerce requires careful e-commerce adaptation to include mobile access for enhanced services and business communications that are not only anytime, but also anywhere. This chapter presents the importance of, the components and technologies involved with, the future market forecast, and key future trends and issues for m-commerce.

Chapter III: M-Commerce Payment Systems

M-commerce allows customers to buy goods from anywhere and anytime using Internet and mobile environments. The success of m-payments using mobile phones primarily depends on the privacy and security of the underlying systems. The success also depends on the trust among the key players. This chapter surveys basic architectures of m-payment systems and compares their features in the security perspective including methods for authentication, replay detection, double spending prevention, proof of receipt, message confidentiality, user privacy, non-repudiation, unforgeability, preventing overspending, anonymity, untraceability, unlinkability, fairness, refundability, dispute resolution, and divisibility. Also several other success factors critical to m-payments services are explored.

Chapter IV: Policy-Based Security for M-Commerce Networks

In this chapter an overview of a general, policy-based security architecture for securing the confidentiality, authenticity, and integrity of enterprise m-commerce data is presented. The security architecture is designed for operation in mobile environments where it provides authentication and data confidentiality and integrity security services to m-commerce systems based on a flexible and fine-grained encryption scheme customized by a scalable and extensible security policy. This chapter provides an overview of the design and components of this architecture and mentions some protocol implementations built according to the specifications of this architecture.

Chapter V: Global M-Logistics in North America, Europe, and Asia: A Comparative Study of the Diffusion and Adoption of Standards and Technologies in Next-Generation M-Logistics

Organizations have to make the movement of raw materials, goods, and services across geographic boundaries as efficient and effective as possible. In order to enable organizations to immediately react to specific events, disruptions, and exceptions, logistics has to become mobile itself. M-logistics may therefore be seen as an enabler for efficient and effective m-commerce. Little research has been done to examine the potential barriers to the implementation of global m-logistics in different continents. This chapter explores and examines the current status of m-logistics in North America, Europe, and

Asia (mainly China, South Korea, and Japan). The chapter focuses on global m-logistics as an essential function and key factor in efficient and effective global m-commerce.

SECTION II: ISSUES IN EUROPE

This section provides a discussion of the m-commerce issues and technologies within the context and environment of the European continent. These chapters will continue to address important concepts and future trends while providing insight into the unique issues that face users and companies in this area of the world.

Chapter VI: Strategy Aligned Process Selection for Mobile Customer Services

This chapter analyzes how companies define their customer value proposition and how the selection of successful mobile customer services is done in alignment with this strategic positioning. A set of five different strategic goals (price leadership, product quality leadership, customer intimacy leadership, accessibility leadership, and innovation leadership) are derived and this classification is applied to case studies of companies in countries including Switzerland, the United Kingdom, Germany, and The Netherlands.

Chapter VII: Exploring Mobile Service Business Opportunities from a Customer-Centric Perspective

Mobile services have evolved into an important business area and many companies in varying industries are offering different mobile services. This chapter develops a conceptual classification for mobile services that illustrates the characteristics of mobile services and gives indications how to describe mobile business opportunities and categorize services from a customer-centric perspective. The classification scheme, grounded in previous research, is based on the type of consumption, the context, the social setting, and the customer relationship with the service provider. The explorative classification is illustrated with two case studies of existing mobile services in the European market.

Chapter VIII: Exploring the Use of Mobile Data Services in Europe: The Case of Denmark and Greece

Many mobile operators, in pursuit of high returns on investment, upgraded their network infrastructures. They expected that this would stimulate high demand for advanced mobile services similar to those used on the Internet. However, these hopes have not been materialized in the Western world yet. It seems that mobile users are not interested or willing to massively adopt and extensively use the mobile data services (MDS) offered.

In this chapter, user perceptions and experiences from MDS are investigated in Denmark and Greece. Useful insights are provided to both researchers in the mobile domain, by underlining the importance of socioeconomic context in the use of MDS, as well as the key players in the mobile market arena, by informing their marketing campaigns and corporate strategies.

Chapter IX: The Design of Mobile Television in Europe

This chapter provides a detailed and systematic analysis of the issues for bringing mobile broadcasting to market, and of the solutions found in five major pilots throughout Europe.

One of the most anticipated applications in Europe's mobile commerce landscape is mobile TV. It is widely argued that mobile digital television has the potential of becoming one of the next high-growth consumer technologies, provided it is able to master its inherent complexities in terms of the various stakeholders required to cooperate. In the European mobile market, digital TV on a mobile device is not a novelty. This chapter explores a number of standards and technologies related to the offering of high quality broadcasts over mobile devices.

Chapter X: Mobile Business Process Reengineering: How to Measure the Input of Mobile Applications to Business Processes in European Hospitals

In comparison to the large amount of money the European telecommunication industry has invested in Universal Mobile Telecommunications System (UMTS) and third generation (3G) mobile infrastructure, there still is a very slow adoption of mobile applications in different domains. This is a result of a lack of methods to demonstrate and measure the value-creation potential of mobile business applications, and a lack of potential best practices and use cases in different domains. This chapter presents the results of a study examining a hospital's processes of drug supply in the pharmacy of the hospital as well as the meal supply in the kitchen. The economic potential that could be gained by implementing mobile terminals for the supply of drugs and meals is measured. The general conditions for the use of mobile devices in hospitals was considered, as well as the applicability of different kinds of mobile devices. Another question to be answered was where and how mobile terminals could be integrated in existing business processes. The analysis of advantages and risks that could occur during the roll-out of the mobile system was targeted as well.

Chapter XI: Mobile Automotive Cooperative Services (MACS): Systematic Development of Personalizable Interactive Mobile Automotive Services

Telematic services in the automotive sector have been rather unsuccessful in Germany over the past years. The three main reasons for discontinuing mobile services are usually mentioned: (1) the costs for data transfer were too high, (2) the services offered did not fit adequately to the users' needs, and (3) telematic services were too focused on technology and had hardly any economic aspects considered, making it almost impossible to deliver viable and sustainable services. Recent availability of new digital transmission channels such as UMTS or digital radio broadcast (DAB) and the declining prices especially for cellular radio almost eliminated the problem of transmission cost, leaving only two problems to solve. This chapter explores the question of how innovative mobile automotive services be systematically developed and structured and which steps have to be taken for deploying mobile services successfully.

Chapter XII: Cross-Cultural Consumer Perceptions of Advertising via Mobile Devices: Some Evidence from Europe and Japan

Marketing instruments using mobile devices (m-marketing) allow innovative forms of customer relationships and interaction. There is little knowledge about how consumers react to advertising via mobile devices. This chapter analyzes the extent to which consumers differ in their perceptions of advertising via mobile devices across different cultures. In order to achieve comparable results, the study focuses on push marketing activities in the form of text advertising messages sent to consumers in Japan and Austria. Results show that Japanese students regard m-advertising as more entertaining than Austrian students do. This finding might be consistent with the Japanese strong orientation on emotions and entertainment, which might explain their better attitude toward m-advertising. On the other hand, as cultural research has shown Japanese are more liberal concerning privacy, their relatively negative perception of irritation might show a weaker influence on advertising value and attitude toward m-advertising than among the Austrians.

SECTION III: ISSUES IN ASIA PACIFIC

This section provides a discussion of the m-commerce issues and technologies within the context and environment of the Asia-Pacific continent. These chapters will continue to address important concepts and future trends while providing insight into the unique issues that face users and companies in this area of the world.

Chapter XIII: Current Status of Mobile Wireless Technology and Digital Multimedia Broadcasting

This chapter presents an overview of wireless mobile technologies and its applications, with a focus on digital multimedia broadcasting (DMB) technology. Empirical findings are presented along with actual DMB subscriber usage results. The chapter attempts to provide stimulating answers by investigating the following questions: (1) Do users perceive easy access to DMB applications as a satisfactory service offered by DMB service providers? (2) Do users perceive high-quality DMB program contents as a satisfactory service offered by the DMB service providers? (3) Are there differences between different age groups in terms of their perception of DMB phone prices, phone usage time, program contents, and services?

Chapter XIV: Understanding the Organisational Impact and Perceived Benefits of Bluetooth-Enabled Personal Digital Assistants in Restaurants

The hospitality industry, more specifically restaurants, has recently started to exploit the benefits of mobile technologies. This chapter explores the perceived benefits of using PDAs in a restaurant in a business-to-employee (B2E) context. The findings indicated that the most common perceptions are increased efficiency: speedier service: better usability and ease of use: enhanced reputation/image; and increased accuracy. Most of the negative perceptions were related to the technical shortcomings of the technology such as unreliable transmission of data, system crashes, short battery life, and limited durability of the devices. The chapter concludes with recommendations for future practice and research.

Chapter XV: Strategies of Mobile Value–Added Services in Korea

As the growth of the mobile market decreases and the market competition increases, mobile carriers have been trying to find new business models to retain their profits and expand their business boundaries. Development of value-added services provides a growth opportunity to mobile carriers. This chapter discusses the motivation of mobile value-added service in terms of value chain and mobile adoption. Value-added services presented in Korea are introduced: short messaging service, personalized call-ring service, mobile music service, mobile video service, mobile payment, and mobile games. The major characteristics of those value-added services are discussed within the context of "4Cs": customization, content-focused, connectedness, and contemporary. This chapter also discusses DMB as a new expecting value-added service and the impacts of value-added services on mobile market.

Chapter XVI: M–Commerce Market Development Scenarios in Korea: Focus on Changes and Their Mega Trends

The growth curve of the m-commerce market is similar to that of the mobile voice market or broadband Internet service in Korea. In this chapter, trends based on technological, social, and political changes and the development scenarios of the m-commerce market are discussed. A review of the technological, social, and policy changes that have occurred in Korea is presented. Four scenarios are discussed: (1) gloomy market scenario, (2) dream market scenario, (3) market collapse scenario, and (4) rainbow compromise scenario. An analysis of the trends that could create an m-commerce market in Korea and a study of the development scenarios provide some insight to communication service providers in Korea and other countries.

Chapter XVII: Individual Telecommunications Tariffs in Chinese Communities

The chapter addresses the mobile service pricing and affordability issues in China. The goal is to assist fast diffusion and sustainable development of mobile communication services in China through pricing mechanisms. Although the industry has been on a fast track since the early 1990s, a large number of people still lack basic services; most of them are from rural areas where the tariffs of mobile services are prohibitively high compared to their incomes. Furthermore, people in the urban areas, especially in south-eastern provinces of China, are demanding a wider scope of personalized value-added services. Community-based individual tariffs and a business model which suits the community culture rooted in Chinese tradition is described.

SECTION IV: ISSUES IN THE AMERICAS

This section provides a discussion of the m-commerce issues and technologies within the context and environment of the American continent. These chapters will continue to address important concepts and future trends while providing insight into the unique issues that face users and companies in this area of the world.

Chapter XVIII: M-Commerce in the U.S. and China Retail Industry: Business Models, Critical Success Factors (CSFs), and Case Studies

This chapter investigates the current trends of m-commerce in the retail industry in an effort to establish a greater understanding and awareness of the technology, problems, business models, applications, and critical success factors (CSFs) it provides to consumer subscribers and business users. The retail segment is expected to stimulate the future growth of m-commerce with the potential to purchase goods and services, exchange financial transactions, and establish home delivery in a matter of minutes with the touch of a button and no geographical limitations. This unique business opportunity, with all of its accomplishments, potential, and uncertainties is the central focus of this discussion. The chapter concentrates on questions such as: Is m-commerce widely adopted in other countries? What kinds of technology are enabling this spread of m-commerce in the retail industry? How do the CSFs for m-commerce affect the retail business? What are some different types of m-commerce applications? What does the future hold for m-commerce in the retail industry and beyond?

Chapter XIX: Perception of Mobile Technology Provision in Health Service

This chapter investigates the user interface perception and resources for mobile technology (MT) support in health care service activities. MT is an emerging and enabling technology in health care, although there is little evidence from the perspective of health representatives on the effect of having a suitable MT system infrastructure for each service. Moreover, the implementation of new technology competes with funding available for health institutions resources and introducing all of them is prohibitive. A case study using a multi-criteria approach was investigated involving three categories of hospitals in Chile, and empirical data was collected comprising diverse health sector representatives. The main contribution is the proposed research decision-making model using the analytic hierarchy process (AHP) to evaluate and compare information and communications systems such as fixed, wireless, or computer-assisted provisions for health-related activities and the identification of the high-priority dimensions in the health care service. The study revealed that mainly private hospitals have access to advanced network and Internet access; hence the technical basis for developing new applications.

Chapter XX: The Implementation of Wi-Fi Technology in Higher Education in the United States

Wi-Fi technology can keep everyone connected all the time and is changing the way people work, play, and communicate. People around the world are using Wi-Fi technology to work, study, play, travel, shop, and bank. Wi-Fi technology is also quickly gaining a foothold on many institutions as a means to achieve mobility and anywhere, anytime access. Wi-Fi technology opens a new dimension of computer networking in higher education. Wi-Fi technology is affecting not only the classroom environment and technology access, but also the actual activities of learning and teaching. This chapter provides the general picture of Wi-Fi technology implementation in the global setting and in higher education in the United States and then examines the following aspects of Wi-Fi technology: Wi-Fi standards, Wi-Fi security, the adoption of Wi-Fi, Wi-Fi to support teaching and learning, challenges of Wi-Fi implementation, and future trends and directions.

Acknowledgment

We would like to first and foremost thank our family members for their love, understanding, and support. Editing a peer-reviewed academic book is a long journey with dozens of weekends that cannot be spent with family members. As a result, their names deserve to be recognized here: Ruth Day, Xian Ru Zhang, and Xiao Yun (Rose) Shi.

We would like to thank Professor Richard Watson who kindly arranged time to write the Forward for this book.

We thank the MIS Department in the College of Business, Ohio University for the support to help arrange teaching schedules so that one co-editor could be off for a quarter to concentrate on editing this book. Otherwise, this book might not have been completed in 2007.

We would also like to thank Meg Stocking, assistant executive editor of IGI Global, for her support. Working with her is a pleasant experience.

Last but not least, we thank many faculty members and others who took their valuable time out of their working schedules to review the book chapters:

Chang Liu, North Illinois University
Jim Quan, Salisbury University
Qing Hu, Florida Atlantic University
Kristin Dowler, College of Business, Ohio University
Hongyan Ma, Salisbury University
Kanliang Wang, Xi'an Jiaotong University
Eric Lu, Pennsylvania State University

Section I
Emerging M–Commerce Issues and Technologies

Chapter I
From Mobility to True Nomadicity and Ubiquity:
Discussing Fluidity, Metaspaces, Micromobility, and Multiple-Profiling

Erkki Patokorpi
Åbo Akademi University, Finland

Franck Tétard
Åbo Akademi University, Finland

ABSTRACT

It is becoming blatantly clear that some key concepts used in computer science and information systems literature—most notably those of nomadicity, mobility, and interaction—cannot any more satisfactorily capture the present-day reality of advanced mobile technology environments. A paradigm shift from a strapped mobility to truly nomadic digital environments is underway. Peter Wegner, Carsten Sørensen, and Leonard Kleinrock, among others, have aspired to describe and explain the workings of this emerging field of very advanced information and communication technology environments. Building on their ideas of digital nomadicity, fluidity, and interactivity, we propose the concepts of metaspace, transient hierarchies, and multiple-profiling to round up a vision of truly nomadic and ubiquitous computing environments. It will be argued that along with geographical and technological barriers or boundaries the barriers created by local and parochial techno-social systems have to be taken into consideration in order to make us truly nomadic. A key question in the near future is how the user of advanced mobile technology could be empowered to have more control over the multiple spaces he or she inhabits and the numerous boundary crossings that he or she is forced to perform.

INTRODUCTION

Mobile technology has been characterized as mobile, interactive, ubiquitous, localized, and personalized (see e.g., Carlsson & Walden, 2002; Keen & Mackintosh, 2001). More recently, concepts like context-aware, virtual, and multisensory have been used in this context, but these features usually assume, among other things, a more advanced, fully working third generation (3G) network or other more advanced mobile technology environments that are not yet generally in place, and if in use, only tentatively so (Anckar, Carlsson, & Walden, 2003). However, this state of affairs has not prevented some visionaries from stealing a glance at things to come. These visionaries argue that we are entering a new world of digital nomadicity, transgressing the confines of a more static type of mobile communication and collaboration. Although we are still partly trapped in the old world of fixed computing platforms, accessed by users with the same (personal) device from the same IP address, the world of radical mobility—true nomadicity—is just round the corner (see esp. Kleinrock, 2001).

The terms *paradigm* or *paradigmatic* have been used for instance by Sørensen (2002, 2003) and Sørensen and Pica (2005) to refer to the significant difference between the old idea of mobility and fluidity (fluid interaction); and by Kleinrock (2001) to refer to the shift from nomadicity in a disconnected world to a transparent, adaptive, and integrated nomadicity. The word *paradigm* should not be understood in a strict Kuhnian sense, though. First, the new vision of true nomadicity is still without a sharp and systematic enough conceptual apparatus in order to seriously challenge the old paradigm. Second, and more importantly, we are dealing with here a technological entity, a construct that did not exist before. The construct has changed the world (reality), so the conceptual shift does not entail a sudden *Gestalt* switch while the research object stays the same, which is generally the case in Kuhn's (1962) examples. Rather,

in the case of digital nomadicity the concepts have ceased to describe reality in a satisfactory manner as technology has evolved. In this context, we would rather speak of an epistemic rupture, a breaking point in our conceptual arsenal and discourse.

In this paper we analyze some central conceptual tools used by writers on advanced mobile technology (esp. nomadicity and mobility). In line with Peter Wegner, Leonard Kleinrock, and Carsten Sørensen, we argue that these concepts are not any more satisfactory as tools of scientific research into advanced information and communication technology (ICT), or even as tools of popular understanding. To conclude with, we will present and discuss some candidates for conceptual tools (fluidity, metaspace, micromobility, and multiple-personalization) that might better catch the social and technological properties of true nomadicity and ubiquitous computing. Taking the advice of Orlikowski and Iacono (2001), we seek to meaningfully combine both the technological and sociocultural aspects of the matter. It should be noted that we are not so much interested in what kind of a new breed of man (e.g., Castells, 2001) or new organizations (e.g., Järvenpää & Leidner, 1999) our society is giving birth to but in the actual human-computer and machine-to-machine interaction and its epistemic conditions.

NOMADICITY

"We are all nomads," says Kleinrock (1996). And he continues: "but we lack the systems support to assist us in our various forms of mobility" (p. 351). For Kleinrock, nomadicity means two different things. First, nomadicity is used to describe a vision of a perfectly connected environment: "The essence of a nomadic environment is to automatically adjust all aspects of the user's computing, communications, and storage functionality in a transparent and integrated fashion" (Kleinrock, 1996, p. 351). This sentence is presently widely used as a definition of nomadic computing. Being on the move, in transit, is here seen as a normal part of the life of digital nomads. However, Kleinrock also uses "nomadicity" to refer to a situation where a mobile user gets disconnected because the environment does not support perfect connectivity. The title of his paper underlines this second meaning of nomadicity: "Nomadicity: Anytime, Anywhere in a Disconnected World." The second meaning has since been adopted by the mobile computing community so that by the phrase "go nomadic" is meant the phenomenon of a temporary disconnection: "It is desirable that mobile devices be able to cope with temporary disconnection (or "going nomadic") as it is known in the mobile computing literature" (Hawick & James, 2003, p. 134; see also Alanko, Kojo, Liljeberg, & Raatikainen, 1999).

In a more recent paper, Kleinrock (2001) starts off with the assumption that most users of computing, communication, and services are people on the move, and that sudden changes in connectivity and bandwidth should be treated as the norm rather than the exception. Here the word nomadicity is systematically used to refer to a phenomenon in which the state of being on the move is the normal state and not a break from the normal. And, when mobile devices get disconnected, they get disconnected rather than "go nomadic." Kleinrock underlines the need for a better infrastructure and a more advanced system support for nomadic users so that the computing environment adjusts itself to the user rather than the other way round. Computing should become as transparent and convenient a product as electricity (on the utility model see Rappa, 2004). According to Kleinrock (2001), we are on our way to a world of true nomadicity.

OLD SCHOOL OF MOBILITY, LOCALIZATION, AND PERSONALIZATION

Portable computing—in the form of laptops, mobile phones, PDAs, and handheld computers—set the so-called knowledge workers free from the physical confines of the office. Along this line of thought, mobility has traditionally meant the ability of the user to move anywhere, anytime and yet stay connected, independently of the geographical constraints. For instance, Kopomaa (2000) talks about urban nomads and their "placeless use" of mobile devices. For Dahlbom and Ljungberg (1998), mobility implies that the user is away from his/her usual stationary point of activity (the office, for example), facing a changing and unpredictable context that deviates from the normal situation of use. Consequently, most of the research on mobility has dealt with technology issues such as limited battery life, unreliable network connections, volatile access points, risk of data loss, portability, and location discovery (Wiberg & Ljungberg, 2001). This sort of technologically oriented view on mobility has been aptly summarized by Messeter, Brandt, Halse, and Johansson (2004, p. 30) as follows: "Even if connectivity and location-based services receive a lot of attention in the mobile technology industry, the dominating rhetoric still revolves around providing the functionality of the conventional office environment 'anytime and anywhere', regardless of contextual factors." This kind of mobility Kakihara and Sørensen (2001, 2002) call spatial mobility: people in the post-industrial era are geographically independent "nomads" supported by various technologies.

Let us call it contextual mobility when context is, in some form, taken into account. Positioning (e.g., GPS, GLONASS, Galileo) is the single most important technology that makes contextual mobility possible. Apart from outdoor systems mentioned previously there are indoors systems, which attain an accuracy of a few centimeters, whereas outdoor systems usually have an accuracy ranging from one meter to hundreds of meters (see e.g., Liljedal, 2002; Priyantha, Miu, Balakrishnan, & Teller, 2001; Spriestersbach & Vogler, 2002). The most researched area in mobile context studies is the physical location of the mobile user. Examples include context-aware applications that enable users to discover resources in their physical proximity (Harter, Hopper, Steggles, Ward, & Webster, 1999; Priyantha et al., 2000), active maps that automatically change as the user moves (Schilit, Adams, & Want, 1994), and applications whose user interface adapts to the user's location. Another aspect of context that is frequently discussed in research literature is related to the orientation of device position indoors (Bahl & Padmanabhan, 2000). Dix et al. (2000), too, underline the importance of the physical locality and context in mobility: Localization in mobile systems like mobile guides means that the interaction is based not on the device properties alone but on a device in a context—context includes the infrastructure context, the system context, the application domain context, and the physical context. In other words, the location where the device is being used has an important impact on the nature of the information presented and on the whole interaction. All the same, this type of discussion focuses on the technological aspects of mobility. Some writers take a step further, trying for instance to make sense of both persons and devices moving in space (see e.g., Floch, Hallsteinsen, Lie, & Myrhaug, 2001; O'Hare & Gregory, 2000), and of the value that such technologically supported connectedness while moving creates in m-commerce or in work (Anckar & Eriksson, 2003).

To sum up so far, in the early days of mobility, most mobile applications still sought to hide the location of use. Mobility meant first of all to be able to move anywhere, anytime and still stay connected—to be able to stay happily oblivious about location. In contrast, context-aware design, to name one example, tries to exploit location, making some aspects of it an integral part of the interaction between the user, the mobile system, and the mobile device. Sørensen (2002, 2003) and his associates (Kakihara & Sørensen, 2001, 2002; Pica & Kakihara, 2003) have vigorously propagated for an even more expanded view on mobility, one which would better take into account the fact that not just devices and persons move but that also objects, spaces, and symbols do so. This fact entails that over and above the spatial context, we consider the social and virtual contexts of use.

Personalization is a feature that is frequently connected to mobile devices. Compared to PCs, mobile devices like cellular phones and PDAs are very personalizable. Mobile devices are truly personal in the sense of being rarely shared by other people. They are also traceable, which makes it possible to link an individual with a particular device and therefore tailor for instance services to suit the individual in question. By personalization is also meant the malleability of the technology, allowing either the user himself/herself to mold and adjust some of the device and interaction features or the technology learned about user preferences and automatically adapt to them (see e.g., Lim, Wang, Ong, & Hwang, 2003; Smyth, 2003). Research on personalization has been meager and it has focused on personalization methods (computer science) and marketing applications. Personalization from the user's point of view has received little attention (Karat, Blom, & Karat, 2003).

Researchers consistently stress the importance of personalization as the key to enhanced usability of mobile services. When machines universally talk to one another, personalized user interfaces seem to be the only way to reasonably cater to individual information and service needs (Omojokun & Isbell, 2003). As was mentioned earlier, the capability of accessing relevant information regardless of time and place was the main attraction for users just a few years ago: You could call or receive a call while lost in the woods but you could receive a call while paying your respects at a funeral. However, it does matter whether one is in the woods or at a funeral and one would like one's system to be able to tell those two apart. Time and place have not become less important but more important than ever, but our personalization techniques are not yet up to the challenge (Lyytinen & Yoo, 2002a; Sørensen, 2002).

INTERACTIVITY

Traditionally computability is seen in line with the algorithmic model. According to Wegner (1997), equating computability with the behavior that Turing machines are able to do (i.e., to compute mathematical functions) falls short of satisfactorily describing the behavior of object-oriented and distributed or decentralized multi-agent systems. Wegner and Goldin (1999) (Goldin & Wegner, 2004) say that the interaction of this sort of advanced computing systems is similar to dialog, question-answering, and two-person games in the sense that inputs are dynamically dependent on prior outputs, whereas in a Turing machine the inputs are history-independent and reproducible. Keil and Goldin (2003) characterize decentralized multi-agent systems as open systems that are constructed and constrained by the environment rather than designed. A termite colony is an example of a decentralized multi-agent system in nature. Without design (i.e., an internal representation of a shared goal) as well as without a capacity for planning and coordination, the termites as a colony are capable of building a nest. If Wegner and Goldin are right, we have to revise our thinking not only of human-computer interaction but also of interaction within computers and computing systems.

Wegner and Goldin's (1999) claim that there is a new paradigm of interactive computation has not been accepted by all and sundry. Prasse and Rittgen (1998) dismiss Wegner's claim of interactive computing systems being open systems by saying that "if the external resources are integrated into the system, the system no longer interacts with the environment and we get a new closed system" (p. 359). We think, however, that this is stretching the system theory too far; the line between two phenomena or systems may be fuzzy but that does not mean that the line (interpreted as a line between a system and the environment) is not real but merely a mental construct: It is not in the eye of the beholder. Interestingly enough, some sociologists deny that human-computer interaction is really interaction. Stone (1996), for instance, says that interaction requires at least two conscious beings that are able to interpret, not just respond. However, in interaction between humans or two conscious beings, too, interaction entails that both parties play according to the rules (respond in a relevant manner), or act partial recursively, as Prasse and Rittger (1998) put it. If I am engaged in a conversation and then run away, I am not engaged in a conversation any more. At least the definition of machine-to-machine and human-computer interaction should not be stronger than a hard-line, sociological definition of interaction between humans.

UBIQUITY: AN EMERGING PARADIGM

The term *ubiquity* (Lat. *ubique*, everywhere) conveys the idea that computing will be available everywhere and at all times. Ubiquitous computing and communication means intelligent environments in which various distributed computing units are linked together by heterogeneous communication links (see e.g., Abowd & Mynatt, 2000).

Ubiquitous mobile computing, in order to be really ubiquitous, entails that different networking technologies work seamlessly together (see e.g., Chen & Petrie, 2003). As a rule, coupling is made between cellular data networks and wireless local area networks (WLANs). WLANs are quicker and cheaper to maintain and operate than cellular networks. Cellular data networks again have wider coverage but are more expensive and slower. By combining the two, the user gets both high speed and anytime-anywhere mobility. The problem nowadays is that most integrated WLAN-cellular networks are parasitical annexes to cellular networks, without smooth and effortless connecting between different WLANs as the user moves from one place to another. Typically a WLAN-cellular network user needs to reconnect when he/she moves from a public WLAN to a private WLAN. There is no shortage of architectural models for integrating different networks. Logging in or signing in is both time consuming and prone to errors. Consequently, a central problem in the integration is to manage connecting without having to login into several WLANs as the user moves about. When moving about the mobile device, the user can apply four principal strategies of reconnecting to a resource. The resource, say a news service, moves the resources with the mobile entity. This does not work with a database for instance. A copy is transferred with the moving mobile entity. This does not work when the copy is frequently modified. The reference instead of the resource is modified to refer to the remote host hosting the resource; rebinding the mobile entity to an equivalent resource in the new locality. For instance, a news service can be accessed in a new locality for up-to-date local news (Bellavista, Corradi, Montanari, & Stefanelli, 2003). Luo, Jiang, Kim, Shankaranarayanan, and Henry (2003), to mention just one example, have presented a model in which the user needs to sign in and authenticate him/herself just once. Kanter's (2003) Geobots service is another model, applying intelligent agents to automatically negotiate between competing local WLAN operators and GPRS access networks. Binding is not a simple matter, though context and location awareness help in choosing the suitable binding strategy. Notwithstanding, we are told that seamless network infrastructure is just round the corner.

The term nomadicity implies that the user carries the technology with him/her, whereas ubiquity implies that the world itself is computerized. Presently, these two lines of development are converging. Other terms related to ubiquitous and nomadic computing are for instance ambient intelligence, distributed and context-aware systems, tangible interaction, mobile informatics, and pervasive computing (Kristensen, May, Jensen, Gersbo-Møller, & Maersk, 2003; Lyytinen & Yoo, 2002b; Patokorpi, 2006). In this paper we consider all of the previous as slightly different perspectives to the same general phenomenon: very advanced mobile ICT environments.

FLUIDITY, METASPACE AND MICROMOBILITY

In this chapter we seek to make sense of the alleged new paradigm by presenting and discussing some candidates for conceptual tools. Carsten Sørensen, Daniele Pica, and Masao Kakihara have borrowed the concept of fluidity from topology to describe the social patterns of interaction in advanced mobile ICT. They claim that fluidity describes better than the network metaphor the movement from one space to another. From a technological point of view, an integrated network of networks enables interactional stability, and interactional stability enables mobility regardless of the physical context as well as the continuous flow of virtual and real objects from one space to another across diverse networks, that is, fluidity. Pica and Kakihara (2003) and Kakihara and Sørensen (2002) have characterized this feature of a nomadic environment as the duality of mobility:

Figure 1. Transient hierarchies and metaspaces

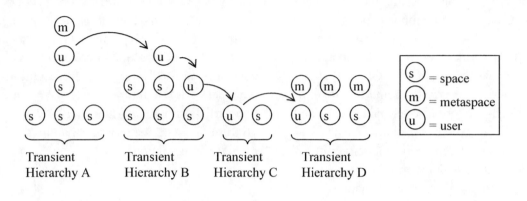

the dual possibility both to break loose from the physical (spatiotemporal) context and to enrich our contact with it by adding a virtual layer to it. From a sociological point of view, within a nomadic or ubiquitous environment—which by definition provides a transparent, integrated, and convenient support for mobility—mobile devices synchronously bring real and virtual environments together, allowing us, the users, to be in both at the same time.

The cyberspace is a space of spaces. We suggest that there is a metaspace, a kind of a dominant (though transient) reference point in the fluid topology. Someone or something is usually to some extent, some of the time in control of the relations between the different spaces of cyberspace. Someone or something configures or shuts out connections or in some other way steers the flow of interaction. For instance, different countries have different levels of access to the Internet (the digital divide); bandwidth varies at different locations; digital fences have been set up to prevent violations of copyright; private blocking software is blocking out sites; encryption and firewalls restrict access; different applications have built-in asymmetries or someone

or something may control and configure applications so that the parties to an interaction are in an asymmetrical relation to one another (see e.g., Bar, 2001; Boyle, 1997). It is commonplace that we are not equal in the cyberspace, and our models should be able to reflect this fact.

In our opinion, there are distinguishable metaspaces that form the upper level of transient hierarchies of a fluid interaction. As the name indicates, these transient hierarchies change in the course of interaction, but most of the time there is a dominant space that somehow controls or overrides other spaces. A flat (egalitarian) space of spaces is rare. The transient hierarchies of fluid interaction are presented graphically in Figure 1.

Figure 1 depicts how the user moves or evolves across different transient hierarchies in the course of fluid interaction. Hierarchies are presented as circles, representing the user, the different spaces, and metaspaces. In Transient Hierarchy A, the user is not in control of the interaction; however, he or she takes control of the interaction as he or she moves to Transient Hierarchy B. One may of course change one's position *within* a transient hierarchy, for instance from a metaspace position to the bottom of the hierarchy (i.e., from Transient Hierarchy B to Transient Hierarchy D). Transient Hierarchy C depicts an egalitarian position.

Fluidity is a metaphor or a regulative idea, which needs to be checked and balanced against the messy backdrop of reality. One could say that the concepts of metaspace and transient hierarchies function here also as such checks and balances. Anyone who has taken part in a videoconference has got an intuitive understanding of metaspaces and transient hierarchies at work on a small scale. In other words, this chapter partly is an effort to pin down fluid interaction into something concrete, so that we do not lose sight of the technological limitations and the practical details of the situated actual human-machine and machine-to-machine interaction.

One more thing delimiting digital interaction is micromobility. Luff and Heath (1998) (see also Fagrell, Ljungberg, & Kristoffersen, 1999; Perry, O'Hara, Sellen, Brown, & Harper, 2001; Wiberg & Ljungberg, 2001) have observed that distributed collaboration, that is, mobile team work, runs into problems as the digital artefacts undergo small changes when transported from one space to another. The functional view on mobility (the rhetoric of "anytime, anywhere") generally turns a blind eye to micromobility, making all spaces equivalent. Unfortunately, in reality a paper document differs from its digital version on a PC screen, which in turn differs from a digital version of it on a mobile device screen. Consequently, the three manifestations of the same general object (document) often cannot perform a similar enough function in all three contexts of use to enable collaboration as intended. As Luff and Heath's (1998) observations indicate, complete fluidity is a distant and perhaps even an unrealizable dream. Even commonplace objects would need to be augmented by giving them virtual features or intelligence, and also the more mundane aspects of interaction would need to be successfully digitally enhanced and supported by ubiquitous computing. Lyytinen

and Yoo (2002a) have addressed the same general issue when talking about the problems of digital convergence, calling for technical and managerial solutions to them. We believe that metaspaces, transient hierarchies, and micromobility open up a field of empirical study into the conditions and practices of digital interaction (e.g., communication, collaboration, and learning), capturing the mixture of social-technological and real-virtual aspects of interaction.

MULTIPLE-PROFILING

Nomadic and ubiquitous environments are prone to be markedly intrusive and insensitive to the user's desires and intentions. Fluidity implies that the user, owing to the extreme flux or fluidity of multiple spaces or contexts, often is not in control of the terms of interaction. Personalization technologies are supposed to level the way for better user control and usability in context. Unfortunately, many ambitious models of context—for instance within computer science—approach context mainly from the computing system perspective (Chen, 2003). As a result, these models have a distinct element of the "big brother." The same issues could be approached from a user perspective. In this way the big brother aspect could be tuned down. From the user's perspective the following aspects of context seem to be of fundamental importance:

1. Who am I?
2. What is this place?
3. Who are these people in this place?
4. What devices and artifacts are around or carried by these people?
5. Why are these people, artefacts, and devices in the environment?

Despite appearances the first question is the most important of all. Nothing determines the suitability of a service or mode of interaction better than the role or identity of the user in a given context. The user should know or at least easily find out his or her own role in the situation, and also be able to change his or her role at will. Social roles, identity, and anonymity are determinants of human behavior and interaction over which the user needs to have some control. The transparency of the user's actions to the user him/herself is a goal to be strived for but difficult to attain in design (Kramer, Noronha, & Vergo, 2000; Purao & Krogstie, 2004). In addition to the system context, the designer has to take into account the geographical, the (relative) locality, the temporal, the social, and the virtual contexts (Avital, Robey, Sawyer, & Sorensen, 2004; Junglas & Watson, 2003; Lee & Sawyer, 2002; Prasopoulou, Panteli, & Pouloudi, 2004). Not even this suffices because, as Varshney (2004) points out, "different users could act quite differently even in the same context" (p. 70).

We believe that multiple-profiling (or multiple-personalization) might be of some assistance in meeting personalization requirements in a truly nomadic environment. Multiple Personality Disorder (MPD) is a codified psychopathological state in which an individual manifests many (multiple) personalities per body. Usually one (or several) of these alter-personalities may be conscious of some other alters residing in the same body (see e.g., Allison, 1998). Applied to cyberspace, multiple-personalization means that when moving from one space to another the user changes personality, that is, profile, to fit the space he or she is in at that particular moment. The user can change profiles by modifying an old one or by purchasing or borrowing a new (ready-made) one, or the modification may take place automatically (i.e., to trump up a profile for the occasion). A ready-made profile is a software programm riding on the data stream, and its job is to configure (e.g., to decide what personal information to give, choose the level of user expertise) and personalize the systems, applications, and networks encountered. The change of profile in a fluid cyberspace

is a frequently recurring event, which needs to be negotiated. Negotiation is performed either automatically or by intelligent agents or by users or by a combination of these (see Figure 1: the arrows indicate a change of profile). One should observe that a change of profile usually means a change of hierarchical position, over and above the change in position that follows from a transition from one space to another. The advantages of multiple profiles are significant. The user is not locked into a certain role or *persona* but can quickly, easily, automatically, and, if need be, purposefully "by hand" change his or her profile to meet the requirements of the context and situation of use.

BOUNDARY CROSSING IN EVERYDAY LIFE

As Weiser (1991) predicted, computing is disappearing to the background. The fact that it disappears from the center of attention helps the user focus on what he or she really is doing, that is, focus on the real task at hand and not the tools. Foregrounding (i.e., deciding what the real task at hand is) is extremely difficult to master since background knowledge is largely tacit and increasingly embedded in the technological infrastructure. As we know from human interaction in general, keeping some knowledge at the background and uncodified is not something neutral but may be a significant exercise in discursive power (Duguid, 2005). Therefore, the user and not the technology should be in charge of how, when, and which things move from the background to the foreground or vice versa (Abowd & Mynatt, 2000). As a rule, the user is unable to interpret the technical infrastructure underlying the interface. The user should be able to do so because technologies most likely have at least partly inherent values and consequences. Technologies are not infinitely malleable locally (Brey, in press; Kallinikos, 2002; Longford, 2005; Winner, 1986). It means that even if the user could make sense of the underlying technical layers, he or she has relatively few (physical or social) means of modifying them. Unfortunately, our digital media literacy in general is lacking not just in "reading" skills but much more so in "writing" (e.g., programming) skills, which prevents users from exploiting the already small potential for molding technology. Gleason and Friedman (2005) argue that we should be able to predict the consequences of our use of the information society technologies (ISTs) in the same way as we in the physical world are expected to predict the potential impact of our tools to others. Technology has to be domesticated (Punie, Bogdanowicz, Berg, Pauwels, & Burgelman, 2003). Rather than the technological and economic considerations, the user and his or her needs, capabilities, and routines in the everyday life should inform design: "Ambient Intelligence will be aware of the specific characteristics of human presence and personality" (Punie, 2003, p. 6). This sort of sociological everyday life approach, advocated by Punie and his colleagues, starts from human concerns, trying to identify barriers for the use of ISTs in everyday life. Hence any attempts at helping the user cross all sorts of barriers and boundaries—however petty they may seem—in his or her everyday use of the ISTs are highly welcome.

In order to further illustrate some central concepts discussed so far, we will present a few simple examples that we encountered in several research projects (mobile learning project and mobile physicians) and in the Finnish mobile telecommunications market (Multi-Sim and Dual-Sim).

The first example originates from a research project on mobile learning. In this project, several students used PDAs during several weeks in an IS course given at the Åbo Akademi University. Students borrowed the devices during the project and used the mobile system in parallel with their own mobile phones. The mobile system could be used to retrieve course materials, interactively discuss course matters, and to check if other course participants were remotely available for interaction. The students reported that the use of the PDA in parallel with their own mobile phones appeared to be a problem because it was not possible to synchronize information (e.g., personal contacts) between the two devices (Patokorpi, Tétard, Qiao, & Sjövall, 2007). The students had to juggle between two different information spaces and to choose the information space they needed depending on the situation, while the devices did not support such transition from space to space.

Our second example relates to a project where mobile physicians, who act in both civil and military medicine, use a mobile medical database, using the same mobile device. The mobile medical IS, used in this research, is designed by Duodecim Publication Ltd. It is a set of medical information and knowledge databases. It contains the Evidence-Based Medicine Guideline (EBMG) (available in both English and Finnish) with Cochrane abstracts, a pharmacology database, Pharmaca Fennica, with a wireless update service for a complete medicine price list, the international diagnosis code guide (ICD-10) in Finnish, a laboratory guide by the Helsinki University Hospital, an emergency care guide issued by the Meilahti Hospital, a medical dictionary of over 57,000 terms, and a comprehensive database over healthcare-related addresses and contact information (pharmacies, hospitals, health centres). The duties and information needs are different in civil and military medicine. In the project, physicians expressed the need for the possibility to customize the database according to the situation at hand. For example, the defence forces do not use the same drugs as in civil medicine (Tétard, Shengnan, Harkke, & Collan, 2006).

Multi-Sim is a service introduced by a major telecommunications company on the Finnish market in 2006. The service allows customers to use one mobile phone number on two phones, without the need to transfer the SIM card from one phone to another. In practice, the customer has two SIM cards (one main subscription and an additional card) that can be installed in his/her phones. Additionally, the number is shown to the recipient of the call or text message as the same, regardless of whether the main subscription or the additional card is used (TeliaSonera, 2006). The service is very handy for users who need to use different phones in different situations, but still want to be reached through the same number, regardless of which phone they use. This service illustrates the concept of multiple-profiling: The user has the choice to use a different device according to his/her own needs, whereas the system is transparent for the recipients of who will not need to know which device is used.

The Dual-Sim service is expected to be launched in fall 2006. Several manufacturers have produced devices that allow the use of several SIM cards in the same phone; although not simultaneously. The innovation of the new Dual-Sim service will be that both SIM cards will be available at the same time. The service will be handy for people who want to use the same device in several situations, but need to use different connections (for example, one connection for leisure and one connection for work; or one connection including a special set of mobile services and the other including another set of features). This illustrates the concept of multi-profiling: using this service, the user could use the type of connection he/she needs without changing the device or the SIM card.

One promising advance, which can be observed on the telecommunications market, is the launch of new devices that integrate WLAN and 3G technologies (for example, Nokia mobile phones). Beyond the possibility that these devices offer to use different network access depending on the context and the preferences of the user, these new devices will offer seamless integration between different access technologies, so that the shift from one network to the other will be transparent to the user, for example, when a user moves between geographical areas with different network coverage and different network access technology.

The previous examples illustrate how advances in mobile technologies (devices, networks, and software) will enable true nomadicity and extend our understanding of mobility. Although several problems remain, as illustrated in the first and the second examples; we believe that technology advances illustrated in the latter examples will solve several problems by enabling fluidity between different information spaces, giving the user control over the transition from one information space to another and allowing transparency about the different information spaces.

CONCLUSION

In this chapter, we have analyzed some central concepts widely used in ICT literature. In line with Wegner (1997), Kleinrock (2001), and Sørensen (2002, 2003), we argue that these concepts are not any more satisfactory as tools of scientific research into advanced ICT. As the technology has evolved, some of these key concepts have adopted a confusing double meaning. For instance, nomadicity implies both the technological capability to deal with temporary disconnectedness, caused by movement from one connected place to another connected place, and the seamless technological support for nomads, for whom being on the move is the normal state of affairs. Mobility means both to be able to disregard context ("anywhere, anytime") and to enrich interaction by contextual factors. It is beginning to be a widely acknowledged fact that context has not become less important but more important than ever. Consequently, current research is focusing more and more on contextual issues. One decisive factor in contextual mobility is personalization, but, clearly, present personalization techniques are not yet up to the challenge.

Wegner (1997) and his associates question whether the algorithmic model of computing can tell us what is happening for instance in distributed multi-agent systems, which they call interactive systems. Indeed, we live in a largely "man-made" world and there seems to be need for attempts—similar to Wegner's—to conceptually bridge the gap between humans and machines. It seems also clear to us that we need to come to a better understanding of interactivity. Unfortunately, the term interaction is currently carrying excessive intellectual baggage.

We are inclined to think that Wegner, Kleinrock, Sørensen, and their associates are right in claiming that certain very advanced ICT environments constitute an emerging paradigm, whose present-day manifestations include nomadic and ubiquitous computing. In this chapter, we have sought to make sense of the alleged new paradigm by presenting and discussing some candidates for conceptual tools. Sørensen and his associates have proposed the metaphor of fluidity to describe the patterns of social interaction in advanced mobile ICT. We have presented and discussed the concepts of micromobility (borrowed from Luff & Heath, 1998), metaspace, and transient hierarchies. Our objective has been to pin down fluid interaction into something concrete so that we do not lose sight of the technological limitations and the practical details of the situated actual human-computer and machine-to-machine interaction. We believe that the concepts of micromobility, metaspaces, and transient hierarchies open up a field of empirical study into the conditions and practices of digital communication, collaboration, and learning capturing the mixture of social-technological and real-virtual aspects of interaction in cyberspace. Lastly, we have suggested multiple-profiling as one means of meeting personalization requirements in a truly nomadic environment. We believe that a key question in the near future is how the user of advanced mobile technology could be made more aware of as well as empowered to have more control over the multiple spaces he or she inhabits and the numerous boundary crossings that he or she is forced to perform.

REFERENCES

Abowd, G. D., & Mynatt, E. D. (2000). Charting past, present, and future research in ubiquitous computing. *ACM Transactions on Computer-Human Interaction, 7*(1) 29-58.

Alanko, T., Kojo, M., Liljeberg, M., & Raatikainen, K. (1999). Mobile access to the Internet: A mediator-based solution. *Internet Research: Electronic Networking Applications and Policy, 9*(1), 58-65.

Allison, R. B. (1998). Multiple personality disorder, dissociative identity disorder, and internalized imaginary companions. *Hypnos, 25*(3), 125-133.

Anckar, B., Carlsson, C., & Walden, P. (2003). Factors affecting consumer decisions and intents in mobile commerce: Empirical insights. *16th Bled E-Commerce Conference. ETransformation*, Bled, Slovenia.

Anckar, B., & Eriksson, N. (2003). Mobility: The basis for value creation in mobile commerce? In *Proceedings of the SSGRR 2003s Conference*, L'Aquila, Italy.

Avital, M., Robey, D., Sawyer, S., & Sorensen, C. (2004). Social and organizational issues in ubiquitous computing. In K. J. Lyytinen, Y. Yoo, U. Varshney, M. Ackerman, G. Davis, M. Avital, D. Robey, S. Sawyer, & C. Sørensen (Eds.), *Surfing the Next Wave: Design and Implementation Challenges of Ubiquitous Computing, Communications of the AIS, 13*(40), pp. 697-716.

Bahl, P., & Padmanabhan, V. N. (2000). Radar: An in-building rf-based user location and tracking system. In *Proceedings of the IEEE Infocom*, Tel-Aviv, Israel.

Bar, F. (2001). The construction of marketplace architecture. In The BRIE-IGCC E-conomy Project Task Force on the Internet (Eds.), *Tracking a transformation: E-Commerce and the terms of competition in industries* (pp. 27-49). Washington, DC: Brookings Institution Press.

Bellavista, P., Corradi, A., Montanari, R., & Stefanelli, C. (2003). Dynamic binding in mobile applications: A middleware approach. *IEEE Internet Computing, 7*(2), 34-42.

Boyle, J. (1997). *Foucault in cyberspace: Surveillance, sovereignty, and hard-wired censors.* Retrieved January 18, 2005, from www.law.duke.edu/boylesite/foucl.html

Brey, L. (in press). Theorizing the cultural quality of new media. *Téchne: Journal of the Society for Philosophy and Technology.*

Carlsson, C., & Walden, P. (2002). Mobile commerce: Some extensions of core concepts and key issues. In *Proceedings of the SSGRR International Conference on Advances in Infrastructure for e-Business, e-Education, e-Science and e-Medicine on the Internet*, L'Aquila, Italy.

Castells, M. (2001). *The Internet galaxy: Reflections on the Internet, business, and society.* UK: Oxford University Press.

Chen, H. (2003). *An intelligent broker architecture for context-aware systems.* PhD dissertation proposal. Retrieved May 1, 2006, from http://umbc.edu/~hchen4/

Chen, Y.-F. R., & Petrie, C. (2003). Ubiquitous mobile computing. *IEEE Internet Computing, 7*(2), 16-17.

Dahlbom, B., & Ljungberg, F. (1998). Mobile informatics. *Scandinavian Journal of Information Systems, 10*(1&2), 227-234.

Dix, A., Rodden, T., Davies, N., Trevor, J., Friday, A., & Palfreyman, K. (2000). Exploiting space and location as a design framework for interactive mobile systems. *ACM Transactions on Computer-Human Interaction, 7*(3), 281-321.

Duguid, P. (2005). "The art of knowing": Social and tacit dimensions of knowledge and the limits of the community of practice. *The Information Society, 21,* 109-118.

Fagrell, H., Ljungberg, F., & Kristoffersen, S. (1999). Exploring support for knowledge management in mobile work. In *Proceedings of the 6th European Conference on Computer Supported Cooperative Work*, Copenhagen, Denmark.

Floch, J., Hallsteinsen, S., Lie, A., & Myrhaug, H. I. (2001). *A reference model for context-aware mobile services.* Retrieved July 29, 2003, from www.nik.no/2001/06-floch.pdf

Gleason, D. H., & Friedman, L. (2005). Proposal for an accessible conception of cyberspace. *Journal of Information, Communication & Ethics in Society, 1,* 15-23.

Goldin, D., & Wegner, P. (2004). *The origins of the Turing thesis myth* (Tech. Rep. No. CS-04-13). Providence, RI: Brown University.

Harter, A., Hopper, A., Steggles, P., Ward, A., & Webster, P. (1999). The anatomy of a context-aware application. In *Proceedings of the ACM/IEEE MobiCom.*

Hawick, K. A., & James, H. A. (2003). Middleware for context sensitive mobile applications. In C. Johnson, P. Montague, & C. Steketee (Eds.), *Workshop on Wearable, Invisible, Context-Aware, Ambient, Pervasive and Ubiquitous Computing* (Vol. 21). Adelaide, Australia. Conferences in Research and Practice in Information Technology.

Järvenpää, S. L., & Leidner, D. E. (1999). Communication and trust in global virtual teams. *Organization Science, 10*(6), 791-815.

Junglas, I. A., & Watzon, R. T. (2003). *U-commerce: A conceptual extension of e- and m-commerce.* Paper presented at the International Conference on Information Systems, Seattle, WA.

Kakihara, M., & Sørensen, C. (2001). Expanding the "mobility" concept. *ACM SIGGROUP Bulletin archive, 22*(3), 33-37.

Kakihara, M., & Sørensen, C. (2002). Mobility: An extended perspective. In *Proceedings of the*

Hawai'i International Conference on System Sciences, Big Island.

Kallinikos, J. (2002, December 14-16). Re-opening the black box of technology: Artifacts and human agency. In *23rd ICIS* (pp. 287-294). Barcelona, Spain.

Kanter, T. G. (2003). Attaching context-aware services to moving locations. *IEEE Internet Computing, 7*(2), 43-51.

Karat, C.-M., Blom, J., & Karat, J. (2003). Designing personalized user experiences for E-Commerce: Theory, methods, and research. In *CHI 2003: New Horizons* (pp. 1040-1041).

Keen, P. G. W., & Mackintosh, R. (2001). *The freedom economy: Gaining the M-Commerce edge in the era of the wireless Internet.* New York: Osborne/McGraw-Hill.

Keil, D., & Goldin, D. (2003). Modelling indirect interaction in open computational systems. In *Proceedings of the Twelfth IEEE International Workshops on Enabling Technologies: Infrastructure for Collaborative Enterprises (WETICE'03)*, Linz, Austria.

Kleinrock, L. (1996). Nomadicity: Anytime, anywhere in a disconnected world. *Mobile Networks and Applications, 1,* 351-357.

Kleinrock, L. (2001). Breaking loose. *Communications of the ACM, 44*(9), 41-45.

Kopomaa, T. (2000). *The city in your pocket. Birth of the mobile information society.* Helsinki, Finland: Gaudeamus.

Kramer, J., Noronha, S., & Vergo, J. (2000). A user-centered design approach to personalization. *Communications of the ACM, 42*(8), 45-48.

Kristensen, B. B. May, D. Jensen, L. K., Gersbo-Møller, C., & Maersk, P. N. (2003). *Reality-virtuality continuum systems empowered with pervasive and ubiquitous computing technology: Combination and integration of real world and*

model systems. Retrieved June 5, 2006, from http://scholar.google.fi/scholar?hl=en&lr=&q=cache:hr5pv8eE-EMJ:www.mip.sdu.dk/~bbk/teaching/sw04/reality54.pdf+kristensen+2003+virtual

Kuhn, T. (1962). *The structure of scientific revolutions.* IL: University of Chicago Press.

Lee, H., & Sawyer, S. (2002). Conceptualizing time and space: Information technology, work, and organization. In *Proceedings of the Twenty-Third International Conference on Information Systems* (pp. 279-286).

Liljedal, A. (2002). *Design implications for context aware mobile games.* Retrieved February 18, 2003, from www.interactiveinstitute.se/mobility/Files/Master%20Thesis.pdf

Lim, E.-P., Wang, Y., Ong, K.-L., & Hwang, S.-Y. (2003). In search of knowledge about mobile users. *ERCIM News, 54,* 10-11.

Longford, G. (2005). Pedagogies of digital citizenship and the politics of code. *Téchne, 9*(1), 68-96.

Luff, P., & Heath, C. (1998). Mobility in collaboration. In *Proceedings of the 1998 ACM conference on Computer Supported Cooperative Work* (pp. 305-314).

Luo, H., Jiang, Z., Kim, B.-J., Shankaranarayanan, N. K, & Henry, P. (2003). Integrating wireless LAN and cellular data for the enterprise. *IEEE Internet Computing, 7*(2), 25-33.

Lyytinen, K., & Yoo, Y. (2002a). Issues and challenges in ubiquitous computing. *Communications of the ACM, 45*(12), 63-65.

Lyytinen, K., & Yoo, Y. (2002b). Research commentary: The next wave of nomadic computing. *Information Systems Research, 13*(4), 377-388.

Messeter, J., Brandt, E., Halse, J., & Johansson, M. (2004). Contextualizing mobile IT. In *Proceedings of the 2004 conference on Designing interactive systems: processes, practices, methods, and techniques* (pp. 27-36). New York: ACM Press.

O'Hare, G. M. P. (2000). Agents, mobility and virtuality: A necessary synergy. *Proceedings of International ICSC Symposium on Multi-agents and Mobile Agents in Virtual Organisations and E-Commerce—MAMA 2000.*

Omojokun, O., & Isbell, C. L. (2003). User modeling for personalized universal appliance interaction. In *Proceedings of the 2003 Conference on Diversity in Computing* (pp. 65-68).

Orlikowski, W. J., & Iacono, C. S. (2001). Desperately seeking the "IT" in IT research: A call to theorizing the IT artifact. *Information Systems Research, 12*(2), 121-134.

Patokorpi, E. (2006). Low knowledge in cyberspace: Abduction, tacit knowledge, aura and the mobility of knowledge. *Journal of Human Systems Management, 25*(3), 211-220.

Patokorpi, E., Tétard, F., Qiao, F., & Sjövall, N. (2007). Mobile learning objects to support constructivist learning. In K. Harman & A. Koohang (Eds.), *Learning objects: Applications, implications and future directions,* (pp. 187-222). California: Informing Science Press.

Perry, M., O'Hara, K., Sellen, A., Brown, B., & Harper, R. (2001). Dealing with mobility: Understanding access anytime, anywhere. *ACM Transactions on Computer-Human Interaction, 8*(4), 323-347.

Pica, D., & Kakihara, M. (2003). The duality of mobility: Designing fluid organizations through stable interaction. Paper presented at the *11th European Conference on Information Systems (ECIS 2003),* Naples, Italy.

Prasopoulou, E., Panteli, N., & Pouloudi, N. (2004). Social accessibility and the mobile phone: A temporal perspective. In T. W. Bynum, N. Pouloudi, S. Rogerson, & T. Spyrou (Eds.), *Proceedings of the seventh international conference Ethicomp 2004: Challenges for the Citizen of the Information Society* (Vol. II, pp. 773-784). Mytilene, Greece: University of the Aegean.

Prasse, M., & Rittgen, P. (1998). Why Church's thesis still holds. Some notes on Peter Wegner's tracts on interaction and computability. *The Computer Journal, 41*(6), 357-362.

Priyantha, N. B., Miu, A. K. L., Balakrishnan, H., & Teller, S. (2001). *The cricket compass for context-aware mobile applications.* Retrieved February 18, 2003, from http://nms.lcs.mit.edu/papers/CricketCompass.pdf

Punie, Y. (2003). *What bends the trend? Technological foresight and the socialization of ubiquitous computing.* EMTEL2, KEY DELIVERABLE Work Package 2.

Punie, Y., Bogdanowicz, M., Berg, A.-J., Pauwels, C., & Burgelman, J.-C. (2003, September). *Living and working in the information society: Quality of life in a digital world.* A Final Deliverable of the European Media Technology and Everyday Life Network (EMTEL).

Purao, S., & Krogstie, J. (2004). *Impact of ubiquitous computing.* In K. J. Lyytinen, Y. Yoo, U. Varshney, M. Ackerman, G. Davis, M. Avital, D. Robey, S. Sawyer, & C. Sørensen (Eds.), (pp. 705-707).

Rappa, M. (2004). The utility business model and the future of computing services. *IBM Systems Journal, 43*(1), 32-42.

Schilit, B., Adams, N., & Want, R. (1994). Context-aware computing applications. Paper presented at the *IEEE Workshop on Mobile Computing Systems and Applications,* Santa Cruz, CA.

Smyth, B. (2003). The missing link—User-experience and incremental revenue generation on the mobile Internet. *ERCIM News, 54,* 11-12.

Sørensen, C. (2002). Digital nomads and mobile service. *Receiver. Vodafone.* Retrieved December 11, 2004, from www.receiver.vodafone.com

Sørensen, C. (2003). *Research issues in mobile informatics: Classical concerns, pragmatic issues and emerging discourses.* Retrieved January 5, 2005, from is.lse.ac.uk/staff/sorensen/downloads/Sorensen2003.pdf

Sørensen, C., & Pica, D. (2005, April 1). Tales from the police: Rhythms of interaction with mobile technologies. *Information and Organization, 15*(2), 125-146.

Spriestersbach, A., & Vogler, H. (2002). *Location-awareness for improving the usability of mobile enterprise applications.* Retrieved February 18, 2003, from http://www.sapdesignguild.org/community/readers/reader_mobile.asp

Stone, A. (1996). *The war of desire and technology at the close of the mechanical age.* The MIT Press.

TeliaSonera. (2006, January 30). [Press release]. Retrieved April 25, 2006, from http://wpy.observer.se/wpyfs/00/00/00/00/00/06/D7/7B/wkr0007.pdf

Tétard, F., Shengnan, H., Harkke, V., & Collan, M. (2006). Smart phone as a medium to access medical information: A field study of military physicians. In *Proceedings of Helsinki Mobility Roundtable.*

Varshney, U. (2004). *Technology issues in ubiquitous computing.* In K. J. Lyytinen, Y. Yoo, U. Varshney, M. Ackerman, G. Davis, M. Avital, D. Robey, S. Sawyer, & C. Sørensen (Eds.), (pp. 699-702).

Wegner, P. (1997). Why interaction is more powerful than algorithms? *Communications of the ACM, 40*(5), 81-91.

Wegner, P., & Goldin, D. (1999). *Interaction, computability, and Church's thesis.* [Draft]. Retrieved October 29, 2004, from http://www.cse.uconn.edu/~dqg/papers/

Weiser, M. (1991). The computer for the twenty-first century. *Scientific American, 625*, 94-104.

Wiberg, M., & Ljungberg, F. (2001). Exploring the vision of "anytime, anywhere" in the context of mobile work. In Y. Malhotra (Ed.), *Knowledge management and virtual organizations* (pp. 157-169). Hershey, PA: Idea Group.

Winner, L. (1986). *The whale and the reactor: A search for limits in an age of high technology.* IL: University of Chicago Press.

Chapter II
The Future of M–Commerce:
The Role of Bluetooth and WiMax

David C. Yen
Miami University, USA

Sean Lancaster
Miami University, USA

ABSTRACT

This chapter discusses the growing significance of m-commerce with special focus on Bluetooth and WiMax. There is a detailed investigation of the components involved with, and the marketplace for, m-commerce transactions. The chapter concludes with the future opportunities and obstacles for m-commerce. The authors hope that the reader will gain a better understanding of, not only of m-commerce, but the impact of Bluetooth and WiMax.

INTRODUCTION

As m-commerce continues to grow in overall use and importance for modern business, it is critical to examine future opportunities, trends, questions, and related concerns. By understanding the future implications and outlooks, m-commerce venders, IT/IS developers, and users can continue to pursue this incredible mobile or wireless movement. Additionally, the increasing adoption of short range technologies like Bluetooth, as well as long range technologies like WiMax, are increasingly aiding m-commerce. These technologies have increased the number of applications for mobile users and strengthened the future of m-commerce. It is important to note that m-commerce is not only expected to expand its share of the e-commerce market, but also to expand the overall e-commerce market through rapid evolution of m-commerce services. M-commerce requires careful e-com-

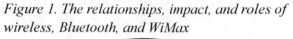

Figure 1. The relationships, impact, and roles of wireless, Bluetooth, and WiMax

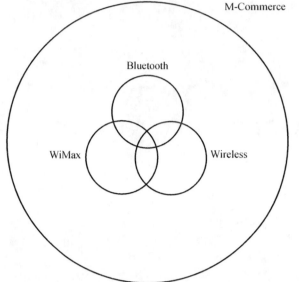

merce adaptation to include mobile access for enhanced services and business communications that are not only anytime, but also anywhere. This chapter will present the importance of, the components and technologies involved with, the future market forecast, and key future trends and issues for m-commerce.

Learning Objectives

* Understand m-commerce and its role in modern business
* Investigate specific m-commerce technologies
* Examine the future trends impacting m-commerce
* Understand the relationship between Bluetooth, WiMax and m-commerce (see Figure 1)

BACKGROUND

A busy executive on a PDA, an anxious driver using a cell phone, and a college student walking to class listening to his or her Mp3 player; all of the aforementioned are common sights in today's world. All are dependent on wireless technology. Wireless has changed many aspects in our lives, including how we conduct business.

M-commerce is the ability to conduct e-commerce transactions over wireless media. Examples of m-commerce include buying and downloading a ring tone to your cell phone, acting on the real-time stock quote on your PDA, or subscribing to have last night's news and highlights sent to your mobile device.

M-commerce requires similar steps as a physical transaction. An m-commerce transaction is more than just checking an e-mail message from a wireless device. A buyer and seller must agree on an item and price, delivery of the product must be made, and payment to the seller must be completed.

That being said, mobility must still be involved during the transaction and a wireless device must be used by the buyer, the seller, or both. Common examples include cell phones; palm pilots or PDAs; or blackberrys. Even more so, the wireless device should be connected to a wireless ISP and not just an extension of a hardwired LAN.

Wireless applications such as pagers, cellular phones, and satellite television have been around for years. Increasingly today, mobile data communication is viewed as an emerging area for many industries, and companies are increasing their investment accordingly. While many recent developments in the wireless industry have been "flops" (including Mobitex messaging, Cellular Digital Packet Data services), the development and acceptance of the Wireless Application Protocol (WAP) has given wireless carriers and mobile service providers sufficient confidence to introduce a new generation of wireless applications like Bluetooth and WiMax.

The PC Industry

Wireless communication has had great impact on the personal computing industry. Most desktop and laptops come readily equipped for wireless devices. WiFi (802.11) and Bluetooth are commonly used in a multitude of applications. Access to hotspots and wireless clouds are routine connections for personal computers.

Another significant impact to the PC industry is that wireless communication becomes a key feature of palmtop computers. 3Com's palm computers now allow users to access their e-mail and to access over 100 different Web sites.

The Communication Service Industry

Most common carriers offer wireless telephone service now. Cell phones are readily used for a variety of reasons ranging from business, to social, to family connections. Recently, Sprint and MCI have been more active on wireless service than their primary competitor, AT&T, which has been more focused on "wired" fiber optic networks.

As more applications over IP networks become possible, there should be even greater impact on the communication service industry. A convergence of television, telephone, radio, and video applications will allow companies who offer wireless bandwidth to compete with large groupings of products and packages.

Other Industries

The microprocessor industry has also responded to the increasing demand for wireless products. In December of 1999, Intel created a new "wireless communications and computing group" that focuses on creating cellular and wireless communication products and technologies. Advanced Micro Devices (AMD), one of the leading providers of wireless communications, has recently formed an alliance with Motorola.

Firms looking to innovate wireless processors that can quickly and efficiently perform the needed tasks while consuming reasonable levels of power. Speed of execution and battery life have become critical components for wireless devices.

Global Society

TIA's 2006 telecommunications Market Review and Forecast (Flanigan, 2006) found that there were more than 194 million wireless subscribers in the United States in 2005. That figure is expected to grow to 270 million by 2009. Most of them subscribe to mobile telephone services, but an increasing number of subscribers take advantage of wireless services for palmtop computers and Web accesses from their mobile phones.

The term the *wireless Web* is used to describe Web sites that can be viewed from these mobile devices. Today, wireless users are viewing the scores of their favorite teams, researching stocks, reading the current headlines, watching videos, and purchasing goods and services.

E-commerce companies work on providing their services available through wireless devices. Online bookstores such as Amazon.com and Barnesandnoble.com are among the first retailers to let handheld users order products. One of the most well known e-commerce companies that take advantage of wireless technology is Peapod Inc., an online grocery store. Peapod believes that services provided through wireless communication are important to their customers, because most people do not have PCs in their kitchens. They currently offer services for the Palm VII platform and plan to expand the service to mobile phones in the future.

M-COMMERCE ISSUES

Businesses should be interested in adapting their e-commerce infrastructures and including m-commerce applications for a variety of reasons. Predominantly, as the wireless title pronounces, m-commerce offers the freedom and flexibility of not needing to be plugged in and tethered to a desk or office. Business can be conducted without the use of the bulky desktop and office environment. An additional benefit of m-commerce is the convenience that goes along with that freedom. This allows business to be extended beyond the traditional norms and truly be conducted from anywhere at anytime.

Along with the aforementioned benefits is the ability to better tap into your data to drive efficient and timely decision making. This allows for businesses to offer higher levels of customer support and to catch and act on potential problems sooner than by relying on hardwired communication. In fact, a true wireless infrastructure, where the business is capable of sending wireless communication and the consumers are enabled to receive, offers enormous one-one marketing capabilities. Wireless environments allow for closer to real-time communications as messages can be received on the fly (Zeng, Yen, & Hwang, 2003).

The increased speed, convenience, and ubiquity of wireless communication should not be underestimated. Consider the move from traditional telephones to cordless phones, and to today's cell phones. Telecom users have shown a preference for the freedom that wireless devices offer.

However, as with any emerging technology, there are a number of critical issues that must be planned for in order to effectively implement a wireless infrastructure. A major downfall for m-commerce, to this stage, is the small size of wireless devices. Whether it is a small display or a tiny keypad, viewing and interacting with wireless content is at a disadvantage versus the high resolution and common keyboards associated with desktop computing. It is easy to recognize the quick clicking of students frantically sending text messages to friends (Bai, Chou, Yen, & Lin, 2005).

Another negative of wireless applications is the potential lack of security. A business must implement and communicate a comprehensive wireless security plan to ensure that its own architecture is not at risk. In addition, these firms must provide a secure wireless environment to their customers and trading partners. The increased freedom and flexibility offered by wireless do come partnered with increased risk of cybercrime.

Finally, as wireless is a relatively new innovation, users will need to have education, training, and continued experience. Wireless operators must struggle with the negative perceptions of the wireless link. Moreover, the complexity of technical standards, the difficulty and the accompanied expense of roaming outside a given carrier's territory, and the limits to how much information can be displayed attractively on tiny screens are regarded as major obstacles to the operations with relative simple inquiries and responses. Thus, educating the end users about the implications of doing m-commerce on a cell phone or PDA will be a crucial factor for the technology more widely accepted (Yen & Chou, 2000).

A number of key m-commerce characteristics are profiled in Table 1.

Table 1. Characteristics of m-commerce

Currentness	Allows for real-time communication from any time or location
Accessibility	Enables users to stay in contact with desired parties
Personalization	Allows for one-one marketing opportunities and personalized data communications
Convenience	Aside from allowing access from any time or location, m-commerce applications are increasingly easy to use
Localization	Allows users to find information on a specific location when used in conjunction with technologies like global positioning systems (GPS)

M-COMMERCE: COMPONENTS

M-commerce applications use a variety of components. These components are critical in allowing customers to conduct transactions. A diagram of the relationship between the components is provided in Figure 2. The major components involved are a Web merchant server, a content conversion server, a wireless access protocol server, a digital payment server, a wireless payment proxy, and a subscriber management system (Zeng et al., 2003).

Web Merchant Server. Similar to a brick-and-mortar store for consumers, a Web merchant server is a virtual storefront on the Internet. It maintains and displays the listing of products, descriptions, prices, and availability.

Content Conversion Server. A content conversion server is responsible for taking the existing HTML from a Web page and converting it to a wireless enables format, like WML. This component works as an important gateway to link the Web merchant server and the various wireless devices.

WAP Server. A WAP server connects WAP-enabled hardware, like PDAs and phones with

Figure 2. The interpretative relationship of m-commerce components

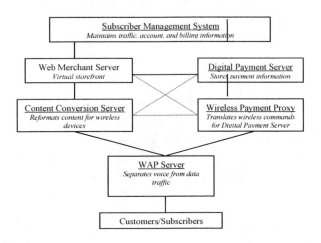

applications hosted on the server. In addition, it routes content based on whether it is voice or data traffic (Leavitt, 2000).

Digital Payment Server. A digital payment server electronically stores consumer's payment information: credit cards, shipping locations, and so forth. This server is essential to the convenience of one-click shopping as it automatically supplies the necessary details to complete the transaction (Karnouskos & Fraunhofer, 2004).

Wireless Payment Proxy. Wireless payment proxy converts wireless commands from mobile devices into commands that can be understood by digital payment servers.

Subscriber Management System. The subscriber management system maintains the traffic, account, and billing information for a firm's wireless operations ensuring a stable and effective m-commerce experience (Zeng et al., 2003).

M-COMMERCE: TECHNOLOGY

Technological innovation has been critical to the adoption of m-commerce. The following sections profile important network and service technologies.

Network Technologies

Network technologies have greatly evolved over the years. TCP/IP enabled the shift from circuit-switched to packet-switched networks. Cellular networks have moved from analog to digital technologies. This evolution over the years has been categorized as first-generation (1G), second-generation (2G), 2.5G and third-generation (3G) wireless. Finally, these technologies encompass short-range communication, including bluetooth and ultra wideband shortwave, as well as local area networks and metropolitan networks, such as WiFi and WiMax (see Figure 3).

Figure 3. An overview of wireless networking technologies

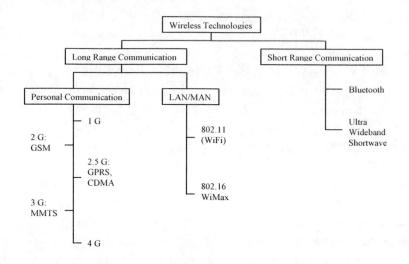

GSM

GSM is a 2G standard for mobile communication. The European Telecommunications Standards Institute (ETSI) membership and technical teams built the GSM standard and The Third Generation Partnership Project (3GPP) now owns GSM along with its own successor standards.

GSM operates in the frequency range of 900/1800 MHz in Europe and 1900 MHz in the US. GSM operates in over 200 countries worldwide providing almost complete coverage in Western Europe, and growing coverage in the Americas, Asia, and elsewhere. For more information visit (http://www.gsmworld.com).

General Packet Radio System (GPRS)

General Packet Radio System (GPRS) is a 2.5G technology that enables higher bandwidth for mobile wireless applications. GPRS allows for multimedia graphics and video to take a larger role in wireless developments. From a historical perspective, GPRS was a crucial step in the move from GSM to Universal Mobile Telephone System (UMTS), from 2G to 3G wireless.

Code Division Multiple Access (CDMA)

A competing standard to GSM, Code Division Multiple Access (CDMA) is the proprietary wireless standard of Qualcomm and Ericsson. Unlike GSM, CDMA is much more common in the United States than elsewhere in the world. CDMA is considered a "spread spectrum" technology, meaning that it spreads the data from a wireless signal over a much greater bandwidth. A CDMA call may start with a standard rate of 9.6 kbps before spreading to a transmitting rate of approximately 1.23 Mbps.

UMTS

UMTS is a European 3G cellular technology. Under optimal conditions, UMTS can deliver content at a bandwidth of 2 Mbps. However, 384 Kbps is a more realistic expectation in a populated area. Because of the dramatic performance loss, UMTS does have its critics and the adoption of this standard has been slower than originally expected (Holma & Toskala, 2000).

Fourth Generation (4G)

Fourth generation (4G) is considered the future for wireless traffic. The Institute of Electrical and Electronics Engineers (IEEE) considers 4G to be "3G and beyond." Specifically, 4G is expected to provide significant improvements to streaming high quality audio and video formats to wireless devices. A 4G network will be a true packet switched network.

4G wireless is not one single technology, but a combination of many technologies all packed into one. It will incorporate technologies from WiFi, Bluetooth, and cellular signals to TV and radio broadcasts, and satellite communication. 4G will have the capability to integrate all these technologies into one seamless worldwide network, and all will be able to connect at lightening fast speeds. It will also be small enough that it will allow just about anything from a laptop to a dog collar to have a transceiver in it and be assigned its own IP address. Japan has set out to be the leader in 4G and they expect to have it by 2007 and be able to transfer at speeds up to 100 Mbps (Dursch, Yen, & Huang, 2005).

Bluetooth

Bluetooth is a wireless technology that can be used for short-range communication between different Bluetooth-enabled devices. Common examples of Bluetooth devices include wireless video game controllers, PDAs that can be synched to their docking station, and mobile phone headsets. Bluetooth works in the unlicensed 2.4 GHz industrial, scientific, and medical (ISM) band and uses frequency-hopping spread-spectrum (FHSS) communication, which transmits data over different frequencies at different time intervals. This is accomplished by making "hops" to different frequencies through the ISM band. A device makes about 1,600 hops per second, which is spaced out over 1 MHz (Ersala & Yen, 2002).

Ultra Wideband Shortwave

Ultra wideband is a wireless technology that sends brief, intermittent pulses of high bandwidth communications. Like Bluetooth, it suffers from offering connections at a very short range. However, its high bandwidth capability gives it promise for m-commerce applications.

WiFi

IEEE developed the 802.11x standards for wireless local area networking (LSN). These standards have become quite popular and coined WiFi by users and the media. The 802.11a band operates in the 5 GHz frequency band and is limited to primarily line of sight communication. 802.11b and 802.11g both operate on the 2.4 GHz frequency band and therefore are subject to interference from common household devices such as microwaves and cordless phones. The IEEE has had great success innovating and adding to the original standard improving both available bandwidth and acceptable operating distance. Despite the improvements, WiFi is still viewed as a LAN technology.

WiMax

The IEEE developed the 802.16 with the idea of creating a wireless networking technology suitable for coverage of large metropolitan areas, sometimes referred to as metropolitan area networks (MAN). WiMax, while a wireless standard, joins other high broadband competitors like DSL and cable. It offers great potential as it is the first wireless standard that offers higher bandwidth capabilities than cellular providers.

Service Technologies

Wireless Application Protocol

The purpose of wireless application protocol (WAP) is to provide operators, infrastructure, terminal manufacturers, and content developers a common environment that should enable development of value-added services for mobile phones. Essentially, WAP is the technology that makes it possible to link wireless devices (such as mobile phones) to the Internet by translating Internet information so it can be displayed on the display screen of a mobile telephone or on other portable devices. WAP is an open, global specification developed by WAP forum that has over 500 members. Motorola, Nokia, Ericsson, and the U.S. software company Phone.com (formerly Unwired Planet) were the initial partners that teamed up in mid 1997 to develop and deploy WAP. WAP is an attempt to define the standard for how content from the Internet is filtered for mobile communications. Content is now readily available on the Internet and WAP was designed as the way of making it easily available on mobile terminals.

Unstructured Supplementary Services Data

Unstructured Supplementary Services Data (USSD) is a means of transmitting information via a GSM network. It is to some extent similar to the Short Message Service (SMS), which refers to the ability to send and receive text messages to and from mobile telephones. In contrast to SMS, which is a store and forward service, USSD offers a real-time connection during a session.

The direct radio connection stays open until the user or the application disconnects it. A USSD message can have up to 182 characters. It is relevant for real-time applications, such as mobile stock trading, where a confirmed information transmission is needed. USSD is a WAP bearer service. It is said that USSD will grow with the further market penetration of WAP. We see it used mainly for mobile financial services, shopping, and payment.

M-Commerce: Applications

M-commerce offers many beneficial applications to businesses and consumers. Consumers are able to stay well informed with up-to-the-minute details of the topics of their choice. Text messaging allows people to stay in contact with each other for both business and pleasure. When higher wireless bandwidth is added into the mix, consumers will be able to demand and expect a richer mobile experience.

Consumers will also have access to a larger number of vendors, as they can now find localized products and firms. An example would be to use your mobile phone to find the nearest restaurant while walking down a city block.

For businesses, m-commerce offers a number of positive applications. For example, inventory can be managed with greater degree of confidence when using mobile devices. The ability to identify and track products from anywhere anytime can help firms better answer supply chain questions. This in turn will allow businesses to better satisfy their customers and build healthy business-business relationships with their trading partners.

Additionally, businesses will be able to collect data about their customers to better understand their needs. As consumers use their mobile devices for business transactions, companies will have an additional avenue to market and support their products.

THE MARKET FOR M-COMMERCE

The following section examines the major stakeholders of m-commerce: customers, technology providers, Web designers and developers, and service providers (see Figure 4).

Figure 4. The market for m-commerce

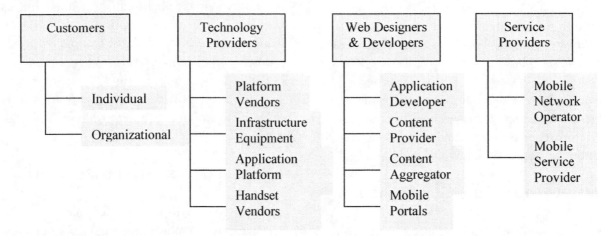

Customers

Customers, individual and organizational, play a large role in the adoption of m-commerce. As they become the everyday users of wireless devices, their satisfaction and comfort are of the utmost importance. A Nokia study on wireless value-added services found that the primary adopters of wireless technology include:

- Teens (18 years and under)
- Students (19-25 years old)
- Young business people (25-36 years old)

It should be noted that the main consumers of m-commerce devices are under the age of 36. These numbers should expand in the future as wireless applications are accepted by larger segments of the population ("Four in ten users," 2002).

Businesses and organizations also use m-commerce products. Similar to the previous section on m-commerce applications, the businesses most likely to posses m-commerce platforms include:

- Businesses that use m-commerce for direct sales to the customer; for example, investment firms selling stocks via wireless devices.

- Firms that have a high demand for real-time, in-house communication. An example of this category of business would include a consulting firm utilizing wireless devices to keep better track of employees.
- Organizations that have a mobile work force; for example, a shipping company using mobile devices to track its deliveries (Bai et al., 2005).

Business customers may use m-commerce applications to check schedules and e-mail, use in-house applications like customer relationship management (CRM) or enterprise resource planning (ERP), or scan products and their associated bar codes or radio frequency identification (RFID) tags.

Technology Providers

Technology providers include the businesses that sell and support the m-commerce platforms, firms that sell the equipment used for the infrastructure of a wireless network, companies that create connecting software and middleware for wireless applications, and the firms that manufacture the actual devices.

Technology Platform Vendors

Mobile devices require similar software and hardware components as other computing devices. Technology platform vendors create the operating systems and specialized applications needed by wireless handhelds, laptops, and cell phones. This industry is largely based around two companies, Microsoft and Symbian, and their respective operating systems, Windows CE and Palm.

Infrastructure Equipment Vendors

Wireless networks require specialized components to create a reliable and efficient communications infrastructure. Companies such as Ericsson, Lucent, Motorola, and Nokia have helped shape the m-commerce environment their products. This is an industry that has seemingly been in a constant state of innovation, with the new and improved products and protocols emerging.

Application Platform Vendors

The wireless application protocols needed to connect different m-commerce applications to help the mobile industry grow and expand. Industry interest groups like the WAP Forum, the Bluetooth Special Interest Group, and the Mobile Data Initiative help to forge agreements and standards to help connect a variety of applications over mobile networks. Additionally, companies like Nokia, Ericsson, and Dr. Materna create and market their own forms of middleware that can ease the connectivity of their products (Bai et al., 2005).

Device Vendors

Handheld computers, cellular phones, and mobile computers are an obvious m-commerce technology provider. There has been a great shift to multi-function devices in this industry, as customers demand products that can mix and match the ability to make phone calls, surf the wireless Web, connect to wireless applications, even listen to music and take pictures. The companies in this industry scramble to offer the right components, but more importantly the right features for consumers. Successful design of these devices is essential to strong consumer loyalty (Cyr, Head, & Ivanov, 2006).

Web Site Designers and Developers

Web designers and programmers play a central role in creating applications suitable for the wireless environment. In the past, these applications have largely been limited by a lack of bandwidth and the limitations of the wireless devices. Both of these characteristics have greatly improved for today's m-commerce designs.

Application Developers

Wireless application developers design and code mobile applications. There is a wide array of tools that can be used in this process. The WAP, The Wireless Markup Language (WML), and the Handheld Devices Markup Language (HDML). In addition, there is a mobile version of Java termed J2ME.

Content Providers

Wireless content providers help to provide Web content to mobile devices. Firms recognizing the attractiveness of using the wireless Web to communicate with consumers have shown a willingness to make available a sometimes limited, or in some case a full featured, version of their Web content. A key challenge for the organizations is to create a suitable version of their content, especially in conjunction with the previously discussed limitations of wireless devices and bandwidth (Saha, Jamtgaard, & Villasenor, 2001).

Content Aggregators

Content aggregators are firms that gather similar content on a topic and make it available to wireless users. For example, a mobile news site may offer subscribers wireless updates of the current headlines. This firm gathers top stories before making them available on mobile devices. Yahoo, AOL, and CNN are all examples of wireless content aggregators.

Mobile Portals

Mobile portals create personalized and localized content to users by providing e-mail, calendar, communication tools, and dynamic information. These portals become the one stop for many wireless users, as they can access a variety of applications from a single location. In addition to being content aggregators, Yahoo and AOL are also mobile portals.

Wireless Service Providers

This section will focus on the firms that supply wireless access. These companies operate and manage mobile networks for subscribers.

Mobile Network Operators

Vodaphone, T-Mobile, Verizon, and NTT Do-CoMo are all examples of mobile network operators. These firms have launched an infrastructure to transport mobile content and data to wireless devices. While some of these firms are traditional cell phone coverage providers, others are moving in and serving more directly as wireless ISPs (Bai et al., 2005).

Mobile Service Providers

Mobile service providers are the firms that provide access to mobile networks. In some cases, the operators and service providers are the same.

For example, Verizon supports and grants access to its mobile network. In other cases, the service providers are simply reselling access over the mobile network, while typically supplying their own content. Vonage has recently announced plans to launch a mobile version of its product (Kharif, 2007).

FUTURE TRENDS

M-commerce is a recent development and it is anticipated that it will exhibit strong growth in the next decade.

Market Forecasts

A 2006 wireless telecommunications industry profile by Datamonitor found the global market value of wireless telecommunications services to be $401.9 billion. This figure is expected to grow to $567.8 billion by 2010 (Global Wireless Telecommunications Services, 2006). These numbers clearly demonstrate scope and potential of wireless networks and mobile applications.

An interesting trend is that Asia and Europe have seen stronger growth of wireless services than the Americas. The United States has been much slower to accept and adopt mobile communications and m-commerce than other areas of the world. For this to change, there will need

Figure 5. Global wireless telecommunications services market segmentation (Source: Global Wireless Telecommunications Services, 2006)

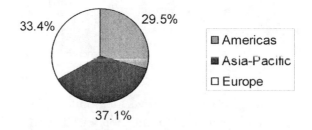

to be continued education of consumers and the emergence of uniform standards with critical applications. A summary of Datamonitor's (Global Wireless Telecommunications Services, 2006) findings is given in Figure 5.

Future Issues

M-commerce is still emerging as a field, industry, and discipline. While there has been some disappointment that it has not evolved faster, there is still great hope for the future. In order for it to reach its promise consumers must continue to accept and even demonstrate a preference for the wireless medium. In addition, firms must continue to deliver products, services, and features that build loyal customer relationships. Finally, two important areas for innovation include security and enterprise applications.

Acceptance of Wireless Technology

In the past, wireless services and devices have been improved upon. We now see products focusing on cross-functional capabilities. This trend will continue but must be echoed by the demands of consumers. The marketplace will drive innovation and lead to more sophisticated products and services.

Customer Loyalty

Wireless firms seek a loyal customer base. Currently, consumers remain loyal through contracts and service agreements that lock them into their current vendors. There is opportunity for the industry to establish service levels that satisfy customers to the extent that they no longer shop for new vendors (Bai et al., 2005).

Enterprise Applications

As the business market grows for mobile applications, firms will seek to implement ERP, CRM, and supply chain management (SCM), and other business intelligence (BI) applications over their wireless infrastructure. This will greatly improve the effectiveness of m-commerce's impact on internal and external decisions like inventory management, customer support, and one-one marketing.

Mobile Security Will Become a Hot Issue

Security has always been a concern for wireless devices. This will continue with increased scrutiny as users accept and adopt mobile solutions. In order for m-commerce to reach its potential, users must trust that the wireless environment is safe and secure to conduct business and to complete financial transactions.

TECHNOLOGY PUSH: BLUETOOTH

Bluetooth is a wireless technology used for short-ranged communication between multiple Bluetooth-enabled devices. An example would include connecting a wireless PDA, camera, or similar device to a desktop computer. The wireless connection would instantly update changes made to either device. Bluetooth works in the unlicensed 2.4 GHz (ISM) band focusing on industrial, scientific, and medical applications. It uses FHSS communication, which transmits data over different frequencies at different time intervals. This is accomplished by making "hops" to different frequencies through the ISM band. A device makes about 1,600 hops per second, which is spaced out over 1 MHz (Ersala & Yen, 2002).

Unlike most devices, Bluetooth-enabled devices communicate with each other automatically. There is no need to specify what type of action is to take place or when it is to happen. When two devices are within range of each other, they will communicate back and forth to determine if there is any information to be passed. During initial communication, it is necessary to create a relationship between unknown devices; this process is referred to as pairing. During the paring process, a secret PIN is created that is only known by the two devices that are communicating. It is better for the user to manually enter a PIN, and make it complex, in order to make the code hard to break (Dursch & Yen, 2004).

Bluetooth has several advantages; one of the most notable is its ease of use. As with every other wireless technology, Bluetooth frees up the user from being bogged down by wires. With an increasing number of peripheral devices, all the wires can become overcrowded and, at times, confusing. If not all the wires and slots are color-coded, it can become very difficult to figure out the location that each wire is plugged into, even for a professional. With Bluetooth, all these wires disappear, saving the user the time that would be spent trying to figure out how to get all the devices connected. When two Bluetooth devices come within range of each other, they automatically make a connection and decide if there is any information that needs to be passed, or if one needs to control the other.

Not only is the fact that Bluetooth devices use wireless communication an advantage, but also that the communication is done automatically. This reduces user interaction time, and tasks can be accomplished more efficiently. Within a wired environment, if the user wanted two devices to be synchronized, data would need either to be reentered by hand or connect the devices by wires. If the user would forget to do the synchronization, the data would eventually become outdated and could lead to data discrepancies. Because of the automatic communication between Bluetooth devices, the user does not need to worry about forgetting to synchronize, so the data between devices would always match and be up-to-date (Ferro & Potorti, 2005).

Another advantage of Bluetooth is its added security features. The fact that it is a short-range technology (about 3 meters), adds some security in

itself, because someone would need to be close to the communicating devices to be able to intercept the signal. As discussed earlier, the authentication process is also much more in-depth and harder to crack than that of other wireless standards.

Even though Bluetooth's short range helps security, there is still the possibility that someone can intercept the signal. The signal that Bluetooth devices send out, is sent in every direction, and can travel through walls. Intercepting the signal could be just as easy as sitting in the next room and listening to someone's conversation. With the increasing speeds of computers and programs, hacking equipment can be made to quickly and easily crack any code. With a wired network, a hacker needs to somehow tap into the company's network. This makes it harder for hackers because they need a physical connecting, whereas with Bluetooth all they need is a receiver that can catch the radio signals being sent out. As this technology continues to grow and mature, there will be better security measures, and someday may be as secure as some of the wired technologies.

The short range poses another disadvantage for Bluetooth. Only being able to transmit to distances up to 30 feet away can be very limiting in an office or production setting. Users cannot go too far away from the device that they are communicating with without losing the signal. If a company were spread out over separate buildings, Bluetooth would not work without help from another networking technology, such as a wired system.

Another disadvantage of Bluetooth is its speed. Today there is a greater need than ever for fast speeds to transfer large quantities of data. Bluetooth is only capable of transferring at speeds of 1 Mbit per second, but the SIG is working on a newer version that would allow speeds to reach 10 Mbits per second. If companies need to continuously exchange large files, Bluetooth would not work for their demands. Bluetooth is only meant for small amounts of data to be transferred at one time.

Bluetooth is already used in a number of real-world applications. Personal area networks use

Bluetooth to connect peripherals with desktop and laptop units. Wireless headphone and speaker units to use in conjunction with cell phones are also increasingly more common and use Bluetooth. Most importantly for m-commerce, Bluetooth offers a method of transferring financial data for wireless transactions.

TECHNOLOGY PUSH: WiMax

While Bluetooth was limited in both range and carrying capacity, WiMax is greatly enhanced in both areas. WiMax is a wireless technology that can be used to communicate over much longer distances, up to 30 miles. For this reason the technology is considered a metropolitan area network (MAN), offering the potential to cover large geographic areas. Even though this standard reaches a much larger area than others do, it provides sufficient latency. In addition, WiMax offers bandwidths exceeding 70 Mbits per second.

WiMax is seen as a broadband solution. Whereas the cost of laying cable lines or even extending telecom networks for DSL, are quite high, WiMax offers a cheaper and more scalable solution. For this reason, the standard is seen as a solution to "last mile" problems. Furthermore, its bandwidth potential exceeds cellular networks so it affects other wireless and not just hard-wired solutions (Ghosh, Wolter, Andrews, & Chen, 2005).

A disadvantage of WiMax at the current moment is in its actual adoption. It is seen primarily as an access technology. While it does compete with hard-wired fixed broadband solutions, it cannot match the performance of all, although the hard-wired solutions are not as cost effective.

Additionally, WiMax is sometimes seen as a competitor with the much more established WiFi. In reality, the two technologies would be best used in conjunction with each other. Meshing WiMax and WiFi together, using WiMax as a large area, high-speed backbone and WiFi for LAN needs is a complementary solution (Goth, 2004).

Figure 6. The relationships, impact, and roles of wireless, Bluetooth, and WiMax

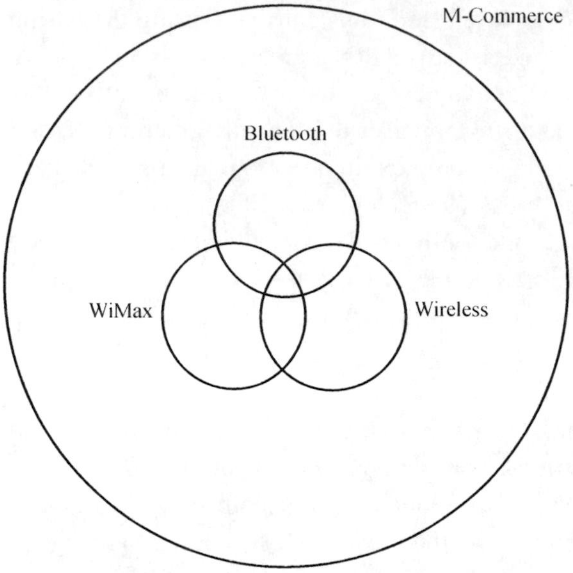

As the world embraces IP-based solutions like television over IP, radio over IP, and voice over IP (VOIP), there is great potential for a high bandwidth, large area wireless networking method. For m-commerce, WiMax offers tremendous potential with both its range and bandwidth. Its ability to mesh with other mobile technologies is vital to providing consumers with a wireless networked solution.

Both Bluetooth and WiMax satisfy and contribute to separate applications of m-commerce. Both have the ability to significantly boost mobile implementations and applications.

CONCLUSION

There is no question that m-commerce will continue to grow. It is successfully being used. Its reliance on improving standards, both hardware and software, have allowed it to not only develop but to be improved. As more businesses adopt m-commerce solutions, and as additional consumers utilize the flexibility of mobile devices, additional applications will be in demand. M-commerce will also be positively impacted as more Bluetooth and WiMax applications and devices are developed. M-commerce will receive an additional boost as these applications mature and are meshed together on mobile networks. Consumers will have options other than be tied to a desktop plugging into the wall. M-commerce is an area of past growth and future potential for the IT industry.

REFERENCES

Bai, L., Chou, D. C., Yen, D., & Lin, B. (2005). Mobile commerce: Its market analyses. *International Journal of Mobile Communications, 3*(1), 66-81.

Cyr, D., Head, M., & Ivanov, A. (2006). Design aesthetics leading to m-loyalty in mobile commerce. *Information & Management, 43*(8), 950-963.

Dursch, A., & Yen, D. (2004). Bluetooth technology: An exploratory study of the analysis and implementation frameworks. *Computer Standards and Interfaces, 26*(4), 263-277.

Dursch, A., Yen, D., & Huang, S. (2005). Fourth generation wireless communications: An analysis of future potential and implementation. *Computer Standards and Interfaces, 28*(1), 13-25.

Ersala, N., & Yen, D. (2002). Bluetooth technology: A strategic analysis of its role in global 3G wireless communication era. *Computer Standards & Interfaces, 24*(3), 193-206.

Ferro, E., & Potorti, F. (2005). Bluetooth and Wi-Fi wireless protocols: A survey and a comparison. *Wireless Communications, IEEE, 12*(1), 12-26.

Flanigan, M. (2006). *TIA's 2006 telecommunications market review and forecast.* Telecommunications Industry Association. Retrieved from www.tiaonline.org

Four in ten users want to carry out mobile commerce. (2002). *Card Technology Today, 14*(5), 7-8.

Ghosh, A., Wolter, D. R., Andrews, J. G., & Chen, R. (2005). Broadband wireless access with WiMax/802.16: Current performance benchmarks and future potential. *IEEE Communications Magazine, 43,* 129-136.

Global Wireless Telecommunication Services. (2006). London: Datamonitor PLC. Retrieved April 12, 2007, from Business Source Premier database.

Goth, G. (2004).Wireless MAN standard signals next-gen opportunities. *IEEE Distributed Systems Online, 5*(8), 4.

Holma, H., & Toskala, A. (2000) *WCDMA for UMTS: Radio access for third generation mobile communications.* New York: Wiley.

Karnouskos, S., & Fraunhofer, F. (2004). Mobile payment: A journey through existing procedures and standardization initiatives. *IEEE Communications Surveys, 6,* 44-66.

Kharif, O. (2007, February 20). Coming up: Vonage wireless? *BusinessWeek.com.* Retrieved April 20, 2007, from http://businessweek.com/technology/content/feb2007/tc20070220_452876.htm

Leavitt, N. (2000). Will WAP deliver the wireless Internet? *Computer, 33*(5), 16-20.

Saha, S., Jamtgaard, M., & Villasenor, J. (2001). Bringing the wireless Internet to mobile devices. *Computer, 34*(6), 54-58.

Wu, J., & Wang, S. (2005). What drives mobile commerce? An empirical evaluation of the revised technology acceptance model. *Information and. Management, 42*(5), 719-729.

Yen, D., & Chou, D. C. (2000). Wireless communications: Applications and managerial issues. *Industrial Management & Data Systems, 100*(9), 436-443.

Zeng, E. Y., Yen, D., & Hwang, H. (2003). Mobile commerce: The convergence of e-commerce and wireless technology. *International Journal of Services Technology and Management, 4*(3), 302-322.

ADDITIONAL READING

Kane, J., & Yen, D. (2002). Breaking the barriers of connectivity: An analysis of the wireless LAN. *Computer Standards & Interfaces, 24*(1), 5-20.

Varshney, U., & Vetter, R. (2000). Emerging mobile and wireless networks. *Communications of the ACM, 43*(6), 73-81.

Yen, D., & Chou, D. C. (2001). Wireless communication: The next wave of Internet technology. *Technology in Society, 23*(2), 217-226.

Chapter III
M–Commerce Payment Systems

Valli Kumari Vatsavayi
Andhra University, India

Ravi Mukkamala
Old Dominion University, USA

ABSTRACT

With mobile operators having a large customer base and e-payments getting popular, there is a shift of focus on the huge potential that the mobile commerce (m-commerce) market offers. Mobile payment (m-payment) service is the core for the success of m-commerce. M-payments allow customers to buy digital goods from anywhere and anytime using Internet and mobile environments. Ubiquity, reachability, localization, personalization, and dissemination of information are the characteristics that favor m-payments and encourage the consumers and merchants to use them. This chapter examines various aspects of m-payments like architectures, limitations, security, and trust issues. It also discusses and compares the existing payment procedures of several different companies providing m-payment services. While exploring the advantages of shifting to m-payments, the problems that have to be dealt with when adopting new solutions are discussed. Finally, the chapter concludes by identifying a common set of requirements criteria for successful global m-payments.

INTRODUCTION

M-commerce allows customers to buy goods from anywhere and anytime using the Internet and mobile environments. The content for which the payment is made may be digital goods (e.g., downloading software, e-books, and tickets) or services (e.g., auctions, games, booking tickets, trading, healthcare, and auto parking).

Mobile-phone-based services are becoming an important target for business. M-payment is about using the mobile phone for making payments. This provides a good experience combining convenience with flexibility to the customer while making payments. The customer does shopping online and uses the mobile phone to pay for a product or service or make transactions. There is no need to carry a personal wallet. A customer is required to give a unique code for recognition by

Figure 1. Cellular subscriber growth in USA (Mercator Advisory Group Report 1, 2006)

Year	Approx. Customers (millions)	Approx. annual Revenues in $(billions)
1995	45	20
1999	75	42
2001	125	64
2005	230	100

Figure 2. Mobile phone penetration and subscribers in Asia (Mercator Advisory Group Report 2, 2006)

Country	Mobile subscribers (millions)	Mobile penetration
China	400	31%
Japan	90.7	71%
South Korea	37.5	77%
Taiwan	22.7	99%
Malaysia	19.5	81%
Hongkong	6.8	99%
Singapore	4.3	97%

the bank when making payments. The payment is made only after validation is done. Shopping is finished, after delivery of the goods depending on the type of goods and mode of delivery. Requirements of mobility by consumers and businesses show a need for rise in the m-payment services. M-payments are an important aspect of M-Commerce that allow and enable secure payments and settling credit and debit claims.

In 2002 and 2003, due to the hype and later crash of new technologies, companies resisted investments in new technologies; since then the number of mobile device users has grown dramatically. According to Lombardi (2006) as of December 2005, there were more than 2 billion mobile connections globally. According to the Mercator Advisory Group (2006), almost 208 million Americans in the year 2005 were cell phone subscribers, as shown in Figure 1.

In China, according to China's Ministry of Information, the number of mobile phone users has passed 400 million in February 2006 and by 2009 it is expected to pass 600 million (Nystedt, 2006). In the European Union (EU) more than 80% of the population has mobile phones (Damsgaard & Marchegiani, 2004). With consumers spending in excess of £700 million during 2005 in the UK, and German consumers spending an average of €4.50 each month on mobile downloads, it is a lucrative market. According to Telecom Regulatory Authority of India (TRAI), there are 90 million cell phone subscribers in India. Mobile phone penetration has almost saturated a few Asian countries as shown in Figure 2 (Mercator Advisory Group Report 2, 2006).

Thus m-commerce has the potential for explosive growth and that m-payments could be the next "killer application" for business (Aswin, 2003). Though the m-payment market did not live up to the expectations because of multiple service providers and a variety of payment solutions and technologies, it has gained a reasonable level of acceptance. Obviously any customer would adapt to a new payment technology if thorough solutions to his prime concerns of cost, convenience, and security are provided. Mostly the transactional costs that the customer will have to pay should be negligible when compared to the cost of the transaction. Finally, the m-payment vision is to transform the mobile phone into a personal mobile wallet holding credit cards, debit account information, and mobile cash for transactions (Ding & Unnithan, 2004).

A few m-payment applications suggested in the literature are (Gross, Fleisch, Lampe, & Miller, 2004):

- automated point-of-sales payments (vending machines, parking meters, and ticket machines);
- attended point-of-sale payments (shop counters, taxis);
- mobile-accessed Internet payments (merchant wireless application protocol [WAP] sites);

- mobile assisted Internet payments (fixed Internet sites using phone instead of credit card); and
- Peer-to-peer payments between individuals.

Several m-payment schemes have been successful, but all have been limited in implementation and geography (Bradford, 2003). In order that consumers and merchants accept m-payments globally, an interoperable set of standards and payment systems is needed. Implementing m-payment infrastructure and consumer adoption is fairly complex and is exemplified by the retraction of several m-payment mediators like Paybox (Jones, 2003).

In this chapter, several issues faced by m-payment systems are discussed along with their implementations, successes, and failures. The perspectives and challenges in providing effective m-payment solutions are discussed. Initially, the requirements and the need for m-payments are discussed. Later, categorization of m-payments based on various criteria is given. Then, various existing successful payment system processes and the technical and security issues are discussed. A comparison of these systems is given. Based on these observations a common set of requirements criteria for successful global m-payments is suggested.

E-PAYMENTS TO M-PAYMENTS

Introduction

Any payments made through an electronic terminal to order, instruct, or authorize a financial institution to debit or credit an account is called as an *electronic payment*. Mobile Payment Forum (www.mobilepaymentforum.com), defines "*mobile payment* as the process of two parties exchanging financial value using a mobile device in return for goods or services."

An electronic payment requires a connection

Figure 3. Expected popularity of m-commerce/m-payments region wise (Little, 2004)

Year	Europe	Asia & Australia
2004	2%	0%
2006	6%	43%
2008	51%	71%

to the Internet to fulfill the payment. In m-payment, the mobile device uses a wireless connection to interact with multiple parties involved in the transaction. There are several factors that are driving the merchants to shift to m-payment-based solutions. One of the main reasons is that the device used by the consumer for making payments is usually the personal trusted device. The other possible reason could be to tap the potential mobile services market. The services can be offered round the clock as m-payments are location independent and can be used anytime and anywhere.

Already, the m-payments market started becoming popular around the world. Based on the table shown in Figure 3 the penetration of m-payments services is greater in Asia and Australia when compared to Europe and the USA (Little, 2004). Currently, Japan is the only country in the world that has fully adopted m-payments to exchange e-mail, search for restaurants, train schedules, store photos, and listen to music.

Key Players in M-Payments

The key players in the payment process are (Stallings, 2000):

- **Consumers:** A consumer or a customer is an authorized party, allowed to make payments through his/her mobile device. He/she is usually registered with mobile network operators or financial institutions usually called issuers. A consumer holds an account with them from which credits and debits are made.
- **Merchants:** A merchant is an organization

Figure 4. Simple m-payment process (MeT, 2003)

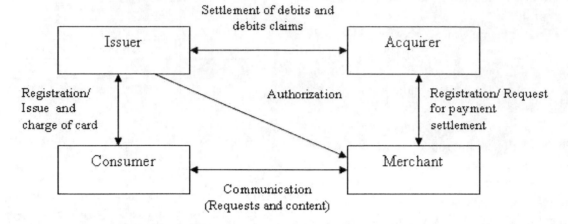

or a person that has goods or services to sell to the consumer. A merchant is usually associated with an acquirer.

- **Issuer:** An issuer is usually a financial institution or a mobile network operator, who maintains the accounts of consumers and makes payments on behalf of the consumer.
- **Acquirer:** An acquirer is a financial institution or a mobile network operator who maintains the account on behalf of merchant and performs transfer of funds on his behalf.
- **Certification authority:** It is an authority that issues X.509 v3 certificates to banks, consumers, and merchants. These certificates allow in distribution of public keys of banks, consumers, and merchants.

M-payment process (Figure 4) has the following steps in general:

1. **Registration:** The consumer registers with an issuer for the payment service.
2. **Payment submission:** The merchant communicates to the user about the goods and services. The consumer selects goods and submits payment.
3. **Authentication:** The merchant authenticates the consumer and requests authorization by contacting the issuer.

4. **Authorization:** The issuer sends authorization information. The merchant sends this information to acquirer. Acquirer and issuer settle the claims by performing appropriate debits and credits.
5. **Confirmation:** The consumer gets confirmation message after the transaction is completed.

Now we discuss the general requirements, advantages, and limitations of m-payments systems.

Why M-Payments?

In this section reasons that support a shift from e-payments to m-payments are given:

- **Personalization and convenience:** Consumer uses the mobile device which is easy to carry and is usually a personal device. This ensures traceability and trust for merchants.
- **Established airtime payment process:** E-payment is already an established process. Payment for airtime too is an established one. Hence payment service costs can be computed in an amicable way.
- **Mobile operators know the customers and hence can act as third party:** As the

consumer registers with the mobile operator, consumer's whereabouts and identity are known. Thus, the mobile operator can act as a third party for all transactions between merchant and consumer.

- **Allows both voice and text communication:** Mobile devices allow both voice and data to be communicated. This enables multiple services to be offered to consumers.
- **Ubiquity:** Accessibility from any part of the world; transactions can be done instantaneously irrespective of time and place.
- **Security:** SIM card and PIN ensure more security of transactions when compared to e-payments. As mobile network operators know the consumers, the transactions done by the consumers are authenticated and hence more secure.
- **Localization:** Depending on the geographical area from which the device is being operated, the services according to the local customs and preferences may be provided to the consumers.
- **Existing consumer base and Less time to adapt:** Existing customer base of e-commerce is a potential for m-commerce,

Figure 5. Benefits of m-commerce/m-payment for consumers (Little, 2004)

Benefits	Importance (1 to 5 point scale)
Less limitations in time and space	4.4
Avoiding counting and carrying coins	3.5
Customer security	3.4
Life style	3.1
Cost effective payment method	2.7
Avoiding carrying different cards	2.6
Customer anonymity	2.6
Avoiding carrying different currencies	2.1
Access to additional source of credit	2.1

and the time and effort required to shift to m-commerce is less.

- **Availability in remote towns and villages:** Mobile services can reach remote villages and towns and would give the merchants access to a wide range of consumers.
- **Person-to-person (P2P) transactions:** Interpersonal (P2P) transactions are easy with mobile phones.

In addition, Figure 5 lists a set of benefits ordered by priorities assigned by a group customers when asked about why they prefer m-payments (Little, 2004).

Issues with M-Payments

Most of the limitations of m-payments are due to the mobile device constraints. For instance keyboard, display, memory, processing, and bandwidth are some of the limited resources which prevent implementation of highly secure and efficient m-payment solutions. But as the capabilities of mobile devices are increasing, possibly in future the aforementioned limitations may soon be void, as large screens and broad band access may make them attractive.

Other than the device restrictions, the issues that are restricting m-payments solutions from being adopted are:

- **Anonymity:** Sharing data with many parties keeps the customers away from online payments, even though it is convenient, they wish to be anonymous.
- **Possibility of theft:** The mobile device gets lost more easily than a credit card. So, consumers may refrain from using the mobile device as a wallet.
- **Signal reception:** Quality of signal reception can be limited (e.g., in buildings). This may prevent transactions from being carried out or completed with less reliability.

- **High costs:** As currently, there are no interoperable global solutions for m-payments settlement of roaming becomes complex. Usually, the mobile operators or banks have a high credit risk. Other than these costs, the service provider investment is high for implementing and upgrading the solutions.
- **Hardware and software flexibility:** Hardware and software used for the m-payment solutions is relatively inflexible.

Requirements for M-Payments

The success of m-payments entirely depends on consumer and merchant willingness to adopt the payment process. The different characteristics based on which consumers and merchants would choose the payment model are broadly classified into three categories: strategic, operational, and participant characteristics (Kreyer, Pousttchi, & Turowski, 2002). The identification of strategic characteristics allows the choice of a payment model based on payment scenario or the size of the payment. Operational characteristics depend on the type, mode, frequency, time, and basis of payment. The participants are the key players mentioned in the previous sections and their characteristics might also lead to choice in the payment system to be adopted. Based on Ondrus and Pigneur (2006) and considering customer and merchant perspectives, the following are the general characteristics required of effective and successful m-payments.

- **Ease of use/convenience:** The payment process should be simple to learn and convenient to use to enable more consumers to prefer the payment method.
- **Low cost to implement:** For the merchant and the service provider, process should take less investment in terms of infrastructure and technologies upgrading.
- **Reliability:** The process should be reliable and less prone to fraudulent activities.

- **User/market acceptance:** A user obviously gets inclined more to use a widely accepted payment process. Thus maturity of the process is the key factor that counts for an m-payment's success. Existing solutions should be used where applicable. Any payment solution should offer better profits to all parties concerned.
- **Security:** End to end security has to be guaranteed. In this process the essential security services like authentication, confidentiality, integrity, and non-repudiation should be possible. Banks should be able to authenticate their customer while providing banking and payment services. No party should deny having done any transaction, thus enabling non-repudiation. The details about the transactions should not be visible to third parties, thus achieving confidentiality. The messages sent and received during transactions should not be modifiable and should ensure integrity. In addition to these, many users wish to remain anonymous while making payments (Nambiar & Lu, 2005).
- **Flexibility:** The system should be flexible in nature, that is, it should be possible to enhance and include new features, as the requirements of the customers and technologies change day to day. Open and non-proprietary solutions, if used, will make the solutions more flexible.
- **Speed:** In spite of the fact that mobile devices have their own limitations with respect to memory and computing power the payment transactions should be completed at desirable speeds. The ACID properties (atomicity, consistency, independence, durability) should hold good for the transactions.
- **Scalability:** The payment solutions should be scalable in nature.

Generally speaking, it is observed that unless security is high, and the payment solution is convenient and simple, the customer would not be convinced to adopt the m-payment solution. After the customer wishes to use the mobile device for payment he/she would choose a solution only if it is broadly accepted, costs less, and the customer is free to choose the handset, the bank, and the mobile network operator independent of each other. The additional services opted by the customer are usually anonymity, traceability, convertibility, and portability.

On similar lines the merchant requirements include, guaranteed payment for services provided, customer relationship and high diffusion into the customer community. And the cost to adopt the solutions should be less. Based on these requirements factors, an assessment of several successful and unsuccessful payment systems is done in the later sections.

Security in M-Payments

Most of the time the level of security required is based on transactions amount. There are a few cases where no security is required at all, say for picopayments. In such low-valued transactions the cost of implementing security is more than the worth of the transaction and hence no security may be provided. But if the consumer requires that irrespective of the value of the transaction, any transaction should be made only by him/her, then a PIN may be used for encryption. It is known only to the consumer and no one else can perform the transaction. In cases where the transactions will have to be authenticated, digital certificates (X.509 v3) based keys may be used for both authentication and encryption. A more advanced and reliable technique to make transactions secure are the use of smart cards. By using smart cards high levels of security can be achieved.

Many communication security protocols are used for m-payments. WAP (McKitterrick & Dowling, 2003) provides a mechanism for displaying Internet information on a WAP-enabled mobile device. The basis for WAP 1.x security is Wireless Transport Layer Security (WTLS)

standard, which is on the other hand based on TLS. WAP 2.0 provides enhanced security as it encompasses several standards that ensure security at application level, transport level, and management level. Several standards used in WAP are: (1) WAP Identity Module (WIP) which is a tamper resistant smart card chip stored on mobile device and is capable of storing Public Key Infrastructure (PKI) keys; (2) WMLSCrypt, WML Script Crypto API is an application programming interface that uses security functions in WMLS Crypto Library (WMLSCLib) and WIM for providing basic security services; and (3) Wireless PKI (WPKI) is an optimized extension of traditional PKI for wireless environment.

CATEGORIZATIONS OF M-PAYMENT SYSTEMS: A SURVEY

In this section, several categorizations are given to enable a better understanding of the m-payment systems. These categorizations can then be used to develop a requirements framework for global m-payment systems.

Payment Systems Categorization

In this section we give a broad overview of different categorizations proposed in the literature (Buhan, Cheong, & Tan, 2002; Kountz, 2002; Ondrus, 2003; Schwiderski-Grosche & Knospe, 2002).

Categorization Based on Money Model

- **Token based:** A token is issued for exchange of money. This token represents monitory value. This instead can be used for a goods purchase, and this token is then en-cashed with the issuing financial institution.
- **Notational:** The value equivalent to some cash is stored in an account with a financial institution and is exchanged by authorization.

Categorization by Proximity

- **Remote payments:** Remote mobile transactions span from the purchase of ring tones and logos sent to the mobile phone, for purchasing goods, services, and content during a browsing session with online mobile merchant sites (Ondrus, 2003). In remote transactions there are at least four parties involved: (1) merchant, (2) acquirer, (3) issuer, and (4) customer. A customer registers with the issuer. This enables the merchant to trust the customer. The customer visits the Web site through a mobile network and selects the item to be purchased, the payment method, and confirms the request through a PIN. The customer then receives the acknowledgement receipt. The goods are then delivered to the appropriate place.
- **Local payments:** Local payments are usually done through communication protocols like Radio Frequency Identification (RFID) and Blue tooth, Infrared, WLAN 802.11. Local payments are usually made when using vending machines or through a parking fee or toll gate fee. Europay, MasterCard, & Visa(EMV) is also used for mobile environments.

Categorization Based on Time of Payment

- **Pre-paid systems:** With prepaid accounts the customer pays before obtaining the content.
- **Pay-now systems:** In this system a customer's account is debited at the time of payment.
- **Post-pay systems:** In this system a merchant's account is credited before the

customer's account is debited.

Categorization by Seller/Buyer Origin

- **P2P m-payments:** In a P2P payment system there are three parties involved: consumer, merchant, and the P2P payment service provider. The consumer and merchant hold an account with the service provider. The service provider keeps track of funds available to both the consumer and merchant. With P2P, if the consumer has deposited the appropriate funds at the P2P payment service then the transaction is approved and the purchase amount is deducted from the consumer's account and added to the merchant's account. The most popular P2P service is PayPal.
- **Business-to-consumer (B2C) m-payments:** B2C payment services are usually used for services like mobile ticketing and mobile gaming.
- **Business-to-business (B2B) m-payments:** The demand for retail m-commerce may drive the B2B payments and applications. Banks can use the infrastructure used for retail m-payments and brokerage services for corporate customers too. While corporate customers' payment information is stored in bank servers, the retail payment information is stored on a phone chip, card readers attached to the phone, or on a central server accessed via internet (Aswin, 2003).

Categorization Based on Applications Installed

Mobile wallet is a trusted application installed in the mobile phone, which allows cards, tokens, tickets, reminders, and receipts to be stored. Most of the global payments are card based. It is possible that in the future multiple virtual cards issued by different parties will have to be dealt with by the mobile devices. The wallet also helps in making remote and local payments possible. The wallet can be secured using a PIN and other such mechanisms. It is also possible to access other security elements like WIM from wallet applications (MeT, 2003). There are two categories based on whether devices are installed with applications or not (Seah et al., 2001).

- **Device without payment applications:** The wallet is held in a remote site, like in PayBox. The charges are debited from the subscriber's account.
- **Device with payment applications:** Payment applications are installed in the devices in this category.

Categorization by Clearing and Settlement Method

- **Bilateral:** Bilateral payments are limited to just one mobile operator and one bank, which restricts participation to the mutual customers of just these two organizations.
- **Multilateral:** Multilateral payment offsets the debits and credits accumulated by each member against the other members in the process of transactions. The advantage of multilateral clearing or payments is that multiple currencies can be supported.
- **Using intermediaries:** A third party can be used as an intermediary to settle payments.

Categorization by Mode of Registration

- **Registration required:** A few services require the consumers to register with the payment solution provider, by giving some personal information.
- **Registration not required:** A few payment systems do not require any prior customer registration.

Categorization by Type of Transaction

- **Pay per view (PPV):** It is a service where conditional access is given to use a particular program. A popular service is a pay television program for which a consumer pays a separate fee for each program like a movie or a sporting event.
- **Pay per unit (PPU):** The payment made is made whenever a unit of goods is bought like when buying a ring tone. Each time the ring tone is downloaded, a payment has to be made.
- **Subscription:** Instead of viewing a program just once, a service can be subscribed for a given period of time.

Categorization by Scenarios

- The following are the scenarios mentioned by Kreyer et al. (2002). M-commerce (all service), e-commerce (all kinds of B2C transactions like purchasing goods via the Internet using debit/credit cards), stationary merchant (face to face [F2F] conventional purchase like a purchase in super market, auto parking using cash or debit/credit cards), and customer-to-customer (C2C) (transfer of money between individuals through cash or offline transactions).

Categorization Based on Payment Amount (Size of Amount)

- **Pico-payments:** The transaction is done for very small amounts. A survey (Kreyer et al., 2002) reported that consumers prefer payments with mobile devices when the amounts are small to average.
- **Micro-payments:** The transaction is done for average amounts.
- **Macro-payments:** The transaction has large value.

Categorization by Type of Purchase

- Physical goods, digital/electronic goods, rights: The digital products can be general services or entertainment content or services.
  General Services:
  - Messaging services (notification etc.)
  - Directory enquiries (phone numbers, addresses, etc.)
  - Commercial content (news, etc.)
  - Off-line applications (dictionary, road maps)

  Entertainment:
  - Messaging content (voice greetings, etc.)
  - Online games (multiple choice, etc.)
  - Online services(like chatting)
  - Off-line games (Pac man)

Categorization Based on Validation Payments

- **Online validation:** A trusted third party is used to establish a trust relationship between two or more entities unknown to each other. All the transactions are validated by the trusted third party.
- **Off-line:** No third party is involved in transactions between merchant and the consumer.
- **Semi-online:** There is some involvement of the trusted party, but not at each payment.

Categorization by Technology Used

- **SMS based:** All the SMS-based payments are made through text messaging to a given number, amount, and the destination of the payment. A popular SMS based payment is PayPal Mobile.
- **WAP:** The simplest form of WAP-based payment is the basic key-entered transaction. Using a mobile device, the payment application prompts a merchant through a series of screens for key, entering the transaction amount, card number, and expiration date to receive an authorization. This method is the lowest cost of entry for a mobile merchant, but it is less secure.
- **Dual-slot/dual card phone:** A SIM card is inserted like in ItiAchat payment system in the traditional slot of the mobile phone and the payment card is inserted in the second slot.
- **Special payment software:** A few payment solutions require specific applications to be installed.

Categorization Based on Solution Provider

The provider could be a financial service provider like Mobile operators, Banks, Ecash providers, or payment service providers like IBM, Unwire, and so forth.

Categorization by Geography

A few solutions are specific to a region, while a few others are applicable to consumers in several nations. Thus, a few solutions support just single currency, while others allow exchange of currencies. Hence the categories are:

- Domestic/Cross-border
- Single currency/multiple currency

Categorization by Location of Payers' Account Details

A few categorizations focus on the whereabouts of money stored on a smart card (hardware based), electronic money stored on mobile device in a file format (software based) device, and money kept in a background account.

- Network/server based
- Client based (device/card)

Categorization Based on User Preferences

According to Zmijewska, Lawrence, and Steele (2004), m-payments should be categorized based on user preferences, as user-centric categorizations will allow system providers to see how their systems are perceived by the consumer, comparing those of their competitors. The dimensions that were proposed are: change of phone requirement, registration requirement, available phone operating company to which the company has to subscribe, available applications, communication of consumer's number to start transaction, communication of transaction details to user, acceptance of transaction by user, confirmation to customer, payment occurrence, brand visible of consumer, value of payment, registration fee, transaction cost for consumer, and time of transaction.

Kreyer et al. (2002) proposed a morphological box of m-payment characteristics, though exhaustive, it is quite difficult to assess a given payment system. The characteristics given are: payment scenarios, payment heights, involved parties, receiver of customer data, the need for pre-registration, technology required, basis of payment, payment frequency, deduction time, and method for settlement.

M-PAYMENT SYSTEMS

We discuss a few existing mobile systems (Carat, 2002; Meister, 2005; Ondrus & Pigneur, 2006; Zmijewska et al., 2004) in this section.

Vodafone M-Pay Bill

Vodafone m-Pay Bill is a simple, easy to use system that supports virtual point-of-sale (POS) for micro and small payments. Bill is charged via customer's phone bill or from prepaid airtime. There are three entities in this system: customer, merchant, and m-Pay Bill server. The Vodafone customer

registers for m-Pay Bill online by entering their mobile phone number, PIN, and other credentials. The amount is then charged along with the phone bill or deducted from prepaid airtime.

The only problem with the system is that the customer data is maintained in a server and is shared with other service providers for interoperability and thus this prevents privacy. Though there is no joining fee, the customer needs to register as a member.

TextPayMe

TextPayMe (https://www.textpayme.com) allows P2P payments to be sent from both the mobile phone and the Web browser. TextPayMe aims to solve the unattended parking market, simple F2F transactions with merchants, and transfer of funds between individuals for tasks as simple as splitting dinner bills. The only requirement is that the phone should be able to send and receive text messages. No installations are necessary. Even if the mobile device is lost, the consumer need not worry as enough steps are taken to prevent fraud. The payment steps are as follows. The customer needs to initially select a credit card or bank account as the source of funds. The customer sends an SMS to TextPayMe with a mobile number specified. Then the mobile phone authorization process can be initiated. A phone call is received after that asking for a PIN to authorize the payment and complete the transaction. Cancellation of the transaction is also possible.

TextPayMe claims providing a convenient and secure solution that works with virtually every mobile phone model across all major carriers in the United States. Currently, TextPayMe users are limited to sending and receiving a maximum of USD $500 a month.

M-Pay

PBS, Orange, and Gemplus support the m-pay system (http://www.m-pay.com). A WAP-enabled phone is required to use this system. It is based on server-based credit/debit cards and a WAP-based mobile phone or PC and the Internet. Initially the customer has to register with the payment server. A PIN is allocated which is installed on a SIM card in the mobile phone. The customer then sends a purchase request via SMS to a merchant. This message is sent to the payment server. The payment server authorizes the payment request by sending a confirmation request to the customer. The customer confirms by entering the PIN. The server then debits the amount from the appropriate account. Confirmation is then sent to the payment gateway, which in turn generates a receipt and sends it to the merchant.

To use the m-pay system, the customers will have to register for free. Customers will then have to buy airtime and the amount is automatically drawn from their credit/debit card account. The advantage of this system is that customer's sensitive information is not put online. The system also claims fraud prevention mechanisms. The user's identity is defined on a SIM card in the mobile phone and is further secured by entering a special PIN either on a phone or payment terminal. The payment terminal and payment center authenticate mutually with a digital signature based on the Elliptic Curve Cryptography (ECC) cryptographic system (public key cryptography using elliptic curves). Data encryption is performed according to a validated digital signature. End-to-end encryption is available for third parties, such as banks.

Paybox

Paybox.net (http://www.paybox.de) AG was founded in July 1999 and launched in 2000 by Deutsche Bank, Debitel AG. It covers Germany, Austria, Spain, Sweden, and the UK. This is used for P2P and also real and virtual POS payment via mobile phone. Registration with Paybox is needed and Paybox provides the user with a PIN. The consumer communicates his/her phone number

to the merchant. The merchant communicates this phone number and the price to Paybox via a free phone number. Paybox calls the payer and asks for payment authorization (merchant name and amount are repeated). The payer authorizes by using a PIN. Paybox informs Deutsche Bank as credit institute to settle the payment using a common payment instrument. All the settlements are done via the customer account and hence can be used for various payment frequencies. The procedure is almost the same with Internet payments. Both users and merchants are charged a small fee. Paybox works with any mobile phone independent of financial institution and mobile operator. Paybox is suitable for both micropayments and macropayments. Paybox also promises fraudulent detection techniques. The disadvantage is that Paybox uses interactive voice response (IVR) to make voice calls to the customer. There is no data privacy and no proof of transaction. Transactions are possible with only Global System for Mobile Communications (GSM)-enabled phones. According to Jones (2003), Paybox started too early. Though it was a failure for a brief period of time, the concept resulted in raising interest in the m-commerce market. Technically speaking it was strong, but the other key players were not prepared for the technology. The system ensures secure encryption and the authentication and authorization is done via GSM voice channel using CallerID and mobile subscriber integrated services digital network (MSISDN) for authentication and a Paybox PIN for authorization.

i-Mode

This payment procedure was initiated by NTT DoCoMo, the largest network provider in Japan (http://www.imode.com). This works in m-commerce and e-commerce payment scenarios. The user has to dial a premium number and his/her bills are settled via the phone bill. NTT DoCoMo serves as telco and payment provider and settles the accounts with the merchants. This procedure was also initiated in Europe in 2002 by NTT-Do-CoMo and KPN Mobile. NTT-DoCoMo claims 30 million subscribers in just 4 years around the world.

OboPay

OboPay (http://www.obopay.com) was launched in April 2006. This Palo Alto based startup claims to be the first U.S. company to allow cell phone users to make purchases as well as sending and receiving funds on their mobile phones. Their main targets are theatre tickets and restaurant bills. Obopay relies on a java client on the phone instead of SMS or text message payments like Pay-Pal Mobile and TextPayMe. While this provides for a richer and more secure interface, Obopay is of use only to people who have phones that support Java. It is supported by major carriers Cingular and T-Mobile. Five different handset manufacturers are represented in this group (i.e., Nokia, Motorola, Kyocera; Samsung, and Sony Ericsson). They are currently targeting all of the handsets that are used by the consumers and all the major carriers.

The service allows for P2P payments between phones. Users are also to be issued a debit card attached to the account for real-world payments, including ATM withdrawals. After installing the application on the mobile phone, any amount can be sent to a receiving person. A small transaction fee is also charged.

To use OboPay, an account has to be created and an application has to be downloaded. Once the account is created, request for payments from friends and family, checking the balance, and viewing payments is possible. After creating the account a debit card is received through the mail. The debit card can be used at an ATM or to make purchases in retail. Obopay is associated with MasterCard. The amount of money in the phone is the same as in the debit card. So balances can be checked anywhere and anytime. All the transactions done are stored and hence can be tracked.

LUUP

LUUP (http://www.luup.com) is a new m-payments company in the UK. It is also called LUU-PAY in Germany. It allows consumers to use their mobile phone like a wallet to shop with retailers or send and receive money on a P2P basis—with cash, debit/credit card, and bank account functions built-in. The service is independent of mobile phone operators. LUUP is fully integrated with the UK and German banking systems allowing funds to be accessed from credit cards, debit cards, and bank accounts. One of the major benefits of LUUP is its ability to handle payments between individuals. LUUP users who want to transfer money to a friend or split a restaurant bill can send money with one SMS to anyone with a mobile phone. If the recipient is not a LUUP user, they will receive an SMS with the amount sent to them and an invitation to sign up for a LUUP wallet. Once the LUUP wallet has been credited the recipient can save their money in their account, use it for purchases at LUUP merchants, or transfer it to their bank account. The transaction costs for merchants are very small. Additionally, the purchase process is transparent to consumers who can view all LUUP account activity online in real time helping solve consumer concerns about unfair charges.

LUUP uses 128-bit SSL encrypting, IP, and user password-based client authentication to protect personal data. Online purchases and high value P2P payments are confirmed using a PIN code. Personal information, including credit card details, is not made visible to the merchants.

LUUP is an m-payment solution first launched in Norway under the Contopronto name in July 2002. By May 2006, more than 10,000 customers held LUUP accounts each in the UK, Germany, and Norway. As announced by the media in April 2006, five top mobile operators in UK are planning to launch a service called Pay4It which may challenge LUUP.

MobiPay

Mobipay (Carat, 2002) can be used for payment to stationary merchant or mobile merchant; for payment on the Internet or at a vending machine; for P2P payments; and to recharge mobile telephone pre-paid accounts. A customer's registration with Mobipay is associated with the consumer's telephone number. All the operations are carried out by this number and are authorized by the customer. Usually the authentication is done by a PIN. Once the operation is successful, the transaction charges are remitted through issuer cards or through any client associate. A message is sent to confirm the payment. The Mobipay security system is based on personal Mobipay number, PIN, and encrypted communications through the network.

Paiement CB sur mobile

A France Telecom Mobile launched Paiement CB sur mobile in 2000. The system was previously called as Iti Achat. The system is bank centric and hence is an inter-operator system. This system uses dual slot mobile phones and WAP Internet phones. This M-payment solution is offered to France Telecom mobile subscribers (Itineris network) by using dual slot mobile phones, one of the slots being for chip-based Cartes Bancaires (CB) debit/credit cards. This system allows customers to pay for their purchases on their mobile phones without having to type in their debit or credit card numbers. Users can also reload their prepaid phone accounts and pay utility bills using the CB charge cards.

The customer orders goods by entering his/her mobile phone number (typing it on the merchant Web site in the case of using the Internet or saying it over the mobile phone to the catalog sales merchant). Then the customer receives an SMS with purchase details. If the customer wants to proceed with the purchase, he/she inserts a payment card and types in the PIN. When the transaction is authorized by the bank, a confirmation message is then sent by the bank via SMS to the customer's mobile phone. The merchant receives payment confirmation.

Bibit

Bibit has support from several key companies like Microsoft, IBM, Oracle, Intershop, Mercantec, Allaire and KPN Mobile, and so forth. It covers more than 15 countries. Bibit is specialized in international Internet payments, allowing the consumer to pay a foreign Internet retailer using a payment method which is customary in his/her own country. The consumer is thus able to pay in their own currency using a familiar method, while the retailer is paid in his/her own currency. A customer chooses the product in a virtual shop. The customer is then redirected to the Bibit Payment Service. The customer makes a choice of the payment method. After a successful payment, Bibit notifies the merchant that the order can be shipped. The service is free for consumers. Bibit's back-office informs merchants of all transactions, irrespective of the payment method used. All software is Java-based. All communication to and from Bibit's server is SSL encrypted. Bibit's Mobile Payment Suite can be used to accept payments on a variety of mobile devices. The solution consists of an application that runs on a mobile device, connected to the Internet. The application takes order and credit card details and performs a real-time authorization of the transaction. In most European countries this is possible using standard technology such as GPRS. This means that one single solution can be used in more than one country.

PayPal Mobile

PayPal (http://www.paypal.com) has more than 100 million accounts around the world. PayPal allows sending and receiving payments online securely and easily with a bank account and an

Figure 6. Comparison of different payment systems

Payment System	Payment Initiation	Payment Authorization	Payment Base	Possibility of Interoperability	Security	Cost and Convenience
TextPayMe 2005	SMS	PIN	Bank Card	To be provided in future	Fraud management available	Free
PayPal Mobile 2006	SMS IVR Debit Card	PIN	PayPal account Bank card	Based on PayPal account only, hence not applicable	PIN based security	Fee based on transaction amount
Obopay 2006	Application on handset SMS Debit Card	PIN	Bank Card	Possible	Unauthorized access is prevented. SSL and PIN based security	Sender has to pay the fee
Paiement CB sur mobile 2000	SMS Credit/debit card	PIN	Bank account Debit/credit card	Possible	Secure because of dual chip slot	New handset required registration is free Transaction cost is equal to phone call
LUUP 2002	SMS	PIN	Cash credit/debit card Bank account	Interoperable	SSL based	Nominal transaction fee, no registration fee
Vodafone m-Pay Bill 2002	WAP SMS IVR	PIN	Phone bill Prepaid airtime	Only for Vodafone registered users but interoperable in different countries	No privacy, as personal data is shared with other networks if necessary	No registration fee and transaction fee
mpay 2001	WAP Credit/debit SMS	PIN (SIM card based)	Credit/debit card	Possible	Uses certificates based on SIM cards, so secure.	registration free confirmation costs
i-mode 2002	Phone	PIN	Phone bill	Possible	Levels of Security provided	New handset required Separate fee
Paybox 2000	IVR	PIN	Debit card Bank account	Interoperable with other networks	Personal data on server but is not shared	Annual subscription Transaction fee

e-mail address. It allows payments to be made to the merchants without sharing any financial information with merchants, thus ensuring privacy.

Previously, payments via Paypal were settled via a credit card. This worked for all the payment scenarios. The customer has to register with PayPal and reveal his/her credit card details. If a device like a PDA is used, specific software must be installed. Paypal is now also used for m-payments. The service is called PayPal Mobile. Money can be sent in two ways: (1) by texting to a given number with the amount and recipient's phone number or (2) calling a number and following a set of instructions specified in the scheme. To use PayPal Mobile, customers first activate their telephones by logging into their PayPal accounts. After registering their mobile telephone numbers, users must choose a secure PIN which protects every m-payment. PayPal Mobile users make payments by sending a text message to PayPal. PayPal calls the user back to confirm the m-payment and then sends the money to the recipient. In the case of a text-to-buy purchase, after the merchant receives the payment, the item is shipped to the address already saved in the user's PayPal account.

Comparison

In Figure 6, a comparison of different payment systems is made based on security, cost, convenience, interoperability, payment initiation/authorization, and base. Any customer would accept the payment model if it has high security, is easy to use, and the technology based on which the system works is an already known one. Customers are already used to SMS, credit, and debit cards. Interoperability is about support for different networks, different mobile operators, and different financial institutions. Security is about ensuring confidentiality, integrity, authentication, and availability.

FUTURE TRENDS

The failure of acceptance of many innovative payment procedures like eCash and the German GeldKarte show that there is a wide set of criteria to be satisfied for the system to be successfully adopted by customers (Kreyer et al., 2002). Based on the surveyed articles, it is found that there are no globally accepted payment systems, but there are some trial projects running. In order for B2B and B2C m-commerce to be widely accepted, standard payment procedures should exist. The consumer acceptance depends on cost, security, privacy, and convenience. The reason stated against m-payments in several surveys found in the literature was that security is a big concern across all ages with respect to contactless payment technologies.

The design of m-payment systems should target the e-commerce scenario as already it has proved to be successful. And also m-commerce may initially focus on micropayments, until customers get adjusted to it. It is not possible to make consumers shift all of a sudden to m-payments leaving traditional payments. Local practices followed for payments may be difficult to shift. Relatively, teenagers adapt to new technologies faster than aged people. Cash is still a predominant payment device, but that percentage reduces significantly with age.

The main problems to be faced by a global payment system are that the wireless network infrastructure varies, and customer needs are usually dependent on the region and culture.

Another challenge for m-payment providers is to provide a secure environment and convince the consumers and the merchants about the security (Lee, Kou, & Hu, 2005). Most of the security challenges posed by m-commerce are the problems due to Internet and problems due to WAP. Most of the security solutions provided today are based on PKI keys. The different security issues that have to be taken care of are privacy of data, confidentiality, integrity, authentication, non-repudiation, accountability, system availability, and customer protection.

The technical difficulties can however be overcome through software and hardware solutions and standardizations. With proper intermediaries and interoperable standards, a global m-payment solution is always possible.

Requirements for a Common M-Payments Model

Any future payment system should support these steps at the minimum: (1) Registration for the payment service, (2) Transact and authorize, (3) Proof of completion of transaction, and (4) Dispute resolution.

While in Ding and Hampe (2003) and Schwiderski-Grosche and Knospe (2002), several critical success factors are discussed for successful m-payment systems, we consider ease of use, security, divisibility, transferability, interoperability, privacy, popularity or brand, cost, and standardization as critical factors for success of m-payments. The system should be flexible and open for wider acceptance. Smart-card-based payments are more secure and trustable. PKI keys combined with smart cards enhance trust in the transactions.

Any future payment type should support multiple types of payment methods like credit cards, charge cards, debit cards, direct debit to bank account, and account-based stored value. Banks should not insist the customers to use a particular network service provider. The system should be independent of mobile network operators, bank, and type of device used. The customers should be given an open choice to choose a combination of network service provider and the bank, only then the m-payments will be most widely adopted.

Evolving Standards and Technologies

There are scores of standards for handheld devices and also a lot of network standards like Bluetooth, 802.11a, 802.11b, HyperLAN2, and 802.11g WLANs. Though currently most of the WANs follow 2G or 2.5G, 3G systems will dominate the wireless cellular services. The standards proposed for 3G are CDMA 2000 proposed by Qualcomm and WCDMA proposed by Ericsson. The WCDMA system is capable of internetworking GSM networks and is strongly supported by EU, which calls it UMTS. CDMA 2000 is widely deployed in United States. Other than these, there are a few m-payment specific standards, organizations, and forums. For almost all the standards bodies, the common issues are: (1) security, (2) interoperability, (3) convenience, and (IV) ease of use.

- **Mobile Payment Forum:** It creates a framework for m-commerce using payment card accounts (www.mobilepaymentforum. com). Mobile Payment Forum is also working on standardization of the phases in the m-payment life cycle, namely device setup and configuration, payment initiation, authentication, and payment completion.

- **Mobile Electronic Transactions:** MeT focuses on aspects of digital signatures and PKI for mobile devices (http://www. mobiletransaction.org). The main objective is to ensure the interoperability of mobile transaction solutions.

- **Mobey Forum (Mobile Financial Services):** It focuses on how to use the end-user mobile phone as a personal trusted device. This addresses security issues for mobile execution of financial services: payment, remote banking, and brokerage (http://www. mobeyforum.org). Mobey Forum facilitates aims at facilitating business and security requirements; evaluation of potential business models and technical solutions and by making recommendations to standard bodies; handset manufacturers; payment schemes; network operators; regulators; and technology suppliers in order to speed up the implementation of solutions.

- **PayCircle (Payment group):** PayCircle addresses a business-enabling infrastructure for Web services with the focus on micro payment (http://www.paycircle.org).

- **Radicchio:** Radicchio promotes digital signature and PKI for the mobile environment (http://www.radichchio.org).

- **GMCF:** GMCIG enables security and interoperability for mobile macro payments (http://www.gmcf.org). The Global Mobile Commerce Forum (GMCF) promotes the development of m-commerce services. Its membership includes operators, content providers, suppliers, financial institutes, and other organizations involved with m-commerce. The aim of GMCF is construct standards to facilitate the implementation and use of m-commerce applications and devices.

- **Liberty Alliance Project:** (http://www.projectliberty.org/) For secure interoperability, the Liberty Alliance, a consortium representing organizations from around the world, was created in 2001 to address the technical, business, and policy challenges around identity and identity-based Web services.

- **Oasis PKI Forum:** (http://www.pkiforum.org/) The OASIS PKI Member Section is a group of OASIS members who work together to advance the use of the PKI as a foundation for secure transactions in e-business applications. It was formed in November 2002 with the migration of PKI Forum to OASIS.

- **Open Mobile Alliance:** (http://www.openmobilealliance.org/) The mission of the Open Mobile Alliance is to facilitate global user adoption of mobile data services and ensure service interoperability across devices, geographies, service providers, operators, and networks.

FUTURE RESEARCH

In order to make consumers and merchants naturally get adapted to m-payments, a global and interoperable set of standards for payments needs to be created. It is not just the technical issues that need to be researched, but developing business models that would benefit network operators and banks along with customers and merchants is equally important. A lot of fraudulent activities have been identified in recent literature. The virus, theft of devices, and so forth are a big problem for payments. Hence, fraud management is one issue that can be looked into. Security policies of different countries are a major hindrance to global m-payments. The issues and challenges that arise out of interoperability problems and security problems can be researched further. Anonymity and privacy are important topics in security, which are related to customer personal data, transactions, and content purchased. Mobile operators already have a large customer base. Several operators may collude to share the customer base through the involvement of intermediaries. The trust factor comes into play whenever an intermediary plays an important role in any transaction. Hence, trust in m-commerce is also an important topic when we speak about global m-payments. Trust and security must lie on both the merchant and customer sides.

CONCLUSION

M-payments are quickly catching up in almost all parts of the world. Various m-payment methods have been proposed and implemented in the literature. This chapter has attempted to give an overview of existing m-payment systems, their payment procedures, and limitations. The identified requirements in general, to adopt m-payments are: convenience; cost to implement and use; reliability; user and market acceptance; security; flexibility; speed of transaction; response; and scalability. The issues of concern with most of the existing m-payments are: anonymity, possibility of theft, poor signal reception in certain areas, and inflexible hardware and software solutions. The age of customers, culture, region, type of purchase, size of amount, devices used, and the network operators influence the use of m-payments in a global context. The issues and challenges that arise out of interoperability problems can be solved through proper standards derivation and common security policies. Standards should consider payments in different perspectives. The chapter also includes several payment categorizations based on different issues to enable derivation of better standards.

REFERENCES

Aswin, R. (2003). *From e-commerce to m-commerce: The wireless proposition, HSBC's guide to cash and treasury management in Asia.* Retrieved October 29, 2006 from www.infosys.com/industries/banking/ white-papers/ 11_Wireless_RoongtaHSBC.pdf?page=bcmwphsbc

Bradford, A. (2003). *Consumers need local reasons to pay by mobile.* Retrieved October 29, 2006 from http://www.gartner.com/resources/115600/115603/115603.pdf

Buhan, D., Cheong, Y. C., & Tan, C. (2002). *Mobile payments in m-commerce.* Retrieved October 29, 2006 from http://www.capgemini.com/tme/pdf/MobilePaymentsinMCommrce.pdf

Carat, G. (2002). *E-Payment systems database: Trends and analysis.* Retrieved October 29, 2006 from http://epso.jrc.es/Docs/Background-9.pdf

Damsgaard, J., & Marchegiani, L. (2004). Like Rome, a mobile operator's empire wasn't built in a day! A journey through the rise and fall of mobile network operators. In J. Marjin, et al. (Eds.), *ICEC'04, ACM Sixth International Conference on Electronic Commerce* (pp. 639-648).

Ding, M. S., & Hampe, J. F. (2003, June 9-11). Reconsidering the challenges of mPayments: A roadmap to plotting the potential of the future M-Commerce Market. Paper presented at the *16th Bled eCommerce Conference eTransformation*, Bled, Slovenia.

Ding, M. S., & Unnithan, R. C. (2004). Mobile payments (m-payments)—An exploratory study of emerging issues and future trends. In P. C. Deans (Ed.), *E-commerce and m-commerce technologies.* Hershey, PA: Idea Group.

Gross, S., Fleisch, E., Lampe, M., & Miller, R. (2004). *Requirements and technologies for ubiquitous payment.* Retrieved October 29, 2006 from http://www.vs.inf.ethz.ch/res/papers/MKWI_UPayment.pdf

Jones, N. (2003, January 28). *Pay box retrenches, but its technology remains active.* Retrieved October 29, 2006 from http://gartner11.gartnerweb.com/resources/112800/112827/112827.pdf

Kountz, E. (2002). Mobile commerce: No cell, no sale? *Card Technology, 7*(9), 20-22.

Kreyer, N., Pousttchi, K., & Turowski, K. (2002). *Characteristics of mobile payment procedures.* M-Services 2002. Retrieved October 29, 2006 from ftp.informatik.rwth-aachen.de/ Publications/CEUR-WS/Vol-61/paper1.pdf

Lee, C-W., Kou, W., & Hu, W-C. (2005). Mobile commerce security and payment methods. In W-C. Hu, C-W Lee, & W. Kou (Eds.), *Advances in security and payment methods for mobile commerce.* Hershey, PA: Idea Group.

Lombardi, C. (2006, April 10). *Cell phone subscriptions surge in India.*

Retrieved October 29, 2006 from http://news.com.com/Cell+phone+subscriptions+surge+in+India/2110-1037_3-6059482.html

McKitterrick, D., & Dowling, J. (2003). *State of the art review of mobile payment technology.* Retrieved October 29, 2006 from http://www.cs.tcd.ie/publications/tech-reports/reports.03/TCD-CS-2003-24.pdf

Meister, R. (2005, June 27). *The situation of M-Commerce after Simpay's retreat.* Retrieved October 29, 2006 from http://www.payboxsolutions.com/327_397.htm

Mercator Advisory Group Report 1. (2006). *A research report on mobile payments in the United States: SMS and NFC implementations enter the market.* Retrieved October 29, 2006 from http://www.paymentsnews.com/mercator_advisory_gr/index.html

Mercator Advisory Group Report 2. (2006). *A research report on predicting mobile payment success in Asia.* Retrieved October 29, 2006 from http://www.mercatoradvisorygroup.com/index.php?doc=emerging_technologies&action=view_item&id=137&catid=5

MeT. (2003). *MeT white paper on mobile transactions.* Retrieved October 29, 2006 from http://www.mobiletransactions.org/pdf/R200/white_papers/MeT_White_paper_on_mobile_transactions_v1.pdf

Nambiar, S., & Lu, C. (2005). M-payment solutions and m-commerce fraud management. Mobile Commerce Security and Payment methods. In W-C. Hu, C-W. Lee, & W. Kou (Eds.), *Advances in security and payment methods for mobile commerce.* Hershey, PA: Idea Group.

Nystedt, D. (2006, February 24). *China passes 400 million mobile phone user mark.* Retrieved October 29, 2006 from http://www.infoworld.com/article/06/02/24/75849_HNchinaphoneusers_1.html

Ondrus, J. (2003). *Mobile payments: A tool kit for a better understanding of the market.* Retrieved October 29, 2006 from http://www.hec.unil.ch/jondrus/files/papers/mpayment.pdf

Ondrus, J., & Pigneur, Y. (2006). A multi-stakeholder multi-criteria assessment framework of mobile payments: An illustration with the Swiss public transportation industry. In *Proceedings of the 39th Hawaii IEEE International Conference on System Sciences* (pp. 1-10).

Schwiderski-Grosche, S., & Knospe, H. (2002). Secure mobile commerce. In C. Mitchell (Ed.), *Special issue of the IEE Electronics and Communication Engineering Journal on Security for Mobility, 14*(5), 228-238. Retrieved October 29, 2006 from http://www.isg.rhul.ac.uk/~scarlet/documents/Secure%20m-commerce%20ECEJ.pdf

Seah, W., Pilakkat, S., Shankar, P., Tan, S. K., Roy, A. G., & Ng, E. (2001). *The future mobile payments infrastructure: A common platform for secure m-payments.* Retrieved October 29, 2006 from http://www.itu.int/ITU-D/pdf/4597-13.3bis-en.pdf

Stallings, W. (2000). *Network security essentials: Applications and standards.* Pearson Education.

Zmijewska, A., Lawrence, E., & Steele, R. (2004, July 12-13). Classifying m-payments—A user-centric model. In *Proceedings of the International Conference on Mobile Business 04,* New York.

Chapter IV
Policy–Based Security for M–Commerce Networks

Wassim Itani
American University of Beirut, Lebanon

Ayman Kayssi
American University of Beirut, Lebanon

Ali Chehab
American University of Beirut, Lebanon

ABSTRACT

In this chapter we present an overview of a general policy-based security architecture for securing the confidentiality, authenticity, and integrity of enterprise mobile commerce (m-commerce) data. A policy-based architecture protects data based on content and sensitivity and highly surpasses the performance of bulk encryption protocols such as secure sockets layer (SSL) and transport layer security (TLS) by utilizing a customizable, policy-driven approach. This approach makes use of the structure of enterprise data objects (Web pages, relational database entities, directory hierarchies, log files, etc...) to provide flexible, multi-level, and fine-grained encryption and hashing methodologies. This makes policy-based security protocols a very efficient choice for operation in wireless m-commerce environments characterized by low-bandwidth networks and supporting limited-resource devices with low memory, battery, and processing power.

INTRODUCTION

With the emergence of the wireless application protocol (WAP Forum, 2000) in 1998, which provided users of mobile devices with an optimized wireless protocol to access the Internet and to browse specific Web content, and with the introduction of specialized wireless programming models such as Java 2 Mobile Edition (J2ME) (Lawton, 2002), the .Net Compact Framework (Neable, 2002), and the Binary Runtime Environment for Wireless (QUALCOMM Incorp., 2004), businesses started accepting a new set of clients represented in cell phones, two-way pagers, PDAs, and palmtops. Enterprise application software is witnessing a rapid proliferation and an increased user base supported by the ubiquity, accessibility, and flexibility provided by wireless networking and mobile computing and communication (Shim, Varshney, Dekleva, & Knoerzer, 2006).

New m-commerce applications are becoming possible (Smith, 2006) and many existing e-commerce applications can be modified to fit into the mobile environment. M-commerce offers several advantages for today's businesses by allowing them to reach existing and new clients through new and extended channels, such as mobile communications and wireless channels. It also allows companies to offer new and enhanced applications and services that are unique to the wireless world. Using a mobile device, the user can interact with m-commerce applications in real time, anywhere and at any time, without being bound to one location. In the same sense, m-commerce vendors and application service providers can access their users through location or positioning systems, such as global positioning systems (GPS), which could lead to a suite of valuable location-based applications and services. In addition and due to the fact that mobile devices are not usually shared among users, huge opportunities exist for developing personalized applications and services that can be offered by application providers to individual users.

Although the adoption of m-commerce services is showing some acceleration, great concerns are raised about the security of the sensitive data over the wireless links where confidentiality, authenticity, and integrity are potentially compromised by unauthorized access. Mobile applications have special and unique requirements compared to Internet applications. Usually, mobile applications operate over low bandwidth networks with high latency and frequent disconnections using devices that vary greatly in capabilities and resources. For these reasons, the protocols used in securing mobile enterprise applications have to be designed

specifically for operation in wireless environments and must address the needs and requirements of a large variety of devices which are, in their majority, severely constrained in terms of processor speed, memory resources, storage capacity, and battery power. This diversity makes the implementation of a unique security standard that encompasses the whole device range infeasible. A least-common denominator security standard that targets devices with limited memory and slow processors would be unfair for powerful devices and would not meet their security requirements, and in the same sense, a security standard that addresses high-end devices would neither fit nor perform efficiently on limited-resource devices. What is needed is a security protocol that can be customized and configured to perform the security operations flexibly, taking into consideration the memory capabilities and the processing power of the device, the wireless network latency, and the specific requirements of the enterprise application. This ensures the efficient operation of the same application on a wide range of devices and wireless networks. Moreover, this protocol must be extensible, scalable, and capable of evolving to meet new challenges and to adapt to new application requirements.

In this chapter we present an overview of a general, policy-based security architecture for securing the confidentiality, authenticity, and integrity of enterprise m-commerce data. A policy-based architecture protects data based on content and sensitivity and highly surpasses the performance of bulk encryption protocols such as the SSL protocol (Freier, Karlton, & Kocher, 1996) and the TLS protocol (Dierks & Allen, 1997) by utilizing a customizable, policy-driven approach. This approach makes use of the structure of enterprise data objects (Web pages, relational database entities, directory hierarchies, log files, etc...) to provide flexible, multi-level, and fine-grained encryption and hashing methodologies. This makes policy-based security protocols a very efficient choice for operation in wireless m-commerce environments.

The rest of this chapter is organized as follows: the next section discusses some solutions for securing m-commerce applications. The third section provides an overview of the design and architecture of a general policy-based security system, and the fourth section presents a formal and platform independent analysis of the policy-based system performance and shows the cost savings offered over traditional m-commerce security systems. The fifth section points out some protocol implementations utilizing the policy-based security architecture presented. Conclusions are presented in the final section.

M-COMMERCE SECURITY SOLUTIONS: AN OVERVIEW

This section provides an overview of current solutions dealing with the security of wireless networks and applications. It examines the degree to which the solutions are effective in securing mobile systems, considers the topics that require greater consideration and refinement, and shows the advantages that a policy-driven security solution offers over these security solutions.

Transport Layer Solutions

At the transport layer, security protocols are categorized into two main architectures depending on their conformance to current Internet protocols. The first architecture uses non-standard Internet protocols to secure data in the wireless part of the network and then switches to standard Internet protocols in the wired parts of the network (WAP Forum, 2000). This use of non-standard Internet protocols on the wireless device is related to the fact that Internet protocols in their current form were too heavy for implementation on low-memory and limited-power wireless devices. This lack of compatibility between the wireless protocols and the wired protocols necessitates the presence of a proxy or gateway that performs the protocol switching operations.

The second architecture insists that compliance with current Internet protocols can be achieved by implementing these protocols in a way that respects the limited resources on the wireless device and that takes into consideration the characteristics of the wireless network (Dawkins, Montenegro, Kojo, & Magret, 2001). This architecture does not require a gateway between the client and the server.

The WAP (WAP Forum, 2000) makes use of the first model. WAP uses the wireless transport layer security protocol (WTLS) as its security protocol at the transport layer. WTLS is based on the TLS protocol and optimized to be used efficiently within the limitations of wireless communications. WTLS is responsible for securing data on the wireless network between the mobile phone and the WAP gateway, while the SSL protocol secures the communication on the wired network between the WAP gateway and the Internet Web server. This architecture has the advantage of being well-suited for operation in restricted wireless environments since its wireless protocols are especially designed for such environments; however, the incompatibility with standard Internet protocols and the need for using a gateway to perform protocol conversion raises serious security concerns and prevents WAP 1.x from providing end-to-end security (Soriano & Ponce, 2002). This is due to the fact that the protocol conversion mechanism leaves data in an unencrypted form at the gateway during the protocol switching process, which risks the confidentiality of data at the gateway. Any intruder who gains access to this gateway can intercept the data after it is decrypted and before it is encrypted again by SSL. Moreover, the gateway represents a single point of failure by being the only entry point to the Internet for a large number of wireless clients.

It should be noted that enhancements in WAP (WAP Forum, 2002) fix the gateway security problem by providing a new alternative approach that does not use a gateway at all by adding support for the standard Internet communication protocols such as IP, TCP, and HTTP. Thus, the WAP-enabled mobile phones become Internet-enabled devices. However, WAP-based applications have experienced a decline in their user base lately due to a number of weaknesses in WAP, which in-device applications (such as J2ME- and .NET-based applications) can overcome.

The second TLS approach relies on using Internet-based security protocols end-to-end and thus eliminating the need for using a protocol conversion gateway. Being the de facto security protocol on the Web, SSL is the natural choice to be used in providing the end-to-end security of this approach. SSL has proved to be very successful in securing e-commerce applications. It operates by establishing a secure channel on top of TCP, where it provides server authentication using certificates, confidentiality, and message integrity. Optionally, there is support for cryptographic client authentication. Despite its success in securing Internet applications, SSL, in some of its parts, is too compute- and memory-intensive for wireless devices, thus Sun Microsystems has developed a light-weight SSL implementation called KSSL (Gupta & Gupta, 2001) which is a client-side implementation of SSL version 3.0, supporting the RSA-RC4-128-MD5 and RSA-RC4-40-MD5 cipher suites.

SSL is divided into four sub-protocols; these are Handshake, Record, Alert, and Change Cipher Specification. The *handshake protocol* is the most complex part of SSL. Its purpose is threefold; first, it allows the client and server to negotiate encryption and message authentication code (MAC) algorithms to be used in protecting the actual data transfer. Second, it allows the client and server to establish a set of cryptographic keys, which will be used by the Record layer to conventionally encrypt the SSL record data using the agreed-upon algorithms. Third, the handshake protocol authenticates the server and may optionally authenticate the client. The handshake protocol uses public key operations to create a master secret that is shared by the client and the server. It is this master secret that will be used to generate the symmetric cipher keys and the MAC keys. These public key operations as well as the parsing of certificate chains used to authenticate the server impose a major performance bottleneck that is particularly evident in mobile devices. For this reason, the SSL specification also supports an abbreviated SSL Handshake which makes use of previous session communication between the same client and server, such as reusing the master secret of the previous session, to avoid parsing server certificates and performing public key cryptographic operations. This improves the performance of the handshake mechanism significantly. The Record layer is responsible for securing the actual data transfer by assuring its confidentiality and integrity using the algorithms and keys negotiated and established by the handshake protocol. The *alert protocol* is used to allow one side to alert the other to exceptional conditions, while the *change cipher specification protocol* is needed to indicate the completion of the handshake operation and the start of the symmetric ciphering and MAC operations.

The SSL implementation on J2ME devices (KSSL) provides a major advantage by enabling these devices to communicate directly and securely with the large number of Internet Web servers supporting SSL. The main concept behind KSSL is represented in reusing previous session results such as certificate parsing results and master secrets, in order to avoid repeated SSL handshakes. This helps in avoiding complex, resource-intensive, public-key operations on the client device. Moreover, KSSL does not implement client authentication since it requires CPU-intensive private-key RSA operations. KSSL, and its related classes, increase the size of the J2ME virtual machine by approximately 25%, and it is the recommended protocol to support HTTPS (HTTP over SSL) in the MIDP 2.0 specification.

Despite the advantage provided by KSSL in securing m-commerce applications, some comments are worth mentioning here. First, KSSL's performance is considered unacceptable when the client needs to communicate with different servers or when browsing sensitive content. This is due to the fact that in such cases the full handshake SSL operation needs to be carried out every time the client connects to a new Web server. The full handshake takes 10-13 sec on a CDPD wireless network using a 20 MHz Palm PDA (Gupta & Gupta, 2001). This performance bottleneck can be avoided when the client communicates with the same server repeatedly by performing an abbreviated handshake that makes use of the previous session's certificate parsing result and master key, hence bypassing resource-intensive, public-key operations. However, storing the master secret and reusing it repeatedly in generating the symmetric ciphering keys raises some concerns about the security of this master key on the mobile device which can be easily snooped or stolen. This is a very important issue to consider since nearly all the security of SSL depends on keeping the master secret private. An attacker who knows the master secret can compute all the cryptographic keys that are used to protect the connection.

A second comment about the operation of SSL is its non-differentiation when performing the encryption operations on the mobile device. In other words, SSL indiscriminately encrypts all the network data without regard to its type or sensitivity. To SSL, network data is of one type, and there is no categorization of this network data based on sensitivity. Thus when using SSL, all the network data is encrypted by the same cryptographic key strength, which can be unnecessary or even undesirable for some wireless applications. This fact about SSL will become more evident and pressing as the m-commerce network expands; thus the need will arise for a configurable security model with flexible encryption schemes to meet a range of different requirements.

The application-layer security model presented in this chapter has given great attention to this issue. A "one-size-fits-all" solution such as KSSL is not feasible in the diverse wireless world where no assumption can be made about the capability and performance of mobile devices or about the operation of applications on wireless networks. It is only the user and the service provider who can determine the actual needs and requirements of their applications. For this reason, the security operations are based on an externally customizable and differential security policy which groups network data according to sensitivity and content and takes into consideration the processing power and memory capabilities of the client device. This flexibility ensures efficient operation of the same application on a wide range of devices and wireless networks.

Application-Layer Solutions

On the application layer, some solutions propose using the Extensible Markup Language (XML) (Bartel, Boyer, Fox, LaMacchia, & Simon, 2002; Imamura, Dillaway, & Simon, 2002) as the format for data communication between mobile clients and back-end servers and to provide end-to-end security by securing the XML documents transferred between the client and the server. Such proposals relied on several XML security protocols that have been proposed to support communication data security in XML applications. Of these security protocols one can mention the XML encryption protocol (Imamura et al., 2002), which provides applications with the ability to encrypt certain sections of an XML document, or even the whole document, by using symmetric ciphering techniques, whose keys are referenced in the document; the XML digital signature protocol (Bartel et al., 2002), which specifies how to digitally sign an XML document and the Security Assertion Markup Language (OASIS, 2002), which specifies how to embed authentication and authorization information in an XML document.

One example of a commonly used XML-based technology is Web Services (Weerawarana, Curbera, Leymann, Storey, & Ferguson, 2005). Securing Web Services is usually done by using a combination of the XML security protocols presented earlier in this section. The most significant specification dealing with the security of Web Services is the one produced by OASIS (OASIS, 2006). This specification proposes the addition of a standard set of simple object access protocol (SOAP) extensions to ensure the privacy and integrity of the SOAP messages produced and consumed by the Web Service. On the other hand, Web Services data can also be protected by utilizing point-to-point SSL channels to secure the entire connection. The SSL approach, in addition to having large overhead and slow response times, does not suit the distributed nature of the Web Services architecture and complicates the routing of the SOAP XML messages between the client and service across different intermediary entities (IBM & Microsoft, 2002).

In spite of all the advantages provided by the Web Services technology in building distributed applications that are simple to develop and use and that are based on a standard and platform-independent, XML-based messaging architecture, its area of application is drastically bounded and restricted in m-commerce applications and environments. This is a direct result of the poor response times and the high protocol overhead imposed on the low-bandwidth wireless network infrastructures and the battery-powered mobile devices. The tagged structure of XML (International Telecommunication Union [ITU], 2001) makes it a rather heavy language for the limited wireless bandwidths and imposes extra network traffic and overhead that is not necessary in a wireless environment. Adding cryptographic security

to the Web Services architecture will make the response times even worse due to the additional complexity imposed by the XML cryptographic algorithms.

In a policy-based security architecture, the format of the network data is implementation-dependent and there is a clear and clean separation between the data format used to transport the data between the communicating parties and the implementation of the security operations. This makes the security solution applicable to a range of data formats without being bound to a single one and allows for the effort to be concentrated on assuring security and guaranteeing optimal performance without making any assumptions about the format used in transporting the network data.

Another application-layer security solution is Tiny SESAME (Al-Muhtadi, Mickunas, & Campbell, 2002). It is a light-weight implementation based on the Secure European System for Applications in a Multi-vendor Environment (SESAME) architecture (Vandenwauver, Govaerts, & Vandewalle, 1997). SESAME is designed for operation in distributed systems where it provides access control, authentication, and data confidentiality and integrity. It supports the Kerberos authentication mechanism and extends it with additional services such as asymmetric public key cryptography and access control and authorization certificates.

Tiny SESAME has the advantage of being based on standardized protocols such as Kerberos and SESAME; however, two main reasons make it unsuitable for operation in wireless environments. First, SESAME regularly employs public-key/Kerberos operations to securely authenticate network entities and to establish trust relationships. These operations impose a heavy load on mobile devices and require intensive CPU and memory resources that lead to unacceptable response times in mobile applications. Second, Tiny SESAME's light weight is achieved through the use of a dynamically reconfigurable, component-based architecture where resources can be loaded dynamically at runtime. This dynamic resource loading, although it helps in reducing the memory requirements of the application, increases network traffic, and raises significant security risks on low-end mobile device platforms that lack the standard security verification and access mechanisms for controlling the operation of dynamically loaded resources. The absence of such security mechanisms is due to their complex and memory-consuming algorithms that cannot be supported on low-end devices. For this reason, dynamic resource loading is eliminated from low-end platforms such as J2ME/CLDC, which makes the implementation of Tiny SESAME only possible on high-end devices.

POLICY-BASED SECURITY DESIGN AND ARCHITECTURE

This section provides an overview of the design and architecture of a general policy-based security system for m-commerce. It details the components and processes involved in building an efficient, policy-based, and customizable security system. Figure 1 presents an abstract view of the different components comprising this security architecture. A functional description of each component is presented next.

Figure 1. An m-commerce policy-based architecture

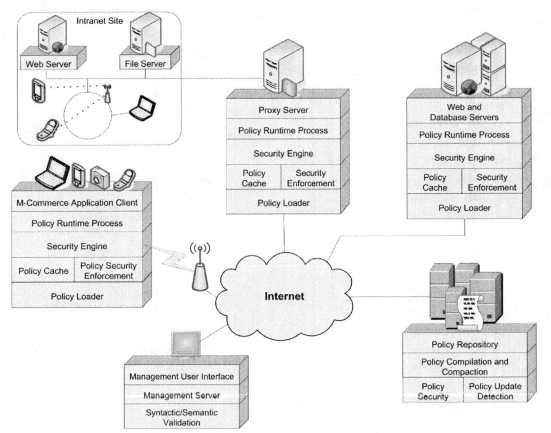

The Security Policy

The security policy specifies the security behavior and operation of the m-commerce enterprise application. It identifies which m-commerce data should be secured and in what way. In other words, the security policy consists of a set of conditions and rules over which the policy is applied, and a set of actions that are executed in the event of satisfying the policy conditions. The source information of this policy is present in a centralized policy repository on a file server, database server, or a directory server. A policy-based security system operates on the network devices by seamlessly employing a security engine component to transparently control the network data encryption/decryption operations. The security services supported by the security engine are controlled and configured based on the information present in the policy configuration file which provides the primary information source that the security engine consults for taking security decisions at runtime. Based on this design paradigm, the security system can provide end-to-end security services for all the sensitive m-commerce information flowing on the network.

Utilizing a customizable security policy in the architecture enhances to a great degree the scalability, flexibility, and customization of the security system. Moreover, it facilitates the process of managing and administering the different elements composing the security architecture. This is considered very vital in today's complex and intricate m-commerce systems where the process of managing and securing the different network nodes is not in any way a simple task.

To be effective, the security policy should be characterized by intuitiveness and simplicity in specification to make the job of the security administrator easy. On the other hand it should also be optimized for operation and interpretation by the network devices functioning according to the specification of this policy. Since the two requirements are somewhat contradicting, two security policy levels are usually specified; a high-level security policy consisting of high-level syntactic constructs that can be easily implemented by a human operator, and a low-level security policy which is a compiled binary representation of the high-level policy, optimized for operation on network devices and auto-generated by a high-level policy compiler.

The high-level security policy usually consists of two main parts: the first part specifies a set of security-related attributes and configuration parameters, while the second part identifies the scope and strength of the encryption and hashing operations to be applied on the fields of the m-commerce data. The security-related attributes and configuration parameters specified in the first part are required by the security engine component to control the confidentiality, integrity, and key management operations. The security engine is the component responsible for taking security decisions and carrying out security-related operations to secure the network data. The following is a possible list of attributes supported by security policy:

- **Encryption algorithm:** Specifies the encryption algorithm to be used for securing the privacy of the m-commerce data.
- **Hashing algorithm:** Specifies the hashing algorithm to be used in securing the integrity of the m-commerce data.
- **Key management algorithm:** Specifies the key management algorithm for sharing the initial secret key between the different communicating entities in the network.
- **Session keys lifetime:** Specifies how frequently the encryption keys should be regenerated. It should be noted that the lifetime of session keys has a major impact on the security of the system and its performance. As the lifetime decreases, the security increases since the network data in this case will be encrypted by frequently changing keys which reduces the risk that

an attacker will gather useful information about the encrypted network data, and makes successful analysis less probable. However, this increase in security comes at the expense of performance. The inclusion of the *session keys lifetime* attribute in a security policy is very important since it gives enterprise users a great deal of flexibility in setting this attribute according to the security requirements of their application and the capabilities of their mobile devices.

Many other attributes may be included depending on the m-commerce application security and performance requirements. It is worth emphasizing that a policy-based architecture, in theory, can generically support any number of encryption, hashing, and key management algorithms. However, increasing the number of supported algorithms is practically infeasible due to the overhead of protocol implementations on limited-storage devices.

The second part in the security policy controls the scope and level of the security operations to be applied on the network data. The scope specifies what data is to be encrypted depending on a certain criteria related to the sensitivity of this data. For example, any data pattern matching a credit card number or a banking account format should be encrypted. The level parameter specifies the level of encryption to be applied on the data. The number of encryption levels that the policy-based architecture can provide depends on the different key lengths supported by the encryption algorithm used. Usually the following four encryption levels are provided: a *High_Security* level which is equivalent to 256-bit AES (Daemen & Rijmen, 2001) encryption; a *Medium_Security* level which is equivalent to 192-bit AES encryption; a *Standard_Security* level which is equivalent to 128-bit AES encryption; and a *No_Security* level which represents no encryption or security on the field.

It should be noted that as the key length increases, the security of the system and the processing requirements of the algorithm increase.

The Policy Loader

In order for the policy information present in the policy repository to be utilized by the mobile devices, there has to be a mechanism for loading this policy information from its central location to the network device runtime system. In a policy-driven, security architecture, the policy loader component is responsible for carrying out the policy loading operation.

A very important criterion when designing the policy loader component is the policy loading time. This is the time at which the mobile device requests loading the security policy to initialize the policy runtime process. Two design alternatives are usually considered. The first one is to load the security policy at application startup (eager loading), while the other is to load the security policy at the time it is first needed (lazy loading). The drawback of the first approach is that it adds to the application startup time and requires the application user to explicitly issue the policy loading command, which contradicts an essential design goal of keeping the security architecture details as transparent as possible to the application and its users. On the other hand, the second approach has the disadvantage of increasing the time needed for carrying out the first operation requiring the security policy, since it now includes the time needed for loading the security policy from the policy repository. It is worth mentioning here that in most cases the security policy will not be loaded from the policy repository, but rather from a local copy present in the mobile device cache. This will dramatically enhance the policy loading time.

The Policy Runtime Process

The policy runtime process is a compact, internal representation of the security policy in the memory of the mobile device. This runtime process is initialized at policy loading time and is the primary source that the security engine consults for taking security decisions and carrying out security-related operations at runtime.

Policy Security

The security policy contains sensitive information that controls the various security operations in an m-commerce application. Any malicious modification to this information may lead to dangerous security attacks. As an example, consider the scenario where the security policy is maliciously modified to specify that no data is to be encrypted. Thus, assuring the integrity of the policy information must be given exceptional attention. MACs and digital signatures are two common mechanisms to guarantee the authenticity of the policy information downloaded from the central policy repository to the mobile devices.

Policy Caching

Policy caching on the network devices is an important feature that must be considered when designing the policy loader. Caching improves the policy loading time by using a local copy of the security policy instead of loading it remotely from the policy repository every time it is requested. However, due to the possible modification of the policy configuration by users and administrators, good care should be taken to ensure that the policy information is kept up-to-date in the local cache. For this reason, whenever the policy loader component requests the policy information, the policy repository component checks if the policy configuration has been modified. If the policy has changed, the policy repository sends the updated version to the device; otherwise it asks the policy loader on the client to load the policy information from the local cache. The process of detecting the modification of the policy configuration is implementation-dependent. Message digests can

be used to check for possible updates in the policy configuration.

Policy Compaction and Compilation

The high-level policy information present in the policy configuration file should be designed to be human-readable so that it can be easily configured by users and system administrators using simple text editors. Transferring this information as-is over the network to the mobile device will not only produce unnecessary increase in the network traffic, but will also increase the storage requirements due to the policy caching mechanism, and the processing load on the mobile device due to the large number of string operations necessary to parse and interpret the policy information. For this reason, a policy-based architecture utilizes a policy compactor component, which is responsible for parsing the policy configuration file and compiling it into a compact binary, low-level representation before transmitting it to the mobile device. This compact binary representation consists of a set of simple data structures that can be easily processed.

Policy Repository

The policy repository is the central location used to store the security policies generated by security administrators using policy administration utilities. The policy repository could be a directory server, a file server, a relational database server, and so forth. LDAP-based directory servers are the most popular for managing the storage of security policy representations. It should be noted that the policy repository may be used to store human-readable, high-level security policies or compiled low-level security policies.

The Policy Administration Utility

A security policy configuration file can be created using a simple text editor or using a policy administration utility. The policy administration utility is a human-friendly, graphical user interface application that facilitates the creation and management of security policy configuration files. It helps the security administrator create and administer security policy files rapidly without requiring knowledge of the exact details of the policy file syntax. This assists in constructing valid and error-free policy configuration files. The policy administration utility plays a major role in checking the syntactic and semantic structure of the policy file and determining whether this policy file is compatible with the device and network resources and other security performance constraints.

The Security Engine

The security engine is the most important component in the security architecture due to the great role it plays in providing, directly or indirectly, the essential security services needed for protecting the m-commerce application and securing its data. The security engine is responsible for providing authentication and data confidentiality and integrity services. The security engine participates in carrying out an efficient and secure key management mechanism and ensures the storage security of the ciphering keys and other sensitive parameters on the mobile devices. The security services supported by the security engine are controlled and configured based on information present in the policy runtime process, which provides the primary information source the security engine consults for taking security decisions at runtime. The security engine is the only component that can be accessed by the application. The interaction between the security engine and the application is done through an application programming interface (API) that hides the complexity of security programming and operations from the application developer.

As shown in Figure 1, the policy-based security architecture can be implemented to operate on a proxy server to provide the data assurance to an entire intranet site or LAN. This scenario is suitable for providing policy-based security services to mobile devices with limited resources that are not capable of running the security engine in their address space.

SYSTEM PERFORMANCE MODEL

This section presents a formal mathematical analysis of the performance of a policy-based security architecture. Most of the equations presented in this performance analysis are conducted in a platform-neutral manner without relying on any device hardware or operating system. In the rest of this section we will use the following notation:

- N is the number of encryption levels supported by the policy-based security architecture (this depends on the number of key lengths supported by the encryption algorithm).
- T is the number of bytes exchanged between two network entities in an m-commerce session.
- E_T is the number of bytes encrypted in an m-commerce session.
- μ_i is the percentage of bytes encrypted by the ith encryption level based on the specifications of the security policy.

Percent Decrease in Encrypted Bytes

PDE is the percent decrease in encryption operations resulting from the use of policy-based encryption mechanisms. Compared to bulk encryption, the percent decrease in encryption operations is obtained as follows:

$$PDE = \frac{T - E_T}{T} \times 100$$

The percent decrease in hash operations can be obtained in a similar manner.

Performance Gain

We now calculate the performance gain achieved due to the policy-based security. We define W_i to be the number of bytes encrypted by the ith encryption level.

The percentage of bytes encrypted according to the ith encryption level is obtained as follows:

$$\mu_i = \frac{W_i}{T} \times 100$$

Let Ψ_i be the cost of an encryption operation using the ith encryption level. This cost may be the number of CPU cycles to perform an encryption operation or the RAM footprint consumed by an encryption operation, or a function of both. It should be noted that the values of the different Ψ_i s are platform-dependent but $\Psi_1 < \Psi_i < \Psi_N$ since the complexity, and therefore cost, of encryption increases with the size of the encryption key. Assume that the traditional security approach of securing all m-commerce network traffic uses an encryption strength equivalent to Ψ_r; we define:

$$J = \sum_{i=1}^{N} \frac{\mu_i}{100} \times \Psi_i$$

The performance gain G, resulting from the use of policy-based security mechanisms relative to the traditional approach which encrypts all traffic will be:

$$G = \frac{\Psi_r - J}{\Psi_r} \times 100$$

If the policy-based architecture uses a three-level encryption scheme (low, medium, and high)

utilizing an encryption algorithm with three key sizes such as AES (128, 192, and 256 bit keys) then the percentage of bytes encrypted according to the high, medium, and low encryption levels are respectively obtained as follows:

$$\mu_3 = \frac{W_3}{T} \times 100$$

$$\mu_2 = \frac{W_2}{T} \times 100$$

$$\mu_1 = \frac{W_1}{T} \times 100$$

If the traditional security approach of securing all m-commerce traffic uses an encryption strength equivalent to the medium encryption level that is, $\Psi_r = \Psi_2$, we will have:

$$J = \frac{\mu_1}{100} \times \Psi_1 + \frac{\mu_2}{100} \times \Psi_2 + \frac{\mu_3}{100} \times \Psi_3$$

and

$$G = \frac{\Psi_2 - J}{\Psi_2} \times 100$$

PROTOCOL IMPLEMENTATIONS

Many security protocols utilizing the policy-based security architecture are available. Some protocols are designed to secure general m-commerce network traffic and storage data (Itani & Kayssi, 2003; Itani & Kayssi, 2004; Itani, Kayssi, & Chehab, 2005b), while others are specifically oriented towards other e-commerce applications such as protecting relational database data entities (Itani, Kayssi, & Chehab, 2006a), Web-based network traffic (Itani, Gaspard, Kayssi, & Chehab, 2006), and safeguarding the process of business transaction logging in wireless environments (Itani, Kayssi, & Chehab, 2005a). The protocol implementations and their functional relationships are presented in Figure 2. It should be noted here that the hierarchical structure representation of the policy-based security protocols in Figure 2 is done based on the functional dependency of the child protocol on its parent protocol or protocols. For example, the relational database security protocol at the bottom of the hierarchy tree in Figure 2 relies on the general security protocol for providing the data confidentiality and integrity security services for transport data marshaling over the enterprise network links and on the audit log security protocol (which in turn depends on the general storage security protocol) for protecting the privacy and authenticity of the stored enterprise data (Itani, Kayssi, & Chehab, 2006b). All these protocols employ a variety of the components described in a way specific to the targeted application and suiting its requirements and constraints. A considerable performance gain is realized when implementing these protocols in real m-commerce environments, since some protocols are able to achieve a 200 to 300 percent increase in performance gain over traditional bulk encryption protocols.

Figure 2. Policy-based security protocol implementations

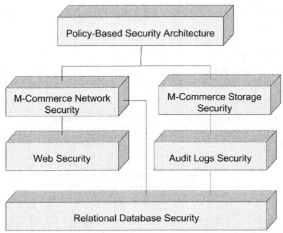

CONCLUSION

In this chapter we presented a policy-driven security architecture for protecting m-commerce network data. The security architecture is designed for operation in mobile environments. It provides authentication and data confidentiality and integrity services to m-commerce systems, based on a flexible and fine-grained encryption scheme customized by a scalable and extensible security policy. This chapter provided an overview of the design and components of this architecture, presented a performance model, and mentioned some protocol implementations built according to the specifications of this architecture.

REFERENCES

IBM & Microsoft. (2002). *Security in a Web services world: A proposed architecture and roadmap*. Retrieved from http://www-128.ibm.com/developerworks/library/specification/ws-secmap/

Al-Muhtadi, J., Mickunas, D., & Campbell, R. (2002). A lightweight reconfigurable mechanism for 3G/4G mobile devices. *IEEE Wireless Communications.*

Bartel, M., Boyer, J., Fox, B., LaMacchia, B., & Simon, E. (2002). *XML-signature syntax and processing.* W3C Recommendation. Retrieved from http://www.w3.org/TR/xmldsig-core/

Daemen, J., & Rijmen, V. (2001). Rijndael, the advanced encryption standard. *Dr Dobb's Journal, 26*(3), 137-139.

Dawkins, S., Montenegro, G., Kojo, M., & Magret V. (2001). End-to-end performance implications of slow links. *RFC3150.* Retrieved from http://www.faqs.org/rfcs/rfc3150.html

Dierks, T., & Allen, C. (1997). The TLS Protocol[Version 1.0]. Internet-Draft. Retrieved from http://tools.ietf.org/html/draft-ietf-tls-protocol-00

Freier, A., Karlton, P., & Kocher, P. (1996). The SSL protocol [Version 3.0]. Internet-Draft. Retrieved from http://www.netscape.com/eng/ss13/draft302.text

Gupta, V., & Gupta, S. (2001). Securing the wireless Internet. *IEEE Communication, 39*(12), 68-74.

IBM & Microsoft (2002). *Security in a Web Services World: A Proposed Architecture and Roadmap.* Retrieved from, http://www-128.ibm.com/developerworks/library/specification/ws-secmap/

Imamura, T., Dillaway, B., & Simon, E. (2002). *XML. Encryption, syntax and processing.* W3C Recommendation. Retrieved from http://www.w3.org/TR/xmlenc-core/

Itani, W., Gaspard, C., Kayssi, A., & Chehab, A. (2006). PRIDE: Policy-driven Web security for handheld wireless devices. In *Proceedings of IEEE GLOBECOM 2006*, San Francisco.

Itani, W., & Kayssi, A. (2003). J2ME end-to-end security for m-commerce. In *Proceedings of the IEEE Wireless Communications and Networking Conference.* New Orleans, LA.

Itani, W., & Kayssi, A. (2004). SPECSA: A scalable, policy-driven, extensible, and customizable security architecture for wireless enterprise applications. In *Proceedings of the Workshop on Information Assurance (WIA04).* Phoenix, AZ.

Itani, W., Kayssi, A., & Chehab, A. (2005a). PATRIOT—A policy-based, multi-level security protocol for safekeeping audit logs on wireless devices. In *Proceedings of IEEE/CreateNet First International Conference on Security and Privacy for Emerging Areas in Communication Networks (SecureComm).* Athens, Greece.

Itani, W., Kayssi, A., & Chehab, A. (2005b).

SPARTA: A secure, policy-driven architecture for content distribution and storage in centralized wireless networks. In *Proceedings of Fist International Workshop on Security, Privacy, and Trust in Pervasive and Ubiquitous Computing (SecPerU'05).* Santorini, Greece.

Itani, W., Kayssi, A., & Chehab, A. (2006a). An enterprise policy-based security protocol for protecting relational database network objects. In *Proceedings of the 2006 International Wireless Communications and Mobile Computing Conference (IWCMC 2006).* Vancouver, Canada.

Itani, W., Kayssi, A., & Chehab, A. (2006b). SE-CERN: A secure enterprise backup and recovery protocol for mission-critical relational database servers. In *Proceedings of the Innovation in Information Technology Conference (IIT 06),* Dubai, UAE.

International Telecommunication Union (ITU). (2001). *ASN.1 encoding rules: XML encoding rules (XER). ITU-T Recommendation X.693.* Retrieved from http://www.itu.int/ ITU-T/studygroups/com17/languages/X.680-X.693-0207w.zip

Lawton, G. (2002). Moving java into mobile phones. *IEEE Computer, 35*(6), 17-20.

Neable, C. (2002). The .NET compact framework group. *IEEE Pervasive Computing, 1,* 84-87.

Organization for the Advancement of Structured Information Standards (OASIS). (2002). *SAML 1.0 Specification.* Retrieved from http://www.oasisopen.org/committees/download.php/1383/oasis-sstc-saml-1.0-pdf.zip

Organization for the Advancement of Structured Information Standards (OASIS). (2006). Web services security: SOAP message security 1.1 (WS-Security 2004). Retrieved from http://www.oasis-open.org/committees/download.php/16790/wss-v1.1-spec-os-SOAPMessageSecurity.pdf

QUALCOMM Incorp. (2004). *Starting with BREW.* Retrieved from http://brew.qualcomm.

com/brew_bnry/pdf/developer/resources/gs/starting_brew.pdf

Shim, J. P., Varshney, U., Dekleva, S., & Knoerzer, G. (2006). Mobile and wireless networks: Services, evolution and issues. *International Journal of Mobile Communications, 4,* 405-417.

Smith, A. (2006). Exploring m-commerce in terms of viability, growth and challenges. *International Journal of Mobile Communications, 4,* 682-703.

Soriano, M., & Ponce, D. (2002). A security and usability proposal for mobile electronic commerce. *IEEE Communication, 40*(8), 62-67.

Vandenwauver, M., Govaerts, R., & Vandewalle, J. (1997). Overview of authentication protocols: Kerberos and SESAME. In *Proceedings 31ˢᵗ Annual IEEE Carnahan Conference on Security Technology.*

WAP Forum. (2000). *Wireless application protocol architecture specification.* Retrieved from http://www.wapforum.org/what/technical_1_2_1.htm

WAP Forum. (2002). *WAP 2.0 technical white paper.* Retrieved from http://www.wapforum.org/what/WAPWhite_Paperl.pdf

Weerawarana, S., Curbera, F., Leymann, F., Storey, T., & Ferguson, D. F. (Eds.). (2005). *Web services platform architecture: SOAP, WSDL, WS-policy, WS-addressing, WS-BPEL, WS-reliable messaging, and more.* Prentice Hall.

Chapter V
Global M–Logistics in North America, Europe, and Asia:
A Comparative Study of the Diffusion and Adoption of Standards and Technologies in Next Generation M–Logistics

Frank Teuteberg
Osnabrueck University, Germany

Jochen Friedemann
Osnabrueck University, Germany

ABSTRACT

Mobile logistics (m-logistics) may be seen as an enabler for efficient and effective mobile commerce (m-commerce). Recent developments in mobile computing and communication standards and technologies allow more flexible operations and real-time monitoring in a supply chain. This chapter explores and examines the current status of m-logistics in North America, Europe, and Asia (mainly China, South Korea, and Japan). The chapter focuses on global m-logistics as an essential function and key factor in efficient and effective global m-commerce. Diffusion and adoption models as well as factors influencing the diffusion and adoption of standards and technologies in m-logistics are discussed. Our comparative study shows that all of the investigated regions have begun to adopt next-generation mobile logistics standards and technologies.

INTRODUCTION

Organizations have to make the movement of raw materials, goods, and services across geographic boundaries as efficient and effective as possible. Logistics is responsible for this movement. It has a unique position in linking external suppliers and customers. Moreover, it is an essential function and key factor in global commerce. In order to enable organizations to immediately react to specific events (e.g., a traffic jam), disruptions, and exceptions logistics has to become mobile itself (e.g., a truck driver has to be able to revise tour plans using GPS and mobile devices when unexpected events occur). M-logistics may therefore be seen as an enabler for efficient and effective m-commerce.

On the other hand, m-logistics increases the amount of m-commerce transactions. With growing international trade, the cross-country and cross-continental movement of raw materials and finished goods increases. The management and monitoring of activities in a supply chain and topics like supply chain integration become global issues. Cost reduction pressures and reduced time-to-market drive the need for real-time information about the location and status of goods and services in a supply chain. Purchasing; sourcing; tracking and tracing; and supply chain management will therefore increasingly become global activities.

Recent developments in mobile computing and communication standards (e.g., Universal Mobile Telecommunications System [UMTS] in Europe, i-mode supervised by NTT DoCoMo in Japan) and technologies ranging from automatic identification (Auto-ID) technologies (e.g., radio frequency identification [RFID]) for the automatic identification of goods, wireless sensors, localization technologies (e.g., satellite tracking systems such as GPS in North America and GPS or Galileo in Europe), on-board systems in vehicles, and mobile devices for automatically sending and receiving information about unexpected events allow more flexible operations and real-time monitoring in a supply chain.

Little research has been done to examine the potential barriers to the implementation of global m-logistics in different continents. This chapter explores and examines the current status of m-logistics in North America, Europe, and Asia (mainly China, South Korea, and Japan). The chapter focuses on global m-logistics as an essential function and key factor in efficient and effective global m-commerce.

In the second section we introduce standards and technologies enabling m-logistics. Diffusion and adoption models as well as factors influencing the diffusion and adoption of standards and technologies in m-logistics are discussed in the third section. In the fourth section we discuss the influence and interrelation of these factors based on a number of studies reviewed in this chapter. Finally, we draw some conclusions and point out some future trends in m-logistics.

STANDARDS AND TECHNOLOGIES IN NEXT GENERATION M-LOGISTICS

We define next generation m-logistics (NGML) as the application of mobile information technologies and information systems, including Auto-ID technology, GPS, wireless computing, sensor networks, and mobile devices for the communication, coordination, and management of business transactions in supply networks and for the localization and automatic identification of products and raw materials. On the one hand these technologies should enable the efficient tracking of goods through the entire supply network by the use of Auto-ID technology. On the other hand mobile access to data warehouses, scheduling and route-planning systems, and so forth has to be provided to logistics managers using data supplied by Auto-ID systems as well as organizational software (e.g., enterprise resource planning systems). The use of handheld devices alone, for instance, to monitor and plan supply networks is not NGML. In the following subsections we introduce emergent technologies for NGML.

Four technologies currently have a strong impact on NGML: (1) localization, (2) Auto-ID, (3) sensor, and (4) mobile network technologies. These technologies help answer the central question:

"Where is which object, and what is its current state?"

In the subsequent sections, we give a brief overview of these technologies.

Mobile Communication Standards

In the European Union, all member states agreed to apply a mobile communication standard called Global Mobile Communication System (GSM). In the USA and Asia, however, competing standards still exist. For example, Japan and China adopted both the GSM and the Code Division Multiple Access (CDMA) standard.

GSM provides data rates of 9.6 KBit/s. Due to this insufficiently low data rate the European Union recently agreed to apply the new UMTS standard. Through third-generation mobile networks like UMTS, data transfer rates are theoretically now available up to 2 MBit/s.

Nevertheless, in today's enterprises the use of mobile devices such as mobile phones or smart phones is often limited to making calls and using the short message service (Van Akkeren & Harker, 2003, p. 223), although today's mobile phones still support Java- or wireless application protocol (WAP)-based applications. Besides data transfer rates, enterprises are often concerned about security, service continuity, and cost (Marshall, Signorini, & Entner, 2004, p. 8). With *Mobile IPv6*, for example, the implementation of strong authentication and encryption features (IP Security) will improve security in mobile networks (Nokia, 2001, p. 4). Furthermore, a unique static IP address can be assigned to the mobile device, so ubiquity and seamless roaming will be possible within supply networks.

Mobile Computing Technologies for Localization

Trucks using GPS are able to transmit positional information back to the carrier's home office to enhance, for example, customer services and asset management. GPS, first introduced in the United States in the 1970s, is based on 24 high-altitude satellites in orbit (approx. 12,500 miles above the earth).

GPS is a widely used system that uses the lateration technique with one GPS receiver and four visible GPS satellites to determine the latitude, longitude, and altitude of objects (transceivers).

Proximity is a commonly used localization technique, where cellular access points are monitored to determine the position of smart cards/mobile device owners. Lateration and angulation of ultrasonic signals are other frequently used localization techniques, which rely on distance or angle measurements between certain fixed points by means of signal strengths (Hightower & Borriello, 2001).

An alternative to GPS and the Russian GLONASS is the Galileo positioning system, built by the European Union. The Galileo satellite system should be operational by 2010 (two years later than originally planned). In September 2003, China joined the Galileo project, followed by South Korea in January 2006. The goal of the Galileo project is to provide greater precision to all users than is currently available by GPS.

Mobile Sensor Technologies

Mobile sensor technology is able to detect changes to the environment. For example, thermal, acoustic, visual, infrared, magnetic, seismic, or radar sensors allow the monitoring of conditions such as the temperature, humidity, vehicular movement, noise levels, the presence or absence of mechanical stress levels, or current characteristics such as the speed, direction, or weight of an object (Akyldiz, Su, Sanakarasubramaniam, & Cayirci, 2002). In global m-logistics sensor technologies such as temperature sensors, for example, improve the monitoring of perishables in cool supply chains.

Figure 2. RFID standards (low, high, ultra high, and microwave frequency)

Automatic Identification: RFID and EPC

Auto-ID technology such as a barcode, smart cards, biometric systems or RFID is used to identify personnel, products, or delivery units (Bose & Pal, 2005). The most common Auto-ID technology today is RFID.

RFID tags are small computer chips that are attached to entities (e.g., products) which store

the entity identifier and entity-related data (Bohn, 2006). An antenna is connected to the RFID tag so that chips can be read out by means of RFID tag readers without the need of line of sight. RFID systems are therefore a good alternative to barcode systems, since they do not need human intervention or direct line of sight between the tag and the reader.

Currently several organizations aim to establish international standards for the use of RFID. The Auto-ID Center, for example, established the Electronic Product Code (EPC) network (Auto-ID infrastructure), which usually consists of the components as illustrated in Figure 1 (cf. Angeles, 2005, pp. 52-56). The chip on an RFID tag contains the so-called EPC, serving as a unique identifier. The EPC is identified by means of RFID readers (step 1). The EPC is usually transmitted to a so-called Savant server that filters and bundles data from the RFID tag readers (step 2) to query a so-called object naming service (ONS), where more information on the objects can be found (step 3). The ONS receives a URL that references an EPC information service delivering product-related

Figure 1. Auto-ID infrastructure

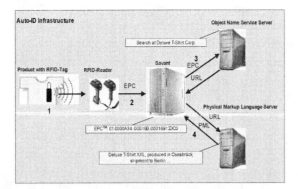

data (e.g., product name, supplier, etc.) of the observed objects (e.g., containers, pallets, packages, articles) as Physical Markup Language (PML) messages (step 4). PML (Flörkemeier, Anarkat, Osisnki, & Harrison, 2003) is a language used to describe objects on EPC networks.

However, a multiplicity of competitive RFID standards exists worldwide which differ substantially with regard to their suitability for different applications as well as with regard to their diffusion. Figure 2 gives an overview of these standards. The four numbers in each circle stand for low, high, ultra high (UHF), and microwave frequency standards used in RFID applications worldwide.

DIFFUSION AND ADOPTION OF STANDARDS AND TECHNOLOGIES IN M-LOGISTICS

Diffusion and Adoption Models

To describe the diffusion of innovations the framework introduced by Rogers (1995) is commonly used in economics, business administration, sociology, and related sciences, where the spread of technology throughout a society is described by an S-curve. Consumers are categorized into five groups: (1) innovators, (2) early adopters, (3) early majority, (4) late majority, and (5) laggards. The innovators introduce technology which will then be adopted by the early adopters. As the early adopters are a minor group of customers, diffusion will initially be quite slow. When the early majority and later the late majority adopt the innovation, the diffusion curve rapidly increases. The laggards are the last group to adopt a technology, at which point the curve reveals slow growth (Rogers, 1995). Figure 3 shows the ideal type of diffusion curve.

In information systems the most common model to measure and explain adoption is the technology acceptance model (TAM), introduced

Figure 3. Ideal type of a s-shaped diffusion curve

by Davis (1989). It explains the actual use of a certain technology by *perceived usefulness* and *perceived ease of use* on the one hand and attitudes towards usage and behavioral intention on the other. By perceived usefulness "the degree to which a person believes that using a particular system would enhance his or her job performance" (Davis, 1989, p. 320) is meant. Perceived ease of use defines "the degree to which a person believes that using a particular system would be free of effort" (Davis, 1989, p. 320).

This model has been modified several times either to adopt it for special technologies or to extend it by other variables. For example, Malhotra and Galletta (1999) added social influence. Anckar, Carlsson, & Walden (2003) modified the TAM to describe the acceptance of m-commerce and mobile Internet. Their general purpose was to specify the multidimensional constructs of perceived usefulness and perceived ease of use to gain more explanatory power (Anckar et al., 2003, p. 896). They surveyed different benefits and barriers of m-commerce, to explore key drivers and inhibitors. The findings were that drivers and inhibitors differ across customer segments. For example, adopters perceive network limitations as important barriers while current non-adopters tend to name high costs as the greatest barrier (Anckar et al., 2003, p. 897).

Fife and Pereira (2005) introduced the global acceptance of technology (GAT) model and applied it to explain differences in mobile data use

Table 1. Models and studies of technology diffusion and acceptance reviewed for this chapter

Study/Model Name, Author (Year of introduction)	Core Constructs	Definitions / Findings
Diffusion of Innovations, Rogers (1995)	• S-shaped diffusion curve • Five categories of adopters	• Innovators: venturesome, educated, multiple info sources, greater propensity to take risks • Early adopters: social leaders, popular, educated • Early majority: deliberate, many informal social contacts • Late majority: skeptical, traditional, lower socio-economic status • Laggards: neighbors and friends are main info sources, fear of debt
TAM, Davis (1989)	• Perceived ease of use • Perceived usefulness • Attitudes towards usage • Behavioral intention	• **PEU:** degree to which a person believes that using a particular system would enhance his or her job performance • **PU:** degree to which a person believes that using a particular system would be free of effort
Factors affecting consumer adoption decisions and intents in mobile commerce, Anckar et al. (2003)	• Differentiation between key drivers and inhibitors of mobile commerce adoption.	Drivers and inhibitors differ in their importance between customer segments
GAT, Fife and Pereira (2005)	• Perceived relative value • Usability • Cultural socialization drivers • Technology catalyst	• **PRV:** the social and/or economic advantage that users think they can derive from adopting a new technology • **Usability:** consistent with existing and past experiences and the mind-set of the adopter(s) • **CSD:** the tacit or explicit social rules that govern interaction between individuals in a society • **TC:** in many cases, authority-based decisions have tended to promote faster adoption • High impact of socio-cultural norms
UTAUT, Venkeshar et al. (2003)	• Performance expectancy • Effort expectancy • Social influence • Facilitating conditions	• **PE:** degree to which an individual believes that using the system will help him or her make gains in job performance • **EE:** degree of ease associated with the use of the system • **SI:** degree to which an individual perceives that other important people believe he or she should use the new system • **FC:** degree to which an individual believes that an organizational and technical infrastructure exists to support use of the system
Technical change and the rate of imitation, Mansfield (1961)	Growth of the number of adopters of an innovation will conform to the logistic curve, and the diffusion rate will be linearly related to the profitability of the innovation	• Most diffusion processes conform to the S-shaped growth curve
A model of the diffusion of technology into SMEs, Thomas (2000)	External source channels of technology transfer mechanisms involved in the transfer of technology into the innovative SME	• S-shaped diffusion curve • Spillovers through formal and informal networks

across cultures. Their framework consists of four concepts: (1) the *perceived relative value*, (2) *usability*, (3) *cultural socialization drivers* and (4) the *technology adoption catalyst* (Fife & Pereira, 2005, pp. 10-13). They build upon Rogers' framework (Rogers, 1995) and the *unified theory of acceptance and use of technology* (UTAUT) (Fife & Pereira, 2005, p. 3). Their study shows that socio-cultural norms have a relatively high impact upon the acceptance of mobile data services (Fife & Pereira, 2005, p. 22).

The UTAUT was introduced by Venkatesh, Morris, Davis, & Davis (2003). Based on an empirical comparison of eight models of technology adoption, including Rogers' framework (Rogers, 1995) and the TAM, they stated four concepts to determine the use of technology: (1) performance expectancy, (2) effort expectancy, (3) social influence, and (4) facilitating conditions (Venkatesh et al., 2003, p. 447). The UTAUT combines approaches of well-accepted models of technology acceptance. Venkatesh et al. empirically tested it and found it capable of explaining 70% of the variance in intention (Venkatesh et al., 2003, p. 471).

These models were all able to explain the diffusion of innovations or the adoption of technology by consumers to a certain extent. But the standards and technologies that are the subject of this chapter are primarily to be adopted by companies and organizations. For this reason, none of the models presented previously fits the needs of this chapter satisfactorily. Nonetheless, studies by Mansfield (1961) examining the diffusion of industrial innovations in steel, coal, railway, and brewing industries and by Thomas (2000) setting up a model of the diffusion of technology into small and medium-sized enterprises show that the diffusion of technology throughout companies and organizations also follows an S-shaped curve. This can be explained by network economies. The more companies are already applying a technology, the greater the knowledge is about it. And greater demand will lead to lower costs. There is

therefore less risk to adopt this technology. Later on, when the technology is more widely used, it could be a significant competitive disadvantage not to apply it in one's own company. Table 1 gives an overview of studies and models of technology diffusion and acceptance reviewed for this chapter.

At present, however, there is no model which can be fully adopted to describe the diffusion of NGML standards and technologies. Due to the fact that NGML is still very new and quite "research-based" it would not be of use to state a new model here. It would be impossible to fully test it, as the later steps of diffusion could not be measured.

We therefore decided to compare current adoption and diffusion according to criteria introduced in the next section. The earlier studies and models described previously and summarized in Table 1 should be kept in mind when reading the next section.

Factors Influencing the Diffusion and Adoption of Standards and Technologies

Regulatory, socio-cultural and economical factors will be used to measure the adoption and diffusion of standards and technologies for m-logistics, as well as the potentials for further development, throughout different regions.

Regulatory Factors

UHF enables more effective use of Auto-ID technologies for logistics, which is why the availability of globally accepted UHF frequencies will be used as a factor. The regulation of frequencies has a direct impact on the technology acceptance catalyst mentioned in the third section.

The other two regulatory factors are the total number of EPCglobal subscribers in relation to the size of the inspected region and the growth in EPCglobal subscribers. The EPCglobal network was introduced in the second section. It is the major organization for developing Auto-ID related standards for business purposes. The extent to which a region's companies and institutions aim to participate in this development is therefore a strong indicator of the diffusion and adoption of Auto-ID technologies as an enabler for NGML. The will to participate in developing standards shows the respective company's interest in applying Auto-ID technology.

Socio-Cultural and Demographic Factors

Applying socio-cultural factors is related to Fife and Pereira's (2005) findings.

Socio-culturally, the general acceptance of mobile devices and especially mobile Internet use is important. Having no or bad experience might complicate the adoption of mobile devices for this purpose by managers or field staff. Positive experience with mobile Internet or mobile device use increases factors like the perceived ease of use or usability mentioned in the third section. Positive experiences decrease factors like the *effort expectancy* of deciders and staff members.

Extreme consumer concerns about Auto-ID technologies threatening privacy may complicate the roll-out of RFID-based logistic services in a region. This might cause regional authorities to set up restrictive laws which would have a negative impact on the technology catalyst.

We will further analyze the research landscape according to mobile supply chain management as another socio-cultural factor. Having strong research activities increases a region's ability to get used to new standards and technologies. To analyze this factor, a research database on mobile supply chain management literature developed by the authors of this chapter will be used. A literature survey of the publications listed in this database will be given. Particular attention will be given to the location of the authors' primary places of work (e.g., university, research center), if applicable.

The research database is available at http://www.mobilescm.de.

Economic Factors

The first economic factor is the revenues of third-party logistics (3PL) providers. The logistics market is dominated by 3PL providers. In 2005 the percentage of firms using 3PL ranged between 73% in the USA and 83% in the Asia-Pacific region (Langley, Van Dort, Ang, & Sykes, p. 10). According to CapGemini's 10th Annual 3PL Logistics survey (Langley et al., 2005, p. 29), RFID and asset tracking is the most important future requirement for IT-based services of 3PL providers. These providers will therefore force the adoption of Auto-ID technologies for logistics. They might therefore influence the technology adoption catalyst mentioned in the third section.

The extent to which 3PL providers have adopted RFID is another major factor, as this may be seen as an indicator of the future adoption of RFID in the overall economy of a specific region. This is due to the s-shaped diffusion curve. Having the 3PL providers and some major retail companies acting as innovators, other companies will also be willing to apply NGML. This will lead the 3PL providers to further investigate how to supply NGML solutions. Having standardized NGML solutions offered by 3PL providers, the majority of companies might apply NGML.

The third economic factor is the *end user ratio,* the quotient of end users and solution providers subscribed to EPCglobal. A low end user ratio shows that there are far more solution providers than end users interested in global RFID standards. This indicates that the standards are not that well adopted in the specific region and that only solution providers who aim to gain international companies are forced to participate. We assume that a high end user ratio represents higher adoption of the technology, which increases demand and leads to further adoption, as more vendors will enter the market. For this reason, the end user ratio is supposed to be cyclic. Having a high end user ratio means high demand, which will increase the number of vendors and therefore decrease the end user ratio.

This factor is again related to the s-curve of diffusion. Initially, the end user ratio will be relatively low, indicating less demand. When early adopters enter the market, some might want to participate in the development of standards, which will increase the end user ratio.

Table 2 gives an overview of the factors used.

Figure 4 gives an overview of the factors used and their interdependencies. The lines in Figure 4 show indicator relations, whereas arrows signal interdependencies. All of the factors indicate the extent of the diffusion and adoption of NGML standards and technologies. Some factors also have an impact on adoption and diffusion. Adequate regulation of UHF supports further adoption. High experience in mobile Internet use eases the adoption of mobile Internet for NGML. Consumer concerns might hinder the implementation of NGML solutions. Strong and educative research might decrease consumers' concerns. A high number of EPCglobal subscribers might support further research, as EPCglobal does some research itself. Growth in EPCglobal subscribers might force the regulation of UHF bands, as EPCglobal supports the use of UHF for Auto-ID. Research might increase the adoption of RFID by 3PL providers by developing solutions

Figure 4. Factors and their interdependencies

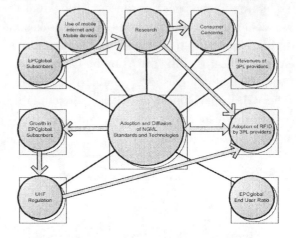

that are easy to apply. Global regulation of UHF would also drive the adoption of RFID by 3PL providers as implementation costs could sink, due to standardized frequencies.

Organization and corporate culture is another factor influencing the adoption and diffusion of standards and technologies by enterprises. On the other side, technology may affect the organization itself (for example through rationalization). This chapter is focussed on economic regions more than single companies. Nevertheless, significant differences in organization and corporate culture could lead to different speeds of adoption throughout the inspected regions.

We apply empirical surveys to compare the inspected regions according to the defined factors. However, empirical surveys have a number of shortcomings including, for example, high non-response rates, coverage errors, or a lack of control over the way questionnaires are completed. On the other hand, the authors of this chapter cannot see a better alternative to the empirical approach to obtain a general overview of the diffusion and adoption of standards and technologies in global m-logistics.

Table 3 gives a general overview of the studies reviewed in this chapter.

Table 2. Factors influencing the diffusion and adoption of standards and technologies for NGML

Factors	
Regulatory	• UHF availability • EPCglobal members • EPCglobal members' growth
Economical	• End user ratio • Revenues of 3PL providers • Adoption of RFID by 3PL providers
Socio-cultural	• Use of mobile Internet • Privacy and other concerns • Research

Table 3. Research design of reviewed studies

Empirical Study	Research Method	Duration	Sample Size	Focus Group	Questionnaire	Research Topics
Mobile supply chain event management (Teuteberg & Weberbauer, 2006)	Internet-based	Dec. 15 2005-March 15 2006	63 completed questionnaires	German companies (esp. logistics service providers)	Standardized questionnaire with closed questions	RFID, Diffusion and adoption of mobile computing technologies in supply chain event management
3PL surveys (Lieber & Bentz, 2005)	Questionnaires	2004	Asia: 11 completed questionnaires Europe: 13 completed questionnaires North America: 23 completed questionnaires	3PL providers operating in the specific regions	Standardized questionnaire with closed and open questions	Market situation, Adoption of RFID, Future trends
RFID and consumers (CapGemini, 2005)	Internet-based	November 2004	2,000 respondents	Consumers	Standardized questionnaire with closed and open questions	Consumers' knowledge and perception regarding RFID
2005 third-party logistics (Langley et al., 2005)	Internet-based	Summer 2005	1,091 respondents	3PL users	Standardized questionnaire with closed questions and expert interviews	Key trends and views of the 3PL industry from the perspective of the customers

FINDINGS

Regulatory Factors

UHF Regulation

The availability of UHF bands for RFID and logistics applications is determined by governmental or other official regulation. The USA allocated these frequencies at an early stage.

The overall image in Asia is also positive. Countries like Japan, South Korea, and India have already regulated the frequencies for RFID use. China and many other countries aim to do so by mid-2006. In Europe there are conflicts between existing regulations and the proposed UHF regulations. This can be seen in Spain, France, and Italy (Barthel, 2005, p. 17).

In total, 70% of the global economy already has adequate UHF regulations, and 13% will be regulated by mid-2006 (Barthel, 2005, p. 17).

EPCglobal Subscribers

By January 2006 the EPCglobal network had a grand total of 848 members. The three biggest regions were the USA/Canada, Europe, and Asia. A few remarks have to be made here. The European members of EPCglobal are mainly to be found in Central Europe and the UK. There is a lack of members in China. The USA/Canada region is the clearly biggest one. It has a total number of 568 subscribers, which is around 67% of the total subscribers.

Asia has 119 subscribers (14% of all subscribers), whereas Europe has 109 members (13%) (EPCglobal, 2006).

Considering that Asia is much larger and more highly populated than Europe and the fact that there are virtually no EPCglobal subscribers in China—one of Asia's fastest growing countries—Asia must be benchmarked worse than Europe at this point.

In 2003 there was not a single company applying RFID (Min, Zhou, Jui, Wang, & Chen, 2003, p.16). Min et al. (2003, p.11) found 33% of Chinese companies who were excited about RFID technology to be potential early adopters.

Growth in EPCglobal Subscribers

By August 2004 EPCglobal had 292 subscribers. This represents a total growth in subscribers of 290% in 1.5 years. In the Asia-Pacific region a growth of 565% from 26 to 147 subscribers (including Australia) was measured. In Europe the number of subscribers increased by 232%. In USA/Canada a growth of 263% was noted. It is obvious that the Asian industry is rapidly approaching EPCglobal Standards (EPCglobal, 2004, 2006).

Economic Factors

Revenues of 3PL Providers

A 2004 survey focusing on the North American 3PL market reports $17 billion revenues for 2003 in total, based on the answers of 23 CEOs (Lieber & Benz, North America, 2005, p. 3).

For the Asia-Pacific region another survey reports $4.5 billion revenues for 3PL for 2003 (Lieb & Benz, Asia-Pacific, 2005, p.3). It should be noted that this includes Australia, hence the value has to be decreased slightly.

The survey examining the European 3PL market had a very low response rate with regard to revenues, but six reporting providers together had a total revenue of above $9 billion in 2003 (Lieb & Benz, 2004, p. 3).

Kilie and Klaus (2006, p. 10) give an overview of the world's top 10 logistics providers' revenues in 2004. Three of these are located in Central Europe (Germany and Denmark), three in Asia (Japan and China), and three in the USA. One, which is located in Russia, will not be considered here.

The U.S. providers account for € 61.2 billion revenues, which makes up around 37% of the top 10 providers' revenues (€ 163.9 billion in total). European providers account for € 54.2 billion revenues (33%). The three Asian companies together report € 36.2 billion (22%) (Kilie & Klaus, 2006, p. 10).

Adoption of RFID by 3PL Providers

The aforementioned surveys conducted by Lieber and Benz (2005) in 2004 also inspected the embrace of RFID by 3PL providers.

The North American survey showed that 85% of 3PL CEOs regard RFID as *very significant* or *significant*. The CEOs reported that on average 12% of their customers were already applying RFID, and another 10% on average were undertaking pilot studies. For both values the range was between 1 and 50%. Nearly all CEOs proposed that their companies would broaden their service offerings to support RFID applications (Lieber & Benz, North America, 2005, pp. 11-13).

Sixty-seven percent of Asian CEOs who responded regarded RFID as *very significant* or *significant*. According to customers, an average of 15% already applying RFID was reported with a range of 5 to 40%. Twelve percent on average of the customers were conducting RFID pilot studies, ranging from 2 to 30% (Lieber & Bentz, Asia-Pacific, 2005, pp. 9-11).

Ninety-two percent of the European CEOs who took part in the survey regarded RFID as *very significant* or *significant*. On average 11% of customers were already applying RFID, and another 11% were undertaking pilot studies (ranges 1 to 50% and 2 to 50%) (Lieber & Bentz, 2004, pp. 14-15).

The Mobile Supply Chain Event Management Survey (Teuteberg & Weberbauer, 2006, p. 20) reports around 23% of companies in Germany were already applying Auto-ID solutions in 2006 and another 20% were undertaking pilot studies.

End User Ratio

In 2006 272 end users and 296 solution providers were subscribed to EPCglobal in USA/Canada. This leads to an end user ratio of 0.92. For 2005 the end user ratio was 0.94 (130/138). In August 2004 it was measured at 0.64 (EPCglobal, 2004, 2005, 2006). This indicates that USA/Canada has passed the first step of diffusion and has now reached a point where more vendors try to participate as demand increases.

For Europe the 2006 end user ratio was 0.85 (50/59), the 2005 ratio was nearly 1.0 (32/33). The 2004 ratio was 0.47 (EPCglobal, 2004, 2005, 2006); the findings for Europe are therefore similar to those of the North American region.

The Asia-Pacific end user ratio set out at 0.44 in 2004 then fell to 0.18 in 2005, and reached 0.38 in January 2006 (EPCglobal, 2004, 2005, 2006). This indicates that RFID has only been adopted by a few Asian end users and that mainly vendors interested in international market shares aim to drive the development.

Socio-Cultural and Demographic Factors

Mobile Phone Penetration and Use of Mobile Internet

Several studies show extreme differences in the use of mobile Internet services throughout the three investigated regions. Srivastava (2004, p. 237) shows that the three countries having the highest share of mobile Internet subscribers of total mobile phone subscribers in 2002 were Japan (79.2%), South Korea (74.9%), and China (33.9%). The highest proportion reached in a European country is 20.0% in Finland. Germany and France have 13.8 and 11.7%, respectively.

Only 8.9% of mobile phone subscribers in the USA are reported to be mobile Internet subscribers.

In 2004 the EU-15 nations had the highest number of mobile phone subscribers per 100 in-habitants (96.75), followed by the South-East Asian states (Japan: 71.58, South Korea: 76.09), while the USA had a penetration rate of 62.11 (International Telecommunications Union, 2005, pp. 2-4).

Henten, Olesen, Saugstrup, & Tan (2004, p. 206) state that there is an immense lack of success for mobile data and Internet services in Europe compared to Japan and South Korea, which is mainly caused by high prices for frequency bands and the over-hyping of WAP-based implementations by European service providers at the beginning of the century, which has not been adopted by customers.

These findings show that in Asia (especially in Japan and South Korea) mobile Internet use is nearly ubiquitous, which eases the use of mobile services for logistics management. In the USA and Europe use of mobile Internet services for logistics could be rejected by deciders and staff members due to a lack of experience or bad experiences with initially offered services.

Consumer Concerns

Currently there are no studies available regarding privacy concerns regarding RFID by Asian customers. Asia will therefore not be benchmarked here.

A CapGemini (2005, p. 12) survey about consumers' attitudes towards RFID shows that there are slightly higher concerns about RFID affecting privacy in the USA than in Europe. Sixty-nine percent of responding U.S.-American consumers are afraid that personal data stored on RFID tags may be read by third parties, 59% of Europeans share these fears. Sixty-five percent of American consumers fear that they might be tracked via product purchases, with 55% of their European counterparts thinking the same. Sixty-two percent of American consumers and 57% of Europeans would like to see privacy protection regarding RFID become law.

The same survey shows that 41% of American and 39% of European consumers believe that RFID would increase the cost of goods (Cap-Gemini, 2005, p.6).

These findings show some strong concerns regarding RFID, with 42% of American and 52% of European consumers said to have a favorable perception of RFID (CapGemini, 2005, p. 5).

Diffusion of the M-Logistics Concept in the Scientific Community

Over the last 5 years a steadily increasing number of scientific papers in the area of m-logistics have been published.

In this section, we provide a literature review of the current status in m-logistics research with regard to the continents of Europe, the USA, and Asia. In order to do this, we have analyzed 101 scientific papers and more than 15 research projects in this emerging research area described in a research database which is available at http://www.mobilescm.de. The purpose of this database is to document today's state of the art of m-logistics research.

The conceptual data model underlying our research database reflects the objectives of the database mentioned previously. Figure 5 shows a simplified model of this data model.

The journals in Table 4 were seen as relevant for research in m-logistics and have been considered in our literature review.

The majority of these journals are published by well-established scientific publishers, whose headquarters are normally located in the USA or Western Europe. Most of these journals now have international boards of editors and organizational sections in many countries all over the world.

The distribution of the articles in our research database across the analyzed period 1999-2006 is illustrated in Table 5.

A high number of publications were issued after the year 2002. Thus the research topic m-logistics has increasingly been considered interesting in recent years. This conforms to the higher interest of Auto-ID technology in mass media and the results of the 3PL surveys discussed in the third section.

One-hundred-one publications (journal articles) issuing mobile logistics have been inspected according to their main author's primary place of work.

Figure 5. Data model of the research database

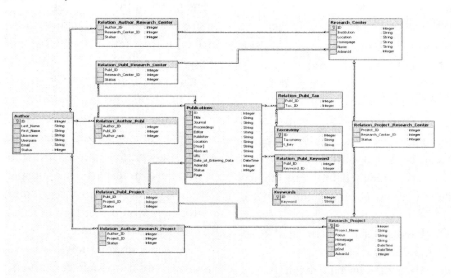

Table 4. Journals publishing articles in m-logistics

Journal	Number of Publications
Industrial Management & Data Systems	9
Communications of the ACM	7
Mobile Networks and Applications	6
International Journal of Physical Distribu¬tion & Logistics Management	6
Journal of Manufacturing Technology Manage¬ment	5
British Food Journal	4
International Journal of Retail & Distribu¬tion Management	4
Supply Chain Management: An Interna¬tional Journal	4
Int. Journal of Adv. Manuf. Technology	4
ACM SIGMOBILE Mobile Computing and Communi¬cations Review	3
BT Technology Journal	3
Information System Management	3
Journal of Facilities Management	3
Journal of Operations Management	3
Logistics Information Management	3
The International Journal of Flexible Manufactur¬ing Systems	3
Electronic Commerce Research and Applications	2
European Journal of Operational Research	2
International Journal of Mobile Communications	2
Journal of Intelligent Manufacturing	2
Others	23

Table 5. M-logistics publications per year (Status: May 2006)

Year of Publication	Number
2006	6
2005	31
2004	22
2003	19
2002	9
2001	6
2000	5
1999	3

The required information was available for 90 publications via the printings themselves or Internet research. If teams of authors from different regions were found, the paper was classified to the region in which the majority of authors was located.

Our literature review showed that a total of 53 researchers were located in Europe (59%), 26 worked in the USA or Canada (29%), and 11 were conducting their research in Asia (12%).

Furthermore, we analyzed the publications according to the applied research methodologies in relation to their authors' origin. Due to their limited quantity, the Asian publications were not analyzed at this point. A differentiation was made between the following research methodologies in our literature review: simulations, empirical surveys, and prototyping.

A clear difference arises: While 17% of European papers chose a prototyping approach (developing systems for m-logistics) and another 10% were dealt with simulation, prototyping was only used in 10% of the American publications, and only 4% applied the simulation concept. On the contrary, 13% of American publications reported results of empirical surveys, while only 4% of Europeans did so.

Summarization of Findings

Table 6 summarizes our findings described in the previous sections.

Table 6. Adoption and diffusion of m-logistics

Factors		Europe	USA/Canada	Asia (esp. Japan, South Korea, China)
Regulatory factors	UHF Regulation	Conflicts with existing regulations in Spain, France, and Italy; Adequate regulation in place or planned for the rest	Adequate regulation in place	Adequate regulation in place in Japan and South Korea; planned in China
	EPCglobal Subscribers by January 2006	109	568	119
	Growth in EPCglobal subscribers from August 2004 to January 2006	232%	263%	565%
Economic factors	Revenues of 3PL providers in the specific market	> $9 bn	$17 bn	$4.5 bn
	Revenues of the three largest logistics and transportation companies	$54.2 bn	$61.2 bn	$36.2 bn
	3PL providers regarding RFID as very significant or significant	92%	85%	67%
	EPCglobal end user ratio by August 2004, January 2005 and January 2006	0.47/ 0.97 / 0.85	0.64 / 0.94/ 0.92	0.44/ 0.18/ 0.38
Socio-cultural and demographic factors	Mobile cellular subscribers per 100 inhabitants (selected values)	EU-15: 96.75 Europe total: 71.61 Highest: 138.17 (Luxembourg)	USA: 62.11 Canada: 46.72	Japan: 71.58 South Korea: 76.09 China: 25.76 Hong Kong: 118.77 Asia Total: 18.72
	Mobile Internet subscribers as a percentage of all mobile subscribers (highest values)	20% (Finland)	8.9% (USA)	79.4 % % (Japan)
	Consumers with privacy concerns regarding RFID	57%	62%	Not available
	Consumers with a favorable perception of RFID	52%	42%	Not available
	Percentage of m-logistics researchers located in region	59%	29%	12%

CONCLUSION AND FUTURE TRENDS

Our comparative study shows that all of the investigated regions have begun to adopt next-generation m-logistics standards and technologies. The large number of EPCglobal subscribers and especially the growth rates indicate that this will be the future's standard setter for business purposes of Auto-ID technology.

The growth in EPCglobal subscriptions and the development of the end user ratio over the past 1.5 years leads to the conclusion that NGML has left the status of being only observed by innovators, trying to gain new market shares or researchers. Some early adopters have already begun to apply NGML solutions. The results of the 3PL findings indicate that RFID-based solutions will gain greater importance in future years.

Some differences throughout the investigated regions were determined. First the South-East Asian nations have a much higher affinity to mobile Internet services. Thus companies located there are likely to be far more sophisticated in developing applications for mobile devices and engineering mobile business processes. This might lead to a competitive advantage of Asian industries in providing information systems for NGML.

On the other hand Europe and the USA/Canada have greater experience in Auto-ID technologies. This is indicated by the much higher percentage of research activities and the adoption of RFID by 3PL providers in these regions.

Moreover, our study showed that NGML has globally left the "embryonic" status, and that standards and technology are being adopted by a number of companies in the different regions. A lot of global players are currently working on hardware, software, and business models for RFID and NGML. For example IBM, Microsoft, SUN, Oracle, and SAP are working in the field of software applications and consulting as well as CapGemini, Accenture, and other major consultancies. Metro, Tesco, and Wal-Mart, some of the world's largest retailers, are strongly driving the development of Auto-ID systems for logistics and retail purposes. Hardware providers like Intermec, Texas Instruments, and Phillips Semiconductor are also actively forcing new developments.

The 3PL surveys discussed in the fourth section show an expected increase in demand for RFID-based logistics solutions in future years.

For the further adoption and diffusion of standards and technologies in m-logistics the following challenges still have to be met:

- **Security:** Security issues concerning mobile devices still remain unsolved (Luck, McBurney, Preist, & AgentLink community, 2003, p. 13). Today's Auto-ID systems, for example, are vulnerable to hijack attacks, which have to be addressed when developing more secure communication protocols.

- **Trust and privacy:** Not only security but also trust and privacy issues concerning Auto-ID have to be solved (Twist, 2005, p. 231).

- **Available resources:** Mobile devices require significant resources. Smart phones and PDAs have limited resources, so resource-intensive tasks should be executed by stationary computers.

- **Information overflow:** The mass of products, machine data, and other resources that have to be scanned and transmitted in an EPC network have to be managed in time-critical processes due to constraints in available bandwidth and computing power (Angeles, 2005, p. 55).

- **Lack of standards:** There is still a diverse range of competitive standards worldwide (e.g., diverse RFID standards; codes for product identification; data exchange formats and mobile computing standards; etc.), which differ substantially with regard to their suitability for different industries, as well as with regard to their diffusion. These standards are still being improved and constantly expanded.

The most important issue will be the acceptance of global data standards for NGML as differences in frequency bands, and so forth may be solved by technical solutions like multi-frequency readers. This would slow the adoption/development of NGML due to higher costs but would not have an impact because of the lack of possibilities for easy data interchange along global supply networks.

ACKNOWLEDGMENT

This work is part of the research project "Mobile business processes and user interfaces based on Wireless Internet" (Mobile Internet Business) funded by the German Federal Ministry of Education and Research (http://mib.uni-ffo.de).

REFERENCES

Akyldiz, I., Su, W., Sanakarasubramaniam, Y., & Cayirci, E. (2002). Wireless sensor networks: A survey. *Computer Networks Journal, 38*(4), 392-422.

Anckar, B., Carlsson, C., & Walden, P. (2003). Factors affecting consumer adoption decisions and intents in mobile commerce: Empirical insights. In *Proceedings of the 16th Bled eCommerce Conference* (pp. 886-902).

Angeles, R. (2005). RFID technologies: Supply-chain applications and implementation issues. *Information Systems Management, 22*(1), 51-65.

Barthel, H. (2005). *EPCglobal—RFID standards & regulations.* Paper presented at the *Radio Frequency Identification (RFID) Applications and Public Policy Considerations, OECD Foresight Forum,* Paris.

Bohn, J. (2006). Prototypical implementation of location-aware services based on super-distributed RFID tags. In W. Grass, B. Sick, & K. Waldschmidt (Eds.), *Proceedings of the 19th Inter-national Conference on Architecture of Computer Systems* (LNCS 3894, pp. 69-83).

Bose, I., & Pal, R. (2005). Auto-ID: Managing anything, anywhere, anytime in the supply chain. *Communications of the ACM, 48*(8), 100-106.

Davis, F. D. (1989). Perceived usefulness, perceived ease of use, and user acceptance of information technology. *MIS Quarterly, 13*(3), 319-340.

CapGemini Consulting Inc. (2005). *What European consumers think about radio frequency identification and the implications for business.*

EPCglobal—The source—Global round-up. (2004, August). Retrieved May 9, 2006, from http://www.epcglobalinc.org/thesource/2004_08/html/global_roundup.html

EPCglobal—The source—Global round-up. (2005, January). Retrieved May 9, 2006, from http://www.epcglobalinc.org/thesource/2005_01/html/global_roundup.html

EPCglobal—The source—Global round-up. (2006, January). Retrieved May 9, 2006, from http://www.epcglobalinc.org/thesource/2006_01/html/global_roundup.html

Fife, E., & Pereira, F. (2005). Global acceptance of technology (GAT) and demand for mobile data services. In *Proceedings of the Hong Kong Mobility Roundtable (CD).*

Flörkemeier, C., Anarkat, D., Osisnki, T., & Harrison, M. (2003). *PML core specification 1.0* (White Paper). Cambridge, MA: MIT, Auto-ID Center.

Henten, A., Olesen, H., Saugstrup, D., & Tan, S.-E. (2004). Mobile communications: Europe, Japan and South Korea in a comparative perspective. *The Journal of Policy, Regulation, and Strategy for Telecommunications, Information and Media, 6*(3), 197-207.

Hightower, J., & Borriello, G. (2001). Location systems for ubiquitous computing. *IEEE Computer Magazine, 34*(8), 57-66.

International Telecommunications Union. (2005). *Mobile cellular subscribers per 100 people.* Retrieved May 9, 2006, from http://www.itu.int/ITU-D/ict/statistics/at_glance/cellular04.pdf

Kilie, K., & Klaus, C. (2006). *Neuvermessung der Logistik: Aktuelle Ergebnisse aus der Studie Die „Top 100 der Logistik" 2006.* Retrieved May 9, 2006, from www.logistik-inside.de/fm/2239/LDL_Top_00Exec_2006.pdf

Langley, C. Jr., Van Dort, E., Ang, A., & Sykes, S. R. (2005). *2005 third-party logistics. Results and findings of the survey* (Research Report), CapGemini, Georgia Institute of Technology, SAP, DHL.

Lieber, R., & Bentz, B. A. (2004). *The year 2004 survey: CEO perspectives on the current status and future prospects of the European third party logistics industry* (Report). Boston: Northeastern University, College of Business Administration.

Lieber, R., & Bentz, B. A. (2005a). *The year 2004 survey: CEO perspectives on the current status and future prospects of the third party logistics industry in the Asia-Pacific region* (Report). Boston: Northeastern University, College of Business Administration.

Lieber, R., & Bentz, B. A. (2005b). *The year 2004 survey: CEO perspectives on the current status and future prospects of the third party logistics industry in North America* (Report). Boston: Northeastern University, College of Business Administration.

Luck, M., McBurney, P., Preist, C., & AgentLink community. (2003). *Agent technology: Enabling next generation computing.* Retrieved May 9, 2006, from http://www.agentlink.org/roadmap/

Malhotra, Y., & Galletta, D. F. (1999). Extending the technology acceptance model to account for social influence: Theoretical bases and empirical validation. In *Proceedings of the Thirty-Second Annual Hawaii International Conference on System Sciences 1* (pp. 6-19).

Mansfield E. (1961). Technical change and the rate of imitation. *Econometrica, 29*(4), 741-766.

Marshall, P., Signorini, E., & Entner, R. (2004). *An analysis of UMTS as a mobile data solution for the enterprise market.* Retrieved May 9, 2006, from http://www.attwireless.com/media/downloads/umts/umts2004analysis.pdf

Min, H., Zhou, F., Jui, S-l., Wang, T., & Chen, X. (2003). *RFID in China* (White Paper). Fudan, China: Fudan University, Department of Microelectronics, Auto-ID Center.

Nokia. (2001). *Introducing mobile IPv6 in 2G and 3G mobile networks* (White Paper). Retrieved May 9, 2006, from http://www.nokia.com/BaseProject/Sites/NOKIA_MAIN_18022/CDA/Categories/Business/NetworkSecurity/Firewalls/IPv6/_Content/_Static_Files/mobileipv6in3gnetworks.pdf

Rogers, E. M. (1995). *Diffusion of innovations* (4th ed.). New York: The Free Press.

Srivastava, L. (2004). Japan's ubiquitous mobile information society. *The Journal of Policy, Regulation, and Strategy for Telecommunications, Information and Media, 14*(4), 234-251.

Teuteberg, F., & Weberbauer, M. (2006). *Mobile supply chain event management: Eine empirische Studie zum aktuellen Stand in deutschen Unternehmen* (Research Report).

Thomas, B. (2000). *A model of the diffusion of technology into SMEs.* WEI Working Paper Series 4. Garmogan, University of Carmogan, Welsh Enterprise Institute.

Twist, D. C. (2005). The impact of radio frequency identification on supply chain facilities. *Journal of Facilities Management, 3*(3), 226-239.

Van Akkeren, J., & Harker, D. (2003). Mobile data technologies and small business adoption and diffusion: An empirical study of barriers and facilitators. In B. Mennecke & T. Strader (Eds.), *Mobile commerce: Technology, theory and applications* (pp. 218-244). Hershey, PA: Idea Group.

Venkatesh, V., Morris, M. G., Davis, G. B., & Davis, F. B. (2003). User acceptance of information technology: Toward a unified view. *MIS Quarterly, 27*(3), 425-478.

Section II
Issues in Europe

Chapter VI
Strategy Aligned Process Selection for Mobile Customer Services

Ragnar Schierholz
University of St. Gallen, Switzerland

Lutz M. Kolbe
University of St. Gallen, Switzerland

Walter Brenner
University of St. Gallen, Switzerland

ABSTRACT

In this chapter we analyze how companies define their customer value proposition and how the selection of successful mobile customer services is done in alignment with this strategic positioning. We derive a set of five different strategic goals (price leadership, product quality leadership, customer intimacy leadership, accessibility leadership, innovation leadership) and apply this classification to case studies we analyzed. We show interdependencies between the strategic premises and the processes selected for being supported by mobile technology, resulting in typical properties which qualify processes for mobilization. These are used to derive guidelines for strategy aligned process selection when implementing mobile customer services.

INTRODUCTION

Mobilizing Customer-Oriented Business Processes

Technological advancements in mobile communications enable new ways of doing business (Feldman, 2000, pp. 26; Stafford & Gilleson, 2003), often referred to as mobile business (MB) or mobile commerce (MC). While Turowski and Pousttchi (2003, p. 3) do not distinguish between the two but rather use the term *mobile commerce,* Lehner (2003, pp. 6-8) and Zobel (2001, pp. 2-3) define *mobile business* as the application of mobile technologies to improve or extend business processes and open new market segments and distinguish it from mobile commerce. Here, the latter is rather a subordinate field of MB, focusing of the handling of transactions. In this chapter we will follow the understanding of Lehner and Zobel and concentrate on the application of mobile technologies to support customer-oriented business processes.

The research field dealing with the interaction of businesses with their customers and the related back-end processes within the businesses, such as marketing, sales, and service processes has often been referred to as customer relationship management (CRM) or, when supported by Internet technologies, e-commerce CRM (eCRM) (Romano & Fjermestad, 2002, 2003). Gebert, Geib, Kolbe, & Brenner (2003) classify CRM processes as knowledge-intensive processes, managing knowledge for customers (e.g., knowledge about products and services), knowledge from customers (e.g., customer experience with products and services), or knowledge about customers (e.g., knowledge about customers' preferences and histories). Geib, Reichold, Kolbe, & Brenner (2005) provide a framework identifying major CRM processes in the fields of marketing, sales, and service and point out their interdependencies.

An empirical analysis addressing 1,000 subjects with CRM responsibility in large companies (82% with a revenue > € 100 million) and 89 respondents (9%) was conducted in the authors' research team. Eight percent of the respondents indicated that they already have a mobile CRM solution, a further 22% are currently working on a mobile CRM solution, and 30% are planning to do so (Dous, Salomann, Kolbe, & Brenner, 2004).

Combining the concepts of CRM and MB allows new types of interaction between companies and customers. To leverage investments in IT, the investment has to be aligned with the business strategy (Bakos & Treacy, 1986; Brynjolfsson & Hitt, 2000; Hitt & Brynjolfsson, 1994; Weill & Broadbent, 1998; Weill, Subramani, & Broadbent,

2002). A recent survey conducted by the German Society for Management Research investigated major success factors and success barriers for MB initiatives. The top success barrier was a lack of strategic vision and the initiatives' alignment with corporate strategy (Wamser & Buschmann, 2006).

Obviously, companies face the question of how to select the right MB investment to support their business strategy and how to identify potentials that can be exploited using mobile communication and transaction channels. Depending on the strategic premises different alternatives of mobilizing customer-oriented business processes must be chosen (Weill & Vitale, 2002). The goal of this chapter is to provide assistance in making this decision.

Research Goals and Structure

In this chapter we show interdependencies between the strategic premises and the processes selected for being supported by mobile technology. We explicitly do not analyze the process of defining the strategy but rather rely on existing work of strategy research. Therefore we answer the questions:

- *What are the typical characteristics of business processes chosen for mobile technology support?*
- *What are the interdependencies between these characteristics and the companies' market strategy?*

First, the second section gives an overview of existing research in the field of MB and CRM and identifies the gap of customer-focused research the authors see. In the third section we briefly describe 10 cases, where companies have successfully introduced mobile solutions to support business processes in alignment with their strategic positioning towards customers. In the fourth section we introduce the classifications of different strategic focuses from Crawford and Mathews (2001) and Treacy and Wiersema (1994). We derive a set of five different strategic goals which are specifically focused on the company's interaction with the customer and apply this classification to the analyzed cases. We analyze the selection of processes for the support by mobile technology in the cases and identify the relationship between the strategic premises according to the framework derived from Crawford and Mathews (2001) and Treacy and Wiersema (1994). This results in typical properties which qualify processes for mobilization. The final section summarizes the findings and gives an outlook on further research to be done in this field.

Research Methodology

Our research approach follows the concept of case study research as described by Eisenhardt (1989), Stake (1995), and Yin (2002). The cases (see the third section) have been selected from available published material, in the case of the Helsana health insurance, cologne public transport authority, eBay, and Lufthansa airline the authors have been involved in-depth through a long-term research partnership. Selection was based on the following criteria: a) availability of information about the company's strategic orientation towards customers, b) the case deals primarily with the introduction of mobile technology (be it cellular, synchronization, or other), and c) the process(es) affected by the introduced technology is a customer-oriented business process as defined in the process model developed by the authors' research team and described in Geib et al. (2005). Data were collected by analysis of the published available material about the projects and the companies in general as well as by semi-structured interviews with employees involved in the projects. Only the core aspects from the previously published cases are summarized in this chapter.

The data from each case was analyzed following the strategy suggested by Yin (2002).

The analysis had the primary objective of understanding the process selection and the influence which the corporate strategy had in this process. The findings finally have been integrated into a generalization of strategy's implications for the process selection and design.

BACKGROUND

Mobile Business

Technological advancements in mobile communications enable new ways of doing business (Raisinghani, 2002), often referred to as mobile business or mobile commerce. While Turowski and Pousttchi (2003) do not distinguish between the two but rather use the term *mobile commerce*, Lehner (2003) and Zobel (2001) define *mobile business* as the application of mobile technologies to improve or extend business processes and open new market segments. They differentiate between MB and MC, the latter being a rather subordinate MB field focusing on the handling of transactions. With a similar understanding of the term, Möhlenbruch and Schmieder (2001) conceptualize MB in analogy to electronic business and distinguish fields such as mobile supply chain management, mobile procurement, mobile customer relationship management, and so forth (see Figure 1). We follow this more general understanding and concentrate on mobile CRM (mCRM), which we define as mobile technologies' application in order to support CRM processes such as marketing, sales and service delivery.

The research development in MB and MC can be compared to the development in electronic business and e-commerce. It can be structured into multiple stages. The first stage begins with the technological foundation in IT and infrastructure. It is followed by simple consumer-focused application and service concepts along with business models for technology and base service providers. These applications and services are being advanced fur-

Figure 1. Conceptualization of mobile business (cp. Möhlenbruch & Schmieder, 2001)

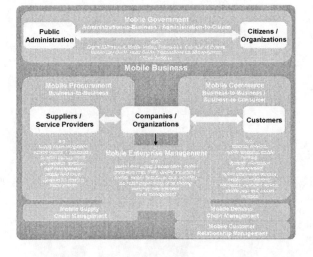

ther, until they reach a maturity level appropriate for business use. Finally the technology is applied to support business processes and entire business models for businesses other than technology and base services are developed. The shift of focus in MB from simple applications for end consumers to advanced applications for business is a condition that hints for mobile technologies to be disruptive technologies in the sense of Christensen (1997): "technologies [that] underperform established products in mainstream markets [...] but [...] have other features that a few fringe (and generally new) customers value. Products based on disruptive technologies are typically cheaper, simpler, and, frequently, more convenient to use" (p. 15). Funk (2003) analyzes this issue in great detail.

The subject of MB and related subjects has gained a substantial interest in the research community, which can be seen in the emergence of new journals focusing on this particular subject (e.g., the *International Journal of Mobile Communications* or the *International Journal of Mobile Computing and Commerce*), conferences explicitly dedicated to the subject (e.g., the International Conference on Mobile Business sponsored by the IEEE being held for the fifth time in 2006) or special issues of well-established journals in the field of IS (see Liang & Wei, 2004; Mylonopoulos & Doukidis,

2003; Schierholz, Kolbe, & Brenner, in press; Urbaczewski, Valacich, & Jessup, 2003).

Current research has certainly passed the mere technology-focused stage, even though advancements in technology are still a subject (e.g., Fritsch & Rossnagel, 2004; Turowski & Pousttchi, 2003). Consumer applications and services are well established and drive impressive markets as well (Funk, 2003, p. 20). Past and current research is further advancing this field as well (Ali, Torabi, & Ali, 2006; Amberg, Figge, & Wehrmann, 2003; Figge, 2001, 2002; Figge, Schrott, Muntermann, & Rannenberg, 2002; Kunze, Zaplata, & Lamersdorf, 2006; Mallat, Rossi, & Tuunainen, 2004; Paavilainen, 2002; Rannenberg, 2004; Reichwald, 2002; Sheng, Nah, & Siau, 2005; Silberer, Wohlfahrt, & Wilhelm, 2001; Stender & Ritz, 2006; Tarasewich, 2003; Titkov, Poslad, & Tan, 2006).

There is a plethora of publications regarding typical benefits of mobile technologies and MB or MC. The subject has been approached both from a more technical point of view as well as from a business perspective. Therefore, we derive two classifications of typical benefits from available literature. The first classification focuses on the technical benefits of mobile technologies (see Table 1).

While these benefits are proven, they must be transformed into improvements of business performance in order to justify investment in MB technologies. Table 2 gives an overview of typical business process benefits which can be realized by leveraging technological benefits in alignment with business process goals and requirements.

In order to actually improve the business performance through IT investments, these investments and the expected benefits should be aligned with the business performance metrics and the overall strategy (Bakos & Treacy; 1986; Brynjolfsson, 1993; Brynjolfsson & Hitt, 2000; Hitt & Brynjolfsson, 1994; Kohli & Devaraj, 2004; Weill, 1992; Weill & Vitale, 2002; Weill et al., 2002). Despite the accepted importance of

Table 1. Classification of technical benefits of mobile technologies

Benefit	Definition	References
Ubiquity	Mobile technologies allow for IS to become accessible from virtually any place and at virtually any time.	Anckar & D'Incau, 2002a, 2002b; Balasubramanian, Peterson, & Jarvenpaa, 2002; Clarke III, 2001; Laukkanen, 2005; Laukkanen & Lauronen, 2005; Lehner, 2003, 11ff.; Pousttchi, Turowski, & Weizmann, 2003; Wohlfahrt, 2001
Context sensitivity	Mobile technologies allow for the contextualization of IS. The context may include the identification of the individual user as well as geographic position and physical environment.	Clarke III, 2001; Laukkanen, 2005; Laukkanen & Lauronen, 2005; Lehner, 2003, 11ff.; Pousttchi et al., 2003, 11ff.; Siau, Sheng, & Nah, 2004; Skelton & Chen, 2005; Wamser, 2003; Wohlfahrt, 2001
Interactivity	Mobile technologies allow for greater interactivity in IS, since they typically provide an "always online" connectivity and have shorter set-up times (e.g., for booting, "instant on").	Anckar & D'Incau, 2002a, 2002b; Clarke III, 2001; Hartmann & Dirksen, 2001; Laukkanen, 2005, 11ff.; Laukkanen & Lauronen, 2005; Lehner, 2003
Convenience and familiarity	For certain tasks, mobile technologies can offer a higher degree of convenience as compared to standard desktop or laptop PCs. This is partially due to limited functionality, thus reduced complexity and higher ease of use. For example, most users are capable of using most features of their cell phones (voice and text communication, address book, etc.), while most users only use a fraction of their PCs functionality.	Anckar & D'Incau, 2002a, 2002b; Gebauer, 2002; Gebauer & Shaw, 2004; Kenny & Marshall, 2000; Lehner, 2003, 11ff.; Perry, O'Hara, Sellen, Brown, & Harper, 2001; Siau, Sheng, & Nah, 2004; Van der Heijden & Valiente, 2002; Wohlfahrt, 2001
Multimediality	Mobile technologies have gained multimedia functionality over the years, for example, most cell phones shipped today include a digital camera, current models even with sufficient resolution for quality snapshots.	Han, Cho, & Choi, 2005; Kung, Hsu, Lin, & Liu, 2006; Pousttchi et al., 2003; Wamser, 2003; Wolf & Wang, 2005

strategy alignment of IT investments there is only little research addressing the strategic aspects of applying MB (Amberg & Remus, 2003; Clarke III, 2001; Sadeh, 2002; Sheng et al., 2005; Wamser & Buschmann, 2006). Even fewer research addresses strategic potentials of *mobile business to businesses* whose core competencies are outside of the technology or base service field, such as financial service providers (Looney, Jessup, & Valacich, 2004).

Customer Relationship Management

The origins of CRM can be traced back to the management concept of Relationship Marketing (RM) (Levitt, 1983). RM is an integrated effort to identify, build up, and maintain a network with individual customers for the mutual benefit of both sides (Shani & Chalasani, 1992, p. 34). RM is of largely strategic character and lacks a holistic view

on business processes, although they are regarded as important (Parvatiyar & Sheth, 2000).

Advances in IT had a significant influence on CRM, focusing mainly on the IS layer in the past. The goal was to support the existing isolated approach of dealing with customer relationships. With the CRM philosophy aiming at creating an integrated view of the customer across the enterprise, these systems were connected and today form the building blocks of comprehensive integrated CRM systems.

We consider CRM to view the customer relationship as an investment, which is to contribute to the bottom line of the enterprise. The design and management of customer relationships is to strengthen the competitive position of an enterprise by increasing the loyalty of customers. While this extends beyond the use of IT, IT is still an important enabler of modern CRM.

Apart from the strategy-oriented concept of RM and systems oriented concepts, there are

Table 2. Classification of business benefits of mobile business

Benefit	Definition	References
Flexibility	The ubiquity and interactivity of MB applications allows for the break-up of process structures. Activities in processes, which were previously bound to location or time constraints, can now be dispatched more flexibly. Unforeseeable events can be responded to more flexibly and timely, since decision makers and action takers can be informed and immediately wherever they are and can be involved in the emergency response interactively.	Anckar & D'Incau, 2002a, 2002b; Fleisch, 2001; Fleisch & Bechmann, 2002; Fleisch, Mattern, & Österle, 2002; Gebauer, 2002; Gebauer & Shaw, 2004; Hartmann & Dirksen, 2001; Humpert & Habbel, 2002; Laukkanen, 2005; Laukkanen & Lauronen, 2005; Nah, Siau, & Sheng, 2004, 2005; Perry et al., 2001; Reichwald & Meier, 2002; Siau et al., 2004; Van der Heijden & Valiente, 2002; Wamser, 2003; Wohlfahrt, 2001
Organizational efficiency	The ubiquity and interactivity of MB applications allows for higher operational efficiency since the gaps between information's point of creation and its point of action can be bridged. For example, field agents can enter information electronically and directly to corporate IS, thus duplicate entry can be eliminated and back-end processing of the information can begin immediately. Information is available ubiquitously and immediately and can be used in geographically dispersed processes and activities.	Anckar & D'Incau, 2002a, 2002b; Fleisch & Bechmann, 2002; Fleisch et al., 2002; Gebauer, 2002; Gebauer & Shaw, 2004; Hartmann & Dirksen, 2001; Humpert & Habbel, 2002; Kadyte, 2005; Laukkanen, 2005; Laukkanen & Lauronen, 2005; Nah et al., 2004, 2005; Perry et al., 2001; Siau et al., 2004; Skelton & Chen, 2005; van der Heijden & Valiente, 2002; Wamser, 2003; Wohlfahrt, 2001
Individual productivity and effectiveness	Context sensitivity and interactivity as well as convenience and familiarity of MB applications allow for a greater level of effectiveness of business processes and a higher individual productivity. Interactive and context-sensitive offerings can increase the effectiveness of marketing campaigns. Interactive and ubiquitous control mechanisms can increase effectiveness of machines since they can send alerts in case of errors. Similarly individual productivity of employees can be increased since they can use waiting time more effectively (e.g., in airport terminals).	Anckar & D'Incau, 2002a, 2002b; Gebauer, 2002; Gebauer & Shaw, 2004; Kadyte, 2005; Nah et al., 2004, 2005; Perry et al., 2001; Siau et al., 2004; Skelton & Chen, 2005; Van der Heijden & Valiente, 2002; Wamser, 2003; Wohlfahrt, 2001
Transparency	Ubiquity and interactivity of MB processes allow for the increase of process transparency. This decreases costs for process control and customer satisfaction. Transparency of information can lead to higher market transparency and thus more efficient market mechanisms, for example, customers can compare prices online while in a retail store.	Chen, 2005; Kadyte, 2005; Laukkanen, 2005; Laukkanen & Lauronen, 2005; Reichwald & Meier, 2002; Wamser, 2003; Wohlfahrt, 2001
Entertainment	Especially multimediality but also ubiquity and interactivity increase the entertainment gained from MB applications. Entertainment content typically is multimedia-based in nature, thus entertainment devices need to be multimedia enabled. Additionally, mobilization of everyday life leads to more mobile and spontaneous entertainment needs.	Anckar & D'Incau, 2002a, 2002b; Dickinger, Arami, & Meyer, 2006; Han et al., 2005; Humpert & Habbel, 2002; Park, 2006; Reichwald & Meier, 2002; Wolf & Wang, 2005; Wong & Hiew, 2005

Figure 2. Mobile business value chain (Zobel, 2001, p. 122)

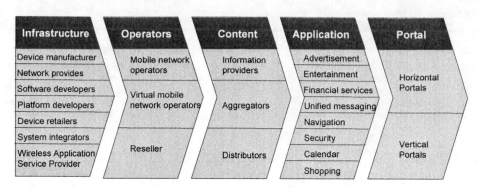

several CRM approaches with special focus on business processes (Schulze, Thiesse, Bach, & Österle, 2000). However, these approaches are based on the separation of the functional areas of marketing, sales, and service, which by itself does not provide a cross-functional process view.

CRM processes typically require not only transactional data, which can be automatically collected and stored in relational databases, but also a significant amount of knowledge. Also, CRM processes are typically complex and only structured to a certain extent. Hence, they can be considered knowledge-intensive processes (Eppler, Seifried, & Röpnack, 1999). Besides developing an integrated view of CRM processes, it is therefore critical to address the management of knowledge flows from and to the customer across all communication channels as well as to enable the use of the knowledge about the customers.

Customer Focus in Mobile Business

When trying to achieve strategy alignment of mobile solutions in CRM, the analysis of the customer value proposition (i.e., the market strategy) is a crucial step. Some researchers have given guidance for a company's positioning in a mobile value chain, but guidance on how to analyze different customer value propositions and how to support

these by mobile support for business processes still is lacking.

Zobel (2001) introduces a value chain of MC (see Figure 1). It begins with network infrastructure providers, providing, for example, IP infrastructure and devices. On the second stage, operators provide mobile infrastructure for such cellular networks. On the third stage, content is provided, for example, by news agencies, media owners, and so forth. On the fourth stage mobile applications (such as payment solutions, security solutions, etc.) are built on top of the network infrastructure and content. Players on this stage are service operators (e.g., mobile ticketing services), transaction clearing centers, and so forth. Finally an interface to the MC is provided by mobile portal providers. A similar value chain can be found in Paavilainen (2002). For each stage, Paavilainen explains strategies and business models showing opportunities for market players.

Published MB value chains do not cover the user of the output of the value chain though. Works analyzing consumer value have mostly focused on mobile services provided via the mobile network operator. What is lacking in published research is a concept how businesses should go about using mobile solutions in customer processes, for example, companies offering mobile services such as banking or businesses using mobile sales support to improve and extend the way they are doing business. In these cases, the strategic options of the MB value chain are less important, because these businesses are primarily positioned in a different industry's value chain. For example, Lufthansa is primarily an airline and as such positions itself strategically in the airline industry's value chain rather than as a mobile content provider, even though part of its service offerings is mobile content for customers. Also, while still very important, consumer value of the services are not the only aspect in the decision process, because the strategic goals of the company offering the service provide the business background and thus have to be taken into account as well. There is little research published on how companies can support their strategic customer value proposition using mobile services. This is the focus of this chapter.

Strategic Frameworks

A substantial amount of research has been done in the field of business strategy or strategic management. While many of the foundational works were developed in the 1960s through the 1980s (Andrews, 1969; Ansoff, 1965, 1969; Anthony, 1965; Chandler, 1962, 1977; Mintzberg, 1980, 1987; Porter, 1979, 1996, 1998; Wernerfelt, 1984), it has been argued how far these frameworks are still helpful in facing today's business challenges. Cummings and Angwin (2004) analyze this in detail and come to the conclusion that the traditional frameworks are somewhat helpful still, but need to evolve to handle multi-dimensional today's strategies. Hartline, Maxham, and McKee, 2000; Rust, Inman, Jia, and Zahorik (1999); Rust, Zeithaml, and Lemon (2000); Rust, Lemon, and Zeithaml (2004); and Colgate and Danaher (2000) suggest a stronger focus on the customer. Luo and Seyedian (2003) go along with this argumentation suggesting a contextual marketing strategy.

Crawford and Mathews (2001) break the customer strategy concepts down to an operational applicability and describe the strategic aspects of customer focus for business strategy. In an empirical research addressing 5,000 American consumers, they find that consumers do not simply look for lowest prices, best products, and best services, but rather have a desire for more complex values (rather than simple value). They discovered the following five attributes which customers demand and successful companies focus on (Crawford & Mathews, 2001, p. 23):

- **Price:** Customers want a transparent, fair price (not necessarily the lowest price).
- **Customer service:** Customers want a hassle-free fulfillment of their basic needs and want to be recognized as individuals.
- **Accessibility:** Customers want simple access to the products, including clearly distinguished products and clear channels to interact with businesses.
- **Customer intimacy:** Customers want a unique experience in the interaction with businesses, that is, they want personalized offers and they want to be treated as a human individual.
- **Product quality:** Customers want an overall good product, not necessarily the single-one best product, but the best value for their money.

Crawford and Mathews (2001, p. 26) point out four levels to which a company can perform concerning these attributes. These range from level 0, where a customer avoids the company; level 1, where a customer trusts the company for everyday business; level 2, where a customer prefers the company over others to; level 3, where the customer only accepts this company, even if it means, for example, waiting for a product not yet shipped.

Crawford and Mathews (2001, p. 33) suggest that reaching level 3 in all attributes is unrealistic. They propose the successful strategy to be selecting one attribute to focus on to achieve level

3 (dominant position in the market), to focus a secondary attribute to reach level 2 (differentiating from competitors), and to maintain level 1 (market average) on the remaining three attributes.

In a different study analyzing multiple cases from market leaders in several branches (such as Casio, Kellogg's, FedEx) Treacy and Wiersema (1994) identify the following three main strategic goals (Treacy & Wiersema, 1994, p. 29):

- **Operational excellence:** Focus on the combination of quality, price, and ease of purchase without being exceptionally innovative in products or customer service.
- **Product leadership:** Focus on exceptional innovation in product features.
- **Customer intimacy:** Focus on the intimate one-to-one relationship to the customer.

Combining the results of Crawford and Mathews (2001) and Treacy and Wiersema (1994) it becomes obvious that the aspects of "Product Quality" (Crawford & Mathews) and "Product Leadership" (Treacy & Wiersema) as well as "Customer Service" and "Customer Intimacy" are almost identical in concept. Further more, the aspect of "Price" (Crawford & Mathews) is included by "Operational Excellence" (Treacy & Wiersema). Thus the list of attributes can be consolidated to:

- Price
- Customer intimacy
- Accessibility
- Product quality

STRATEGY ALIGNED MOBILE BUSINESS: INSIGHTS FROM THE REAL WORLD

In order to identify interdependencies between corporate market strategy (following the framework explained previously) and the selection of business processes to be supported by mobile solutions, we analyzed 10 cases. As mentioned in the second section, the cases have been published before and the analysis was mainly based on the published material. In the following each of the cases will be briefly summarized, pointing out the aspects of most relevance to our analysis. For further details about the cases, please refer to the original publications. For each of the cases, we briefly describe the company background, followed by the specific challenge that lead to the introduction of a mobile solution to support a business process. We also briefly describe the implemented solution and the characteristics of relevance for our analysis.

Helsana/Progrès: Mobile Marketing

Company Background

Helsana (http://www.helsana.ch) is the largest health insurance provider in Switzerland with about €2.5 million annual premium yield (2002). Its brand Progrès (http://www.progres.ch) represents affordable offerings for young customers. The brand strategy focuses on *maximum availability* and *competitive prices*.

Challenge

- There is only a short time frame for contract switching, thus high marketing efforts by all competitors overload the customers' perception.
- Customers show a high price sensitivity and low interest in the product itself thus they need a spontaneous and instant trigger.

Solution

Customers can retrieve an offer for Progrès insurance within 1-2 seconds via SMS, allowing Helsana to:

- Increase the visibility of its brand against the intensive activities of competitors
- Emphasize the innovative image of the Progrès brand
- Leverage the situational context once the customer is focused on the offer by other marketing activities (18,000 requested premiums resulted in 10,000 calls into the customer call center and 3,500 contract closures in 2003)

For further details about this case, see Reichold, Schierholz, Kolbe, and Brenner (2003) and Reichold, Schierholz, Kolbe, and Brenner (2004).

Gossard G4Me: Mobile Marketing

Company Background

Gossard (http://www.gossard.co.uk) is a manufacturer of lingerie products. Gossard's strategy focuses on *a strong, intimate bond* to customers in the market for string thongs by shifting the brand image towards the self-image of their primary target group: young, modern women and on *a premium, luxury product.*

Challenge

- To position the Gossard brand in a market for products with a strong personal bond requires an in-depth knowledge about customers.
- This conflicts with the goal of a non-invasive, opt-in, and privacy-preserving marketing campaign.

Solution

By launching marketing campaigns and providing giveaways such as coupons to respondents via SMS Gossard could build up a database with high-quality and detailed information about customers in their target group. Thus, Gossard has succeeded in:

- Gaining an in-depth understanding about their customers' desires
- Building a means to address customers for personal products on a very personal channel/medium such as a cellular phone
- Boosting the affectivity of traditional marketing campaigns such as TV spots with an interactive element, reaching an eight months sales target in just eight weeks

For further details about this case, see Lerner and Frank (2004, pp. 72-73).

Cologne Public Transport Authority: Mobile Sales

Company Background

The Cologne public transport authority is a publicly owned organization which runs the public transportation (buses, local trains, underground trains) in the agglomeration of Cologne, Germany and the surrounding suburbs. With the liberation of the market for public transport as required by the European Union, it will have to compete for the contract, thus it has launched a campaign to improve their image as an *innovative service provider* with *a high customer service level.*

Challenge

- Apart from tickets being sold on subscription, still many tickets for public transport are sold individually, for example, via ticketing machines at bus stops or in trains.
- The image of the public transport authority has been reported as rather mixed. While the core service of public transport has been accepted as good, the level of customer service, for example, flexibility and innovativeness, have been reported as low.

- Providing high level, individual service to anonymous customers buying at ticketing machines is impossible.

Solution

A mobile ticket has been introduced by which customers can order a ticket for public transportation by simply calling a free 1-800 number. The ticket is delivered as a text message to their mobile within seconds. Customers need to register before they can use the service (except for one free trial ticket per mobile phone number). With this new system, it is possible:

- To allow discounts for customers who repeatedly buy single tickets (e.g., customers who by the third single ticket within one day, receive a full-day pass, and save about 20% of the fare)
- To create customer profiles and individualize services for customers
- To improve the Cologne public transport authority's image as an innovative service provider

eBay in Germany: Mobile Transactions

Company Background

eBay is probably the most well-known online auction platform in the world. Customers range from professional sellers (power sellers) to occasional private sellers to private buyers. eBay's customer value proposition focuses on *global reach, variety of traded items, efficient information services,* and *low trading fees and item prices.* eBay experiences impressive growth rates, in many figures constantly around and above 30%.

Challenge

- eBays biggest challenge currently is to maintain the large growth rates in a more and more saturated market. eBay tries to maintain this growth by acquiring new members (which is hard to achieve in almost saturated markets), activation of passive members and maximizing activity of active members. Currently, all member activity is dependent on the member's access to a Web-enabled PC, since eBay is a typical Web application.

Solution

In order to increase the reach of the platform and the activity of existing members, eBay introduced an SMS-based bidding process in Germany. Members who have placed the highest bid on an item can register for an alerting service, which notifies them when another member has placed a higher bid or when the auction is over and they won. Also, in response to the message about a higher bid, the recipient can place a new bid via SMS. With this new interaction channel, eBay members:

- Receive up-to-date information on auctions they personally participate in wherever they are
- Can respond to higher bids by other members and thus stay active in their auctions even when not in reach of Web-enabled PC

Eneco: Mobile Field Force

Company Background

Eneco (http://www.eneco.nl) is a Dutch energy supplier with about €2 billion annual turnover (2002). The corporate strategy aims to achieve customer loyalty by supplying a *high level of customer service* and a *reliable energy supply at affordable rates (i.e. in this case competitive price).*

Challenge

- Field force agents have no access to crucial information while in the field.
- Customers' issues cannot be resolved immediately due to lack of information.

Solution

Agents are provided with a PDA-based mobile application connecting them to the corporate IT via a mobile middleware module. This improves customer service by:

- Allowing for real-time processing of billing-relevant data collected by agent
- Better coordination of and information supply for agents on-site
- More visited customers per agent and a higher on-site solution rate

For further details about this case, see Lerner and Frank (2004, pp. 18-20).

SOS Médecins: Mobile Field Force

Company Background

SOS Médecins (http://www.sosmédecins.ch) is an initiative of more than 50 doctors in the Geneva region, providing medical treatment at home, in emergencies, and otherwise. SOS Médecins' strategy focuses on *best possible medical service (i.e., in this case product quality)* and *maximum availability.*

Challenge

- Doctors have no direct access to the patient's records, thus the need for time-consuming

calls to the central office instead of treating patients
- The scheduling of doctors' routes proves inefficient due to lack of location information
- The travel routes of doctors prove inefficient due to lack of navigational support

Solution

By providing doctors with a PDA- GPRS-based solution, secured via VPN technology, SOS Médecins provides doctors with most current patient records and navigation support as well as optimized the scheduling efficiency and thus achieved to:

- Increase the time each doctor can effectively treat a patient
- Decrease the delay between the patient's call and the doctor's arrival
- Improve medical treatment itself

For further details about this case, see Lerner and Frank (2004, pp. 54-56).

Verizon: Mobile Sales Force

Company Background

Verizon (http://www.verizonwireless.com) is the largest wireless telecommunication provider in the U.S., serving about 39 million customers; generating an annual revenue of $22.5 billion (2003). Verizon's strategy aims to show its ability to *innovate* while providing *the best service* in consulting their business customers according to their particular, individual needs.

Challenge

- In an innovative field like MB, Verizon needs to demonstrate ability to deliver innovative solutions.

- To maintain the solutions' innovativeness Verizon needs to reduce time-to-market for its products and services as much as possible.

Solution

Verizon equipped its own sales force with mobile corporate data access, for example, to its CRM application, and thereby:

- Improved customer service and consulting due to better and more proactive information availability for sales agents
- Improved its visibility as an innovator by demonstrating wireless solution know-how on-site

For further details about this case, see Lerner and Frank (2004, pp. 36-37).

Novartis: Mobile Info Services

Company Background

Novartis (http://www.novartis.ch, http://www. novartis.co.uk) is a Swiss pharmaceutical manufacturer with $24.8 billion annual turnover and $5 billion annual profit (2003). Novartis' Consumer Health business unit positions itself as an innovative company having a *positive impact on people's lives (i.e., customer intimacy)*, making *available the right information at the right time (i.e., accessibility)*.

Challenge

- Novartis wants its brand to be seen as a partner helping lower the burden of allergies in everyday life.
- The "Aller-eze" product should be seen as the main product in the anti-allergy (especially hay fever) market, that is, customers'

creating the association between the two intuitively.

Solution

To introduce the new anti-allergic product "Aller-eze" Novartis' British affiliate launched a mobile marketing initiative. By offering a subscription service providing patients with timely, location-specific allergy warnings and hints for patients, Novartis succeeded in:

- "Aller-eze" being perceived as a partner providing daily support, easing the pain of allergy patients
- Emphasizing the innovative image of Novartis as a whole

For further details about this case, see Lerner and Frank (2004, pp. 74-75).

Lufthansa: Mobile Info Services

Company Background

Lufthansa is one of the largest airlines and a founding member of the star alliance, the largest network of cooperating airlines in the world. It considers itself a *full-range service provider addressing all customer segments* with different product variations. Price-sensitive customers can book *cheap rates with low service level,* business customers can book *flexible rates with high service level* and luxury customers are treated with *exclusive service*. Lufthansa also cultivates an innovative image, for example, by adopting new technologies early.

Challenge

- Events such as delays or cancellations create new information which is viable for customers, which are traveling and therefore mobile by nature.

- Cost pressure in the airline industry in general requires the airline to streamline processes and to raise operational efficiency.
- Procedures such as check-in are time critical, since there is only a short time frame for the handling. Additionally, especially business customers are typically in a hurry and appreciate shorter handling procedures.

Solution

Lufthansa offers multiple mobile services, with different service levels for different customer segments. Services include general information such as timetables (available freely for customers and non-customers), flight-related information such as alerts about delays and gate changes (available to all customers), and mobile check-in service (available to premium customers only). With these services, Lufthansa was able:

- To further differentiate the service levels for different customer segments, for example, allow for a more flexible check-in procedure for premium customers
- Streamline the customer handling procedures since customers are informed about flight-related events proactively instead of having to request or search the information
- To demonstrate its innovation capabilities by leveraging a new technology earlier than most competitors

For further details about this case, see Schierholz, Glissmann, Kolbe, and Brenner (2006).

Lotto NL: Mobile Gaming

Company Background

Lotto NL (www.lotto.nl) is a publicly owned lottery service in the Netherlands. Its strategy is to *cover the entire market* with a mix of service

channels, *providing anywhere-anytime access to lottery services.*

Challenge

- A high market saturation in traditional channels requires an exploitation of new market segments/channels to allow for revenue growth.

Solution

By allowing customers to take part in lottery games via SMS Lotto NL:

- Lowers customers' efforts to take part in lottery games and thus engages more customers
- Leverages and enhances the traditional marketing activities such as TV spots by providing instant access to its services

For further details about this case, see Lerner and Frank (2004, pp. 34-35).

STRATEGY'S IMPLICATIONS FOR PROCESS SELECTION AND DESIGN

Looking at the cases of Verizon, Helsana/Progrès, Cologne Public Transportation Authority, Gossard, and Lufthansa, we identified an attribute to include in addition to the ones listed in the framework as introduced in the second section. These cases show that especially new technologies (such as currently mobile technology) can be a means for businesses to demonstrate innovative capabilities. In current literature, we also found approaches, suggesting innovativeness to be an important strategic attribute of market strategy (Kim & Mauborgne, 1999; Micheal, Rochford, & Wotruba, 2003). Thus, we added the attribute of innovativeness which can be supported by the application of MB technologies. This results in the following common strategic focus attributes/goals which make up the strategic framework used for our analysis:

- **Price:** Offering low, transparent, and fair prices compared to the market
- **Customer intimacy:** Offering hassle-free service on a personal level, establishing a one-to-one relationship with customers
- **Product quality:** Offering the best product features in the market
- **Accessibility:** Offering simple, anytime-anywhere-anyhow access to products
- **Innovativeness:** Being perceived as an in-novator or early-adopter of new, innovative technologies

Table 3 summarizes the prioritization of these attributes across the analyzed cases; applying the classification from Crawford and Mathews (2001) of primary focus, secondary focus, and no focus (i.e., the company pursues market average performance).

Obviously, the strategic framework as introduced in the second section and which has been extended here can be used to classify the mobile

initiatives in the analyzed cases. The following common aspects of the selected customer-oriented processes, depending on the strategic orientation, can be observed.

Comparing the correlations between strategic focus and process selections for mobile support in the case studies, the following observations can be made. Companies focusing primarily on price were not found in the sample, companies who focus on price as the second distinguishing attribute have chosen processes where either process steps could be eliminated by removing media breaches (Eneco) or processes where mobile technology allows for better price transparency and the communication of the price on an individual basis (Progrès). Most companies have the focus on customer intimacy. These companies have chosen processes where mobile technology allows for customer support in spontaneous or emergency situations (eBay, Novartis, Lufthansa) or processes where contextualization (mostly personalization) allowed for a convincing one-to-one interaction (Gossard, Cologne PTA). Only SOS Médcins focuses on product quality, their product is a service offering which is improved by better information support to mobile service

Table 3. Overview of strategic focus in the analyzed cases

	Price	Intimacy	Product	Accessibility	Innovation
Progrès	●	⊘	⊘	○	●
Gossard G4Me	⊘	○	●	⊘	●
Cologne PTA	⊘	○	⊘	⊘	●
eBay in Germany	●	⊘	⊘	○	●
Eneco	●	○	⊘	⊘	⊘
SOS Médcins	⊘	⊘	○	●	⊘
Verizon	⊘	●	⊘	⊘	○
Novartis	⊘	○	⊘	●	⊘
Lufthansa	⊘	○	⊘	⊘	●
LottoNL	⊘	●	⊘	○	⊘

Legend: ○ = primary focus   ● = secondary focus ⊘ = no focus (market average)

agents (doctors). Companies who focus on accessibility have used mobile technology to offer their customers a direct and interactive interaction channel, either for requesting/receiving information or individual offers (Progrès, eBay, Novartis) or to order services or products or perform other transactions (eBay, LottoNL). Companies who focus on innovation have chosen processes which have a high external visibility and which occur frequently (Progrès, Cologne PTA, eBay, Verizon, Lufthansa).

Strategic Focus on Price

A strategy focused on competitive and transparent price can be supported, when business processes are mobilized in which information is passed on and the point of creation (PoC) and the point of action (PoA) of the information differ. For example, Eneco could raise operational efficiency, and thus lower operational costs of their field force by supporting them with mobile devices, which were connected and integrated with Eneco's billing system and other IS which provide them with information to help them in solving customer incidents on-site.

Strategic Focus on Customer Intimacy

A strategy focused on customer intimacy and the best customer experience can be supported when business processes are mobilized that support the customer in spontaneous situations or where anonymity can be overcome by using a personalized mobile medium. Here a customer experiences that the company is there to help and provide knowledge for the customer when he/she needs it. Also, the generation of personalized knowledge about the customer can be well supported by mobile solutions, since the devices used in such solutions, such as cellular phones, usually have a strong personal touch. For example, Novartis could support its customers with crucial information,

personalized to the location and allergic profile of each individual customer and the Cologne public transport authority could provide personalized discounts on repeated purchases.

Strategic Focus on Accessibility

A strategy focused on accessibility is probably the most obvious one to be supported by mobile technology, even though again the support of physical products seems to be hard. A strategy focusing on accessibility should leverage mobile technology's potential to extend the communication channels the customer can use to obtain a service from a business to location- and time-independent media such as cellular phones. For example, Lotto NL could extend its reach to occasional gamblers, who were not taking part in the lottery because of the burden of having to obtain a lottery ticket from a store or from an Internet-connected PC. By offering the purchase of lottery tickets via cellular phones, customers can now purchase lottery tickets anytime (i.e., independent from office hours of points of sale), anywhere (i.e., independent of where the next point of sale is located at), and anyhow (i.e., it is the customer's choice via which channel to purchase).

Strategic Focus on Innovativeness

A strategy focusing on the demonstration of innovativeness of a company can be supported by MB at least nowadays, when mobile technology has not yet become a commodity. To support an innovative image of a company the processes obviously have to be externally visible to have an impact on the company's image. For example, Verizon chose the sales agents because they have immediate customer contact and thus can best show Verizon's ability to put innovative products into operational use. Also, addressing young customer market segments can be well supported with innovative marketing based on technologies considered "cool" by these customers as the cases Helsana/Progrès and Gossard illustrate.

Strategic Focus on Product Quality

The analyzed cases indicate that a strategy focused on quality of product is hard to support unless the product is either closely related to mobile technology or is a knowledge-intensive service product. For example, Verizon could support the product quality and how this quality is perceived by customers by showing its products and services on-site via its own sales agents. The knowledge aspect played an important role in the case of SOS Médecins, where the product of medical service has been greatly enhanced by providing the doctor with complete and current knowledge about the visited patient.

OUTLOOK

The MB industry will mature further. On the one hand, the technological evolution will bring about more sophisticated devices and networks, which allow for more sophisticated applications and services. On the other hand, the market will likely experience a shakeout leading to more clearly distinguished roles in the value chain. Currently, especially in Western Europe, many mobile network operators try to control the entire value chain, leaving little room for other partners, claiming large parts of the profit potential and thus rendering the applications of MC and MB relatively unattractive. Price competition and a maturing market will likely cure this phenomenon.

CONCLUSION AND FURTHER RESEARCH

The analysis presented in this chapter shows how the alignment of the use of MB technology with corporate strategy can be achieved, with special respect to business processes in customer interaction. We have identified five different strategic focuses and explain which criteria the processes

should fulfill to provide the best support to the corporate strategy when being mobilized, thus promise to realize their full potential (i.e., the best ROI of the related IT investments).

Since the analysis so far is based on 10 cases, which are not representative for a general target audience, the framework should be further validated by further cases studies and quantitative empirical research. Other aspects that should be addressed by further research include a detailed method for process selection, business process redesign, and technology selection to provide businesses with a structured method on how to achieve best effects with the application of MB technology.

REFERENCES

Ali, S., Torabi, T., & Ali, H. (2006). A case for business process deployment for location aware applications. *International Journal of Computer Science and Network Security, 6*(8a), 118-127.

Amberg, M., Figge, S., & Wehrmann, J. (2003). A cooperation model for personalised and situation dependent services in mobile networks. In A. Olivé, M. Yoshikawa, & E. S. Yu (Eds.), *Advanced conceptual modeling techniques* (2784 ed.). Berlin, Germany: Springer.

Amberg, M., & Remus, U. (2003). Multi-channel commerce: Hybridstrategien und controlling. In W. Uhr, W. Esswein, & E. Schoop (Eds.), *Wirtschaftsinformatik 2003/Band II* (pp. 795-817). Heidelberg, Germany: Physica-Verlag.

Anckar, B., & D'Incau, D. (2002a). Value creation in mobile commerce: Findings from a consumer survey. *Journal of Information Technology Theory and Application, 4*(1), 43-64.

Anckar, B., & D'Incau, D. (2002b, January 7-10). *Value-added services in mobile commerce: An analytical framework and empirical findings from a national consumer survey.* Paper presented at the 35th Annual Hawaii International Conference on System Sciences, Big Island.

Andrews, K. (1969). Toward professionalism in business management. *Harvard Business Review, 47*(2), 49-60.

Ansoff, I. (1965). *Corporate strategy: An analytical approach to business policy for growth and expansion.* New York: McGraw-Hill.

Ansoff, I. (Ed.). (1969). *Business strategy.* Harmondsworth, UK: Penguin.

Anthony, R. N. (1965). *Planning and control systems.* Boston: Harvard University Press.

Bakos, J. Y., & Treacy, M. E. (1986). Information technology and corporate strategy: A research perspective. *MIS Quarterly, 10*(2), 106-120.

Balasubramanian, S., Peterson, R. A., & Jarvenpaa, S. L. (2002). Exploring the implications of m-commerce for markets and marketing. *Journal of the Academy of Marketing Science, 30*(4), 348-362.

Brynjolfsson, E. (1993). The productivity paradox of information technology: Review and assessment. *Communication of the ACM, 12*(36), 66-77.

Brynjolfsson, E., & Hitt, L. M. (2000). Beyond computation: Information technology, organizational transformation and business performance. *Journal of Economic Perspectives, 14*(4), 23-48.

Chandler, A. (1962). *Strategy and structure.* Boston: Harvard University Press.

Chandler, A. (1977). *The visible hand.* Boston: Harvard University Press.

Chen, M. (2005). A methodology for building mobile computing applications: Business strategy and technical architecture. *International Journal of Electronic Business, 2*(3), 229-243.

Christensen, C. M. (1997). *The innovator's dilemma: When new technologies cause great firms to fail.* Boston: Harvard Business School Press.

Clarke III, I. (2001). Emerging value propositions for m-commerce. *Journal of Business Strategies, 18*(2), 133-148.

Colgate, M. R., & Danaher, P. J. (2000). Implementing a customer relationship strategy: The asymmetric impact of poor versus excellent execution. *Journal of the Academy of Marketing Science, 28*(3), 375-387.

Crawford, R., & Mathews, R. (2001). *The myth of excellence: Why great companies never try to be the best at everything.* New York: Crown Business.

Cummings, S., & Angwin, D. (2004). The future shape of strategy: Lemmings or chimeras? *Academy of Management Executive, 18*(2), 21-36.

Dickinger, A., Arami, M., & Meyer, D. (2006, January 4-7). *Reconsidering the adoption process: Enjoyment and social norms—Antecedents of Hedonic mobile technology use.* Paper presented at the 39th Hawaii International Conference on System Sciences, Kaua'i.

Dous, M., Salomann, H., Kolbe, L., & Brenner, W. (2004). *CRM—Status quo und zukünftige Entwicklungen.* Switzerland: Universität St. Gallen.

Eisenhardt, K. M. (1989). Building theories from case study research. *Academy of Management Review, 14*(4), 532-550.

Eppler, M., Seifried, P., & Röpnack, A. (1999, April 8). *Improving knowledge intensive processes through an enterprise knowledge medium.* Paper presented at the ACM SIGCPR conference on computer personnel research.

Feldman, S. (2000). Mobile commerce for the masses. *IEEE Internet Computing, 4*(6), 74-75.

Figge, S. (2001, May 3). *Situation dependent m-commerce applications.* Paper presented at the Conference on Telecommunications and Information Markets—COTIM, Providence, RI.

Figge, S. (2002). Die open mobile architecture—Systemumgebung für mobile Dienste der nächsten Generation. *Wirtschaftsinformatik, 44*(4), 375-378.

Figge, S., Schrott, G., Muntermann, J., & Rannenberg, K. (2002, June 16). *EARNING M-ONEY—A situation based approach for mobile business models.* Paper presented at the European Conference on Information Systems, Neapel, Italy.

Fleisch, E. (2001). *Business perspectives on ubiquitous computing.* St. Gallen, Switzerland.

Fleisch, E., & Bechmann, T. (2002). *Ubiquitous computing: Wie "intelligente Dinge" die Assekuranz verändern.* St. Gallen, Switzerland.

Fleisch, E., Mattern, F., & Österle, H. (2002). *Betriebliche anwendungen mobiler technologien: Ubiquitous commerce.* St. Gallen, Switerzland.

Fritsch, L., & Rossnagel, H. (2004). SIM-based mobile electronic signatures: Enabling m-business with certification on demand. *Card Forum International, 8*(1), 38-40.

Funk, J. L. (2003). *Mobile disruption: The technologies and applications driving the obile Internet.* Hoboken, NJ: Jon Wiley & Sons.

Gebauer, J. (2002, June 17). *Assessing the value of emerging technologies: The case of mobile technologies to enhance business to business applications.* Paper presented at the 15th Bled Electronic Commerce Conference, Bled, Slovenia.

Gebauer, J., & Shaw, M. J. (2004). Success factors and impacts of mobile business applications: Results from a mobile e-procurement study. *International Journal of Electronic Commerce, 8*(3), 19-41.

Gebert, H., Geib, M., Kolbe, L. M., & Brenner, W. (2003). Knowledge-enabled customer relationship management. *Journal of Knowledge Management, 7*(5), 107-123.

Geib, M., Reichold, A., Kolbe, L. M., & Brenner, W. (2005, January 3). *Architecture for customer relationship management approaches in financial services,* Big Island, HI.

Han, S.-Y., Cho, M.-K., & Choi, M.-K. (2005, July 11). *Ubitem: A framework for interactive marketing in location-based gaming environment.* Paper presented at the Proceedings of the Fourth International Conference on Mobile Business (mBusiness), Sydney, Australia.

Hartline, M. D., Maxham, J. G., & McKee, D. O. (2000). Corridors of influence in the dissemination of customer-oriented strategy to customer contact service employees. *Journal of Marketing, 64*(2), 35-50.

Hartmann, S., & Dirksen, V. (2001). Effizienzsteigerungen von unternehmensinternen Prozessen durch die Integration von Komponenten des M-Business. *Information Management & Consulting, 16*(2), 16-19.

Hitt, L., & Brynjolfsson, E. (1994, December). *Creating value and destroying profits? Three measures of information technology's contribution.*

Humpert, F., & Habbel, F.-R. (2002). Mobile Dienste für die Öffentlichkeit. *HMD Praxis der Wirtschaftsinformatik, 226,* 37-43.

Kadyte, V. (2005, July 11). *Process visibility: How mobile technology can enhance business-customer care in the paper industry.* Paper presented at the Proceedings of the Fourth International Conference on Mobile Business (mBusiness), Sydney, Australia.

Kenny, D., & Marshall, J. F. (2000). Contextual marketing—The real business of the Internet. *Harvard Business Review, 78*(6), 119-125.

Kim, W. C., & Mauborgne, R. (1999). Creating new market space. *Harvard Business Review, 77*(1), 83-93.

Kohli, R., & Devaraj, S. (2004). Realizing the business benefits of information technology investments: An organizational process. *Misqe, 3*(2), 53-68.

Kung, H.-Y., Hsu, C.-Y., Lin, M.-H., & Liu, C.-N. (2006). Mobile multimedia medical system: Design and implementation. *International Journal of Mobile Communications, 4*(5), 595-620.

Kunze, C. P., Zaplata, S., & Lamersdorf, W. (2006, June 13). *Mobile process description and execution.* Paper presented at the 6th IFIP WG 6.1 International Conference on Distributed Applications and Interoperable Systems, Bologna, Itlay.

Laukkanen, T. (2005, July 11). *Comparing consumer value creation in Internet and mobile banking.* Paper presented at the Proceedings of the Fourth International Conference on Mobile Business (mBusiness), Sydney, Australia.

Laukkanen, T., & Lauronen, J. (2005). Consumer value creation in mobile banking services. *International Journal of Mobile Communications, 3*(4), 325-338.

Lehner, F. (2003). *Mobile und drahtlose Informationssysteme: Technologien, Anwendungen, Märkte.* Berlin, Germany: Springer.

Lerner, T., & Frank, V. (2004). *Best practices mobile business* (2nd ed.). BusinessVillage.de.

Levitt, T. (1983). After the sale is over... Author(s): Source: ; Sep/Oct83, Vol. 61 Issue 5, p87, 7p. *Harvard Business Review, 61*(5), 87-94.

Liang, T.-P., & Wei, C.-P. (2004). Introduction to the special issue: Mobile commerce applications. *International Journal of Electronic Commerce, 8*(3), 7-17.

Looney, C. A., Jessup, L. M., & Valacich, J. S. (2004). Emerging business models for mobile brokerage services. *Communications of the ACM, 47*(6), 71-77.

Luo, X., & Seyedian, M. (2003). Contextual marketing and customer-orientation strategy for e-commerce: An empirical analysis. *International Journal of Electronic Commerce, 8*(2), 95-118.

Mallat, N., Rossi, M., & Tuunainen, V. K. (2004). Mobile banking services. *Communications of the ACM, 47*(5), 42-46.

Micheal, K., Rochford, L., & Wotruba, T. R. (2003). How new product introductions affect sales management strategy: The impact of type of "newness" of the new product. *Journal of Product Innovation Management, 20*(4), 270-283.

Mintzberg, H. (1980). Structure in 5's: A synthesis of the research on organization design. *Management Science, 26*(3), 322-341.

Mintzberg, H. (1987). The strategy concept II: Another look at why organizations need strategies. *California Management Review, 30*(3), 11-24.

Möhlenbruch, D., & Schmieder, U.-M. (2001). Gestaltungsmöglichkeiten und Entwicklungspotenziale des Mobile Marketing. *HMD Praxis der Wirtschaftsinformatik, 220,* 15-26.

Mylonopoulos, N. A., & Doukidis, G. I. (2003). Mobile business: Technological pluralism, social assimilation, and growth [Special issue]. *Internation Journal of Electronic Commerce, 8*(1), 5-22.

Nah, F. F.-H., Siau, K., & Sheng, H. (2004). *Values of mobile technology in education.* Paper presented at the Tenth Americas Conference on Information Systems, New York.

Nah, F. F.-H., Siau, K., & Sheng, H. (2005). The value of mobile applications: A utility company study. *Communications of the ACM, 48*(2), 85-90.

Paavilainen, J. (2002). *Mobile business strategies: Understanding the technologies and opportunities.* London: Addison-Wesley.

Park, C. (2006). Hedonic and utilitarian values of mobile Internet in Korea. *International Journal of Mobile Communications, 4*(5), 497-508.

Parvatiyar, A., & Sheth, J. N. (2000). The domain and conceptual foundations of relationship marketing. In J. N. Sheth & A. Parvatiyar (Eds.), *Handbook of relationship marketing* (pp. 3-38). Thousand Oaks: Sage.

Perry, M., O'Hara, K., Sellen, A., Brown, B., & Harper, R. (2001). Dealing with mobility: Understanding access anytime, anywhere. *Transactions on Computer-Human Interaction, 8*(4), 323-247.

Porter, M. E. (1979). *How competitive forces shape strategy.* Boston: Harvard Business School Press.

Porter, M. E. (1996). What is strategy? *Harvard Business Review, 74*(6), 61-78.

Porter, M. E. (1998). *Competitive advantage: Creating and sustaining superior performance.* New York: Free Press.

Pousttchi, K., Turowski, K., & Weizmann, M. (2003). *Added value-based approach to analyze electronic commerce and mobile commerce business models.* Paper presented at the International Conference of Management and Technology in the New Enterprise, La Habana, Cuba.

Raisinghani, M. (2002). Mobile commerce: Transforming the vision into reality. *Information Resources Management Journal, 15*(2), 3-4.

Rannenberg, K. (2004). Identity management in mobile cellular networks and related applications. *Information Security Technical Report, 9*(1), 77-85.

Reichold, A., Schierholz, R., Kolbe, L. M., & Brenner, W. (2003, September 1). *M-Commerce at Helsana health insurance: Mobile premium calculator.* Paper presented at the Dexa '03, Prag.

Reichold, A., Schierholz, R., Kolbe, L., & Brenner, W. (2004). Mobile-commerce bei der Helsana: Mobile Prämienerstellung. In K. Wilde & H. Hippner (Eds.), *Management von CRM-Projekten*: Gabler.

Reichwald, R. (2002). *Mobile Kommunikation: Wertschöpfung, Technologien, neue Dienste.* Wiesbaden: Gabler.

Reichwald, R., & Meier, R. (2002). Generierung von Kundenwert mit mobilen Diensten. In R. Reichwald (Ed.), *Mobile Kommunikation—Wertschöpfung, Technologien, neue Dienste* (pp. 207-230). Wiesbaden, Germany: Gabler.

Romano, N. C., & Fjermestad, J. (2002). Electronic commerce customer relationship management: An assessment of research. *International Journal of Electronic Commerce, 6*(2), 61-113.

Romano, N. C., & Fjermestad, J. (2003). Electronic commerce customer relationship management: A research agenda. *Information Technology and Management, 4*(2-3), 233-258.

Rust, R. T., Inman, J. J., Jia, J., & Zahorik, A. (1999). What you don't know about customer-perceived quality: The role of customer expectation distributions. *Marketing Science, 18*(1), 77-92.

Rust, R. T., Lemon, K. N., & Zeithaml, V. A. (2004). Return on marketing: Using customer equity to focus marketing strategy. *Journal of Marketing, 68*(1), 109-127.

Rust, R. T., Zeithaml, V. A., & Lemon, K. N. (2000). *Driving customer equity: How customer lifetime value is reshaping customer strategy.* New York: The Free Press.

Sadeh, N. (2002). *M-Commerce: Technologies, services, and business models.* New York: John Wiley & Sons.

Schierholz, R., Glissmann, S., Kolbe, L. M., & Brenner, W. (2006, July 6). *Mobile systems for customer service differentiation—The case of Lufthansa.* Paper presented at the 10th Pacific Asia Conference on Information Systems, Kuala Lumpur, Malaysia.

Schierholz, R., Kolbe, L. M., & Brenner, W. (in press). Mobile customer relationship management: Foundations, challenges and solutions. *Business Process Management Journal.*

Schulze, J., Thiesse, F., Bach, V., & Österle, H. (2000). Knowledge enabled customer relationship management. In H. Österle, E. Fleisch, & R. Alt (Eds.), *Business networking: Shaping enterprise relationships on the Internet* (pp. 143-160). Berlin, Germany: Springer.

Shani, D., & Chalasani, S. (1992). Exploiting niches using relationship marketing. *The Journal of Consumer Marketing, 9*(3), 33-42.

Sheng, H., Nah, F. F.-H., & Siau, K. (2005). Strategic implications of mobile technology: A case study using value-focused thinking. *The Journal of Strategic Information Systems, 14*(3), 262-190.

Siau, K., Sheng, H., & Nah, F. F.-H. (2004). *Value of mobile commerce to customers.* Paper presented at the Tenth Americas Conference on Information Systems, New York.

Silberer, G., Wohlfahrt, J., & Wilhelm, T. (Eds.). (2001). *Mobile commerce. Grundlagen, Geschäftsmodelle, Erfolgsfaktoren.* Wiesbaden, Germany: Gabler Verlag.

Skelton, G. W., & Chen, L.-d. (2005). Introduction to m-business applications: Value proposition, applications, technologies and challenges. In G. W. Skelton & L.-d. Chen (Eds.), *Mobile commerce application development* (pp. 1-21). Hershey, PA: Idea Group Inc.

Stafford, T. F., & Gilleson, M. L. (2003). Mobile commerce: What it is and what it could be. *Communications of the ACM, 46*(12), 33-34.

Stake, R. E. (1995). *The art of case study research.* London: Sage.

Stender, M., & Ritz, T. (2006). Modeling of B2B mobile commerce processes. *International Journal of Production Economics, 101*(1), 128-139.

Tarasewich, P. (2003). Designing mobile commerce applications. *Communications of the ACM, 46*(12), 57-60.

Titkov, L., Poslad, S., & Tan, J. J. (2006). An integrated approach to user-centered privacy for mobile information services. *Applied Artificial Intelligence, 20*(2-4), 159-178.

Treacy, M., & Wiersema, F. (1994). *The discipline of market leaders.* Reading: Addison-Wesley.

Turowski, K., & Pousttchi, K. (2003). *Mobile commerce: Grundlagen und Techniken.* Berlin, Germany: Springer.

Urbaczewski, A., Valacich, J. S., & Jessup, L. M. (2003). Mobile commerce—Opportunities and challenges. *Communications of the ACM, 46*(12), 31-32.

Van der Heijden, H., & Valiente, P. (2002, June 6-8). *The value of mobility for business process performance: Evidence from Sweden and The Netherlands.* Paper presented at the European Conference on Information Systems, Gdansk, Poland.

Wamser, C. (2003). Die wetbbwerbsstrategischen Stoßrichtungen des Mobile Commerce. In J. Link (Ed.), *Mobile commerce* (pp. 65-93). Berlin, Germany: Springer.

Wamser, C., & Buschmann, D. (2006). *Erfolgsfaktoren des Mobile Business.* Rheinbach: Deutsche Gesellschaft für Management Forschung (DMGF).

Weill, P. (1992). The relationship between investment in information technology and firm performance: A study of the valve manufacturing sector. *Information Systems Research, 3*(4), 307-333.

Weill, P., & Broadbent, M. (1998). *Leveraging the new infrastructure—How market leaders capitalize on information technology.* Boston: Harvard Business School Press.

Weill, P., Subramani, M., & Broadbent, M. (2002). Building IT infrastructure for strategic agility. *MIT Sloan Management Review, 44*(1), 57-65.

Weill, P., & Vitale, M. (2002). What IT infrastructure capabilities are needed to implement e-business models. *MIS Quarterly Executive, 1*(1), 17-34.

Wernerfelt, B. (1984). A resource based view of the firm. *Strategic Management Journal, 5*(2), 171-180.

Wohlfahrt, J. (2001). One-to-one marketing in mobile commerce. *Information Management & Consulting, 16*(2), 49-54.

Wolf, H., & Wang, M. (2005, July 11-13). *A framework with a peer fostering mechanism for mobile P2P game.* Paper presented at the Proceedings of the Fourth International Conference on Mobile Business (mBusiness), Sydney, Australia.

Wong, C. C., & Hiew, P. L. (2005, July 11-13). *Mobile entertainment: Review and refine.* Paper presented at the Proceedings of the Fourth International Conference on Mobile Business (mBusiness), Sydney, Australia.

Yin, R. K. (2002). *Case study research. Design and methods* (Vol. 5, 3rd ed.). London: Sage.

Zobel, J. (2001). *Mobile business und m-commerce—Die Märkte der Zukunft erobern.* München, Germany: Hanser.

Chapter VII
Exploring Mobile Service Business Opportunities from a Customer–Centric Perspective

Minna Pura
HANKEN—Swedish School of Economics and Business Administration, Finland

Kristina Heinonen
HANKEN—Swedish School of Economics and Business Administration, Finland

ABSTRACT

Mobile services have evolved into an important business area and many companies in various industries are offering mobile services. However, formal classifications or user-centric categorizations of mobile services are still scarce. This chapter develops a conceptual classification for mobile services that illustrates the characteristics of mobile services and gives indications on how to describe mobile business opportunities and categorize services from a customer-centric perspective. The classification scheme, grounded in previous research, is based on the type of consumption, context, social setting, and customer relationship with the service provider. The explorative classification is illustrated with two case studies of existing mobile services in the European market. The theoretical contribution to service management research involves how to describe mobile services from a customer perspective. Managerially, the classification helps marketers, service developers, and stakeholders to evaluate, differentiate, group, and market mobile service offerings more effectively.

INTRODUCTION

Mobile services differ from traditional services in their ability to provide service offerings regardless of temporal and spatial constraints. The benefits of mobile services are often summarized by four factors: (1) ubiquity, (2) convenience, (3) local-ization, and (4) personalization that differentiate mobile services from online services (Clarke & Flaherty, 2003). Mobile services are also different from traditional interpersonal services that are delivered face-to-face, or from other types of e-services, such as wireless online services, where the service delivery is linked to a specific fixed local area network or specific location. Mobile services can be accessed on the move, where and whenever the need arises. In this paper, mobile services are defined as "all services that can be used independently of temporal and spatial restraints and that are accessed through a mobile handset (mobile phone, PDA, smart phone, etc.)" Examples of most popular BtoC mobile services in Europe include logos, ring tones, games, address inquiry, account balance inquiry, paying for parking, vending machines, subway tickets, finding the nearest service location, maps, directions, and so forth.

Although an increasing number of academic studies are starting to focus on mobile services from a service management perspective rather than a technology perspective (e.g., Balasubramanian, Peterson, & Järvenpää, 2002; Heinonen & Andersson, 2003; Nysveen, Pedersen, & Thorbjørnsen, 2005a, 2005b; Pura, 2005), formal classifications or categorizations of mobile services are still scarce. Previous studies clearly indicate that specific categorizations are needed, and especially categories of mobile services have been called for (e.g., Rodgers & Sheldon, 2002). Additionally, so far theories used to analyze mobile business stem from information systems literature and often treat mobile services as a category as such compared to Internet and brick and mortar services. Aspects that would allow us to categorize different types of mobile services have remained largely unexplored, and future research has been encouraged in the field (Okazaki, 2005).

Many service classifications in earlier literature stem from traditional service environments that distinguished services from products. They attempt to offer managerial insights on how to organize and classify services in order to serve customers better. Lovelock's (1983) service classification of traditional interpersonal services is one of the notable classifications. It suggested a need to move away from the industry-specific classifications by exploring managerially relevant service characteristics. However, previous service

classification models incorporating several fields of industry are quite generic, and more specific classifications are needed to depict the nature of the new electronic channels, especially in order to identify the specific characteristics of mobile services.

Some attempts have already been made to develop service categorizations that depict the special nature of electronic services in general (e.g., Angehrn, 1997; Dabholkar, 1996; Meuter, Ostrom, Roundtree, & Bitner, 2000). However, they have not acknowledged the mobile nature of delivering services. For example, Meuter et al.'s categorization of technology-based service encounters does not include services provided through a mobile interface. Hence, existing e-service categorizations do not identify the special nature of mobile services in comparison to other e-services.

Furthermore, most existing mobile service categorizations tend to focus on the providers' perspective rather than the customer or user perspective (e.g., Giaglis, Kourouthanassis, & Tsamakos, 2003; Hyvönen & Repo, 2005; Mitchell & Whitmore, 2003; Mort & Drennan, 2005). Although some previous research on mobile services does incorporate a customer perspective of mobile services, the focus of this group of studies has not been on classifying mobile services, but on some specific aspect of mobile services, such as intentions (e.g., Nysveen et al., 2005a, 2005b) or motivations (Pura & Brush, 2005) to use, segments of users, value (Anckar & D'Incau, 2002; Van der Heijden, 2004), user acceptance (Van der Heijden, Ogertschnig, & Van der Gaast, 2005), or sociability (Heinonen & Andersson, 2003; Järvenpää & Lang, 2005). To our knowledge, there are no studies that specifically attempt to provide a solid ground for categorizing mobile services, and most existing mobile service categorizations are mainly a by-product of the study. The study by Nysveen et al. (2005b) represents an exception, as it was one of the first to compare adoption of different types of mobile services, but the grounds for service categorization remain to be explored further. Thus, further conceptualizations are needed in this area.

The aim of the chapter is to develop a conceptual classification for mobile services that illustrates the characteristics of mobile services and gives indications on how to describe mobile business opportunities and categorize services from a customer-centric perspective. The chapter contributes mainly to service marketing research with its classification of mobile services, and hence it differs from most studies on mobile services positioned in information systems research. By focusing on mobile service value from a customer perspective and building on previous research of mobile services, we propose a classification of mobile services based on the type of consumption, context of use, social setting, and relationship with the provider. These concepts are described more in detail by breaking them down into classification grids that differentiate mobile services from one another by describing the aspects in a two-dimensional way. The resulting typology and suggested managerial questions, as well as the preliminary set of questions for evaluating perceptions of service users, give implications for further empirical research in the mobile area. They also help managers and service developers to differentiate and group their mobile service offerings in a meaningful way that is especially useful for marketing purposes. Managerial challenges and questions related to each aspect are also discussed.

The chapter has the following structure. First, we introduce the theoretical background and discuss how the chapter combines views from previous service management literature. The main thrust of the chapter consists of the proposed framework and two case studies that illustrate the practical use of the framework. We also discuss the solutions based on the case studies and suggest recommendations for evaluating business solutions based on the classification scheme. We conclude the chapter with future trends, suggestions for future research, and concluding remarks

that summarize the contribution of the chapter. While discussing previous theories, we provide concrete examples of existing European mobile services in each category of the classification grid. Furthermore, two case studies (a mobile fishing permit and a mobile adventure game) are used to illustrate how the framework can be applied to assess specific mobile services.

THEORETICAL BACKGROUND

What distinguishes different mobile services from each other and from services offered through other channels? What kind of value do users perceive in different mobile services? Based on a review of previous research in the service management and relationship marketing literature, as well as on literature on mobile services and mobile technology, we can identify four main aspects that represent and summarize the special nature of mobile services (see Table 1).

- What is the type of consumption?
- What is the temporal and spatial context of service use?
- What is the social setting in service use situations?
- What is the relationship between the customer and the service provider?

Based on a review of the literature, we argue that these aspects are of key importance with regard to categorizing mobile services from a customer-centric perspective, and hence we build the classification of mobile services on these four aspects. Next we describe in more detail the four aspects that form the foundation of our conceptual framework and provide examples of existing mobile services. The two case studies will further elaborate on how these four factors are linked together into a hierarchical framework that illustrates the business opportunities from a customer point of view.

Although these four key aspects have been indicated in earlier literature by several individual authors, as summarized in Table 1, so far the four aspects have not been discussed in conjunction with each other. However, many of the previous studies do focus on one or two of the aspects in different combinations, and hence the studies indicate the importance of integrating them into one conceptual framework.

Next, the four key areas are discussed individually and combined into a classification framework presented later in Figure 5. Each area includes two dimensions and they are illustrated in four schemes.

Type of Consumption

Different types of services are used for many purposes based on customers' individual consumption values (Sheth, Newman, & Gross, 1991). Different channels may be used for various types of tasks (Neslin et al., 2006). Motivations for consumption are often divided into hedonic and utilitarian value in the marketing literature (Babin, Darden, & Griffin, 1994; Chaudhuri & Holbrook, 2002; Koivumäki et al., 2006; Van der Heijden, 2004). Utilitarian value refers to extrinsic motivation that exists in goal-directed service use (Babin et al., 1994). Hedonic value means intrinsic motivation that exists in experiential, fun, and

Table 1. Relevant research on mobile services

Authors	Focus	Type of Consumption	Context	Social setting	Relationship
Isoniemi & Wolf 2001	Segments of mobile service users			●	●
Anckar & D'Incau 2002	Value creation in mobile commerce	●	●		
Balasubramanian et al 2002	Mobile commerce		●		
Pura (2003b)	Nature of loyalty in mobile services		●		●
Heinonen & Andersson 2003	Use of mobile services			●	
Nysveen et al 2005 a,b	Intentions to use mobile services	●		●	
Pura & Brush 2005	Motivations for mobile service use	●	●		
Pura 2005	Value and loyalty in mobile location-based services	●	●		
Järvenpää & Lang 2005	Mobile technology			●	
Van der Hejden et al. 2005, Koivumäki, Ristola and Kesti 2006	User acceptance of mobile information services	●	●		
Laukkanen & Lauronen 2005	Customer value creation in mobile banking	●			
Lin & Wang 2006	Loyalty in m-commerce	●			

Figure 1. Consumption types

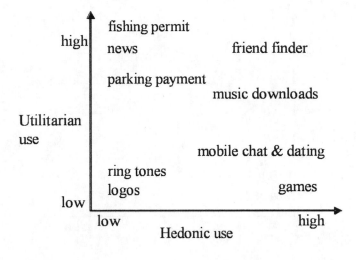

enjoyable service use as such (Novak, Hoffman, & Duhachek, 2003). Similar categorization into goal-directed and experiential services has been used also in the mobile field (Nysveen et al., 2005b; Okazaki, 2005). It has been suggested that hedonic value refers to entertainment needs and utilitarian value to efficiency needs (Anckar & D'Incau, 2002; Cotte, Tilottama, Ratneshwar, & Ricci, 2006; Pura & Brush, 2005). The use of new technology to access the services can be seen as fun and exciting, as such services can also create both utilitarian and hedonic value.

The first classification scheme depicting consumption types is based on utilitarian and hedonic use. In this study, utilitarian use denotes the level of goal-oriented value a user receives from using the service. Examples include information-based services, for example, news, weather reports, timetables, traffic information, and search services (address and number inquiry, nearest service location, search for stolen vehicles, routes, etc.) are examples of services that create high utilitarian value and help users to achieve a goal effectively and conveniently. Transaction-oriented payment services (mobile banking, parking payment, pay-

ing for fishing permit) are also used for utilitarian reasons, such as saving time and providing an efficient and convenient way to do transactions (Laukkanen & Kantanen, 2006; Laukkanen & Lauronen, 2005).

In this study, highly hedonic use involves services that create fun experiences and that are used for the sake of the experience. Examples include entertainment-oriented services such as mobile chat, games, and music downloads.

Finding examples for the category that presents low value both on utilitarian and hedonic aspects is not easy, but they may include many of the most popular services currently offered by the majority of mobile service providers: logos, ring tones, pictures that may be perceived "nice to have", but something that you can also manage without.

Temporal and Spatial Context

The temporal and spatial context of service use also differentiates mobile services from other types of services (e.g., Anckar & D'Incau, 2002; Balasubramanian et al., 2002; Mennecke & Strader, 2003; Yoo & Lyytinen, 2005). It influ-

Figure 2. The temporal and spatial criticality of service

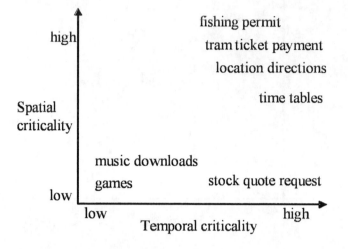

encesthe value of mobile services (e.g., Heinonen, 2006; Nysveen et al., 2005b; Pura & Brush, 2005; Van der Heijden, 2004) and, as the criticality of time and space of service use is a factor mostly considered in previous literature (Mennecke & Strader, 2003), it is essential also when categorizing mobile services. Balasubramanian et al. (2002) proposed a space-time matrix for tasks that could be used in the mobile environment. Other researchers have also used time and location to conceptualize products and services based on the relative immediacy of the task of the user and the relative location of the user when the service is used (Heinonen, 2004a, 2004b, 2006; Mennecke & Strader, 2003; Pura, 2003c).

We use a similar approach and introduce a classification scheme based on temporal and spatial criticality. In this scheme, temporal criticality depicts a time dimension of how urgently the customer needs the service. Spatial criticality indicates whether the use situation is location noncritical, that is, if the service can be used anywhere, for example, at work or at home, where there are other alternatives to the mobile device such as fixed Internet connections. Alternatively, the use location can be critical, that is, the customer is on the move using the service in the street or in other places where there are no other alternatives to the mobile service, or location-based information is needed.

Although temporal and spatial elements of the use context represent a main benefit of technology-based services (Meuter et al., 2000) and mobile services in particular, it can be argued that a broader perspective on the use context should be considered. This larger context incorporates aspects other than time and space, namely the social setting where the service is used (Celuch, Goodwin, & Taylor, 2007). Researchers have acknowledged sociability as a purpose for using mobile technology (Yoo & Lyytinen, 2005), and it has been suggested that social aspects influence the use of mobile services (e.g., Heinonen & Andersson, 2003) or intentions to use them (Nysveen et al., 2005b). Traditionally, social pressure of others to use new technology has gained attention in the mobile context (Kleijnen, Wetzels, & De Ruyter, 2004; Venkatesh, Morris, Davis, & Davis, 2003). However, the social setting itself has not explicitly been taken into consideration

Figure 3. The social setting

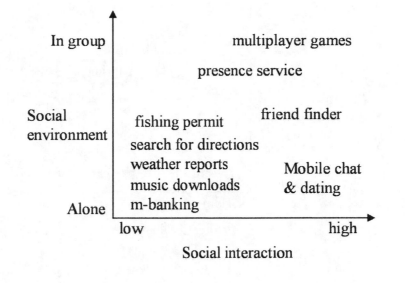

in this field. In a retail context, social setting has been defined as "the social setting focuses on the presence or absence of others, together with their social roles, role attributes and opportunities for interaction" (Nicholson, Clarke, & Blakemore, 2002, p. 134) This definition also applies well to the social setting where mobile services are used, because it encapsulates opportunities for interaction with friends and family through to the presence of other people at work and even proximity to total strangers. The social setting can enhance or inhibit the use of mobile services in a certain situation (Isoniemi & Wolf, 2001). The social setting is expected to have a greater influence on the usage of services in the mobile environment than the Internet, because mobile services are often used in a social environment that involves interpersonal influence (Mort & Drennan, 2005).

The type of social setting in which mobile services are normally used is very important in defining what kind of interactivity or possibility of lack of interactivity is offered by specific mobile services (Okazaki, 2005). The third classification

scheme depicting the social setting is based on the social environment and social interaction involved when using the service. The social environment denotes the environment in which the user is when the need to use the service arises. It is depicted by the continuum alone vs. in-group, as illustrated in Figure 3. The social environment in a group may motivate to socialize with people by playing multiplayer games, location-based games that involve social interaction. Alternatively, social environment with other people present may also motivate people to use mobile services, because they can be used discretely without disturbing others, for example, ordering tickets or paying for parking during a meeting at work. Similarly, one reason for using mobile services in the presence of strangers, for example, on public transport is the need to create a personal space for social interaction, communicating with friends discretely in mobile chat rooms without disturbing others, or playing a game in order to kill time. These types of services are normally used alone.

The other axis in Figure 3 depicts the desired state of social interaction through the mobile

Figure 4. Relationship

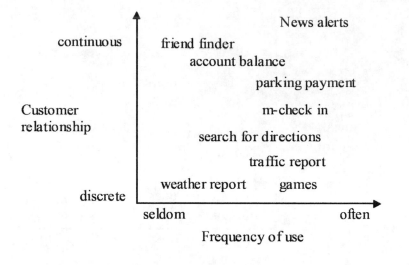

service, named social interaction. Mobile banking services are an example of services that are typically intended for use in situations involving low social interaction with others. Because of the private nature of the financial information, the user normally wishes to be left alone. In contrast, people who use mobile chat services or search the whereabouts of their friends or family members seek social interaction (high social interaction).

A similar conceptualization has been previously mentioned by Nysveen et al. (2005b), who differentiate between machine-interactive and person-interactive services. In our opinion, machine-interactive services, that is, interactivity between the medium and the user, are services that aim at low social interaction and thus people wanting to be alone. In contrast, person-interactive services that occur between people through a medium are, in our model, services that aim at using services in a highly social setting, or that aim at interaction with other people either through the mobile media or in a real environment, for example, playing multiplayer mobile games in a group.

The social setting is the core of the benefit offered by newly launched mobile phone "presence" services that enable the person to specify criteria of how he/she wishes to be contacted at a specific time and social environment. It is also possible to indicate wishes for social interaction. For example, the user can indicate his/her current environment to others wishing to contact him/her: "I am now at a meeting, but can read text messages." Others can check who else is available for free-time socializing or work-related negotiating at that specific time, or how some particular person is best reached in the near future. This way they can acknowledge the other person's social environment and wishes for the level of social interaction, and proceed in an appropriate manner (for more information on presence applications, see e.g., http://europe.nokia.com/A4170049).

Relationship Between Customer and Service Provider

The relationship between the customer and service provider represents another important aspect of mobile services. Relationships can be used to categorize mobile services, because mobile services are especially effective in reaching individual customers, and they involve different types of relationships (Pirc, 2006). It has been argued that mobile services are considered more personal than any other remote service (Kleijnen, De Ruyter, & Andreassen, 2005), and that they can easily be personalized for specific customers (e.g., Watson, Pitt, Berthon, & Zinkhan, 2002). However, since customers cannot be expected to engage in a long-lasting relationship with every service provider, companies need to customize their service offerings according to the desired depth or length of relationship between the service provider and the customer (Pura, 2003a).

Thus, relationships represent the fourth classification scheme. The two ends of the customer relationship axis can be described as discrete transactions or continuous relationships (see Figure 4). In his study on relationship switching in a mobile service context, Pirc (2006) defined the mobile service relationship as involving either contract or pre-paid transactions. Discrete trans-

actions can be seen as episodes that represent a set of different interconnected actions, and at the other extreme, there is a continuous relationship based on a set of interconnected sequences (Holmlund, 1997). Whereas the former constitutes a customer's discrete transactions, a continuous relationship often involves some kind of agreement between the customer and service provider. Subscription-based services entail opportunities for closer relationships with the service provider. However, most services offered in Europe today are based only on occasional transactions initiated by the customer and invoiced on the customers' monthly telephone bill (Pura, 2003b).

In this study on mobile services, continuous relationships are mainly related to services that are based on a contract. For example, mobile check-in requires a membership in an airline loyalty program. Services like checking for account balances, receiving an short message service (SMS) from the library when books are due, an SMS reminder the day before the dentist appointment, or ordering a security alert message to a mobile phone if someone happens to break

Figure 5. Classification of mobile services

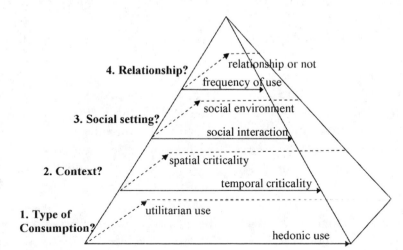

in the summer cottage, all involve a subscription with a specific company and therefore represent continuous relationships.

In contrast, many services are offered primarily to unidentified occasional users. For example customers without prior relationships with a specific company can use m-payment for public transport, buying a fishing permit, logos, and weather reports, or buying products from vending machines. These types of services represent discrete transactions.

Frequency of use represents another perspective on the relationship between the customer and service provider. It is relevant when considering that a service that is paid continuously (continuous relationship) is not necessarily used often, or that a discrete relationship still can involve very regular use. The frequency of use may be linked to spontaneous and mobility needs (Anckar & D'Incau, 2002) and need for planning and improvising (Järvenpää & Lang, 2005). Some mobile services are used infrequently, when the need arises in a specific situation, for example, a real-time weather report may be found necessary while sailing and when the weather conditions are changing. Similarly, a fishing permit can be first purchased while at sea, without having to plan in advance where and when to go fishing. These types of services may be accessed via other channels in normal situations, but when other channels are not available, mobile services are used. This means that some services are used infrequently and sporadically. Furthermore, discrete services can be used without permission from the other party. In contrast, some other services are used often, for example, mobile games. Games are often included in a service portfolio offered by mobile portals and these types of services may be used based on a monthly subscription. However, this does not necessarily mean that the services are also used often.

The previous examples illustrate that creating value to the user by offering mobile services requires consideration of several aspects. These aspects may influence the choice to use mobile services instead of other electronic or traditional service delivery channels. In an attempt to offer a classification framework for mobile services, we summarize the previous grids into a framework that is discussed next.

Classification of Mobile Services

Based on previous research, we now combine each of the classification schemes and introduce a framework for classifying mobile services by focusing on mobile service value (Figure 5). It is proposed that the assessment of the mobile service offering is hierarchical, based on the service value for the customer.

Hence, the four levels are related to each other and each level contributes to offering value-in-use to the customer. 1) The type of consumption related to the specific mobile service represents the underlying core of the value proposition; why the mobile service is used, whereas the following three levels provide additional value to the user relating to more specific aspects of mobile service use situations and service providers. The next consideration is 2) the context; when and where services may be used, that is, the temporal and spatial context of use, followed by the 3) social setting in which they may be used, and finally, 4) the relationship between the customer and service provider. These aspects represent factors that distinguish mobile services from other types of electronic or interpersonal services.

Thus, all four levels should be taken into account when categorizing and designing mobile services, pricing services, and segmenting services into bundles that offer similar value propositions. The pattern of each mobile service as depicted by the positioning in the classification framework can then be used for grouping similar services together and targeting service bundles to potential user groups. Next, we will illustrate how the classifying framework can be used to assess current or future mobile services.

We will present two case examples that are different in nature.

CASE STUDIES

The case studies illustrated in this chapter describe mobile services that are aimed at a specific interest group rather than the mass of people using a mobile device. We believe that the maturing global mobile market will slowly evolve into offering more targeted services for niche interest groups. This requires developing an understanding of hedonic and utilitarian needs, context of use, social setting, and the requirements of customers in their relationship with service providers. Better understanding of these issues should result in more effective marketing strategies by segmenting customers and different markets and targeting the services and marketing messages to the right potential user groups. The first case study used to depict the use of the conceptual framework is a mobile transaction service that allows purchase of a lure-fishing permit by text message, and the second case study describes a mobile adventure game. Next, the case studies are described in detail and summarized in the classifying framework to illustrate the differing nature of these two mobile services.

Case 1: Mobile Fishing Permit

To the authors' knowledge, a mobile fishing permit is currently a unique service offered in Northern Europe. The basic idea of the service is that the customer orders a regional fishing permit by text message when the need arises. The service has been offered as a pilot service in Northern Finland since 2003. Two documents are required when fishing by means other than basic angling or ice fishing. The first is a receipt for payment of the fishing management fee, the second the actual fishing permit. The actual fishing permit is region-specific and must be purchased before fishing. It can be bought traditionally in post offices

Figure 6. Mobile fishing permit (Nikulainen, 2003)

or by electronic banking and in the region also with the help of a mobile service. The permit fee is charged on the monthly phone bill. A receipt for the transaction is received as a text message. The provincial lure fishing fee is about 27 euros for a year or 6 euros for seven days.

The service has several implications for different stakeholders: unauthorized fishing is in decline, because of the convenient way of paying for the permit. Furthermore, easy remote controlling of permits through mobile devices saves controlling resources. The service has been successful and a large proportion of the permits have been purchased via a mobile device. This is an example of a niche service targeted at a hobby-related interest group. Since the pilot has been successful, similar services could be developed for various purposes, for example location-based services for hunters and pet owners.

Case 2: Mobile Game: Can You Confront Your Worst Nightmare?

Mobile games [1] have developed quickly in less than a decade. Nevertheless, the unique capabilities of wireless mobile devices have not yet been exploited much, with the exception of highly developed markets like Japan and Korea (Hämäläinen, 2006). The majority of the popular mobile games played in North America and Europe are basic games targeted at casual players, such as Tetris

Table 2. Description of the Darkest Fear™ 3: Nightmare game

Darkest Fear™ 3: Nightmare is the final part of Rovio Mobile's award winning Darkest Fear™ horror trilogy. The game offers completely new lightning effects like never seen on mobile. Thomas Warden has found his daughter Helen while searching for survivors of the horrible events at Grim Oak's Hospital. A monstrous bacterium has taken over her body, giving Helen unique powers but also making her extremely sensitive to light. Now it is up to you to find the ingredients for an antidote. As Thomas, you are forced to come up with ways to lighten your pathway with fire sparkles, water reflections and burning objects. When controlling Helen however, light is the deadliest of enemies. The game's ingenious puzzles, horrifying atmosphere, fifteen different endings and Helen's new monster abilities offer a unique experience. The game throws flesh-eating creatures, prowling zombies and three monstrous bosses against you. Can you confront your worst nightmare?

ROVIO MOBILE   Copyright © 2006 Rovio Mobile Ltd.

(Copyright: 2006 Rovio Mobile Ltd. Used with permission)

Figure 7. Mobile game: Darkest Fear 3: Nightmare (horror/adventure/puzzle) (Source: Rovio & N70 image retrieved from the Nokia press site)

(Copyright: 2006 Rovio Mobile Ltd. Used with permission)

and the Who Wants To Be A Millionaire quiz (Segerstrale, 2006). As the mobile industry is working to provide faster access and improved ease of use, combined with more transparent and user-friendly pricing, game developers can start envisioning games that make best use of the features of mobile devices and combine those with the recent developments in the Web and Internet environment (Hämäläinen, 2006).

Rovio Mobile (www.rovio.com) is a Finnish mobile game developer and publisher founded in late 2004 by industry veterans. It is acknowledged as a leader in both product quality and game play innovation. The Rovio games are an example of developments into gaming solutions that have adopted views from PC and console-based game contexts. Rovio games are aimed at a demanding niche target group that looks for more action and experiences than the basic mobile games usually provide. The company focuses on developing strategy, adventure, role-playing and action games, and the games are story-driven, easy to pick up, and offer in-depth, extensive gaming experiences. A newly launched Rovio adventure game titled Darkest Fear 3: Nightmare is used to illustrate the classification scheme. A more detailed description of the course of the game may be found in Table 2 and a screenshot of the game is illustrated in Figure 7.

Rovio Mobile games are being sold through wireless application protocol (WAP) portals. The games can be ordered by clicking the "buy" tag on a WAP-page, or alternatively by sending an SMS that downloads a link to the mobile device screen in SMS format. The games are usually downloaded over the air (OTA), using the operator's network, directly to the user's mobile phone. In some cases games can be preinstalled or downloaded over Bluetooth to the phone. The game is usually charged on the users' monthly phone bill. However, alternative payment methods, such as credit card or PayPal, may also be used in different markets.

Logic of the Case Analysis

The proposed conceptual framework presented in Figure 8 is expected to ease constructive evaluation of mobile service business opportunities and to describe new services by clarifying the intended target group and the type of situations in which the services will most likely be used. We illustrate the possible applications by evaluating the case study services with the help of the framework.

The Fs in the framework in Figure 8 represent the fishing permit service and the Gs represent the adventure game case. They are located on the four grids in places where they are most likely positioned from a customer perspective, in most typical use situations. The positioning of the fishing permit and adventure game was done by the authors, and it is based on discussions with service users and our perceptions of typical users of the specific services in typical usage situations. The service providers were able to comment on our preliminary suggestions and changes were made accordingly.

DISCUSSION OF THE SOLUTIONS BASED ON THE CASE STUDIES

The framework presented in Figure 8 helps to clarify the value of the mobile service from a customer's point of view. A presentation follows of a managerial list of questions about issues to consider while planning or evaluating a mobile service. The value of the fishing permit can be

Figure 8. Classification of the case study examples

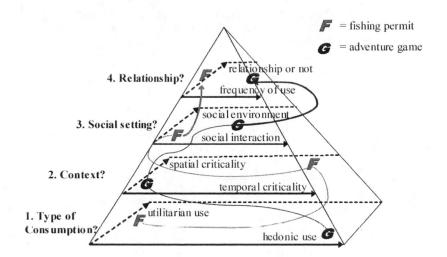

Table 3. Summary of the positioning of the case studies in the classification framework

MANAGERIAL QUESTIONS	FISHING PERMIT	ADVENTURE GAME
1. Type of consumption • Is the service used for efficiency needs to achieve a task? (utilitarian) • Is the service used just for its own sake, for experience? (hedonic)	Utilitarian task of paying for permit effectively	Hedonic, fun experience
2. Temporal and Spatial Context • When and where is the service used? (spatial) • How spontaneously is the service used? (temporal)	In time and place critical situations, while at sea. A need for personal permit is mainly spontaneous.	The user can play a game anywhere, anytime in non-time and place critical situations. Games are usually played often, but can be used also sporadically e.g. while waiting and 'killing time'
3. Social Setting • Is the service used alone or in a group? (social environment) • Is the service normally used for creating personal space or mainly for the purpose of socializing? (social interaction)	The service is normally used alone, avoiding social interaction especially with the permit controllers.	This game is usually used alone with no network connectivity, but can create social interaction.
4. Relationship • How does the service support the different phases of customer relationship from new customer acquisition to customer retention? (relationship or not) • Does the nature of the service support better regular customers or mainly sporadic use of services on the move? (frequency of use) • How do customers prefer to pay for services? (discrete transactions / subscription-based use) • Does the delivery of the service require permission from the customer, peer customers, other stakeholders? (e.g. location-based information and advertising)	The permit is a discrete transaction for new customers. It is used sporadically while fishing. It is a discrete transaction that is paid once a year or for a week. It does not require permission, but continuous users could opt-in for e.g. reminders from the provider when the permit expires.	Because Rovio does not offer games directly to end-customers, but uses mobile portals as distribution channels, customers do not necessarily know the Rovio brand while playing the game. New customers are acquired via portals. Games are often used regularly. This game is a discrete transaction, because it is delivered to the end-users via mobile portals and invoiced on the monthly phone bill.

communicated as a convenient, easy, and quick way to buy the permit. The service should be mainly marketed proactively, so that the potential customers know where to get it when the need arises spontaneously, on the move. Reaching potential users in the natural environment, alone, out of the reach of other media, is demanding. Nevertheless, regarding the social appreciation of others, fishing communities can be effective peer marketers. Payment on the mobile phone bill seems an appropriate choice, since it is a discrete transaction. However, there is also potential for continuous subscriptions for current permit holders, because payment on the phone invoice is more convenient than paying for a permit the traditional way in a post office.

The adventure game case represents another type of service that is purely hedonic in nature. Therefore, the consequences of use important in the previous example, such as convenience, speed, and good value for money, are not that important in a gaming context. Instead, people evaluate the service based on how entertaining the game is and what experiences they go through while playing the game. Games are mostly accessed via mobile portals anywhere and any time the inspiration arises to play a game. Therefore the portal plays an important role in reaching the customers wherever they are. The customer relationship is also formed primarily with the mobile portal, and payment for the service is thus dependent on the customers' type of contract with the portal. Furthermore, in a portal context, service marketers face a challenge in attracting potential customers while competing with other interesting services offered.

It should be noted that the mobile service examples mentioned in the classification grids may be placed in several positions, depending on the use situation and the individual customer's preferences. For example, the mobile fishing service as a discrete transaction meets especially well the needs of tourists or occasional fishermen, who may not otherwise pay for the permit. However, fishermen who go regularly to the same place to

fish may consider using the mobile service only if it is a more convenient way to pay for the permit than the traditional ways. These regular service users may also consider spatial and temporal issues less critical, but may face more social pressure to pay for the permit in the local community. Similarly, games are normally used in non-temporally and spatially critical situations, for example at home. However, games can also be played at highly context-critical places, if they are mostly used while waiting for public transport or while traveling on it. Furthermore, basic games are used alone. However, the multiplayer games present opportunities for use of games in a group, even when the group of people is not geographically in the same place.

A summary of the main managerial questions for mobile business stakeholders and conclusions on how the two case examples of mobile services are positioned in the framework are presented in Table 3. The classification exercise can be done for different types of services, and it is expected to give indications on how to group similar services together and how to communicate the value of the service to the customers.

In order to be able to position different services relative to each other, we also propose a preliminary practical approach for evaluating, comparing, and positioning different mobile services. Therefore, a short set of eight possible questions is presented in Table 4. The questions were developed based on previous literature and they should give indications as to what aspects of mobile services are important to the user. A Likert scale or other type of scales could be used to illustrate the positioning of a service relative to other services. However, it should be noted that a low vs. high figure on the scale does not necessarily mean that one service is better than the other, but only indicating that they differ in how and when they are used.

The proposed set of questions illustrated in Table 4 should be developed further and tested with mobile service users. The eight questions

Table 4. Proposed approach for evaluating different services

PROPOSED QUESTIONNAIRE ITEMS		SCALE	
1. Type of consumption			
The added value gained by using the service effectively is...	*low*	☐☐☐☐☐	*high*
The added value gained by enjoying the use experience as such is...	*low*	☐☐☐☐☐	*high*
2. The temporal and spatial criticality of service			
How critical is the place where the service is used?	*low*	☐☐☐☐☐	*high*
How urgent is time of service use or service delivery?	*low*	☐☐☐☐☐	*high*
3. The social setting			
The social environment where the service is primarily used is...	*alone*	☐☐☐☐☐	*In group*
The social interaction with other users related to service use is...	*low*	☐☐☐☐☐	*high*
4. The relationship			
The type of the relationship between the user and the service provider is...	*discrete*	☐☐☐☐☐	*continuous*
The service is used...	*seldom*	☐☐☐☐☐	*often*

summarize the four important factors that influence the use of mobile services: (1) type of consumption, (2) temporal and spatial criticality, (3) social setting, and (4) relationship between the customer and service provider. The results of this type of questionnaire should ease the task of differentiating mobile services from each other with regard to the factors that are important to customers.

RECOMMENDATIONS BASED ON THE CLASSIFICATION SCHEME

The proposed classification schemes of mobile services contribute to marketing practice in several ways. The proposed categorizations have implications for communication, design, and pricing of mobile services and for segmenting customers using the services. They provide

insights for marketers on how to differentiate and group mobile services based on criteria that are relevant from a customer's point of view. The framework might be used to evaluate potential customer perceptions of specific mobile services and to understand the types of mobile services that customers are likely to perceive valuable and use in different situations.

Thus, in the end, the customers will evaluate the overall value of the services based on the type of consumption, context of use, social setting, and relationship with the provider. The classification framework helps service providers to assess the critical success factors of mobile services compared to other electronic channels from a customer-centric viewpoint and to identify situations where the service is mostly used. As such, the classification schemes can be used to develop strategies to create value in the mobile channel in situations in which it represents most added value for the customers compared to other channels.

Because customers may use services for various reasons, customers may be segmented based on the relative balance of what is important to the customer in different situations. These key benefits can be communicated to the right customer segments in order to attract the right customers. To date, mobile services are quite often marketed as a bundle of services that people can use via their mobile devices. However, this type of homogenous communication undermines the real potential of using mobile services for different needs and preferences, in different situations. Different types of services should be marketed based on their potential value to the customer.

The **hedonic vs. utilitarian** categorization of the service types gives implications on how to communicate the value of some specific services or service types to the customers. Hedonic value is often gained from entertainment-related services, for example, games, and thus can be communicated as fun and an enjoyable service experience. This can be facilitated with pictures and describing what kinds of feelings the entertaining content is expected to evoke in the user. Utilitarian services represent information-based services, such as weather reports, timetables, and search services that aim at achieving a task effectively, maybe saving time and finding information easily. Therefore the communication of the value of these services should also reflect the consequences of use; effectiveness; saving time and effort; good value for money compared to alternatives; and convenience of accessing the service regardless of temporal and spatial constraints.

Moreover, the **context** of use has several implications. The fact that there may be other alternative services that the customer can use influences pricing and service design. Mobile services that are offered as the only alternative can be priced higher than services that are competing with other service delivery alternatives. Correspondingly, when there are other service

alternatives, the mobile service must be priced competitively.

Furthermore, it is important that services aimed for urgent or highly critical spatial context are designed in a simple way, so that the customer can use the service easily without extra effort or time needed. Point-of-sale advertising, for example, at subway stations, informing how to pay for the subway ticket with the mobile phone, are good examples of how the use of mobile services can be promoted on the spot. Services used in an urgent situation need to rely on logical user interfaces and customers' recall of how to access the services. In this respect, word-of-mouth may have an important role in marketing strategies. Moreover, marketers need to acknowledge that the customer's location may change even during a mobile service use session and network availability may pose some problems, for example, if sitting on a train. Ability to save information for later use or for continuing to use the service at a later stage may therefore be a useful feature. On the other hand, services aimed at less time and place-critical contexts, where the customer has more time to use the service, can be designed with additional service elements to increase the value of the service. It is easier to reach customers in a state when they have time to read instructions and marketing communication. They may also have access to other channels, for example, digital television, the Internet, radio, and magazines that can serve as cross-marketing channels.

The social setting of mobile service usage situations also has implications for marketing strategies. Social pressure from friends and family may exist when using services, especially in group usage situations. Moreover, services used for socializing purposes have high interaction with participants, and therefore marketing efforts should seize the opportunity of using these networks of customers interacting with each other. The interaction may even result in sharing downloaded digital content and received messages (Maier, 2005; Van Camp, 2005) Motivating current customers to spread positive word-of-mouth is often an essential part of service providers' marketing strategy in mobile environments (Barnes, 2002).

Customers who have an ongoing **relationship** with a specific service provider are more attractive to companies than customers who use services in an ad hoc manner. Obviously, it is less expensive to cross-sell to existing customers than to attract new customers. However, it is important to understand that there may also be customers with an ongoing relationship, who still use the service infrequently. In addition, there may be unidentified users who may use the service regularly and wish to stay anonymous. The discrete use of services is often a benefit sought compared to other service channels for people who do not wish to reveal their identity or use services discretely without others noticing (e.g., adult entertainment, chat services, searching for others' taxed income information, car owner information based on the registration plate, etc.). Avoiding personal contact has also been suggested as a motive for using mobile services, which offers new perspectives on how to market these services. They may often be an alternative to other channels that require personal interaction. In the mobile context, people can act anonymously and plan better what to say and how to respond to others' comments than in personal interaction situations (Aminuzzaman, 2005). Thus, a viable option of seeing services as connecting people is to market some mobile services as a planned choice of avoiding personal contact and offering a way to interact anonymously and discretely with the service provider.

In addition, a much-debated issue in the literature is how to invoice services so that customers feel they gain value for money. Many companies have ended up offering alternatives to access the services, either with transaction-based invoicing on the phone bill; a short trial subscription for free or for a small amount of money; or a monthly subscription. The choice depends on the nature of the service and no definite recommendation can be made (Munnukka, 2005). However, service providers should also acknowledge that the best payment method for the service provider, one that creates steady and secure cash flows (subscription-based or payment from a service account), may not always be the preferred way from the customer's point of view. Invoicing per usage on the monthly phone bill is regarded as convenient and may even motivate people to use mobile services (Pura, Viitanen, & Liljander, 2003). Alternative pricing strategies are common in different markets. For example in the gaming context, some offer subscription models such as i-Mode. Some offer try-and-buy solutions, where the game is distributed free and the first level or one minute of game play is free. Afterwards, the game needs to be registered and paid for. The Darkest Fear game case example presented in this study is invoiced on the monthly phone bill after downloading the game. These transaction-based invoicing methods are common in Europe. Eighty-three percent of the services used in the focal market are post-paid. However, other new methods are being tested, such as a mobile wallet and chip cards in the mobile phone that can be used as debit cards. On a global scale, we believe that pre-paid contracts are more common, and therefore package deals and monthly subscriptions are also more common than in the market in question. Nevertheless, we suggest that the classification grid can be used in all markets, regardless of how the service is paid for, because the relationship grid in the framework encourages constructive analysis of the payment and contract options.

FUTURE TRENDS AND SUGGESTIONS FOR RESEARCH

The typology and the proposed set of questions give indications for further empirical research in the mobile sector. On a global scale, mobile services are currently primarily offered by network operators and service portals. However, especially in markets where the majority of services are post-paid based on transactions, the role of individual service and content providers may become more important in the future. This kind of development impacts on all the layers of the classification framework presented in this study. The customer relationship with the service provider in particular could evolve into a more personal relationship, and information about real use of services and customer attitudes towards individual services could be tracked more accurately. In general, the transaction vs. relationship nature of service use requires further research. Some research results on the loyalty of mobile services indicate that customers who are restricted by a contract to stay with a service provider are more likely to switch service providers after the contract period is over than those who do not have a contract (Fullerton, 2005; Libai & Nitzan, 2005). Thus, subscription-based services may create a falsified feeling of loyal customers who are only committed to use the same service provider because of constraints that prevent them from changing providers. Fullerton (2005) even claims that customers' feelings of being stuck in the relationship tend to override the positive feelings of attachment to the provider.

Moreover, the discrete transactions are very important as they also potentially represent a door opener to more frequent use of services and can be used to increase the awareness of the service provider. Mobile services represent a new range of services for many customers, and offering customers the opportunity of trying new mobile services and thus indicating the potential benefit of the mobile device is expected to be successful.

Future research needs to empirically explore and develop reliable scales for measuring the proposed conceptualization, in order to validate the proposed classification schemes. Although future research may need to structure the clas-sification schemes according to industries, we feel that it is important to move beyond the traditional industry-specific classification towards a more generalizable and ultimately more descriptive categorization of mobile services.

CONCLUSION AND CONTRIBUTION

In this chapter, we focus on what users value in mobile services and how mobile services are used in typical use situations, in order to better understand the underlying reasons why mobile services are used. This chapter extends past classification schemes of traditional interpersonal services and e-services by examining the characteristics of mobile services and focusing on service value from a customer perspective. Based on a literature review, we introduce four different classification schemes that can be used to understand the consumption type, use context, social setting, and customer relationship. The resulting classification framework gives a holistic view of mobile services from a value-in-use perspective, and it is considered essential in differentiating and grouping mobile service offerings in a meaningful way. It also describes the distinct characteristics of mobile services that should be considered in developing, assessing, and planning marketing communication of mobile services.

The classification scheme differs from existing research on mobile services in the respect that emphasis is moved away from the prevailing focus on what developments of mobile applications are technologically possible. The focus is on what may be offered and how customers perceive the value of these offerings. This service- and customer-oriented perspective on mobile services is hence achieved by acknowledging why current and potential customers might use services in concrete situations, and how services might create value for customers. Because the focus is on different characteristics that describe mobile services, the classification schemes can also be used to explore new avenues for mobile services and to create new types of services.

In conclusion, the classification scheme can be used to evaluate potential customer reactions to specific mobile services and to understand the types of mobile service that customers are likely to try and use.

ACKNOWLEDGMENT

The authors would like to thank the Foundation for Economic Education for its financial support. We also appreciate the comments of the reviewers who have reviewed previous versions of this paper. Our sincerest thanks also to Jan Bonnevier who provided us with the Rovio Mobile Ltd case information and to Lauri Haapanen for providing information about the mobile fishing permit. Both authors have contributed equally to the chapter.

REFERENCES

Aminuzzaman, S. (2005). Is mobile phone a socio-cultural change agent? A study of the pattern of usage of mobile phones among university students in Bangladesh. In *Proceedings of the International Conference on Mobile Communication and Asian Modernities II, Information, Communications Tools & Social Changes in Asia,* Beijing, China.

Anckar, B., & D'Incau, D. (2002). Value creation in mobile commerce: Findings from a consumer survey. *Journal of Information Technology Theory & Application, 4*(1), 43-64.

Angehrn, A. (1997). Designing mature Internet business strategies: The ICDT Model. *European Management Journal, 15*(4), 361-369.

Babin, B. J., Darden, W. R., & Griffin, M. (1994). Work and/or fun: Measuring hedonic and utilitarian shopping value. *Journal of Consumer Research, 20*(4), 644-656.

Balasubramanian, S., Peterson, R. A., & Järvenpää, S. L. (2002). Exploring the implications of m-commerce for markets and marketing. *Journal of the Academy of Marketing Science, 30*(4), 348-361.

Barnes, S. J. (2002). Wireless digital advertising: Nature and implications. *International Journal of Advertising, 21*(3), 399-421.

Celuch, K., Goodwin, S., & Taylor, S. A. (2007). Understanding small scale industrial user Internet purchase and information management intentions: A test of two attitude models. *Industrial Marketing Management, 36,* 109-120.

Chaudhuri, A., & Holbrook, M. B. (2002). Product-class effects on brand commitment and brand outcomes: The role of brand trust and brand affect. *Brand Management, 10*(1), 33-58.

Clarke, I., & Flaherty, T. (2003). Mobile portals: The development of m-commerce gateways. In B. E. Mennecke & T. J. Strader (Eds.), *Mobile commerce, technology, theory and applications* (pp. 185-201). Hershey, PA: Idea Group.

Cotte, J., Tilottama, G. C., Ratneshwar, S., & Ricci, L. (2006). Pleasure or utility? Time planning style and Web usage behaviors. *Journal of Interactive Marketing, 20*(1), 45-57.

Dabholkar, P. A. (1996). Customer evaluations of new technology-based self-service options: An investigation of alternative models of service quality. *International Journal of Research in Marketing, 13,* 29-51.

Fullerton, G. (2005). How commitment both enables and undermines marketing relationships. *European Journal of Marketing, 39*(11/12), 1372-1388.

Giaglis, G. M., Kourouthanassis, P., & Tsamakos, A. (2003). Towards a classification framework for mobile location services. In B. E. Mennecke & T. J. Strader (Eds.), *Mobile commerce: Technology, theory, and applications* (pp. 67-85). Hershey, PA: Idea Group.

Hämäläinen, M. (2006). Enabling innovation in mobile games—Going beyond the conventional. In *Proceedings of Mobility Round Table,* Finland: Helsinki School of Economics.

Heinonen, K. (2004a). Reconceptualizing customer perceived value: The value of time and place. *Managing Service Quality, 14*(2/3), 205-215.

Heinonen, K. (2004b). Time and location as customer perceived value drivers. (doctoral thesis No. 124), HANKEN, Swedish School of Economics and Business Administration, Finland.

Heinonen, K. (2006). Temporal and spatial e-service value. *International Journal of Service Industry Management, 17*(4), 380-400.

Heinonen, K., & Andersson, P. (2003). Swedish mobile market: Consumer perceptions of mobile services. *Communications & Strategies, 49,* 151-171.

Holmlund, M. (1997). Perceived quality in business relationships (Doctoral dissertation No. 66). HANKEN, Swedish School of Economics and Business Administration, Finland.

Hyvönen, K., & Repo, P. (2005). Mobiilipalvelut suomalaisten arjessa (Mobile Serives in the everyday life of Finns). In J. Leskinen, H. Hallman, M. Isoniemi, L. Perälä, T. Pohjoisaho & E. Pylvänäinen (Eds.) *Vox consumptoris—Kuluttajan ääni,* . Kerava: Kuluttajatutkimuskeskus.

Isoniemi, K., & Wolf, G. (2001). Three segments of mobile users. In *Proceedings of the Seamless Mobility Workshop,* Stockholm, Sweden.

Järvenpää, S. L., & Lang, K. R. (2005). Managing the paradoxes of mobile technology. *Information Systems Management, 22*(4), 7-23.

Kleijnen, M., De Ruyter, K., & Andreassen, T. W. (2005). Image congruence and the adoption of service innovations. *Journal of Service Research, 7*(4), 343-359.

Kleijnen, M., Wetzels, M., & De Ruyter, K. (2004). Consumer acceptance of wireless finance. *Journal of Financial Services Marketing, 8*(3), 206-217.

Koivumäki, T., Ristola, A., & Kesti, M. (2006). Predicting consumer acceptance in mobile services: Empirical evidence from an experimental end user environment. *International Journal of Mobile Communications, 4*(4), 418-435.

Laukkanen, T., & Kantanen, T. (2006). Customer value segments in mobile bill paying. In *Proceedings of the 3rd International Conference on Information Technology: New Generations 2006 (ITNG 2006),* Las Vegas, NV: IEEE Computer Society Press.

Laukkanen, T., & Lauronen, J. (2005). Consumer value creation in mobile banking services. *International Journal of Mobile Communications, 3*(4), 325-38.

Libai, B., & Nitzan, I. (2005). Customer profitability over time in the presence of switching costs. In *Proceedings of 14th Annual Frontiers in Services Conference,* Arizona: The Center for Service Leadership, W.B. Carey School of Business, Arizona State University.

Lin, H-H., & Wang, Y-S. (2006). An examination of the determinants of customer loyalty in mobile commerce contexts. *Information & Management, 43,* 271-282.

Lovelock, C. H. (1983). Classifying services to gain strategic marketing insights. *Journal of Marketing, 47,* 9-20.

Maier, M. (2005, March 1). *Song sharing for your cell phone.* Retrieved November 10, 2006, from http://money.cnn.com/magazines/business2/business2_archive/2005/03/01/8253120/index.htm

Mennecke, B., & Strader, T. (2003). *Mobile commerce: Technology, theory, and applications.* London: Idea Group.

Meuter, M. L., Ostrom, A. L., Roundtree, R. I., & Bitner, M. J. (2000). Self-service technologies: Understanding customer satisfaction with technology-based service encounters. *Journal of Marketing, 64*(3), 50-64.

Mitchell, K., & Whitmore, M. (2003). Location based services: Locating the money. In B. E. Mennecke & T. J. Strader (Eds.), *Mobile commerce, technology, theory and applications* (pp. 51-66). Hershey, PA: Idea Group.

Mobile game. (n.d.). Retrieved September 28, 2006, from http://en.wikipedia.org/wiki/Mobile_game

Munnukka, J. (2005). Dynamics of price sensitivity among mobile service customers. *Journal of Product & Brand Management, 14*(1), 65-73.

Neslin, S. A., Grewal, D., Leghorn, R., Shankar, V., Teerling, M. L., Thomas, J. S., et al. (2006). Challenges and opportunities in multichannel customer management. *Journal of Service Research, 9*(2), 95-112.

Nicholson, M., Clarke, I., & Blakemore, M. (2002). One brand, three ways to shop: Situational variables and multichannel consumer behaviour. *The International Review of Retail, Distribution and Consumer Research, 12*(2), 131-148.

Nikulainen, K. (2003). *Fishermen hooked in mobile in Oulu (Oulussa kalastajat iskivät mobiilikoukkuun).* Retreived January 26, 2006, from http://www.digitoday.fi/page.php?page_id=11&news_id=20035391

Novak, T. P., Hoffman, D. L., & Duhachek, A. (2003). The influence of goal-directed and experiental activities on online flow experiences. *Journal of Consumer Psychology, 13*(1&2), 3-16.

Nysveen, H., Pedersen, P. E., & Thorbjørnsen, H. (2005a). Explaining intention to use mobile chat services: Moderating effects of gender. *Journal of Consumer Marketing, 22*(5), 247-56.

Nysveen, H., Pedersen, P. E., & Thorbjørnsen, H. (2005b). Intentions to use mobile services: Antecedents and cross-service comparisons. *Journal of the Academy of Marketing Science, 33*(3), 330-46.

Okazaki, S. (2005). New perspectives on m-commerce research. *Journal of Electronic Commerce Research, 6*(3), 160-64.

Pirc, M. (2006). Mobile service and phone as consumption system—The impact on customer switching. In *Proceedings of the Helsinki Mobility Round Table.* Helsinki: Helsinki School of Economics.

Pura, M. (2003a). Case study: The role of mobile advertising in building a brand. In B. Mennecke & T. Strader (Eds.), *Mobile commerce: Technology, theory, and applications* (pp. 291-308). London: Idea Group.

Pura, M. (2003b). Linking perceived value and loyalty to mobile services. In *Proceedings of the ANZMAC 2003,* Adelaide, Australia.

Pura, M. (2003c). Measuring loyalty to mobile services. In *Proceedings of the Third International Conference on Electronic Business (ICEB),* National University of Singapore.

Pura, M. (2005). Linking perceived value and loyalty in location-based mobile services. *Managing Service Quality, 15*(6), 509-538.

Pura, M., & Brush, G. (2005). Hedonic and utilitarian motivations for mobile service use. In *Proceedings of SERVSIG,* National University of Singapore.

Pura, M., Viitanen, J., & Liljander, V. (2003). Customer perceived value of mobile services. In *Proceedings of the 32th EMAC Conference,* Glasgow: University of Strathclyde.

Rodgers, S., & Sheldon, K. (2002). An improved way to characterize Internet users. *Journal of Advertising Research, 42(*5), 82-94.

Segerstrale, K. (2006). *Enabling innovation in mobile games—Going beyond the conventional.* Helsinki: Helsinki.

Sheth, J., Newman, B., & Gross, B. (1991). *Consumption values and market choices, theory and applications.* South-Western.

Mort, G. S., & Drennan, J. (2005). Marketing m-services: Establishing a usage benefit typology related to mobile user characteristics. *Journal of Database Marketing & Customer Strategy Management, 12*(4), 327-41.

Van Camp, S. (2005, May 1). 15 minutes with Derek Pollock on markets for tablet PC. *Adweek Magazines' Technology Marketing.*

Van der Heijden, H. (2004). User acceptance of hedonic information systems. *MIS Quarterly, 28*(4), 695-704.

Van der Heijden, H., Ogertschnig, M., & Van der Gaast, L. (2005). Effects of context relevance and perceived risk on user acceptance of mobile information services. In *Proceedings of 13th European Conference on Information Systems.* Regensburg, Germany: Institute for Management of Information Systems at the University of Regensburg.

Venkatesh, V., Morris, M., Davis, G., & Davis, F. D. (2003). User acceptance of information technology: Toward a unified view. *MIS Quarterly, 27*(3), 425-478.

Watson, R. T., Pitt, L. F., Berthon, P. R., & Zinkhan, G. M. (2002). U-commerce: Expanding the universe of marketing. *Journal of the Academy of Marketing Science, 30*(4), 333-47.

Yoo, Y., & Lyytinen, K. (2005). Social impacts of ubiquitous computing: Exploring critical interactions between mobility, context and technology. *Information and Organization, 15,* 91-94.

ENDNOTE

[1] The definition of a mobile game on Wikipedia ("Mobile game," n.d.) reads: "A mobile game is a computer software game played on a mobile phone, smartphone, PDA or handheld computer. Mobile games may be played using the communications technologies present in the device itself, such as by text message (SMS), multimedia message (MMS) or GPRS location identification. More common, however, are games that are downloaded to the mobile phone and played using a set of game technologies on the device."

Chapter VIII
Exploring the Use of Mobile Data Services in Europe:
The Cases of Denmark and Greece

Ioanna D. Constantiou
Copenhagen Business School, Denmark

Maria Bina
Athens University of Economics and Business, Greece

ABSTRACT

Mobile data services seem a promising revenue source for the stakeholders that have heavily invested in mobile communications infrastructures. However, in the Western world those services have not reached the mass markets yet. This chapter focuses on two markets that are representative of the European socioeconomic environment, Greece and Denmark, with the aim to investigate and compare mobile data services use through the means of an online survey. We depict two user groups and observe their behaviors in both countries. The results indicate differences in locations and frequency of services use that can be attributed to specific socioeconomic characteristics. However, certain similarities exist in the experience derived from mobile data service use since users believe that services cannot cater to their specific needs. We conclude by underlining the current challenges faced by mobile service providers in order to increase mobile data services use and summarizing user groups' characteristics.

INTRODUCTION

Mobile communications markets have been in the spotlight for the last decade due to the impressive increase of users in most countries around the world. This dynamic environment led practitioners and academics to numerous predictions and speculations for the industry's growth potential. Many mobile operators, in pursuit of high returns on investment, upgraded their network infrastructures (e.g., third generation [3G]). They expected that this would stimulate high demand for advanced mobile services similar to those used on the Internet, such as infotainment content and e-commerce transactions. However, these hopes have not been materialized in the Western world yet. It seems that mobile users are not interested or willing to massively adopt and extensively use the mobile data services (MDS) offered.

In the IS research, there has been considerable attempts to explore, understand, and analyze diffusion of innovation and technology acceptance through models and theories that offer constructs or factors affecting adoption and use based on individuals' expectancies and attitudes (Venkatesh, Morris, Davis, & Davis, 2003). This research domain has inspired many academics who have applied these models and theories in mobile communications markets in order to interpret or predict future trends and identify drivers and inhibitors for MDS adoption. In these research efforts, consumer behavior has been analyzed using conceptual frameworks inspired by the *technology acceptance model* (TAM) (Davis, 1986) or *diffusion of innovation theory* (DoI) (Rogers, 2003). Moreover, it has been pointed out that a cross-disciplinary integration of the four research directions on diffusion, adoption, uses, and gratification as well as domestication, was needed for understanding individuals' mechanisms for adopting MDS (Pedersen & Ling, 2003).

Following the same reasoning, Carlsson, Carlsson, Hyvønen, Puhakainen, and Walden (2006) applied a modified TAM model as an explanatory framework for mobile devices/services adoption. In addition, Lu, Yao, and Yu (2005) extended the TAM for wireless Internet adoption by incorporating concepts such as social influences and personal traits. Similarly, Wu and Wang (2005) enriched TAM with constructs regarding perceived risk, cost, and compatibility, while Yang (2005) added individual characteristics, such as innovativeness, past adoption behavior, and knowledge about technology, as external antecedents of TAM constructs. Furthermore Kim, Chuan Chan, and Gupta (2005) developed the *value-based adoption model* including benefits as well as sacrifices in the adoption process of mobile Internet, whereas

Massey, Khatri, and Ramesh (2005) identified technology readiness and wireless Web site interface usability as key factors influencing the uptake of mobile commerce and services. This indicative, though non-exhaustive, listing of research efforts underpins how the domain of MDS adoption and diffusion has acquired an important position within the research agenda of IS researchers.

Overall, past research has mainly focused on investigating in detail the impact of several attributes on MDS adoption and use. However, in this emerging market landscape, it becomes pivotal to understand the types of existing users and their perceptions of MDS use. At this point, it is important to keep in mind that the MDS market is a voluntaristic setting, where the potential user chooses to adopt or not the service based on his/her individual perceptions about it. Thus, different behavioral characteristics and experiences of the users may affect usage patterns (Constantiou, Damsgaard, & Knutsen, 2007). Moreover, exploring different end-user types and behavioral patterns may provide a comprehensive market segmentation that can be used to improve matching of consumer needs to appropriate service offerings. In this line, there have been few research attempts to categorize mobile users based on characteristics such as their demographics and level of innovativeness (Constantiou, Damsgaard, & Knutsen, 2004).

In this chapter, we draw on earlier categorization research and focus on exploring users' perceptions and experiences from MDS. To this end, we adopt the categorization proposed by Constantiou, Damsgaard, and Knutsen (2005) and investigate MDS users in two European countries, namely Denmark and Greece. Our comparisons are based on the results from a global survey on MDS use that was conducted during November 2004. In particular, we apply the proposed categorization on two samples representing two countries with different information and communications technologies (ICT) market structures.

The chapter's contribution is twofold. First, it provides suggestive evidence on the applicability of the proposed categorization in different economic contexts. Second, it facilitates the uncovering of similarities and differences on MDS usage patterns between user categories in the two countries that can be interpreted based on national socioeconomic characteristics. Thus, we offer useful insights to both researchers in the mobile domain, by underlining the importance of socioeconomic context in the use of MDS, as well as the key players in mobile market arena, by informing their marketing campaigns and corporate strategies.

The remainder of this chapter explores mobile users' perceptions and experiences from MDS use. The next section offers a brief review of user categorization research in mobile markets and introduces the segmentation applied in this study. The following section describes the research design and depicts the MDS adopter segments and the hypotheses regarding inter-group similarities and differences. The empirical data is analyzed and discussed focusing on the group profiles, the MDS usage patterns, and the experiences in the next section. Finally, the chapter concludes with a summary of the resulting MDS adopter categories and highlights on the research and managerial insights offered by this research.

RESEARCH ON THE DEMAND SIDE OF MOBILE MARKETS

Research Efforts on User categorization in Mobile Markets

DoI explores adoption as a direct result of the five elements that characterize an innovation: (1) relative advantage, (2) compatibility, (3) complexity, (4) trialability, and (5) observability. These elements relate to the relative rate of adoption in a social system (Rogers, 1995). In turn, the rate of adoption refers to the relative speed with which

members of a social system will adopt a new idea. In addition, innovativeness is a behavioral characteristic of individuals that relates to the time it takes to adopt an innovation relative to others in a social system.

Rogers has identified five categories of adopters: (1) innovators, (2) early adopters, (3) early majority, (4) late majority, and (5) laggards, all of whom co-exist in a social system. These groups are characterized by different socioeconomic profiles and are defined based on their degree of innovativeness (Rogers, 2003). The categorization of the adopters' population into different groups has a pivotal role within the context of diffusion of innovation research (Wolfe, 1994) since it is commonly believed that a "copy-behavior" or "imitation principle" guides the adoption process (Rogers, 1995): from innovators to early adopters and so forth. However, Rogers' categorization is not immaculate; it suffers from the "individual-blame bias" (2003) and it implies that innovators and early adopters benefit more from the adoption than the early and late majority, or the laggards. Furthermore, researchers have questioned the validity of Rogers' prescribed adoption pattern under the light of the current ICT environment; for example, Moore (1999) introduced "The Chasm," a critical stage between early adopters and the majority that needs to be crossed for an innovation to be massively adopted. Moore's chasm was introduced to explain why adoption for many innovations suddenly stops at the early adopters' category (e.g., wireless application protocol [WAP]).

Moreover, in the case of communications services that exhibit network effects (Katz & Shapiro, 1985, 1992), the value for users increases almost exponentially with the number of other users following Metcalfe's law (Shapiro & Varian, 1999). Additionally, value increases by indirect network effects generated from complementary offerings available over the network (Katz & Shapiro, 1992). Thus, whether innovators and early adopters are benefited more than all others, as posited by Rogers, becomes quite doubtful. For example, the value of short message service (SMS) due to connectivity increased slowly with the first adopters, but then as the number of connected users grew it increased substantially. Furthermore, the wide use of SMS creates business opportunities for content providers to offer new services through SMS (e.g., voting for a contest), which in turn generates extra value to mobile users through indirect network effects. In sum, the value of mobile communications is not only attributable to the offering as such but also to the user's benefits from network effects. In the light of network effects, the role of innovators and early adopters according to Rogers is very important from an economic and business perspective. These groups may constitute the critical mass (Carter, 1998) enabling MDS to take off faster.

Although Rogers' categorization is not explicitly used in current MDS research, it is reflected in a number of recent studies. Gilbert and Kendall (2003) collected data from Singapore and Malaysia and outlined five adopter categories based on their intention to use WAP services, their specific service requirements as well as their demographics. In particular, "mobile professionals" required services useful in relation to work such as calendaring, e-mail and access to intranet/extranet; "sophisticates" focused on material style services; "socialities" were more interested in interpersonal contact; "technotoys" were driven by a need to know technological developments hands-on; and "lifestylers" focused on the always-mobile way of living. In addition, two segments unlikely to adopt mobile services were also identified; "misers" were the ones unwilling to pay, while "laggards" were the last to know and adopt new technologies. In recent research Gilbert and Han (2005) combined findings from adopter categorization of mobile gaming and entertainment services to dedicated, social, and casual gamers with cross-country comparisons of the five adopter categories described in Gilbert and Kendall (2003) to delineate a dynamic

needs-based segmentation of the MDS adopter population. The proposed segmentation separates five adopter groups (mobile professionals, sophisticates, socialities, technotoys, and lifestylers) based on their degree of expectation for intrinsic or extrinsic rewards from using MDS and their individuality, or collectivity when learning and taking up a new technology.

In the same line, Aarnio, Enkenberg, Heikkilä, and Hirvola (2002) identified five adopter categories that had all adopted SMS text messaging and e-mail. In their research, advanced forms of SMS services were used by "innovative opinion leaders" representing 12% of the sample, "early adopters" (14%) and "late adopting students" (40%). Moreover, the "innovative opinion leaders" were the only category using WAP and data transmission services. Mort and Drennan (2005) combined evidence from a careful screening of related literature and empirical data on MDS usage patterns to identify five groupings of MDS adopters: "innovators" who tend to adopt technological innovations like MDS earlier than all others, "techno-confidents" who have high mobile self-efficacy and belief in their ability to use MDS effectively, "shopping lovers" who have strong emotional orientation towards shopping, "belonging seekers" who tend to use MDS as a vehicle for receiving others' approval, and "consulters" who tend to ask friends or significant others for advice for using communication services such as pictures, SMS, and multimedia message service (MMS). Okazaki (2006) offered an alternative approach based on a two-step procedure for identifying clusters of mobile Internet adopters. Both demographic and attitudinal variables describing individual mind-sets towards MDS innovation features were used as input to the analysis, which resulted to the uncovering of young people as the core segment exhibiting a strong positive inclination for taking up MDS.

Furthermore, a European study conducted in Finland, Germany, and Greece during 2001 (Vrechopoulos, Constantiou, Mylonopoulos,

& Sideris, 2002; Vrechopoulos, Constantiou, Sideris, Doukidis, & Mylonopoulos, 2003) proposed a basic two-group classification: "mobile users"—those using traditional (e.g., voice services) or "more sophisticated" data services (e.g., MMS)—and "mobile shoppers" those using at least one of the content (information and news) or transaction (physical goods or services such as travel, ticketing, banking, or entertainment purchasing) services. These two groups were found to differ on perceptions of the importance of key attributes affecting consumer behavior such as price, service quality, user interface, security, and personalization.

This research was followed up in Denmark during 2004 through a survey focusing on investigating technology and service use, innovativeness as well as technology service requirements of mobile users (Constantiou Damsgaard & Knutsen., 2004, 2006). The outcome was a broad segmentation between "basic" and "advanced users." "Basic users" were found to have matured in terms of their perceptions of the key attributes affecting MDS use and did not differ significantly from "advanced users." However, significant differences between the two user groups were traced in terms of innovativeness and technology-service requirements. Thus, it becomes clear that studying the adoption pattern of an innovation like MDS, developed and marketed within the complex and continuously evolving ICT landscape, involves improving our knowledge on the different categories of MDS users and potential users and the ways they interact with each other to allow the diffusion of MDS to take place.

The Applied Market Segmentation

To deepen their understanding of mobile users, Constantiou et al. (2007) refined their early broad segmentation and provided a more detailed categorization of mobile users. Accordingly, four mobile user categories were delineated based on the learning steps taken towards specific service use:

1. **Talkers:** Users of voice services only
2. **Writers:** Users of SMS in addition to voice services
3. **Photographers (PH):** Users of MMS services in addition to voice and SMS
4. **Surfers (SU):** Users of data services in addition to SMS, MMS, and voice services

Consequently, "talkers" have taken a primary learning step in terms of mobile communications use, whereas "writers," "photographers," and "surfers" have experienced one, two, or three additional changes in their behavior. Constantiou Damsgaard & Knutsen. (2005) concluded that the groups were different in terms of innovativeness, technology, and service use as well as technology service requirements. These results underline the differences observed in terms of learning steps taken by each group. In this chapter we focus on the two latter categories, namely, "photographers" and "surfers." These two categories consist of MDS users who are the main target group of mobile service providers in order to generate high revenues (Constantiou Damsgaard & Knutsen, 2007).

THE RESEARCH APPROACH

The Research Context

In this chapter we investigate and compare the behaviors of MDS users originating from two European countries, namely; Greece and Denmark. Demark is among the most advanced European countries in mobile communications (e.g., Denmark holds the first place in the Information Society Index). In particular, broadband penetration in Denmark was 25% (Organisation for Economic Co-operation and Development [OECD], 2005) and Internet use reached 75% of the population during 2005 (Eurobarometer, 2006). Besides, the Danish mobile communications market is one of the most progressive in terms of liberalization (e.g., 13 mobile operators resulting in extensive price wars on contracts for SMS and voice services) and has high mobile penetration (95%) (i.e., SIM cards as percentage of the population).

Greece is less advanced in the ICT sector. It exhibits low broadband penetration of 1,4% (OECD, 2005) and low Internet use at home (25%) (Eurobarometer, 2006). Nevertheless, mobile communications penetration has reached saturation with 109% (i.e., SIM cards as percentage of the population) though the market is characterized as an oligopoly with only four mobile network operators (Kopf, 2005).

We believe that those two countries are useful examples of dynamic and mature mobile communications markets that have different structures. Additionally, they have differing ICT market growth rates, both of which are representative within the European context. Furthermore, they represent two traditional geographic poles: the Scandinavian and the Mediterranean territories. Thus, we can investigate emerging trends in MDS use that may be prominent and repeated in other European markets as well.

The Survey Instrument

Empirical data for the research presented in this article were collected within the 2004 Worldwide Mobile Data Services Survey (WMDS), a global Web-based survey designed to explore consumer behavior and the market environment for MDS around the world through cross-cultural and longitudinal trend analysis. WMDS is a rigorous academic study conducted annually since 2001. Ten countries (Australia, China, Denmark, Finland, Greece, Hong Kong, Japan, Korea, Taiwan, and USA) took part in WMDS during 2004. The survey theme was the effects of quality of life on MDS use. All countries are expected to use a jointly developed core set of questions on their

surveys to facilitate cross-comparison of results, while each country is also free to include additional questions of local significance if required.

The Danish and Greek research teams adopted a common approach that led to the design of a survey instrument including 31 questions organized in different categories such as mobile communication usage patterns, mobile data services use, pricing considerations, assessment of quality of life, and demographics. Furthermore, both research teams followed similar processes for pilot testing (trials conducted using university staff) and revising the questionnaire before its official launch on the Internet. The survey ran during November 2004.

Our target groups were respondents that were MDS users and had prior experience with networked technologies and services such as the Internet and the use of online consumer services. In particular, we focus on Internet users since this group can be depicted as MDS early adopters (Constantiou Damsgaard & Knutsen, 2007). Moreover, according to Carter (1998) and Rogers (2003) early adopters are the target groups that should be addressed with specific strategies at the introductory phase of a new product or service in order to create the critical mass. Thus, we explore a sample including respondents with an early adopter profile to identify behavioral patterns that may significantly affect the diffusion process.

The samples are not representative of the total Danish or Greek populations since they include self-selected Internet users who are also mobile users. According to Hair, Bush, and Ortinau (2000), as well as Kinnear and Taylor (1996), self-selected sampling is suitable for exploratory research and when *ex ante* knowledge of the population characteristics is not sufficiently present. The sample is influenced by Internet and mobile penetration as well as the advertising effort put up by the two research teams that included a balanced mix of press announcements and Internet pages hosting links to the survey (e.g., information portals and university Web sites). The resulting sample consists of 673 and 683 usable responses in Denmark and Greece respectively. Respondents who have used MDS at least one reached 78% of the Danish sample and 57% of the Greek sample. This suggests that MDS penetration has been faster in Denmark than in Greece. It remains to be seen whether this penetration is associated with sophisticated usage patterns in terms of frequency of use or it has yet to be transformed to an actual users' pool.

The Sampling Categorization

The available samples in both countries encompass all mobile users who have or have not used MDS. However, for the purposes of this research, we focus only on those mobile users who have at least once in their life used one or more of the commercially available MDS in both countries—in total, 42 services.

The statistical analysis performed in both data sets denotes low penetration scores for the majority of MDS categories. In particular, in a scale from 1 (never) to 7 (very often), the most popular MDS in Greece is taking photos and/or sending them

for printing through MMS that scores a mean value of 3.44, while among Danish respondents the most popular service is receiving weather forecasts with a mean score of 2.26. Our research focuses on the top-scoring MDS in both data sets. In other words, our focus is on the services whose mean value is greater than 2.0 (Table 1). It appears that MDS market penetration is clearly very low in both countries. Moreover, Table 1 indicates that Greek and Danish consumer preferences for MDS exhibit similarities. Both top-ranking MDS are related to entertainment- and communication-oriented services, some of which are mobile extensions of Internet services (e.g., e-mail). This observation may be valuable for mobile marketing strategy design at a cross-national level. In addition, the strong preferences in both countries for logos, wallpapers, and ringtone-related services are yet another demonstration of the increasing importance that these services have acquired as means of expressing individual identity, inner values, and emotions (Hjorth, 2005).

Adhering to the categorization in "photographers" and "surfers" proposed by Constantiou et al. (2005) we formed an initial hyperset of MDS

Table 1. Top-ranking MDS in Greece and Denmark

RANK	GREECE	DENMARK
1	Taking photos and sending them to a third party for printing through MMS	Getting weather updates
2	Updating logos/wallpapers and/or ringtones	Updating logos/wallpapers and/or ringtones
3	Downloading logos/wallpapers and/or ringtones	Downloading logos/wallpapers and/or ringtones
4	Searching for infotainment content (movie updates, restaurants, concerts, etc.)	Exchanging e-mails through the mobile phone with colleagues
5	Getting weather updates	Searching for infotainment content (movie updates, restaurants, concerts, etc.)
6	Exchanging e-mails through the mobile phone with colleagues	Exchanging e-mails over my mobile phone with friends
7	Exchanging e-mails over my mobile phone with friends	Downloading updates for the software or firmware installed on my mobile phone
8	Downloading games for my mobile phone	Exchanging e-mails over my mobile phone with family members
9	Downloading and/or listening to music on the mobile phone	Taking photos and sending them to a third party for printing through MMS

users by selecting all respondents who have used one or more of the proposed MDS at least once in their life (i.e., corresponding values of the MDS greater than 1). Photographers were found within the initial hyperset by selecting respondents who have used at least one in the MMS-related service, while their use of the remaining MDS is seldom (value < 3). Surfers are frequent users of MDS. They were found within the initial hyperset by selecting respondents whose frequency of use of MDS scores values greater than 3. Thus, we delineated four groups including "photographers" and "surfers" in both Denmark and Greece.

The Hypotheses

After the identification of the four groups, the next step in our research involved investigating their differences in terms of frequency of MDS use in various locations, purpose of MDS use, and experience from using MDS by formulating the corresponding hypotheses. According to the research efforts in the mobile domain, these behavioral characteristics of users are pivotal in understanding MDS market adoption and use dynamics.

Recent research has shown that the purpose of MDS use is different among categories of users and this may affect their adoption and usage patterns (Aarnio et al., 2002; Anckar & D'Incau, 2002; Gilbert & Kendall, 2003). A major dichotomy in terms of MDS use is between functional uses of mobile services, with the objective to increase work productivity, and efficient allocation of time during the day and entertainment, or hedonic use, among individuals who perceive the mobile device and the services enabled over it as an entertainment or lifestyle tool. In fact, Lee, Kim, Lee, and Kim (2002) have empirically shown that cultural differences can be at the heart of this differentiation in MDS purpose of use. We asked respondents to indicate on a 1-7 scale whether they use MDS more for personal- or business-related purposes.

Thus, we investigated respondents' purpose of MDS use by setting the hypothesis:

H_0^I: There are no significant differences between the four groups in their purpose of MDS use.

Moreover, there is a large stream of research focusing on location-based services (Rao & Minakakis, 2003) that underlines the role of physical locations in the adoption of MDS. A broad classification of physical locations includes school/university, work, home, public places (e.g., streets and shops), and transit or transportation means (including waiting time). Recent research efforts on consumer choices of MDS by Blechar, Constantiou, and Damsgaard (2006b) underlined the importance of physical location on actual service use. In particular, the individual's decision to use a service may be affected by his/her physical location. For example, when the user has available Internet access (i.e., school, work), he/she may choose this infrastructure over mobile networks to access a service (e.g., e-mail, news). We asked respondents to mark on a 1-7 scale their frequency of MDS use in various locations, namely, workplace, school, in public (e.g., shopping, street), in transit (including waiting time), or at home. We explored the frequency of MDS use in different physical locations by hypothesizing that:

H_0^{II}: There are no significant differences between the four groups on the frequency of MDS use in different locations

Finally, experience from MDS use that relates to perceived content quality has been postulated as a key determinant of future use (Andreou et al., 2005; Cronin & Taylor, 1992, 1994). We asked respondents to reveal their experience from MDS use through four constructs. Two constructs are related to overall experience; "I am satisfied with my decision to use mobile data services," "Mobile data services provide excellent overall service." Another construct is based on earlier documentations of the relation between pleasure or joy from using a technology and its adoption (Davis, Bagozzi, & Warshaw, 1989); "I feel that my experience with using mobile data services has been enjoyable." The fourth construct captures user evaluation of MDS; "Compared to the money, effort and time I have to spend on mobile data services, their overall ability to satisfy my wants and needs is high" based on the empirical documentation that consumer's choice of a service is influenced by a cognitive process comparing the cost and benefits involved (Thaler, 1985). We explored users' experiences by hypothesizing that:

H_0^{III}: *There are no significant differences between the four groups on the experience from MDS use.*

The aforementioned hypotheses are expected to shed light on the observed low usage of MDS

in both countries that has not reached the mass market and is not frequent.

ANALYSIS OF RESULTS

Group Profiles

Having delineated the four groups in the two countries, we start by depicting their demographic characteristics (Table 2).

Table 2 indicates that "surfers" are in both countries a considerably larger group than "photographers," which is in line with the purpose of this survey targeting users of MDS. Greek "photographers" are students with relatively low annual income whereas the respective Danish group includes mainly men working in the private sector with high annual income. Greek "surfers" are young people with quaternary education work-

Table 2. The groups' demographics

		PH_{GR}	PH_{DK}	SU_{GR}	SU_{DK}
Group	size	62	50	185	103
Gender	male	60%	94%	59%	92%
	female	40%	6%	41%	8%
Age	<18	5%	0%	8%	0%
	18-24	32%	10%	22%	9%
	25-34	50%	70%	47%	52%
	35-49	8%	18%	21%	32%
	>50	5%	2%	2%	7%
Education	Primary, secondary, and no tertiary	34%	14%	31%	28%
	Tertiary	32%	66%	27%	46%
	Quaternary	34%	20%	42%	26%
Occupation	Private sector	45%	80%	62%	77%
	Students	50%	6%	28%	13%
	Public-semi public	5%	14%	10%	10%
Annual Household Income	<20,000 €	40%	2%	37%	10%
	20,001 €-40,000 €	26%	6%	37%	6%

ing in the private sector that have medium annual income. Danish "surfers" are mainly men with tertiary education working in the private sector that have relatively high annual income. The Danish sample seems to be overrepresented by men. This trend is in line with previous research on this market indicating that "surfers" in Denmark are mainly men (Constantiou Damsgaard & Knutsen, 2005). Overall, the demographics structuring of the four groups is in accordance with previous research findings regarding the role of age and gender in the adoption of MDS (Anckar & D'Incau, 2002; Ling, 2004). In addition, the difference in annual income underlines the differences in the economic structure of the two countries.

Additional questions were also asked to explore the groups' characteristics in terms of MDS usage patterns. We asked "photographers" when they started using MMS. We observed different distributions between countries and groups. Upon performing chi-square tests we found significant differences between "photographers" experience with MMS use. In particular the highest percentage of Greek "photographers" (29%) started using MMS less than three months ago, whereas the majority of the Danish group (42%) started using them more than 24 months ago. We also asked them how much time they spent on MMS use on a monthly basis. The majority of Greeks (62%) and Danish (60%) use MMS for less than 9 minutes monthly. This is not a surprising result since "photographers" are only sending and receiving MMS which is not a time intensive activity.

Turning to "surfers" usage patterns, the Greek group is divided into two subgroups (30% each) with an MDS use period of either less than three or more than 24 months ago, whereas the majority of the Danish group (53%) have used MDS for more than 24 months. In terms of time spent on MDS monthly, the majority of Greeks (52%)

Table 3. Group purpose and context of MDS use (significant contrast values identified with the Games Howell post-hoc comparison procedure)

	PH_{GR}	PH_{DK}	SU_{GR}	SU_{DK}	Asympt. F	P-value	Significant Contrast Values
Location (1: never, 7: very often)							
Workplace	2.56	2.93	3.64	4.06	8.76	0.00	PH_{GR} - SU_{GR} PH_{GR} - SU_{DK} PH_{DK} - SU_{DK}
School/University	1.52	2.48	2.25	3.00	5.60	0.00	PH_{GR} - SU_{GR} PH_{GR} - SU_{DK}
Public place	2.78	3.08	3.68	3.57	4.43	0.00	PH_{GR} - SU_{GR} PH_{GR} - SU_{DK}
In transit	2.72	3.81	4.00	5.08	21.14	0.00	PH_{GR} - PH_{DK} PH_{GR} - SU_{GR} PH_{GR} - SU_{DK} PH_{DK} - SU_{DK} SU_{GR} - SU_{DK}
Home	3.49	3.21	4.59	3.63	12.33	0.00	PH_{GR} - SU_{GR} PH_{DK} - SU_{GR} SU_{GR} - SU_{DK}
Purpose (1: only business, 7: only personal)							
	5.19	5.00	4.47	4.16	6.36	0.00	PH_{GR} - SU_{GR} PH_{GR} - SU_{DK} PH_{DK} - SU_{DK}

and the highest percentage of Danes (27%) state less than 9 minutes. However, 25% of the Danish respondents state 10-29 minutes of monthly MDS use. Thus, in relative terms, Danish "surfers" use MDS more frequently. This result may relate to the fact that Danish respondents have longer experience with MDS.

Mobile Data Services Usage Patterns and Experiences

We then explored the purpose and the context of MDS use by performing a series of ANOVA tests and post hoc comparisons to identify significant contrast values between groups (Table 3).

According to Table 3, "photographers" purpose of use does not significantly differ. It seems that they mainly use MMS for personal reasons. This finding is in line with the main property of MMS which is to improve person-to-person communications (Yrjänäinen & Neuvo, 2002) and enhance the creation and maintenance of personal and group memory (Van House, Davis, Ames, Finn, & Viswanathan, 2005). However, "surfers" significantly differ from "photographers" since they use MDS in a more balanced mix of business and personal purposes. This result may relate to their profile (i.e., people working on the private sector) and the wide variety of MDS available covering both purposes. Thus, they appear to be more mature users who are capable of distinguishing among the various functions of mobile data services and achieve higher added-value from using them.

In terms of frequency and place of use, there are significant differences among all groups. A general observation is that the frequency of use for "photographers" is lower than "surfers." Besides, Danish "surfers" mainly use MDS while in transit or when waiting for transportation means and Greek "surfers" mainly at home. This can be partially explained by the relatively high Internet penetration at home in Denmark and low in Greece. It is empirically documented

through longitudinal field studies that MDS are perceived by users as close substitutes of Internet services (Blechar, Constantiou, & Damsgaard, 2006a; 2006b). A similar trend is also observed for "photographers."

Moreover, in places like school, university, or work, where Internet access is available, we observe low frequency of use. These observations indicate that the user may compare the two access means and the Internet may be preferred over mobile networks. This choice may relate to the perceived value derived from the reference price and situation of the mobile user (Blechar et al., 2006a). For example, when accessing news the user may find mobile network access more expensive compared to the Internet that is perceived as free of charge at the university or at work. This comparison may induce the user not to use the former means.

Furthermore, we asked respondents to comment on their experience from using MDS.

Observing Table 4 shows that "photographers" experience with MDS does not significantly differ between the two countries and is rather neutral. This observation may be explained by the fact that they only use MMS and, thus, their experience is relatively narrow in scope and not intense. The average experience and satisfaction observed may relate to the nature of MMS, which has a very short duration and simplicity in content provided. In addition, we found average scores for the last construct comparing the user's perceived costs incurred from MMS use to the benefit derived. This result implies that the "photographers" do not perceive MMS as a high value-adding service which may in turn affect the decision to adopt other MDS service as well.

"Surfers" experiences between the two countries significantly differ. It appears that Greeks have more positive experience than Danes. This may relate to content per se that is offered in Greece by a wider variety of independent service providers (i.e., an operator with high market share provides access to i-mode platform that allows

Table 4. Group mean values and the results of ANOVA tests

Experience from MDS use (1: Not at all , 7: Quite a lot)	PH$_{GR}$	PH$_{DK}$	SU$_{GR}$	SU$_{DK}$	Asympt. F	P-value	Significant Contrast Values
I am satisfied with my decision to use mobile data services	4.32	3.54	5.15	4.10	18.81	0.00	PH$_{GR}$ - SU$_{GR}$ PH$_{DK}$ - SU$_{GR}$ SU$_{GR}$ - SU$_{DK}$
I feel that my experience with using mobile data services has been enjoyable	4.45	3.56	4.82	3.88	12.42	0.00	PH$_{DK}$ - SU$_{GR}$ SU$_{GR}$ - SU$_{DK}$
Mobile data services provide excellent overall service	3.94	3.78	4.43	4.57	4.27	0.01	PH$_{DK}$ - SU$_{DK}$ SU$_{GR}$ - SU$_{DK}$
Compared to the money, effort, and time I have to spend on mobile data services, their overall ability to satisfy my wants and needs is high	3.56	3.34	4.07	3.65	3.63	0.13	

mobile users accessing independent content providers) than in Denmark (i.e., the operators offer their own content services and accessing third party providers in not encouraged in technical and economic terms). Besides, Greeks may value MDS use more since in specific locations with high observed frequency of use such as home there are no other data communications means (e.g., Internet). Moreover, the significantly lower evaluations of Danish surfers may also explain the relatively lower use of MDS that we observe in this sample.

However, both groups indicate neutral experience when asked to compare their satisfaction in terms of wants and needs with money, time, and effort related to MDS. This finding suggests that respondents are not generally satisfied from the use of MDS when comparing the costs incurred and the benefits derived. This result highlights the challenges faced by mobile service providers both in terms of content and variety of services that can cover users' needs and wants as well as improving the technical characteristics, (e.g., interface, network availability) to decrease the cost incurred in terms of money, effort, and time spent.

The low satisfaction may in turn affect their willingness to pay for MDS. We asked respondents to calculate how much of their total monthly expenditure was related to MDS use. In this question there are no significant differences between the two countries' "photographers" since the majority of Greeks (82%) and Danish (66%) stated less than 15 Euros. This in turn relates to the fact that MMS is offered on a relatively low flat price per use in both countries. Turning to "surfers," there are also no significant differences between the two countries on monthly expenditure for MDS, since the majority of Greeks (50%) and Danish (39%) state less than 15 Euros.

In sum, although our research suggests that there are differences in several aspects of MDS use in the two countries under study, it appears that both markets are rather immature. Several steps need to be taken for MDS use to reach a critical mass.

CONCLUSION

This chapter aimed at offering an empirical argumentation regarding the particularities of the MDS adoption trajectory in two European countries, namely Denmark and Greece. To this end, the analysis presented in the previous sec-

Table 5. Group characteristics

	PH$_{GR}$	PH$_{DK}$	SU$_{GR}$	SU$_{DK}$
Demographic profile	students low income	men working in private sector high income	individuals working in private sector medium income	men working in private sector high income
Experience with MDS	<3 months	>24 months	> 3 months	>24 months
Expenditure on MDS	<15 Euros	<15 Euros	<15 Euros	<15 Euros
Monthly time spent on MDS	<9 minutes	< 9 minutes	<9 minutes	>9 minutes
Purpose of MDS use	personal	personal	personal and business	personal and business
Place and frequency of MDS use	Home, sometimes	Transit, sometimes	Home, often	Transit, often

tions was structured around the application of a segmentation specific marker to distinguish two broad genres of MDS adopters in the two countries under scrutiny, "photographers" and "surfers." Although these groups are meant to reflect advanced MDS users, groups' mean frequencies of specific service use are relatively low indicating that the adoption process is still at a nascent stage in both countries. Furthermore, our research investigated key attributes and parameters in MDS usage patterns through the development and empirical testing of three hypotheses set up to explore intra- and inter-country group differences relating to purpose and location of, as well as experience from using MDS. Table 5 highlights the primary findings from our categorization research.

It appears that while the socioeconomic differences among the two countries can partially explain the emerging usage patterns, there is a common trend between advanced mobile service users. They are not satisfied with service offerings because they cannot generate the expected benefits. This also implies lower willingness to pay for MDS. It seems that in current market settings there are limited opportunities to generate high revenues from MDS as expected. There is no critical mass of MDS users to generate benefits from network effects. These findings set new challenges

for mobile service providers. They may have to alter their development and marketing efforts to increase exposure and personalization of service offerings to meet their customers' needs.

This chapter identified country-related differences between advanced mobile service users that mainly affect the context of MDS use. In particular, different infrastructural development indicates that in Greece MDS may substitute Internet services at home, whereas in Denmark MDS are used when there is no Internet access available (e.g., in transportation means). It is important to underline the possible substitution effect between Internet services and MDS that is reflected by the low usage rates at locations where there is Internet access (e.g., work).

Furthermore, the significant differences between the two groups at a country level relate to the fact that "surfers" have taken an extra learning step and are actual MDS users whereas "photographers" are technologically advanced users that have not adopted MDS yet. This may relate to negative experiences. Thus, mobile service providers should develop different marketing strategies pushing "photographers" to adopt MDS while maintaining and increasing "surfers" current use.

MDS represents a new category of information and communication services and applications that combine well-known and established Internet features (e.g., instant access to information, communication, or entertainment facilities) with the particularities of the mobile device as the access medium. The understanding MDS adoption occupies an important position within the IS research stream and researchers have attempted to explore the challenges associated with MDS consumer acceptance using a wide portfolio of theories and methods. Research findings are then applied to explain why markets are still struggling to increase MDS adoption rates above certain thresholds that will enable the stakeholders (enterprises and consumers) to capitalize on MDS value elements. Results of this chapter contribute to this area by offering some initial insights on why the MDS market suffers from low use rates in European countries.

Furthermore, our work highlights the need for incorporating cross-cultural surveys and comparisons of MDS usage patterns since it confirms early observations regarding the non-universalism of the MDS adoption process. MDS geography is not only characterized by the Europe-Asia dichotomy, since important differences can be traced within countries belonging to the same periphery, such as Denmark and Greece. Thus, future research needs to take into account not only individual traits and behaviors but also the wider socioeconomic or cultural context within which MDS use takes place.

REFERENCES

Aarnio, A., Enkenberg, A., Heikkilä, J., & Hirvola, S. (2002). *Adoption and use of mobile services. Empirical evidence from a Finnish survey.* Paper presented at the 35th Annual Hawaii International Conference on System Sciences (HICSS-35'02), Big Island, HI.

Anckar, B., & D'Incau, D. (2002). Value creation in mobile commerce: Findings from a consumer survey. *Journal of Information Technology Theory and Application, 4*(1), 43-65.

Andreou, A. S., Leonidou, C., Pitisillides, A., Samaras, G., Schizas, C. N., & Mavromoustakos, S. M. (2005). Key issues for the design and development of mobile commerce and applications. *International Journal of Mobile Communications, 3*(3), 303-323.

Blechar, J., Constantiou, I., & Damsgaard, J. (2006a). Understanding behavioural patterns of advanced mobile service users. *Electronic Government: An International Journal, 3*(1), 93-104.

Blechar, J., Constantiou, I. D., & Damsgaard, J. (2006b). Exploring the influence of reference situations and reference pricing on mobile service user behaviour. *European Journal of Information Systems, 15*(3), 285-291.

Carlsson, C., Carlsson, J., Hyvønen, K., Puhakainen, J., & Walden, P. (2006). *Adoption of mobile devices/services—Searching for answers with the UTAUT.* Paper presented at the 39th Annual Hawaii International Conference on System Sciences (HICSS-39'06), Big Island, HI.

Carter, J. (1998). Why settle for early adopters? *Admap, 33*(3), 41-44.

Constantiou, I. D., Damsgaard, J., & Knutsen, L. (2004). *Strategic planning for mobile services adoption and diffusion: Empirical evidence from the Danish market.* Paper presented at the Mobile Information Systems (MOBIS), Oslo, Norway.

Constantiou, I. D., Damsgaard, J., & Knutsen, L. (2005). *Beware of Dane-geld: Even if paid, m-service adoption can be slow.* Paper presented at the European Conference on Information Systems (ECIS), Regensburg, Germany.

Constantiou, I., Damsgaard, J., & Knutsen, L. (2006). Exploring perceptions and use of mobile services: User differences in an advancing market. *International Journal of Mobile Communications, 4*(3), 231-247.

Constantiou, I. D., Damsgaard, J., & Knutsen, L. (2007). The four evolution steps to advanced mobile services' adoption. *Communications of the ACM, 50*(6), 51-55.

Cronin, J., & Taylor, S. (1992). Measuring service quality: A reexamination and extension. *Journal of Marketing, 56*(3), 55-68.

Cronin, J., & Taylor, S. (1994). SERVREF vs. SERVQUAL: Reconciling performance-based and perceptions-minu-expectations measurement of service quality. *Journal of Marketing, 58*(1), 125-131.

Davis, F. (1986). *Technology acceptance model for empirically testing new end-user information systems: Theory and results*. Boston.

Davis, F. D., Bagozzi, R., & Warshaw, P. R. (1989). User acceptance of computer technology: A comparison of two theoretical models. *Management Science, 35*(8), 982-1003.

Eurobarometer. (2006). *Safer Internet*.

Gilbert, A. L., & Han, H. (2005). Understanding mobile data services adoption: Demography, attitudes or needs? *Technological Forecasting & Social Change, 72*, 327-337.

Gilbert, A. L., & Kendall, J. D. (2003). *A marketing model for mobile wireless services*. Paper presented at the 36th Hawaii International Conference on System Sciences (HICSS'03), Big Island, HI.

Hair, J. F. J., Bush, R. P., & Ortinau, D. J. (2000). *Marketing research: A practical approach for the new millennium*: McGraw-Hill International Editions.

Hjorth, L. (2005). Postal presence: A case study of mobile customisation and gender in Melbourne. In P. B. Glotz, S. & Locke, C (Eds.), *Thumb culture: The meaning of mobile phones for society*. Bielefeld, Germany: Transcript-Verlag.

Katz, M. L., & Shapiro, C. (1985). Network externalities, competition, and compatibility. *American Economic Review, 75*(3), 424-440.

Katz, M. L., & Shapiro, C. (1992). Product introduction with network externalities. *Journal of Industrial Economics, 40*(1), 55-83.

Kim, H.-W., Chuan Chan, H., & Gupta, S. (2005). Value-based adoption of mobile Internet: An empirical investigation. *Decision Support Systems, In Press*.

Kinnear, T. C., & Taylor, J. R. (1996). *Marketing research: An applied approach* (5th ed.). McGraw-Hill.

Kopf, W. (2005). *The European mobile industry—A case for consolidation?* T-Mobile International AG & Co. KG.

Lee, Y., Kim, J., Lee, I., & Kim, H. (2002). A cross-cultural study on the value structure of mobile Internet usage: Comparison between Korea and Japan. *Journal of Electronic Commerce Research, 3*(4), 227-239.

Ling, R. (2004). *The mobile connection. The cell phone's impact on society* (3rd ed.). Morgan Kaufmann.

Lu, J., Yao, J.-E., & Yu, C.-S. (2005). Personal innovativeness, social influences and adoption of wireless Internet services via mobile technology. *Journal of Strategic Information Systems, 14*(3), 245-268.

Massey, A. P., Khatri, V., & Ramesh, V. (2005). *From the Web to the wireless Web: Technology readiness and usability*. Paper presented at the 38th Annual Hawaii International Conference on System Sciences (HICSS-38'05), Big Island, HI.

Moore, G. A. (1999). *Crossing the chasm* (2nd ed.). Oxford: Capstone.

Mort, G. S., & Drennan, J. (2005). Marketing m-services: Establishing a usage benefit typology related to mobile user characteristics. *Database Marketing & Customer Strategy Management, 12*(4), 327-341.

OECD. (2005, December). *Telecommunications and Internet policy: OECD broadband statistics.*

Okazaki, S. (2006). What do we know about mobile Internet adopters? A cluster analysis. *Information & Management, 43*(2), 127-141.

Pedersen, P. E., & Ling, R. (2003). *Modifying adoption research for mobile Internet service adoption: Cross-disciplinary interactions.* Paper presented at the 36th Hawaii International Conference on System Sciences (HICSS'03), Big Island, HI.

Rao, B., & Minakakis, L. (2003). Evolution of mobile location-based services. *Communications of the ACM, 46*(12), 61-65.

Rogers, E. M. (1995). *Diffusion of innovations* (4th ed.). New York: Free Press.

Rogers, E. M. (2003). *Diffusion of innovations* (5th ed.). New York: Free Press.

Shapiro, C., & Varian, H. (1999). *Information rules: A strategic guide to the network economy.*

Thaler, R. H. (1985). Mental accounting and consumer choice. *Marketing Science, 4,* 199-214.

Van House, N., Davis, M., Ames, M., Finn, M., & Viswanathan, V. (2005, April 2-7). *The uses of personal networked digital imaging: An empirical study of cameraphone photos and sharing.* Paper presented at the CHI 2005, Portland, OR.

Venkatesh, V., Morris, M., Davis, G. B., & Davis, F. D. (2003). User acceptance of information technology: Towards a unified view. *MIS Quarterly, 27*(3), 425-478.

Vrechopoulos, A. P., Constantiou, I. D., Mylonopoulos, N., & Sideris, I. (2002). *Critical success factors for accelerating mobile commerce diffusion in Europe.* Paper presented at the 15th Bled E-commerce Conference, e-Reality: Constructing the e-Economy, Bled, Slovenia.

Vrechopoulos, A. P., Constantiou, I. D., Sideris, I., Doukidis, G. I., & Mylonopoulos, N. (2003). The critical role of consumer behavior research in mobile commerce. *International Journal of Mobile Communications, 1*(3), 329-340.

Wolfe, R. A. (1994). Organizational innovation: Review, critique and suggested research directions. *Journal of Management Studies, 31*(3), 405-432.

Wu, J.-H., & Wang, S.-C. (2005). What drives mobile commerce? An empirical evaluation of the revised technology acceptance model. *Information & Management, 42,* 719-729.

Yang, K. C. C. (2005). Exploring factors affecting the adoption of mobile commerce in Singapore. *Telematics and Informatics, 22,* 257-277.

Yrjänäinen, J., & Neuvo, Y. (2002). Wireless meets multimedia. *Wireless Communications and Mobile Computing, 2*(6), 553-562.

Chapter IX
The Design of
Mobile Television in Europe

Pieter Ballon
Vrije Universiteit Brussel, Belgium

Olivier Braet
Vrije Universiteit Brussel, Belgium

ABSTRACT

Mobile television is potentially the most anticipated mass-market mobile application across Europe. This chapter examines the business model design of mobile TV by the various stakeholders currently piloting mobile broadcasting in the European national markets. It adapts a generic business model framework to systematically compare five recent pilots of the two mobile broadcasting technologies that are currently trialled most intensively in Europe, that is, digital video broadcasting-handheld (DVB-H) and digital audio broadcasting-Internet protocol (DAB-IP). The article illustrates the cross-impact of cooperation agreements between the various stakeholders with technological, service-related, and financial design choices. It also provides insights as to the likely business models in the upcoming commercialisation phase of mobile broadcasting in Europe.

INTRODUCTION

One of the most anticipated applications in Europe's mobile commerce and multimedia landscape is mobile TV. It is widely argued that mobile digital television has the potential of becoming one of the next high-growth consumer technologies (Kivirinta, Ali-Vehmas, Mutanen, Tuominen, & Vuorinen, 2004; Södergard, 2003), provided it is able to master its inherent complexities in terms of the various stakeholders required to cooperate (Shin, 2006). It has a clear and easily understand-able value proposition towards the majority of end users: TV on a mobile device. Also, the technology lies at the crossroads of two powerful socio-technical trends: the ubiquity of mobile phones, and new forms of accessing media content.

In the European mobile market, digital TV on a mobile device is not a novelty. Initial TV services on mobile phones consist of streaming video over the cellular network. Third generation (3G) cellular networks (i.e., Universal Mobile Telecommunications System [UMTS]) already allow for streaming video for a considerable time.

In several European countries, a wide selection of rich video content is available over UMTS, with large markets such as Italy, the UK, and France as front-runners. The downside of this solution is that without network capacity investments the video images degrade in quality if there are too many simultaneous users, since content needs to be streamed to each user in a point-to-point fashion. Therefore, streaming content over cellular is a costly option for serving a mass audience. The Multimedia Broadcast Multicast Service (MBMS) standard could circumvent this by offering a multicast and a broadcast mode for existing cellular networks, but its implementation time path is currently unclear.

An alternative is offered by new point-to-multipoint digital TV standards such as DVB-II, DAB-based standards, and Media-FLO. These are able to offer high quality live broadcast TV, allowing mass-market service delivery in a more scalable way and at more attractive operational costs (but still considerable capital expenditures). However, since the current uptake of mobile video content over 3G is quite slow, some operators have expressed doubts as to whether investments in these new network technologies are necessary and are counting on the fact that their 3G property will be sufficient for the coming years.

Other major technology choices faced by prospective European mobile TV operators include whether or not to combine any new mobile broadcasting technologies with uplink technologies such as *global system for mobile communications* (GSM) and UMTS in order to ensure more flexibility and interactivity in the service offering, and whether new mobile broadcast standards should "piggy-back" on top of existing networks—*digital video broadcasting-terrestrial* (DVB-T) and DAB networks, respectively, - or whether they should be built as stand-alone networks.

The technological outlook on mobile broadcasting will be sketched briefly in the second section of this chapter. However, we aim to demonstrate that the main design choices to be addressed are not only, even not predominantly, techno-economic in nature. It is our assertion that the cross-impact of strategic cooperation and competition issues (e.g., related to control over this new market by broadcasters, content aggregators, or cellular network operators), market expectations (e.g., related to speed of uptake, service offerings, degree of interactivity), and legacy situations (e.g., related to existing networks and customer relations) will to a large extent determine the outcome of mobile digital TV in Europe (see Shin, 2006 for a similar argument on digital multimedia broadcasting [DMB] development in Korea). A four-level design framework, along with a detailed enumeration of mobile TV design issues, is presented in the third section.

To test both technological maturity and marketability of the new service, many mobile broadcast test and experimentation platforms (TEPs)[1] in the form of field trials and market pilots have been started in Europe since 2004. Two multicasting standards are being trialled quite intensively in the European area, that is, DVB-H and DAB-IP/DMB. Their commercialisation is expected to start in earnest from 2007 on, with small-scale commercialisation already available in 2006 in a few countries..

We selected and analysed five of the largest and most documented pilots (four DVB-H pilots and one DAB-IP pilot) using publicly available info, telephone interviews, and e-mail interactions with key pilot participants. The fourth section contains the results of the case analysis in terms of the design choices made, how these were interlinked, and which cooperation schemes were devised. Where possible, the consequences of the design choices for the commercialisation phase are indicated. Finally, the final section offers some concluding remarks in terms of the models and strategies encountered in European mobile TV pilots.

TECHNOLOGY OUTLINE

The mobile broadcast landscape consists of three primarily non-proprietary standard families (Integrated Services Digital Broadcasting-Terrestrial [ISDB-T], DAB-based standards and DVB-H) developed by industry associations, and of the proprietary Media-FLO technology developed by Qualcomm. This section focuses on the DVB-H and DAB-based standards, as these are currently being piloted intensively throughout Europe. For a deeper analysis, see the rather extensive technological literature available on this subject (e.g., Curwen, 2006; Faria, Henriksson, Stare, & Talmola, 2006; Skiöld, 2006; Weck & Wilson, 2006).

The DVB-H Standard

DVB-H enjoys strong and organised support in Europe, as witnessed by the large amount of trials and pilots currently carried out, and by the forceful backing by European telecommunications giant Nokia, but it also has its supporters abroad. For instance, Intel Corporation, Modeo, Motorola, Nokia, and Texas Instruments created the Mobile DTV Alliance in January 2006 to promote the growth and evolution of DVB-H in the U.S.A.

As an extension of the DVB-T standard, DVB-H is relatively straightforward to implement, with several adjustments that make the standard more suitable for mobile communication. DVB-H uses significantly less bandwidth than DVB-T, approximately 300 kilobits versus 3 Megabytes per channel. Also, DVB-H saves on battery power by using the technique of time slicing, inserting the different video channels into the transmitted transport stream in bursts of data. The additional level of forward error correction (MPE-FEC) inserted in the DVB-H front end contributes to the robustness of the DVB-H signal.

DVB-H detractors regularly dispute the performance of DVB-H. They add that DVB-H channel switching is slow, unlikely to be able to deliver the stated data rates, and is susceptible to signal variations and problems with synchronisation. In fact, even DVB-H supporters acknowledge that the up to 6 seconds to switch channels is an issue, but claim that it is not insurmountable. DVB-H receiver manufacturers are confident they can drive down the channel switching to approximately 1.5 seconds as already achieved with DVB-T receivers.

Data on the amount of channels that DVB-H can carry as opposed to DAB-based standards varies. Currently, DVB-H seems to be able to offer considerably more channels, with between 10 and 20 channels per multiplex being offered in various trials, versus around 5 channels for DMB and DAB-IP.

DAB-IP, T-DMB, AND S-DMB

DAB-based standards include DAB-IP, terrestrial digital multimedia broadcasting (T-DMB), and S-DMB. DAB-IP can be described as a DMB I addition to DAB digital radio. More specifically, the network platform consists of DAB enhanced packet mode (EPM), in conjunction with an IP application. EPM was standardised by the WorldDAB Forum and enables video and other services—that are more sensitive to errors than the native audio services carried by DAB—to be carried.

DMB is an European Telecommunications Standards Institute (ETSI) standard developed in Europe that delivers mobile television services using the Eureka-147 DAB standard with additional error correction. Within the DMB sphere, a distinction is made between T-DMB and S-DMB. DAB-IP and T-DMB are both based on the DAB transport layer, contrary to S-DMB. T-DMB uses the terrestrial network in Band III and/or Band L while S-DMB uses the satellite network in Band L. To complicate matters, S-DMB is actually not directly related to the DAB standard, but was developed in Korea using the System E

International Telecommunication Union (ITU) standard based on code division multiple access (CDMA). S-DMB can deliver 13 video channels in a typical spectrum allocation.

T-DMB supporters argue that the scarcity of available spectrum will cripple the implementation and acceptance of DVB-H and MediaFLO, whereas T-DMB, due to its association with DAB, already has most of the required spectrum and infrastructure in place. T-DMB backers claim that it requires even less power than DVB-H or MediaFLO. Other reasons quoted by the T-DMB camp on why their standard is more suited than DVB-H for mobile digital TV are: lower channel switching time (around 1.5s), 30 frames per second (fps) versus just 15 fps on DVB-H (with traditional TV delivering between 25 and 30 fps), and the usage of 1.5 MHz channels requiring less power and circuit complexity (DVB-H uses 5 to 8 MHz channels).

However, as argued previously, DAB-based standards seem to be disadvantaged vis-à-vis DVB-H in terms of the number of channels per multiplex.

Principal Technical Components

In a complete mobile broadcast system (including an uplink for interactive applications), the following functional roles and their constituting technical components can be distinguished:

- **Business support system:** Back office system for billing and help desk support.
- **Content aggregation:** Entails the collection of content in a content management system
- **Broadcast service provisioning:** Provides frequency allocation, IP encapsulation, and multiplexing
- **Broadcast network operating:** Entails network transmission of the content.
  - Note that, although the technical literature often groups IP-encapsula-

Figure 1. General technical architecture of mobile broadcasting (based a.o. on Digitag, 2005 and Pieck, 2005)

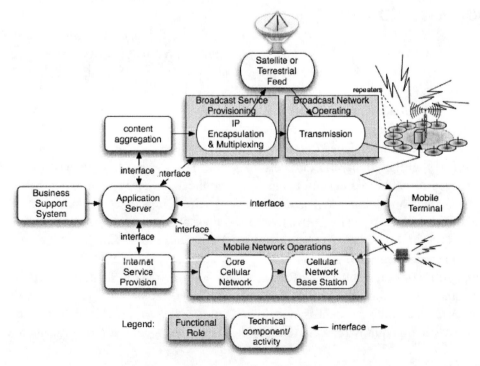

tion, multiplexing, and the ownership + management of the transmitters into one actor—the broadcast network operator (BNO)—we will distinguish these roles, because in the business models these roles may be performed by different actors (see later on).

○ Therefore, the functions performed *before* the transmission will be referred to as broadcast service provisioning. All functions connected with the transmission of the DVB-H signal will be referred to as broadcast network operating.

• **Mobile network operations:** Provide the return channel through its cellular network.

• **The application layer:** provides for communication between the broadcast content and the mobile network operator (MNO) return channel.

• **The mobile terminal:** Has to be equipped with the suitable receiver in order to access the (free, subscribed or pay-per view) content.

METHODOLOGY AND DESIGN ISSUES

As illustrated by the technical architecture, cooperation between various stakeholders is necessary in order to bring mobile broadcasting to the market. Even though there might be significant differences between the pilot and the commercialisation phase, it may be assumed that the cooperation models currently employed in pilots to a certain extent foreshadow the business models that will arise in the commercialisation phase (see also Dittrich & Van den Ende, 2006). In line with current thinking on strategic management and business model design (Ballon, 2007; Barney, 1991, 1997; Faber et al., 2003; Haaker, Bouwman, & Faber, 2004), our case analysis focuses on four business model design phases, which are equally relevant to the

cooperation models used in the different pilots. These phases can be defined as follows:

1. **Organisation design phase:** The organisation design involves defining a business scope (what customers will we try to reach and how), identifying distinctive competences, and making business governance decisions (make versus buy decisions).

2. **Technology design phase:** The technology design involved defining the technology scope (which technical design are we trying to develop and how), identifying the systemic competences that will contribute to the business strategies, and deciding on the IT governance (how will we develop or acquire the needed technical competences).

3. **Service design phase:** The service design involves choosing a specific value proposition towards the user, which implies choosing for a specific strategic scope.

4. **Financial design phase:** In a final phase, the financial modalities are formalised in binding contracts that clearly describe each partner's responsibilities, and the financial or other benefits they will receive in return.

Figure 2 illustrates how these design steps occur (chrono)logically, but cross-decisions are also possible, as illustrated by the horisontal and vertical arrows.

The framework presented previously emphasises organisation design as the starting point of any business modelling or cooperation modelling. This is especially relevant in cases such as mobile TV where convergence between various stakeholders and sectors increases the strategic importance of organisational design significantly. The focus of this chapter will be on cooperation models between stakeholders in the pilot phase of bringing mobile TV to the market. Therefore, a generic mobile TV value network model is constructed on which these models are subsequently mapped. They are described with the use

Figure 2. Business modeling cycle

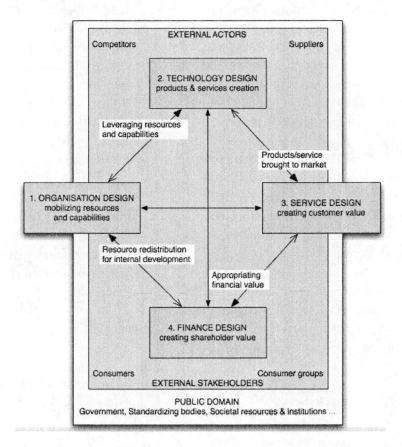

of three main building blocks: business actors, business roles, and business relationships (see also Ballon et al., 2005). *Business actors* can be physical persons or corporations that participate in the creation of economic value, through the mobilisation of tangible or intangible resources within a business value network. *Business roles* are logical groups of business processes that are fulfilled by one or more actors. Business actors provide value to or derive value from the business roles they play. Finally, *business relationships* are the contractual exchanges of products or services for financial payments or other resources.

Organisation Design

The organisation design dimension concerns the relationships that are adopted between cooperat-ing industrial partners to produce value for end customers. It entails which roles the partners take on, what resources each actor brings to the pilot and will bring during future commercialisation, and what kinds of cooperations arise during the delivery of specific mobile content services.

Figure 3 presents a generic value network for mobile digital TV delivery. The black arrows represent business relationships in the form of delivered services. The blue rectangles depict the different service deployment phases. The white rectangles are the business roles that actors can adopt. Each discrete role can be performed by a discrete actor, in which case the actor's name is inferred from the business role. Very often actors will perform more than one business role. Each configuration of roles, actors, and relationships constitutes a different cooperation model.

Absent from Figure 3—since this cannot be inferred from the mobile TV pilots—is the upwardly flow of revenues. Although the services flow more or less chronologically from the upper layers to the lower layers to the end users, the revenues may not. Most often, the infrastructure players receive their revenues in advance, that is, when the network operator purchases the networking gear. It is then up to the network operator to leverage this infrastructure into tempting service offerings towards the end users. To formulate this differently, one can say that there exists asynchronicity between the supply chain and the value chain. Because of the possible disconnect between a network operator's expenses and expected revenues, there are cases of vendor financing, where the infrastructure manufacturers supply credit lines to the network operators so they can foot the initial capex bill.

The following business roles were distinguished:

Service Development Phase

In this phase those business roles are situated that are necessary for the development and integration of the mobile digital content and of essential technical components such as the transmission infrastructure and the terminal devices.

- **Content development:** Development of the content that will be distributed. The distribution and branding of the content to the end user can be done directly by the content developer (which is rare) or via a content aggregator (which is common).
- **Content aggregation:** The acquisition, branding/marketing, and scheduling of the content that will be delivered to the broadcast service provider.
- **Network infrastructure development:** The designing and manufacturing of the network equipment, to be purchased and installed by the network operators (both mobile and broadcast network operators (BNOs).
- **Network infrastructure integration:** The installation of the network equipment acquired from network equipment manufacturing, at the request of the mobile and BNOs.
- **Application development:** The development of applications that will be used in the application layer.
- **Application integration:** The integration—when necessary—of application components into a platform or bundle.
- **Mobile device development:** The design and manufacturing of the end-user mobile devices with which the mobile content can be consumed.

Service Delivery Phase

In this phase the business roles are situated that transport and deliver the products and services to the end user, or prepare them to be sold through middlemen.

- **Broadcast service provision:** Preparation, encapsulation, encryption (with Digital Rights Management [DRM]), and multiplexing of the content so it can be delivered to the mobile devices via the BNO. An actor called the *datacast service operator* usually performs this role.
- **Broadcast network operation:** Operation (but not necessarily ownership) of the broadcast network. This can be combined with other networks. If a business actor, for example, already operates a DVB-T network, they could be a more logical party to operate the DVB-H network.
- **Mobile network operating:** The operation and management of the mobile cellular network. This business role will be relevant if mobile broadcasting is integrated with a mobile cellular network.

Figure 3. Generic mobile digital TV value network

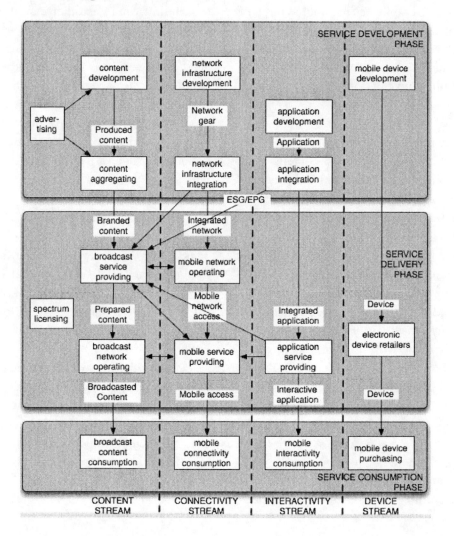

- **Mobile service providing:** This role constitutes a layer between the MNO and the end user. Most often, this role together with the role of mobile network operation is performed by a single actor, which we call an MNO. A *mobile virtual network operator* (MVNO) stands for a special case of a business actor that provides network services to customers without owning the physical network infrastructure, but does sell mobile services to end users.
- **Application service providing:** The daily management and ownership of the (interac-

tive) application service platform built by the application integrator.
- **Electronic device retailing:** The selling of handsets to end users. MNOs can also perform this role through the subsidisation or marketing of specific devices.

Service Consumption Phase

In this final phase the roles are situated that are related to consumption. Usually they are performed by a single actor (the end user), but they can also be unbundled, for example, in the case of a company buying a mobile device or mobile connectivity for its employees but not paying for the content or application consumption by the employees. One of the key questions is to what extent the different services will be combined into a single bill (and thus offered by a single customer owner). The roles are:

- **Broadcast content consumption:** The consumption of the broadcast content.
- **Mobile connectivity consumption:** The consumption of mobile connectivity services.
- **Interactivity consumption:** The return channel will usually but not necessarily run over a MNO's network. If broadcasters decide to sell mobile digital TV services to mobile TV-only devices, they could opt, for example, to use the fixed Internet as a (non-synchronised) return channel, instead of the mobile network.
- **Mobile device purchasing:** The act of purchasing the mobile device, be it a cellular plus DVB-H-enabled device or a stand-alone mobile TV terminal.

It should be noted that no single "service provider" role is included in Figure 3. Most business model literature assumes a unique service provider entity that ensures customer acquisition, billing, and customer care—in short, that possesses "customer ownership." However, in a potential unbundled market, it has to be envisaged that every provider, operator, retailer, or aggregator role can establish such a relationship with the end customer. Therefore, our design approach does not define customer ownership and the activities it entails as a specific role, but will rather treat it as an attribute that can be associated with several roles.

Technology Design

This section will describe the specific technology designs of each pilot, such as the network standard adopted for the pilot and what technological application choices were made. The following criteria were used to describe the technology design.

a. **Technical network architecture and device design:** This first criterion describes the network standard(s) that were adopted during the pilot, and that will possibly be adopted during commercialisation. For example, the pilot participants could choose to build a standalone DVB-H network or a hybrid network such as a DVB-H network

Table 2. Potential mobile TV services

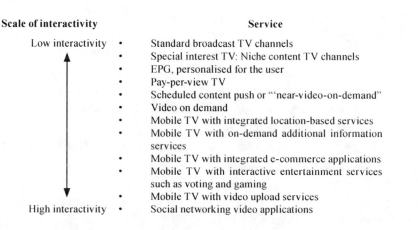

on top of a DVB-T network, and combinations of DVB-H or DAB-based standards with second generation (2G), 2.5G, or 3G networks as return channel. Also, the end user device used during the pilot is indicated.

b. **Interactivity:** This criterion refers to the kinds of interactive applications and functionalities that were developed during the pilot. This could include one button voting, voting via short message service (SMS), upload functionalities, or other forms of interactive applications.

c. **Content protection:** This entails the encryption or other security technology used, in order to protect the broadcasted content from being intercepted and/or re-used via other channels.

d. **Electronic service guide (ESG):** This criterion describes the technical standard chosen for the ESG. While the Electronic Program Guide (EPG) refers to the visual interface shown to the end user, the ESG is a structured document that contains information on all available services. With an ESG one can for instance describe whether a delivered service concerns a video game, home banking, or shopping.

Service Design

The service design dimension describes the specific characteristics of the developed end-user services, such as the degree of user interactivity allowed during the consumption of the services, and the different service bundles presented to the end user.

The potential services that can be delivered within a mobile digital TV value network to the end users can be situated along a continuum ranging from very low interactivity to high interactivity (see Table 2), which will influence the degree to which the mobile broadcast channel needs to cooperate with a mobile return channel.

Mobile phones have proven to be excellent conduits for interactivity using SMS. While SMS voting proves to be very popular while watching TV programs, the limitation of SMS lies in the simplicity of the interaction. For more sophisticated applications—such as allowing viewers to participate in game shows alongside the televised contestants—SMS is not convenient.

Local services can provide viewers with information on a city or region, such as weather forecasts, trailers of movies featured locally, and a teletext guide. With an interactive channel, viewers can request specific information. However, because a standard middleware interface is currently lacking, some further development is necessary before viewers will be able to trigger interactive services directly from the broadcast system.

As a rule, most TV content services listed previously will be delivered most efficiently over a mobile broadcast network. In contrast, interactive services will usually be delivered following a point-to-point distribution model over UMTS or, if the slower speeds are acceptable, over General Packet Radio Service (GPRS) or via SMS (Pilz, 2005). However, it is important to note that broadcast standards such as DVB-H can be used as stand-alone solutions for the delivery of low-interactivity services including near-video-on-demand.

Interactivity may be especially important when trying to reach the first adopter market segment. This segment is generally acquainted with on-demand content consumption such as personal video recorders (PVR), cable TV video-on-demand services, and the Internet and might consider a pure broadcast offering as a step back towards scheduled programming, with fixed viewing times of each show. Pre-downloaded content, which can be consumed when the end user has time to "snack" content, might prove to be at least equally popular. Nokia actually has a service called "Nokia Media Charger," that allows for push delivery of rich content.

The following criteria were used to describe the ways in which the service package was presented to the end users.

a. **User involvement:** This refers to the degree of interactivity experienced by users. User involvement can vary from low (no end-user involvement/interaction) to middle (user can give input, e.g., vote), to high (user can generate and post his/her own content). The degree of user involvement depends on the network characteristics, the chosen return channel, and the implementation of interactive technologies from the technology design.

b. **Product bundles:** This criterion describes the kind of product bundle that is offered to the end user. This can be a *package* (user takes a subscription on a collection of channels and does not have the authority to add or delete channels), *modules* (user can take a subscription on individual channels or theme packages), *individual views* (user can chose individual shows), or *hybrid* (mixes of the aforementioned bundles). Other product bundles that are possible are bundles with existing TV channels, bundles including new channels for specific mobile content, bundles with digital radio, bundles with interactive services, and so on.

Finance Design

Finally, the financial design criteria in this context relate to the costs of the network build-out, the revenue sharing agreements, and the business-to-consumer billing formulas.

Figure 4. Helsinki pilot cooperation model

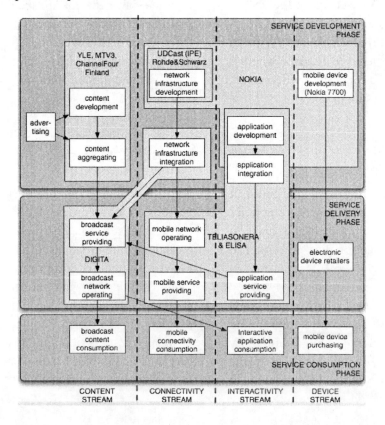

In most pilots, no revenues were generated, and no revenue-sharing agreements were negotiated. However, during the interviews some executives provided information on how these financial matters might be resolved during commercialisation, and this information is included in the pilots' descriptions.

The following criteria were used to describe the financial design decisions:

a. **Cost sharing agreements:** This first financial criterion describes how different actors carry the costs of the service roll-out. Three cost categories are taken into account. First, the **device cost** refers to the primary purchase cost of the handsets and to what degree the consumer has to pay the entire cost of the handset, or whether device subsidies are al-

lowed. Second, the **network infrastructure costs** refer to the cost of building the transmission infrastructure. Third, the **content and application costs** refer to which partner carries what part of the content and/or application development cost. Besides the traditional approach, where content is aggregated by a traditional broadcaster, and applications are developed by or on behalf of a MNO, these efforts (and subsequent costs) could also be borne by other actors. For instance, a MNO could develop mobile TV content by purchasing and aggregating programs under his own brand, or even by building or acquiring a TV station of one's own.

b. **End-user billing:** This criterion describes the ways in which the user pays for the services provided. The billing formula will

Figure 5. Berlin pilot cooperation model

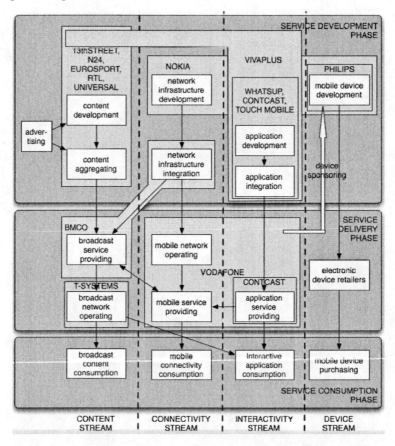

depend on the kinds of product bundles offered, but does not follow directly from that criterion. For example, being able to select individual shows does not necessarily imply pay-per-view pricing. Three basic end-user billing models can be distinguished: subscription based, pay-per-use, and free-to-air with advertisements. Between these three pure forms of revenue generation, any number of hybrid combinations can also arise.

c. **Revenue-sharing agreements.** The last criterion describes the ways in which the service supplier(s) agree on how the revenues generated through end-user billing are distributed throughout the value network, including the broadcasters, other content providers, and the MNOs.

CASE STUDY ANALYSIS

This section systematically compares a selection of European pilots using the framework defined previously. Five of the largest and most documented pilots (four DVB-H pilots and one DAB-IP pilot) were selected, that is, in Helsinki, Berlin, Paris, Oxford, and London. They were analysed using publicly available info, telephone interviews, and e-mail interactions with key pilot participants.[2] First, the organisational design of each pilot is addressed, highlighting the respective cooperation model. Next, the technical, service and financial design repercussions of these models are outlined.

Figure 6. Paris pilot cooperation model

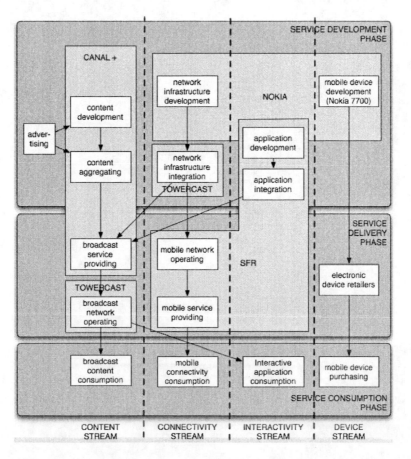

Organisation Design

In this section the organisational cooperation that arose between the different pilot partners during the pilots is illustrated. Each figure is accompanied by a list of the roles performed by the business actor involved. When information could be obtained about the business roles and value networks during the future phase of commercialisation, the text expands on this issue. The information presented here is based on interviews with executives and publicly available pilot presentations.

Figure 4 illustrates the cooperation model adopted during the Helsinki trial. Note that the visual overlapping of one business actor by another, such as Nokia encapsulating UDCast and

Rohde & Schwartz in Figure 4 does not imply that UDCast is a department of Nokia, but that different actors mutually performed different segments of the business role of "network infrastructure development" in the example below.

In Finland the MNOs Teliasonera and Elisa retained customer ownership during the pilot by offering the TV content service to the end users and offering help desk support. Nokia used the pilot to focus on the further development of its mobile service platform (later branded as Mobile Broadcast Solution or MBS 3.0). Digita (a unit of the French media group TDF) is the builder and owner of the DVB-T network in Finland. It used the pilot to learn about the pitfalls of rolling out a DVB-H transmission network. This practical

Figure 7. Oxford pilot cooperation model

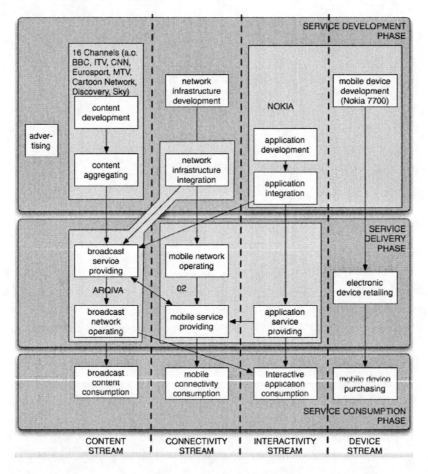

Figure 8. BT Movio London pilot cooperation model

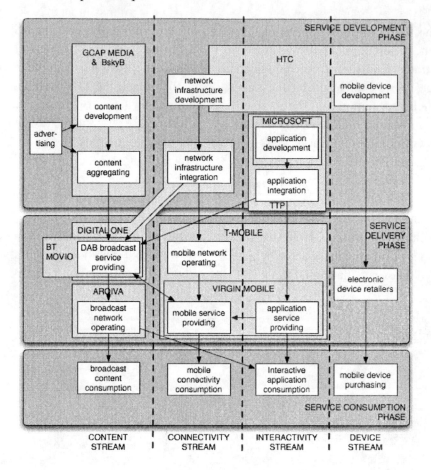

experience proved fruitful when in March 2006 Digita won the Finnish DVB-H license beating Elisa, TeliaSonera, and Telemast Nordic. In May 2006 Digita announced that it had signed a contract with Nokia to use its DVB-H platform for the service. By the end of this year, Digita plans to reach 30% of the population by providing coverage in the Helsinki region as well as the cities of Turku, Tampere, and Oulu. Digita will hold the license for a period of 20 years.

During commercialisation, it is foreseen that Digita will adopt two business roles: broadcast service providing and broadcast network operating. Digita will be solely responsible for the

management of the DVB-H digital multiplex and the transmission network, but will not offer mobile TV services directly to any end customers. The license includes a condition under which the license holder is obliged to sell network capacity to service operators. Digita will as BNO utilise an open network model for the DVB-H network, by offering access to the broadcast network to all service providers under equal, fair, and transparent terms. The role of *network infrastructure integration*, performed alone by Digita during the pilot given the lower complexity of the pilot context, will during commercialisation be jointly performed by the MNOs and Digita.

The basic cooperation model in the pilot, where Digita functioned as a common broadcast service provider for competing mobile operators, will nevertheless be replicated in the commercialisation phase, in which Digita will provide open access to its DVB-H platform to various service providers. Also, while functional roles related to broadcasting will remain in the hands of Digita, and will not be taken up by mobile operators, these mobile operators (and possibly other service providers) will most probably leverage their existing customer base to act as integrated service providers towards the customer (see also the sections on service and financial design). Figure 5 illustrates the cooperation model adopted during the Berlin trial. The role of broadcast network operator was taken by T-Systems, being already the DVB-T network operator in Berlin. During the pilot phase, half of a T-Systems DVB-T multiplex was used for DVB-H transmission, while the other half continued to provide commercial DVB-T programmes without any problems. This did cause the number of available TV programs to be restricted to four channels. BMCO provided network infrastructure integration and broadcast service provisioning. GPRS was used as the return channel (Sattler, 2005). Vodafone retained customer ownership and partially outsourced application service provision to Contcast. The development of the Berlin City Guide, ring tones downloading, and Get the Clip applications entailed cooperation between content aggregators and application developers.

During the commercialisation phase, it is expected that MNOs such as Vodafone will apply for a license to broadcast DVB-H. They will need to cooperate with an actor that has a media license, which is the local government's responsibility. While in Germany the spectrum license is handed out by the Bundesnetzagentur on a national level, the media licenses have to be applied for locally, namely each of the 15 regulators of the 16 federal states.

Already in the cooperation model used during the trial, and different from the Finnish model, there is a split between the BNO (T-Systems, the current DVB-T network owner) and the broadcast service provider (a consortium including Vodafone), which can be explained by the fact that two competing network operators are involved as network owner and network user, respectively. Figure 6 illustrates the cooperation model adopted during the Paris trial.

Until now, four multicasting pilots have been conducted in France, of which one was based on the DAB-IP standard, and three others based on the DVB-H standard. While the pilot under review here combined Towercast, Nokia, SFR, and Canal+Group, the other pilots used Sagem phones (instead of Nokia), and had TDF as BNO (instead of Towercast). The other pilots also involved more MNO partners (Orange, SFR, and Bouygues Telecom), and more content aggregators (TF1, TPS France Television, Radio France, and RTL, among others).

During the pilot described here, a DVB-H only pilot network was built and operated solely by Towercast. Also during the pilot, Nokia worked together with SFR for the development of the service platform. Canal+Group retained customer ownership.

During commercialisation, the DVB-H network is not expected to be built by the MNOs, but by TDF or Towercast, who are currently involved in constructing a DVB-T network. In France, no DVB-T operating licenses have been issued yet. Before analogue switch-off only one multiplex per French region is expected to be in place. In the commercialisation phase, it is expected that Canal+Group will come to market with an offering that will also target devices that only have mobile TV functionalities, without an integrated mobile phone. According to the interviewed executives, MNOs that come to market with a DVB-H brand will always choose a service that targets DVB-H + mobile phone terminal devices and will not introduce a second line of terminal devices that do not have integrated mobile telephony.

Again, it is interesting to see that the co-operation model in the pilot, in which broadcaster Canal+Group took an important role and combined the roles of content aggregation and broadcast service providing, will be mirrored in the commercialisation phase, in the sense that the broadcaster will probably come up with specific offers towards end customers, and thus will be competing with MNOs for the mobile TV market. Figure 7 illustrates the cooperation model adopted during the Oxford trial.

A DVB-H-only pilot network was built by Arqiva, while O2's network bandwidth was used as mobile telephony channel. Arqiva is also the company developing and implementing the digital terrestrial network for BBC, one of the digital terrestrial license holders in the UK.

During the pilot, all actors involved focused on their core competence. Nokia delivered the service platform software to Arqiva and mobile terminals to O2. The content suppliers provided content for the DVB-H broadcast, but did not interfere with the broadcast service provisioning side. The MNO O2 focused on mobile network operating, application service provisioning, and mobile service provisioning. The BNO Arqiva did have a more expanded role when compared to the Berlin or Paris pilot, in that it simultaneously performs the roles of broadcast provisioning and network operating. In the next pilot, Arqiva is restricted to broadcast network operation.

The Oxford pilot cooperation model is similar to the Helsinki pilot, in the sense that Arqiva provided and operated the platform on which an MNO offered its services. The difference with the Helsinki trial is that no competing MNOs were involved in the Oxford pilot. There is little information on the commercialisation trajectory envisaged, but it may be expected that the MNO will want to retain full customer ownership. Figure 8 illustrates the cooperation model adopted during the London DAB-IP trial.

During the pilot, BT Movio, which leases 20% (later 30%) of the spectrum capacity on Digital One's DAB network, led the network build-out effort and acted as middleman between the content aggregators and the MNOs. The radio and TV content were delivered over the DAB-IP transmission network built by Arqiva, while T-Mobile's network was used as the return channel for additional interactivity and mobile telephony. T-Mobile offered Virgin Mobile, mobile network access, allowing Virgin Mobile to adopt the role of MVNO.

During commercialisation, BT Movio will probably act as a middleman between the owner of the broadcast network (which will be GCap Media, see next section on financial design) and the content aggregators, by offering a bundled wholesale package of broadcast access plus bundled content to the MNOs.

The pilot cooperation model already demonstrated the BT Movio wholesale model by leasing capacity from existing DAB network owner and granting access to MNOs and MVNOs under specific terms, as will be continued in the commercialisation phase.

Technology Design

The first technology design choices to be made concern the end-user devices and the network standards adopted during the pilots.

Three out of four of the DVB-H pilots built a DVB-H only pilot network, while in Berlin the network was built on top of DVB-T, which had an effect on the amount of TV content channels that could be used in Berlin. The Nokia 7710 was the dominant device during the four DVB-H pilots. Only the Berlin pilot also conducted tests with another device, the Philips HoTMAN2. The London pilot used a smart phone developed jointly by BT, TTP, and HTC, and adopted the DAB-IP network standard.

Most users considered the Nokia 7710 as too big and unpractical. The Nokia N92 that is now

---

arriving in the market is user friendlier, according to interviewed executives.

In most cases it is currently unknown what specific network technology choices will be made for the commercialisation phase. For instance, most pilots opted for DVB-H stand-alone configurations and many interviewees stressed the need for as many channels to be available as possible. On the other hand, the fact that in most cases DVB-T or DAB network owners were actively involved in the pilots seems to suggest that the mobile broadcast networks will be combined as much as possible with existing infrastructure.

Another design decision is whether the interactive applications that were developed during the pilots will have a direct effect on the degree of end-user interactivity in the service design (see section 5.2). Limited, "red button" interactivity was present in most pilots. The Paris pilot, in which broadcaster Canal+Group was the main actor, stands out as the only pilot where no extended forms of interactivity were developed, and where the focus remained primarily on downstream content delivery. The partners involved in the Berlin pilot developed the most interactive applications, that is, one-button voting for music videos, push of cinema trailers (users could then book cinema tickets directly through an interactive application), and the download of ring tones (a list of ring tones corresponding to currently played songs was broadcasted. Ring tones could be downloaded via the cellular network).

Concerning content protection, Berlin and Oxford did not implement content protection, considering the pilot context a controlled situation. While Helsinki adopted Nokia's content protection solution, Paris opted for the alternative conditional access through a SIM-card solution. Within the DAB-IP pilot, the industry participants opted for Windows Digital Rights Management solution. Interviewees stated that the choice of standards to be adopted during the commercialisation phase is an issue that will have to be cleared with the content owners beforehand. All observers agree

that the choice of DRM is highly strategic and closely connected to the organisational design. If there is no lock-in by a SIM card, this might prove more interesting for actors who do not have a vested interest in mobile networks. Operators that do not have investments in a mobile network will not opt for a SIM-based solution, since this ties the customer to a MNO. Technical arguments can be given on why the SIM-based solution is still suitable in an age of convergence. SIM is a proven solution that provides a high level of security and reliability. But with the advent of converged services, using one service to tie the customer to a series of other services is experiencing pressures from non-MNO players.

Concerning the ESG, within the DVB-H field there are two camps with regard to the ESG standards (Yoshida, 2006). Nokia implemented its own version of the Open Mobile Alliance's OMA-BCAST specification on its DVB-H handsets, in a move against proponents of digital video broadcast-convergence of broadcast and mobile services (DVM-CBMS). Because of this rift, the two camps are promoting different ESGs. The Finnish and German Pilot adopted Nokia's non-standardised ESG, while in Paris the competing solution was chosen. Interviewed executives, even from pilots where the Nokia ESG was used, expressed doubts whether the Nokia non-standardised solution will be broadly adopted. In the DAB-IP pilot BT Movio developed a proprietary ESG.

Service Design

Given the aforementioned organisational and technological design decisions, the business actors then proceeded to offer the test users access to a variety of service packages. The service bundles that were offered mostly consisted of TV content, but in some cases content was enriched with interactive applications.

The Helsinki pilot ran from March until July 2005. Five hundred test users received a basic package, which consisted of seven "free to air" television channels and three radio stations. In addition to the basic package users could subscribe to a supplementary package of seven premium service television channels. For some special events, like the Formula 1 Grand Prix in San Marino and Monaco, users had the possibility to buy one day's access in a pay-per-view model for $.50 a day.

The Berlin pilot started in July 2004 and took 8 weeks, during which the 20 test users had access to four television channels, one interactive channel and an interactive city guide of Berlin. The four television channels, with exception of the news channel, concentrated on the entertainment potential of mobile television.

In Paris, the pilot was conducted from September 2005 until June 2006, with 250 users. Access was provided to 10 television channels, four radio stations, and one channel that offered short programs to watch on mobile television (SFR TV). The user had also the possibility to subscribe individually to three additional channels or to choose the entire package of the three channels (Canal+, Sport+, and CineCinema Premier). Furthermore the user could watch additional content through a pay-per-view model.

In the Oxford pilot, which started in June 2005 and ran for 6 months, 400 users were offered 16 television channels among which 12 free-to-air channels, three pay-TV channels and one made-for-mobile channel: ShortsTV, a channel which offers short programmes developed for mobile television.

In the London pilot, BT Movio and Virgin Mobile let 1,000 users test their mobile digital TV service in the region of London, inside the M25 highway area. The users of this pilot were able to access three television channels and 52 radio stations.

It was already discussed shortly whether forms of interactivity were offered to the end user. Usage of an EPG is considered as the most basic form of interactivity. Additional types of interactivity were found in Berlin, Oxford and London.

In the Finnish pilot the focus was on TV content delivery, and interactivity was limited to the use of the EPG and some on-demand downloads (Sandell, 2005). In Berlin users were able to consult movie trailers and book cinema tickets for Berlin movie theatres through the What's Up application. The Vivaplus application was an interactive music channel where users could vote for music clips. Finally, users could download ring tones that were delivered over the cellular network. In Paris, besides the interactions with the EPG some on-demand downloads were possible. In Oxford users were able to record short content to their mobile device. In the London trial, the degree of interactivity was not very high. Although the user could use the red button functionality, a proportion of them were afraid to use it because of lack of good communication towards the user, concerning the price of each interaction.

The section on financial design will detail the customer ownership models in the pilots. It can already be stated here that most interviewees agreed that cooperation between business actors on the service design level is necessary in order to offer the consumer an integrated package.[3] It would be too confusing for consumers if they have to buy access from a separate firm, and their content from another firm. The consumer will expect that the purchase of network access will come together with a reasonable amount of basic content. Therefore, the MNOs (supposing most do retain full customer ownership) will have to negotiate content deals in order to be able to offer attractive packages.

The youth market (ages 18-35) is considered as the most important market segment for mobile TV (Page, Watt, & Menon, 2005), so it is expected that content aggregators geared towards the youngest demographic segment such as music TV stations, will have important bargaining power as part of entering the bouquet. Jason Hirschhorn, MTV's chief digital officer, has stated that MTV would enter into discussions with operators over an advertising-based business model (Best, 2006).

While the chances are slim that telecom operators will massively start developing or commissioning the development of content on their own, it is very probable that the content aggregators will also develop interactive applications or services alongside their TV content. But as a rule it is foreseen that existing content aggregators will provide most of the video content, while MNOs will mainly develop the interactive services. Therefore, cooperations between the MNOs and the broadcast service platform will have to be guaranteed for interactive applications that can run over DVB-H.

Concerning time-shifting services, design choices between near-video on demand (near-VOD), VOD, and PVR have to be made. MNOs appear to favour VOD most, since this offers an opportunity to utilise their 3G property. Near-VOD, where content is downloaded at an earlier point in time (e.g., overnight) ranks second, but PVR creates tensions with the content aggregators. In reality, it is feasible that a hybrid solution will be implemented to circumvent the content industry's doubts about copyright protection. In this solution, content can be downloaded at an earlier time, but a one-time activation over a mobile network is then necessary to unlock the downloaded content. Content providers do not prefer lock-in by a SIM-based solution, since this hampers the amount of platforms they can offer their content on. Ideally, only one encryption scheme is used across several platforms.

Financial Design

In this final section, the financial design decisions taken during the pilots and the possible repercussions on the commercial financial design are described. Three design criteria are considered: (1) the sharing of the infrastructural cost, (2) the pricing of the product bundle offered to the end users, and (3) the revenue sharing arrangements (if any) among the different partners involved. It needs to be noted that during the pilots little to no revenues were generated, except in the Helsinki pilot and the London DAB-IP pilot. Therefore both revenue and cost-sharing agreements were rare to nonexistent during the pilots. Contacts with executives from the different pilots did however offer some insight into the financial arrangements that could arise during commercialisation. If not mentioned otherwise, the pilot costs incurred were carried by each individual pilot participant individually.

Concerning who will bear the cost of network roll-out during commercialisation, the discussions are still ongoing within most pilot consortia. In most countries there seems to be a movement away from cooperative models that were considered in a number of pilots, where various partners jointly funded the DVB-H roll-out, towards a wholesale model, where a single entity deploys and funds the roll-out of the network, and then gets the right to resell it. Some variation can arise on who will be able to resell access to the platform to interested parties. The wholesalers are not necessarily the actors with existing DVB-T or DAB networks (see BT Movio). In Germany, where T-Systems is currently building out the DVB-T network, the situation is still unclear on who will apply for the service licenses, and who will fulfil the role of reseller.

Only during the Finnish, French, and the London BT Movio pilot the end users were billed (and only some in the French case). No specific total amounts were made publicly available of the revenues collected, though. The pricing plans of the partners does show that all the MNOs are planning on retaining customer ownership. Only in France Canal+Group is counteracting this logic by also planning to include a mobile digital TV subscription in its pay-TV bundle. It is expected that some pay-TV business actors in other European countries (e.g., Sky in the UK) will follow this example.

Concerning customer ownership, most MNOs are aiming to leverage their intimate customer relations during the DVB-H roll-out. But in each country any actor that has a customer base such as pay-TV broadcasters (France) or MVNOs (UK) may wish to be able to extend their service offering towards their customers.

Given the informal character of the pilots, no revenue-sharing arrangements were negotiated. Interviewed executives did express numerous hypotheses on what they thought would probably happen during the commercialisation phase. However, it was clearly expressed that the revenue split would be primarily between the end user service provider ("the customer owner") and the broadcast service provider ("the spectrum owner"). Although only a limited amount of data were available on the financial design from the pilots and the subsequent commercial roll-outs. However, at least some information could be obtained on the commercialisation phase. It appears that the license holder (or the party that leases spectrum from the license holder) on the one hand, and the customer owner (the actor that sells the subscription/service to the end customers) on other hand will divide the lion's share of revenues between them. Some anxiety among the content aggregators that occupy neither of these roles about revenue-sharing agreements that might be suboptimal for them was already reported in a few pilots.

CONCLUSION

This chapter aimed to provide a detailed and systematic analysis of the issues for bringing mobile broadcasting to market, and of the solutions found in five major pilots throughout Europe. We focused on organisation design, and in particular on the cooperation models employed by various stakeholders during the pilot phase.

Various cooperation models were found, specifically regarding the roles of broadcast service provider and BNO. It became clear that pilot cooperation models in this sense already foreshadow envisaged business models in commercialisation

phase. However, some significant differences were found and reported in this chapter, particularly regarding the (types of) actors assuming the new and important role of broadcast service provider, and on the (types of) actors assuming customer ownership.

In Helsinki and Oxford, the role of BNO and the role of broadcast service provisioning were performed by one actor. In the other cases different actors performed these two roles. This split of responsibilities is expected to persist in many cases during commercialisation, with BNOs, content aggregators, MNOs, and intermediaries all taking an interest in broadcast service provisioning and/or spectrum ownership.

The business responsibility of customer ownership includes customer acquisition, end-user billing (including handling bad debt), and customer care (help desk support). The BNOs did not retain customer ownership in any pilot, nor did the broadcast service providers or the content aggregators (such as broadcasters), except in France where a content aggregator (pay-TV channel owner Canal+Group) retained customer ownership alongside one MNO (SFR). This scenario is expected to repeat itself during French commercialisation.

Concerning technical design, a majority of European pilots has chosen the DVB-H standard, although a sizeable minority opts for DAB-IP/DMB. It is not entirely clear to what extent the new mobile technologies will be tied in with the existing DVB-T and DAB networks, but given the cost advantages and the involvement of current DVB-T and DAB network owners, coupling, at least to a certain degree, seems probable in most countries. It also became clear that organisational arrangements (e.g., whether MNOs or broadcasters respectively took the lead in the project) affected technical design decisions such as the selected standard for the ESG, or the degree of interactive applications.

In terms of service design, the pilots experimented with a wide variety of product bundles, subscription and pay-per-view schemes, and usually—but not necessarily—including some forms of interactivity. The combination of basic packages with premium packages was widespread throughout the pilots.

Regarding network roll-out, there seems to be a move away from the cooperative models (i.e., various partners jointly funding the roll-out) that were at one time considered in various pilots, towards a wholesale model, where a single entity deploys and funds the entire roll-out and then resells access to various service providers. These wholesalers are often actors currently owning or building out DVB-T or DAB networks, although not necessarily so, as the BT Movio example demonstrates. In Germany, where telco T-Systems is currently building out the DVB-T network, the situation is still unclear. In most cases, the MNOs seem to limit their involvement in the infrastructural effort to opening their network for the placement of repeaters necessary for full coverage.

Most of the MNOs aimed to leverage their current customer base into the mobile broadcasting arena. But other types of actors with an established customer base such as pay-TV broadcasters (France) or MVNOs (UK) also showed interest in acquiring access to the platform, or acquiring a service license, in order to offer mobile TV services directly to customers themselves.

Finally, from the information available, it appears that the spectrum owner (i.e., the license holder or the actor that leases spectrum from the license holder) on the one hand, and the customer owner (the actor that sells and guarantees the service to the end customer) on the other hand will divide the lion's share of revenues among them. Several content aggregators that neither own spectrum nor have direct customer ownership have expressed fears that revenue share agreements may turn out to be suboptimal for them. The evidence gathered here suggests that these fears may well materialise.

ACKNOWLEDGMENT

This article is based on results from the MADUF project (IBBT project 0052), which is funded by the IBBT (Interdisciplinary Institute for BroadBand Technology) of Flanders, Belgium, as well as by various partner companies. The authors gratefully acknowledge their interview partners for the information provided on various mobile TV pilots, as well as Dr. Jo Pierson, Katrien Dreessen (both IBBT-SMIT), and the other MADUF partners involved for their insightful comments and suggestions.

REFERENCES

Ballon, P. (2007, August). Business modelling revisited: The configuration of control and value. *The Journal of Policy, Regulation and Strategy for Telecommunications, Information and Media.*

Ballon, P., Pierson, J., & Delaere, S. (2005, September 4-6). *Open innovation platforms for broadband services: Benchmarking European practices.* Paper presented at ITS (International Telecommunications Society) 16th European Regional Conference, Porto, Portugal.

Ballon, P., Pierson, J., & Delaere, S. (2007) Fostering Innovation in Networked Communications: Test and Experimentation Platforms for Broadband Systems. In S. Heilesen & S. S. Jensen (Eds.) *Designing for Networked Communications: Strategies and Development.* Hershey: Idea Group Publishing, pp. 137-167.

Barney, J. B. (1991). Firm resources and sustained competitive advantage. *Journal of Management, 17*(1), 99-120.

Barney, J. B. (1997). *Gaining and sustaining competitive advantage.* Reading, MA: Addison-Wesley.

Best, J. (2006, February 16). Is free the way forward for mobile TV? *Silicon.com*. Retrieved from http://networks.silicon.com/mobile/0,39024665,39156508,00.htm

Braet, O., Ballon, P., & Dreessen, K. (2006). *Cooperation models for DVB-H rollout*. Final Report for IBBT-project MADUF ("Maximize DVB-H Usage in Flanders").

Curwen, P. (2006). Mobile television. *Communications & Strategies, 62,* 183-195.

Digitag (2005) *Television on a handheld receiver: Broadcasting with DVB-H*. Geneva: DigitAG :The Digital Terrestrial Television Action Group.

Dittrich, K., & Van den Ende, J. (2006, June 18-20). *Organizational forms for the development of new broadband services: A dynamic model for the degree of integration between collaborating firms*. Paper presented at the DRUID Summer Conference 2006, Copenhagen, Denmark.

Faber, E., Ballon, P., Bouwman, H., Haaker, T., Rietkerk, O., & Steen, M. (2003, June 9-11). *Designing business models for mobile ICT services*. Positioning paper for workshop on concepts, metrics & visualization. In *Proceedings of the Bled E-commerce conference,* Bled, Slovenia.

Faria, G., Henriksson, J., Stare, E., & Talmola, P. (2006). DVB-H: Digital broadcast services to handheld devices. *Proceedings of the IEEE, 94*(1), 194-209.

Haaker, T., Bouwman, H., & Faber, E. (2004). Customer and network value of mobile services: Balancing requirements and strategic interests. In R. Agarwal, L. Kirsch, & J. I. DeGross (Eds.), *Proceedings of the 25th international conference on Information systems (ICIS 2004)* (pp. 1-14).

Kivirinta, T., Ali-Vehmas, T., Mutanen, T., Tuominen, T., & Vuorinen, M. (2004). *Forecasting market demand for mobile broadcast services in Finland* (Rep. No. 51530C). Finland: Helsinki University of Technology.

Page, M., Watt, M., & Menon, N. (2005). *Mobinet 2005—Raising the stakes*. Retrieved from http://www.atkearney.com/main.taf?p=5,3,1,121,1

Pieck, R. (2005, September 14). *DVB-H broadcast to mobile devices*. Retrieved from http://www.newtec.be/fileadmin/webfolder/whitepaper/DVB-H_White_Paper.pdf

Pilz, K. (2005). *TV goes mobile with DVB-H—Swisscom's approach developing a market entry scenario with DVB-H based products*. Retrieved from http://www.ipdc-forum.org/resources/documents/6-Swisscom.pdf

Sandell, L. (2005). *FinnishMobileTV: Analysis on logfile data, April-June2005*. Retrieved from www.mobiletv.nokia.com/download_counter.php?file=/pilots/finland/files/Finnpanel_press_all_channels.pdf

Sattler, C. (2005, November 8). *BMCO newsletter*. Retrieved from http://www.bmco-forum.org/

Shin, D. H. (2006). Prospectus of mobile TV: Another bubble or killer application? *Telematics and Informatics, 23,* 253-270.

Skiöld, D. (2006). An economic analysis of DAB and DVB-H. *EBU Technical Review*. Retrieved from http://www.ebu.ch/en/technical/trev/trev_305-skiold.pdf

Södergard, C. (Ed.). (2003). *Mobile television: Technology and user experiences: Report on the Mobile TV project* (VTT publications 506).

Weck, C., & Wilson, E. (2006, January). Broadcasting to handhelds: An overview of systems and services. *EBU Technological Review*. Retrieved from http://www.ebu.ch/en/technical/trev/trev_305-wilson.pdf

Yoshida, J. (2006, March 2). Protocol spat threatens to fragment DVB-H market. *EE Times*. Retrieved from http://www.eetimes.com/news/latest/business/showArticle.jhtml?articleID=181500546

ENDNOTES

[1] For a conceptualization and overview of European TEPs, see Ballon, Pierson, and Delaere (2007).

[2] Detailed references are in the original research report Braet, Ballon, and Dreessen (2006).

[3] It was not within the scope of this chapter to assess the way the new service was experienced by the end users. Most pilots reported favourably on the way their service was received by the end users. Nevertheless, some critical results can be quoted. Users were not happy with some of the first generation devices such as the Nokia 7710, which were considered too heavy and clumsy. Also, users complained when there were not enough channels available, a result recorded during BT Movio's DAB-IP pilot (three TV channels) and the German pilot (four TV channels). Finally, the BT Movio pilot proved that users were reluctant to use interactive applications if the pricing model was unclear.

Chapter X
Mobile Business Process Reengineering:
How to Measure the Input of Mobile Applications to Business Processes in European Hospitals

Dieter Hertweck
University for Applied Sciences Heilbronn, Germany

Asarnusch Rashid
Research Center for Information Technology Karlsruhe, Germany

ABSTRACT

There is an ongoing debate about the value of mobile applications for the optimization of business processes in European hospitals. Thus finding satisfying methods to measure the profitability of mobile applications seems to be of great importance. Prior research had its focus mainly on general value dimensions concerning the medical sector or the usability and design aspects of hospital information systems. Conterminous to that, the authors chose a strictly process-oriented approach. They modeled the requirements of future mobile systems as an output of a profitability analysis based on activity-based costing. The cost savings defined as the difference between former and future business processes were used as an incoming payment for an ROI analysis. In a nutshell, the authors present a case study that highlights the value of their analyzing method as well as the enormous benefit of mobile applications in the area of food and medical supply processes in German hospitals.

INTRODUCTION: INCREASED DEMAND FOR EFFICIENT PROCESSES IN HEALTH CARE

Apart from the long-term decline of the population, a great challenge in the contemporary discussion turns out to be the increasing aging of the population in European industrial societies. This raises various difficulties for our welfare systems and reveals the necessity of long-term adjustment to this development. Aging describes the process of composition of the population shifting for the benefit of elderly people.

Thus, the decisive item is not the increasing number of the elderly but rather their increasing proportion of the population. For example as latest simulations for the development of the German population (Statistisches Bundesamt, 2003) reveal, the proportion of 65-year-old and older people will rise from 17.1 % today to 29.6 % in 2050. At the same time the percentage of geriatric people (80 years and older) will increase to 12 % which means a triplication.

This development causes serious problems in welfare and tax systems that are based on the income of a workforce. Less young people have to pay the pensions and health care of the elderly.

Furthermore, the productivity of our highly automated industry leaves an increasing number of people unemployed. So the real challenges of over aged European industrial societies will be to enhance the productivity of the existing education and health care systems.

And as productivity is defined as the relationship between output and input factors, there was an intensive discussion going on during the last 2 years about the input factor dimension. Even though the German health care system was able to perform quite well the last decades, from an input point of view the costs and resources to maintain the system were increasing dramatically (see Figure 1).

This development is not typical for the German health care system only; you will find similar developments in all Organsiation for Economic Co-operation and Development (OECD) countries around the world as published at the OECD fact book (OECD, 2006).

One major initiative to stop this cost explosion was the release of a law for financing the clinical sector in 2002. According to this law, a hospital does not get paid for the duration a patient is being treated, but for the respective type of disease. The treatment of every illness is linked to a fixed price—documented in the Diagnosis Related Group (DRG)—the hospital is then paid by the health insurance companies. This system results

Figure 1. Expenses of the German health care system

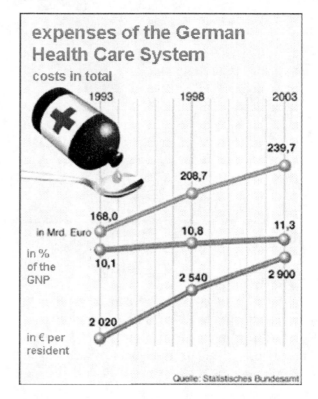

in the effect that a hospital can only earn good money by improving the business processes in the treatment of the patient, without loosing quality. Since this time on, a big competition between hospitals and different clinical departments to enhance there business process productivity has taken place. Best practices achieving business processes improvements are defined as clinical pathways.

As a parallel to other new deregulation decisions invented by the government, new types of market players like, for example, the Rhön Clinical enterprise emerged. They act as business redeveloper, buying unproductive hospitals and now, by standardizing and optimizing their processes in relation to given DRGs to transfer them to profitable businesses.

This development has only just begun, but the trust in the potential of the business process

Figure 2. Chart of the Rhön clinical enterprise

optimizer is still unbowed, if you take a look to the 3 year curves of their stocks (see Figure 2).

Further potentials in optimizing business processes in the clinical sector are dependent on several issues like:

- Deployment of best practices
- Availability of new technologies that enable high qualified staff to perform the processes in a new way
- Permanent will to benchmark and improve existing business processes

If you look on the infrastructural dimensions of business processes in hospitals today, you can still find a lot of weaknesses linked to the traditional clinical organization, like:

- A very low degree of computerization for support and administrational processes, deeply based in history where traditional administration leaders of the hospitals were not very powerful in comparison to their medical colleagues
- A very poor degree of existing IS integration between different hospital departments,

which still causes a lot of medical problems and costs
- A very traditional hierarchical organization with powerful medicinal stuff, but seldom trained in economy
- A very restrictive type of regulation based on the influence of different interest groups and their negotiations in the past

On the other hand, good medical work needs a lot of different information just in time and close to the location, where the patient gets their treatment. From this point of view, one major success factor in business process improvement in the future will be based on technologies that are supposed to be able to transport a big variety of information from different data sources to the medical employee while they are treating their patients, analyzing their physical conditions, or support them with meals and medicine. This is a major reason why the elaborated use of mobile applications in hospitals will be essential for their future success in business

The focus of this paper will be showing you the economic potential of mobile applications, especially their capacity in leveraging the performance of supporting processes like meal and drug supply and how to measure these benefits.

BACKGROUND: THE ECONOMIC POTENTIAL OF MOBILE APPLICATIONS IN A CLINICAL ENVIRONMENT (RELATED WORK)

As mentioned before, it is perhaps, supposed to be a question of organizational survival if the hospitals in European countries are able to decrease there costs far to a level of where they are today. We also argue that only the invention of new, innovatively designed business processes will lead to this target.

But to what degree will and can mobile applications be part of value-added business processes? And how can we measure this value?

If we look at the related literature, we will find two different kinds of studies.

Studies that Deliver Theoretical Basics and Frameworks to the Topic of Value Generation of Mobile Applications

A good example for this kind of research was published by Nah, Siau, and Sheng (2005). Following their definition, value can be defined as: "the principles for evaluating the consequences of action, inaction, or decision" (p.85). The output of their study was a procedure modeled in Figure

3, which was meant to help creating a means-ends objective network including a distinction between basic and fundamental objects as shown in Figure 4.

The methodological way to gain these networks was based on interviews between researcher and employee in the field. A major result can be seen in Figure 4. The strength of this kind of research surely is the identification of relevant factors, which reveals the possibility of enhancing productivity of mobile applications for the whole enterprise.

On the other hand, their weakness can be seen in the fact that efficiency of an application system can only be measured in relationship to a supported business process, its core activities, and the output produced. A second weakness of their approach was more methodologically. The productivity model of the resulting means-ends objective network of the application system might be based on subjective cognitions, given by the interviewee during the interview situation, instead of time and cost savings measured in a real-world user scenario. A measurement of saved costs between the initial business processes and the redesigned one is not addressed.

Studies Focused on the Business-Oriented Design of Mobile Applications

This approach focuses on the question, what are the basic requirements or architectural patterns

Figure 3. Procedures of value-focused thinking

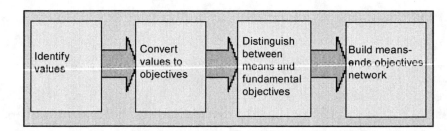

Figure 4. The means-ends objective network

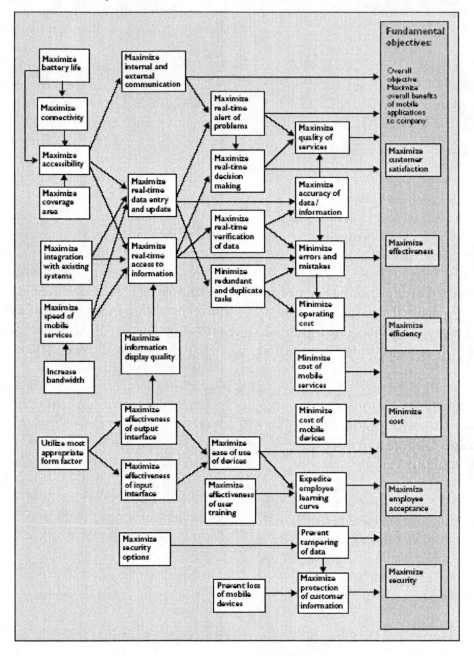

that drives the value of a mobile application system in relationship to supported business processes. In addition we can divide this related work in studies that start from an existing business process that has to be improved, and into studies that derive mobile application systems from target processes. There are various studies in the computer sup-ported cooperative work (CSCW) area, which try to enhance the performance of existing business processes by supporting them with fitting mobile system architectures.

A typical research work in this area was published by Shiffman et al. (1999). He shows the benefits of different services (see Figure 5)

Figure 5. Delivered services by a mobile application (Shiffman 1999)

Delivered Service	Service Description
Recommendation	the determination of appropriate guideline-specified activities that should occur under specific clinical circumstances
Documentation	the collection, recording, and storage of observations, assessments, and interventions related to clinical care
Explanation	the provision of background information on decision variables and guideline-specified actions (e.g., definitions, measures of quality or cost) and the rationale that supports guideline recommendations, including evidence and literature citations
Presentation	the creation of useful output from internal data stores
Registration	the recording and storage of administrative and demographic data to uniquely identify the patient, provider(s) and encounter
Communication	the transmission and receipt of electronic messages between the clinician and other information providers
Calculation	the manipulation of numeric and/or temporal data to derive required information
Aggregation	the derivation of population–based information from individual patient data

delivered by a mobile application to a screening workflow for asthma deceases in child care. They described what kind of information management services should be delivered by a pen-based mobile application system to support decision-making workflows in a hospital. Although they get very deep into the interrelationships between system functionalities and the quality of business process support, they did not measure the resulting influence of the system in cost, time, and quality.

Another study from a more transaction network design perspective was published by Morton and Bukhres (1997). It focuses on the improvement of existing transactions in an ambulance scenario. Morton and Bukhres developed a network architecture that enables a hospital to use mobile applications successfully in the ambulatory service. A major challenge in this scenario is the fact, that a mobile host, for example, in an ambulance car could not be online all the time. So they developed an architectural solution, based on a so called base station agent (BSA) that is responsible for the monitoring of transaction of the mobile host during its execution. This architectural innovation developed from existing business processes by interviewing experts and measuring transaction time, which enables the ambulance to use mobile applications for accelerating their transaction times—a very successes critical benchmark in the area of lifesaving.

Different to Shiffman (1999), and Morton and Bukhres (1997), Wang, Van de Kar, and Meijer (2005) published a study that focuses on a mobile application system design, derived from a future target process. Their design methods are based on the collaborative business engineering (CBE) method from Hengst and De Vreede (2004), and tested for the design of a mobile online information system based on a PDA that supports the conductor on the railway delivering actual information and services to railway customers on the train. The output of their kind of research was a very good system design, derived from the requirements of the new, targeted business processes. Although their research design delivers the opportunity to do a business process benchmark between the performance of the current and the target process, an economically motivated measurement of the improvements was not operated in that research study either.

Conclusion: The Integrated Approach

Recurring to related researches as mentioned before, we were looking for a third way that started from an approach as published by Wang et al. (2005) for the necessary system design but also was combined it with a classical activity-based costing analysis. The aim of our approach was to gain data, which enabled us to measure the efficiency of the new designed and mobile application supported business processes. We found a suitable method named mobile process landscaping (MPL) developed by Köhler and Gruhn (2004) that supported our research in the mentioned way. MPL includes eight steps shown in Figure 6.

However, based on our long-years experience in the area of business process modeling at the Research Centre for Information Technologies (FZI) and a conclusion drawn in the unpublished doctoral thesis of Högler[1] (2006) we improved the MLP method and adapted it to the mobile business process development and profit analysis of a hospital nursing 300,000 patients a year.

We executed the analysis in the five major steps described in Figure 7:

Step 1: Identification of highly valuable business processes in the business process map of the hospital (see Figure 8).

Highly valuable processes should have a significant cost-saving potential as well as a high degree of distributed activities, so that mobile application support may deliver a remarkable benefit. In our case these processes were easily to be identified, as they were delivered from

Figure 6. Major steps of mobile process landscaping (MPL)

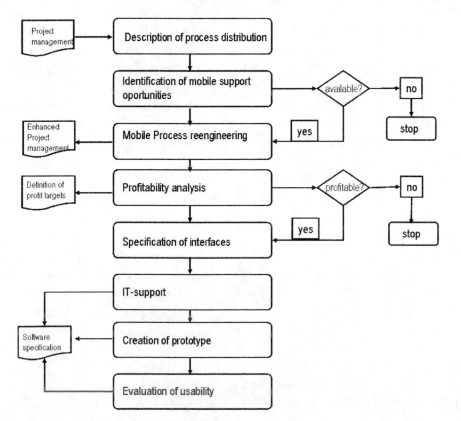

Figure 7. FZI mobile process reengineering approach

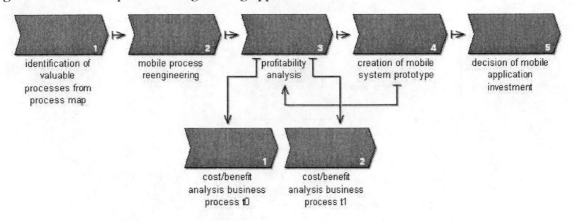

external service providers, too. Benchmarks for meal and medical supply process performance were far ahead from the performance delivered in the observed hospital.

After quick-win business processes in the area of medical and meal supply had been identified as valuable, and the strategic decision made by the management to still internally deliver these services in the future, a second step in research had to be done—the analysis of the mobile potential of the identified supporting processes as well as the reengineering potential on an activity level (see Figure 7).

Step 2: Identification support opportunities on an activity level and the reengineering potential

The analysis of mobile potentials can be operated in two ways:

a.   The first one will be *the identification of activities in an existing process, which could possibly be supported by mobile applications (improvement approach)*. Typical indicators for supportable activities are:
   • the necessity of having access to actual information at a point work that is not yet connected to a network (information quality and delivery function), and

• the necessity to improve existing data input procedures by delivering high qualitative information back to an integrated hospital information system electronically instead of manually (service quality function).

b.   The second one will be *to reach predefined outputs of a needed service with totally new, less cost-intensive mobile business processes (reengineering approach)*.

Especially the design of totally new business processes supported by mobile technologies in regard to their later implementation efforts, costs, and maintenance quality is a central research task the FZI has been working on for years now.

The application of steps 3 to 5 of the FZI Mobile Business Process Reengineering Approach (MBPRA), shown in Figure 7, will be described in the case study in chapter 3. It includes the operation of a profitability analysis, and the design of a mobile system prototype fitting into the reengineered business processes. Once the prototype will be able to reach serious savings of activity-based costs, the investment decision for the implementation of the whole system has to be made.

A major focus in our case study will be regarding the question of data quality, which is necessary for modeling and simulating business

Figure 8. Business process map of the hospital

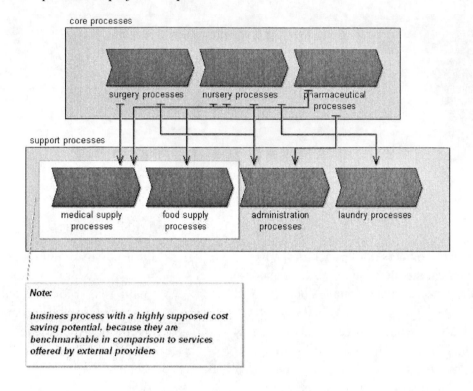

Figure 9. Example of a business process with reengineering potential

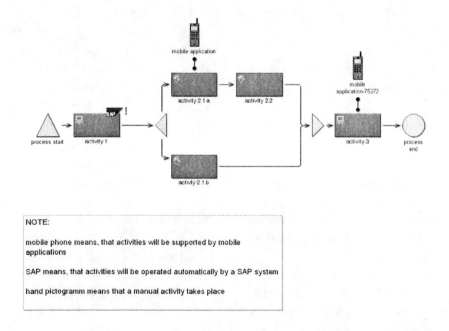

processes in a way that allows the delivery of detailed information about their cost structure and process performance.

CASE STUDY: MOBILE TERMINALS FOR DRUG AND MEAL SUPPLY

This study was carried out from January until June 2004 at FZI by order of Karlsruhe City Hospital, the largest hospital under public law in the vicinity of Karlsruhe with more than 1,500 beds and 14 clinical departments, handling approximately 300,000 patients per year. The departments are allocated campus-like to numerous buildings. In this study the hospital's processes of drug supply in the pharmacy of the hospital as well as meal supply in the kitchen were examined. Key stakeholders were nurses, physicians, pharmacists, assistant medical technicians (MTAs), assistant pharmaceutical technicians (PTAs), cooks, cooking assistants, diabetes consultants, haulage service, and the controlling and executive committee.

Used Methodology

As every model of reality is as good as its input, our profitability analysis of mobile business processes was highly dependent on the data quality. As long as time for delivery or processing of activities was supposed to be measured or informal stocks at the wards to be detected, it does make sense to use a mixture of traditional ethnographic and focused ethnographic approach (see Figure 10) as claimed by Knoblauch (2005). In our role as researchers we were involved as participants in the working process, which is not the case in focused ethnography, where the researcher normally acts as an observer. But all the other techniques we used were based on the ethnographic approach of Knoblauch.

The challenge was to gather high qualitative data and transfer it to linear cost models, like

Figure 10. Comparison between conventional and focused ethnography

Conventional Ethnography	Focused Ethnography
Long-term field visits	Short-term field visits
Experientially intensive	Data/Analysis intensity
Time extensity	Time intensity
Writing	Recording
Solitary data collection and analysis	Data session groups
Open	Focused
Social fields	Communicative activities
Participant role	Field observer role
Insider knowledge	Background knowledge
Subjective understanding	Conservation
Notes	Notes and transcripts
Coding	Coding and sequential analysis

Lazarsfeld, Jahoda, and Zeisel (1933) practiced it in their early studies. We used the following data gathering methods:

- **Participating observation:** we worked together with nurses and a druggist as well as kitchen and health care staff for 8 days and night shifts to get a deep understanding of the business processes including the used resources and materials.
- **Inventories:** Inventories of the formal and informal medical stocks at the drug store and the wards
- **Inside interviews:** 34 non-closed expert interviews with different process owners in the hospital (nurses, pharmacist, IT operators, IT management, IS consultants, cooks, diet cooks, garbage man)
- **Outside interviews:** 4 non-closed expert interviews with experts from other hospitals that had just invented mobile systems in the same processes to validate their own gathered data.

Initial Situation/Preface

Previous to this study the hospital was faced with the choice of an investment and integration of mobile devices on wards and pharmacy. These processes were chosen from the process map, because they promised a high potential for optimization. In 2003 the project team "Mobile Computing" was founded by the head of the pharmacy, the chief information officer, and the chief executive officer. In a pilot project they started to develop and test a mobile system in the pharmacy and on two selected stations (oncology and nephrology, each with more than 20 beds) in cooperation with a software company. The aim of the Mobile Computing project was improving the drug supply by reducing administrative activities just as avoiding sources of error by the dint of mobile terminals and their integration into the supply workflow. At the time the study was performed, the Mobile Computing project was in the productive test phase. In case of a positive result, it was planned to roll-out the system on all stations. The study's objective therefore was to provide a basis of decision making about the roll-out by dint of an economic analysis.

In order to examine the portability of the mobile system the study was made up of two scenarios. The first scenario dealt with the processes of drug supply, where, within the scope of the Mobile Computing project, the possibility of comparing past and new situations in a real environment was given. In the scenario two processes of the meal supply were chosen to demonstrate the ability of the mobile system being extendable. In contrast to the scenario, one of the analyses was limited to the investigation of a business process without any mobile devices due to the fact that there was no test implementation of a mobile system for the meal supply. The analysis of the future processes (with mobile devices) had to be designed with experiences gained from interviews of other hospitals using mobile devices for meal supply already.

By implementing the mobile system, traditional paper-based processes were supposed to be adopted and optimized where exchanging information should be converted from paper-based to electronic-based processes as far as possible. Improvements in workflow by automating administrative jobs (e.g., validity check, sorting of forms, calculating order quantity, etc.) and minimizing sources of error were expected.

In scope of the drug supply the orders were previously taken at the station's PC or at the pharmaceutical rack using PDAs and sent to the enterprise resource planning (ERP) system and the pharmacy's IS via docking station. In the pharmacy, the orders could be processed directly on the PDA by a wireless LAN (WLAN) without the necessity of using paper-based media.

At the meals supply process the paper-based order form was displaced by the digital entry via mobile devices. If necessary, the chosen data could be linked to the patient's incompatibilities or objections. The software was to check up on all data on their plausibility automatically and to send alerts in the case of incomplete or false orders. In the kitchen, all steps for receiving and handling meal orders were automated. Based on the demand of ingredients, the kitchen's staff sent all orders to the supplier. Additionally, the patient nameplates were printed and cut to mark the meal tablets.

Objectives

Of highest interest in this study was the economic potential that could be gained by implementing mobile terminals in a hospital whereat the profitability of the mobile system for the chosen processes for the supply of drugs and meals described previously had to be measured. For this reason processes of the past and future situation were to be documented and compared in order to ascertain possible profit and loss.

Another target was the development of a methodology for the evaluation of economic potentials achieved by the integration of mobile devices into clinical and economical pathways as well as for its testing. For this purpose the general conditions for the use of mobile devices in hospitals had to be considered and the applicability of different kinds of mobile devices to be detected. Another question to be answered was where and how mobile terminals could be integrated in existing business processes. The analysis of advantages and risks that could occur during the roll-out of the mobile system was targeted as well.

Central questions that had to be addressed in the study were:

- How could costs and efficiency of supply processes be measured (with and without the support of mobile devices)?
- What advantages and risks could be expected during the roll-out of mobile systems?
- What profit and loss could result from implementing the mobile system?

Scenario 1: Drug Supply

In the hospital all medicaments like drugs, infusions, and so forth were delivered by the hospital's own in-house pharmacy. The pharmacy is in charge of ordering, producing (in special cases), storing, and delivering drugs to the hospital stations. Pharmacist, MTA, PTA, and warehouseman have to work together closely. The pharmacist is responsible for quality control and consulting services in case of questions about drugs (e.g., compatibility, unlicensed drugs, etc.) for the hospital's physicians and nurses. Furthermore he/she has to determine the demand for drugs and in special cases produce special pharmaceuticals and infusion bags. Usually, wards order drugs every day.

Former Situation in Drug Supply

The processes of the former situation in the hospital's drug supply are presented in Figure 11. After the prescription had been inserted into the patient record by the responsible doctor, nurses ordered lacking medicaments by an order form. Before that, they had to walk along the medicine shelves on their wards and write down name and amount of the needed medicaments on a notepad. Afterwards they went over their notes and transferred them on the order forms mentioned previously. Due to the numerous classifications of medications (usual medication, infusion, dispensing, cytostatica, anesthetic, etc.) there were eight different types of forms available. The order form had to be signed by the responsible doctor and transported to the pharmacy finally by being thrown in the pharmacy's letter box, faxed, or in urgent cases by using pneumatic post.

In the pharmacy, the pharmacist first sorted the incoming order forms according to their type of form and to their posting station and checked the details on the order forms. Detected discrepancies had to be straightened out by telephone. In case of missing compulsory data (e.g., signature of the doctor) order forms were to be sent back to the station. In case of valid details drugs were collected and put in boxes together. Before delivery the drugs were registered in the ERP system of the pharmacy by scanning the barcode. The so called "Hol- und Bringdienst" ("catch and delivery service") performed the delivery to the stations. Additionally, nurses are able to fetch ordered drugs at the pharmacy counter.

Information was transmitted by paper-based information media like order forms and notepads as well as by fax, letter box, pneumatic post, telephone, and the staff itself (nurses, pharmacist).

Weak points in the former situation could be identified in several processes. Inefficient activities were the sorting of the order forms, queries by telephone because of non-explicit or uncompleted details, the recording of the anesthetic, output, and

Figure 11. Processes of the drug supply in the hospital (former situation)

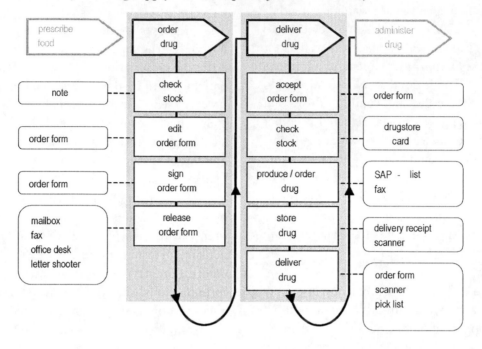

sale to hospital staff member as well as orderings from drug maker and wholesaler.

Using pneumatic post (ca. 40-60 times per day) required several time-consuming activities such as loading and unloading the sleeves. Furthermore the pneumatic post system often revealed little reliability and additionally caused high costs for maintenance (see Figure 12 and 13).

The material costs contain those for paper and printing, order forms, occupancy costs for archival storage of order forms, and of thrown away drugs because of the drugs were out of date/expired. The term factor represents the frequency of the respective activities per day. Costs can be calculated by multiplying labor costs by factor.

Present Scenario with Mobile Devices in the Drug Supply

In the present scenario processes of ordering drugs (see Figure 14 and 15) are supported by PDA (personal digital assistant) and by a Web-based order

entry system. Nurses now walk along the drugs shelves on their station and fill out the order form directly on a PDA without any use of notepads. With the barcode scanner extension nurses just need to scan the barcode of the drug's package and choose the amount by pull-down menu. In order to save time, the barcodes labels itself are stuck on the shelves' front side, so that there is no more need of taking the drug packages out. Via docking station at the station's computer the order forms are directly transmitted to the ERP system of the pharmacy. A Web front end enables nurses to check, correct, and activate the order. The responsible doctor merely has to check the Web-based order form and sign with his/her personal password to ratify its validity.

The team of the pharmacy now gains access to the order form in an electronic way. By computer and PDA they can view and work on all order forms on the display. Due to the pharmacy's WLAN connectivity the staff has ubiquitous access without any need to sort the order forms. The

Figure 12. Cost of material for drug supply (traditional supply system)

	amount	unit price	cost of operation/per year
Drug documentation form	14064	0,0636 €	900 €
Archiving costs (drug store)	15 m²	72 €	1.600 €
Drug expiry costs	1	4.770 €	4.770 €

Figure 13. Personnel cost of drug supply (traditional supply system)

Drug order (each station)	duration [min.]	factor	costs [per day]
Fill out order form	6,36	1	3,08 €
Subscription by doctor	1,79	1	0,86 €
Walking to the mail box	2,18	1	1,05 €
Prepare pneumatic post	1,07	1	0,52 €
Edit returning form	0,45	1	0,22 €
Total costs of drug order (per station)			5,73 €
Drug delivery (pharmacy)	duration [min.]	factor	costs [per day]
Empty mail box and pneumatic post	64,11	1	51,73 €
Sort order forms	17,14	1	6,77 €
Correct orders, making inquiry calls	31,57	1	19,82 €
Store pick lists	9,00	1	3,80 €
Writing and attaching notes	2,39	1	1,50 €
Automated order	8,50	1	3,59 €
Restructure drug cards	12,00	1	5,06 €
Accounting of narcotics	0,50	6,31	2,63 €
Check of the narcotic accounts	30,00	1/30	0,83 €
Accounting of the sales to clinical employee	60,00	1/7	3,62 €
Data entry of Zytostatika in PC	90,00	1	75,00 €
Zytostatika-data exchange with ERP system	45,00	2/30	2,68 €
Register orders for wholesaler	14,00	1	11,67 €
Dictate wholesaler orders to secretary	20,00	1	16,67 €
Empty stock from employee drug sale	5,63	1/7	0,34 €
Additional efforts of employee drug sale	30,00	1/7	1,81 €
Preparation of order forms	2,03	1	0,80 €
Register industrial orders	10,79	1	4,56 €
Archiving of clipboard	27,22	1	11,49 €
Managing call backs of single charges	46,21	1/7	5,50 €
Total costs of drug delivery (pharmacy)			229,85 €

staff can walk along the shelves of the pharmacy and collect all ordered drugs. By scanning the barcode on the drug package the delivery items are automatically registered.

Review of the Process Improvements in the Drug Supply

The mobile system offered numerous forms of relief and advantages. It is possible to remedy the deficiencies of the former situation without IT support and to avoid disadvantages of stationary computer systems. Communication costs (telephone conversations) between pharmacy and station could be limited by eliminating unreadable handwriting and incomplete details. In the pharmacy numerous activities could be automated or usefully supported.

Because of several circumstances the field of application was limited in some issues. For example, ordering and delivering anesthetic had to be excluded from the mobile system, as dealing with anesthetic had to use paper-based documentation by statute. Another area where the mobile system was discussed to be applied was the pharmacy's stock control. But as the use of drugs could not be registered exactly (e.g., returned drug packages, which were partially used and no more needed), improvement of stock control by the mobile system was not possible either, nor was it to be expected that the amount of drugs that had to be disposed for exceed of expiration date could obviously be reduced.

Scenario 2: Meal Supply

In the hospital there exists one kitchen that supplies personnel, patients, and their dependants with meals. Patients get meals three times per day. One day before each meal, for example, lunch, nurses on the stations ask patients about their wishes for lunch the next day and transmit the orders to the kitchen. Thus, the kitchen's staff is able to plan and organize every meal up to 24 hours before.

Figure 14. Processes of the drug supply in the hospital (present situation)

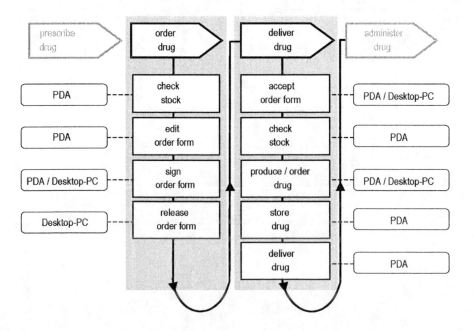

Figure 15. Cost of personnel for drug supply (present situation)

	duration [min.]	factor	costs [per day]
Drug order (each station)			
Fill out order form	2,00	1	0,97 €
Synchronize PDA/Scanner	1	1	0,48 €
Confirrm order	2,00	1	1,16 €
Subscription by doctor	1	1	0,82 €
Edit returning form	0,07	1	0,03 €
Total costs of drug order (per station)			2,98 €
Drug delivery (pharmacy)			
Print out pick-list	1	1	0,40 €
Send messages (e.g., quries, information)	0,60	1	0,31 €
Automated order	1,43	1	0,60 €
Accounting of narcotics	1	1	0,83 €
Check of the narcotic accounts	1	1	0,42 €
Data entry of Zytostatika in PC	10,00	1	8,33 €
Register orders for wholesaler	4,00	1	3,33 €
Register industrial orders	9,25	1	3,90 €
Archiving of clipboard	5,00	1	2,11 €
Managing call backs of single charges	8,00	1/7	0,95 €
Empty stock from employee drug sale	3,00	1/7	0,18 €
Synchonize PDA	1	5	2,56 €
Total costs of drug delivery (pharmacy)			23,94 €

Former Situation in the Meal Supply

Without the implementation of a mobile system, the supply of meals is a slow process (see Figure 16), afflicted with different kinds of errors. Orders are taken on the basis of menus and forwarded to the kitchen via meal vouchers. In the past these vouchers had been sorted, checked superficially, and afterwards were read in with a special PC-linked scanner. The associated software counted the orders per station and furthermore checked the vouchers' plausibility. Having gathered all orders the production schedule for the next day was printed and handed out to the cooks.

Future Scenario with Mobile Devices in the Meal Supply

On the basis of a new mobile system, the traditional paper-based processes can be adopted and improved (see Figure 17). The orders will be taken at the station's PC or directly at the patient via PDA. The name of the patient is chosen out of a patient administration system, linked to the chosen meal and via PC or docking station sent to the ERP system and the kitchen. If necessary, the chosen data can be linked to the patient's incompatibilities or objections. The software will check all data on their plausibility automatically and send alerts in case of incomplete or false orders. Additionally, it will check the patient's administration software in order to verify which patients have left the hospital or have changed the station.

Review of the Process Improvements in the Meal Supply

These meal vouchers as well as false orders and insufficient deliveries emerge as the most important cost drivers within the old system. For example, it takes up a great deal of time to complete the meal vouchers, to arrange and to correct them as well as to import the vouchers into the system; errors emerging are redundant or needless orders that can not be cancelled. Further cost drivers are coordinative telephone calls between kitchen and hospital stations that have to be ascribed to the relocation or early release of patients, for example. 80-100 telephone calls per day are necessary due to short-term changes of orders.

These cost drivers add up to approximately 720,000 € each year for ordering activities between the kitchen and all stations of the hospital. This sum includes material costs like order vouchers and wasted meals due to mistakes as well as personnel costs for placing and taking the daily order.

With the help of the mobile system described previously, many of the former cost drivers in meal supply could be eliminated. Having implemented the mobile system, further costs for materials will only arise from the production of tablet cards and non-preventable false deliveries of meals. Non-preventable situations are, for example, when it is not foreseeable after which meal a patient will be released the next day or whether a meal can be taken after a surgery.

In Figure 18 and Figure 19 the costs accruing in the kitchen due to the old IS are listed.

The costs for materials compound of actualizing the software and the contract for maintenance of costs for paper and those for spare meals which

Figure 16. Processes of the meal supply in the hospital (former situation)

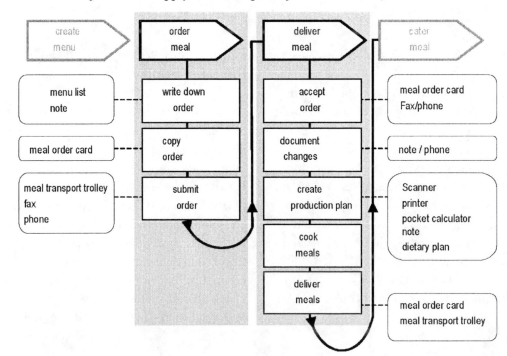

Figure 17. Processes of the meal supply with the mobile system (future situation)

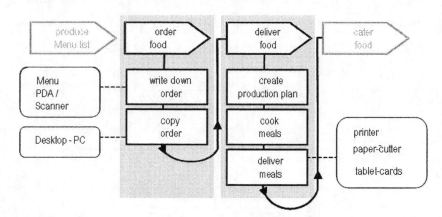

Figure 18. Material costs for meal supply (traditional scenario)

Invest (indispensable)	amount	unit price	Total costs
Software update (license paper based system)	1	3.100 €	3.100 €
Software update (installation)	1	5.200 €	5.200 €
Software update (training costs)	1	1700 €	1700 €
Additional operation costs (per year)	amount	unit price	Total costs
Software material costs	1.336.746,00	0,018 €	23.968 €
Software maintenance contract costs	1	911 €	911 €
Waste of meals	29.975	4 €	120.000 €

can be ascribed either to preventable or non-preventable wrong orders.

Aside from retrenching working expenses, the mobile system also provides an obvious surplus in quality. In contrast to the former system, the patients' incompatibilities like, for example, allergies or possible objections can now be considered with much less effort. Figure 20 shows the personnel costs of the meal supply supported by the mobile system.

Economic Results

Process improvements were performed iteratively in several steps. During the process improvement, ideas and visions of staff members were considered and the experience gained in cooperative hospitals as well as in Mobile Computing projects in other lines of business were taken into account. Approved methodologies and rules for process improvement by Greiling and Hofstetter (2002, p. 96 et sqq.) were included. The profitability was calculated by the *net present value* (NPV) method (see Figure 21), where n means the time horizon of the project and t numeralizes the years. The term *discount rate* refers to a percentage used to calculate the NPV and reflects the time value of money at an actual average between 3% and 6%.

By dint of the methodology current and target processes of the traditional and the mobile sys-

Figure 19. Cost of personnel for meal supply (traditional supply system)

Meal supply process (per station)	duration [min.]	factor	costs [per day]
Produce collection of different menu	10,00	1/7	0,69 €
Discuss menu with involved employee	5,00	1/7	0,35 €
Prepare meal voucher	10	3	14,52 €
Sort meal voucher	1	3	1,45 €
Inform kitchen	2,14	1,00	1,04 €
Total costs of meal order process (per station)			18,04 €
Meal delivery process (kitchen)	duration [min.]	factor	costs [per day]
Retrieve meal voucher from stock	3	3	3,10 €
Sort meal voucher	120	3	123,86 €
Correct meal voucher	10	3	10,32 €
Prepare inward meal voucher for ambulant patients	5	1	1,72 €
Prepare meal voucher for staff.	5	1	1,72 €
Count token coins of staff	1	1	0,34 €
Operate inward statistics	20	1	6,88 €
Operate discharge statistics	20	1	6,88 €
Operate statistics for additional delivered fruits	2	1	0,69 €
Transport meal voucher to administration office	3	3	3,10 €
Start meal software	1	3	1,03 €
Scan paper-based meal voucher	35	3	36,13 €
Print out production plan	2	3	2,06 €
Save data	7	1	2,41 €
Total costs meal delivery (kitchen)			200,24 €
Meal delivery process (diet kitchen)	duration [min.]	factor	costs [per day]
Check and correct special diet meal voucher	45	1	19,86 €
Calculate portions for diet	30	1	13,24 €
Calculate ingredients	30	1	13,24 €
Label plates for special diets	30	1	13,24 €
Total costs meal delivery (diet kitchen)			59,57 €

tem were modeled and documented, their costs and use in terms of activity-based costing were determined and compared within the scope of a profitability analysis.

The costs for the optimized drug and meal supply are scheduled in Figure 22. Just as in the drug supply, the one-of expenses for the mobile system comprise of costs for investment and the non-recurring operating expenses. There is also a strong emphasis on staff's training activities to guarantee a maximum acceptance by the staff and a smooth IS implementation.

The investment into the mobile system and the scanner alternative gets profitable at least within one year (see Figure 23 and Figure 24), based on the assumption that operation expenses

Figure 20. Cost of personnel for meal supply (with the mobile system)

	duration [min.]	factor	costs [per day]
Meal supply process (per station)			
Discuss menu with involved employee	2,50	1/7	0,17 €
Synchronize PDA	1,00	3,00	1,45 €
Confirm meal order	2,00	1,00	0,97 €
Total costs of meal order process (per station)			2,59 €
Meal delivery process (kitchen)			
Count token coins of staff	2,00	1,00	0,69 €
Print out production plan	1,00	3,00	1,03 €
Print out tablet cards	1,00	3,00	1,03 €
Cut tablet cards	10,00	3,00	10,32 €
Total costs meal delivery (kitchen)			13,07 €
Meal delivery process (diet kitchen)			
Calculate portions for diet	5,00	1,00	2,21 €
Calculate ingredients	1,00	1,00	0,44 €
Total costs meal delivery (diet kitchen)			2,65 €

Figure 21. Formula of the net present value according to Grob (1999)

$$NPV = (\sum_{t=1}^{n} \frac{Cash\ Flow_t}{(1 + Discount\ Rate)^t}) - Initial\ Investment$$

are lowered strongly and risks narrowed down. The discount rate is chosen on 10% by an initial investment of 200,000 €. In contrast the payback period is reached within 3 years time, if the implementation of the mobile system is not followed by an appropriate reengineering of the relevant processes. These facts can be ascribed to the integration of autonomous subsystems by mobile devices as well as to the removal of errors. Besides, parallel processes result in the decrease of labor time. Additionally, the mobile devices enable the controlling department to gather more and reliable data for the measurement of costs.

CONCLUSION

In comparison to the big amount of money, the European telecommunication industry has in-

vested in Universal Mobile Telecommunications System (UMTS) and third generation (3G) mobile infrastructure; there still is a very slow adoption of mobile application in different domains, which might result from a lot of different reasons. Two major reasons surely apply: (1) lack of methods to demonstrate and measure the value creation potential of mobile business applications, and (2) the lack of potentially best practices and use cases in different domains.

If we go back to methodologies for measuring the value of mobile-supported business processes, we might be able to demonstrate that it is possible to show the benefits by business process modeling, design, and simulation methods, followed by an activity-based costing and traditional investment appraisal.

However, to do this in a proper way, there was a lot of effort necessary, for example, ethnographic studies and field work for the time of about 2 weeks, participating in the drug and meal supply processes, and recording and analyzing data.

On the other hand the quality of the resulting process model with time and cost data is strongly dependent on the quality of input. But if we look at

Figure 22. Cost of material for mobile system in drug and meal supply

	amount	unit price	Total costs
Invest			
PDA Symbol SPT1846	5	1.200 €	6.000 €
PDA Symbol SPT1550	181	500 €	91.000 €
Printer (kitchen, tablet cards)	2	5.000 €	10.000 €
Paper cutter (kitchen)	2	5.000 €	10.000 €
Printer (pharmacy)	3	750 €	2250 €
WLAN access points	2	200 €	400 €
Software development (ward)	1	39.000 €	39.000 €
Software development (kitchen)	1	32.000 €	32.000 €
Software development (in general)	1	1.000 €	1.000 €
Software development (sales tax.)	1	16.000 €	16.000 €
Course of training (pharmacy)	1	5.000 €	5.000 €
Course of training (station)	108	310 €	33.000 €
Course of training (kitchen)	1	200 €	200 €
Installation (pharmacy)	5	10 €	50 €
Installation (ward)	108	4 €	400 €
Installation (kitchen)	5	80 €	400 €
Additional running costs (per year)			
Costs of lost/ broken PDA (Symbol SPT1846)	0,5	1.200 €	600 €
Costs of lost/ broken PDA (Symbol SPT1550)	20	500 €	10.000 €
Costs of paper (pharmacy)	14.000	0,004 €	50 €
Costs of paper (kitchen)	400.000	0,004 €	1.600 €
Costs of hiring server (electronic data processing center)	1	10.000 €	10.000 €
Costs of data traffic (electronic data processing center)	108.000 MB	0,03 €	3.240 €

the investment done in total and the potential savings, the time for research was worth its money.

The process-oriented research approach derived from the MPL method was able to deliver useful results. It was a further enrichment in comparison to research methods that focus on mobile system design (Wang et al., 2005) only, or on abstract means-ends objective networks that describe general value dimensions of mobile applications (Nah et al., 2004).

The business processes that had been chosen from the process map of the hospital turned out to be very fertile for optimization with mobile

applications. An ROI of an investment of 200,000 € in mobile systems could be paid back in a time frame of 1 (progressive calculation) or maximum 3 years (conservative calculation).

Hospitals stand to benefit in different ways from implementing a mobile system: There is a high ROI and efficiency gain caused by the use of mobile terminals. The restructuring of processes can reduce running time and thus the workload of health care and administrative personnel. By minimizing the number of errors that do occur during the recording and editing of orders, expenses for the drug and meal supply processes

Figure 23. Value calculation with the net present value method

Invest (Total)	274.750 €
PDA Symbol SPT1846	6.000 €
PDA Symbol SPT1550	91.000 €
Printer (kitchen)	10.000 €
Paper cutter	10.000 €
Printer (pharmacy)	2.250 €
WLAN access points	400 €
Software development	116.000 €
Training and installation costs	39.100 €
Single savings	10.000 €
Additional operation costs (per year)	25.250 €
Savings per year (material costs)	
Meal voucher and maintenance	24.900 €
Waste of meals	30.000 €
Drug order forms	900 €
Costs for needed archiving space	1.000 €
Savings per year (personnel costs)	
½ x diet cook	21.000 €
3x cook assistants	99.000 €
Labor time (general)	591.000 €
Total savings per year (material and personel costs only)	176.800 €
Total savings per year (with additional savings of labour time)	767.800 €
Period	3 years
Bank rate	10 %
„net present value" (NPV) (without process time)	108.700 €
„net present value" (NPV) (with process time savings)	1.581.000 €

can be reduced, too. Information processing can be automated by the use of mobile electronic systems, thus the waste of material, labor time, and storage space for files (actually an important expense factor) can be significantly decreased.

Another remarkable improvement caused by the new mobile system is the extraction of very detailed information that can be used by the controlling department for the measurement of process performance, process costs, and occurring errors. Furthermore, by setting data in relation to patients, applications can be developed to share patient-oriented information including high traceability and a high transparency in supply processes. For example in drug supply a mobile system can provide new possibilities for enhancing the medication: The hospital's pharmacy now plans to enhance the existing mobile system to a unit dose system, in which every patient gets their individual medication, beginning at the bed-side prescription by PDAs to the patient-related packaging and ending at the patient-related billing.

Nevertheless, economic potentials can be reduced significantly by the wrong choice of mobile terminals. This fact was revealed by the analysis of the barcode scanner alternative. Though the same processes are supported, the scanner alternative proved to be a less appropriate solution. Although barcode scanner costs half the price of PDAs, they cannot verify the input quality of data, nor display inconsistency checks or warnings. Furthermore, they are not able to alert staff members in case of patients' incompatibilities against drugs or meals. All input can only be checked at the wards' PC.

Figure 24. Schematic diagram of the profitability analysis

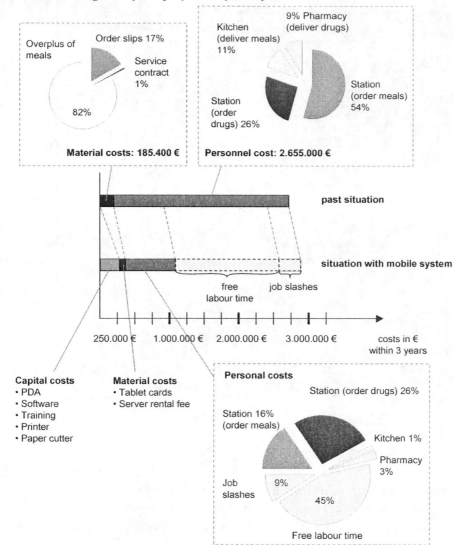

This means, that in case of occurring problems, data has to be recollected again. Comparing the drug supply process scenario operated by the PDA or scanner supported alternative, it becomes clear that barcode scanners lead to additional expenses and to an increasing personnel workload.

In the context of the drug order and supply processes it has not become clear yet if the implementation of intelligent mobile devices can result in measurable advantages in comparison to the implementation of a scanner-supported scenario. This phenomenon is based in the short spatial distance between the ward PCs and the drug cupboards.

But it would make no sense to operate these processes without the PDA system, as it has no measurable negative effects and all different processes can be supported by one system. This lowers the break in barriers for the staff members, who have to be trained only in one system with only one kind of mobile device.

If we go further in the business process map of the hospital, we surely will find other business processes that could be supported by the available mobile system, like, for example, the coordination process for the hospitals laundry.

Once the system's use is established among staff members, the next step might be to support medical business processes, too, if it ends up in a higher efficiency. But before doing that, business process performance analysis will be essential. Nowadays there already exists mobile applications for medical business processes, like decision support systems, e-learning, and telemedical communication systems. One of the prominent mobile systems in Germany is the Stroke Angel system (Holtmann, Rashid, Weinhardt, Gräfe, & Griewing, 2006) in which paramedics use PDAs in emergency ambulance vehicles in case of a stroke to send information about their patient to the targeted hospital. Medicals in this hospital can begin their analysis and make preliminary preparations.. Furthermore, paramedics fill out checklists by PDAs that enable hospitals to make a more precise analysis and collect data for improving the emergency management. Up to present there exists no business process performance analysis, neither of the rescue service nor of the emergency units, in hospitals.

A lot of German hospitals are still not able to tell you how much a treatment belonging to a given and predefined DRG costs. Modeling the existent business processes and enriching them with process costs and time data will be a major first step of improvement—the utilization of mobile applications for performance leverage the second.

Otherwise a hospital might go bankrupt by delivering services in a high quality but to very uncompetitive costs. For example, if a hospital is very famous for its kidney surgery and is planning to enhance it without knowing the cost/benefit structure it is possible to cause serious trouble if the profit contribution is negative, as happened to a competitor of the clinic we had research on.

However, to introduce mobile business process modeling, simulation, and redesign together with activity-based costing will be a major contribution of European hospitals to reduce the costs of their health care systems. Supporting or redesigning distributed clinical processes with mobile applications will be substantial items. This should be an inspiring signal for the telecommunication companies in OECD countries to become an informed partner for the health care sector with fitting mobile information applications and consultancy services.

REFERENCES

Get Process AG. (2006). *Income process designer.* Retrieved May 25, 2006, from http://www.get-process.de

Greiling, M., & Hofstetter, J. (2002). Patienten-behandlungspfade optimieren—Prozessmanagement im Krankenhaus. Baumann Fachverlag, Kulmbach (Germany).

Grob, L. (1999). *Einführung in die Investitionsrechnung* (3rd ed.). München, Germany: Vahlen.

Hengst, M. den, & De Vreede, G. J. (2004). Collaborative business engineering: A decade of lessons from the field. *Journal of Management Information Systems, 20*(4), 87-115.

Högler, T. (2006). Framework für eine holistische Wirtschaftlichkeitsanalyse mobiler Systeme. In *Proceedings of the MKWI Multikonferenz Wirtschaftsinformatik 2006,* Universität Passau, Germany.

Holtmann, C., Rashid, A., Weinhardt, C., Gräfe, A., & Griewing, B. (2006). Time is brain—Analyse der Rettungskette im Schlaganfall. In *Proceedings of the 5th Workshop of the GMDS Workgroup Mobiles Computing in der Medizin,* Frankfurt, Germany: Shaker Verlag.

Köhler, A., & Gruhn, V. (2004, February 2-3). Mobile process landscaping am Beispiel von Vertriebsprozessen in der Assekuranz. Mobile economy: Transaktionen, Prozesse, Anwendungen und Dienste. In *Proceedings of the 4th*

Workshop Mobile Commerce, Universität Augsburg, Germany.

Knoblauch, H. (2005). Focused ethnography. *Qualitative Social Research, 6*(3). Retrieved May 24, 2006, from http://www.qualitative-research. net/fqs-texte/3-05/05-3-44-e.htm

Lazarsfeld, P., Jahoda, M., & Zeisel, H. (1933). *Die Arbeitslosen von Marienthal. Ein soziographischer Versuch über die Wirkungen langdauernder Arbeitslosigkeit.* Germany: Suhrkamp Leipzig.

Morton, S. & Bukhres, O. (1997). Utilizing mobile computing in the Wishard Memorial Hospital ambulatory service. In B. Bryant, J. Carroll, J. Hightower, and K. M. George, (Eds) *Proceedings of the 1997 ACM Symposium on Applied Computing* (SAC '97) (pp. 287-294). San Jose, California, United States. New York, NY: ACM Press.

Nah, F., Siau, K., & Sheng, S. (2005). The value of mobile applications: A utility company study. *Communications of the ACM, 48*(2), 85-90.

Organisation for Economic Co-operation and Development (OECD). (2006). *OECD fact book: Total and public expenditures in health.* Retrieved May 25, 2006, from http://thesius.sourceoecd.org/ vl=5439459/cl=16/nw=1/rpsv/factbook/data/10-01-04-t01.xls

Shiffman, R. N., Karras, B. T., Nath, S., Engles-Horton, L., & Corb, G. J. (1999, August). Pen-based, mobile decision support in healthcare. *SIGBIO Newsl, 19*(2), 5-7.

Statistisches Bundesamt. (2003). *Im Jahr 2050 wird jeder Dritte in Deutschland 60 Jahre oder älter sein.* Retrieved May 25, 2006, from http://www.destatis.de/presse/deutsch/pm2003/p2300022.htm

Wang, Y., Van de Kar, E., & Meijer, G. (2005). Designing mobile solutions for mobile workers: Lessons learned from a case study. In *Proceedings of the 7th international conference on Electronic commerce ICEC'05.*

ENDNOTE

[1] She will publish her PhD thesis including improvements of the MPL method this year. First results had been presented in 2006 at the German Conference of Information Systems (WKWI).

Chapter XI
Mobile Automotive Cooperative Services (MACS):
Systematic Development of Personalizable Interactive Mobile Automotive Services

Holger Hoffman
Technische Universität München, Germany

Jan Marco Leimeister
Technische Universität München, Germany

Helmut Krcmar
Technische Universität München, Germany

ABSTRACT

In this chapter we describe the systematic development and implementation of mobile services in the automotive sector. This includes a design framework that represents different requirements of automotive service engineering. The framework is used following a corresponding process model which combines iterative service development with classical prototyping. The framework and the process model are applied to a new mobile service MACS MyNews, a personalizeable, interactive news service, allowing the driver to be the editor and end user of his/her newscast at the same time. In order to design this service, we start with designing service scenarios. For these service scenarios a matching value-added network is derived, technologies for service provisioning are chosen, and a prototype is implemented. The service is then evaluated especially concerning driving safety. A final user evaluation helps the designers choose whether or not to include the service in series production before planning the service roll-out.

INTRODUCTION AND BACKGROUND

Mobile services in the automotive sector have been rather unsuccessful in Germany over the past years. Of all car manufacturers that offered services in this field only BMW and Fiat still offered mobile services in their cars in 2004/2005. The three main reasons for discontinuing mobile services are usually mentioned: (1) the costs for data transfer were too high (Frost & Sullivan, 2003), (2) the services offered did not fit adequately to the users' needs (Fuhr, 2001), and (3) mobile services were too focused on technology (Werder, 2005) and had hardly any economic aspects considered making it almost impossible to deliver viable and sustainable services.

But things are changing: The recent availability of new digital transmission channels such as theUniversal Mobile Telecommunications System (UMTS) or digital audio broadcast (DAB), digital radio and the declining prices especially for cellular radio (i.e., mobile phone fees) almost eliminated the problem of transmission cost, leaving only two problems to solve. This is the starting point for the project MACS, a research project funded by the German Federal Ministry of Education and Research FKZ 01 HW 0207, and its central research question: "How can innovative mobile automotive services be systematically developed, structured and which steps have to be taken for deploying mobile services successfully?"

In order to address the problem of designing services that meet the end users' needs, the first step is to find and evaluate service scenarios that seem promising for new mobile services. Based on the scenarios found, the process of deriving a business model out of those scenarios has to be defined. Extracting common factors from these scenarios and models and finding common interfaces for mobile services are necessary for allowing a large and heterogeneous group of service providers to offer their products in the future. From an economic point of view there are several requirements a systematic design of mobile automotive services has to be able to deliver:

- Defining service scenarios and use cases which are comprehensible for the average car user and that are to be frequently used (in contrast to, e.g., emergency call services).
- Integrating mobile broadband services (DAB/UMTS/etc.) into mobile automotive services allowing data exchange at high data rates and thus enabling more powerful services in the years to come.

The following presented MACS design framework for developing mobile automotive services was designed to meet these criteria and to incorporate a wide variety of different solutions from different technical domains of mobile services. One of the main challenges for such a design framework which is unique to automotive mobile services, is the lifecycle mismatch between the car and the software in the car (Hartmann, 2004). While the average lifetime of a car is roughly 10 years, new technology and software comes to market every 2 to 3 years, thus making the manufacturing lifecycle complicated to manage (Mohan, 2006). The technological aspects, for problems imposed by the car as the service carrier, addressed by the MACS design framework thus are:

- Design and implementation of mobile services completely integrated into the car's infrastructure and operational concept
- Design of a modular infrastructure for mobile services, which is independent from individual car manufacturers' platforms in order to enable independent service providers to develop own services and reduce development costs
- Ensuring drivers' safety when using mobile services through responsible usage of different channels of user interaction (e.g., visual vs. audible content) in excess to complying with the current legal requirements

Figure 1. MACS "research radar" for mobile services, based on Ehmer (2002)

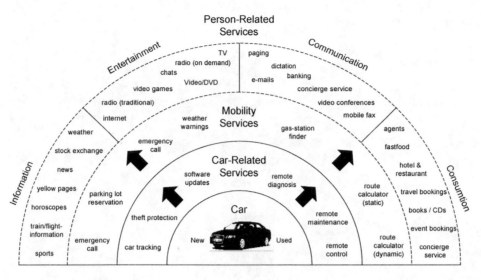

In order to be able to develop mobile automotive services successfully it is furthermore necessary to integrate both technical and economic views in one design framework. We will consequently present the MACS design framework which is composed of a set of guidelines for mobile service development as well as an example for a technical platform for service deployment in cars. To show the feasibility of that solution a specific mobile service—MACS MyNews—has been selected from a previously developed "research radar" of possible mobile services (see Figure 1) and it has been prototypically built according to the criteria derived from domain requirements.

THE MACS DESIGN FRAMEWORK

One of the main arguments in the past years when criticizing research in the field of mobile services was that most research conducted was too technical or technology-driven without offering usable solutions to existing needs or problems of drivers. Besides that there were hardly any viable business models for the developed mobile services.

In order to design attractive, usable, technically stable, and economically promising mobile services, both the economical as well as the technical perspective have to be taken into account. For that reason the MACS design framework (Figure 2) is divided into the following subsets or views, each describing one step in the life cycle of a mobile service:

- **Service scenario** which is targeted by the provider
- **Service network** of partners for service provision
- A selection of **technologies** used for the service
- **Prototype and platform** for service evaluation and assessing transferability to related services
- Consideration of **safety aspects** for ensuring the driver's safety
- Planning of **live service** deployment

No service whatsoever can be successful if it is not created according to the targeted users' needs. Similarly a service that offers useful functional-

Figure 2. MACS design framework

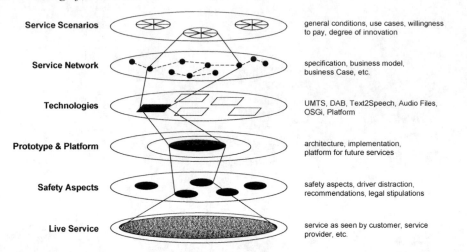

Service Scenarios — general conditions, use cases, willingness to pay, degree of innovation

Service Network — specification, business model, business Case, etc.

Technologies — UMTS, DAB, Text2Speech, Audio Files, OSGi, Platform

Prototype & Platform — architecture, implementation, platform for future services

Safety Aspects — safety aspects, driver distraction, recommendations, legal stipulations

Live Service — service as seen by customer, service provider, etc.

ity, but is not really usable for the customer will have to be redesigned. In order to enhance the chances of an economically promising service a targeted user group, partners needed for providing the service, and ways to successfully deploy the finished product have to be determined.

The "service scenarios" define the general set-up of the targeted environment and the use cases of mobile services. They are being studied in order to be able to determine more detailed information, like customer requirements or the willingness to pay for selected services. For finding the needed partners for the "service network" the service scenarios are being analyzed to determine the interaction between the different partners and how they should be organized in a network for value creation.

Since the provision of the mobile service as well as the service itself are technology centered the analysis of the economical aspects alone is insufficient for service design. The selection of proper technologies, both fulfilling economic requirements and supplying a sustainable platform for the service, are essential. To ensure a viable selection of technologies and allow the creation of an infrastructure, which is able to

compensate the lifecycle mismatch between car and technology, the process steps "technologies," "prototype & platform," and "safety aspects" are being examined. Initially the input coming in form of business cases is being matched with the available technology. Following this a prototype for demonstration and evaluation against safety guidelines is built. After being found safe the deployment of a "live service" is the final step in the whole process, merging the ideas generated and the prototypical implementations so far to a service offered to the public that should be usable, useful, technically stable, and economically sustainable.

Applying such a framework for a systematic iterative development of mobile automotive service confronts the developer with several challenges:

- Strategies for the service scenario have to be matched with the available technologies
- The service network design has to reflect the strategies for the service scenario
- People from different domains have to be able to work together, that is, understand each others' languages and rationales

- Functionality has to be built up iteratively and it has to be evaluated continuously against specific criteria and refined according to the results obtained

A solution for most of these aspects, which are not unknown in IS research, is presented, for example, by Hevner, March, Park, and Ram (2004) in form of the design science IS research process. At every point in the process of service design the previous step in the design framework defines the respective environment, composed of needs for which a solution is being searched and the setting in which the found solution has to work.

Whenever possible best practices already existing for a specific topic are being extracted from the domains' knowledge base and applied to the problem. Analogical to the "build and evaluate" loops found in iterative process models like the waterfall model (Royce, 1970) or in design science (Hevner et al., 2004), the assumptions being made in one process step of the model are evaluated in the following layer, such delivering input for a new "build" iteration. This is true in the form of additional requirements in the requirements elicitation phase conducted for each process (i.e., information flowing top-down) as well as for evaluation feedback for the process (i.e., information going bottom-up).

After a satisfactory solution has been found for the current layer the information gained in that process step is being applied to the preceding step (maybe causing a new iteration phase there), the change in knowledge, that is, the learning, is added to the respective domain's knowledge base.

APPLICATION OF THE MACS DESIGN FRAMEWORK

In the following section we will apply the MACS design framework to the exemplary service MACS MyNews. MACS MyNews was selected from a variety of services based on its high customers'

benefit, the relative ease of price building for the service, the availability of technology needed for offering the service, and last but not least the very high degree of innovation of that service in the automotive sector. We will highlight the findings on each stage on the way towards a deployable mobile automotive service.

Employing only the standard methods of vertical or horizontal prototyping for mobile services built in multiple iterative steps are inefficient or hardly useable. Floyd (1983) describes vertical prototyping as implementing system functions in their intended final form, only including selected functions, while in horizontal prototyping the functions are completely available, with part of their effect being omitted or simulated.

In the case of mobile services, a horizontal approach forbids the integration into the car's infrastructure. Evaluating mobile services in their target environment would be impossible. A tight integration using a vertical approach on the other hand does not allow to test the handling of the actual service, an evaluation of the safety implications is impossible.

A solution for this dilemma is to combine the two prototyping methods: functionality that is special or even unique to the service, like the ability to present personalizeable news or interact with the system via voice commands, is being implemented (vertical approach). Most of it in a form that is similar to what the user would experience while using the final service, but not necessarily in a way that would be used for technical realization for the final product (horizontal approach). This reduces the complexity of the approach from developing in a highly proprietary embedded system (i.e., in the car's infrastructure and on its infotainment unit) to presenting the user an approximation of the innovations important to the service in a way he or she would expect to see in his or her car.

Combining the iterative nature of the MACS design framework with its distinct phases described previously with the diagonal prototyping approach results in the MACS development model depicted in Figure 3.

The heart of the following process model is an iterative process adapted from the generic spiral process model (Boehm, 1988, p. 61; Wigand, 1998). It is combined with elements of prototyping. In opposition to the original spiral model, a stronger focus is placed on scenario discussions, the display of mock-ups and prototypes, and the active involvement of users. Requirements are collected and adapted within each iteration. Figure 3 shows the MACS process model that was used during the development of the MACY MyNews service.

Beginning with the planning phase, the activities for the respective iterations are scheduled. Afterwards the needed input for the tasks is analysed and the appropriate requirements are either deducted from the prior field studies and expert interviews (iteration 1) or simultaneously collected through user and expert involvement (iteration 2-4). The rendered part of the system is evaluated after the engineering phase is completed. Using the previously deducted general requirements

(see above), the translation of the socio-technical and economic needs into system design is done iteration by iteration with the assistance of users and experts. After cycling through the phases a total of four times, the MACS MyNews service is operative since May 2006 and will be presented to the broader public by end of 2006.

MACS Service Scenarios

Defining the service scenario is the first step when planning the development and deployment of a new mobile service. It mainly consists of a thorough analysis of the target environment, including both the prospect customers as well as the competitors in the field. The desired outcome of this step is the definition of a service scenario in which the environmental factors and the proposed business model are evaluated. The service scenario is the starting point for selecting partners for future service provision and technologies for the service implementation.

The three elementary questions derived from the literature (Kotler & Keller, 2005) needed to

Figure 3. MACS development process model

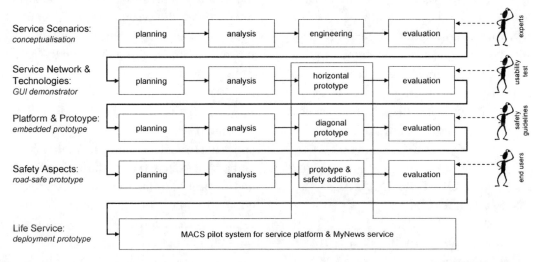

identify a service scenario and players involved in the service network are the following:

- **Who** are my targeted customers (target group)
- **What** am I offering (value proposition)
- **How** will the service be delivered (service production and delivery, this will be addressed in the service network level)

"Who would be interested in offering a mobile service?" Despite the lack of success of in-car mobile services in the past years, researches results reveal both declining average prices for in-car mobile systems and rising numbers of subscribers for mobile services, ranging from enhanced navigation systems to digital entertainment (e.g., Lawrence, 2005). Furthermore Lawrence compiles figures from various research groups, that indicate an expected rise in subscriber numbers in the German market from below 5 million in 2004 to substantially over 15 million in 2009. A Roland Berger Strategy Consulting survey "How to hit a moving target" (Heidingsfelder, Kintz, Petry, Hensley, & Sedran, 2001) even projected 31 million mobile service subscribers by the end of the decade. Thus mobile services still could represent a promising way of generating new revenue streams in after-sales processes for both car manufacturers and independent service providers (Parnell, 2002), also offering an interesting strategy for value-added services for "premium" car manufacturers.

Parallel to identifying who would probably be interested in offering a new service an even more important issue is: "Who is interested in using or buying a mobile service?" For MACS we identified usage scenarios of mobile services that result from the everyday use of our cars. In the morning and evening commuters join professional drivers on the streets on their way to work or back home. In doing so, almost 2/3 of German job holders commute by car, 4 out of 5 when the distance to work is greater than 10 km. The time spent in the car varies, but more than half of the commuters need up to 30 minutes for one way, for 1/5 the trip takes up to one hour and more (Statistisches Bundesamt Deutschland, 2005). Working on at least 200 days a year travel times easily top 8 whole days spent on the road for a majority of German commuters during one year. Similar situations are found globally, for example, average travel time of commuters in the U.S. is 25 minutes (Reschovsky, 2004; United States Census Bureau, 2003), so the following assumptions made for the German market will probably be rather similar for the U.S. and other markets.

The next question after knowing who could offer and who could use a service is: "What kind of service is useful for the target group?" Growing needs for information and time being a scarce and precious resource, providing interesting and "valuable" information for the driver while he/she is in the car appears to be promising. Drivers usually do not completely focus on their task of driving, but are distracted by other tasks like listening to music and so forth. Thus personalizable and interactive mobile information services could enable drivers to use time in their cars more efficiently—this is the setting for MACS MyNews.

MACS MyNews should be a solution for organizing the daily routine in the car more efficiently: a personalizable, interactive news service allowing people to be the editor, producer, and consumer of their very own newscast, thus minimizing redundancies and overlapping times. The vision of MACS MyNews is to completely liberate drivers from ordinary radio stations and their news program. MACS MyNews should therefore provide the user with news items which are up to date and ready for presentation all the time, not only every half or full hour as the radio stations' newscasts. MACS MyNews should enable every user to be the editor of "his/her" newscast, since they can not only specify the topics they are interested in, but also set the sequence in which the topics are being presented, assign weights to topics to define how much information they want in that category and more. News could be started when the user would like to hear the latest news, not just every full and half hour. The user could also interact with the news service, that is, if the user has to refuel his/her car he/she can pause the news; if the user missed a detail of a message he/she could listen to it again instantly, skipping forward and backward like with a CD or MP3 player is also possible.

Summarizing the service scenario obtained here is straightforward: MACS MyNews should be a service designed for commuters and professional drivers. It should be designed to replace the radio stations' news casts, offering to use the commuting times more efficiently through a tailored information supply.

MACS Service Network

After determining what kind of service should be supplied to which target group, the next step is the definition of a service network. This comprises the necessary partners needed to offer the service as it has been defined in the service scenario. The outcome of this process step is used in iterative loops together with the following selection of possible technologies to define a network of partners for providing a service according to the definition in the service scenario.

By asking what kind of service could be offered the partners that have to be integrated in the service network are the ones in charge of creating the value for the customer. In the case of a news service those partners will most likely supply the newscasts. Defining the targeted customer base allows the selection of a partner in the automotive sector that makes sense for service deployment: people driving a high end limousine might not very likely be interested in mobile games, but rather in a stock market live ticker. Asking how the service is going to be delivered finally should close the gap between creation and consumption of the service

It is very noteworthy that especially the first and last questions cannot be answered right away. In both cases certain technological conditions that are being worked out in the following process step have to be considered to answer the questions correctly. The most pragmatic approach is to revise the assumptions and ideas for the service network and the technological aspects iteratively until a solution is found that offers a sound technological basis as well as a promising service.

The following example illustrates how the service network for MACS MyNews was derived by analyzing the service scenario and technological implications: The news being used by the MACS MyNews service is delivered to commuters by various content providers. They are being selected, aggregated, and edited by the service provider and transmitted to the car where they are displayed. The main data channel to the customer is digital radio (DAB) for the news messages. Additional value-added services, such as more detailed information or multimedia files, can be downloaded on a pay-per-use basis via mobile phone, provided by a mobile network operator. The partners needed for offering the MyNews services thus are one or several content providers, a car manufacturer, network providers for digital radio, and cellular networks as well as one controlling instance that is in charge of service provisioning: the overall service provider.

The service provider plays a very central role and is in charge of:

- Selecting content providers
- Aggregating and editing their information (for use while driving)
- Selecting network providers for data transfer
- Ensuring the integration into the car's infrastructure
- Coordinating the efforts of the partners

The service provider is also the single point of contact for the customer subscribing to the MACS MyNews service, being responsible for customer

Figure 4. Proposed MyNews service network

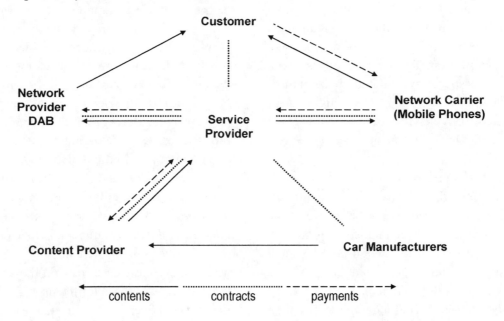

management as well as offering a first-level support to the customer.

The topology chosen for the MyNews service network is a star-shape with the service provider as the central instance and single contractor for all other partners. The other partners are arranged in a way that represents their position for supplying the mobile service. The base is formed by the car manufacturer that offers the basic platform for service deployment and the content providers delivering the raw material for MACS MyNews. The middle layer is composed of the central service provider, aggregating and editing the contents before they are being transmitted to the customer, and the network providers needed for delivering the content to the customer. The customer as the end consumer of the service output is the tip of the MACS MyNews service network.

MACS Technologies

The development of the technical domain have to be made considering the economic considerations and, as mentioned for the previous step "service network," decisions or restrictions in one of the domains often have implications for the other. Using the described service scenario and integrating the service network partners the outcome of this process step are the technological fundamentals of the future service.

The logical separation of mobile services into three areas (creation/aggregation, transmission, and display of information) as seen in the service network is also applicable for technological considerations:

- The data formats are important for data creation or aggregation since all the information needed for supplying the service has to be representable by the format.
- The data format as well as the usage scenario has a great impact on the decision how the data should be delivered to the car. Along with different pricing models and costs for the transmission, the volume of data in combination with the data rate at which the information is being transmitted can be limiting factors for one or another channel. In the worst case a change of the assumptions made for the service scenario and service network is needed.

- The available amount of data and its quality influence the possible ways of user interaction in the car. While the information itself might be transferred in form of (compressed) text files that are being read to the user with a text-to-speech system it might be of more value for the customer to have higher quality audio or video files of pre-recorded text, which is slower in transmission.

The following example for MACS MyNews points out how the iterative decision process between the definition of the service and the selection of matching technologies. To reduce complexity only the technology used for content transmission is being presented here. MACS MyNews is supposed to deliver the latest news in a personalizeable form for commuters on their way to work or back home. That means:

- Personalized news selected are most likely only a subset of the news available
- Time until the first item is presented after start-up should be as short as possible
- The same is true for latency between news items
- A basic version of MACS MyNews is supposed to be provided free of charge

Those assumptions from the service scenario and a possible business case greatly affect the selection of the media format (audio/video or text) used in MACS MyNews and the channel used to transmit them. While audio contents provide a high sound quality, their production (i.e., a speaker recording them) is more expensive compared to automated aggregation of texts, which are later synthesized by a text-to-speech engine. The transmission of audio content also is more expensive than the transmission of texts, since the same amount of information (i.e., a news item) uses a multiple of storage space, bandwidth, and time to transmit.

Even very highly encrypted audio files cannot be transferred over digital radio as it is available today at a reasonable rate. In the worst case, that is, when the desired information had just been transferred, the user would have to wait for up to 2 hours before that particular information would be retransmitted (based on the assumption of 2 hours of audio files, CSA-Celp encoded [61Mbit] broadcasted via 8kbit/s digital radio). This problem can be circumvented either by using text files, which are smaller and faster in transmission thus reducing the waiting time by a factor of 30, or by using broadband cellular services where the user queries for the information and receives only the news he/she is interested in. Since the MACS MyNews business case rests on the assumption that basic news is free for the user, the latter option cannot be realized as the user would have to pay the fees for data transmission over his/her cell phone. This means that in order to supply news in near real time after entering the car, text files have to be broadcasted.

The very brief and generic examination of the different possible technologies for data transmission and data representation for MACS MyNews alone shows the diversity of general technical conditions a service provider has to cope with in the design phase of the product. After the technologies promising to be the most viable have been chosen the next step is to evaluate that decision in form of a functional prototype in the next steps.

MACS Prototype and Platform

The preceding steps delivered the requirements for the new mobile service as well as possible partners in providing service and a selection of technologies that are to be used for providing the service. In order to be able to evaluate the service itself (e.g., user acceptance), the implementation (e.g., as to safety, usability, and perceived usefulness), and the practicability of the chosen technologies (e.g., technical proof of concepts), a prototype of

Figure 5. MACS service platform architecture

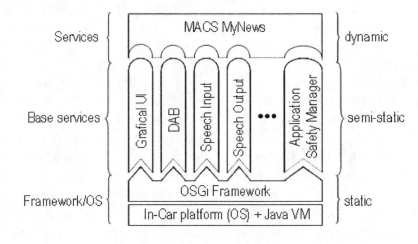

the planned service has to be built. The outcome of the evaluation using this prototype will then be used for applying changes to the preceding levels in the MACS design framework as well as for the following considerations of safety aspects.

To be able to successfully implement mobile services in a car a service platform has to be available. Its two main purposes are to allow the easy integration of services into the car's infrastructure and thus allowing the developer to focus on the development of the services' business logic. In order to determine which services would be needed and how to structure the service platform as a framework for mobile services, an approach mixing domain analysis (i.e., automotive mobile services) (Aksit, Tekinerdogan, Marcelloni, & Bergmans, 1999) and "best practice" analysis (Boone, 1999), with the Siemens "Top Level Architecture" (TLA) in mind, proved to be useful and applicable.

The functionality of the MACS framework should be differentiated into "base services," each one grouping related methods logically and communicating among each other via the OSGi framework (Barr & Mata, 2000; OSGi Alliance, 2005). Those base services could represent either an interface to the car infrastructure, ensure the usage safety of the mobile services, or provide architectural building blocks on top of existing frameworks such as the OSGi framework (OSGi Alliance, 2005).

The OSGi framework offers many inbuilt services such as component life cycle management and dynamic service discovery of services, ensuring a robust end-to-end solution for embedded devices (Wong, 2001). Remotely upgrading the system or adding new features or services also poses no problem for OSGi-based solutions (Palenchar, 2002). Furthermore the OSGi platform has a large user base and is used by car manufacturers such as Audi and BMW as well as tier one supplier such as Siemens VDO.

Since the base services mentioned previously are very specific to a car's infrastructure, they form an application programming interface (API) for the car's devices. Every car manufacturer would have to implement this API according to public and open specifications, allowing others to supply end-user software for the manufacturer's cars. Of course the embedded platform in a car may not be extended easily or quickly, thus the base services also enable the system designer to add or alter functionality even between platform life cycles (life-cycle mismatch, Hartmann, 2004).

For MACS MyNews several of the proposed base services have been implemented in order to allow realistic user evaluations. The user interface base service offers information output to a graphical display (i.e., textual output or graphical/video output) as well as the output of texts via a text-to-speech engine and different audio formats. On the input side the platform currently supports the (car manufacturer's specific) haptic input device as well as speech recognition. A universal cell phone adapter and a broadcast adapter allow exchanging data with services in the car or simply provide information on services in the car.

During the testing phases only the broadcast adapter is being used to receive data via digital radio broadcast. The technical specifications for unidirectional services (only using broadcast technology) and bidirectional services as worked out in the context of the DIAMOND project (Hallier, 2001, Hallier 2001a) served as foundation for the creation and definition of functionality merged in the broadcast adapter and the universal cell phone adapter. A very basic implementation of the *application safety manager* blocks detailed information from being shown on the display while driving.

An implemented a preliminary diagonal prototype (i.e., showing the unique features in the correct environment) is necessary for the following safety verifications for creating a service that is usable in a moving vehicle.

MACS Safety Aspects

The safe usage of mobile services also while driving is the single most important aspect for mobile automotive services. The premise is never to distract the driver from the main task—driving. For that reason safety considerations already had an influence on the design of the service in the previous design steps, but also (and mainly) on the design of the mobile service platform in the car. One of the MACS project partners, the Institute of Ergonomics at the Darmstadt University of Technology, compiled a compendium of safety guidelines for mobile services from the current state of the art as found in the literature (e.g., in Becker, 1996; Tijerina, 2000; Tijerina, Parmer, & Goodman, 2000), as well as current laws and evaluated the MACS MyNews prototype against these guidelines.

In order to ensure driving safety for the automotive mobile services two main aspects have to be taken into account. First, the services are supposed to be usable in a safe way even while driving and second, the services have to comply with local legislation (Becker, 1999). The first step to achieve safety is to offer user interfaces that are qualified for usage while driving. This is why user input on the MACS platform is not limited to using a haptic input device, which means taking one hand off of the steering wheel, but allows the usage of a speech recognition engine, where the user uses voice commands (Färber & Färber, 1984). The same is also true for output devices: The MACS service platform not only offers the visual man-machine interface for the output of information but also a speech synthesis engine to output texts using the audio channel. The driver can thus focus on the street and does not have to look at the screen for information retrieval.

In order to assure a safe level of user interaction a special component, the application safety manager, controls the quantity as well as the format of information that may be delivered to users at any time. An internal rating function weights sensor information and incorporates the amount and the nature of information that is to be presented into the determination of how to present which information. Services using the MACS reference platform thus are flexible to avoid user distraction (e.g., limiting the output to only critical messages if the driver is under stress) and ensure that all services comply with current law (e.g., using text-to-speech instead of displaying written text while driving).

In order to be able to evaluate the risk potential of the prototypically implemented MACS

Figure 6. Taped road test usage scenario (TU Darmstadt)

MyNews using the service platform the Institute of Ergonomics conducted a road trial test, comparable to Wikman, Nieminen, & Summala (1998), with several test persons. The usage of MACS MyNews during those road trials were defined using different usage scenarios. On one hand the driving situation varied, that is, the road trials took place on motorways/freeways, on the highways, and on city roads. On the other hand the mode of user interaction was changed: The test persons were to operate the MyNews service using the haptic man-machine interface or using speech commands.

As a comparing parameter for the actual risk potential the car radio had to be operated in the same situations using only the haptic interface, as a speech recognition engine is not yet available for the radio. After each of those scenarios the subjective stress and distraction was evaluated using questionnaires the test persons had to fill out. In order to be able to objectively analyze the scenarios the general traffic situation (density of traffic, etc.), the man-machine interface (both input device and display) and the face of the driver were recorded by four video cameras mounted in the test vehicle. That enabled us to determine, for example, if the driver stayed in the lane, how often and for how long the driver looked at the screen in the middle of the dashboard, and how often and for how long the driver took his/her

hands off of the steering wheel to use the haptic input device.

The evaluation of the road trials is not yet completed, but first evaluations of the questionnaires give strong evidence that the drivers felt comfortable using the service while driving and did not make any difference between using MACS MyNews and the familiar car radio as to a distraction from the driving task. Minor changes concerning details of the interface design have been extrapolated from that feedback and have been included in another iteration of the prototyping process step.

MACS Live Service: Some Preliminary Conclusions

The final step and conclusion of a successful development process of a mobile service is the deployment of a live service. In order to achieve a successful introduction into the market all process steps have to be re-evaluated quickly and checked for inconsistencies. These steps are currently (early 2006) being done.

The service scenario built at the very beginning evaluated the general conditions and pointed out usage scenarios and use cases. Since some time has passed since all that information was collected a review of the assumptions made has to ensure that they are still valid, for example, the targeted customer base is still available and willing to pay for the service, and so forth. A detailed business plan and an up-to-date *strengths weaknesses opportunities threats* (SWOT) analysis are mandatory for a successful and sustainable mobile service.

In order to be able to offer the service derived from the service scenario a service network was designed, also considering major technological implications. For all roles in the service network specific partners have to be found. If these partners cannot be found a start-up or spin-off company could be considered. In the current case the most likely candidate for such a spin-off is to fill the role of service providers themselves, which is about to be founded by a car manufacturer (maybe in corporation with content providers).

Since the field of technologies is very dynamic it might be possible to find better or cheaper solutions for the tasks to be solved for the service in the future. Examples for the fast changing environment are the availability and prices for mobile broadband connectivity using UMTS in Germany. While UMTS services seemed to be far away in Germany back in the fall of 2003 (Dernbach, 2003), today more than half of the people in Germany can use the high speed mobile network (Teltarif, 2006). As of 2006, almost all of the German network providers offer flat fees for data services over their UMTS networks for about $50 per month and prices are about to decline in the future.

The service platform and the service itself exist in early 2006 as a prototype. Before the actual service can go live for the mass market the needed interfaces, also derived from the technologies that are coming into operation, have to be finally determined together with the car manufacturers. Since the target system, the car, is a safety-critical environment even more special precautions have to be taken in order to ensure a safe operation at all times. One approach to ensure that automotive software meets requirements, for example, response times, is proposed by Botaschanjan, Kof, Kühnel, and Spichkova (2005). In their development model traditional testing phases for software components are exchanged with software verification processes that are proving that critical functionalities are working properly and cannot be affected by other subsystems.

Driver safety is the most critical issue when offering a live service. The proposed service platform, however, if implemented correctly, liberates the service developer from coping with those problems. The platform is a fast and reliable way of controlling services' output to the driver at any time. Rules for the output can be adjusted to reflect the current legal situation at anytime, so for the deployment of the service those rules have to be defined according to the current jurisdiction. The safety guidelines worked out by the Institute of Ergonomics are a good starting point for re-evaluating the upcoming life service.

Last but not least: the service framework not only allows the developers to work with standardized and open interfaces, it also enables the service provider to deal with the lifecycle mismatch between the car's and the software's life cycles and keep the services offered up to date. Innovative technologies in the automotive sector, such as Wireless LAN or WiMax, will have to be supported by the framework as soon as possible in order to allow the adoption of services and the creation of novel services using the distinct properties offered by new technologies. In the case of Wireless LAN, services may be altered so it is possible to receive data additionally via W-LAN access points offering location-based information.

OUTLOOK

The application of the development framework and the development process initially proposed using MACS MyNews as an exemplary service proved the practicability and usefulness of the approach. Especially the interconnections between the different layers of the framework could thus be handled. The MACS MyNews service worked as expected, the results obtained at the various stations in the development were often presented to the public to not only receive evaluation feedback for the service itself, but also for checking for the development framework and the development process itself.

One of the main results learned through these presentations was that the users' evaluation of the usefulness of the service as well as the service usability is highly dependent on the setting in which the service is being presented. The most obvious example was one person who complained about the "unacceptable" quality of the text-to-speech engine when evaluating a GUI mock-up of the service on a PC, but complimented us on the very same component when he tried the service integrated in the car.

This lead us to the conclusion that the platform described in the development process for mobile services should be extended to offer a rapid prototyping environment enabling software developers to show services in the car very early in the development process. Such an in-car GUI demonstrator also helps to communicate and coordinate the service development among engineers and management. It also enables the research of very new terrain of user interaction in the car, like an intelligent avatar based co driver system.

REFERENCES

Aksit, M., Tekinerdogan, B., Marcelloni, F., & Bergmans, L. (1999). Deriving frameworks from domain knowledge. In M. E. Fayad, D. C. Schmidt, & R. E. Johnson (Eds.), *Building application frameworks—Object-oriented foundations of framework design* (pp. 169-198). New York: John Wiley & Sons.

Barr, J., & Mata, R. (2000). OSGi: Spec basics, interface issues. *Electronic Engineering Times, 1144,* 112.

Becker, S. (1996). *Panel discussion on introduction of intelligent vehicles into society: Technical, mental and legal aspects. Mental models, expectable consumer behaviour and consequences for system design and testing.* Paper presented at the IEEE Intelligent Vehicles Symposium.

Becker, S. (1999). Konzeptionelle und experimentelle Analyse von Nutzerbedürfnissen im Entwicklungsprozess. In Bundesanstalt für Straßenwesen (Ed.), *Informations- und Assistenzsysteme im Auto benutzergerecht gestalten. Methoden für den Entwicklungsprozess.* (pp. 64-72). Bergisch Gladbach: Verlag für neue Wissenschaft.

Boehm, B. W. (1988). A spiral model of software development and enhancement. *IEEE: Computer, 21*(5), 61-72

Boone, J. (1999). Harvesting design. In M. E. Fayad, D. C. Schmidt, & R. E. Johnson (Eds.), *Building application frameworks—Object-oriented foundations of framework design* (pp. 199-210). New York: John Wiley & Sons.

Botaschanjan, J., Kof, L., Kühnel, C., & Spichkova, M. (2005, May). *Towards verified automotive software.* Paper presented at the 2nd International ICSE workshop on Software Engineering for Automotive Systems.

Dernbach, C. (2003). *UMTS-Start in Deutschland nicht in Sicht.* Retrieved April 20, 2006, from http://www.heise.de/newsticker/meldung/print/39973

Ehmer, M. (2002). Mobile Dienste im Auto—Die Perspektive der Automobilhersteller. In R. Reichwald (Ed.), *Mobile Kommunikation: Wertschöpfung, Technologies, neue Dienste* (pp. 459-472). Wiesbaden, Germany: Gabler.

Färber, B., & Färber, B. (1984). *Sprachausgaben im Fahrzeug. Handbuch für Anwender.* Frankfurt am Main: Forschungsvereinigung Automobiltechnik e.V.

Floyd, C. (1983). *A systematic look at prototyping.* Paper presented at the Approaches to Prototyping, Namur, Belgium.

Frost & Sullivan. (2003). *Customer attitudes and perceptions towards telematics in passenger vehicles market.*

Fuhr, A. (2001). *Die Telematik ist tot—es lebe die rollende Schnittstelle.* Paper presented at the Euroforum Jahrestagung "Telematik," Bonn.

Hallier, J., Betram, G., Koch, H., Perrault, O., Kuck, D., Korte, O., & Twietmeyer, H. (2001a). *DIAMOND: Technical specification for bi-directional services.*

Hallier, J., Kuck, D., Perrault, O., Rucine, P., Twietmeyer, H., Korte, O., Capra, L., Betram, G., Fernier, M., & Schulz-Hess, T. (2001). *DIA-MOND: Technical specification for uni-directional Services*

Hartmann, J. (2004). Wo viel Licht ist, ist starker Schatten - Softwareentwicklung in der Automobilindustrie. *Automatisierungstechnik, 52*(8), 353-358.

Heidingsfelder, M., Kintz, E., Petry, R., Hensley, P., & Sedran, T. (2001). *Telematics: How to hit a moving target—A roadmap to success in the Telematics arena*. Detroit/Stuttgart/Tokyo: Roland Berger.

Hevner, A. R., March, S. T., Park, J., & Ram, S. (2004). Design science in information systems research. *MIS Quarterly, 28*(1), 75-105.

Kotler, P., & Keller, K. L. (2005). *Marketing management* (12 ed.). Upper Saddle River, NJ: Prentice Hall.

Lawrence, S. (2005, January). Wireless on wheels—The latest advances in telematics. *Technology Review,* 22-23.

Mohan, L. R. (2006). Driving down the fast lane: Increasing automotive opportunities the EMS provider way. *Frost & Sullivan Market Insight* Retrieved April 29, 2006, from http://www.frost.com/prod/servlet/market-insight-print.pag?docid=67150588

OSGi Alliance. (2005). *About the OSGi service platform.* Technical Whitepaper. San Ramon, CA: Author.

Palenchar, J. (2002). OSGi networks ready to roll. *TWICE.* retrieved January 15, 2005 from http://www.twice.com/article/CA198367.html

Parnell, K. (2002, Fall). Telematics drives the new automotive business model. *Xcell Journal.*

Reschovsky, C. (2004). *Journey to work: 2000.*

Royce, W. W. (1970). *Managing the development of large software systems.* Paper presented at the International Conference on Software Engineering, Monterey, CA.

Statistisches Bundesamt Deutschland. (2005). *Leben und Arbeiten in Deutschland - Ergebnisse des Mikrozensus 2004.* Wiesbaden, Germany.

Teltarif. (2006). *UMTS: Wo sind die neuen Netze schon verfügbar?* Retrieved April 30, 2006, from http://www.teltarif.de/i/umts-coverage.html

Tijerina, L. (2000, May). *Issues in the evaluation of drive distraction associated with in-vehicle information and telecommunication systems.* Retrieved May 5, 2006, from http://www-nrd.nhtsa.dot.gov/departments/nrd-13/driver-distraction/PDF/3.PDF

Tijerina, L., Parmer, E. B., & Goodman, M. J. (2000). *Individual differences and in-vehicle distraction while driving: A test track study and psychometric evaluation.* Retrieved April 5, 2006, from http://www-nrd.nhtsa.dot.gov/departments/nrd-13/driver-distraction/PDF/4.PDF

United States Census Bureau. (2003). *2003 American community survey.* Washington DC: Author.

Werder, H. (2005). *Verkehrstelematik als Element der Verkehrspolitik.* Paper presented at the its-ch, Olten, Switzerland.

Wikman, A.-S., Nieminen, T., & Summala, H. (1998). Driving experience and time-sharing during in-car tasks on roads of different width. *Ergonomics, 41*(3), 358-372.

Wigand, R., Picot, A., & Reichwald, R. (1998). *Information, organization and management: Expanding corporate boundaries.* Chichester.

Wong, W. (2001). Open services gateway initiative: OSGi links devices and clients. *Electronic Design,* p. 86.

Chapter XII
Cross–Cultural Consumer Perceptions of Advertising via Mobile Devices:
Some Evidence from Europe and Japan

Parissa Haghirian
Sophia University, Japan

Maria Madlberger
Vienna University of Economics and Business Administration, Austria

ABSTRACT

This chapter tries to answer the question on how international consumers differ in their perceptions of mobile advertising (m-advertising). In order to answer this research question a survey among mobile phone users was carried out in Austria and in Japan. These two countries have been selected because they show a high dissimilarity in culture in historical terms but also in the degree of technological development and usage. Both countries experienced a similar economic development and show comparable living standards. Furthermore, Japan and Austria are leading markets for advanced mobile technology in their geographic areas. On the basis of the literature review, variables picturing perceptions of m-advertising are defined, hypotheses in comparing consumer perspectives in the respective countries are presented, and results of the MANOVA analysis are shown and discussed. Finally, the paper presents theoretical and managerial implications, limitations, and recommendations for future research on this issue.

INTRODUCTION

Permanent Internet access enabled by mobile devices like mobile phones or PDAs is becoming more and more widely used. Mobile technologies open up new challenges for companies which want to benefit from mobile commerce (m-commerce).

One of the most important commercial applications in this respect is marketing. Marketing instruments using mobile devices (m-marketing) allow innovative forms of customer relationships and interaction. They can lead to the development of numerous m-commerce-based services (Venkatesh, Ramesh, & Massey, 2003). In m-commerce, a mobile phone can serve as a "portable entertainment player, a new marketing tool for retailers and manufacturers, a multi-channel shopping device, a navigation tool, a new type of ticket and money, and a new mobile Intranet device" (Funk, 2004, p. 2).

Compared with computer-based e-commerce, m-commerce is a very new area of development. As a consequence, m-commerce applications have been subject to academic research to a much lesser extent. Many potential applications of m-commerce are still under researched. One of them is the application of mobile devices for advertising purposes. One important exception is the empirical study by Okazaki (2004) who investigated Japanese consumers' perceptions of wireless ads. Beyond that, there is only little knowledge about how consumers react to advertising via mobile devices. This gap becomes even wider when this issue is addressed on an international basis. By now, no findings on cross-country differences in the context of m-advertising are available. In contrast, online advertising accessed via desktop computers is well researched. For example, Web-based research in cross-cultural context revealed that users' cultural background strongly influences their perception of visible advertising design elements and colors (Del Galdo & Neilson, 1996; Marcus & Could, 2000). World Wide Web advertisers react to this by creating locally oriented Web sites (Cyr & Trevor-Smith, 2004).

The current trend in e-commerce toward globalization may be observed in m-commerce as well. This makes a cross-cultural investigation on consumers' perceptions of m-commerce applications a critical research issue. The research project described in this chapter has been carried out in order to analyze to what extent consumers differ in their perceptions of advertising via mobile devices across different cultures. In order to achieve comparable results, the study focuses on push marketing activities in the form of text advertising messages sent to consumers.

MOBILE-ADVERTISING AND ITS TECHNOLOGICAL DIMENSIONS

Together with the development from seller markets to buyer markets in the consumer goods sector, technological innovations were a key driver for a paradigm shift in marketing theory in the 1980s and 1990s (Dwyer, Schurr, & Oh, 1997; Groenroos, 1994; Gummesson, 1987). Although there are critical arguments on this approach as well (Brodie, Coviello, Brookes, & Little, 1997; Fournier, Dobscha, & Mick, 1998), this marketing practice has gained importance. Information technology plays a key role in this development as data warehousing and data mining are necessary sources of information for obtaining knowledge about the customer (Parvatiyar & Sheth, 2000).

In general, advertising is defined as "any paid form of non-personal presentation and promotion of ideas, goods or services by an identified sponsor" (Kotler, 2003, p. 590). Advertising via mobile devices or m-advertising is defined as *the usage of interactive wireless media (such as mobile phones and pagers; cordless telephones; personal digital assistants; two-way radios; baby crib monitors; wireless networking systems; GPS-based locators; and maps) to transmit advertising messages to consumers with the overall goal to promote goods and services.* M-advertising can be carried out on the basis of a number of technologies. Besides Web-based approaches that apply mobile Internet, messaging-based push advertisements can be used. Since the target consumer can be clearly identified by the advertiser, these advertising messages may include time and location sensitive, personalized information that can be transmitted via text messages or via e-mail on the mobile Internet.[1] There are different synonyms for m-advertising, such as wireless advertising (Krishnamurthy, 2003) or wireless advertising messaging (Petty, 2003).

Information systems are also vital in order to address each consumer on an individual basis (Peppers, Rogers, & Dorf, 1999). The opportunities of one-to-one marketing on the Web can be extended in m-commerce to context-specific marketing on allowing a higher degree of individualization. In particular, online activities can be closely linked with off-line activities. Some examples of potential m-advertising measures illustrate that, in practice, more innovative campaigns are possible. Advertising messages can be sent considering the *location* of the recipient, for example, containing a coupon with a price reduction on a certain product to a consumer who is in a particular shop. In addition, consumers' shopping needs can be accommodated with location-dependent offers and promotions (Stafford & Gillenson, 2003), like advertisements showing the menu of the day at a nearby restaurant or allowing access to a branded online game while waiting for the train at a railway station. All these advertising activities can also be used to create perceivable benefits for the consumers.

Like classical Web-based advertising, m-marketing activities allow personalization and interactivity. But m-advertising also has some distinctive features that enhance as well as limit advertising opportunities for marketers and lead to considerable differences compared to Web-based advertising. Besides the different optical appearances of m-advertising messages due to screen size, the linkage between online and off-line activities becomes more relevant. The recipient's context serves as an integrative part of the communication as messages can be adapted to the consumer's current location and time.

Personalization of Advertising Message Content

Marketing activities performed via mobile devices provide potential for personalization, because the transmission tools usually carry the user's assigned identity (Lee & Benbasat, 2003). Marketers can so use consumer feedback to customize their messages and offerings and collect information about consumers' preferences to improve future products and services (Stewart & Pavlou, 2002). The advantages of doing so are obvious. Potential customers can be addressed in a very individual way and relationships with the user improve because users are generally receptive to advertising that is personalized and relevant to their lifestyle (DeZoysa, 2002). Advertising can be carried out very precisely and with a clear focus on the target group (Varshney & Vetter, 2002). Using mobile devices to transmit messages to consumers also enables marketers to collect information on their current location. Consequently, advertising activities can be adapted to time and location-related consumer interests. In Japan, Internet-based services like city maps or train schedule information are commonly downloaded via mobile phones.

Information that is transferred in the context of m-commerce can thus be related to three situational aspects: (1) location, (2) time and location, and (3) context.

Location-Related Information

This takes into account where the recipient is situated during message transmittal. Consequently, consumers' shopping needs can be accommodated with location-dependent offers and promotions (Stafford & Gillenson 2003). In contrast to many Web-specific advertising instruments, which are limited to desktop computers, m-advertising allows their application at any location, for example, shops, pubs, cafes, public transportation, and other locations where a personal computer usually is not available. This allows a considerably improved customization of the advertising message. For example, a company can send an advertising message with a coupon for a price reduction on a certain product to a consumer who stays in a certain store. Such promotion campaigns have been carried out successfully via Web-based coupons where consumers could redeem coupons obtained on the Web in the physical store (Madlberger, 2004).

Time and Location-Related Information

This takes time-specific settings into account. In these settings, a firm can transfer information to remind recipients of a happening in the near future, for example, an event or a time-dependent service (e.g., a dinner at a restaurant). Hence, this kind of information might encourage the recipient to move to a specific location at a certain point of time.

Customer-Context-Specific Information

This can be related to time or the recipient's location, but it is primarily focused on the actual situation of a recipient. In a setting, in which an individual is waiting or being bored (e.g., waiting for a train, waiting at a hospital), he/she might be more likely and willing to grasp information or access the Internet than during a period of activity. In such a situation, the perception of an advertising message might be higher.

Limitations of M-Advertising

Although m-advertising offers attractive and innovative opportunities, it also has important *limitations,* which make m-advertising rather impractical in its current form. These limitations imply that today's application opportunities are still far away from the aforementioned scenarios. Most limitations are due to technical attributes of the mobile devices. In order to be portable, mobile devices today have limited processing power, low bandwidth, and unfavorable input/output devices. It is expected that many of these drawbacks will be overcome in some years, but screen size will remain limited (Lee & Benbasat, 2003) and will be an obstacle to extensive m-advertising messages. Beyond the mobile device's limitations, today's technology is also characterized by limited capacity, for example, the maximum length of SMS

texts or network operating systems. Design and content of m-advertising messages are therefore restricted to constraints in data volume and visual presentation.

CROSS CULTURAL PERCEPTIONS OF M-ADVERTISING

Mobile Development in Japan and Europe

In Japan, mobile phones started to gain popularity among young consumers as early as in the mid-1990s. In 1999, market leader NTT DoCoMo launched its mobile Internet-based i-mode service. The i-mode service allows mobile phone users constant access to the World Wide Web and enables subscribers to view Web pages via their mobile phones. Furthermore, they can send and receive mobile e-mails and can be directly addressed with advertising messages. As of the end of 2002 the proportion of mobile Internet users among mobile phone owners was 79.2 %. This was the highest percentage worldwide (Ministry of Public Management, Home Affairs, Post, and Telecommunications [MPHPT], 2003). Mobile phones also have quickly become a new advertising tool for more than 100 Japanese retailers and manufacturers that use mobile Internet as an instrument to target customers with discount coupons, to conduct surveys, or offer free samples (Funk, 2004).

The Austrian mobile phone market shows one of the largest penetration rates in Europe. In 2002, 6.8 million mobile phone users were registered (83.6%); in March 2004 penetration reached a level of 89.7% (Telekom Austria, 2004). GPRS and the Universal Mobile Telecommunications System (UMTS) (the European pendant to the Japanese mobile Internet) were introduced in 2003 (Merrill Lynch, 2002). In March 2004, the number of Austrian GPRS users increased to 840.000 (Telekom

Austria, 2004). The most popular non-voice-based service, however, is short message service (SMS), which is a part of the older Global System for Mobile Communications (GSM) standard. Basic SMS messaging, which counts for almost 10% of mobile telecommunications revenue, is not or to a very small extent related to mobile Internet. The frequent usage of SMS in Austria is mainly due to its usability, whereas other services like e-mail download and the usage of mobile Internet applications are considerably less applied. One major reason is consumers' lack of technology knowledge (Gutmann & Sochatzky, 2003).

Perceptions of M-Advertising in Japan and Austria

An important goal of any advertising activity is the achievement of certain reactions by the recipients. In order to get insights into how customers react to these campaigns, it is necessary to measure the mechanisms that drive consumers' reactions. Advertising research has revealed that the success of an advertising campaign strongly depends on how the customer reacts to a message. Effectiveness of advertising campaigns depends on numerous constructs; the most important ones are attitude toward advertising and attitude toward an advertising message (Gardner, 1985; Lutz, 1985; MacKenzie & Lutz, 1989; Moore & Hutchinson, 1983). On the basis of literature research in empirical results concerning Web-based advertising (Ducoffe, 1995, 1996) we derived four more variables picturing the effectiveness of m-advertising. These constructs are entertainment, informativeness, irritation, and credibility and will be discussed in the following.

Entertainment of M-Advertising

Feelings of enjoyment evoked by advertisements positively influence people's attitude toward the advertisement (Shavitt, Lowrey, & Haefner, 1998).

Entertainment fulfills the consumers' needs for "escapism, diversion, aesthetic enjoyment or emotional release" (McQuail, 1983). It can be used to involve customers more deeply and make them more familiar with the advertised product or service (Lehmkuhl, 2003). In Japan, mobile communication providers have very strongly promoted mobile Internet as a means of entertainment for many years. Japanese consumers regard their mobile phones not as mere communication tools anymore, but as portable entertainment players (Haghirian, Dickinger, & Kohlbacher, 2004). In contrast, in Europe and the United States, mobile Internet-based services are chiefly positioned as a convenient service for business professionals (Funk, 2004). As Johansson & Nonaka (1996) point out, advertising in Japan is more fantasy oriented but less logic. Advertising messages are often implicit, intuitive, and rather emotional. This is also true for m-advertising. Consequently, we assume that Japanese perceive m-advertising messages as more entertaining than Austrians.

H1: Japanese perceive m-advertising as more entertaining than Austrians.

Informativeness of M-Advertising

Information is considered a very valuable issue in m-marketing because recipients react very positively to advertising transferring incentives (Varshney, 2003). Marketers generally want to convey information via advertising messages (Gordon & De Lima-Turner, 1997). When it comes to m-advertising, the consumers want the message's content to be tailored to their interests (Robins, 2003). They prefer messages that are relevant for them (Milne & Gordon, 1993). In contrast to Europeans, Japanese prefer information to flow freely (Hall & Hall, 1987). Information plays an important role in Japanese society. A larger quantity of information is collected and transmitted within the Japanese society than in a Western society. Japanese are avid information gatherers, hence information exchanged refers to all kinds of data, including information that would not be relevant in Western countries (Johansson & Nonaka, 1996). Therefore we assume that m-advertising messages are considered a source of information to a higher degree by Japanese.

H2: Japanese perceive m-advertising as more informative than Austrians.

Irritation of M-Advertising

Advertisements might also evoke negative feelings. One important effect is irritation. If people feel indignity when being addressed by advertisements, their attitudes can be negatively influenced (Shavitt et al., 1998). A typical reaction is ignoring the message. Like any advertising message, m-advertising may provide an array of information that can confuse the recipient (Stewart & Pavlou, 2002). Moreover, as it is sent to a consumer's mobile phone, it can be perceived as an intrusion into his/her privacy. Many consumers are still uncomfortable with mobile business and are skeptical whether such business models are feasible and secure (Siau & Shen, 2003). M-advertising might affect users' feeling of being watched or recorded by organizations or other individuals (Rust, Kannan, & Peng, 2002). This leads to feelings of insecurity. Privacy concerns differ across cultures. Japanese are generally considered members of a collectivistic culture, where also information about individuals is frequently and openly shared. Hence, people share information that would be considered very private by Western standards (Hall & Hall, 1987). In contrast, Austrians belong to an individualistic culture where personal information is not freely distributed (Hall & Hall, 1987; Hofstede, 1980). Hence, we conclude that Austrians will be more easily irritated by m-advertising messages intruding into their lives than Japanese consumers are.

H3: Japanese perceive m-advertising as less irritating than Austrians.

Credibility of M-Advertising

Advertising credibility refers to "consumers' perception of the truthfulness and believability of advertising in general" (MacKenzie & Lutz, 1989, p. 51). An advertisement's credibility is particularly influenced by the company's credibility and the bearer of the message (Goldsmith, Lafferty, & Newell, 2000; Lafferty, Goldsmith, & Newell, 2002). In Japan, companies use social group allegiances to create value-added options for customers. They believe that the best way to perform advertising is to present a buyer who is satisfied with the product. Thus, they try to establish a mutual supportive relationship between buyer and seller (Johansson & Nonaka, 1996). This concept is strongly based on Japanese groupism and collectivistic features of Japanese society. Hence, Japanese are in general more trustful than their Western counterparts (Downes, Hemmasi, Graf, Kelley, & Huff, 2002). Companies they buy from are considered trustful partners. We thus conclude that Japanese perceive m-advertising messages as more credible than Austrians.

H4: Japanese perceive m-advertising as more credible than Austrians.

Perceived Advertising Value

Ducoffe (1995) argues that advertising value is a measure for advertising effectiveness and "may serve as an index of customer satisfaction with the *communication products* of organizations" (p. 1). The perceived value of advertising is "a subjective evaluation of the relative worth or utility of advertising to consumers" (Ducoffe, 1995, p. 1). Japanese retailers generally try to create value with their m-advertising messages, mainly because conveying service and product information to consumers readily and on time is a crucial aspect of advertising in Japan (Schneidewind, 1998). M-advertising messages contain information about bargains and new products or carry incentives to increase customers' convenience. We thus conclude that Japanese perceive m-advertising as more valuable than Austrians.

H5: Japanese perceive m-advertising as more valuable than Austrians.

Attitude Toward M-Advertising

Attitudes are "mental states used by individuals to structure the way they perceive their environment and guide the way they respond to it" (Aaker, Kumar, & Day, 1995, p. 254). An attitude toward an advertisement is defined as consumers' "learned predisposition to respond in a consistently favorable or unfavorable manner toward advertising in general" (MacKenzie & Lutz, 1989, p. 54). As it is known from the *theory of reasoned action* (TRA) (Ajzen & Fishbein, 1980) and the *theory of planned behavior* (Ajzen, 1991), attitudes have a considerable impact on behavior (Churchill & Iacobucci, 2002). A major influencing factor on attitude toward an advertisement is the general attitude toward the advertising medium (Larkin, 1979). A positive attitude toward mobile phones also reflects on attitude toward m-advertising. In Japan, 45% of mobile consumers state that their mobile phone is essential in their lives (NTT Docomo, 2001). Mobile phones play an important role in Japanese everyday life. The consumers show an extraordinarily positive attitude toward their mobile phones (Haghirian et al., 2004). The situation in Europe is different. People use their mobile phones chiefly for communication and to a lesser extent for handling contents, and mobile phones are also an integrative part of everyday life.

H6: Japanese show a more positive attitude toward m-advertising than Austrians.

RESEARCH METHODOLOGY

In order to analyze differences in users' attitudes and the mentioned antecedents, we conducted an empirical survey in Japan and in Austria. The study focused on messaging–based, push mobile advertisements, such as SMS and MMS. We included only the owners and users of mobile phones in the survey. In order to reflect general differences in user perceptions, we carried out both surveys with undergraduate students. This was done in order to obtain homogenous samples concerning socio-demographic structure and in order to cover a very relevant target group of mobile phone users.

In Japan, data collection was conducted in summer 2004. The respondents were undergraduate business students of two different Japanese universities. Out of 450 questionnaires handed out, 420 were returned; 367 of them provided usable answers for this investigation. In Austria, data collection took place in fall 2003. In an Austrian university, 408 undergraduate business students were surveyed. Out of 550 questionnaires handed out, 448 were returned; 408 of them provided usable answers for the investigation. Table 1 provides an overview of the demographic distribution of the Japanese and Austrian respondents. As data shows, there are differences in the gender and age structure between the responding undergraduates in the two countries.

In the survey, a standardized questionnaire was developed in English and then translated into German and Japanese by native speakers. After a back-translation into English and a comparison of the two English versions, two pre-tests (Austria: 30 students, Japan: 35 students) were conducted and adaptations were integrated into the questionnaires.

The scales for informativeness, entertainment, irritation, and advertising value were derived from the Web-based advertising scales of Ducoffe (1996). The scale measuring attitude toward m-advertising was based on Alwitt and

Table 1. Demographic attributes of the investigation samples

Age of Respondent	Austrian sample (n=408)		Japanese sample (n=367)	
	Female	**Male**	**Female**	**Male**
18-20 years	6.4%	1.0%	16.3%	37.1%
21-25 years	39.0%	34.8%	13.0%	28.3%
older than 26 years	7.2%	11.6%	1.9%	3.3%
Total	**52.6%**	**47.4%**	**31.3%**	**68.7%**

Table 2. Cronbach alphas of scale items

Measures	Scale Origin	Items	Alpha Japan	Alpha Austria
			n=367	n=408
Entertainment	Ducoffe, 1996	6	.86	.84
Informativeness	Ducoffe, 1996; Lastovicka, 1983	7	.78	.88
Irritation	Lastovicka, 1983; Ducoffe, 1996	5	.62	.65
Credibility	MacKenzie and Lutz, 1989	4	.79	.77
Attitude toward advertising	Alwitt and Prabhaker, 1992	8	.76	.72
Perceived advertising value	Ducoffe, 1996	2	.83	.90

Prabhacker's (1994) scale measuring consumer attitudes toward TV ads. The credibility scale based on Mackenzie and Lutz's (1989) scale for measuring advertisement credibility. All measures were assessed via 5-point Likert-type scales ranging from "strongly agree" (1) to "strongly disagree" (5). Sample questions can be found in the appendix. Table 2 provides an overview of the reliabilities (Cronbach's alphas) of the investigated items. All variables, except the irritation scale in both samples, show alpha levels above .7.

The factor analysis was performed by main component analysis with Varimax rotation. Only factors with eigenvalues < 1 were further used.

STUDY RESULTS

The analysis of the hypotheses developed in the previous section was conducted via MANOVA tests. Table 3 summarizes the results of the comparative analysis of the Austrian and Japanese sample.

Entertainment of m-advertising is perceived more positively by Japanese than by Austrians, hence Hypothesis 1 is supported by the data (F=20.51). Like mobile phones in general, also advertisements received via them are considered a source of entertainment to a larger extent in Japan. Concerning the informativeness of m-advertising, the MANOVA results indicate no significant difference between Japanese and Austrian students, Hypothesis 2 is therefore rejected (F=.86). Although Japanese advertisers send a large amount of consumer-relevant information via m-advertising messages, the surveyed recipients do not perceive them as more informative. Hypothesis 3 indicates that Japanese are less irritated by m-advertising messages than Austrians. In this respect, Austrian and Japanese students differ significantly (F=132.2). But in contrast to Hypothesis 3, it is the Japanese students who perceive m-advertising

Table 3. Hypotheses tests via MANOVA

	F-Ratio	Country	Mean	Standard Deviation	Hypothesis
Entertainment (H1)	20.51**	Japan	3.96	.87	Supported
		Austria	4.2	.80	
Informativeness (H2)	.86	Japan	3.7	.91	Rejected
		Austria	3.7	.86	
Irritation (H3)	132.2**	Japan	2.1	.84	Rejected
		Austria	2.9	.92	
Credibility (H4)	.355	Japan	4.0	.80	Rejected
		Austria	3.9	.81	
Attitude toward m-advertising (H5)	50.62**	Japan	3.8	.83	Supported
		Austria	4.2	.88	
Advertising value of m-advertising (H6)	30.03**	Japan	3.7	.93	Supported
		Austria	4.1	.85	

**p<0.001, 1= Strongly Agree, 5= Strongly Disagree

more irritating than Austrian students. Therefore we reject Hypothesis 3. In the light of the high group orientation of Japanese (Hofstede, 1980), these results are rather unanticipated. One explanation could be a larger number of messages received by Japanese students that influences the degree of irritation. In the context of credibility, the analysis shows that Japanese students score slightly lower on this variable. But the difference is not significant, hence Hypothesis 4 is not supported either (F=.355).

Both dependent variables, advertising value, and attitude toward advertising are rated more positively by the Japanese respondents. Therefore we accept Hypothesis 5 (F=30.03) and Hypothesis 6 (F=50.62) according to the MANOVA analysis. M-advertising messages are obviously regarded as more valuable and are therefore being appreciated to a higher extent by Japanese students. This result is consistent with the observation obtained by Haghirian et al. (2004) who are stating that Japanese consumers generally perceive mobile phones and their impact on daily life as very positive.

DISCUSSION

This investigation is a pioneer in analyzing cross-cultural differences in the perception of m-advertising. Figure 1 shows the differences between perceptions of m-advertising of the two respective markets.

In general, the study reveals that Japanese and Austrian students do not rate m-advertising very positvely. Looking at attitude toward m-advertising, it can be observed that Japanese students' display show a mean agreement of 3.8. The Austrian sample even shows a mean of 4.2, hence being located between the two most negative answer categories. The difference between these two means is highly significant (p = .01). Almost the same result is achieved for advertising value of m-advertising. Here, Japanese's mean value is 3.7, Austrians' mean value is 4.1. Again, this difference is highly significant at a .01 level. Obviously, m-advertising is not popular among students in both countries.

Having a closer look at the antecedents, we can see that also here the two groups have different perceptions. There are significant differences in terms of entertainment and irritation. Japanese

Figure 1. Perceptions of m-advertising in Japan and Austria (Means)

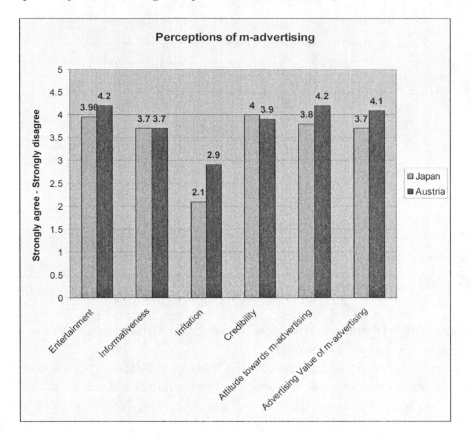

students regard m-advertising as more entertaining than Austrian students do. This finding might be consistent with Japanese strong orientation on emotions and entertainment what might explain their better attitude toward m-advertising. On the other hand, as cultural research has shown that Japanese are more liberal concerning privacy, their relatively negative perception of irritation might show a weaker influence on advertising value and attitude toward m-advertising than among the Austrians.

But there are probably additional differences that could explain the different perceptions between the two samples. They can be separated into technical issues, socio-demographic issues, and legal issues.

Technology

The two countries are in different stages of mobile technology adoption and diffusion. These differences occur both on the supply side and the demand side. Concerning the supply of m-advertising messages, in Japan, m-advertising is a popular and frequently used instrument for addressing consumers. Mobile Internet, which can largely contribute to a value added to m-advertising, is commonplace in Japan but not widespread in Austria. Hence, m-advertising is mainly carried out by SMS and does not offer any value that exceeds textual information. M-advertising plays a minor role in Austria.

From the demand side's point of view, user adoption of mobile technologies is extraordinarily high in Japan. Like in other Asian countries, consumers are very technology oriented. They integrate the mobile Internet into their daily activities very intensively. For example, it is common to download information about train schedules or baseball results and navigate through urban Tokyo using a mobile Internet map. Users regard mobile Internet and its services as a very important and helpful asset and therefore regularly use it. In Austria, mobile technology adoption is at an early stage of diffusion. As long as technologies are still being introduced into a market, their benefits are often nebulous to consumers (Balasubramanian, Peterson, & Jarvenpaa, 2002). Many Austrian consumers are less educated on the functions and usability of mobile devices. This results in a lower willingness to use these services. In addition, many Austrian mobile phone users stick to their phones for several years. As a consequence, they have hardware devices that do not support advanced, Internet-based applications. These differences might have, in general, a strong influence on attitudes and perceived value of m-advertising.

Socio-Demographic Issues

The two samples differ from each other concerning the socio-demographic structure. In the Japanese sample, there are considerably more respondents younger than 20 years (53.4%) than in the Austrian sample (7.4%). In contrast, the largest portion of the Austrian respondents was the age group of 21 to 25 years (73.8% compared with 41.4% in Japan). Respondents older than 26 years accounted for 18.6% in the Austrian sample, but only 5.2% in the Japanese sample. In the light of the observation that young users are early technology adopters, these differences could be another explaining factor for the better attitudes and value perceptions of Japanese. In previous research, age turned out to show a moderating influence on consumers' acceptance of wireless finance services (Kleijnen, Wetzels, & De Ruyter,

2004). Similarly, the Japanese sample contains more male users, whereas the Austrian sample consists of more female respondents. Hence the effect of gender could also be observed, although this influence is considered to become less relevant with increasing technology adoption. But, as Nysveen, Pedersen, and Thorbjornsen (2005) show, gender affects the relevance of antecedents of the intention to use mobile chat services, hence there might also be significant differences in the respect of m-advertising.

Legal Issues

Finally, legal regulations form different conditions for m-advertising in both countries. In Europe, marketers must obtain consumers' explicit agreement before they may send advertising messages to personal communication media (the same is true for e-mail, fax, or telephone advertising). In contrast, Japanese companies need not rely on consumers' explicit agreement to provide them with m-advertising messages. The legal regulations can hinder fast distribution of m-advertising in Europe. Consequently, consumers are less used to m-advertising, which can negatively influence their perceptions of this way of advertising.

FUTURE TRENDS AND IMPLICATIONS FOR PRACTITIONERS

Low Overall Perception of M-Advertising

M-advertising is currently not a popular marketing instrument. Although it allows context-sensitive messages and a high level of customization, it obviously does not provide much added value to the surveyed students. As this effect is observed in two culturally different countries, this problem seems to be located at a higher level. It seems that being able to send customized advertising messages to consumers, which was and is considered one of the most profitable aspects of m-advertising, has turned out to be a major hindrance in consumers' acceptance of mobile devices as a carrier of product and service information. The following aspects could be obstacles to a more positive perception of m-advertising.

Privacy Concerns

Customer privacy has always been a critical issue in marketing. But it has experienced a greater significance in recent years with the rise of Internet-based commercial transactions (Rust et al., 2002). Most consumers are still quite uncomfortable with the concept of mobile business and they are skeptical whether these businesses are feasible and secure (Siau & Shen, 2003). Privacy issues are therefore very important when using mobile devices in addressing the consumers. Before receiving advertising messages via a mobile device, consumers need to empower a marketer to send promotional messages in certain interest categories to them. Typically, this is done by asking the consumer to fill out a survey indicating his or her interest when registering for a service. After that, the marketer can match advertising messages with the interests of the consumer (Krishnamurthy, 2001). Although this procedure of permission marketing is obligatory by law in European countries, the benefit and value of this approach should be made clear to the users. In order to convince users to subscribe to advertising newsletters, firms should clearly point at the benefits that are associated with such m-advertising campaigns. This implies certainly the necessity to provide real value added to the customers.

Mobile Phones as Private Items

Originally meant to connect the world of business, the mobile phone has been increasingly applied by private households and therewith entered the domestic sphere. Accordingly, the mobile phone has changed its identity: It has lost its internal coherence and its connotations of being a mobile technology (Fortunati, 2001). Consumers regard their mobile phone a very private item. Mobile technologies are considered "personal" technologies, attached to a particular body or person (Green, Harper, Murtagh, & Cooper, 2001). Consequently, individuals are very sensitive towards receiving messages from unknown persons or organizations. Data control by unknown individuals can easily lead to annoyance among receivers (Whitaker, 2001).

Frequency of Messages

The number of advertising messages received via mobile devices is an important factor influencing the advertising value for the consumer (Haghirian & Dickinger, 2004). Ducoffe (1995) states that informativeness and entertainment of the advertising information should decline with repetition, because the information will be learned by the audience and thereby lessening its value. As the quantity of promotional messages rises, the attitude of the individual towards the promotional vehicle also worsens and leads to tedium from consumers' point of view (Ha, 1996; Tellis, 1997).

Implications

The analysis shows that the Japanese sample rates m-advertising significantly better than the Austrian respondents. In Japan, where the adoption of mobile technology is by far more advanced and also the number of m-advertising messages received per customer is higher, the perception of m- advertising seems significantly better. This may lead to the conclusion that mobile devices as communication channels for marketers will become more popular once consumers become more familiar with the underlying technology.

Future Trends

If firms can derive valuable services from these future opportunities, m-commerce will become a significant part of the advertising industry. Cyriac Roeding, the European chair of the Mobile Marketing Association indicates that "as bandwidth increases, advertisers will have to be innovative in their campaigns to overcome the limitations of handsets with small screens" (DeZoyza, 2002).

However, m-advertising is currently still in its infancy. Both the supply side and the demand side of m-advertising are not yet ready for a broad usage of m-advertising. As the study in Japan shows, an advanced technological basis is not sufficient for a wide acceptance of m-advertising. Technology is an enabler but not a guarantee for a positive development of m-advertising. The future development of m-advertising should be regarded in a larger context, especially in the light of e-commerce. Unlike e-commerce, m-commerce did not experience the extreme phases of hype and disappointment in the early 21st century. This is due to the later development of m-commerce. Hence it is not surprising that many people are skeptical about another trend in the new economy after the disastrous failures in the dot-com world. But if conclusions from e-commerce development are drawn, one could also assume a more positive future in m-commerce. Like the e-commerce history shows, technology acceptance and the implementation of intelligent Internet-based business models requires some time. Firms have to develop business models that follow the classical rules of business governance, consumer behavior, and profit generation. The same will be true for m-commerce, which is just a part of e-commerce. With increasing convergence of media, the boundaries between different devices—computers, mobile devices, TV sets—will lose relevance.

Consumers will thus only accept this form of advertising, if they can get a concrete added value. One of the key potentials for m-commerce

will be the advanced possibilities of technology usage (see the *M-Advertising and its Technological Dimensions* section). As the results of the study shows the design of the advertising message is by no way trivial and message characteristics need to be developed carefully. If companies decide to send out m-advertising messages, they should be both entertaining and informative. Marketers can not only rely on the fact that an advertising message sent via a mobile device will be read and remembered automatically. The mobile device may be an attention getter, but an attention getting device that is unrelated to the message will not attract consumers interested in the message or the product (Ogilvy, 1963).

CONCLUSION

Like any empirical investigation, this study has several limitations, which calls for further research in this area. These limitations address a lack of comparability of the investigated samples, cultural differences in interpreting the survey items, possible biases in response styles, and differences in socio-demographic respondent structure. From a technological point of view, the study's results cannot be generalized to m-commerce in total as only selected technologies and mobile devices have been considered. Hence, in order to gain deeper insights into attitudes and m-advertising value, other technologies, especially Internet-based approaches, should be considered. In addition, environmental conditions should be addressed in further research. Such issues are legal regulations, technology diffusion, and costs related to sending and receiving m-advertising messages.

Considering future research, this study offers several research avenues. First, empirical research should address the role of demographics in attitudes toward m-advertising. As earlier research in e-commerce and m-commerce has shown, there are considerable differences between men and women as well as across different age groups. Second, the relevance of informativeness of a m-advertising message should be revisited. In contrast to Web advertising, m-advertising can provide valuable, time and location-oriented information for consumers. Future research must also clarify cross-cultural perceptions on informativeness of m-advertising. Another issue is the "evergreen" discussion of standardization vs. adaptation of global advertising activities. The impact on standardization or adaptation of global m-advertising needs to be further investigated in order to develop normative recommendations for advertisers and international marketing researchers.

REFERENCES

Aaker, D. A., Kumar, V., & Day, G. (1995*). Marketing research*. New York: Wiley.

Ajzen, I. (1991). The theory of planned behaviour. *Organizational Behavior & Human Decision Processes, 50*(2), 179-211.

Ajzen, I., & Fishbein, M. (1980). *Understanding attitudes and predicting social behavior*. Englewood Cliffs, NJ: Prentice Hall.

Alwitt, L. F., & Prabhaker, P. R. (1994). Identifying who dislikes television advertising: Not by demographics alone. *Journal of Advertising Research, 34*(6), 17-29.

Balasubramanian, S., Peterson, R. A., & Jarvenpaa, S. L. (2002). Exploring the implications of m-commerce for markets and marketing. *Journal of the Academy of Marketing Science, 30*(4), 348-361.

Brodie, R. J., Coviello, N. E., Brookes, R. W., & Little, V. (1997). Towards a paradigm shift in marketing? An examination of current marketing practices. *Journal of Marketing Management, 13*(5), 383-406.

Churchill, G. A. J., & Iacobucci, D. (2002). *Marketing research; Methodological foundations*. South-Mason, OH: Western Publishing.

Cyr, D., & Trevor-Smith, H. (2004). Localization of Web design: An empirical comparison of German, Japanese, and United States Web site characteristics. *Journal of the American Society for Information Science and Technology, 55*(13), 1199-1208.

Del Galdo, E., & Neilson, J. (1996). *International user interfaces*. New York: Wiley.

DeZoysa, S. (2002, February). Mobile advertising needs to get personal. *Telecommunications International*.

Downes, M., Hemmasi, M., Graf, L. A., Kelley, L., & Huff, L. (2002). The propensity to trust: A comparative study of United States and Japanese managers. *International Journal of Management, 19*(4), 614-621.

Ducoffe, R. H. (1995). How consumers assess the value of advertising. *Journal of Current Issues and Research in Advertising, 17*(1), 1-18.

Ducoffe, R. H. (1996). Advertising value and advertising on the Web. *Journal of Advertising Research, 36,* 21-36.

Dwyer, F. R., Schurr, P. H., & Oh, S. (1987). Developing buyer-seller relationships. *Journal of Marketing, 51*(2), 11-27.

Fortunati, L. (2001). The mobile phone: An identity on the move. *Personal and Ubiquitous Computing, 5*(2), 85-98.

Fournier, S., Dobscha, S., & Mick, D. G. (1998). Preventing the premature death of relationship marketing. *Harvard Business Review, 76*(11), 43-51.

Funk, J. L. (2004). Key technological trajectories and the expansion of mobile Internet applications. *Info—The Journal of Policy, Regulation and Strat-*

egy for Telecommunications, 6(3), 208-215.

Gardner, M. P. (1985) Does attitude toward the ad affect brand attitude under a brand evaluation set? *Journal of Marketing Research, 22,* 192-198.

Goldsmith, R. E., Lafferty, B. A., & Newell, S. J. (2000). The impact of corporate credibility and celebrity credibility on consumer reaction to advertisements and brands. *Journal of Advertising, 29*(3), 43-54.

Gordon, M. E., & De Lima-Turner, K. (1997). Consumer attitudes towards Internet advertising. *International Marketing Review, 14*(5), 352-375.

Green, N., Harper, R. H. R., Murtagh, G., & Cooper, G. (2001) Configuring the mobile user: Sociological and industry views. *Personal and Ubiquitous Computing, 5*(2), 146-156.

Groenroos, C. (1994). From marketing mix to relationship marketing: Towards a paradigm shift in marketing. *Marketing Decision, 32*(2), 4-20.

Gummesson, E. (1987). The new marketing. Developing long-term interactive relationships. *Long Range Planning, 20*(4), 10-20.

Gutmann, A., & Sochatzky, C. (2003). *Mobile applications for teenagers.* Unpublished masters thesis, Vienna University of Economics and Business Administration, Austria.

Ha, L. (1996). Observations: Advertising clutter in consumer magazines: Dimensions and effects. *Journal of Advertising Research, 36*(4), 76-84.

Haghirian, P., & Dickinger, A. (2004). *Identifying success factors of mobile marketing.* ACR Asia-Pacific 2004, Association of Consumer Research, 28-29.

Haghirian, P., Dickinger, A., & Köhlbacher, F. (2004, November). Adopting innovative technology—A qualitative study among Japanese mobile consumers. In *Proceedings of the 5th International Working with e-Business Conference (WeB-2004),* Perth, Australia.

Hall, E. T., & Hall, M. R. (1987). *Hidden differences; Doing business with the Japanese.* New York: Anchor Books, Doubleday.

Hofstede, G. (1980). *Culture's consequences.* Beverly Hills, CA: Sage.

Johansson, J. K., & Nonaka, I. (1996). *Relentless—The Japanese way of marketing.* New York: Harper Business.

Kleijnen, M., Wetzels, M., & De Ruyter, K. (2004). Consumer acceptance of wireless finance. *Journal of Financial Services Marketing, 8*(3), 206-217.

Kotler, P. (2003). *Marketing management.* Upper Saddle River, NJ: Pearson Education.

Krishnamurthy, S. (2001). A comprehensive analysis of permission marketing. *Journal of Computer Mediated Communication, 6*(2). Retrieved from http://www.ascusc.org/jcmc/vol6/7issue2/krishnamurthy.html

Krishnamurthy, S. (2003). *E-Commerce management.* Mason, OH: Thomson Publishing.

Lafferty, B. A., Goldsmith, R. E., & Newell, S. J. (2002). The dual credibility model: The influence of corporate and endorser credibility on attitudes and purchase intentions. *Journal of Marketing Theory and Practice, 10*(3), 1-12.

Larkin, E. F. (1979). Consumer perceptions of the media and their advertising content. *Journal of Advertising, 8*(2), 5-48.

Lastovicka, J. L. (1983). Convergent and discriminant validity of television commercial rating scales. *Journal of Advertising, 12*(2), 14-23.

Lee, Y. E., & Benbasat, I. (2003). Interface design for mobile commerce. *Communications of the ACM, 46*(12), 49-52.

Lehmkuhl, F. (2003, January 6). Küsse und machotests. *FOCUS.*

Lutz, R. J. (1985). Affective and cognitive antecedents of attitude toward the ad: A conceptual framework. In L. F. Alwitt & A. A. Mitchell (Eds.), *Psychological processes and advertising effects: Theory, research and application* (pp. 54-63). Hillsdale, NJ: Lawrence Erlbaum Associates.

MacKenzie, S. B., & Lutz, R. L. (1989). An empirical examination of the structural antecedents of attitude toward the ad in an advertising pretesting context. *Journal of Marketing, 53,* 48-65.

Madlberger, M. (2004). *Electronic retailing.* Wiesbaden, Germany: Deutscher Universitätsverlag.

Marcus, A., & Could, E. W. (2000). Cultural dimensions and global Web user-interface design. *Interactions, 7*(4), 33-46.

McQuail, D. (1983). *Mass communication theory: An introduction.* London: Sage.

Merrill Lynch. (2002). *Wireless matrix—3Q02, quarterly update on global wireless industry metrics.* Author.

Milne, G., & Gordon, M. E. (1993). Direct mail privacy—Efficiency trade-offs within an implied social contract framework. *Journal of Public Policy & Marketing, 12*(2), 206-216.

Ministry of Public Management, Home Affairs, Post, and Telecommunications (MPHPT). (2003). *2003 white paper: Information and communications in Japan.* Retrieved September 29, 2003, from http://www.johotsusintokei.soumu.go.jp/whitepaper/eng/WP2003/2003-index.html

Moore, D. L., & Hutchinson, J. W. (1983). The effects of ad affect on advertising effectiveness. In R. P. Bagozzi & A. M. Tybout (Eds.), *Advances in consumer research* (Vol. 10, pp. 526-531). Ann Arbor, MI: Association for Consumer Research.

NTT DoCoMo. (2001). *Docomo report current trends in mobile phone usage among adolescents* (Company Report). Author.

Nysveen, H., Pedersen, P. E., & Thorbjornsen, H. (2005). Explaining intention to use mobile chat services: Moderating effects of gender. *Journal of Consumer Marketing, 22*(5), 247-256.

Ogilvy, D. (1963). *Confessions of an advertising man.* New York: Ballantine Books.

Okazaki, S. (2004). How do Japanese consumers perceive wireless ads? A multivariate analysis. *International Journal of Advertising, 23*(4), 429-454.

Parvatiyar, A., & Sheth, J. N. (2000). The domain and conceptual foundations of relationship marketing. In J. N. Sheth & A. Parvatiyar (Eds.), *Handbook of relationship marketing* (pp. 3-38). Thousand Oaks, CA: Sage.

Peppers, D., Rogers, M. & Dorf, B. (1999). Is your company ready for one-to-one marketing?, *Harvard Business Review, 77*(1), 151-160.

Petty, R. D. (2003). Wireless advertising messaging: Legal analysis and public policy issues. *Journal of Public Policy & Marketing, 22*(1), 71-82.

Robins, F. (2003). The marketing of 3G. *Marketing Intelligence & Planning, 21*(6), 370-378.

Rust, R. T., Kannan, P. K., & Peng, N. (2002). The customer economics of Internet privacy. *Journal of the Academy of Marketing Science, 30*(4), 455-464.

Schneidewind, D. (1998). *Markt und Marketing in Japan—Shin Hatsubai.* Munich, Germany: Verlag C. H. Beck.

Shavitt, S., Lowrey, P., & Haefner, J. (1998). Public attitudes towards advertising: More favourable than you might think. *Journal of Advertising Research, 38*(4), 7-22.

Siau, K., & Shen, Z. (2003). Building customer trust in mobile commerce. *Communications of the ACM, 46*(4), 91-94.

Stafford, T. F., & Gillenson, M. L. (2003). Mobile commerce: What it is and what it could be. *Communications of the ACM, 46*(12), 33-34.

Stewart, D. W., & Pavlou, P. A. (2002). From consumer response to active consumer: Measuring the effectiveness of interactive media. *Journal of the Academy of Marketing Science, 30*(4), 376-396.

Telekom Austria. (2004, March 29). [Press release]. Mobilkom Austria Group.

Tellis, G. J. (1997). Effective frequency: One exposure or three factors? *Journal of Advertising Research, 37*(4), 75-80.

Varshney, U. (2003). Location management for mobile commerce applications in wireless Internet environment. *ACM Transactions on Internet Technology, 3*(3), 236-255.

Varshney, U., & Vetter, R. (2002). Mobile commerce: Framework, applications and networking support. *Mobile Networks and Applications, 7,* 185-198.

Venkatesh, V., Ramesh, V., & Massey, A. P. (2003). Understanding usability in mobile marketing. *Communications of the ACM, 46*(12), 53-56.

Whitaker, L. (2001). Ads unplugged. *American Demographics, 23*(6), 30-34.

ENDNOTE

[1]   Mobile Internet can be understood as free access to the Internet via mobile devices by means of mobile telecom operators or wireless devices, but it can also denote limited Internet access that is restricted to selected Web sites supported by the mobile telecom operator. In the paper at hand, mobile Internet is related to free Internet access to any Web sites.

APPENDIX 1. SAMPLE QUESTIONNAIRE ITEMS

Message content
Informativeness: Advertising on the mobile Internet is a good source of information.
Entertainment: Advertising on the mobile Internet is entertaining.
Irritation: I do not always understand advertising on the mobile Internet.
Credibility: Advertising on the mobile Internet is believable.
Perceived value of m-advertising
Advertising on the mobile Internet is important.
Attitude toward m-advertising
In general, advertising on the mobile Internet presents a true picture of the product advertised.

Section III
Issues in Asia Pacific

Chapter XIII
Current Status of Mobile Wireless Technology and Digital Multimedia Broadcasting*

J. P. Shim
Mississippi State University, USA

Kyungmo Ahn
Kyunghee University, Korea

Julie M. Shim
Soldier Design LLC, USA

ABSTRACT

The purpose of this chapter is to present an overview of wireless mobile technology, its applications, with a focus on digital multimedia broadcasting (DMB) technology. The chapter also explores the research methodology regarding users' perception on DMB cellular phones and presents empirical findings. Implications for future research are presented. The report attempts to provide stimulating answers by investigating the following questions: (1) Do users perceive easy access to DMB applications as a satisfactory service offered by DMB service providers? (2) Do users perceive high-quality DMB program content as a satisfactory service offered by the DMB service providers? (3) Are there differences between different age groups in terms of their perception of DMB phone prices, phone usage time, program content, and services?

INTRODUCTION

Wireless mobile technology and handheld devices are dramatically changing the degrees of interaction throughout the world, further creating a ubiquitous network society. The emergence of these wireless devices has increased accuracy, ease-of-use, and access rate, all of which is increasingly essential as the volume of information handled by users expands at an accelerated pace. Mobile TV broadcasting technology, as a nascent industry, has been paving a new way to create an intersection of telecommunication and media industries, all of which offers new opportunities to device makers, content producers, and mobile network operators.

There are currently various wireless connectivity standards (e.g., Wi-Fi, Bluetooth, Radio Frequency Identification [RFID], etc.), which have been expanding across all vertical industries, in an era of mobile and ubiquitous computing, which provides access to anything, anytime, and anywhere. Mobile TV technologies have been creating a buzz, as it adds a new dimension to the "on the go" mobility factor—simultaneous audio and video services are broadcasted in real-time to mobile devices in motion, such as mobile TV-enabled phones, PDAs, and car receivers.

There are currently three major competing standards: digital video broadcasting for handhelds (DVB-H), which is going through trial phases in Europe; digital multimedia broadcasting (DMB), which has been adopted in South Korea and Japan; and MediaFLO (QUALCOMM Inc., 2005), which is currently in trial phase in the United States with plans to launch by late 2007. The competition scheme is further intensified given the challenge of how quickly terrestrial and satellite DMB can be deployed and commercialized throughout countries such as Korea, Japan, and Europe. Additionally, there is pressure to recoup the costs with creating the network and catapult the technology to the ranks of industry standard.

The purpose of this chapter is to present an overview of wireless mobile technology, its applications, with a focus on DMB technology. The chapter also explores the research methodology regarding users' perception on DMB cellular phones and presents empirical findings from Study Phases I and II, along with actual DMB subscriber usage results. Implications for future research are presented.

Given that the research topic of DMB has not yet been covered extensively, the use of qualitative methods is considered advantageous when exploring the topic to develop theoretical variables, which may then be employed in quantitative research. Thus, with the difference found between the DMB cellular phone usage experience and traditional cellular phone usage, qualitative methodology was applied to Study Phase I. The project was then triangulated by the use of quantitative methodology in Study Phase II to develop an additional understanding of the DMB cellular phone users' experiences as identified in Study Phase I.

The report attempts to provide stimulating answers by investigating the following questions: (1) Do users perceive easy access to DMB applications as a satisfactory service offered by DMB service providers? (2) Do users perceive high-quality DMB program contents as a satisfactory service offered by the DMB service providers? (3) Are there differences between different age groups in terms of their perception of DMB phone prices, phone usage time, program contents, and services?

WIRELESS MOBILE TECHNOLOGIES: CURRENT STATUS AND CONCEPTS

Over the last decade, wireless technologies have attracted unprecedented attention from wireless service providers, developers, vendors, and users. These wireless technologies provide many connection points to the Internet between mobile phones and other portable handheld devices to ear-pieces and handsets. These technologies include Wi-Fi hotspots, Bluetooth, WiMAX, wireless broadband Internet (WiBRO), RFID, and others. Wi-Fi hotspots, with a distance and penetration of approximately 50 feet, are physical addresses where people can connect to a public wireless network, such as a cafe, hotel, or airport. WiMAX is a metropolitan-scale wireless technology with speeds over 1Mbps and a longer range than Wi-Fi. WiBRO, the Korean version of WiMAX, allows users to be connected to the Internet while in motion, even in cars traveling up to 100 kilometers per hour. It is anticipated that users may one day seamlessly switch between networks multiple times per day, depending on the service offered by a specific network service provider.

Many industries have seen the benefits of these wireless technology applications, of which some will be described here. For local, federal, and state agencies, wireless connections provide for GPS functionality, along with real-time vehicle tracking, navigation, and fleet management. For automated logistics and retail industries, RFID tags will give information on just-in-time inventory or shipment location, security status, and even environmental conditions inside the freight. In the health care industry, the wireless applications include patient and equipment monitoring, and telemedicine through the monitoring of an outpatient's heart via continuous electrocardiograms (ECG). Other applications already on the radar: handsets that function as a blood pressure monitor, a blood glucose meter, and wireless pacemaker. One of the hurdles that wireless solution carriers have to overcome is the cost of the devices, and whether insurance companies are willing to cover or share the costs. The wireless technology allows government officials and emergency response teams to stay informed of critical information in the event of an emergency or a disaster that affects wire line services, much like Katrina; these include advanced warnings and public alerts, emergency telecommunications services, global monitoring for environment, and assistance with search and rescue (SAR).

PC World, an online technology magazine, recently reported that the number of Wi-Fi hotspots reached the 100,000 mark globally.[1] Businesses are realizing the value-added service by offering free or paid wireless services to attract customers. Analysts believe that locations such as school campuses and citywide deployment of WiMax technology will benefit users.

a. **United States:** Wi-Fi integration into retail, hospitality, restaurant, and tourism industries has been instrumental for marketing plans, particularly for franchise venues, including Starbucks and McDonald's.

b. **Asia/Pacific:** An article in *The Australian* (2003, March 4) described that 200 restaurants in Australia have migrated away from taking orders via pen and paper to using wireless handhelds to relay orders to the kitchen/bar staff. In addition to offering this type of service, Japan's NTT DoCoMo introduced its iMode Felica handset, enabling users to scan their handsets as their mobile wallets (m-wallets), eliminating the need to carry a credit card, identification, and keys. The feature allows for conducting financial transactions, purchasing services/products, or opening electronic locks.[2] The issue at hand is the different business models of the wireless carrier and that of the credit card companies.

DIGITAL MULTIMEDIA BROADCASTING: CURRENT STATUS AND CONCEPTS

Digital multimedia broadcasting (DMB) is a process of broadcasting multimedia over the Internet or satellite that can be tuned in by multimedia players, capable of playing back the multimedia program.[3] DMB is an extension of digital audio broadcasting (DAB), which is based on the European Eureka 147 DAB Radio standard. DMB technology has two sub-standards: satellite-DMB [S-DMB] and terrestrial-DMB [T-DMB]. While both S-DMB and T-DMB broadcasts television to handheld devices in motion, the difference lies in the transmission method: via satellite versus land-based towers. These real-time transmissions allow users to view live TV programs, including news, reality shows, or sports games on their DMB cellular phones in the subway.

With mobile growth two or three times that of Europe and North America (Budde, 2002), Japan and Korea have been known for their cutting edge technological innovations and tech-savvy consumers. Korea is one of the world's most broadband-connected countries, with a high penetration rate (Lee, 2003; Shim et al., 2006a; Shim et al., 2006b). The government initiatives have been instrumental in this arena, as the government's hands-on style has created the IT infrastructure necessary to power the latest technological tools. The mobile markets in Japan and Korea have become optimal testing grounds for mobile operators and manufacturers before rolling out products in the rest of the world, given the consumers' insatiable appetite of acquiring the latest technologies, early acceptance behavior, and education fever.

In Asia-Pacific and Europe, considered to be the power houses of the mobile gaming industry, wireless gaming and instant messages have exceeded expectations. In North America, music downloads and e-mails have become essential. As the market for mobile applications, (including short message service [SMS], ring-tones, games,

music, videos) is becoming more saturated, more wireless applications have become integrated into most consumer electronics devices, from digital cameras to video game consoles. With over 85% cellular phone penetration rate, Korea introduced the world's first DMB mobile-enabled phone, or "TV-on-the-go" in 2005. [4] While Japan currently provides S-DMB services designed for car receivers, Korea has been the only country to provide full-blown S-DMB and T-DMB services on cellular phones while in motion (including car receivers) by late 2006. With T-DMB and S-DMB services already launched in Korea, several countries in Europe, and the U.S. are planning to launch DVB-H services by the end of 2007. Informa, a consultancy, says there will be 125 million mobile TV users by 2010.[5]

The history of DMB began with the development of DAB services during the mid-1990s in the U.S. and Europe (Korean Society for Journalism and Communication Studies, 2003; Nyberg, 2004). The current status of Mobile TV services in the U.S., Europe, Japan, and Korea is shown in Table 1 (Shim, 2005b).

As shown in Figure 1, DMB program producers provide a variety of programs and content to

Table 1. Current status of mobile TV services in various countries

Country	USA		Europe		Japan	Korea	
Mobile TV technology	MediaFlo	DVB-H	DVB-H	T-DMB	S-DMB	S-DMB	T-DMB
Receiving device	Car receiver	Car receiver	Mobile TV- phone, Car receiver	Car receiver	Car receiver	Mobile TV- phone, Car receiver	Car receivers
Service launch date	2006	2006	2006	2006	2004	May 2005	Dec 2005

Sources: The Korea Times, (2005, January 18) "Korea's Free Mobile Broadcasting Faces Snag".
KORA Research 2003-10,. (2004, May). "A Market Policy Study on DMB".
M. H. Eom, "T-DMB Overview in Korea," (2006, April). Proceedings of 2006 Wireless Telecommunications Symposium, Pomona, CA,

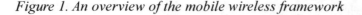

Figure 1. An overview of the mobile wireless framework

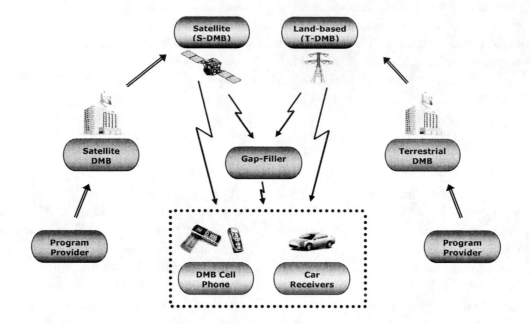

the DMB center, which broadcasts through either satellites or towers. Thus, the DMB cellular phone users receive content and programs through satellites, towers, or "gap-fillers" (small base stations) to ensure there are no reception problems, even in underground subways (Shim, 2005a).

Consumers are increasingly gravitating towards customized devices and features, as a miniaturized interactive entertainment center is packaged into the cellular phone, complete with an MP3 player, multi-megapixel camera, digital video recorder, CD-quality audio, and a selection of satellite broadcast television and audio channels (Olla & Atkinson, 2004) as they can choose from television and audio on-demand and simultaneously make phone calls. The mobile TV-enabled phone, equipped with these features, has become more than integrated into one's lifestyle, as it becomes an extension of the consumer's identity. The handset carriers are in the process of yet again trying to capitalize on producing fashion-forward phones and portable gaming consoles.

DMB data service is a framework of the following groups: data provider, audio/video content producer, DMB producer, advertiser, and customer. A schematic view of DMB data service and the components, shown in Figure 2, provides a basic understanding of the general structure of the DMB business model. The figure also shows interaction of the DMB producer with other groups of DMB data services.

For example, the DMB producer provides various content and programs to customers for a service fee. The DMB producer charges an advertising fee to the advertiser, from whom customers can purchase directly for advertised services via the DMB device. The audio/video content producer and data provider each provide various contents to the DMB producer for a fee. The perceived richness of the medium should have an impact on the use of the communication medium (Daft & Lengel, 1986; Smagt, 2000). The rich media is more appropriate in ambiguous communications situations, which emphasizes

Daft and Lengel's valuable contribution of placing equivocality high in the business and information systems field.

There exists a rich body of knowledge of technology adoption and diffusion, including the digital multimedia broadcasting technology. For example, several theoretical backgrounds, such as institutional theory, technology acceptance model (TAM) (Venkatesh & Davis, 2000), and diffusion of innovation theory (Gharavi, Love, & Cheng, 2004; Rogers, 1983) explain the DMB technology adoption at an individual, organizational, and industry level (Lee, 2003; Shim, 2005a, 2005b). Among the theories, Lee and Shim both describe the major factors behind Korea's information and communication technology diffusion such as: external factors (global economy, government policies), innovation factors (usefulness, ease of use, self-efficacy), and imitation factors (subjective norm of belongingness, word of mouth). The

authors believe that either the diffusion theory (such as external, internal, and mixed influence models), or TAM (such as perceived usefulness and perceived ease of use), or the combination of both can be applied behind DMB cellular phone adoption and diffusion.

RESEARCH METHODOLOGY

A recent study demonstrates a higher number of DMB viewers than regular TV viewers during the daytime (Figure 3). Since the DMB cellular phone captures the content-on-demand aspect, the DMB phone service (S-DMB) are optimal for the on-the-go daytime enthusiasts.

To determine how integral DMB phones have been and will be in consumers' daily lives, the authors conducted qualitative and quantitative analyses. Study Phase I describes the use of the

Figure 2. A schematic view of DMB data service business model

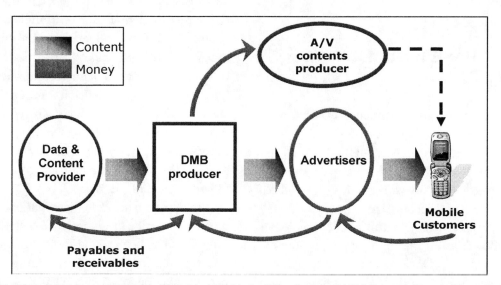

Source: Modified from KORA Research 2003-10. (2004, May). "A Market Policy Study on DMB," Research Report of Korea Radio Station Management Agency.

Figure 3. The percentage of viewing on S-DMB vs. regular TV

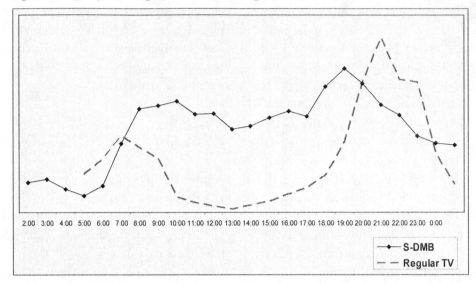

Source: Suh, Y. (2005, November). "Current Overview of S-DMB," TU Media.

qualitative research method, specifically the existential phenomenological method. Study Phase II describes the quantitative research methods including the survey questionnaire (Shim, Shin, & Nottingham, 2002).

STUDY PHASE I: QUALITATIVE ANALYSIS

Although quantitative instruments serve as valid methods to study the perceived use of DMB phones, qualitative research methods, such as interviewing, can reveal the function of variables perhaps overlooked by survey designers. The current project was designed to employ the qualitative technique of existential phenomenology. Thus, it develops an in-depth understanding of the new concept of DMB usage by investigating respondents' reports of their DMB phone usage experiences. With this data collection technique, the respondent is encouraged to describe in-depth the personally experienced phenomenon (Thompson, Locander, & Pollio, 1989).

Existential phenomenology was selected among various qualitative methods, such as case studies and ethnography, because of its attention to a respondent's individualistic, subjective expression of an actual live experience of the situation of interest. Such reflection on a single experience encourages the perceiver to focus on nuances that would likely escape the broader brush of a researcher's selection of choices among a pre-set list of quantitative dimensions or escape even the surface comparison of reports of respondents' experiences. Existential phenomenology encourages the respondent to consider specific and live events. The goal is to discover patterns of experiences (Thompson et al., 1989).

Since the purpose of existential phenomenology is to describe the experience as it is lived, the interview has been found to be a powerful tool for attaining in-depth understanding of another person's experience (Kvale, 1983). Research analysis of interview-derived information is considered valid because the respondents' own words are used to understand their experiences (Feagin, Orum,

& Sjoberg, 1991). Accordingly, respondents in this research were presented with a set of open-ended questions designed to encourage them to discuss and describe their experiences with DMB phone usage. To determine a specific set of key factors that would be of critical concern to DMB users, 19 respondents in Korea were enlisted in Study Phase I.

A purposive sample is deemed appropriate for exploratory research designed to query respondents who have experienced a phenomenon of interest. Thus, the networking technique was utilized to obtain a purposive sample of individuals who had interacted with the DMB cellular phone services. These respondents were then asked to name additional individuals who had experienced DMB services. Thus, aside from the requirement of the respondents' familiarity with the DMB services, demographic characteristics of the sample resulted by random chance.

The majority of respondents were well-educated young professionals with a zealous tech-gadget nature, affluent, computer proficient, and somewhat knowledgeable about DMB services. Although this sample clearly is not representative of the population at large, the sample profile corresponds with what the authors presumed to be identified as a typical DMB service user. Thus, the experiences relayed by these respondents are considered to be a reasonable representation of a random sampling of regular DMB cellular phone users. After respondents were assured of confidentiality and protection of their privacy, each tape-recorded interview lasted 20-30 minutes. Each interview began with open-ended questions posed in a conversational format to encourage the respondent to develop a dialogue with the interviewer, providing the context from which the respondent's descriptions of his or her own DMB service experience could flow freely and in detail. Participants were encouraged to discuss not only their DMB services experiences, but also their attitudes and perceptions regarding negative and positive aspects of DMB services.

Such in-depth descriptions have been found to be beneficial in revealing emotional and behavioral underpinnings of overt user behavior. In reality, the act of a respondent's description of a specific experience in-depth, frequently results in further personal insights that arise through the revival of the experience. The respondents were asked to describe their main reasons for purchasing DMB cellular phones, which varied: "to gain information access," "to spot the latest trends," "for education or entertainment," "to watch TV while commuting," and "for movies, dramas, and shopping." Their personal positive experiences were: "mobility—a deviation from a fixed location point," "high quality reception," "convenience," "accessible anytime/anywhere," "lifestyle change," "great for commuting," and "good for managing time." On the other hand, the negative aspects they experienced included: "expensive device," "reception problem," "low battery hours with limited usage time (e.g., 2-3 hours)." Most respondents reported that the following areas would have great potential for future DMB applications and content: information access, education/learning, e-trading, retail, tourism, and entertainment. In Study Phase II, these themes were reconstructed to set up independent variables for the quantitative analysis.

STUDY PHASE II: QUANTITATIVE ANALYSIS

To determine the extent to which DMB phones are being used as the latest multimedia product, the authors developed a questionnaire. DMB has a wide array of advantages: personalized, live media (television, radio, or data broadcasts) that can be viewed on-demand anytime; the mobility of the phone which receives satellite and terrestrial television broadcast signals even at high speeds or underground; and an interactive handset into which one can speak via the handset while watching TV programs. The research instrument underwent two pretests. The first pretest involved administering the questionnaire to 25 graduate and undergraduate students at a large university in Seoul, Korea. The questions, which concerned price, usage time, program content, and services were modified to reduce the effects of proximity bias on the responses, with several questions reworded for clarity. The second pretest was conducted at a DMB phone service provider company to ensure the content validity. A five-point Likert scale was used for recording the responses.

DMB will not be successful if content and service providers fail to provide high quality service, a variety of content, and reasonable prices for services and handsets (Teng, 2005). Several research studies demonstrated that there are differences among age groups on factors such as technology adoption and usage (Larsen & Sorebo, 2005; Ventatesh, 2000). It is believed that older generations are more anxious about the use of technologies than the younger generations. A number of research studies have supported this belief (Gilbert, Lee-Kelley, & Barton, 2003). Based on the theories and research questions along with Study Phases I and II, the authors developed the following six hypotheses:

H_1: *The user's easy access to DMB service is perceived as a satisfactory service offered by the DMB service provider.*

H_2: *Premium (excellent) content of DMB programs corresponds with a good quality DMB service provider.*

H_3: *There is a difference between different age groups and their perceived value of DMB handset price.*

H_4: *There is a difference between different age groups and their perceived value of DMB phone usage time.*

H_5: *There is a difference between different age groups and their perceived value of DMB program content.*

H_6: *There is a difference between different age groups and their perceived value of DMB services.*

The authors and their research assistants distributed the questionnaire to 300 randomly selected individuals inside the Korea Convention Exhibition Center (COEX) and Korea World Trade Center during January and February 2005. Of the 300 randomly selected individuals' responses, 264 were valid. The two-page questionnaire was divided into three sections with a total of 32 questions. In Section 1, the authors asked the randomly selected participants about DMB services, such as information sources about DMB services, user satisfaction ratings, influential factors when choosing DMB services, DMB applications, and others. The questions in Section 2 covered the participants' perceived values of DMB application services. Section 3 inquired of participants' demographics.

DATA ANALYSIS AND FINDINGS

The 264 usable research instruments collected from the respondents were well represented in terms of gender, age, and occupation. Statistical Package for the Social Sciences (SPSS) was used to calculate descriptive statistics and perform a confirmatory factor analysis. The respondents' primary occupations included: students (51.9%), IT staff (15.2%), government employees (13.3%), professionals (7.6%), self-employees (4.1%), housewives (3%), and others (4%). Approximately 73.8% of the sample respondents indicated that they had either undergraduate (64%) or graduate school (9.8%) education.

The respondents were well represented in terms of gender and age. About 30% of the sample respondents had not heard about DMB. Of the 70% of respondents who had heard about DMB, the main sources included: TV (26%), newspaper (20%), Internet (15%), friends (6%), and others (33%). About one-fifth (20.1%) of the respondents were utilizing DMB services. Of those respondents, 62.2% were satisfied with their current DMB service whereas 30.3% were only satisfied on a mediocre level. In other words, only 7.5% of the current DMB users were not satisfied with their DMB services. The current users accessed their DMB phones for news and information; leisure and tourism; public relations (marketing); shopping; games; and education. The users believed that the DMB services would impact service industries such as tourism and retail.

The results also indicated that among the sample respondents, the non-users felt that the following major factors would be taken into consideration when choosing DMB services for the future: (1) pricing of DMB cellular handset, (2) video quality, (3) program content, (4) quality [of DMB cellular handset], (5) ease of use, and (6) others [e.g., customer service by the DMB cell phone manufacturer or service provider; brand image and perception]. The aforementioned results from the sample respondents were very astonishingly similar to the 19 interviewees' perceived values.

The independent variables that determine DMB services are: price, usage time, and program content. The dependent variable is DMB service. Table 2 provides a definition of each of these variables. The reliability measure (construct validity) for these constructs was Cronbach's coefficient (alpha). Even though the general rule of thumb for reliability is a value of 0.8 (alpha), values of 0.6 or 0.7 may be considered adequate in some cases (Hair, 1998). Overall, the model provides a valid representation of the data and the constructs are reliable. The reliability test generated Cronbach's coefficient alpha of .7343 for the 12 items. From the analysis, it was concluded that the measure of 12 items was reliable. Coefficient alphas for the four constructs are shown in Table 3.

Table 2. Model construct

Table 3. Coefficient alpha for construct

Construct	Variables	Cronbach's alpha
Price	PR1, PR2, PR3	.7970
Access/Usage time	TM1, TM2, TM3	.6218
Program content	CO1, CO2, CO3	.8104
Service	SE1, SE2, SE3	.7081

Table 4. Construct: Factor loadings

Constructs	Loading	Eigenvalue	Communality (%)
PR1	.875		
PR2	.863	2.137	71.223
PR3	.791		
TM1	.792		
TM2	.744	1.710	56.986
TM3	.727		
CO1	.908		
CO2	.907	2.189	72.970
CO3	.737		
SE1	.838		
SE2	.782	1.897	63.219
SE3	.764		

Table 5. Correlation matrix for the constructs

	Price	Usage time	Program content	Service
Price	1.000			
Access/Usage time	.296**	1.000		
Program content	.454**	.497**	1.000	
Service	.266**	.481**	.511**	1.000

** P<0.01

Table 6. Analysis of service performance

Independent Variable	Dependent Variable: Service	
	Beta	t-value
Price	0.008	0.141 (sig = .888)
Access/Usage time	0.300	5.104 (sig = .000)
Program contents	0.358	5.689 (sig = .000)
R²	0.330	
F	42.602	
Sig.	.000	

A series of principal components factor analyses using a VARIMAX rotation were used to assess the unidimensionality in this study. Eigenvalues of at least 1.0 were used to assess the number of factors to extract. The dimensionality of each factor was assessed by examining factor loadings. Factor loadings on construct are shown in Table 4.

Assessing dimensionality involves examining the inter-correlations among the major constructs. A correlation matrix for the constructs is shown in Table 5. The inter-construct correlation coefficients were all positive and significant at less than 0.01 (see Table 5).

The t test was used in the quantitative analysis. The price factor of the DMB phone usage is not an issue if the user perceives the DMB program content to be valuable. Table 6 also showed that DMB service was affected by program content (beta=0.358, t-value=5.689). The users associate easy access/connection time to the DMB services with reliability provided by DMB equipment makers or service providers (beta=0.300, t-value=5.104). H_1 and H_2 were supported. ANOVA and Duncan test were used to evaluate hypotheses H_3, H_4, H_5, and H_6.

DMB PHONE PRICE AND RELATED FEES

The users were asked to rate the importance of price issues of the DMB handset and related service fees when selecting a DMB cell phone. These

Table 7. ANOVA and Duncan Test of DMB phone price and related fees

	Sum of squares	df	Mean Square	F	Sig.
Between groups	11.161	3	3.720	12.583	.000
Within groups	76.879	260	.296		
Total	88.040	263			

7a. ANOVA

Age	N	Subset for alpha = .05		
		1	2	3
Teens	45			4.6889
20s	116		4.2328	
30s	52		4.3269	
40s and older	51	4.0261		
Sig.		1.000	.354	1.000

7b. Duncan Test

issues include price per program content, price per usage time, and price of the DMB handset. The mean response among the teens was 4.46 (on a scale of 1=unimportant and 5=very important); 4.23 for 20s, and 4.33 for 30s. The mean response among the older generations (40s and older) was 4.0. Table 7b showed that there were significant differences among teens and the other age groups (20s, 30s, 40s, and older). And the 20s and 30s age group perceived the DMB phone price and related fees differently, when compared with teens, and the 40s and older age group.

In an effort to explain this unexpected finding, the authors used analysis of variance (ANOVA) to see if there were any significant differences between the DMB handset price/related fees and age group. As shown in Table 7a, the difference is statistically significant (F=12.583, df=3, 260, p=0.000), which demonstrates that the younger generation is willing to pay the current market price for the DMB handset and related services, given that they perceive the content to be useful

and worthwhile. This supports H_3, as it validates that there is a difference between the age groups and their perceptions of DMB phone price.

ACCESS/USAGE TIME

The users were asked to rate the importance of access/usage time issues of DMB services and handset when selecting a DMB cellular phone. These issues include access time, air time, and the time it takes to get familiarized with the DMB handset and services. The mean response among the teens was 4.02 (on a scale of 1=unimportant and 5=very important); 3.82 for 30s, 3.86 for 40s and older. Table 8b demonstrates a slight discrepancy between teens and those in their 20s, but no significant divergences among other age groups (30s, 40s and older). The ANOVA test showed that there was not a significant difference between age groups and their judgments of the importance placed on the DMB access/usage time (see Table 8a). This

Table 8. ANOVA and Duncan Test of access/usage time

	Sum of Squares	df	Mean Square	F	Sig.
Between groups	2.943	3	.981	2.502	.060
Within groups	101.935	260	.392		
Total	104.878	263			

8a. ANOVA

Age	N	Subset for alpha = .05	
		1	2
Teens	45		4.0296
20s	116	3.7328	
30s	52	3.8269	3.8269
40s and older	51	3.8627	3.8627
Sig.		.298	.102

8b. Duncan Test

Table 9. ANOVA and Duncan of program content

	Sum of Squares	df	Mean Square	F	Sig.
Between groups	5.870	3	1.957	6.304	.000
Within groups	80.689	260	.310		
Total	86.559	263			

9a. ANOVA

Age	N	Subset for alpha = .05	
		1	2
Teens	45		4.6963
20s	116	4.2902	
30s	52	4.3013	
40s and older	51	4.3268	
Sig.		.743	1.000

9b. Duncan Test

Table 10. ANOVA and Duncan Test of Service

	Sum of Squares	df	Mean Square	F	Sig.
Between groups	3.428	3	1.143	3.355	.019
Within groups	88.557	260	.341		
Total	91.985	263			

10a. ANOVA

Age	N	Subset for alpha = .05	
		1	2
Teens	45		Teens
20s	116	4.2241	20s
30s	52	4.3782	30s
40s and older	51	4.3137	40s and older
Sig.		.185	Sig.

10b. Duncan Test

does not support H₄, as it validates that there is no difference between age groups and their perceptions of the DMB phone access/usage time. When focusing on strategic moves, the major players in the DMB market do not have to place as much emphasis on the end-users' access/usage time.

PROGRAM CONTENT

The users were asked to rate the importance of program content of DMB handsets when selecting a DMB cellular phone. These issues include video quality of content, audio quality of content, and a selection of content. As shown in Table 9a, the ANOVA test showed that there was a difference between various program contents and age groups (F = 6.30, df = 3, 260, p=0.000). The mean response among the teens was 4.69 (on a scale of 1=unimportant and 5=very important); 4.29 for the 20s age group, 4.30 for the 30s age group, and 4.32 for the 40s age group and older. Table 9b showed significant deviation between teens and

the other age groups (20s, 30s, and 40s and older). The perception on program content for each age group (20s, 30s, and 40s and older) differed from the teens' perceptions. This supports H₅.

SERVICE

The users were asked to rate the importance of DMB services when selecting a DMB cellular phone. These services include after-service of the DMB equipment maker or service provider, performance of the DMB phone device, and the credibility of the DMB equipment maker or service provider. As shown in Table 10a, the ANOVA test showed that there was a difference between the age groups and their approach to the importance of DMB services (F = 3.355, df = 3, 260, p <0.019). The mean response among the teens was 4.54. Table 10b showed that there are significant differences among teens and other age groups (20s, and 40s and older). And each age group's (20s, and 40s and older) perception

Figure 4. Actual DMB statistical usage data by age

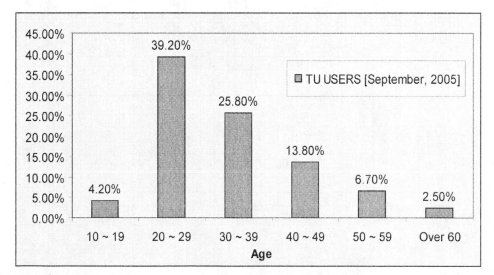

Figure 5. Preferences for various age groups and genders

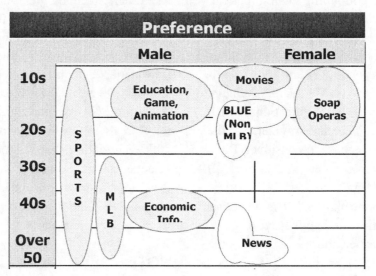

Source: TU Media (2006)

on services deviated significantly from the teens' perceptions. This supports H_6.

As shown previously, all hypotheses (except H_4) were supported.

ACTUAL USAGE AND IMPLICATIONS

Although the exploratory study's results showed teens and the 20s age group as heavy users of DMB services, the actual DMB statistical usage data (see Figure 4) differed. The actual usage data was recently released from TU-Media (S-DMB service provider), which revealed that those in their late 20s, 30s, 40s, and 50s represent a large percentage of users of the following DMB services: soap operas, sports, and music program content (Suh, 2005). The results in Figure 5 show a correlation between preferences across age and gender. While the sports channel was the only preferred program among males to spread across all age groups, soap opera programs were preferred by female teens and those in their 20s. The authors believe that

there are several reasons as to why the younger consumers may not be currently subscribed to S-DMB services: (1) S-DMB handsets (which retails for $600-$800) are too expensive; (2) The teens lack the extra out-of-pocket money to pay for the S-DMB $13 monthly service fee (and $20 activation fee); and (3) The parents do not feel justified in purchasing a DMB handset for their children's TV and gaming purposes. Additionally, most of the school-age children have little time to watch DMB program content due to the academic load. Furthermore, the actual usage results among various demographic groups for T-DMB services, once released, are expected to differ from that of S-DMB services given that T-DMB services are free and advertiser-supported.

CONCLUSION

The mobile TV standards (e.g., DMB, DVB-H, and MediaFLO) and wireless technologies will add a new dimension to the connectivity between enterprises and consumers as well as their access to information and entertainment. Given the demand for ubiquitous computing in an impatient, technology-hungry, instant gratification-seeking population, the desire for mobile TV will continue to grow and soon mobile TV will be synonymous to today's radio in the long run (Kim, 2004). Similar to the interactive TV (iTV) (Tsaih, Chang, & Huang, 2005), the DMB has implications, which include: (1) service and content providers use the DMB as a vehicle for business-to-consumer (B2C) commerce via programs, content, and services; (2) consumers have real-time access to DMB services and programs on mobile phones, PDAs, and other mobile devices anytime and anywhere.

As mentioned earlier, the key issues for the DMB market include: (1) optimal capital investment levels to achieve adequate service coverage for T- DMB and S- DMB services; and (2) appropriate business models, with respect to advertising-supported vs. subscription services. The wireless mobile service industry has very complex issues, which span across technical, logistical, social, and cultural issues (Trappey, Trappey, Hou, & Chen, 2004). Thus, this requires cooperation among the cellular and network service providers, service developers, and equipment makers to collaborate with the government and users to create growth in the cellular telecommunications industry.

Although this research is based on exploratory methods, it still has its limitations. For example, the sample size was collected during the experimental/trial stages of S-DMB services in Korea. The authors reinforce the continuation of this research to solidify findings with an increased sample size of respondents collected during the actual stage of S-DMB and T-DMB services. In addition to this belief, the authors endorse the notion of longitudinal studies conducted to obtain more results. Furthermore, the authors strongly believe that the findings from this exploratory research will be valuable for the DMB service and content providers to gain insight into various age groups and their perceptions.

One of the implications of this paper of wireless mobile technologies and mobile TV is to demonstrate how important the government initiative can benefit less-developed and developing countries. For example, South Korea's Ministry of Information & Communication (MIC) established the "IT839" Strategy—"8" services; "3" infrastructures; "9" growth engines—as a roadmap for Korea's future IT development plan (MIC, 2005). The authors hope that this discussion will be beneficial for the mobile wireless industry and the academia for insight and understanding of the trends of the ubiquitous computing era.

NOTE

* A portion of this chapter is based on an earlier work: Shim, Ahn, & Shim. (2006). Empirical Findings on Perceived Use of Digital Multimedia Broadcasting Mobile Phone Services. *Industrial Management & Data Systems, 106* (2).

REFERENCES

The Australian. (2003, March 4th).

Budde, P. (2002). Asia and Australia telecommunications industry overview. *Annual Review of Communications, 55*, 243-250.

Daft, R., & Lengel, R. (1986). Organizational formation requirements, media richness and structural design. *Management Science, 32*(5), 555-571.

Eom, M. (2006). T-DMB overview in Korea. In *Proceedings of 2006 Wireless Telecommunications Symposium,* Pomona, CA.

Feagin, J. R., Orum, A. M., & Sjoberg, G. (1991). *A case for the case study.* Chapel Hill, NC: The University of North Carolina Press.

Gharavi, H., Love, P., & Cheng, E. (2004). Information and communication technology in the stockbroking industry: An evolutionary approach to the diffusion of industry. *Industrial Management & Data Systems, 104*(9), 756-765.

Gilbert, D., Lee-Kelley, L., & Barton, M. (2003). Technophobia, gender influence and consumer decision-making for technology-related products. *European Journal of Innovation Management, 6*(4), 253-263.

Hair, J. F. (1998). *Multivariate data analysis.* Prentice Hall.

Kim, J. (2004). Terrestrial DMB's effects on the electronics industry. In *Proceedings of 2004 Terrestrial DMB International Forum* (pp. 131-142).

KORA Research. (2004, May). *A market policy study on DMB* (Rep. No. 2003-10).

Korea Radio Station Management Agency. (2004). *A market policy study on DMB.*

Kim Tae-gyu, K. (2005, January 18). Korea's free mobile broadcasting faces snag. *The Korea Times.*

Korean Society for Journalism and Communication Studies. (2003). *A study on satellite DMB.*

Kvale, S. (1983). The qualitative research interview: A phenomenological and a hermeneutical mode of understanding. *Journal of Phenomenological Psychology, 14*(2), 171-196.

Larsen, T., & Sorebo, O. (2005). Impact of personal innovativeness on the use of the Internet among employees at Work. *Journal of Organizational and End User Computing, 17(*2), 43-63.

Lee, S. M. (2003). South Korea: From the land of morning calm to ICT hotbed. *Academy of Management Executive, 17(*2), 7-18.

Ministry of Information and Communication. (2005). *IT 839 Strategy.* Republic of Korea.

Nyberg, A. (2004). Positioning DAB in an increasingly competitive world. In *Proceedings of 2004 Terrestrial DMB International Forum* (pp. 131-142).

Olla, P., & Atkinson, C. (2004). Developing a wireless reference model for interpreting complexity in wireless projects. *Industrial Management & Data Systems, 104*(3), 262-272.

QUALCOMM Incorporated. (2005). *MediaFLO: FLO technology brief.* Retrieved from www.qualcomm.com/mediaflo

Rogers, E. M. (1983). *Diffusion of innovation* (3rd ed.). New York: The Free Press.

Shim, J. P. (2005a). Korea's lead in mobile cellular and DMB phone services. *Communications of the Association for Information Systems, 15,* 555-566.

Shim, J. P. (2005b). Why Japan and Korea are leading in the mobile business industry. *Decision Line, 36*(3), 8-12.

Shim, J. P., Ahn, K. M., & Shim, J. (2006). Empirical findings on the perceived use of digital multimedia broadcasting mobile phone service. *Industrial Management & Data Systems, 106*(2), 155-171.

Shim, J. P., Shin, Y. B., & Nottingham, L. (2002). Retailer Web site influence on customer shopping: An exploratory study on key factors of customer satisfaction. *Journal of the Association for Information Systems, 3,* 53-75.

Shim, J. P., Varshney, U., & Dekleva, S. (2006a). Wireless evolution 2006: Cellular TV, wearable computing, and RFID. *Communications of the Association for Information Systems, 18,* 497-518.

Shim, J. P., Varshney, U., Dekleva, S., & Knoerzer, G. (2006b). Mobile and wireless networks: Services, evolution & issues. *International Journal of Mobile Communications, 4*(4), 405-417.

Smagt, T. (2000). Enhancing virtual teams: Social relations v. communication technology. *Industrial Management & Data Systems, 100*(4), 148-156.

Suh, Y. (2005). *Current overview of S-DMB.* TU Media.

Teng, R. (2005, January). Digital multimedia broadcasting in Korea. *In-Stat Report No. IN-052469WHT.* Retrieved from http://www.cctv.org/InStatPaper.pdf

Thompson, C. J., Locander, W. B., & Pollio, H. R. (1989). Putting consumer experience back into consumer research: The philosophy and method of existential-phenomenology. *Journal of Consumer Research, 16,* 133-146.

Trappey, A., Trappey, C., Hou, J., & Chen, B. (2004). Mobile agent technology and application for online global logistic services. *Industrial Management & Data Systems, 104(*2), 169-183.

Tsaih, R., Chang, H., & Huang, C. (2005). The business concept of utilizing the interactive TV.

Industrial Management & Data Systems, 105(5), 613-622.

Ventatesh, W. (2000). Age differences in technology adoption decisions: Implications for a changing work force. *Personnel Psychology, 53,* 375-403.

ENDNOTES

[1] http://www.pcworld.com/news/article/0,aid,124478,00.asp (2006, January 24)

[2] Wi-Fi Hotstats. *Wireless Review, 22*(8) (August, 2005)

[3] www.scala.com/vignettes/digital-multimedia-broadcasting.html

[4] www.chiefexecutive.net/depts/technology/197a.htm

[5] http://www.economist.com/business/displaystory.cfm?story_id=5356658&no_jw_tran=1&no_na_tran=1 (2006 Jan 5)

Chapter XIV
Understanding the Organisational Impact and Perceived Benefits of Bluetooth–Enabled Personal Digital Assistants in Restaurants

Eusebio Scornavacca
Victoria University of Wellington, New Zealand

Mishul Prasad
Victoria University of Wellington, New Zealand

Hans Lehmann
Victoria University of Wellington, New Zealand

ABSTRACT

The hospitality industry, more specifically restaurants, has recently started to exploit the benefits of mobile technologies. This research explores the perceived benefits of using PDAs in a restaurant in a business-to-employee (B2E) context. The findings indicated that the most common perceptions are increased efficiency; speedier service; better usability and ease of use; enhanced reputation/image; and increased accuracy. Most of the negative perceptions were related to the technical shortcomings of the technology such as unreliable transmission of data, system crashes, short battery life, and limited durability of the devices. The paper concludes with recommendations for future practice and research.

INTRODUCTION

Due to the fast adoption of mobile technologies throughout the world, many academics have enthusiastically predicted a seamless, wireless world where mobile electronic business can occur anywhere and anytime via handheld devices such as cellular phones and PDAs (Andreou et al., 2005; Balasubramanian, Peterson, & Jarvenpaa, 2002; Barnes & Scornavaaca, 2004; Frichol,

2004; Scornavacca & Barnes, 2003; Siau, Lim, & Shen, 2001; Siau & Shen, 2003; Walker & Barnes, 2005).

Much of the literature on mobile business has focused on consumer applications (Scornavacca, Barnes, & Huff, 2006). However, according to studies published by AT Kearney (2003), the international market for B2E applications is expected to grow twice as rapidly as the market for wireless business-to-consumer (B2C) applications.

Worldwide, the hospitality industry has embraced B2E mobile technologies. Several examples of wireless applications can be seen today in hotels, cafes, bars, and restaurants (Microsoft Corporation, 2004). In restaurants, vital tasks such as taking orders from customers using the traditional pen-and-paper method can easily be performed more efficiently with the use of mobile technologies such as PDAs or specialist mobile devices (Microsoft Corporation, 2004). Businesses that implemented mobile technologies reduced operations costs, gained efficiency, and improved service quality (Barnes, 2004; Barnes, 2002; Beulen & Streng, 2002; Parasuraman & Grewal, 2000; Raisinghani, 2002).

The purpose of this case study was to explore the perceived benefits of using wireless PDAs in a restaurant and to verify if managers and employees have the same perceptions. Identifying the differences and similarities on the perceived benefits of different stakeholders can contribute to the improvement and better understanding of the adoption process of mobile technologies in restaurants and other organisations alike.

The next section of this paper reviews the literature pertinent to this study. This is followed by organisational background and research methodology. The results of the research are then provided, along with the case analysis. The paper concludes with suggestions for future research.

MOBILE BUSINESS

There are some fundamental differences between m-business and e-business. Zhang and Yuan (2002) point out that three broad aspects that should be taken into account in order to understand the concept of mobile business: *origin, technology,* and *nature of service.*

- **Origin:** Due to widely expanding networks and nearly free access to the Internet, e-business bridges distances and enables companies to display and sell goods and services cheaply to consumers and businesses around the world. In the Internet world, much is given away free or at a discount in the hope that a way will eventually be found (presumably through advertising income) to turn traffic into profits. Contrarily, m-business is rooted in paid-for service in the private mobile phone industry where business competition is stiff. In the telecom world, users pay for airtime, by the size of the data packet transmitted, and by the service used for what they get. Therefore, due to their different origins, the customer bases of m-business and e-business are quite different.

- **Technology:** The fundamental infrastructure of e-business is the Internet. It has a well-established protocol, TCP/IP, which solves the global Internet-working problem and ensures that computers communicate with one another in a reliable fashion. In contrast, m-business services are constrained by a variety of wireless media communication standards ranging from global (satellite), regional (third generation [3G], IEEE 802,11a/b, I-mode), to short distance (Bluetooth). Cellular carriers use different systems and standards such as global service for mobile (GSM), time division multiple access (TDMA), and code division multiple access (CDMA) to compete with each other. As a consequence, m-business applications tend to be device and carrier dependent. Nevertheless, the boom in e-business applications is actually due to the widespread use of PCs, which have a complete text input keyboard, large screen, substantial memory, and high processing power. Contrarily, mobile devices such as cell phones and PDAs (such as iPAQ and Palmpilot) still present some obstacles such as uniform standards, ease of operation, security for transactions, minimum screen size, and display type.

- **Nature of services:** The Web is widely accessible, enabling search and delivery of rich information. Sophisticated electronic transaction processes can be integrated easily with backend enterprise information systems. In contrast, the delivery of m-business applications relies on private wireless communication carriers. These services are usually delivered to a specific region and are rather simple, more personalised, location-specific, and time sensitive. Also the rapid growth of e-business started from the booming of dot-com companies aimed at online shopping and customer services. Gradually, the emphasis shifted to B2B, and more recently e-business, to take advantage of the real business value of the Internet. In contrast, mobile business started from person-to-person (P2P) communication, and gradually more services were introduced through interactions between people and systems: checking the weather, finding a local restaurant, and so forth. The authors suggest that rather than apply B2C and business-to-business (B2B) classifications to m-business; P2P and person-to-system (P2S) would be more appropriate to address the nature and trend of m-business applications.

All three aspects identified previously highlight the unique characteristics of m-business. Therefore, m-business cannot be simply defined as "e-business via a wireless network." Scornavacca et al. (2006) defined m-business as the use of the mobile information technologies, including the wireless Internet, for communication and coordination within an organisation; between an organisation and other organisations and/or customers; and for management of the firm.

Barnes (2002) analysed the potential impacts that mobile technologies may have on the firm's value chain. As a result, he identified eight core and not mutually exclusive benefits of m-business to the organisations: (1) *business transformation*, (2) *efficiency*, (3) *effectiveness*, (4) *flexibility*, (5) *ubiquity*, (6) *connectivity*, (7) *interactivity*, and (8) *location awareness*. These benefits can be a valuable source of competitive advantage to a business if harnessed correctly.

The first three benefits are considered generic to most IT applications while the remaining five are specific to mobile technologies. In terms of business transformation, Barnes (2002) argues that this can happen at different levels of the organisation by automating processes; networking and sharing information; transforming relationships with other entities; and creating new revenue streams. Efficiency relates mostly to productivity gains or reductions in costs, which are achieved by process automation. Contrarily, effectiveness can be difficult to measure as it is subjective. The gains in effectiveness have come mostly in conjunction with the process transformations in the organisations.

Flexibility refers degree of adaptability and portability of the mobile technologies. Barnes (2002) points out that having mobile technologies in some types of businesses, such as offices and supermarkets, allow rearranging IT equipment without major cabling issues. Having a mobile technology in the organisation gives them flexibility in their environment. Ubiquity refers to creating a real-time environment where a smartphone or PDA can fulfil the need for both real-time information and communication anywhere, independent of the user's location allowing for easier information access. This benefit is realised only if the mobile device is connected through a network.

Connectivity refers to the ability to transmit and receive data wirelessly and at the same time interactivity refers the potential for information to be shared among various devices, thus increasing systems interactivity. Finally, the business benefits enabled by location awareness are now becoming a reality. Location of products and services implies knowing where the user is located at any particular moment. This is the key to offering quick information efficiently when needed. For example, a travelling field technician can be called upon faster to the job site if their location and job status is known. This usually works by having a type of global positioning system (GPS) chip installed on the mobile devices.

As presented previously, the use of mobile technologies can undoubtedly improve the efficiency of the members of an organisation (Barnes & Scornavacca, 2005; Jain 2003; Lehmann, Kuhn, & Lehner, 2004; Walker & Barnes, 2005; Westelius & Valiente, 2004; Yuan & Zhang, 2003). In several cases, as Jain (2003) and Walker and Barnes (2005) reported, mobile technologies replaced inefficient paper data entry processes and enabled the capture of complete and accurate data at the point of origin.

It is clear that different industries (or organisational settings) require distinct levels of mobility (Barnes & Scornavacca, 2005; Jain, 2003; Pica, Sørensen, & Allen. 2004;). The mobility requirements of organisations can be generally divided in three categories (Jain, 2003):

- **Industries with high mobility requirements:** This group involves the organisational settings where users as well as the assets are moving constantly. Examples of such settings include shipping and trucking industries as well as law enforcement agencies (see Pica et al., 2004). Although in agricultural and utility industries assets

are fixed, these assets are spread over a wide geographic region and most tasks are accomplished in the field. For this industry group, mobile technologies are crucial as they liberate mobile employees from wired connections and enable them to accomplish IS-supported tasks needs in a broader temporal and spatial boundary.

- **Industries with medium mobility requirements:** This group involves the settings where users are highly mobile in a restricted perimeter and perform most critical tasks a "base" (e.g., office or kiosk). Examples of such settings include hospitals and restaurants.

- **Industries with low mobility requirements:** Users belonging to this category are rarely mobile and the support of mobile IS hardly influence the fulfilment of their tasks. An example of this setting would be a traditional office setting.

The impact of mobile technologies is triggering the development of B2E applications. B2E has been anticipated as one of the major areas of growth in mobile business (Lehmann et al., 2004). A study conducted in Europe identified some future trends of mobile B2E applications (Lehman et al., 2004). The results of the study showed wireless technologies (i.e., *WIFI*) would be the dominant technology in most large organisations at first, although most small- to medium-sized organisations would have the potential to exploit this particular technology. In addition, it was found that B2E has a large potential to assist service providers.

According to Lehmann et al. (2004), organisations often lack the adequate knowledge regarding the potential opportunities that are emerging from new m-business technologies. In particular, firms may have a lack of clear understanding of the technology per se, which creates problems in the development of their business strategies. Also, there are some concerns regarding how organisations may use m-business technologies to improve business processes (Gilbert & Kendall, 2003).

INNOVATION OF TECHNOLOGY

Many frameworks and models have been developed to explain the adoption behaviour of mobile technologies as well as its potential organisational benefits (Barnes, 2003a; Haque, 2004; Sharma & Deng, 2002; Shim, Beckering, & Hall, 2002; Siau & Shen, 2003; Siau, Sheng, & Nah, 2004).

Roger's (1995) diffusion of innovation model (DoI) has been adapted by many researchers in order to identify adoption behaviours towards mobile technologies (Barnes, 2003a; Lim & Nam, 2003). The DoI model consists of five key characteristics:

- **Relative advantage:** Refers to the degree to which an innovation is perceived as better than the idea it supersedes. An example of this is mobile communications where it has relative advantage over the Internet due to its unique nature. Users are able to access information anytime, anywhere and they can be easily reached, for they are always connected.
- **Compatibility:** Is the degree to which an innovation is perceived as being consistent with the existing values, past experiences, and needs of potential adopters. This refers to the confluence of technology with in the work environment and the impact it has on the social values, needs, and technical expertise with which the new technology can easily be integrated.
- **Complexity:** Means the degree to which an innovation is perceived as difficult to understand and use. Similar to the technology acceptance model's (TAM) perceived ease of use, this model measures the degree of difficulty in using mobile technology.
- **Trialability:** Refers to the degree to which

an innovation may be experimented with a limited basis. This characteristic is used to identify the factors that influence the adoption process when the technology is actually tried and tested. It aims to identify those factors which arise while using a certain technology.

- **Observability:** Relates to the degree to which the results of an innovation are visible to others. This identifies the degree to which a certain technology is noticeable among users. Whether or not it affects people's perceptions and image of the technology.

Barnes (2003a) adapted Roger's (1995) model to the context of m-business. The author added two extra characteristics to the original DoI model: *trust* and *image*.

Trust refers to the degree of reliance users have towards the technology. Some of the most common limitations with mobile technology have been the issues related to trusting the wireless environment. For example, users often do not feel the wireless environment is secure for electronic payments.

Image is concerned with the perceived reputation and status of the technology. When a consumer sees a modern piece of technology used in an innovative way (i.e., waiters carrying PDAs for ordering), this can be attributed to an organisation's status or reputation in the industry; thus contributing toward a positive organisational image.

MOBILE APPLICATIONS IN THE HOSPITALITY INDUSTRY

The hospitality industry is predominantly customer focused especially in the food industry, such as restaurants, bars, and cafes. One of the industry's key objectives is to provide the customer with outstanding quality of service. According to

Parasuraman and Grewal (2000) customers judge service quality by five criteria. These are:

- **Reliability:** Ability to perform the promised service dependably and accurately,
- **Responsiveness:** Willingness to help customers and provide prompt service,
- **Assurance:** Knowledge and courtesy of employees and their ability to inspire trust and confidence,
- **Empathy:** Caring, individualised attention the organisation provides its customers, and
- **Tangibles:** Appearance of physical facilities, equipment, personnel, and communication materials.

Parasuraman and Grewal (2000) point out that the combination of these five factors leads to customer satisfaction and loyalty. Undoubtedly, the applications of mobile technologies can considerably assist restaurants to improve service quality. Therefore it is important for businesses in hospitality to understand customers' perception in their organisation in order to deliver high quality service.

Exploratory studies have shown that m-business technologies can add value to a businesses value chain in many ways (Barnes, 2002). Specifically, wireless devices (i.e. PDAs) have the ability to also significantly improve the efficiency and customer service for restaurants, cafes, and bars. One example is Little Chef, one of the UK's major roadside restaurants. They adopted a wireless restaurant management system in early 2002. The system allows waiters to take customer orders using a handheld device equipped with touch screens and send this information automatically to the point of sale (POS) and kitchen. The key benefits for the organisation include improved staff efficiency, less wastage, and thus increased customer satisfaction (Barnes, 2002).

Another example is Kudos Restaurant and Wine Bar in Australia (Microsoft Corporation, 2004). They implemented a hand-held, POS device to handle customers' orders. The restaurant manager reported that the new technology has brought efficiency, accuracy, and better integration of the different parts of the business. The elimination of errors meant that the staff working in the kitchen and at the bar is getting the accurate information and, consequently, customers are receiving exactly what they ordered. Again, this not only changing the order experience and service quality for the consumer but concurrently changing the way restaurants and others, alike, do business.

ORGANISATIONAL BACKGROUND

The organisation studied is a large Australian franchise restaurant situated in the central business district of Wellington, New Zealand. The restaurant is a busy family restaurant and also has many other stores nation wide. Currently, there is one general manager who runs the entire administrative operation (e.g., sales, stock, wastage, supply chain). Two assistant managers are responsible for supervising 14 staff as well as taking orders from the main floor. The wireless ordering system (Figure 1) connects six PDAs and two POS terminals. Customers' orders are sent via Bluetooth (short-range wireless technology) to the nominated POS terminals. The order is also instantly sent from the terminals to the kitchen or bar staff for preparation. The actual PDA itself has a straightforward touch-screen, graphical menu system that lets the users (employees) navigate easily through it to place the customer's order.

METHODOLOGY

In order to explore the perception and experiences of managers and end users using wireless PDAs in a restaurant, this study used case research methodology. Case research is considered appropriate for researching an area where theories are at formative stages, for emerging technologies, and

Figure 1. Wireless ordering system

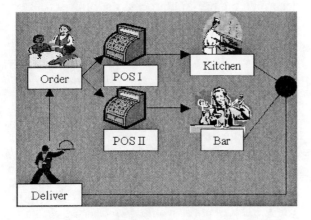

where little research has been completed (Benbasat, Goldstein, & Mead, 1987). Case research is also appropriate for examining practice-based problems, since it allows a researcher to capture the knowledge of practitioners and use it to generate theory (Benbasat et al., 1987; Creswell, 2003; Eisenhardt, 1989).

This study is based on an exploratory single case. The organisation was identified opportunistically. Data collection was based on open-ended interviews that captured the experiences of the employees as well as the general manager. These were face-to-face interviews with the general manager and five of the restaurants employees. Each interview was audio recorded and took approximately one hour. The recordings of the interviews were transcribed and fed back to each participant in order to reduce any possible errors.

FINDINGS

In this section, Figure 2 initially presents the overall perceptions (positive and negative) expressed by the interviewees. This is followed by a comparison between the perceptions expressed by the general manager and the five employees.

Overall Perceptions

A common set of benefits, consistent with the current literature, arose during the interviews (Heitmann, Prykop, & Aschmoneit, 2004; Rao & Parikh, 2003; Roberts & Pick, 2004; Xia & Lee, 2000). All interviewees perceived that the system—in comparison with the old paper-based system—generated material benefits such as error reduction, faster service, cost reduction, and efficiency gains. In addition, the interviewees perceived that the technology was helping them to provide their customers with better quality of service. Furthermore, even though they had no prior knowledge or experience with PDAs, they classified the system as "easy to use." One of the employees mentioned:

It makes my job easier... that's the best value of it because everything's at your hands. It's just all there for you to see and if anyone asks you something then you can just go through the PDA and just tell them. You also don't need to remember every single thing...so memory wise, it helps you out as well. And yeah, it just becomes less stressful.

Also the interviewees noticed that customers were impressed with the technology and that it was positively contributing to the reputation/image of the organisation. One of the floor staff stated:

... A lot of people look at it; they've never seen them before. Most people are like its different, it's quite current, it's new and it's quite up-to-date; it's fresh almost. When you're writing down orders...you're wasting more time where as with this [PDA], customers are quite happy and you go in and quickly take their orders...kids want to see this [PDA] and see you use it and they take interest. Probably 1 in 4 people want to know what it is and how you use it.

The negative perceptions associated with the use of PDAs in the restaurant were predominantly related to technical issues such as battery life, system reliability, and unreliable connectivity. These finding are consistent with findings presented by Roberts and Pick (2004) and Rao and Parikh (2003).

Perceptions Between the Business and the Employees

Overall, the general manager perceived far more value in using the system than the employees. This can be attributed to the fact that he performed a lot more tasks with the system than the others interviewees. The general manager also attributed that the system allowed him to make better decisions due to the large amount of information available. He mentioned:

Probably the biggest way [value] is time saving. I don't have half the mucking around in terms of managing, people, stocks, and everything else. This system gives me such a good breakdown of everything.

Barnes (2003b); Wee and Gutierrez, (2005); and Lehmann et al. (2004) also noticed that wireless technology has the ability to bring great value especially at the operational level of an organisation. It could be speculated that the employees underestimated the business value of the application because they have only limited knowledge and understanding of the overall system. They only used the system to take orders from customers.

Another difference in perception relates to training. The general manager has indicated that the training process was a very important factor for the adoption of the system (Davis & Venkatesh, 1996). However, the employees did not perceive that training was given enough emphasis since most of the training was "self-learned" and is done by trial and error in practicing directly with

PDAs—in a live situation. The general manager described the training process as follows:

...we encourage them [staff] to use it [PDA] themselves. We'd start them in small sections and we give them 2 or 3 tables on a quieter night because part of the thing [training] is for them to become more comfortable. The more comfortable the people are the better service they'll provide the customer. The other thing is that you don't want scare them off. I mean you give somebody one of these and drop them in on a Saturday night...they're never want come back again.

Security was another main concern expressed by the manger, whereas the employees did not see it as an important issue. Generally, PDAs enabled with Bluetooth offer a limited level of security (Coursaris, Hassanein, & Head, 2003).

Figure 2 summarises the positive and negative perceptions towards the system from the general manger's and the employee's perspective.

In order to extend the analysis of the results, the following section discusses the adoption of wireless PDAs in a restaurant using Rogers' (1995) DoI model and TAM as a theoretical guideline (Davis & Venkatesh, 1996).

DIFFUSION OF INNOVATION AND MOBILE TECHNOLOGY

Roger's (1995) model provides a basic guide for examining the impacts of the mobile devices. In accordance with the model, relative advantage, compatibility, complexity, and observability were the main factors that influenced the rate of adoption of the PDAs in the restaurant setting. *Trialability* did not feature as a factor—the restaurant did not trial the technology before acquiring it. The factors are explained as follows:

- **Relative advantage:** The use of PDAs in the restaurant provided advantages in terms of

Figure 2. The perceived benefits between the business and employees of PDAs in a restaurant

	Positive Perceptions	Negative Perceptions
General Manager	Efficiency. Speed. Accuracy – reduced errors. Security. Image. Reliance – usefulness. Cost savings.	Technical. System crashes. Low functionality to support other parts of the business. Beaming Capability. Security. Durability.
Employees	Efficiency. Speed of service. Usability – ease of use. Image/good reputation. Accuracy – reduced ordering taking errors.	Technical. System Crashes (inconsistent). Durability. Beaming capability. Batter power. Number of Terminals. Reliance – difficulty

speed, accuracy, efficiency, and customer service. It was mainly through automating business processes that the technology was perceived as better than the conventional way of working in restaurants.

- **Compatibility**: The PDA system was aligned with the main goals of the restaurant as it increased revenue, saved costs, and provided quality service for its customers.
- **Complexity:** The PDAs had an easy-to-follow graphical interface and a touch screen. It was not difficult to understand how to take orders using the PDAs as it guided the users through the menu system
- **Observability:** The employees found that the PDAs generated a "wow factor" and projected a positive image for their restaurant. These factors were also identified by Barnes (2003b) and Lim and Nam (2003).

The results further indicated that *perceived usefulness* and *perceived ease of use* (Wu & Wang, 2003) of the system were influential factors that directly impacted in the user's attitudes towards the system (Venkatesh, Morris, Davis, & Davis, 2003). The general manager and one employee mentioned that the level of usage of the PDAs always depends on whether the employee is willing or wants to use it (Davis & Venkatesh, 1996).

CONCLUSION

Similar to previous research findings presented in the current m-business literature, efficiency, speed of service, usability (i.e., ease of use), organisational image, accuracy, and productivity were identified as the common set of positives perceptions associated with the adoption wireless technologies in the work domain (Barnes, 2002, 2003, 2004; Laukkanen & Lauronen, 2005; Siau et al., 2001).

The negative perceptions were generally related to the technical factors such as system reliability, connectivity, security, and battery life. Some of these pitfalls could be possibly overcome by the adoption of wireless LAN (WiFi) instead of Bluetooth, which proved to be quite an inadequate technology choice, both from transmission reliability and security perspective. A further improvement requirement would be the implementation of a comprehensive training/tutorial module that employees can work through without being in a live situation.

Relative advantage, compatibility, complexity, and observability were identified as further contributing factors for the adoption of the system. The findings also indicated that, in the early stages of adoption, perceived ease of use and perceived usefulness were the most prominent factors contributing to the user's, that is, the employees', expectations from the system and their positive attitude towards using it.

Most of the differences found between the overall perceptions of the general manager and his staff could be attributed to the nature of the tasks that they accomplish in using the system. The perceived benefits reported by the employees focused on issues mainly related to the substitution of the usual manual (paper based) ordering process by an electronic (wireless) system. On the other hand, the general manager identified benefits mainly related to information management, administrative tasks, and decision support.

LIMITATIONS AND FUTURE RESEARCH

This research was based on a single case study of an organisation within the hospitality industry in New Zealand. The impacts of wireless solutions described in this research must be closely scrutinised in their application to other organisations and contexts.

Further qualitative research should be conducted to investigate the impact of mobile technologies in other organisations within the hospitality industry. This could include exploring mobility in confined spaces, such as restaurants, bars, hospitals, and/or warehouses. In addition, some research could investigate the effect of wireless ordering systems from a customer perspective. Finally, ordering systems based on WiFi technologies could be studied and its results compared with other systems based on Bluetooth.

REFERENCES

Andreou, A. S., Lenidou, C., Chrysostomou, C., Pitsillides, A., Samaras, G., & Schizas, C. (2005). Key issues for the design and development of mobile business services and applications. *International Journal of Mobile Communications, 3,* 303-323.

AT Kearney. (2003). *The new mobile mindset.* Retrieved March 12., 2003, from http://www.atkearney.com/shared_res/pdf/Mobinet_Monograph_S.pdf

Balasubramanian, S., Peterson, R. A., & Jarvenpaa, S. L. (2002). Exploring the implications of m-commerce for markets and marketing. *Journal of the Academy of Marketing Science, 30*(4), 348-361.

Barnes, S. J. (2002). Unwired business: Wireless applications in the firm's value chain. In *Proceedings of the Sixth Pacific Asia Conference on Information Systems*, Tokyo, Japan.

Barnes, S. J. (2003a). Enterprise mobility: Concept and examples. *International Journal of Mobile Communications, 1*(4), 341-359.

Barnes, S. J. (2003b). *M-Business: The strategic implications of wireless communications.* Oxford, UK: Elsevier/Butterworth-Heinemann.

Barnes, S. (2004). Wireless support for mobile distributed work: A taxonomy and examples. In *Proceedings of the 37th Hawaii International Conference on System Sciences,* Big Island, HI.

Barnes, S. J., & Scornavacca, E. (2004). Mobile marketing: The role of permission and acceptance. *International Journal of Mobile Communications, 2*(2), 128-139.

Barnes, S. J., & Scornavacca, E. (2005). *The strategic impact of wireless applications in NZ business.* Paper presented at the Hong Kong Mobility Roundtable, Hong Kong.

Benbasat, I., Goldstein, D. K., & Mead, M. (1987). The case research strategy in studies of information systems. *MIS Quarterly, 11*(3): 369-386.

Beulen, E., & Streng, R.-J. (2002). The impact of online mobile office applications on the effectiveness and efficiency of mobile workers behavior: A field experiment in the IT services sector. In *Proceedings from the International Conference on Information Systems,* Barcelona, Spain.

Coursaris, C., Hassanein, K., & Head, M. (2003). M-Commerce in Canada: An interaction framework for wireless privacy. *Canadian Journal of Administrative Sciences, 20*(1), 54-73.

Creswell, J. W. (2003). *Research design qualitative, quantitative and mixed methods approaches* (2nd ed.). Chennai, India: Sage.

Davis, F. D., & Venkatesh, V. (1996). A model of the antecedents of perceived ease of use: Development and test. *Decision Sciences, 27*(3), 451.

Eisenhardt, M. K. (1989). Building theories from case study research. *The Academy of Management Review, 14*(4), 532.

Frichol, M. (2004). There's no business like e-business. *IIE Solutions, 33*(3), 38.

Gibert, A. L., & Kendall, J. D. (2003, January). A marketing model of for mobile wireless services. In *Proceedings of 36th Hawaii International Conference on Systems Sciences,* Big Island, HI.

Haque, A. (2004). Mobile commerce: Customer perception and it's prospect on business operation. *Journal of American Academy of Business, 4*(1/2), 257.

Heitmann, M., Prykop, C., & Aschmoneit, P. (2004). Using means-end chains to build mobile brand communities. In *Proceedings of the 37th Hawaii International Conference on System Sciences,* Big Island.

Jain, R. (2003). *Enterprise mobile services: Framework and industry-specific analysis.* Paper presented at the Americas Conference on Information Systems 2003, Tampa, FL.

Laukkanen, T., & Lauronen, J. (2005). Consumer value creation in mobile banking services. *International Journal of Mobile Communications, 3,* 325-338.

Lehmann, H., Kuhn, J., & Lehner, F. (2004). The future of mobile technology: Findings from a European Delphi study. In *Proceedings of the 37th Hawaii International Conference on System Sciences,* Big Island, HI.

Lim, J. Y., & Nam, C. (2003). *An empirical study on the factors influencing the adoption of m-payments service in Korea.* Paper presented at the International Telecommunications Society Asia-Australasian Regional Conference, Perth, Australia.

Microsoft Corporation. (2004). *Mobile business solutions case studies.* Author.

Parasuraman, A., & Grewal, D. (2000). The impact of technology on quality-value-loyalty chain: A research agenda. *Academy of Marketing Science, 28*(1), 168.

Pica, D., Sørensen, C., & Allen, D. (2004). *On mobility and context of work: Exploring mobile police work.* Paper presented at the 37th Hawaii International Conference on System Sciences, Big Island, HI.

Raisinghani, M. (2002). Mobile commerce: Transforming the vision into reality. *Information Resources Management Journal, 15*(2), 3-4.

Rao, B., & Parikh, M. A. (2003). Wireless broadband networks: The U.S. experience. *International Journal of Electronic Commerce, 8*(1), 37.

Roberts, K. G., & Pick, J. B. (2004). Technology factors in corporate adoption of mobile cell phones: A case study analysis. In *Proceedings of the 37th Hawaii International Conference on Systems Sciences,* Big Island, HI.

Rogers, E. (1995). *Diffusion of innovations* (4th ed.). New York: The Free Press.

Scornavacca, E., & Barnes, S. J. (2003). M-Banking services in Japan: A strategic perspective. *International Journal of Mobile Communications, 2*(1), 51-66.

Scornavacca, E., Barnes, S., & Huff, S. (2006). Mobile business research published in 2000-2004: Emergence, current status, and future opportunities. *Communications of the Association for Information Systems, 17*(28), 20.

Sharma, S., & Deng, X. (2002). *An empirical investigation of factors affecting the acceptance of personal digital assistants by individuals.* Paper presented at the Americas Conference on Information Systems, Dallas, TX.

Shim, J. P., Bekkering, E., & Hall, L. (2002). *Empirical findings on perceived value of mobile commerce as a distribution channel.* Paper presented at the Americas Conference on Information Systems, Dallas, TX.

Siau, K., Lim, E.-P., & Shen, Z. (2001). Mobile commerce: Promises, challenges, and research agenda. *Journal of Database Management, 12*(3), 4-13.

Siau, K., & Shen, Z. (2003). Mobile communications and mobile services. *International Journal of Mobile Communications, 1*(1/2), 3-14.

Siau, K., Sheng, H., & Nah, F. (2004). *Value of mobile commerce to customers.* Paper presented at the Tenth Americas Conference on Information Systems, New York.

Venkatesh, V., Morris, M. G., Davis, G. B., & Davis, F. D. (2003). User acceptance of information technology: Toward a unified view. *MIS Quarterly, 27*(3), 425-478.

Walker, B., & Barnes, S. J. (2005). Wireless sales force automation: Concept and cases. *International Journal of Mobile Communications, 3,* 411-427.

Wee, J., & Gutierrez, J. A. (2005). A framework for effective quality of service over wireless networks. *International Journal of Mobile Communications, 3,* 138-149.

Westelius, A., & Valiente, P. (2004, June 14-16). *Bringing the enterprise system to the fronline—Intertwinig computerised and conventional communication at BT Europe.* Paper presented at the 12th European Conference on Information Systems, Turku, Finland.

Wu, J.-H., & Wang, S.-C. (2003). *An empirical study of consumers adopting mobile commerce in Taiwan: Analyzed by structural equation modelling.* Paper presented at the Seventh Pacific Asia Conference on Information Systems, Adelaide, Australia.

Xia, W., & Lee, G. (2000). The influence of persuasion, training and experience on user perceptions and acceptance of IT innovation. In *Proceedings from the International Conference on Information Systems,* Brisbane, Queensland, Australia.

Yuan, Y., & Zhang, J. J. (2003). Towards an appropriate business model for m-commerce. *International Journal of Mobile Communications, 1*(1/2), 35-56.

Zhang, J. J., & Yuan, Y. (2002). *M-commerce versus Internet-based e-commerce: The key differences.* Paper presented at the Americas Conference on Information Systems, Dallas, TX.

Chapter XV
Strategies of Mobile Value–Added Services in Korea

Jin Ki Kim
Korea Areospace University, Korea

Heasun Chun
The State University of New York at Buffalo, USA

ABSTRACT

As the growth of the mobile market decreases and the market competition intensifies, mobile carriers have been trying to find new business models to retain their profits and expand their business boundaries. Development of value-added services increases the chances of keeping the growth with mobile carriers. This chapter discusses the motivation of mobile value-added service in terms of value chain and mobile adoption. Six mobile value-added services presented in Korea are introduced: (1) short messaging service (SMS), (2) personalized call-ring service, (3) mobile music service, (4) mobile video service, (5) mobile payment (m-payment), and (6) mobile games. The major characteristics of those value-added services are discussed with "4Cs": (1) customization, (2) content-focused, (3) connectedness, and (4) contemporary. This chapter also discusses digital multimedia broadcasting (DMB) as a new value-added service and the impacts of value-added services on the mobile market. This chapter is concluded with three plausible strategies of mobile carriers: (1) real-time, market-responding strategy, (2) content-focused market strategy, and (3) various bundling service.

INTRODUCTION

Worldwide, the number of mobile subscribers reached 1.7 billion in 2004 (International Telecommunications Union [ITU], 2006). The compound annual growth rate (CAGR) from 1980 to 2004 is 59.54%. The number of subscribers keeps increasing due to the increase of subscription in the under-developed and developing countries. How-ever, recently the growth rate of subscription has decreased. Since 2002, the growth rates dropped to under 20% (See Figure 1). It means that the mobile service market is approaching the mature stage. In several European and Asian countries, penetration ratios are around 80-100%. According to ITU World Telecommunications Indicator 2004, 45 out of 170 countries which reported the penetration ratio of mobile service shows more than 70% (ITU, 2006).

Figure 1. Growth rate of number of mobile subscribers worldwide

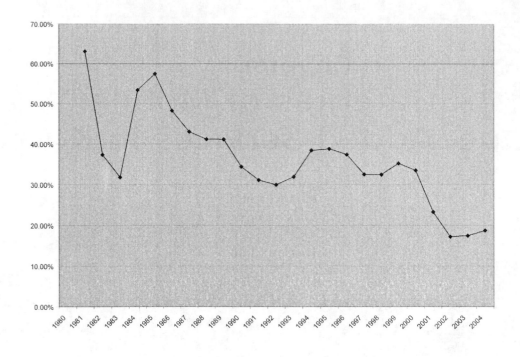

From the perspective of a mobile carrier, the reduced growth rate means a decrease in potential profits. In terms of market competition type, the decrease of growth rate leads to retention-based competition, not to subscription-based competition. From the financial view, the margin would be reduced. Mobile carriers would concentrate on retention of subscribers and on an increase of billing payments per subscriber. For this reason, the focus is now on average revenue per user (ARPU) and attempts are being made to increase ARPU by introducing premium services. Premium services are defined as services that provide added value for which the service provider can charge a premium (Brenner, Grech, Torabi, & Unmehopa, 2005).

What kinds of value-added services can be technically provided? Can they contribute to the profit of mobile carriers? And which kinds of comparative strategies can make sense in the market? Those questions become major issues which should be answered regarding those value-added services.

In this chapter, current trends and strategies of value-added services to keep or increase ARPU of customers for mobile carriers are discussed. This chapter is structured into seven sections as follows: in the second section the motivations of mobile value-added services have been discussed, in terms of value chain and mobile adoption. The case studies on the current value-added services form the content of the third section, including SMS, personalized call-ring service, mobile music service, mobile video service, m-payment, and mobile games. The fourth section highlights the characteristics of current trends of value-added services. DMB for a new value-added service is introduced in the fifth section. In the sixth section, the impacts of value-added services on the mobile market are discussed. Concluding remarks with plausible strategies are presented in the final section.

Figure 2. Third generation value chain (Maitland et al., 2002)

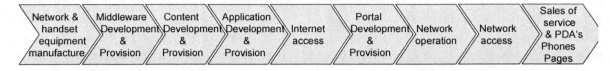

MOTIVATIONS OF MOBILE VALUE-ADDED SERVICES

The telecommunications industry is structured by the economic, regulatory, and technical aspects. The shift from second generation (2G) to third generation (3G) mobile induced several changes in those aspects.

From the economic perspective, the costs of standardization, R&D, the significant costs of the licenses for spectrum, the possibility for network sharing, and the uncertainty surrounding the potential revenue streams for 3G mobile are major concerns. Licensing of spectrum, competition policy, and network sharing agreements are influential factors in the view of regulation. From the view of the technology, the evolution of mobile services has two components. First, voice-only has changed into multimedia-capable communications since the 3G mobile network has more capacity which is devoted to data communications. Data communications on the mobile network have larger portions than before. Second, the closed and dedicated network moved to the open network which is based on the Internet. The 3G mobile network is based on an all IP network.

Those kinds of changes impact the value chain of the mobile service industry which is characterized by a more complex and multi-faceted production platform (or industry value chain). It is necessary to understand the value chain of the mobile industry and its trends of changing in the future in order to check the potential growth of mobile communication services (Maitland, Bauer, & Westerveld, 2002; Sabat, 2002; Steinbock, 2003). Figure 2 shows an example of the value chain of 3G mobile services.

In the market which is diverse and multi-faceted, mobile carriers can take two different approaches: product differentiation and market integration.

Regarding on product differentiations, there are three kinds of options: horizontal, vertical, and cross-market differentiation (Geng & Whinston, 2001).

- **Horizontal differentiation:** Sellers can avoid a price war by targeting different consumer groups with various preferences, tastes, or occupations
- **Vertical differentiation:** Sellers can differentiate their products in a way that consistently affects all consumer valuations
- **Cross-market differentiation by tying:** A seller can use a bundling strategy and its monopoly in one market to attack competitors in another

There are two kinds of integration: vertical and horizontal integration. Mobile carriers can take the benefit from the economy of scale from the horizontal integration. From the view of vertical integration, the development of various value-added services contributes to mobile carriers' leading roles in the new value chain. Multi-faceted and specialized value chain means a possibility of the loss of competitive advantage which mobile carriers had held for a long time. The possibility could lead to losing the leadership in the value chain, and, as the result, losing the market and the profitability. Thus, in order to keep their market leadership, mobile carriers should integrate adjacent components in the value chain.

Provision of value-added services is the first step to forward and backward expansion of business domains in the value chain. Through the process, mobile carriers can learn how to survive in the market in which creativity is a major competitive advantage. Lessons from the learning process can grant mobile carriers a useful chance of expanding their business scope into a broad media industry.

Another clue that shows the importance of value-added services is found in the literature of mobile adoption. Major influential factors on mobile adoption include call quality, tariff level, handsets, brand image, income, and subscription duration (H.-S. Kim & Yoon, 2004; J. K. Kim, 2005; M.-K. Kim, Park, & Jeong, 2004; Middleton, 2002). Switching cost and switching promotion are also found to be critical factors (M.-K. Kim et al., 2004). Under mobile number portability (MNP), the quality of service and price had more affect on customers' intention to retain or churn than before launching the MNP (J. K. Kim, 2005).

Mobile value-added services is one of the components to measure the customer satisfaction for mobile services (J. Lee, Lee, & Feick, 2001). In addition, perceived usefulness, ease of use, price, and speed of use are known as the most important determinants of adoption of multimedia mobile services (Pagani, 2004). In recent studies value-added service is included as one of influential factors (H.-S. Kim & Yoon, 2004; J. K. Kim, 2005; M.-K. Kim et al., 2004).

Table 1. SMS revenues in Korea mobile market (billion dollars) (Source: K.-M. Lee, 2005)

Corporate	2003	2004
SK Telecom	1.87	2.47
KTF	1.03	1.17
LG Telecom	0.43	0.61
Total	3.33	4.25

The market needs have shifted from fulfilling their basic needs, such as call quality, tariff, and handset, to satisfying their upgraded needs, such as various service features, personalized services, and qualified customer services.

Therefore, how to develop value-added service, how to implement them, and how to react to changes in customer preferences will be critical factors that influence the performance of mobile carriers and their strategic positions for future business. To capture strategic implications for developing value-added services, in the following section, we discuss the experiences in the Korean mobile market in which various value-added services were launched and are being developed.

MOBILE VALUE-ADDED SERVICES IN KOREA

Short Messaging Service (SMS)

SMS is a text communication available on mobile phones that permits the sending of short messages. Once a message is sent, it passes through a Short Message Service Center (SMSC) to reach a roaming customer. Multimedia Messaging Service (MMS) is an advanced messaging service of SMS. It extends text messaging to include various multimedia data, such as longer texts, image clips, audio, or video clips. Currently, MMS is popularly used to transmit multimedia data from camera phones to other mobile phones or Internet accounts.

Due to its capacity of transmitting multimedia data through a mobile network, MMS can be applied to various business items. For example, a mobile printing service of camera phone photos is gaining popularity with the development of camera phones. The users who take a picture by camera phones can send their photos by following directions on the browser. Another trend in MMS is convergence with messenger services via fixed communication networks. *Cool Shot*, a joint PC-mobile SMS service of KTF, allows the customer to simultaneously check messages and reply through both SMS and PC pop-up windows (KTF, 2005e). Even when customers do not have SMS-enabled phones, they send their messages by typing text that will be converted as a voice message in the Internet messenger programs. Recently, SMS and MMS offer online billing and payment services in association with Internet banking systems. A customer who registers his/her accounts on Internet banking systems or the bill requester's server can receive electricity or gas bills and confirm the payment through SMS. It has a strong potential in customers' convenience because it does not need to have m-payment chips in their phones. In the near future, MMS is expected to replace SMS, which provides new opportunities to maximize revenues in the value chain of the mobile industry.

SMS and MMS are very rapidly developing from 2002, the first year of MMS services. MMS is expected to continue its sharp increase at an average growth rate of 108.4% from 2002 to 2007. In 2004, the revenue of SMS was 4.2 billion dollars and the number of SMS messages was 332 billion, which was increased by 27.5% and 31.5%, respectively, from a year ago (K.-M. Lee, 2005).

The rapid growth of SMS in Korea is related to various payment plans for heavy users of SMS. KTF and SK Telecom launched *Bigi Egg Unlim-* *ited Text Price Plan* and *Ting Text Price Plan*, respectively, to cater to the trend of teenagers who prefer text-messaging to voice communication, which allows a customer to adjust the rate of phone calls and SMS at \$.02 per SMS and \$.03 per 10 second voice call in his/her price plans (monthly price ranging from 14 to 26 dollars), according to the users needs. SMS are particularly popular among teenagers and young adults. According to Consumer Protection Board (2004), 23% of teenagers are heavy users of SMS, sending over 50 messages per one month, and 87% of teenagers are sending over 10 text messages to their friends and families. The average number of SMS per user is 29.11 per month. The ARPU of SMS was monthly \$2.6 per customer.

Personalized Call-Ring Service

Ring-back tone is typically used to refer to the audible ringing that is heard on the telephone line by the calling party after dialing and prior to the call being answered at the distant end (Wikipedia, 2006b). Recently this form of ring-back tone has transformed as "personalized call-ring service." With personalized call-ring service, callers will hear an audio selection applied to the telephone line that has been previously determined by the called party. Personalized call-ring service is a kind of value-added service which customers can choose their call rings, such as music, voice, and

Table 2. Some cases of exporting personalized call ring services by Korean mobile carriers (Source: KTF, 2005c; SKTelecom, 2004a)

Date	Mobile carrier	Imported mobile carrier (country)	Deal size (million dollars)
Apr-03	SK Telecom	S-Telecom (Vietnam)	1.7
Jun-03	SK Telecom	Mobile-1, SingTel (Singapore)	3
Dec-03	SK Telecom	Smart (Philippines)	1.5 (additional 3.0)
Jul-04	SK Telecom	Telkomsel (Indonesia)	1.5
2005	KTF	PT Mobile-8 Telecom (Indonesia)	2

sound instead of providing a simple mechanic ring-back tone in general.

Personalized call-ring service is operated by servers of mobile carriers. Equipment is installed in the telephone network to enable replacement of the standard ring-back tone with a personalized audio selection. Mobile carriers keep their music source codes which come from content providers. When a user selects a certain music source code, a database of the mobile carrier keeps the sound source code. When a request has been made, the database queries servers by the code and then the sound source is provided to the caller.

The personalized call-ring service is called *Coloring* in Korea because the personalized sound makes personality colored. There are several brand names for that service, such as *Coloring, Tooling, Ring to you, Feeling, Ringo,* and so on. Among them, *Coloring* is the popular name due to that is the first provided brand name. *Coloring* has the largest service which has 8.2 million paying subscribers as of 2006. Users can choose their own sounds by their preferences. They also select sounds by time and numbers of the person called. It is very interesting that *Coloring* which sends sounds to the called party, is more popular than ring-back to which the caller listens. In 2005 the numbers of downloading *Coloring* was 6.8 million which is much more than ring-back which has 4.7 million.

Experience of implementing personalized call-ring services grants Korean mobile carriers a chance of exploiting the international market. Table 2 shows some cases of exporting personalized call-ring services by Korean mobile carriers.

KTF creates a new concept in karaoke with the release of *Magic, Chilo, Joy,* which customize the phone with a song sung by the user through on-line/off-line and fixed/wireless networks. It allows high-quality MP3 musical accompaniment and the option to send karaoke ring tones as a present to another user. Service grows into customer-participation content services in wallpapers, ring-back tones, and so forth (KTF, 2005f).

Personalized call-ring service is contributing to mobile carriers' financial performance. Three mobile carriers have revenues of $8-20 million in 2005. According to a study, the World Cup 2006 is seen as an opportunity to promote 3G which will generate $6.35 billion in revenue, with text-based services and downloads, such as ring tones and logos (3GNewsroom.com, 2006).

As the functionality of mobile handsets has been improved, higher quality of services can be provided. Mobile carriers are trying to develop higher technology. For example, SK Telecom reached an agreement for jointly developing an audio CODEC technology with Coding Technologies (CT) of Germany to increase the service quality of its *Coloring* service (SK Telecom, 2006).

Ring-back tone and call-ring services have a major portion of the digital music market in Korea. The market increased by approximately 80% annually and has about 95% share in this market (see Table 3).

Table 3. Digital music market in Korea (Source: Music Industry Association of Korea [MIAK], 2005)

	2000	2001	2002	2003
Ring back and Call ring services	30.6	62.7	129	176.8
Streaming (WEB, MP3)	9.4	18.8	3.6	4.4
Others (VoD, Mobile)	9.5	8.6	1.5	3.8
Sum (million dollars)	49.5	90.1	134.1	185

Mobile Music Service

Mobile music service refers to a value-added service of mobile telephone service, which users can download music files into their mobile music service-enabled devices. PC, MP3 phone, and MP3 player are popular mobile music service-enabled devices. PC supports download and streaming services through the mobile music Web site and mobile music players. Through an MP3 phone, users can enjoy music by transmitting music files downloaded through its Web site to their mobile phone. When users connect to the wireless Internet service on their mobile phones, users download, stream, and search for the music they want to enjoy. Users can also listen to music by receiving the music files they want in the mobile music service-enabled MP3 players.

Three Korean mobile carriers started providing their own mobile music services, such as *MelOn* (SK Telecom), *Dosirak* (KTF), and *musicOn* (LG Telecom) from November 2004, May 2005, and July 2005 respectively. *MelOn* utilizes Digital Right Management (DRM) technology which prevents illegal distribution and use of wired and wireless integrated networks, platforms, and digital content (SK Telecom, 2004c). *MelOn* service is provided by pay-per-downloading and by monthly flat rate. The number of paying subscribers reached more than 600,000 as of December 2005. *Melon Shop*, a one-stop shopping mall in which customers can purchase items related to music, opened on December 2005 (SK Telecom, 2005a).

KTF launched its music portal service, which offers a unified service allowing users not only to listen to both Korean and foreign music, but to also spice up their phones with ring tones and callback tones. It has a 900,000-tune database and digital rights for 480,000 tunes. KTF has contracts with 90% of Korea's music property rights owners (KTF, 2005d). KTF has attracted 350,000 members to *Dosirak* ("lunchbox" in English) just 2 months after its release; 120,000 are paying subscribers among them (KTF, 2005b).

Most young singers first release their music on the mobile music market. Music producers can gauge the success of a new single through the mobile music market. In addition, technology is advancing to provide various high quality services. A Portable Multimedia Player (PMP) phone that lets users enjoy audio and streaming video through a mobile phone was first made available in November 2005 (SKTelecom, 2005d).

Mobile music market of mobile carriers in Korea is in the growing stage. Annually the increase by $20 million will be forecasted.

Mobile Video Service

3G networks offer the capacity and capability to transmit richer mobile multimedia to users, such as video phone functions, multimedia messages, music on demand (MoD), video on demand (VoD), TV broadcasting, and the Internet. Korea launched the first commercial CDMA 2000 1x EV-DO service in the world that ensures 144Kbps data speed for LAN-quality video streaming service. Korea currently experiences the transfer toward W-CDMA that ensures DVD-quality video streaming services through mobiles.

Table 4. Mobile music market in Korea (Source: Daishin Security, 2005)

	2004*	2005**	2006**	2007**	2008**
Revenue of mobile carriers by mobile digital music (million dollars)	80	88	100	120	140

* *Estimated;* ** *Forecasted*

Figure 3. Fimm's mobile video revenue (Source: Song, 2005)

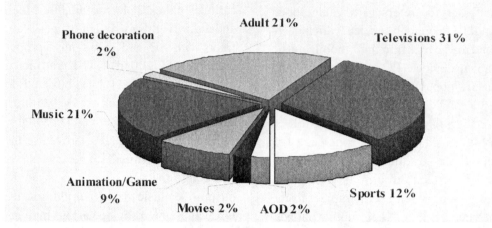

Fimm and *June*, as KTF's and SK Telecom's brand names of premium multimedia services, provide varied multimedia content menus of movie channels with downloadable mobile movies; music channels with music videos and the latest music; and broadcasting channels to receive TV programs.

Sports, adult videos, and short soap operas are most popular contents on mobiles. Retransmission of existing broadcasting channels is also available on mobiles, including terrestrial, cable, and digital satellite channels as real-time services. These services account for 66% of the total revenue of value-added services of KTF. Figure 3 shows *Fimm*'s revenues of mobile multimedia service sector in the fiscal year of 2004. The most dominant revenue resource, mobile television channels, provided 31% of *Fimm*'s mobile multimedia revenue. The second largest sector was adult services and music services, each of which reached 21% of total revenue. This financial result may prove that streaming services are more profitable revenue resources than simple downloadable services, because the revenue of audio-on-demand was only 2%, whereas music streaming service was 21% of total revenue.

In order to retain subscribers, each network operator should secure various contents to cater to the customer's taste. Therefore, each network operator forms a strategic alliance with mobile video contents providers. KTF formed a strategic alliance with Sports Online to supply broadcasting services of American Major League from 2003. This service replayed the main matches from the 2003 major league baseball season through *Fimm*. To produce high-quality mobile movies only for *June*, SK Telecom also formed a strategic alliance with iHQ, a multi-entertainment company, in February 2005 by acquiring 21.66% stake.

Not including wireless data transfer charges, the rate of each downloadable or streaming video is ranging from $0.5 to $1.2. In addition, it is possible to use wireless data service including video streaming and downloading services without limits at a monthly fixed rate of $30. In order to receive television channels of existing broadcasters, the users should pay only additional $6-10. *Fimm Free* service offers 36 channels of Skylife satellite broadcasting and 4 channels of terrestrial broadcastings at $10.

The revenues from mobile video in Korea grew to $59 million in 2003 from $23 million in 2001 (KETI, 2004). In August 2004, over 1.5 million users of mobile-video-enabling devices registered on KTF and the number of users of *Fimm* was over 603,000.

Mobile Payment

M-payment is a payment method for goods or services with a mobile device such as a phone, PDA, or other such device. These devices can be used in a variety of payment scenarios. Typical usage entails the user electing to make a m-payment, being connected to a server via the mobile device to perform authentication and authorization, and subsequently being presented with confirmation of the completed transaction (Wikipedia, 2006a).

The m-payment business has several service paradigms: the payments can be included in the user's mobile phone bill or a separate "mobile wallet" can be used, where the user makes deposits and withdrawals on a mobile money account governed by the mobile operator. Another solution makes use of the mobile phone only as a digital identifier, which is then used to access a digital bank account probably governed by a financial institution rather than the mobile operator.

KTF has launched the world's first exclusive mobile commerce mobile phone, which can easily settle credit card accounts anywhere. The new phone sports an "IC chip" that stores all kinds of credit information. The K-merce phone is used to exclusively settle payments. Users can conveniently settle accounts via IrFM or RF by using the K-merce phone (SPH-X8500). The IC chip card will be issued from the credit card company and inserted into the socket at the back of the phone (KTF, 2002). SK Telecom launched a mobile transaction payment service called Moneta. This system uses an installed IC chip (Smart Chip) in a cellular phone that can be used online as well as off-line (SKTelecom, 2003d). SK Telecom issues an IC chip that has functions such as a membership card, e-money, and ID card, among others. This service offers a prepaid transportation fee payment card function (SKTelecom, 2003b). SK Telecom launched a chip-based mobile banking service in March 2004 with major Korean banks. It would increase synergy effect by establishing a win-win business model between a telecom company and banks. It adopted the SEED for standard security module of a banking IC chip (SKTelecom, 2003a).

In December 2003, SK Telecom started its Liquid Screen Small Payment Service that allows settlement of account charges through ray signals captured on a liquid screen. Any customer who uses a color screening handset can use this service as a method of payment transaction. Users download the exclusive service program which will then generate the rays that flash with special patterns on the cellular liquid screen. This ray acknowledges on a special receiver that it is connected to a PC through the USB port, and is then automatically linked to a server to create a legitimate and secure approval procedure for making payment transactions (SKTelecom, 2003c).

SK Telecom introduced Korea's first mobile bank (m-bank) international roaming service. Customers can use this m-banking service while in Beijing and Shanghai of China, by using their m-bank handsets (SKTelecom, 2004e). SK Telecom issued Moneta IC chip card with all credit card packages issued by Samsung Card (SKTelecom, 2004b). SK Telecom offered an instant mobile lottery purchase service, apartment subscription service, stock trading service, and so forth. (SKTelecom, 2004d). A joint effort by Tong Yang Investment Bank and SK Securities implements an IC chip-based stock trading service. This makes a total of three chip-based mobile financial services. These services offer increased transaction speed, as well as security, compared to a traditional wireless application protocol (WAP)-based mobile stock trading service (SKTelecom, 2004f). Customers are allowed to conduct banking transactions and stock trading with a single chip installed in their mobile phone (SKTelecom, 2005c).

Three Korean mobile carriers make t-money services available for mobile users with Korea Smart Card Co. (KSCC). The service launched in June 2005. The mobile t-money service would allow payment for public transport using t-money

Table 5. Motivations and information sources about mobile games (Source: Ahn, 2004)

Motivations	(%)
Experience on PC game	14
New games	45
Curiosity	36
Advertising and promotions	2
Boredom	63
Friend's recommendation	62
Direct usage experience	**35**
Information Sources	(%)
Friends	72
Game magazines	20
Television programs about mobile games	4
Advertising	3
Game Web site	0

on all three Korean mobile carriers. T-Money is a payment system built by KSCC for public transport in metropolitan areas. Users of this service will not have to go to kiosks to "top off" their transport cards, but rather just use wireless Internet to transfer money from a registered bank account. Users can also check the amount remaining on the transport smart cards and use a refund service (KTF, 2005a). The m-bank service establishes a cooperative business model between a mobile communications operator and a financial firm by the sharing of their roles.

Mobile Games

Mobile games are a gaming service available on mobile devices such as mobile phones, PDAs, and other devices. Through the mobile devices, users can download game programs or use real-time role playing games (RPGs) similar to online games on fixed broadband networks.

In Korea, mobile games are very popular entertainment. Marketing Insight, a consumer research institute, reported that 14 million Koreans play mobile games, accounting for 40% of the total mobile phone users. In addition, around 2.3 million users play mobile games everyday, accounting for 6.2 % of the total mobile phone users (Moon, 2005). Korea's mobile game industry has been sharply increased with annual growth of more than 45 %. The revenues from mobile games in Korea grew to $2.2 billion in 2004 from $1.0 billion in 2002 (Atlas Research, 2004), accounting for the growth rate of 88.4%.

Table 5 shows that 62% of mobile game users are affected by peer-group influence on making a purchase decision of game contents and the average usage time is 1 hour 38 minutes per day, which indicates that mobile games are low-involvement products (Ahn, 2004). It is mainly because most of current mobile phones do not support the real-time interaction, so the users are usually not absorbed in game-playing through mobiles. For these reasons, mobile game users still use simple board games or arcade games more than RPGs or strategic games.

However, according to the development of mobile devices and game contents, the mobile game industry is now evolving into RPGs and 3D games. SK Telecom has launched a mobile game portal site called *GXG* in April 2005 to offer various 3D converting games. 3D games are three-dimensional games that users can enjoy virtual reality as if they are exploring the virtual game place. The representative games of SK Telecom are *Mavinogi, Mu*, and *Ragnarok*, of which price ranges from $3 to 3.7 per each game downloaded. If consumers contract for the *Nate Free Flat Rate Plan* of $14 per month, they can download all *GXG* games without additional call charges. SK Telecom is developing mobile 3D game phones with Qualcomm and Samsung at the average of $400, which is $100-200 lower than current popular game phones such as IM-8300 and IM-8100. KTF also invested $8 million on their mobile gaming portal *GPANG*, in a strategic alliance with NHN that is Korea's second largest Internet portal and that operates *Hangame*, a successful game portal on fixed networks. In addition, KTF has launched additional 100-300 new games every year and has invested in the development of interactive games, since customers are easily bored with simple games. Over 50% of revenue in KTF's mobile game part comes from new games.

The introduction of multimedia online role playing games (MMORPGs) will contribute to expanding the existing mobile game industry. Since heavy users of online games are accustomed to the PCs and consoles which permit real-time interaction with other users, game operators should design their graphics and interaction technologies to attract the online gamers. Once new MMORPGS games through mobile phones attain the awareness from the heavy users, they will enjoy the strong royalty and stable revenues from the heavy online game users. As mobile games evolve into MMORPGs, the ARPU of mobile games will be expected to increase because of the propensity of high royalty and longer usage time in MMORPGs.

CHARACTERISTICS OF MOBILE VALUE-ADDED SERVICES

In the previous section, we discussed six major value-added services in Korea which impact the ARPU of mobile customers. In this section, characteristics of mobile value-added services are discussed.

M-commerce shows the similar aspects to mobile value-added services. Siau, Lim, and Shen (2001) shows that m-commerce has four features, such as ubiquity, personalization, flexibility, and dissemination. Customers can get any information they are interested in, whenever they want regardless of where they are, through Internet-based mobile devices (*ubiquity*). M-commerce applications can be personalized to represent information or provide services in ways

appropriate to the specific user (*personalization*). Mobile users may be engaged in activities, such as meeting people or traveling, while conducting transactions or receiving information through their Internet-enabled mobile devices (*flexibility*). Some wireless infrastructures offer an efficient means to disseminate information to a large consumer population (*dissemination*).

From the market trend in Korea and the discussion about m-commerce, we derived four characteristics of the trends of value-added services in mobile communication market: (1) customization, (2) content-focused, (3) connectedness, and (4) contemporary. We call them the "4Cs" for mobile value-added services.

Customization

Most value-added services have various customized plans to meet different customer needs. This is an effort to satisfy the demand of personalization for customers by their mobile service. This effort helps customers who have concerns about their mobile services and handsets. It increases the involvement of customers with their services. For the call-ring service customers can use a song sung by themselves through online/off-line and fixed/wireless networks.

There are some differences in service preferences among mobile consumer segments. Major segmentation factors are age, gender, and culture. Whereas there is no significant difference between male and female in terms of mobile Internet subscription, gender does affect usage time, ARPU, and their service preferences. Women who have used mobile Internet in 2005 have been overtaking men in usage time. Women use an average of 58.2 mobile Internet minutes a week, compared to an average of 47.4 minutes a week for men (National Internet Development Agency [NIDA], 2005). Female teenagers tend to more frequently use SMS and phone decorations than male teenagers, while male teenagers tend to more frequently use mobile games than vice versa (Consumer Protection Board [CPB], 2004). These results reflect gender differences in mobile usage patterns, which indicate that two groups require distinct segmentation strategies.

Age also influences the amount of use and service preferences. Young adults and teenagers are a distinct segment for mobile service providers. They are more likely to be technology friendly and to try new technology and services when they become available. They usually have a high willingness to pay for entertainment services. However, in terms of mobile banking and some information services, older age groups are more likely to use the services (NIDA, 2005).

To design customized services, mobile carriers in Korea released various service packages and price plans appropriate for each segment. For instance, KTF and SK Telecom provide *Bigi Egg Unlimited Text Price Plan* and *Ting Text Price Plan* as exclusive rating systems for female teenager's communication trends. It allows subscribers aged from 13 to 18 to adjust the rate of phone calls and SMS according to their needs. LG Telecom also released five types of *Human Special Packages* which distinguish each contemporary life style according to various usage patterns.

Figure 4. Data ARPU of Korean mobile carriers (Source: Huh, 2006)

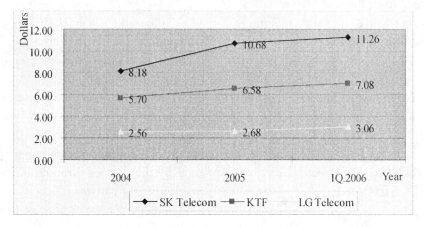

Figure 5. Voice vs. data revenues of Korean mobile carriers (Source: ETRI, 2004)

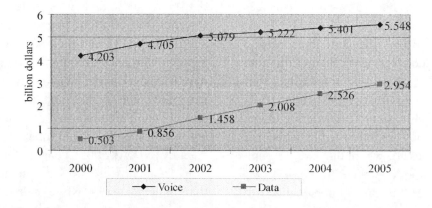

Content-Focused

Mobile service is no more the commonly standardized telephone service. It is more than a voice-only service. It is similar to an Internet portal site. As the success of an Internet portal site depends on whether the site has sufficient information and is updated frequently, the success of mobile value-added service can be made by the capacity which can meet their customer needs. Having key content is more important than a better network. As Figures 4 and 5 show, Korea's mobile industry is moving toward a value-added services market in terms of ARPU. During the last 2 years, voice revenue has been stagnated while data revenue has rapidly increased.

Connectedness

Connectedness can be defined as the psychological need for social relationships. The need motivates people to maintain connection with others so as to keep utilizing reliable peer-to-peer communication technologies. Nardi et al. (2000) reported that people monitor the presence of colleagues through online messenger services even when they have no special intention to communicate with others. In mobile services, the need for social relationship is a still important motivation for people to use the services. From the perspective of consumer's psychology, the desire for connectedness is directly linked to the amount and frequency of mobile service usages, which is capable to raise the revenues in the mobile industry. For example, young adults and teenagers, who have the highest willingness to pay for the services, recognize their mobile phones as a personal device to communicate with friends and peer groups. They are susceptible to peer-group influence and highly consider peer evaluation and social presence when utilizing mobile services. Therefore, they show high demand for peer-to-peer connectedness in their usage pattern of mobile services, such as SMS, messengers, and real-time mobile games.

In this sense, mobile carriers should consider their desire for connectedness when they design a new value-added service. Only the new value-added services enabling "connectedness orientated communication" will be a key business in the mobile market, and the marketing strategies that gratify the needs will contribute to boost the revenues (Rettie, 2003, p. 3). In Korea, three mobile carriers developed membership marketing and promotions exclusive for each segment that allow discounts available for restaurant, amusement parks, movie theaters, shopping malls and more. For example, KTF's successful *Bigi* membership promotion provides the subscribers of *Bigi* price plans with various participation programs such as educational classes and workshops, which generates virtual communities among young subscribers. What is more, the subscribers who contract *Bigi Egg Present call plan* can receive extra phone usage time as gifts from other subscribers. This strategy has been effective in preventing the subscriber loss and in increasing usage frequency.

Contemporariness

The mobile market no longer resides in the infrastructure industry. If mobile carriers can not meet their customers' likeliness in real time, they can hardly survive in this market. It is because the key success factor in this market is how quickly they satisfy the customers' needs, regardless of the technology they provide. As the customers' preferences change very often, the key concern of mobile carriers is how fast they can develop their new value-added services to meet their customer needs.

FUTURE TREND:
DIGITAL MOBILE BROADCASTING

One of future trends in mobile service will be DMB. DMB systems are designed to provide television and radio programs to mobile phones with high-resolution and secure connections. In 2005, Korea launched terrestrial DMB (T-DMB) as a free mobile broadcasting and satellite DMB (S-DMB) as a subscriber-based mobile broadcast. S-DMB started its commercial services in May 2005 with 11 video channels and 21 audio channels and T-DMB started in January 2006 with 7 video channels and 12 audio channels.

The difference from the existing EV-DO services is that it is utilizing a new broadband network to offer mobile real-time broadcasting services, which enables high-speed movements without disconnections. There are two kinds of DMB according to its technology type and network configuration; S-DMB and T-DMB. S-DMB is based on code division multiplexing (CDM) similar to CDMA mobile communication technology and S-Band (2.630-2.655 GHz), whereas T-DMB is based on orthogonal frequency division multiplexing (OFDM) for digital TV standard in Europe and VHF Ch 8 (180-186MHz) and Ch 12 (204-210MHz). Due to stable reception and mobility, DMB is becoming a new value-added service to satisfy consumer demands for mobile broadcasting and to provide the mobile industry, recently experiencing the slow growth rate, with new revenue sources. TU Media, the world's first DMB operator, launched its nationwide S-DMB service in May 2005 and acquired 100,000 customers in 2 months and 22 days and additional 100,000 customers in 4 months. TU Media is collecting more than 2,400 users a day (SK Telecom, 2005b). TU Media now provides 37 channels including 11 video and 26 audio channels.

Since S-DMB and T-DMB services share characteristics of both broadcasting and mobile telecommunication, they were expected to lead to fierce competition in several existing markets, such as broadcasting market, mobile market, and high-speed Internet market. Therefore, the impact of DMB on existing mobile value-added services was controversial and was considered as a challenge for existing network operators to come up with successful revenue models. Current statistics of Korea's DMB reports that new DMB services have helped the continuing growth of mobile industry. The basic effect of introducing DMB turns out to open a new media market, not to transmit existing broadcasting services through mobile phones. In addition, three mobile network operators and existing broadcasters, who composed consortiums for DMB services, benefit from the new services more profit than losses by compensating the decreasing growth rate of voice ARPU. Despite of maturation in mobile phone services, KTF reported that they have attracted 117,000 new DMB subscribers with 200% increased T-DMB's ARPU in the last year, when over all data ARPU increased $.60. SK Telecom also reported that last year's data ARPU was $17, increased by 31 % from 2004 and DMB ARPU was $3.3, which indicated that S-DMB has no negative effect on data ARPU. These results indicate that DMB contributes to the growth of mobile market without cannibalization. New DMB services are allowing three mobile carriers to find the next revenue sources by awakening a dormant market, making the stagnating mobile market a "blue ocean" (W. C. Kim & Mauborgne, 2005).

To promote DMB adoption and usages of mobile services, operators and vendors should secure enough content supply to attract new subscribers. According to KBI's survey (2006), people subscribe for entertainment and killing time, and sports, entertainments, and drama are still popular in DMB services, like traditional broadcasting media. In particular, sports are the top programming choice across all mobile video services including S-DMB, T-DMB, and video downloading through MMS. For all DMB subscribers, the average preference score of sports was 3.35 on a 5-point scale. Also, the gratification score of sports was also 3.35 in S-DMB and 3.5 in T-DMB. During the World Baseball Classic in 2006, sales of DMB mobile phones have surged up to 3,000 per a day, a 200% increase in daily sales (KBS, 2006). According to Visiongain, an industry research company, a 1 month football tournament generates $6.35 billion in revenue only with text-based services and downloads in a 3G network, which implies that sports game relay is a key generator to boost DMB adoption and usages. That is, it will be critical factors of the mobile carriers' performance to secure the supply of sports and entertainment programs.

From the perspective of usage pattern, DMB users are more similar to mobile phone users than traditional broadcasting audiences. Although their program preferences are as same as that of traditional audience, 82.3% of the total respondents have propensity to watch the programs alone, which indicates that people consider DMB media as personal devices. After adopting mobile devices enabling DMB reception, the users utilize their mobile phones longer than before, but reduce the usages of traditional televisions and communication with their families. This means that DMB functions as a revenue generator or a new market exploiter of mobile carriers.

IMPLICATIONS

As the mobile market has shifted from 2G to 3G, a lot of changes took place in the mobile market. The value chain has been divided into several sub-components, which results in various market opportunities. For mobile carriers, the new mobile market has more potentialities through new revenue models. The new potentialities come into view as several value-added services such as mobile video, game, music, and other new services. The advent and growth of value-added services in mobile market has changed the structure of mobile market.

First, the subject of market appeal has changed from new customers to existing customers. At the time when the market has growing enormously, players in this market have more concerns on inducing new customers rather than on the retention of existing customers.

Generally, promoting new subscribers leads to higher financial benefit than keeping existing customers. However, as the current mobile market growth closes to saturation point, the market players concern more about how to retain existing customers and how to increase the net revenue rate from the customers than how to attract new customers. In a saturated market, competition among players has become fiercer and the differences of service quality among competitors have been diminished. Therefore, it is hard for a player to get a significantly competitive position in relation to others. Mobile players in a saturated market should focus on value-added services for existing customers, in order to increase net revenue rate.

Second, as a result of the first implication, market players have shifted from a general strategy to differentiated strategy. Many textbooks on industrial organization (Carlton & Perloff, 2000; Tirole, 2002) explain this kind of change as a dynamics of market structure. When an innovative product or service is introduced in a market, innovators take and use the product or service and offer their services to the public. If the product or service has popularity, the market grows rapidly and encourages potential market players to enter the market. The new entry of players may boost market growth and stimulate the diffusion of product or service in a certain time period. When the market approaches a matured stage, the intensity of competition becomes high and the margins of market players have diminished. At that point, market players need to make a decision for their future business. Typically economists explain there are two kinds of strategies. The first one is a trial to get competitive advantage through cost-saving which is called cost-leadership. The other is exploiting new markets through prod-

Figure 6. Mobile value-added service development strategy

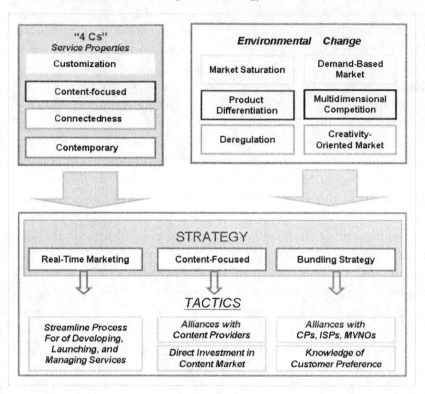

uct differentiations. Mobile carriers are at that place that they need to make a decision. Various value-added services are the examples of product differentiation.

The third one is the change of regulation. Telecommunications service had been classified as a utility until mid-1980s. Even though competition has been introduced partially, the telecommunications market has been under rigorous regulation. It is because telecommunication services have an aspect of natural monopoly in which a bigger company with the economy of scale has the competitive advantage. However, as the value chain of the mobile industry has been divided into several components, the market power of network carriers has been reduced and, as the result, the necessity of market regulation has been diminished. Thus, competition type also has changed from network-based competition to market-based competition.

Fourth, mobile market structure has changed from supply-based to demand-based in the perspective of economics. That means the era in which customers have to wait to enjoy telecom services has passed. There exists excessive supply in this market. The network sunk costs can not be rewarded. The market concern has moved to customers' demand.

Fifth, the telecommunications market is traditionally regarded as a network business that is driven by technology. However, now the market has more concerns about services and marketing. Creativity to meet consumers' needs is much more spotlighted than higher technology.

Sixth, as a result of the change of value chain, the mobile service market has multi-aspect competition rather than the one-dimensional competition in the "old days." Companies from adjacent industries such as ISPs, satellite platform operators, and other broadcasters are entering this converged market and competing with mobile carriers. For instance, iPod of Apple computers providing music services in a mobile environment can be a potential competitor to the mobile carriers, who are trying to provide entertainment with mobility. Therefore, the boundary of the market is going to be vague. In the near future, interconnection between adjacent businesses which were far from the telecom sector becomes a critical competitive factor in the market.

Therefore, it is the time of mobile carriers to come up with new strategies satisfying various demands of their customers.

NEW STRATEGIES FOR MOBILE VALUE-ADDED SERVICES

As we discussed in the previous section, the characteristic of the mobile communications market has changed from common needs to a variety of market needs. Considering service properties and environmental changes, we recommend three new strategies for mobile carriers as the conclusions of our discussion (see Figure 6).

Strategy 1: Real-Time Market-Responding Strategy

The market environment has changed so rapidly. The entry barrier to this market has been lowered. If mobile carriers can not respond the needs of their customers' quickly, the business opportunity no more waits for the mobile carrier. Mobile carriers can not rely on their networks anymore. There are huge numbers of alternate networks that are waiting for the market opportunity.

Mobile carriers should adapt to the market dynamics in order to survive in this market. The development of digital technology accelerates launching new converged services, enables mobile carriers to meet various customer segments, and encourages regulators to change their regulatory frameworks into competition-oriented ones. Thus,

mobile carriers should be prepared to respond to dynamic environmental changes such as competitors' new products, the change of customer preferences, and regulation change.

One of the tactics for this strategy is to streamline the process of developing, launching, and managing the new value-added services. The timing of launching services is a critical factor to gain the market. In particular, certain services have a short life cycle and the market responses are also spontaneous. A systematic and efficient process to develop and launch value-added services is essential.

Strategy 2: Content-Focused Market Strategy

Mobile networks are converging into the IP-based broadband network. The capacity and speed are close to each other. Even though the competition by the network is still going on, the pattern of competition has changed into what mobile carriers can provide on their networks from what kinds of networks they have. If mobile carriers can not have competitive advantage from their networks, they will be trying to keep their markets by product differentiation. That means which content they can provide is more critical. Having "killer" content will be a key success factor.

The transformation from a network company to a network-based content company is a challenge for the traditional mobile carriers. Content, not network will be in the center of strategic decision making. If a company has outstanding content, the company can use any network with network contract and transmit their content to their potential customers. As a result, a company that has excellent content can have bargaining power against a traditional network operator.

Two different tactics come up for the strategy. The first is the alliance with various content providers. Even though it is an indirect method, mobile carriers can respond to market needs more quickly without much risk. However, through this process, mobile carriers can lose their leading role in the value chain of the market. The second is the direct entry to the content market. It can be risky because they do not have sufficient experiences in that market, it can hardly respond to market needs quickly, and they can be exposed to the whole risk of failure of developing killer content. However, mobile carriers can keep their leading role in the value chain and get whole rewards from the success. "Higher risk and higher return," as many mobile carriers already tried to, the combination of two different tactics will be suitable under the recent market environment.

Strategy 3: Various Bundling Strategy

As we discussed before, a characteristic of mobile value-added service is customization. The underlying assumption for that threat is that customers have personalized preference on mobile value-added service. In order to meet their personalized demands, a variety of bundling services should be ready to provide. Without a scheme to mix various service features, it is hard to satisfy customers' personalized needs.

Because "variety" is a key factor in the market of mobile value-added services, mobile carriers should have a strategy to provide a variety of bundled services which meet the specific demands of customers in an efficient way. How many various bundled services mobile carriers have could be a critical competitive advantage in the future mobile market.

In order to provide various bundling services, there are several kinds of tactics.

The first one is the preparedness of a various combination of service features with a strategic network with related companies. Strategic alliances with contents providers, ISPs, and mobile virtual network operators (MVNOs) can be a major strategic decision.

The second tactic is knowledge on customer preferences.

Most content providers or ISPs are less regulated than traditional mobile network carriers. They are small sized and their process of decision making is efficient. Thus they can respond the market more rapidly than network carriers.

Through the state-of-the-art techniques to capture the demands, a quick response mechanism for the changes of customer preferences is necessary.

REFERENCES

3GNewsroom.com. (2006, January 22). *World Cup to promote 3G*. Retrieved from http://www.3gnewsroom.com/3g_news/jan_06/news_6615.shtml

Ahn, S. (2004). Mobile business strategy of SKT. SK Telecom.

Atlas Research. (2004). [Statistics] mobile contents market trend in Korea. *Mobile Contents & Application* (p. 2).

Brenner, M. R., Grech, M. L. F., Torabi, M., & Unmehopa, M. R. (2005). The open mobile alliance and trends in supporting the mobile services industry. *Bell Labs Technical Journal, 10*(1), 59-75.

Carlton, D. W., & Perloff, J. M. (2000). *Modern industrial organization* (3rd ed.). Reading, MA: Addison-Wesley.

Consumer Protection Board (CPB). (2004). *Summary: A survey of teenagers' mobile phone and wireless Internet usage pattern*. Author.

Daishin Security. (2005). *Daishin equity report (SK Telecom)*. Author.

ETRI. (2004). *Korea's mobile services gross revenue*. Author.

Geng, X., & Whinston, A. B. (2001). Profiting from value-added wireless services. *Computer, 34*(8), 87-89.

Huh, W. (2006, May 10). *The gap of data ARPU among mobile carriers.* Retrieved from http://www.fnnews.com/view?ra=Sent0901m_01A&corp=fnnews&arcid=0920722524&cDateYear=2006&cDateMonth=05&cDateDay=10

International Telecommunications Union (ITU). (2006). *World telecommunications indicators.* Author.

KBS. (2006). *Baseball boom in sports and marketing.* Retrieved May 11, 2006, from http://english.kbs.co.kr/life/trend/1388891_11857.html

Korea Electronics Technology Institute (KETI). (2004). *Mobile contents market of 2004 in Korea.* Seoul: Author.

Kim, H.-S., & Yoon, C.-H. (2004). Determinants of subscriber churn and customer loyalty in the Korean mobile telephony market. *Telecommunications Policy, 28*(9-10), 751-765.

Kim, J. K. (2005). *Mobile subscribers' willingness to churn under the mobile number portability (MNP).* Paper presented at the the Eleventh Americas Conference on Information Systems, Omaha, NE.

Kim, M.-K., Park, M.-C., & Jeong, D.-H. (2004). The effects of customer satisfaction and switching barrier on customer loyalty in Korean mobile telecommunication services. *Telecommunications Policy, 28*(2), 145-159.

Kim, W. C., & Mauborgne, R. (2005). *Blue ocean strategy: How to create uncontested market space and make the competition irrelevant.* Boston: Harvard Business School Press.

Korea Broadcasting Institute (KBI). (2006). Trends and strategy of digital multimedia broadcasting in Korea. *KBI Focus, 6*(6).

KTF. (2002, November 4). *KTF launches the world's first mobile payment handset based on IC chip.* Retrieved from http://www.ktf.com/front/IR/eng/

KTF. (2005a, April 27). *3 mobile carriers partner for release of mobile t-money service.* Retrieved from http://www.ktf.com/front/IR/eng/

KTF. (2005b, July 25). *KTF's music portal "Dosirak" finds strong foundation in the market.* Retrieved from http://www.ktf.com/front/IR/eng/

KTF. (2005c, May 25). *KTF expands service in Indonesia.* Retrieved from http://www.ktf.com/front/IR/eng/

KTF. (2005d, May 24). *KTF opens music portal service Dosirak.* Retrieved from http://www.ktf.com/front/IR/eng/

KTF. (2005e, August 17). *Mobile SMS now on PC messengers!* Retrieved from http://www.ktf.com/front/IR/eng/

KTF. (2005f, June 14). *Singing a song, making it my ringtone!* Retrieved from http://www.ktf.com/front/IR/eng/

Lee, J., Lee, J., & Feick, L. (2001). The impact of switching costs on the customer satisfaction-loyalty link: Mobile phone service in France. *Journal of Services Marketing, 15*(1), 35-48.

Lee, K.-M. (2005, September 22). Mobile network operators, 2,354 billion KWON revenue of CID and SMS. Retrieved from http://issuei.com/sub_read.html?uid=1608&section=section1&section2=

Maitland, C. F., Bauer, J. M., & Westerveld, R. (2002). The European market for mobile data: Evolving value chains and industry structures. *Telecommunications Policy, 26*(9/10), 485-504.

Middleton, C. A. (2002). *Exploring consumer demand for networked services: The importance of content, connectivity, and killer apps in the diffusion of broadband and mobile services.* Paper presented at the Twenty-Third International Conference on Information Systems (ICIS), Barcelona, Spain.

Moon, B. (2005, November 8). *Mobile game addiction spreading.* Retrieved from http://www.donga.

com/fbin/output?sfrm=1&u=200511080069

Music Industry Association of Korea (MIAK). (2005). *Statistics of digital music market in Korea.* Author.

National Internet Development Agency of Korea (NIDA). (2005). *Summary: Mobile Internet consumer research 2005.* Author.

Nardi, B., Whittaker, S., and Bradner, E. (2000). Interaction and outeraction: Instant messaging in action. In *Proceedings of Conference on Computer-supported Cooperative Work,* (pp. 79-88). New York: ACM Press.

Pagani, M. (2004). Determinants of adoption of third generation mobile multimedia services. *Journal of Interactive Marketing, 18*(3), 46-59.

Rettie, R. (2003). *Connectedness, awareness and social presence.* Paper presented at the 6th Annual International Workshop on Presence.

Sabat, H. K. (2002). The evolving mobile wireless value chain and market structure. *Telecommunications Policy, 26*(9/10), 505-535.

Siau, K., Lim, E.-P., & Shen, Z. (2001). Mobile commerce: Promises, challenges, and research agenda. *Journal of Database Management, 12*(3), 4-13.

SK Telecom. (2003a, December 9). *SK Telecom establishes the national standard for mobile banking services* [Press release]. Seoul, Korea: Author.

SK Telecom. (2003b, October 27). SK Telecom launches "MONETA Membership Pack Service" for teenagers [Press release]. Seoul, Korea: Author.

SK Telecom. (2003c, December 22). SK Telecom launches "Liquid Screen Small Payment" service [Press release]. Seoul, Korea: Author.

SK Telecom. (2003d, August 12). SK Telecom starts "Moneta Online Payment Service" [Press release]. Seoul, Korea: Author.

SK Telecom. (2004a, July 27). SK Telecom exceeds ten millions US dollars in export sales of call ring (so called Coloring) service solution [Press release]. Seoul, Korea: Author.

SK Telecom. (2004b, August 18). SK Telecom forms strategic alliance with Samsung Card for mobile payment service [Press release]. Seoul, Korea: Author.

SK Telecom. (2004c, November 15). SK Telecom presents a new paradigm for promoting the digital music market [Press release]. Seoul, Korea: Author.

SK Telecom. (2004d, September 30). SK Telecom starts "M-Bank Service" in a joint effort with KB [Press release]. Seoul, Korea: Author.

SK Telecom. (2004e, March 16). SK Telecom starts M-Bank international roaming service [Press release]. Seoul, Korea: Author.

SK Telecom. (2004f, October 18). Stock trading chip service launched as part of a succession of mobile banking service advances [Press release]. Seoul, Korea: Author.

SK Telecom. (2005a, December 15). Melon subscribers hit four million mark [Press release]. Seoul, Korea: Author.

SK Telecom. (2005b, October 14). Satellite DMB customers reach over 200,000 [Press release]. Seoul, Korea: Author.

SK Telecom. (2005c, April 19). SK Telecom introduces mobile multi-use financial chip [Press release]. Seoul, Korea: Author.

SK Telecom. (2005d, October 31). SK Telecom releases the world's first PMP phone [Press release]. Seoul, Korea: Author.

SK Telecom. (2006, February 16). SK Telecom executes an agreement for jointly developing a music file CODEC technology with Germany's CT company [Press release]. Seoul, Korea: Author.

Song, M. (2005). *KT's media business and content strategy*. Retrieved May 3, 2006, from http://ct.kaist.ac.kr/file/seminar/20051025_Song.pdf

Steinbock, D. (2003). Globalization of wireless value system: From geographic to strategic advantages. *Telecommunications Policy, 27*(3/4), 207-235.

Tirole, J. (2002). *The theory of industrial organization*. Cambridge, MA: The MIT Press.

Wikipedia. (2006a). *Mobile payment*. Retrieved from http://en.wikipedia.org/wiki/Mobile_payment

Wikipedia. (2006b). *Ringback*. Retrieved from http://en.wikipedia.org/wiki/Ringback

Chapter XVI
M–Commerce
Market Development
Scenarios in Korea:
Focus on Changes and
Their Mega Trends

Seung Baek
Hanyang University, Korea

Bong Jun Kim
Hanyang University, Korea

ABSTRACT

A growth curve of the mobile commerce (m-commerce) market would be like that of the mobile voice market or broadband Internet service in the past in Korea, and then m-commerce will bring the mobile operators the second revenue. Even though, the subscribers of m-commerce are continues ascent in external appearance, in effect it is have an important problem to though revenue. In this research, after defining the m-commerce market, we will discover trends based on technological, social, and politic changes and the development scenarios of the m-commerce market. We review the technological, social, and policy changes that have occurred in Korea in order to present the mega trends that could affect the m-commerce market most significantly, by finding out the inner and outer arena trends of the m-commerce market. And then, we show four scenarios: (1) gloomy market scenario, (2) dream market scenario, (3) market collapse scenario, and (4) rainbow compromise scenario. We expect that an analysis of the trend that could create an m-commerce market in Korea and a study of the development scenarios will provide some foresight to communication service providers in Korea and overseas countries in order to cope with the future m-commerce market.

INTRODUCTION

The mobile operators in Korea have launched the mobile data service using code division multiple access (CDMA) network technology since 1999, and the overall market has reached 23.4 million subscribers. When the service was launched, the mobile operators and the market researchers had an optimistic view that Korea's m-commerce market would have an explosive increase. This positive expectation was based on the number of the mobile voice service users in Korea. That is, a growth curve of the m-commerce market would be like that of the mobile voice market or broadband Internet service in the past in Korea, and then m-commerce will bring the mobile operators the second revenue. Even though the number of m-commerce subscribers is continuously growing, it does not quite contribute to the operators' revenue so we decided Korea's m-commerce market has stagnated. Due to the saturated mobile voice market, most mobile operators in Korea are experiencing the same difficulty.

The mobile operators have been making an effort to create revenues through m-commerce, and also the use of mobile Internet has become popular. The launch of HSDPA, which is a cellular technology, is one new milestone. Along with these new technologies it has been introduced and

has received much attention in the Korean public. These effects resulted in a positive view for the m-commerce market. Nevertheless, various aspects and assertions about the growing potential and usefulness of m-commerce have been brought up. Korea is a country that supports fixed and mobile Internet to be activated nationwide. But with the complete preparations, what is the reason that m-commerce is not so active in Korea? Ironically, we find the reason in the well-developed, high-speed Internet environment. In Korea, the number of Internet users had been growing rapidly, nearly doubling each year since 1997. What is even more interesting is that most Internet users had subscribed to the high-speed Internet service. In 2001, the number of high-speed Internet subscribers per 100 people was 21.8 people in Korea (about 40% of all Internet users), 4.5 people in the USA (about 9% of Internet users), and 2.2 people in Japan (5% of Internet users). This dramatic expansion of the high-speed Internet service has even received worldwide attention. The International Telecommunication Union (ITU) and the Organisation of Economic Cooperation and Development (OECD) announced that Korea ranked first in the diffusion of high-speed Internet service. Of all households in Korea, 97% have some way of connecting to the Internet and 60% of all households in Korea access the high-speed Internet. Also in Korea the

Table 1. Growth changes in the mobile voice market (Source: Ministry of Information and Communication (MIC), 2006)

	2001	2002	2003	2004	2005	2006.09
Subscriber (1,000 persons)	29,046	32,342	33,592	36,586	38,342	39,703
New subscriber (1,000 persons)	2,229	3,297	1,249	2,994	1,756	361
Increasing rate (%)	8.3%	11.4%	3.9%	8.9%	N/A	N/A
Total sales (billion dollars)	13,506,573	15,007,736	15,532,733	16,502,062	N/A	N/A
New sales (billion dollars)	1,399,665	1,501,163	524,997	969,329	N/A	N/A
Increasing rate (%)	11.6%	11.1%	3.5%	6.2%	N/A	N/A

low-rated Internet cafés are available in the urban area along with the metropolitan area. Therefore "mobility" which is the biggest advantage of the mobile Internet does not bring value to consumers in Korea.

Research Objective

An m-commerce market provides a place to trade tangible and intangible things to consumers. To activate a traditional market, three factors are necessary: tradable products, construction of a market, and the most important factor, consumers. In the m-commerce market, the products are the contents, construction of a market means network and service technology, and the consumers are the consumers. Therefore in this research, after defining the m-commerce market, we will discover trends based on technological, social, and political changes and the development scenarios of the m-commerce market. Rapidly developing digital technology has brought a lot of unexpected changes to consumers' needs and demands, so this research will give implications that will help to outline the direction of changes to the m-commerce researchers and operators.

M-COMMERCE COMPETITIVE STATUS IN KOREA

Definition of M-Commerce

Davison, Brown, and Walsh (2000) defined that m-commerce is exciting because it extends the reach of e-commerce facilities beyond the limitations of the PC or TV to the hundreds of millions of mobile phone users. Flanagan, Fong, Horne, McIntyre, and Robert (2003) defined m-commerce as "a commercial transaction through mobile handsets." KTF, a mobile operator in Korea, defined m-commerce as "a value exchanging activity generated through mobile network" and decided it as a mobile form of e-commerce. Durlacher (1999) defined it very similar to that of KTF, "a trade of monetary value through mobile network." But there has not been a precise definition that works well because the m-commerce market is still growing. In a general definition, m-commerce includes information, entertainment, and commerce, but in the more specific definition, m-commerce means shopping and payment.

In order to define m-commerce, it is necessary to understand the mechanism of a traditional market. In a traditional market, a product exists between a consumer and a producer, and also a payment system exists. Therefore the m-commerce market should be limited to a tangible product market and if it is possible, it could extend to advertising, payment, and reservation system for the product. Secondly, it is necessary to understand the characteristic of "mobility,"—consumers can make a commercial transaction on the fly. In fact, if consumers can make a commercial transaction at home or at work, or at a different place, it is called e-commerce, whether using wired or wireless Internet. A handset which enables a commercial transaction while moving is the norm that can differentiate the m-commerce from the e-commerce. Mobile handsets referred to here

Table 2. General definition of m-commerce in Korea (Source: Customer Protection Board)

General definition		Specific definition
Information	Entertainment	Commerce
News, stock, location, and traffic information	VoD, AoD, content download (such as bell ring, MP3, and online games, etc.)	Financing, payment, shopping, advertising

VoD = voice on demand, AoD = audio on demand

are cellular phones, smart phones, and PDAs. The reasons that a notebook computer is excluded are the following: First, a notebook computer can be connected to the Internet even outside of the building, but it is actually hard to use the Internet in the car or when walking. Secondly, even considering that the semiconductor chip would be developed to be smaller, due to the technology of a battery, it is hard to be "always on" and the seamless location-based service (LBS) can not be served. In this research an m-commerce handset means a handset like a mobile phone that enables consumers to search products, to compare products, and to make payments.

Characteristics of M-Commerce

To predict the m-commerce market understanding of what differentiates the traditional Internet experience from the wireless version such as device, technical character, and recognition of customers is needed. The first circumstance that differentiates wired from wireless surfing is the device's own physical form. Mobile communication technology has undoubtedly made very significant developments in the electronic system field in recent years. All sections of mobile communications are growing rapidly. Apparently the growth of voice applications has benefited us a lot. However, the data applications have lagged behind. Recently the system operators are making provisions to transmit data over the cellular systems, which were primarily designed for voice. The mobile telecommunication industry needs to develop services for the mobile data markets, not only to pay back their investments, but also to stay competitive in the future.

Mobility is at the heart of these wireless systems, where people can transmit and receive information wherever they are and whenever they choose, even when they are moving. The user interface and the size of mobile devices are the main concerns in designing mobile services. A well-designed, single-layered user interface will

be more user friendly than the conventional one and it will have an edge over others. However, it is quite difficult to provide a single-layered user interface on a small screen. Designing mobile services is fundamentally different than designing online services on the Internet. Not only are there differences in underlying technologies, but also in the way people use the services. If these differences are not taken into account, mobile services are likely to fail. If mobile services do not deliver what people want, these services will fail no matter how excellent the underlying technology is. Designing usable interfaces for tomorrow's mobile devices is not trivial but involves a series of challenges in human-computer interaction (HCI). Mobile services require efficient ways to record and access information under circumstances that are often quite different from those where desktop computers are used. Displays on mobile devices are small, means of input are limited, and use contexts are very dynamic. The usability of mobile services consequently suffers from interfaces being very compact and cluttered with information, demanding the user's full attention. Many people say that mobile services are not yet attractive and usable for customers. There clearly is a lack of understanding of real user needs and how mobile Internet can help users satisfy those needs.

Wireless application protocol (WAP) phones are a growing relevant part of the mobile market, and the number of WAP services offered is rapidly increasing. However, usability is crucial for these services which must be easily operated on small screens and keyboards. One of the reasons that many WAP sites have failed is that many service providers simply tried to carry their Web sites over to the mobile Internet. This shows that little thought has been given to the characteristics of mobile Internet and to the specific needs of people who use their mobile devices in real life. Understanding the fundamental differences between mobile and the Web is essential for the success of mobile services. Figure 1 compares a Web interface with a mobile interface. Using the

Figure 1. The interface of wired Internet and wireless Internet

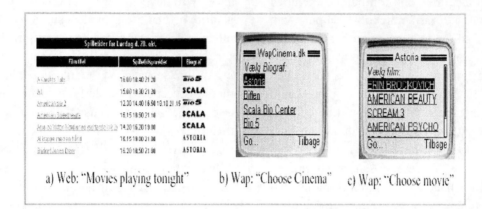

a) Web: "Movies playing tonight"   b) Wap: "Choose Cinema"   c) Wap: "Choose movie"

Web site, users view all relevant information on one page. Whereas, accessing the services from WAP-based phones, users require a lot of clicking in a predefined sequence, due to the division of information into a large number of sub-pages. By following sequential menus, users can find specific mobile services. Generally, interfaces of WAP-based mobile services require minimal attentions and interactions. The usability of mobile services consequently suffers from interfaces being very compact and cluttered with information. It is crucial to design the menus, which can get the user's full attention, to be simple and the required interaction minimal.

Secondly, we think that the difference between e-commerce and m-commerce is based on the following technical characters: (1) mobility, (2) data transfer rate, and (3) switching system. The difference among network technologies provided the wireless users mobility. Traditional Internet and e-commerce applications are notoriously location-unaware. But one attribute of cellular networks is the development of LBS. And the data transferring rate of mobile Internet does not have fast for traditional Internet too. These technical problems limit consumers to use as much information that a fixed Internet could provide. Therefore it can not satisfy consumers who want more information. Finally, there is a difference of switching system. In a wireless communication

network, the packet switching system gives and takes the data. As a result, it is unavoidable to charge consumers high comparatively.

The final difference of wireless and wired Internet is the recognition of the customers. This relationship is very much like the relationship between the desktop computer and a notebook computer. One of the main reason that m-commerce is not quite activated is that a notebook computer is recognized as a second option to consumers. Therefore, it will be important to see a new meaning in the notebook computer. Wireless Web users are also going online with an entirely different mindset and goals than they would have if they were surfing from wired handsets (Zilliox, 2002). Zillox also said that traditional Web surfing often involves either a certain degree of researching or aimless wandering. Mobile device users make moving around, and then wireless users do not have enough time for shopping, Web surfing, and movies.

Wireless Service Status in Korea

Mobile Voice and Data Service

The Korean mobile service market is composed of one dominant carrier (SKT) and two second movers (KTF, LGT). SKT has a market share of

Table 3. Differences between e-commerce and m-commerce

Contents	e-commerce	m-commerce
Information richness	Richness	Poor
A type of information	Both picture and text	Only text
Screen size	Large	Small
Bandwidth	Large	Small
Mobility	Impossible	Possible
Personalized service	A little	Possible
Price	A flat rate	A meter rate

50.9% (as of March 2005) and in sales volume it occupies 58.5% (year of 2004), proving the growth of the market. On the other side, the third ranking mobile operator, LGT occupies 16.8% of the subscribers, and 13.8% of the sales volume, but even with the effect of mobile number portability (MNP), the sales volume dropped. The main reason for aggravated profitability results from the competition in the saturated market. The mobile operators raised marketing expense to draw subscribers from each other, and this bad cycle continuously repeats. Another factor can be the difference between the profit of mobile data service between SKT and LGT. Since 1999, the mobile data service has been provided in the metropolitan area including Seoul, but the revenue difference between SKT, KTF, and LGT is falling apart with the first mover advantage. Recently the main issue in the mobile service market is "convergence." The

convergence between the wired and the wireless; the convergence between telecommunication and media; and more convergence services are expected to be new sources for income to telecommunication operators. Recently the dominant fixed and wireless telecommunication providers, KT and SKT are taking over movie distributors and portal business to strengthen their contents business area for future growth. Thus, in Korea both mobile operators and fixed operators have been preparing for convergence service paradigm.

M-Commerce Service Status in Korea

In 2001 the MIC prepared a program to activate the m-commerce market. The cellular operator, SKT introduced the "Moneta Card" service, which can replace a credit card when using mobile handsets. This service engendered a lot of

Table 4. A subscriber and revenue of mobile operators in Korea. Source: KTOA, MIC, company data from SKT, KTF and LGT

Contents		'01	'02	'03	'04	'05.03	'06.09
SKT	Subscriber	N/A	53.3%	54.5%	50.9%	51.3%	50.5%
	Revenue	58.2%	57.3%	59.9%	N/A	58.5%	N/A
KTF	Subscriber	N/A	31.9%	31.1%	32.3%	32.1%	32.2%
	Revenue	27.1%	28.7%	27.6%	27.7%	26.0%	N/A
LGT	Subscriber	N/A	14.8%	14.4%	16.8%	16.6%	17.4%
	Revenue	12.0%	13.2%	15%	13.8%	14%	N/A

controversy because it was the entry for a mobile operator into the financial market. In Korea the financial transaction regulations prohibit a large enterprise to enter the financial market, such as banks, insurance companies, stocks, and credit card businesses. The intimidated credit card companies delayed the issue of "Moneta Card" and also did not support the installation of the credit card readers, as well as influenced the deactivation of the service. The PCS operator, KTF commercialized the "K.merce" service that enabled e-transactions for the first time in Korea. LGT also started a similar credit card payment service like that of SKT in 2002. These services were in the form of the entry level of m-commerce, focusing on payments and banking services; the users were only 30,000 from SKT and 20,000 from KTF. The m-commerce ended up as an unsuccessful service because of the financial companies' intentional interrupt along with the failure of gaining the consumers' trust.

Customer Needs for Mobile Data Service

According to the Korea Information Society Development Institute's (KISDI) (2004) Mobile Internet Service Usage Behavior Survey the main reasons for not using mobile Internet service were "no needs existing" and "expensive usage fare." Of the total respondents, 59.7% said that they were satisfied with the service, responding "convenient connection." The most frequently used contents were entertainment contents like downloading games or bells and sending pictures. On the other side, mobile shopping and payment were found to be needless contents compared to other contents. These facts give implications that the mobile handset is perceived as a personalized handset and is mostly used on the fly so contents like mobile shopping, which would take some time, is not a preferred use; usually instant services are more attractive.

TECHNOLOGICAL, SOCIAL, AND POLICY CHANGES IN KOREA

Technological Change

Integration of Fixed Voice and Wireless Voice

As the technology develops, fixed-line operators are expanding their business scope to the wireless communication market, whereas wireless operators are entering the fixed-line communication market. There are two backgrounds to the active crossing over of these neighboring markets. First, fixed-voice revenues continue to drop as customers tend to use the mobile service at home or in the office, instead of the fixed service. Second, mobile communication service providers wanted to gain differentiated competitive superiority over their competitors. Korea Telecom (KT), the dominant player in the fixed-line market, commercialized the "One Phone" service based on Bluetooth in 2004 in conjunction with KTF (an affiliated company). The "One Phone" service is based on the concept that customers can place a call with the fixed-line call rate in the hot zone where the receiver is installed and use the wireless voice service at other locations through KTF's mobile communication network. Other mobile operators also commercialized similar services. The third market sharer LG Telecom also provides a similar service with the brand name of "Gibun Zone." However, these two services allow the regular phone rate in a limited area only, and LG Telecom has only limited coverage of the mobile communication network compared with its competitors. Nevertheless, this trend is likely to persist in the Korean mobile communication services market.

Integration of Wired Internet and Wireless Internet

In terms of the technology, the Internet service market has evolved in two directions: (1) wireless technology, and (2) fixed technology. In regards to wireless technology, third generation (3G) (W-CDMA) technology was commercialized by SKT and KTF. Also, they are preparing to commercialize the 3.5G (HSDPA, its brand name, to 3G plus in SKT) technology. For the fixed technology, KT and SKT are preparing to commercialize the WIBRO service based on HPI technology. In other words, the Internet based on the fixed-line network began to supplement "mobility," whereas the Internet based on the mobile network started to provide a service that supplements "transmission speed" to "broadband." Cyworld, which is currently provided by SK Telecom, is the representative case of a wire/wireless portal that combines both the fixed and wireless communication services. Cyworld expands the service coverage from the wired Internet to the mobile Internet, and its users can send pictures or use the bulletin board based on the text through a mobile connection.

Even though SK Telecom's Cyworld is only in the initial service stages of the wire/wireless integrated service, it could end the traditional separation of the fixed/wireless market. As a result, it is expected that classifying the communication service market by service type, as provided by the wire/wireless service providers, would be meaningless, when fourth generation (4G) technology prevails in the market. Offering the wireless broadband Internet service will be the critical success factor of m-commerce in the future.

Generalization of Ubiquitous Technology

The word "ubiquitous" is one of the perspectives for future IT evolution and means that users will be able to use the content by accessing the network at any time and place. To build the ubiquitous society, the wireless broadband network technology

Figure 2. Development of fixed voice and wireless voice

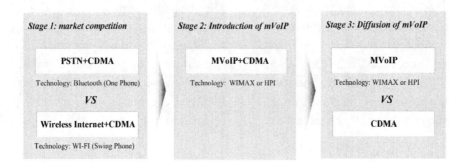

Table 5. Comparison between fixed and wireless technology in Korea

	WCDMA	HSDPA	WIBRO
Download	2 Mbps (384K)	14.4 Mbps	18.4 Mbps
Upload	2 Mbps (128K)	2 Mbps	5.95 Mbps
Service time	December. 2003	June. 2006	Plan to 2006
Service contents	High speed data service, real time video communication		mVoIP, wire Internet contents service
Price	$26 (monthly)	$26 (monthly)	$15~20 (monthly)

is considered as the most appropriate approach, and chip technology will emerge as the one that will be utilized as the infrastructure technology. Radio frequency identification (RFID) has become the core technology to enable LBS. The necessity of LBS is well recognized by individuals, government, and in the safety and commercial transactions of individuals. However, its promotion is likely to encounter considerable obstacles due to human rights issues such as privacy protection. Therefore, the popularization of "ubiquity" might necessitate a process of drawing out social agreements due to concerns over privacy infringements, information access right issues, cyber crimes, and other security issues.

Social Change

Home, Office, and City Network

Humanity's basic desire for communication engenders the need to be able to establish any type of media communication at any time and place, using one convenient device. The preference is for an integrated type of service rather than a functionally separated service, and availability of the multimedia communication services regardless of the device type, time, and place is expected. However, in reality services that are mutually separated have been provided individually or discontinuously. Home appliances that used to have

the stand-alone or off-line types are increasingly wired to the network, which is expected to create a network between digital home appliances and in-house communication devices. The trend has been set by home appliance manufacturers that are actively seeking the development of a new value-added market, since the added value of home appliances such as TVs, audio, and refrigerators is gradually declining. The activities of the home appliance industry to find a new way out through the development of the home network are not limited to individual households only. The formation of new electronic communities such as cyber apartments is expanding the concept of the household to the apartment complex or the small-sized community, like a village. The community network in this area aims for the integration of wire/wireless media as well as integration among the home, office, shopping mall, and entertainment center.

Five-Day Working Week Becomes the Norm

The desire to actually enjoy life is increasing. As the five-day week gains ground, the external activities of consumers increase accordingly and real-time consumption related to the individual's life style also increases. It is expected that the social phenomenon of continuously pursuing something on the move would be the driving

Figure 3. Blueprint of the future society

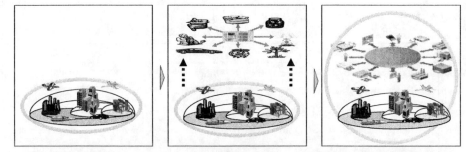

[before 1990] [From 1990 to 2010] [after 2010]

force of creating demand for m-commerce. Kim Sin-base, CEO of SK Telecom, referred to this phenomenon as follows:

The distribution ratio of the pager in Korea was 35% at its peak, whereas it was only 15% in Hong Kong and Taiwan. This shows characteristics specific to us, which cannot be easily explained—the digital nomad. This nomadic characteristic in the digital age has helped the development of the entire industry and market. (Personal communication)

Personalization and Customer Behavior

As IT technologies and services advance, individuals want to increasingly select services that are suited to their personal traits and preferences. Personalization expands the individual's role to production, creation, and distribution of the content, such as mini home pages, blogs, and personal broadcasting stations. It appears that individuals are also more likely to purchase a product according to their personal subjective decision, when reviewing consumption behavior. In the former off-line environment, people tended to be influenced by others rather than follow personalized consumption patterns, since commodity information could not be obtained easily. However, more people now decide to buy a given product online by referring to other peoples' comments or remarks about their usage experience. This trend shows that the usage experience of other consumers has become a critical decision factor when buying a commodity from an Internet shopping mall. That is, due to the characteristics of the Internet shopping mall, where people cannot select a product by touching or visually checking it over, other consumers' evaluations and price comparisons are referenced as the most useful information. As a result, commodity review sites (e.g., Dcinside) that evaluate a commodity based on the consumer's usage experience are emerging rapidly in Korea. The trend of personalized services seems to be affecting the change of direction of the future

m-commerce significantly, because the pull-type self-service, whereby consumers take the initiative by selecting information and making a decision, is likely to prevail, instead of the push-type service by which enterprises provide their goods to the consumer at their discretion.

Diffusion of the Internet Café

The wired broadband Internet service became the common service in Korea as a result of government policy and the low usage rate. Additionally, rapid dissemination of entertainment contents such as online games has led to a social change embodied by the "Internet café." People can use the wired Internet at an Internet café at a moderate price when they are out of the house or office. Presently, it is highly popular in both metropolitan and small- and medium-sized cities. It may be paradoxical, but the high-speed Internet distribution ratio and the proliferation of the Internet café in Korea could be an obstacle to the popularization of m-commerce. That is, people can find an alternative if they have to access the Internet in haste outside of the home or the office, even though they cannot use it on the move. Therefore, people might regard the wireless Internet as the most inconvenient way to access the Internet due to the small screen size, text-based environment, and manipulation difficulty.

Policy Change

From Close Network to Open Network

The MIC established the policy in 2003 that opens the mobile operator's wireless Internet network to other service providers (portal sites and contents providers). In the closed network, other service providers can only use the mobile operator's wireless Internet network. With the introduction of the new policy, they can establish an independent wireless Internet service and select the wireless portal site that they want. The purpose of the open network policy is to allow service providers other than mobile operators to enter the portal and contents business and secure profitability through fair competition, so that the user's "right to choose" can be increased and the share of the mobile Internet market can be expanded to that of the wired Internet market. This policy change is expected to contribute to the promotion of the future m-commerce market, as it will ease the difficulty of off-line businesses like shopping malls and auctions in entering the mobile market.

TRENDS AND THEIR MARKET SCENARIOS

This chapter reviews the technological, social, and policy changes that have occurred in Korea in order to present the mega trends that could affect the m-commerce market most significantly, by finding out the inner and outer arena trends of the m-commerce market.

Based on findings about technological, social, and policy change in this study, interviews with IT experts were performed for two purposes: the first is to verify the validity of variables (predictability and impact on local issues) that were drawn to forecast the direction of m-commerce market in Korea; the second is to determine the other variables that were not considered in composing the m-commerce development scenario. The expert group for this study includes representative IT research centers in Korea (KISDI and ETRI) and senior researcher into telecommunication service providers (Korea Telecom and SK Telecom).

Finding Inner and Outer Arena Trends

Based on the responses from experts with regards to technological, social, and policy changes, 17 trend subjects were drawn out, including 10 inner arena trends and 7 outside arena trends. These trends are classified into the inner area trends that are directly associated with m-commerce, and the outer arena trends that affect m-commerce from a broad perspective.

The inner arena trends include: (1) integration of the wire/wireless voice service; (2) integration of the wire/wireless Internet service; (3) an increase in review site usage, blogs, and bulletin boards; (4) convergence services; (5) online commercial trading; (6) real-time consumption; (7) demand for LBS; (8) risk of cyber crime; (9) efforts for network security; and (10) demand for a personalized service. The outside arena trends have the concept of a "driving force," and include: (11) proliferation of convergence technology; (12) spreading of the ubiquitous technology; (13) entrance into the network society; (14) deepened individualization; (15) popularization of the 5-day working week; (16) increase in the number of Internet cafes; and (17) and increased independent consumption.

To determine the interrelationship between the inner and outer arena trends, the "casual loop" was figured out, based on the interview with experts. As can be seen in Figure 4, the "proliferation of convergence technology [11]" affects the "integration of the wire/wireless voice services [1]," the "integration of the wire/wireless Internet service [2]," and the "increasing convergence services [4]," mutually affects the "spreading of ubiquitous technologies [12]" with each other. The "spreading of ubiquitous technology [12]" affects the "increasing demand for LBS [7]," the "increasing demand for a personalized service [10]," and the "network society [13]."

"Network society [13]" influences the "increasing demand for LBS [7]" and the "increasing risk of cyber crime [8]," whereas the "deepened individualization [14]" affects "increasing real-time consumption [6]," "increasing demand for a personalized service [10]," as well as "increasing independent consumption [17]."

Both the "increasing number of Internet cafes [16]" and "increasing independent consumption

[17]" affect the "increasing online commercial trading [5]." On the other hand, "increasing online commercial trading [5]" is affected by several variables, including "increasing review site usage, blogs, and bulletin boards [3]," "increasing number of Internet cafes [16]," "increasing independent consumption [17]," and "increasing efforts for network security [9]."

Considering the interrelationship between the 17 trends presented, it was found that the mega trends that could affect m-commerce to a large extent are those of convergence, ubiquitous and society, and personalization.

M-Commerce Market Scenarios

According to discussion with relevant professionals in regards to mega trends (convergence, ubiquitous and society, and personalization) and other trends that have a close casual relationship, two uncertainties should be considered in order to forecast the future of m-commerce. The first concerns the direction of government policy: Will the government put more emphasis on service availability or civil rights like privacy protection? The second concerns the central technology that will lead development in the convergence environment: Which one is more beneficial to develop-

Figure 4. Inner and outer arena trends

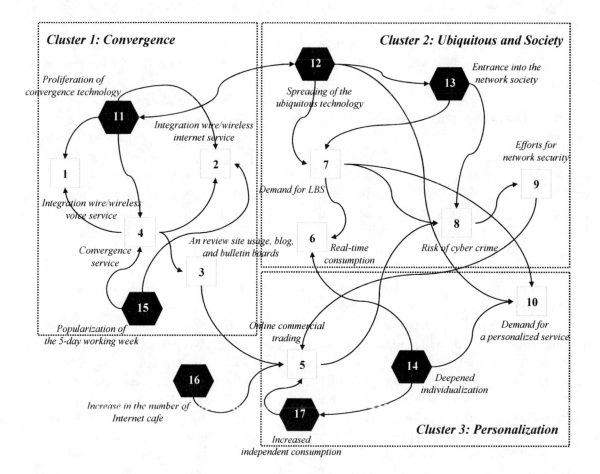

ment—fixed line-based Internet technology or mobile-based Internet technology?

Gloomy Market Scenario

The gloomy market scenario recalls the relationship between desktop PCs and laptops in the personal computer market. In this scenario, service availability is not emphasized, but consumer and civil organizations request privacy protection. Consequently, the offering of personalized services is limited from the ground, and services are not very different from the ones provided by e-commerce. Therefore, consumers are discouraged from using m-commerce as it is relatively more expensive to use. Goods trading will cease at the home, office, or Internet café, and consumers will use the mobile Internet for limited purposes only, such as location tracking of any items that they purchase at the e-commerce market. The m-commerce market will remain as the sub-market of the e-commerce market and as an assistant to it.

Dream Market Scenario

In the dream market scenario, the mobile environment could provide a user interface that is similar to the fixed-line Internet environment, and the value felt by consumers would be increased through the network society as convergence technology develops. Therefore, consumers place greater emphasis on the value that they feel, even though they have to take risks regarding disclosure of personal information and cyber crime. Additionally, the increased usage of review sites, blogs, and bulletin boards will lead to increased demand for the mobile data. In this situation, consumers buy goods at their discretion, which means that the e-commerce market is integrated with the m-commerce market. Consequently, mobile operators could find the best revenue source followed by the mobile voice market.

Market Collapse Scenario

The market collapse scenario is similar to the situation by which the m-commerce market is not created. Consumers feel difficulty in obtaining information about a commodity to buy in the text-based mobile Internet environment, and cyber crime activities increase in commercial trading and financial transactions. Additionally, "Big Brother" becomes a reality as privacy is violated by a certain service provider, which would result in increased interest in privacy protection, as in the gloomy market scenario. Consumers will be more interested in entertainment contents as in the past, instead of the services related with m-commerce, which unfortunately implies the breakdown of the m-commerce market.

Rainbow Compromise Scenario

In the rainbow compromise scenario, an individual's current location can be identified in the network society. Therefore, a personalized service can be provided, which leads to increasing real-time and impromptu consumption. Due to the strength of the e-commerce market and m-commerce market, market players feel that one of them could degenerate into the sub-market. Therefore, they would create a mutually supplementary relationship by providing a customized service which utilizes their competitive advantage in the market.

THE FUTURE OF M-COMMERCE

Although mobile computers have numerous personal and corporate uses, the most notable innovation of mobile technology is the ability to receive Internet access from virtually anywhere (Zilliox, 2002). Despite these strengths, the viewpoints about m-commerce are quite diverse—from viewing the market itself as a gold mine to the most pessimistic standpoint. Almost no one had

Figure 5. M-commerce market scenario

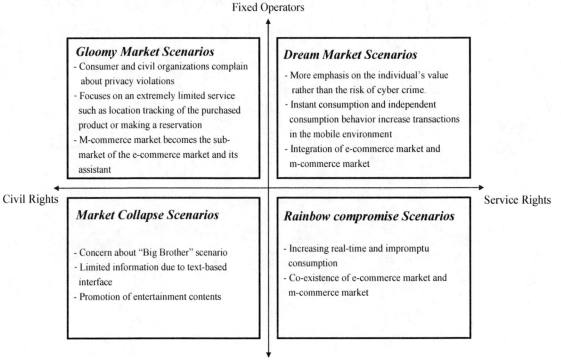

forecast until the mid 1990s, when walkmans and CD players were the norm for listening to music, that the MP3 player would occupy the market share as quickly as we see now. Rapidly changing trends can be caused by diverse consumer demands. However, seen from a different viewpoint, it may be said that the current services do not fascinate consumers. As a result, enterprises could find future competitiveness if they could understand the trends in consumer demand in advance.

The advancement of IT technologies is changing the world market, which is becoming more like a borderless market. Korea took the leading position in wire/wireless IT services and technology, and the Korean communication service market serves as a test bed for other countries like the U.S. and some European countries. Viewed from this perspective, it is expected that an analysis of the trend that could create an m-commerce market in Korea and a study of the development

scenarios will provide some foresight to communication service providers in Korea and overseas countries in order to cope with the future m-commerce market.

REFERENCES

Davison, J., Brown, D., & Walsh, A. (2000). *Mobile e-commerce market strategy*. Ovum.

Durlacher. (1999). *Mobile commerce report.*

Flanagan, S., Fong, J., Horne, S., McIntyre, F., & Robert, P. (2003). *Mobile commerce: Regulatory and policy outlook*, Melbourne VIC 8010: Discussion Paper. Australian Communications Authority.

Ministry of Information and Communication (MIC). (2006). *Wireless telecommunication subscriber report.*

Korea Information Society Development Institute (KISDI). (2005). *The statues of telecommunication industry in Korea* (Issue report). Seoul, Korea: Author.

LGRI. (2005). *The propensity to consume to new generation: White book* (CEO Report).

Zilliox, D. (2002). *The get-started guide to m-commerce and mobile technology.* AMACOM.

Chapter XVII
Individual Telecommunications Tariffs in Chinese Communities

H. Chen
Rotterdam School of Management, The Netherlands

L.-F. Pau
Rotterdam School of Management, The Netherlands

ABSTRACT

The chapter addresses mobile service pricing and affordability issues in China. The goal is to assist fast diffusion and sustainable development of mobile services through pricing mechanisms. Diverse situations exist with a split between a large number of mostly rural people still lacking basic services; and some affluent mostly urban users wanting personalized value-added services. A historical perspective is taken and tariff data are reported. Focussing on content and interactions, solutions are found in community-based individual tariffs; this business model fits especially well with the community culture rooted in Chinese tradition. Such a solution can facilitate the diffusion to all types of users, and also allow community members themselves to satisfy their own demands. Two cases are described: the gaming communities of Lianzhong; and the "Tianfu" rural communication communities in Sichuan province. Concluding remarks are made about existing technologies and standards needed by this approach, and about how to close the gap between the current situation and the envisaged implementation.

INTRODUCTION

In mainland China, the first public mobile operator—China Telecom—started its mobile services in 1987 under heavy government involvement and as a state-owned enterprise, with 700 subscribers. Due to the booming domestic economy, the mobile communications market has developed rapidly since its initiation (see Figure 1). This is reflected in the number of mobile users as well as in the number of mobile operators. In terms of absolute volume, there were about 400 million mobile subscribers at the end of December 2005 (National Bureau of Statistics of China, 2005). In terms of

Figure 1. Mobile subscriber growth in China (1990-2006)

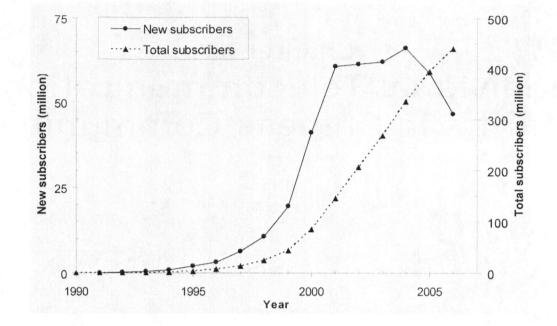

penetration rate, wireless communications had an overall penetration rate of 30.1% among the total population (December 2005). Although fixed telephony had been introduced many years before mobile, it had never enjoyed such a fast growth and the penetration rate was only 26.8% over the whole population in December 2005. There are now four mobile operator groups, two dominant ones: China Mobile and China Unicom; plus two minor ones: China Satcom and China Telecom. Each has subsidiaries at the provincial level.

The sheer number of mobile subscribers implies diverse demands for mobile services. This is further complicated by unbalanced development in regional economics and in urban planning. While people in the more developed areas are demanding more value-added services, people in less developed areas are still lacking basic services. It is challenging, if not impossible, for the service providers (e.g., operators) to elicit such diverse demands from individual users. Furthermore, service creation costs can be prohibitive therefore

leading to high tariffs; which are contradictory to the significantly less affluent purchasing power in the less developed regions. This chapter addresses the mobile service creation and pricing issues in China by introducing community-based individual tariffs. The concept and its business model can help to create mobile services that meet exactly user demands at a group level. More importantly, the concept and its business model allow a user to pay what he/she is willing to pay. Thus community-based individual tariffs can facilitate the fast diffusion as well as sustainable development of mobile services in China.

The chapter is structured as follows: In the second section, the current mobile services and tariff situation in China are analyzed. Without immediately offering a solution, in the third section, we proceed to provide a vision of mobile services in the near future enabled by emerging technologies. The emphasis of these services is on content and interactions in communities. We then introduce community-based individual tariffs and a business model in the fourth section. Two cases to which the concept and model are directly relevant are analyzed in the fifth section. The sixth section discusses the enabling technologies. Conclusions are presented in the final section.

CURRENT MOBILE SERVICES AND TARIFFS IN CHINA

After being on a fast track for nearly 20 years, China's mobile communication market showed signs of slowing down in 2005. First, the number of new subscribers turned out to be lower than the previous year, for the first time (Figure 1). The 2006 data is an estimation based on the number of new subscribers in the first three quarters (National Bureau of Statistics of China, 2006). This is more noticeable in the more developed south-eastern provinces which used to contribute significantly to the overall growth. In the less developed western provinces where the mobile penetration rate is low, the growth is also marginal. Secondly, the growth of average revenue per user (ARPU) from high usage users is offset by the low ARPU from a large number of low usage users, which leads to an overall slowly decreasing ARPU (Ministry of Information Industry of China, 2006).

But the market is far from saturated! Although the growth in basic mobile services in the areas with a high penetration rate has slowed, the demand for value-added services is rising. This is reflected in the huge success and rapid growth of ring tones, short message service (SMS), and multimedia messaging service (MMS)–based, value-added services. People are willing to pay for these services when they meet their requirements (Xu, Gong, & Thong, 2006). However, the limited choice of value-added services on the market can not satisfy the diverse demands from such a huge population. Furthermore, a lack of flexibility in tariffs provides little incentives for service creation.

On the other hand, in the less developed areas representing about 70% of the population with

much lower income, people need communication services that can serve their specific demands at low costs (International Telecommunications Union [ITU], 2005). The lack of flexibility in tariffs makes even the basic communication costs prohibitive when compared to the local income level, let alone the value-added services. Many examples of this mismatch surfaced during the government project "Cun Cun Tong," translated as "connecting every rural village with universal services." Although each connected village is provided with basic telephony service, it is seldom used unless in emergencies and wireless was almost never added. As a consequence, the villagers are still isolated from the outside world; the operators cannot get revenue for their investments in infrastructure. It is a lose-lose situation for both the operators and the users.

In China, mobile tariffs, as part of telecommunication tariffs, are fixed by the Regulations of the People's Republic of China on Telecommunications (State Council of the People's Republic of China, 2000). A telecommunications law was to be promulgated in August 2006 but was postponed. Tariffs are so far divided into three categories:

- Government-set tariffs, which are fixed by the government
- Government-guided tariffs, which are fixed by operators according to benchmark prices and range of the prices as set by the government
- Market-based tariffs, which are fixed independently by operators through market competition

The current regulation prescribes that basic mobile services (voice call, roaming, and long distance call) can follow either government-set tariffs, government-guided tariffs, or market-based tariffs. Value-added mobile services (call forward, line identification, SMS, etc.) can follow government-guided tariffs or market-based tariffs. When there is intensive competition, the

Table 1. Ratio of ARPU to disposable income

	Urban usage	Rural usage
Weighted ARPU (CNY)/month	146.7565	52.79622
Disposable income (CNY/year)	10493	3255
Number of subscribers (million)	94.03	280.41
(Weighted ARPU)*12/Disposable income	16.78%	19.46%

tariffs can be set based on the market mechanism. "State-aid" operators (e.g., China Unicom) are entitled to set price fluctuating within 10% of the government-set tariffs.

However in practice, the tariffs are still mainly guided by the government. The current mobile tariffs are still based on a guideline issued in 1994 by the former Ministry of Posts and Tele-communications. Post-paid users pay a monthly subscription fee of CNY 50 and the tariff is CNY 0.40/minute for local calls, CNY 0.60/minute when roaming. Prepaid users do not pay the monthly subscription fee, but the corresponding tariffs are then CNY 0.60/minute for local calls and CNY 0.80/minute when roaming. There is no difference between developed and less developed regions. Both parties in the communication need to pay, following a U.S. inspired split cost principle (different from the rest of the world's "charges to calling party" rule).

Due to high income disparity in China to-day, the ratio of the ARPU to urban and rural disposable income (see Table 1) is 16% and 19% respectively (2005). (Due to the lack of statistics, we approximate urban users to be the post-paid users, and rural users to be the prepaid users. The weighted ARPU is the average revenue per user, weighted within each population category (urban/post-paid, rural/prepaid). The ARPU data were retrieved from the published annual reports (2005) from two major operators: China mobile www.chinamobilehk.com and China Unicom www.chinaunicom.com.hk. The overall average ARPU is CNY 76/month (2005). The ratio of the overall average mobile usage cost per year, to Chinese GDP per inhabitant CNY 13943 (2005) is 6%. Whereas, the overall mobile penetration rate in China among the total population was approximately 30.1% at the end of 2005, the high usage subscribers represented an estimated 20% of the subscriber base, or 6% of the population. Meanwhile, the majority of the population (69.9%) still cannot afford the expense of even basic mobile communications services.

Both at service level and tariff level, the space for improvement is huge. Besides (de)regulation and policies, we should also consider one major force in the telecommunication industry: technology advances. It can be beneficial if we have a vision of mobile services in the near future enabled by existing and developing technologies; we may then try to bridge the gaps between now and the future in service creation, provisioning, and tariffing.

A VISION OF MOBILE SERVICES CREATION AND PROVISIONING IN THE NEAR FUTURE

About 10 or 20 years from now, advanced personal communication technologies will enable people to stay connected anytime, anywhere with access network alternatives. Users' devices will seam-lessly roam between PAN, WLAN, and WAN, fuelled by new services yet unknown (Frattasi, Fathi, Fitzek, Prasad, & Katz, 2006). With a high penetration rate of wireless devices in most parts of the country, mobile services will be provided quite differently from now on.

While connectivity is the most cherished property as in the year 2000 (Odlyzko, 2001), the key differentiating values of mobile services in the 2030s will be totally different. Through a combination of a large number of users, technology improvements, and operator productivity gains, the pure transport and access tariffs for wireless and mobile will plummet to very low values. Content-based service will generate certain revenue. Content exists in two variants:

1. "Static" from data warehouses with only periodic modifications
2. "Dynamic" from real-time information sensors and other sources, including user-originated content

By profiling and data mining, besides personalization selections, the service providers will know in real time much more about users than they do now. However, in an age with information "overload," static content has only low commercial value; higher commercial value content demands copyright licenses negotiated with the creators, or information access provisions. Advertisement will generate some commission revenue for service providers, but it will probably not be sufficient to support a whole mobile communication industry living from the "law of large numbers" and from very low tariffs.

Mirroring the early trend in video/broadcasting industries for dynamic content, the relative share in tariff bundles of the intellectual property right owners will be larger; the multiplication of dynamic content channels will add price pressure to tariff bundles. Consequently by 2030, the true value of wireless and mobile services will lie in the interactions, where the services are formed as a result of multiparty interactions. These interactions can be divided into three categories:

1. Community-based, human-to-human interactions
2. Cluster-based, machine-to-machine interactions
3. Human-to-machine interactions

Here we focus on the first category. Sociologist Barry Wellman (2001, p. 228) had defined communities as: "Networks of interpersonal ties that provide sociability, support, information, a sense of belonging, and social identity." Because of their business, sociological, or process-linked nature, the communities mentioned previously rely on membership fees (in kind or in money, eventually free) and on managed access privileges, which are essentially similar to current operators customer care administration, but in diverse forms and with more freedom in the organization thereof. More precisely, belonging to a community requires an identity and membership for a user in order to receive services; it also requires a degree of self-care and support to the rest of the community. The community provides collectively information, know-how, and services to members through interactions and access to static or dynamic content.

COMMUNITY-BASED INDIVIDUAL TARIFFS

Community-Based Individual Tariffs for a Set of Communication Services

Community-based individual tariffs mean that each individual sets a tariff for himself/herself for a specific set of services provided by the community, whether the services are user-defined or community-defined. Even if that individual belongs, say to an enterprise, the members of the enterprise may have different individual tariffs, simply because their service demands and content flow (contributions and receipts) are different. Even different users of an identical service (if any such service exists) may value it differently as they decide to belong to different communities of their choice. As a consequence, the users of an identical service may pay different tariffs.

The access to the services inside a community is based on prices and competition, or possibly quasi real-time spot service prices (Meij & Pau, 2006). There are also prices for community peering arrangements, or community-to-community interactions, but these may be on a periodic flat rate basis once a service-level agreement has been enacted between them.

In the aforementioned definition each community ends up supplying a number of services of which only some are initiated by consensus at the community level or by the service manager. A community does not need to own part of or the entire fixed and wireless transmission infrastructure. Such infrastructure can be sourced competitively from an infrastructure owner under a simplified mobile virtual network operator (MVNO) scheme (Varoutas, Katsianis, Sphicopoulos, Stordahl, & Welling, 2006). Also, these community-supplied services are not necessarily entered into Service Level Agreements with other communities or the public at large.

The aforementioned definition says nothing about the transparency of prices and pricing provisions. More precisely, the information disclosure rules are of at least three types, with one between the member and his/her community (especially if this is managed formally), one within a community, and the last one between communities. The information disclosure rules may lead to price equalization but this effect is limited in that it can only happen for the same service, while each community member will have a different and possibly dynamic service usage profile.

The aforementioned definition says nothing about the service provisioning duration the community commits to its members, or which communities commit to themselves. Duration of the

service will be one attribute in the multi-attribute service demand from a user in the community; for example, sporadic uses are possible, just as long term ones, but the difference with the current service offering is that they can be priced differently and made user specific.

Very importantly, per this definition of community-based individual tariffs, when the end user requests a service from a community, he/she is also responsible for the existence and survival of the community through contributions (money, but also information, knowledge). The individual will take and share the risk if the service is underfunded and ceases to exist. So, if the user appreciates the service, he/she may end up paying slightly more than other members, or even more than users of the same service from other communities, to ensure the existence of the service. The person can also consider paying an insurance premium to the community to cover against the risk of service loss. By paying an individually negotiated premium, which may be only a small amount of money, the user maintains his/her access to key services, but also by mutualising this risk across communities and public operators alike, he/she contributes to the survival of the community (Harrington & Niehaus, 2003).

Business Model of a Community

Based on the concepts of community-based individual tariffs, we propose the following business model of a community.

The income base to a community could be made up of a combination of:

1. Membership fees
2. Competitive-specific service usage revenues within the community
3. Service usage revenues generated from non-members
4. Possible premium income from members who select to cover themselves against specific service disruption

5. Flat fees from other communities
6. Contributions in kind (work, information, know-how, knowledge, innovation) by members

On the cost side, they include:

1. Costs of managing community memberships; but this cost does not bear significant marketing and publicity costs, so it will be far less than with today's public operators who often devote one third of their income to such marketing and CRM functions
2. Investments in infrastructures and possibly service access devices
3. Partial service creation expenses, possibly shared with community users or other communities
4. Service provisioning and operations expenses, with in some cases community members being member-employees
5. Flat fees to other communities
6. Last but not least, intellectual property right expenses for service creation and innovation, and from access to information or knowledge shared in the community

We estimate that the community management overhead share will be 25%; the community service creation or usage share will be 60%; and the transport plus access share (to the infrastructure owner) will be 15% of the total costs.

Supply and Demand Analysis

Based on the business model, we first analyze the supply and demand of the community-based services in general; and then put the analysis in the Chinese context.

The supply of services will be abundant, and the price will be low, driven not only by the deregulation and technology advances, but above all by the freedom to define, request, and bear a share of the risk around service and content creation. Still backbone transmission will be essential, as will be different authentication/roaming/settlement/digital right management functions, but it remains to be seen if traditional operators can offer competitive services in terms of flexibility, price, quality, and scalability to what some larger communities may do themselves. What should be kept in mind is that due to exploding traffic demand and competition driven by many community-clients, the revenue from pure transport or access will become minimal compared to the added value of personalized services.

The total demand will be large, as people can personalize their services according to their means and needs, and furthermore because community proliferation may multiply the effect. Compared to the situation with generic public services offered in limited numbers, used by very many, communities offer viable alternatives in terms of revenue and demand. The reason is that within a community, the previous two multiplicity factors are replaced by four:

1. Number of community members
2. Overlapping sub-communities that share some common interests but have some interests and service demands different from others
3. Number of specific services for and made by a sub-community
4. Number of common services to all members in the community

These four distributions allow the replacement of flat rates for all, by individual tariffs, subject to the condition that each community has simple but efficient digital rights management tools, network management and monitoring tools to be able in real-time to quantify equilibrium break-even tariffs (Pau, 2002). People will pay the amount of money and put in their individual contributions, exactly according to how they value the personalized service bundles offered or requested by them.

Two important characteristics of traditional Chinese culture are the emphasis on long-term perspective and collectivism (Hofstede, 2001). Since Confucius, the culture has stressed the enduring relationship with one's "in-group" at different levels from family to nation (Fei, 1992). This serves as a guarantee of reciprocal exchange to maintain the relationships, or "Guanxi" among members of a Chinese community. As a consequence, it discourages free riding of the community resources and makes collaboration and cooperation more appealing to Chinese people; Furthermore, the cultural environment leads to much more diverse communities than Western societies (Kluver & Powers, 1999). For example, the traditional "families and group" notions such as regionalism (xiangtu) and clan loyalties (zong-zu) are widely existing in both rural and urban areas (Wang, 2006). In addition to communities formed based on business, occupation, hobbies, and interests, it is common to find communities which are formed under a same origin, or under a same dialect. There are abundant communities. The service creation and provisioning mechanism of community-based individual tariffs can assist each community in having its own services based on the demands of its members provided their skills level is sufficient. But here the fantastic strengthening of the skill base in China and in some groups drives this into reality. Furthermore services creation, which has the largest proportion in the total service cost, can be linked to the affordability at community level. All these factors contribute to a flourish of mobile services. At the tariff level, the pricing settlement arrangement of individual tariffs makes services affordable to each individual member of various types of communities. Take the example of a family-based community: the membership fee will be very low

(close to zero), similarly within a rural village. But the differences lie in the fact that in a formally organized community, "such as in a village," affordability will be higher as set largely by users themselves in view of their social, economic, and information needs, which may result in non-zero membership fees. Similar analysis can be applied to other aspects of the pricing mechanism of the business model.

The previous analysis shows the potential for community-based individual tariffs in both the service aspect and the tariff aspect. It can be beneficial to the development of mobile services in China between now and 2030. For the less developed western provinces where the majority of people still do not have any mobile service, the concept and business model can help to create affordable services to assist fast diffusion in these areas. For the more developed eastern provinces where people are demanding more value-added services, the concept and business model can assist to achieve sustainable development by creating services that meet the diverse demands.

A real risk remains though in the combination of all or some of the following elements: physical network access coverage, availability of communications infrastructure supporting advanced services, and in the governance at payment intermediaries from banks to rural cooperatives. This last aspect may turn out to be a major stumbling block.

CASE ANALYSES

In this section, we provide analyses on two representative cases: the urban game communities and the rural communication communities. These two cases demonstrate that the concept and business model of community-based individual tariffs are directly relevant to the development of these distinct Chinese communities.

Case 1: Urban Game Communities

History, Background, and Stakeholders

Lianzhong (www.ourgame.com) is a company founded in 1998. It offers online and mobile gaming, which mainly include board games, card games, and arcade games. Many games are deeply rooted in Chinese culture in their traditional forms (e.g., Go, Chinese chess, Tractor) and therefore quickly gain acceptance in their electronic forms. Registered online members have reached 150 million, including more than 1 million paid (premium) members (2004). Registered mobile game members have reached 1 million, with active users of 130,000 per month (March 2006). By providing games and related services, Lianzhong had created one of the largest Chinese game communities.

Besides the big community, a lot of sub-communities have been created in Lianzhong. Lianzhong uses the concept "Jianghu" to provide a fictional environment for the sub-communities. Jianghu is a unique term originated from classical Chinese "wuxia" stories. Metaphorically, Jianghu means wild, romantic, or unsettled region where legends take place. People inside Jianghu are usually associated to different "Menpai" to learn martial arts as well as other knowledge to fight for their own interests. The concepts of Jianghu and Menpai provide a perfect setting for sub-communities. There are over 7,300 sub-communities (in November 2006) that are formed on a different basis, which can be based on location, interests in games, or interests in other aspects such as poems, philosophy, Chinese literature, and so forth. Or some sub-communities are formed under catchy titles. An average sub-community has 600 members, and over 15% are paid premium members.

Deployment, Usage, and Prices

Software needs to be downloaded and installed for each specific game. Online (fixed) versions are free while mobile versions charge about CNY 5-8 per month.

A player needs to register and become a Lianzhong member to play the games. There are two types of memberships: non-paying free membership and paid premium membership. Basic game services are the same for both types of memberships. Lianzhong offers virtual game halls and virtual tables where members can meet and play games; "scores" can be earned with regard to different game results. Lianzhong keeps records of the scores as well as other game statistics for the members. While most of the basic game services are free of charge, Lianzhong also introduces some paid services/functions to let the members have enhanced experiences when playing games or staying in the Lianzhong game community. For example, a member can purchase equipment to be used in games (e.g., a tool that keeps track of all the cards that have been played). Or a member can pay for services offered outside the games (e.g., a service that sends virtual flowers to a player). Paid services are charged in the form of (Lianzhong) credits. Free members and premium members pay slightly different tariffs for a same service/function. The credits need to be bought using real money, which can be done via bank transfer or via mobile phones.

Premium members need to pay CNY 15/35/120, for 30/90/365 days of a premium membership. Premium members, when compared with (non-paying) free members, have certain privileges. For example, they have the privilege of entering a crowded game hall (the virtual game space); they can become a referee in a game. Also premium members are entitled to more services. For example, their names can be listed in the "Hall of

Fame" based on the scores that they have earned in the games while free members do not have this service. Furthermore, premium members can create sub-communities while free members can only choose to join an existing one. Some premium services are free while the others need to pay.

A sub-community can be created by a premium member, who pays a certain amount of credits to Lianzhong and becomes the leader of a sub-community. Membership fees of sub-communities are decided by sub-communities themselves, which can also be free. Lianzhong offers a Web page to each sub-community to advertise itself to potential new members. Each sub-community can have not only fixed game halls for its members to gather, but also a forum to discuss internal affairs. Besides the common game services offered by Lianzhong, each sub-community offers to members its own specific services. These services, most are free, can be game-specific training at different levels. Or they can be tournaments within and between sub-communities. The winners of the tournaments are often awarded with credits, which are either collected from members as registration fees for the tournament or donations from sub-community members. Organizers of a tournament have to submit detailed planning to Lianzhong. The tournament has to be checked and approved manually by a Lianzhong administrator (to prevent possible gambling and other illegal conducts). Actual matches are arranged by the organizers in their own game halls. Lianzhong collects the registration fee (credits) and donations for the tournament and later distributes the rewards to the winners automatically according to the results reported by the organizers. Lianzhong charges a transaction fee for every transfer of credits.

Direct Relevance of Individual Tariffs

The income base of Lianzhong is made up of:

1. (Premium) membership fees
2. Money paid by premium members and free members to buy Lianzhong credits, which are used to play games and to access services in Lianzhong game platform
3. Banner advertisement payments from advertisement companies
4. Payments from title sponsor of various game tournaments
5. Revenue sharing payments from operators for generated network traffic
6. Revenue sharing payments from operator for value added services (e.g., SMS-based VAS)

Lianzhong's costs include:

1. Investment on creating the game platform and developing new games
2. Investment on game servers
3. Service provisioning and operations expenses, which includes payment to staffs, hardware running and maintenance costs, software (game) upgrade costs, access bandwidth leasing cost to last-mile access infrastructure owner, and so forth
4. CRM cost on paid premium members

The introduction of paid (premium) membership/services since June 2000 has brought Lianzhong stable revenue streams. Membership fees once contributed to more than 50% of Lianzhong's income. The introduction of Jianghu and Menpai in 2001 brought Lianzhong faithful members: The virtual settings for the sub-communities suit especially well the Chinese culture and traditions from a game-playing perspective as well as from daily social-life perspective. Members are willing to spend money, contribute their time and efforts to create their own sub-community specific services, which serve as supplements to Lianzhong's common services. These community-created services benefit both the users and Lianzhong.

As a result, Lianzhong became one of the earliest Internet companies in China who made positive profit, that is, CNY 30 million in 2001. After that, it grew steadily until 2004. Due to managerial changes, Lianzhong introduced few new games and services in 2003. Similarly, not much effort was put into community building. As a result, Lianzhong's growth slowed down a great deal in terms of new members and revenues. At the same time, other companies like Shanda (www.snda.com) and Tencent (www.tencent.com) caught up. Lianzhong's profit became negative in several quarters between 2004 and 2005. In 2005, the company underwent a series of restructurings. It outsourced some of its services (e.g., banner advertisement); introduced a series of new games; and put more efforts into community building by introducing more community services for the sub-communities. Lianzhong recovered its growth at the end of 2005.

Case 2: Rural Communication Communities

History, Background, and Stakeholders

Sichuan is one of the poorest provinces in southwestern China, with a farming population of over 76%. Mountainous areas cover 90% of the province's territory. Due to the poor condition in telecommunication and transportation, much of the farm produce can not be traded in time and therefore loses its value. The economic development in Sichuan rural communities was lagging behind other provinces. Thus the "Tianfu agriculture community" was created in the spring of 2003 to help people in these rural communities to acquire and exchange information and to shake off poverty.

The Tianfu community was created as an initiative from Sichuan Unicom (a subsidiary of China Unicom). Thus the communication infrastructure was initially based on Sichuan Unicom's existing network resources, which includes mobile and wireless networks that cover about 70% of the areas in Sichuan province, and fixed networks with less coverage. A call center and a Web portal which integrates information

from several government supported agricultural-related Web sites were added as part of the core infrastructure. The Tianfu community also set up over 1,000 information collection sites all over the rural areas (December 2004). Each site is equipped with a computer and appointed with trained support staffs.

Deployment, Usage, and Prices

To join the Tianfu agriculture community, a user must be a Sichuan Unicom subscriber who owns a user terminal. User terminals can have diverse formats, including be mobile phones, pagers, or other special designed terminals attached to fixed telephone lines. There is no need to install additional software; services are tailored to each specific device. Users here can be an individual user, or a "collective user" when many individuals share one user terminal.

The membership fee of the agriculture community is CNY 2-5 per month, depending on different user terminals. Because of the immense size of the province (485,000 km^2), 21 local (sub)-communities were created based on prefecture-level cities. The purpose is to improve communication efficiency by having more location-dependent information. Members of the Tianfu community can choose to associate with one of the sub-communities during registration.

The Tianfu community provides dynamic content services to its members. There are 10 major categories of content such as local weather forecasts, farming techniques, trading information, plant disease diagnostics and treatment, and so forth. Members can choose more specific sub-categories according to their needs. The related information will be sent to the user terminals each day or in real-time (e.g., weather update). A user pays CNY 2-8 Yuan per month for each category he/she has selected. Some content is created by experts; some content is selected from the agricultural Web sites by the community service managers. Content is also created by the support staffs associated with the information sites; very often, these support staffs are members of the community themselves but are more experienced. They are willing to share their knowledge with other members so that the community as a whole will be better off. The content generated by support staffs can be very relevant and helpful to local people.

Each member can post their supply/demand information to the community Web site or can have their messages sent to user terminals in a specific geographical region. This can be done by dialling the call center and asking a support staff to carry out the operations (the member pays only the communication fee). Or the members can go to an information collection site and use the computer to log on to the community Web portal and go through several simplified steps, with or without the help of a support staff (free of charge now). The information will be checked by one of the Tianfu community administrators before being sent out. Furthermore, as a service to community members, they can also call a service hotline and receive professional assistance on their specific issues from agricultural experts. (The service is free of charge now and members need only pay the communication fee.)

Besides the 21 sub-communities at the prefecture level, other types of sub-communities can be formed among members. A sub-community can be formed based on a smaller geographical region, which can be as small as 3-5 closely located villages. Or it can be formed based on interests, for example a community of peach growers. Sub-communities are created with the help of a system administrator from the Tianfu community, who groups user terminals together in the system and assigns a group account (free of charge now and will be charged in a later phase). Each sub-community needs to appoint its own administrators for daily operations such as adding/deleting a sub-community member, sending information to community members, and so forth. The daily sub-community administration can be

done either via a Web portal, or it can be done by calling the service center and asking a support staff to perform the operations. Each sub-community is charged by Sichuan Unicom based on the communication services it has used (i.e., calls made and messages sent). Each sub-community has its own selection criterion of members; most sub-communities require zero membership fee. Each sub-community can have its own specific services and costs are shared among members. For example, in a peach grower sub-community, members can give their produce a same brand name when the produce meets a community-quality standard and sell them together at a better price. A rice growing community can arrange to share rice reapers among members during harvest seasons.

Furthermore, the content service from the Tianfu community can be offered to users outside the community. A Sichuan Unicom user can subscribe to the content service of the Tianfu community as a value-added service to his/her normal subscription. He/she does not need to register himself/herself to the Tianfu community. The subscription procedure is similar to that of a standard value-added service. Tariffs for content so far are the same as Tianfu community members.

DIRECT RELEVANCE OF INDIVIDUAL TARIFFS

The incomes of the Tianfu community include:

1. Membership fees
2. Subscription fees for content paid by members
3. Subscription fees for content paid by non-members
4. Administration fee for setting up sub-communities

The costs of the Tianfu community are:

1. Investment in information release sites
2. Investment in a call center and a Web portal
3. Running costs of the call center, the Web portal and the information sites, including payment to the support staffs
4. Payment for content generation to the experts (free of charge in the beginning)
5. Payment for "hotline" services to the experts (free of charge in the beginning)

The community does not need to invest in communication infrastructure, as it is owned and run by an operator. Regarding the communication tariffs, the Tianfu community also has a special agreement with Sichuan Unicom. Community members pay only for the communications that they have initiated; receiving calls or SMS is free of charge. The agreement was granted permission from the Sichuan government and Ministry of Information Industry (MII) as a special policy to help rural people.

The services from Tianfu community and sub-communities are partially provided and managed by the members themselves, thus the costs can be linked to the local economic development level and tariffs can be relatively low. This is especially true for collective users who share the cost of "one membership." Secondly, because the goal of the community is to help rural people to shake off poverty, it has been receiving special policies from the local government (e.g., the tariffs arrangement mentioned previously). The community has also been receiving a lot of contributions of this kind from the society, especially the help and advice from the experts. Thirdly, user terminals can take various formats from high end (mobile phones) to low end (pagers), which means the user can choose a suitable one based on his income. Due to the aforementioned reasons, the services are affordable to most of the rural people.

Created as a non-for-profit organization in the spring of 2003, the Tianfu community now has 1.2 million members (August 2006). The number is still expected to increase in the next few years. More than 3 million farmers have benefited directly from the services. As a result, the collective income of the agricultural community has increased and their living standard notably improved. The initiative also won the best e-business award in the World Summit on Information Society 2005. Sichuan Unicom also benefited from the agriculture community, the ARPU from the members are CNY 40. With 900,000 subscribers, the revenue is about CNY 360 million in 2005. Before the introduction of the agriculture community, this revenue was hardly possible. Furthermore, the churn rate of the community member is less than 3%, which is lower than the Unicom average. This implies a stable revenue stream in the coming years.

The two cases analyzed here bear the embryonic form of the community-based individual tariffs. In the Lianzhong case, although the number of services in each sub-community is limited, the service creation, provisioning, and tariffing already illustrate the concepts of community-based individual tariffs. The space for new services is huge. For example, a sub-community can introduce a location-based service that helps in locating a nearby sub-community member in order to play games together. The Tianfu case shows that community-based service creation and provision can meet precisely the demand of its members. It also demonstrates that the concepts and business model can address the affordability issues. Due to the limited functions of some user terminals (e.g., pagers), the services are mainly focused on information exchange via voices and messages. This can be improved when advanced terminals are widely deployed. Following such deployment, the rich set of agricultural-related services envisaged and described by Carrascal, Pau, and Reiner (1995) can be introduced.

TECHNICAL MEANS FOR ACHIEVING INDIVIDUAL TARIFFS

Already today technical means exist to achieve individual tariffs, and the wireless infrastructure industry together with the billing platform industries have shown that the complexity and costs involved in individual user multi-service and multiple access demand monitoring and control are surmountable. In the future, traffic and service aggregation and filtering solutions for communities coupled with service creation platforms will allow this to be done better and cheaper. Moreover, the demand for such solution will grow despite the legacy from existing platforms. Future means are derived from research and standards in the following fields, and include (among others):

Linking the Service Profile of the User to Adaptations in the Billing/rating System

At the time, the user identity, as recorded in the call data records, (with their time stamps and information or quality of service [QoS] labels) is linked to a service tariff table, the default public rates would be replaced for calculation purposes by the individual price list. The reason this is not implemented stems from:

1. The fact that billing systems are not scalable enough, nor powerful enough, nor have enough data storage to execute such operations in general
2. The fact that provisioning such facilities would be largely manual and too costly

Active Networks

Active networks allow network services to be programmed to some extent when the packet processing is distributed and performed by the routers along the path (or tree) to a destination (Information Society Technologies [IST], 2000). Senders at active nodes expecting special processing of their packets by the network simply address the packets to their destination, and routers recognize them as special packets and process them according to a given code. In this code may reside the label or tag representing the individual tariffs; and the code can be distributed to the active nodes at which individual tariffs are expected/executed. The propagation of the tariff labels can be either the node hierarchy control or via additional fields in the routing tables.

Flow Label

In the IPv6 protocol, and not in IPv4, a field is reserved in all packets for a label on each packet. Whereas some have proposed using this field for QoS features, some others (Pau, 2001) have proposed its use in part to encode the individual tariff information for this packet. This approach offers the added advantage over the previous approaches in that the packet to which the individual tariff code applies does not have to originate in some service node, but only in those who have the decoding key to this field. The key itself would be distributed via IPv6 protocol's IPSEC feature with PKE. A standard would have to be designed for the coding of this flow label, when used for this purpose. Some sceptics criticize the data overhead failing to note that the flow label must be carried anyway in IPv6 unless compression is used.

Session Initiation Protocol (SIP)

Session initiation protocol (SIP) is a text-based control protocol intended for creating, modifying, and terminating sessions with one or more participants, it is designed to be independent of the lower-layer transport protocol. In SIP, a P-Charging-Vector header (Garcia-Martin, Henrikson, & Mills, 2003) is defined to convey charging related information. The information inside the vector can be filled in and retrieved by multiple network entities during the establishment of a dialog or stand-alone transaction outside a dialog. In this way, charging related data processing is reduced to session-based.

DISCUSSION

The previous analysis is highly relevant to the cultural, technical, and sociological evolution in China—gradual adoption of community-based individual tariffs, first on connectivity, then on content and finally on interactions, will speed up the diffusion of mobile services for the majority of population in China. While various demands are met individually by user-set affordability, sustainable development in economic aspects can also be obtained. China can avoid the development model among competitive large operators offering a reduced set of standardized services. It can also avoid the competition in the form of price wars, which may hurt the end users in the long term.

One the other hand, the importance of the individual and community pricing scheme is furthermore compounded by the importance in China of regional dialect and regional traditions as well as community demographics.

Community-based individual tariffs can be fuelled by the very fast adoption of new technologies (WLAN, etc.), and cultural linked services (e.g., mobile gaming). Furthermore, the skills base in software for service creation is a prerequisite, the very presence of which in China may further accelerate this evolution.

REFERENCES

Carrascal, M. J., Pau, L. F., & Reiner, L. (1995). Knowledge and information transfer in agriculture using hypermedia: A system review. *Computers and Electronics in Agriculture, 12*(2), 83-119.

Fei, X. (1992). *From the soil: The foundations of Chinese society (A translation of Fei Xiatong's Xiangtu Zhongguo)* (G. Hamilton & W. Zheng, Trans.). Berkeley: University of California Press.

Frattasi, S., Fathi, H., Fitzek, F. H. P., Prasad, R., & Katz, M. D. (2006). Defining 4G technology from the user's perspective. *Network, IEEE, 20*(1), 35-41.

Garcia-Martin, M., Henrikson, E., & Mills, D. (2003). *Private header (P-Header) extensions to the session initiation protocol (SIP) for the 3rd-generation partnership project (3GPP)* (No. RFC 3455): The Internet Engineering Task Force.

Harrington, S., & Niehaus, G. R. (2003). *Risk management & insurance* (2nd ed.). Boston: McGraw-Hill.

Hofstede, G. H. (2001). *Culture's consequences: Comparing values, behaviors, institutions and organizations across nations* (2nd ed.). Thousand Oaks, CA: Sage.

Information Society Technologies (IST). (2000). *Global communication architecture and protocols for new QoS services over IPv6 networks (GCAP).* EU Framework 4 program.

International Telecommunications Union (ITU). (2005). *ITU Internet reports 2005: The Internet of things.* Geneva, Switzerland.

Kluver, R., & Powers, J. H. (1999). *Civic discourse, civil society, and Chinese communities.* Ablex.

Meij, S., & Pau, L.-F. (2006). Auctioning bulk mobile messages. *Computational Economics, 27,* 395-430.

Ministry of Information Industry of China. (2006). *Telecommunication industry development statistics 2005.* Beijing, China.

National Bureau of Statistics of China. (2005). *Statistical communiqué on the 2005 national economic and social development*. Beijing, China.

National Bureau of Statistics of China. (2006). *Monthly data (September): Post and telecommunication services*. Beijing, China: Author.

Odlyzko, A. M. (2001). Content is not king (Vol. 6): Retrieved July 20, 2007 from http://www.firstmonday.org/issues/issue6_2/odlyzko/

Pau, L.-F. (2001). *Note on proposal to IETF as to use of IPv6 flow label for tariffing and encoding thereof*. Ericsson Utvecklings AB.

Pau, L.-F. (2002). The communications and information economy: Issues, tariffs and economics research areas. *Journal of Economic Dynamics and Control, 26*(9-10), 1651-1675.

State Council of the People's Republic of China. (2000). *Regulations of the People's Republic of China on telecommunications*. Beijing, China.

Varoutas, D., Katsianis, D., Sphicopoulos, T., Stordahl, K., & Welling, I. (2006). On the economics of 3G mobile virtual network operators (MVNOs). *Wireless Personal Communications, 36*(2), 129-142.

Wang, T.-Y. (2006). Clan's function and its historical changes. *Journal of Shangrao Normal College, 25*(2), 50-53.

Wellman, B. (2001). Physical place and cyberplace: The rise of personalized networking. *International Journal of Urban and Regional Research, 25*(2), 227-252.

Xu, Y., Gong, M., & Thong, J. Y. L. (2006). Two tales of one service: User acceptance of short message service (SMS) in Hong Kong and China. *The journal of policy, regulation and strategy for telecommunications, 8*(1), 16-28.

Section IV
Issues in the Americas

Chapter XVIII
M–Commerce in the U.S. and China Retail Industry:
Business Models, Critical Success Factors (CSFs), and Case Studies

J. L. Zhang
Huazhong University of Science and Technology, China

J. Quan
Salisbury University, USA

Raymond Frost
Ohio University, USA

Sean McGann
Ohio University, USA

Michelle Ehlers
Ohio University, USA

Wayne Huang
Ohio University, USA

ABSTRACT

The main objective of this chapter is to investigate the current trends and future endeavors of mobile commerce (m-commerce) in the retail industry in an effort to establish a greater understanding and awareness of the technology, problems, business models, applications, and critical success factors (CSFs) it provides to consumer subscribers and business users. A case study is used to illustrate CSFs for successfully implementing m-commerce in organizations.

INTRODUCTION

The retail segment is expected to stimulate the future growth of m-commerce with the potential to purchase goods and services, exchange financial transactions, and establish home delivery in a matter of minutes with the touch of a button and no geographical limitations. This unique business opportunity, with all of its accomplishments, potential, and uncertainties is the central focus of this assessment.

In the emerging wireless arena, it is predicted that everyday consumers will take advantage of the improving mobile technology and mobile e-commerce developments in the retail industry with transactions such as "buying books from Amazon while waiting in the doctors' office, trading stocks from the golf course or ordering CD's of songs on the radio while stewing in traffic" (Davidson, 2002). "Looking at the current expansion in wireless applications, increasing numbers of mobile device subscribers imply that vast opportunities of potential revenue come from the m-commerce retail industry" (Varshney & Vetter, 2001).

It is amazing that the hype in conducting virtual business stemmed from the turning point the Internet has brought to our lives. "First, we have the World Wide Web that brought us informative information, then the introduction of electronic commerce, where consumers have

the convenience of staying home to shop and pay bills. Now, the wireless era has appeared with improved mobile technology and hence the increasing importance of mobile e-commerce, which is also known as m-commerce or wireless e-commerce" (Mennecke & Strader, 2001).

The advent of m-commerce and wireless Internet are thought to be the new wave in the communication industry, which holds a promising future for m-commerce in the retail industry. With the power in the palm of their hands, it is inevitable that mobile users will surpass the notion that mobile devices are solely for one-to-one communication and open doors to a new way of conducting retail business transactions. Figure 1 shows e-commerce/retail as one of the most popular wireless data applications.

This chapter is organized in a manner that will initially depict the credibility and relevance of the research provided throughout the paper, and will be followed by a background information section. The literature review is based on intense m-commerce and wireless company information that was prevalent in peer-reviewed journals, accredited articles, and esteemed conferences in the information technology community.

The background section includes a description of m-commerce and its functionality in the technology market. A framework is presented outlining m-commerce from both the users and

Figure 1. Uptake of wireless data applications, 2000-2005 (in millions) (Source: allNetDevices (www. epaynews.com/statistics/mcommstats.html))

Applications	2000	2001	2002	2003	2004	2005
Messaging	100	230	399	611	916	1268
E-Commerce/Retail	12	36	107	195	318	469
Financial services	50	123	225	357	529	798
Intranet (corporate)	5	20	49	81	129	206
Internet, WAP	4	20	85	183	344	614
Entertainment	61	143	246	372	554	775
Navigation	47	146	239	345	488	785

developers/providers perspective. Statistics are provided as a means of understanding the vast growth and impact that mobile communications has in the retail industry.

Once this introductory information is understood, then it is appropriate to delve into the additional characteristics and functions that thoroughly provide an effective appraisal of the mobile communications market. The remainder of the chapter concentrates on the main research questions to be answered: Is m-commerce widely adopted in other countries? What kinds of technology are enabling this spread of m-commerce in the retail industry? How do the CSFs for m-commerce affect the retail business? What are some different types of m-commerce applications? What does the future hold for m-commerce in the retail industry and beyond?

LITERATURE REVIEW

Literature on the topic of m-commerce is relatively scanty in comparison to the abundance of information on the subject of e-commerce. This is due in part to the fact that m-commerce is in its introductory stage of growth, and a number of literature reviews on the subject matter are still in the publication process. Nonetheless, the literature that was available for this chapter comes from a variety of reliable and highly respected sources in the field of information technology. The journal papers and articles that accounted for the majority of the literature review came from *Communication of the ACM, Harvard Business Review, Computer Networks, and IEEE Communications Magazine*. These journal sources were located by actively exploring business-oriented search engines such as Web of Science and Premier Business Source. The conference proceedings were the *Hawaii International Conference of Systems Science (HICSS)* and the *International Conference on Information Systems (ICIS)*.

In addition to journals and conferences, a number of relevant Internet articles and case studies were employed for a well-rounded approach to m-commerce resources.

Table 1 is included to portray an accurate account of the various research sources that were

Table 1. Summary of reviewed literature papers

Main Research Topic	Literature Review
Introduction including main objective	Davidson, 2002; Varshney and Vetter, Communication of the ACM, 2001; Mennecke and Strader, ICIS, 2001; Muller-Veerse, 2001; Varshney and Vetter, HICSS, 2001; Varshney and Vetter, IEEE, 2001; ClickZ, 2000; CTIA, 1999; Strategy Analytics, 2000; Haskin, 1999; Swatman, Krueger, and Van der Beek, 2006
Worldwide M-Commerce	Muller-Veerse, 2001; M-Commerce Security, 2002; Forbes Magazine, 2002; ResearchPortal.com 2002; Mylonakis, 2005; **Yang, 2005;** Soroor, 2006
CSF of M- and E-Commerce	Lee, 2001; Lindstrom, 2001; Seybold, 2002; E-Business Connection, 2002; KPMG's Nolan Norton Institute, 2000; Ung, 2001; Muller-Veerse, 2001; Tsalgatidou and Pitoura, Computer Networks, 2001; Little, NTT DoCoMo 2001; Christensen and Tedlow, Harvard Business Review, 2000; Andreas, et al., 2005: Chang, Hsieh and Chen, 2006; Huang, Trappey, and Yao, 2006, Scharl, Dickinger, and Murphy, 2005.
Application of M-Commerce	Muller-Veerse, 2001; Varshney and Vetter, IEEE Computer Society, 2002; Wang and Wang, 2005; **Wu and Wang, 2005;** Luarn and Lin, 2005; Awan, 2006; Ondrus and Pigneur, 2006.
Future direction of M- Commerce	PriceWaterhouseCoopers, 2001; Varshney and Vetter, HICSS, 2001; McDonough, 2002; Muller-Veerse, 2001; Naik and Almar, Wall Street Journal, 2002; Shim, Varshney, Dekleva, and Knoerzer, 2006; Ondrus and Pigneur, 2006; Fan and Poole, 2006.

investigated and implemented for each main topic in the chapter. Utilizing a number of different sources with authors' parallel viewpoints on the subject of m-commerce in the retail industry provides a solid foundation for the relevance and credibility of the material presented. Table 1 summarizes relevant literature papers being reviewed for this research.

Definition

According to Mennecke and Strader (2001) m-commerce is the involvement of the delivery of products and services via wireless technologies to enable e-commerce activities at any time or location. It is understood that the transaction that takes place by way of a mobile telecommunications network is for a monetary value. M-commerce represents a subset of all e-commerce transactions, both in business-to-consumer and business-to-business areas (Muller-Veerse, 2001). Understanding the description of m-commerce will be beneficial in determining the main functionality of m-commerce over e-commerce activities.

Functionality

The key utility of m-commerce over e-commerce businesses is the advantage of location functionality. This means that the communication device has the ability to track the physical environment where the user is positioned and provides this information in one way or another (Mennecke & Strader, 2001). In terms of the retail industry, these technological advancements can permit a user to receive information and conduct transactions anywhere and at anytime, while simultaneously a retail establishment can exploit the user as a moving target for advertisements, business promotions, cross selling, store directions, and giving store information based upon the location of the mobile user. Half of the battle to understanding m-commerce is in its functionality and the other half concerns who is involved in the m-commerce process.

Framework

In order to grasp an adequate comprehension of the roles involved in m-commerce, Varshney and Vetter (2001) have proposed a detailed framework outlining m-commerce, from both the users and the developers/providers perspective.

Figure 2 represents the framework for m-commerce, which allows companies to strategize and create m-commerce applications. The framework defines several functional layers, simplifying the design and development so that different parties, for instance, vendors, providers, designers, and so forth can address individual layers. By using this framework, a single entity is not forced to do everything to build m-commerce systems, but can build on the functionalities provided by others. The framework includes a user plane with four levels:

- **Applications.** Many new applications are becoming possible, and many existing e-commerce applications can be modified for a mobile environment.
- **User infrastructure.** The design of new m-commerce applications should consider the capabilities of the user infrastructure—the mobile device
- **Wireless middleware.** With its ability to hide the underlying network's details from applications while providing a uniform and easy-to-use interface, middleware is extremely important for developing new m-commerce applications.
- **Network infrastructure.** In m-commerce, service quality primarily depends on network resources and capabilities.

The framework also provides a developer/provider plane, which addresses the diverse needs and views of application developers, content providers, and service providers (Varshney & Vetter, 2001).

Figure 2. M-commerce framework

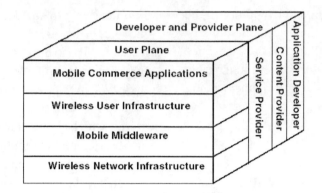

Understanding the framework is valuable if one is interested in the technical aspect of m-commerce, but the following statistics reinforce how m-commerce is penetrating the future of business in laymen's terms.

Statistics

The exponential growth of wireless and mobile networks has brought vast changes in mobile devices, middleware developments, standards and networking implementation, and user acceptance. More than 350 million mobile devices are in use worldwide, 80 million of them in the United States. (Clickz, 2000; CTIA, 1999; Varshney & Vetter, 2001)

According to GartnerGroup, a market research firm, by 2004 at least 40% of consumer-to-business e-commerce came from smart phones using the wireless application protocol (WAP). Some analysts think that the future of electronic retail transactions is going to be via wireless and mobile networks. Emerging developments in wireless and mobile networks will provide new avenues for growth, creating new opportunities in m-commerce. Thus far in the chapter the concentration has been centered on the background information about m-commerce.

ENABLING TECHNOLOGY OF M-COMMERCE

It is impossible to experience a significant growth in the m-commerce retail market throughout the world until the necessary enabling technologies are developed and installed. Tables 2 and 3, compliments of Muller-Veerse (2001); M-Commerce Security (2002); and Mobility Magazine (2002), identify various technology facilitators that have impacted the mobile communications industry and the distinctive characteristics for both network technologies and service technologies.

M-COMMERCE BUSINESS MODELS

M-commerce business models have a tendency to be based on the underlying principles of e-commerce models with their own contexts, situations, and circumstances. The success of a company in terms of its mobile business capacity revolves around its ability to fully implement the following seven essential steps to build an m-commerce business model by Tsalgatidou and Pitoura (2001):

Table 2. Network technologies

Technology Abbreviation (Muller-Veerse, 2001)	Technology Name (Muller-Veerse, 2001)	Characteristics (Muller-Veerse, 2001)	Additional Interesting Facts (M-Commerce Security, 2002)
GSM	Global system for mobile communications	■ Operates in the 900 MHz and the 1800 MHz frequency band ■ Prevailing mobile standard in Europe and most of Asia-Pacific region ■ Provides the critical mass to make it economically feasible to develop a large variety of innovative applications and services	■ GSM is used by more than 215 million people, representing 50% of the world's mobile phone users. ■ Europe and Asia is about 2 years ahead of the U.S. in m-commerce developments
HSCSD	High-speed circuit-switched data	■ Circuit switched protocol based on GSM ■ Able to transmit data up to four times the speed of the typical wireless transmission by using four radio channels simultaneously ■ Typical terminal is the mobile PC ■ Application usage is more like existing mobile connections to the Internet ■ Business travelers are the target market ■ Mainly used for speeding up existing mobile data applications	■ Nokia is currently the only one who can provide PCMCIA modem cards for HSCSD clients ■ It is likely that HSCSD will never reach widespread popularity except for connecting laptops to the Internet
GPRS	General packet radio service	■ Packet-switched wireless protocol that offers instant access to data networks ■ Permits bursts of 115 Kbit/s ■ Provides an "always on" connection between mobile terminal and the network ■ Allows full instant mobile access and enables a wide range of applications	■ GPRS provides a very important role in the adoption of mobile technology because it was packet-based
EDGE	Enhanced data rates for global evolution	■ Higher bandwidth version of GPRS permitting transmission speeds of up to 384 Kbit/s ■ Allow mobile operators to offer high-speed, mobile multimedia applications	■ EDGE is considered the interim data technology between GPRS and UMTS
3G	3rd Generation	■ Generic term for the next big step in mobile technology development ■ Goal is to have one network standard	■ The first 3rd generation network is operated by NTT DoCoMo in Japan

Table 3. Service technologies

Technology Abbreviation (Muller-Veerse, 2001)	Technology Name (Muller-Veerse, 2001)	Characteristics (Muller-Veerse, 2001)	Additional Interesting Facts
SMS	Short message service	<ul><li>Provides the ability to send and receive text messages to and from mobile phones</li><li>Many m-commerce applications will be initiated using SMS and WAP platform</li></ul>	<ul><li>Most popular non-voice service</li><li>90 percent of SMS messages are voice mail notifications and simple person-to-person messaging</li></ul> (*Mobility Magazine*, 2002)
USSD	Unstructured supplementary service data	<ul><li>Means of transmitting information via a GSM network</li><li>Offers real-time connection during session</li><li>Relevant for mobile stock-trading where confirmed info. transmission is needed</li></ul>	<ul><li>Mainly used for financial services, shopping and payment</li></ul> (M-Commerce Security, 2002)
CB	Cell broadcast	<ul><li>Designed for delivery of short messages to multiple mobile users within a region</li><li>Offers one-to-many service</li><li>Mass distribution media mainly for news</li></ul>	<ul><li>Might become a technology used in convergent offerings for E- communities or followers of content such as football, etc.</li></ul> (M-Commerce Security, 2002)
SAT	SIM application toolkit	<ul><li>Allows network operators to send applications over the air as SMS or Cell Broadcast message to update SIM card</li><li>Built in Java for client-server environment</li><li>Targets phones that do not yet fall into the smartphone category</li></ul>	<ul><li>Security is the key feature in SAT</li><li>Mobile banking has been the application with the strongest demand for SAT</li></ul> M-Commerce Security (2002)
WAP	Wireless application protocol	<ul><li>Open, global standard for mobile solutions, including connecting mobile terminals to the Internet</li><li>Permits interactive, real-time mobile service for smartphones and communicators</li><li>Goal is to bring companies from all segments of wireless industry value chain together to ensure product growth and interoperation</li></ul>	<ul><li>Potential for sophisticated services is far greater than other forms of messaging</li><li>WAP is user friendly and easy to use information on mobile phone</li></ul> (*Mobility Magazine*, 2002)
Web Clippings	Web clippings	<ul><li>Formats the delivery of web-based information to Palm devices via wireless communication devices</li></ul>	<ul><li>In the U.S., Web clipping is used on the 3Com's Palm handheld with 75 percent market share</li></ul> (M-Commerce Security, 2002)
MExE	Mobile station application execution environment	<ul><li>Provides a framework on mobile phones for executing operator or service application.</li></ul>	<ul><li>Incorporates java virtual machine into the mobile phone</li></ul> (M-Commerce Security, 2002)

1. Implement core competencies
2. Understand characteristics and constraints of mobile terminals and wireless networks
3. Realize the different context, situation, and circumstances that people use their mobile terminals
4. Utilize the Internet e-commerce models
5. Appreciate the market needs
6. Implement the other actors and players in the field
7. Model previous success stories

The first, second and third factors listed previously will be explained thoroughly in the next main section titled *Critical Success Factors (CSF) of Mobile and E-Commerce*. This section will look at the features of m-commerce that establish its competitive advantages, emphasize its unique business opportunities, and recognize the characteristics, such as personalization and localization, which create value-added services for the users.

The fourth factor talks about the Internet e-commerce models that are stated in the previous section, such as e-shop and e-auction. The fifth factor understands that in order to institute a successful m-commerce business model, it is neces-sary to understand the needs of the marketplace. Companies tend to fail when they do not adhere to the scope of business activities that consumers want and need in the virtual market. For instance, if there is not a great demand for the music industry at the time, then it is only reasonable to deduct that a company furnishing CDs is not going to be very profitable or vital in the market.

The sixth factor understands that depending on how a company uses the actors and players in an m-commerce transaction could alter the type of business model implemented. The following are the main players in an m-commerce transaction:

- **Customers:** The customer is mainly mobile. The place where the transaction is initiated can be different from the place where they receive service, pay, or complete the transaction.
- **Content providers:** Provides specific contents to a customer through a WAP gateway, which can be hosted at the mobile network operator (MNO) or through a portal that can be hosted at the operator's WAP server
- **Mobile portal:** Offers personalized and local services to customers to minimize the required navigation by the user.

Table 4. Adapted from Tsalgatidou and Pitoura (2001)

Business Model	Characteristics	Examples
Content providers	Offer contents by directly contacting customers or via mobile portals	Business is adapted by companies who develop some content for mobile handsets and they offer it to some software companies who subsequently offer it to mobile customers.
Mobile portals	Offer personalized and localized services to mobile customers	Hotel reservations, restaurant bookings, yellow pages, and so forth.
WAP gateway providers	Considered a special case of the ASPs Internet business model. The service they provide is the WAP gateway to service providers who do not want to invest in a WAP gateway.	N/A
Service providers	Provide services to customers either directly or via mobile portal or via a WAP gateway of another company or mobile operator	N/A

- **Mobile network operator:** The role of the operator is vital for the mobile e-commerce. It can vary from a simple mobile network to an intermediary, portal, or trusted third party (Tsalgatidou & Pitoura, 2001).

The seventh factor supports the notion that the greatest form of flattery is imitation. Due to the infancy of m-commerce and its supporting business propositions, one of the best ways to learn is from the previous successes or failures of similar companies. With the advantage of following, an organization working its way into the virtual marketplace has the opportunity to see what business models worked and imitate them or remodel the processes that did not work.

Once a retail business has mastered how to devise an outline for an m-commerce business model, the next step is to become fully aware of the different types of categories that can be implemented and utilized to meet the requirements of the business at hand.

M-commerce business models prevalent in the virtual marketplace are as follows (see Table 4).

CRITICAL SUCCESS FACTORS (CSF) OF MOBILE AND E-COMMERCE

When dealing with m-commerce implementations and business opportunities in the retail industry, it is necessary to understand that while m-commerce may be an extension of an Internet-based, e-commerce channel, there are a number of CSFs that are unique to the wireless retail business arena.

The CSFs section of the paper looks at the basic e-commerce success factors that have been the cornerstone for developing the success factors crucial to m-commerce in the retail industry. First, it is important to mention the e-commerce value creation model and strategies that are the foundation for m-commerce CSFs. Next, a number of CSFs are given and integrated to establish a unified E-tailing Critical Success Factor List acknowledging success factors for surviving today's m-commerce retail competition. In addition, the needs and benefits that are the key targets of m-commerce are explored to see how wireless communication is utilized in the retail industry. Finally, these CSFs and needs/benefits are tested by looking at real-life retail companies and seeing how some of them successfully manipulated m-commerce and those that failed to do so.

Value Creation Model

The following characteristics and Figure 3 are representations of how e-commerce success factors of conducting retail business in a virtual environment have been both a bridge between the business transformation process and a foundation for m-commerce (Lee, 2001):

- Design programs that take advantage of the Internet networks effects and other disruptive attributes to achieve a critical installed base of customers
- Leverage on a single set of digital assets to provide value across many different and disparate markets
- Build trust relationships with customers through e-business communities or e-webs to increase their cost of switching to other vendors
- Transform value propositions and organizational structures for enhanced value creation
- Generate synergy effects on e-commerce products and service offerings

Next, a number of critical success factors are given and integrated to establish a unified e-tailing Critical Success Factor List acknowledging success factors for surviving today's m-commerce retail competition

Figure 3. E-commerce value creation model (Lee, 2001)

Business transformation process	X ⟶ ⊔ ⟶ Y		
Goal	Reach the critical mass by building an installed base of customer	Improve transformation process efficiency	Create numerous innovative information services
Strategy	• Achieve demand-side economies of scale • Increase installed customer base's collective switching costs • Reduce customer's transaction costs (i.e., make it easy for customers to do business with you)	• Apply conventional management techniques (e.g., TQM, process re-engineering) to improve efficiency • Achieve supply-side economies of scale and scope to reduce supply-side switching costs (R&D and setup costs) • Lower transaction costs in the digital economy enables companies to design new organizational structures and to reconfigure value creation systems for enhanced value creation	• Transform value proposition by taking advantage of the demand-side economies of scope • Increase user's (or buyer's) switching costs by offering value across many different and disparate markets

E-Tailing Critical Success Factors

In the e-commerce and m-commerce retail industry there have been a multitude of literature reviews focusing on the implementation of CSFs. Given the abundant number of perspectives and arguments that authors propose, it is necessary to filter through these CSFs to establish a unified list for this chapter. A number of different CSFs will be recognized in this section and then the collective list will be proposed.

According to Lindstrom (2001), the following five attributes are the guidelines that retail companies operating via the Internet must implement in order to endure the competition. These factors may seem simple and like common sense, but all too often they are mismanaged, which explains why only five percent of the e-tailors survive.

- **The full story:** "As consumers, we like to know what we're buying. In the brick-and-mortar buying context, we can use all five senses when distinguishing between items and exercising our preferences—an essential facility when selecting anything we wear, eat or recline on" (Lindstrom, 2001). Unfortunately, e-tailors cannot compete with traditional stores in terms of sensory selling, but what they can do is offer answers to questions consumers might have, extensive high-tech pictures for every angle, information about items right at their fingertips, and other attention-getting techniques. E-tailors need to make up for their lack of sensory selling by helping consumers avoid any obstacles they may come across when shopping online.

- **Keep it simple:** Instead of bombarding consumers with confusing Web sites with limitless amounts of choices, try to keep the site simple and help consumers narrow down their options. "The golden rule is simplicity" (Lindstrom, 2001). Consumers are more impressed about an e-tailor that manages a small amount of inventory extremely well, rather than an abundance of items that are disorganized and overwhelming.

- **Clean up:** It is necessary for an e-tailing store to turn their inventory as fast as possible. "Where a brick-and-mortar store has an inventory turnover rate of six per year, a company like Amazon has to demonstrate a turnover rate of 18. Quick turnover saves money" (Lindstrom, 2001).
- **Be upfront, even about the bad news:** The main reason customers are hesitant to shop online is because of the cost of shipping, but there are ways to avoid losing a customer just be being honest and upfront with them from the start. First, do not ever hide the shipping/handling cost until the end of the transaction. It looks like the e-tailor is trying to be deceiving and this could damage the creditability and brand name of the company. Second, it is possible to include the shipping cost into the price of the product to shun the appearance of added costs.
- **Learn about your customers:** "One key advantage an e-tailor holds over a retailer is the Internet's capacity to enable monitoring of consumer behavior" (Lindstrom, 2001). For instance, Amazon utilizes one-on-one marketing tactics with consumers by tracking their buying trends in order to suggestively sell items on the consumer's next visit similar to previous purchases.

Another researcher, Seybold (2002) has "dissected the e-commerce operations of over 40 online companies and wrote detailed case studies of 16, including Amazon.com, developed this list of eight critical success factors for businesses that are thinking about jumping into e-commerce:

- Target the right customers
- Own the customer's total experience
- Streamline business processes that impact the customer

- Provide a 360-degree view of the customer relationship
- Let customers help themselves
- Help customers do their jobs
- Deliver personalized service
- Foster community

In addition, the E-Business Connection (2002) believes that an e-business model must satisfy the following critical factors:

- **Learn:** About the Internet and related technologies
- **Plan:** Create an e-business plan
- **Your home and neighbors:** Differentiate and position
- **A stamp on the Web:** Create an effective Web site
- **Visitors:** Create and maintain traffic
- **Orientation:** Customer-focused approach
- **Efficiency:** Improve internal processes
- **Security:** Ensure credibility to customers
- **Resources:** Financial support

Another e-commerce study conducted by KPMG's Nolan Norton Institute (2000) suggests the following critical success factors for implementation of e-commerce:

- Start with a needs-based strategy, not a technology solution—not all solutions satisfy all needs or customers; some segments will not use the Web
- Develop an e-commerce strategy that complements the corporate strategy
- Aggregate the disparate investments in e-commerce that are likely to be found in any organization
- Avoid layering costs onto the current distribution network—look for substitution between channels and manage these
- Choose your partners and skills carefully

- Integration across the entire organization is the key to large efficiency gains
- Transparency of implementation and changing process is important, both in terms of acceptance of the change and achieving the expected efficiency gains
- Develop a benefits register and measure your achievements against it

With all of these different CSFs bombarding and overwhelming the e-commerce and m-commerce playing field, it is necessary to incorporate the best factors from every source to institute a well-rounded and harmonized list of e-tailing CSFs.

CSF 1. Start with a Need-Based Strategy, Not Technology Strategy

The e-commerce system must solve a defined business problem or meet a need that can be addressed effectively with Internet technology. There should be a clear link to business objectives and clear benefits in using e-commerce. The e-commerce system must provide something that would not otherwise be available and add value to the business. Organizations must also note that not all technology solutions satisfy all needs or customers; some segments will not use the Web. (Ung, 2001 and Seybold, 2002)

CSF 2. Develop an E-Strategy that Compliments the Corporate Strategy

It is vital that companies define clear e-commerce objectives and be able to align their organization with their business designs and the e-commerce objectives derived from them. Companies should use electronic channels to complement and strength other existing channels. (E-Business Connection, 2002; Ung, 2001)

It is useless to establish an e-business model just for the sake of implementing technology if it does not serve a valid purpose with value-added benefits to the company and users.

CSF 3. Understand and Target the Right Customers

According to Lindstrom (2001), Seybold (2002), and Ung (2001), companies must focus their online effort to target directly to customers who are interested, responsive, and worthwhile, and in addition, the companies must understand the customer's expectations and needs. The m-commerce retail industry would be more effective and profitable if it narrowed its aim to concentrate more on retaining customers who are likely to buy, rather than wooing customers with no interest. The best way to retain customers is to understand and satisfy the user's expectations by listening to their needs and giving them advantages such as endless information at their fingertips and extensive high-tech pictures from every angle.

CSF 4. Use Resources Wisely

When engaging in the virtual marketplace, one of the most important aspects to success is to utilize the resources available to the company in terms of financing, partnerships, and skills. This could include "forming alliances with technology companies who are experts in this area and have the necessary skills and resources to maximize the chances of e-commerce success" (Ung, 2001) or reaching a hand out for government or private funding, financial institution assistance, or other resources available to maximize the potential for success (E-Business Connection, 2002).

CSF 5. Ensure Security and Credibility to Customers

Internet users will only become online shoppers when a company assures the users personal data and funds are secure during the online transaction. To reduce fears of credit card fraud and invasion of privacy, the e-business must provide the customer with a secure, stable and fraud-proof system for the transfer of payments and personal information. Successful transactions build trust and confidence between the company and the customer to foster future transactions and promote goodwill. (E-Business Connection, 2002)

CSF 6. Own a Customer's Total Experience

Lindstrom (2001) and Seybold (2002) believe that an e-business should be designed to elicit the maximum positive response from a customer. The idea is not to waste time or stir-up aggravation. Instead of bombarding consumers with confusing Web sites with limitless amounts of choices, try to keep the site simple and help consumers narrow down their options. "The golden rule is simplicity" (Lindstrom, 2001). Consumers are more impressed about an e-tailor that manages a small amount of inventory extremely well, rather than an abundance of items that are disorganized and overwhelming.

CSF 7. Deliver Personalized Service

One key advantage an e-tailor holds over a retailer is the Internet's capacity to enable monitoring of consumer behavior. (Lindstrom, 2001)

With the ability to utilize one-on-one marketing tactics, a company has the ability to deliver personalized services by tracking user's buying trends in order to suggestively sell items on the consumer's next visit, offering specialized choices or setting up customized accounts.

Real-Life Case Studies

The essential mission of retailing has always had four elements: getting the right product in the right place at the right price at the right time. The way that retailers fulfill that mission has changed as a result of a series of what is called disruptive technologies. A disruptive technology enables innovative companies to create new business models that alter the economics of their industry (Christensen & Tedlow, 2000). In retailing, the most significant disruption has been marked by the usage of e- and m-commerce. There are a number of companies that have taken advantage of these disruptive technological advancements in the retail industry, such as Priceline, MCI's 1-800 Music Now, and Ctrip.com, but only the strong survive. These online retail companies will be analyzed in terms of the functions they perform, the business models they operate, the use of the three streams of business models, and the way that they utilize the CSFs and needs/benefits of m-commerce.

Priceline

The main objectives of Priceline's foundation in the online retail industry revolves around how its technology and its Web site operations has changed the way that people conduct business in terms of shopping for airline tickets, hotels, mortgages, and even cars. Priceline's unique business models and the revolutionary nature of e-commerce is the way that businesses will be redesigned in the future.

The business model that Priceline operates is the e-auction. Priceline obtains its profitability and earns money by automating a bidding process over the Internet. It allows sellers and buyers to barter about the services they can provide and the services they are willing to pay for.

Priceline can measure the success of its business model by evaluating it in terms of the three streams of a business model. Priceline has accomplished *value* by acting as a community where buyers and sellers can access the bids that they want to satisfy the value-added service that they are looking for, for instance marketing name-brand products or flexible price readjustments. Priceline creates *revenue* by advertising, variable pricing strategies, retaining customers by adding value to their total auction experience, and teaming up with big name partners. The *logistics* exploited by Priceline is their unique business operations of providing the means to exchange value, whether it be through buying a product at the right price or selling the product to create common grounds for fulfilling business transactions via the Internet.

Priceline could not have gained all of its accomplishments in the retail industry if it had not been for implementing the CSFs and need/benefits that have established the realms of Priceline's business operations. Priceline has really mastered the art of *understanding and targeting the right customers, customer ownership,* and *convenience.*

"In the traditional model of commerce, a seller advertises a unit of supply in the marketplace at a specified price, and a buyer takes it or leaves it. Priceline turns that model around through customer ownership. They allow a buyer to advertise a unit of demand to a group of sellers. The sellers can then deride whether to fill that demand or not. In effect, we provide a mechanism for collecting and forwarding units of demand to interested sellers—a demand collection system" (Carr, 1999). Priceline permits customers, whether sellers or buyers, to control the ownership of their purchases. They ultimately decide who they want to buy into and the terms and conditions of the sale.

Sellers are attracted to Priceline's electronic business transactions and the convenience of remaining anonymous through the buying process which provides them with two beneficial aspects: brand shield (the brand is not eroded by advertising a lower price) and price shield (the established price is not advertised to the public so other can not demand that same price) (Carr, 1999). These convenience factors

make online shopping easy at Priceline because there are no sacrifices made by either party that could disrupt future selling engagements.

Priceline is familiar with the importance of *owning a customer's total experience and personalization* as well. They expose the truth about consumers in the marketplace: "consumers don't have brand loyalty, but rather brand preference. At a certain price, consumers will sacrifice their preference and switch brands. Priceline recognizes the truth by allowing consumers to disclose the price at which they'll trade of their brand preference" (Carr, 1999). Priceline exemplifies personalization by creating services that customize the end-user experience. They create an ideal tool for marketing product reconfigurations and price readjustments in a way that meets the needs of both the buyers and sellers.

Priceline is no stranger to using *localization, omnipresence, timeliness, and ensuring security and credibility to customers,* much like Amazon, to make shopping safe and available at anytime, anywhere. Priceline serves as a cornerstone for other companies to build off of in terms of its innovative electronic business transactions and exclusive business models.

MCI's 1-800 Music Now

Opening a business in the virtual marketplace is not a business model that all companies can transform into a successful and profitable venture. Some companies, such as MCI 1-800 Music Now, tried to withstand the fierce competition in the Internet e-commerce playing field, but due to poor utility of the CFSs in the m-commerce retail industry these companies were trampled by companies like Amazon, Priceline, and SkyGo.

MCI 1-800 Music Now was an extension of MCI that permitted both telephone and online ordering of CDs. Unfortunately, it was shut down in December 1996 after only operating for one year. The company failure was attributed to a plethora of factors, but the most significant reasons were "(1) weakness in the music industry that year, leading to deep discounting by retailers, (2) the site was not easy to use, consumers seemed to prefer ordering through traditional stores and (3) its prices were relatively high, compared once again to traditional stores" (Slade, Hale, & Dorr, 2002).

The business model that MCI failed to operate was the e-shop. MCI slacked in its ability to earn money due to the factors previously listed.

MCI 1-800 Music Now was unsuccessful at establishing a working business model based on the three streams of a business model. MCI failed to create a *value* proposition for a couple of reasons; they could not create a successful virtual community of music fanatics because at that period in time the music industry was very weak and there was no value-added services being offered, for the site was not easy to use, therefore consumers seemed to prefer ordering through traditional stores. In terms of *revenue*, if there are no value-added, market-making processes being presented to the customers, then it is impossible to be profitable. MCI slacked in its ability to earn money due to the fact that its prices were terribly inflated and customers preferred to shop at the brick-and-mortar stores. In terms of *logistics*, even if MCI had an ingenious idea of selling music via the Internet, with the other two business model streams failing, it is not viable to operate on logistics alone. With no added values to the customers and no source of revenue, it is clear that there is no need for logistics.

It is obvious from these factors that MCI disregarded the importance of applying the CSFs for mobile retail communication. MCI lacked *understanding and targeting the right customers, customer ownership,* and *personalization* because if they would have maintained one-to-one relationships with its customers or maintained a customer database of behaviors and buying trends, or in this case a lack thereof, then MCI would have realized the shortage of music purchasing and weakness in the music industry at that period of time.

MCI is also guilty of poor *convenience* because users complained about the complexity of the interfaces and the confusion in Web usability. They were ultimately turned off by the MCI site and turned to traditional retailers instead. The convenience of technology is supposed to make tasks easier and the quality of life better, but all MCI did was add to the pain of unpleasant activities.

In addition to these faults, MCI's prices were terribly inflated, which did not appeal to the customers who were interested in purchasing music at that time. The consumers figured they could save themselves the trouble of manipulating MCI's site and save money in traditional stores. The only thing MCI had going for itself was *localization*, but it was useless to promote using MCI anytime, anywhere when the customers could not even figure out how to utilize the site. Overall, the lack of CSF implementation lead MCI to deteriorate in the mobile and e-commerce retail industry.

Ctrip.com

Ctrip.com International Ltd. is a leading consolidator of hotel accommodations and airline tickets in China. The company's business philosophy defines its name CTRIP: Customer, Teamwork, Respect, Integrity, and Partner. The company aggregates information on hotels and flights and enables customers to make informed and cost-effective hotel and flight bookings. It acts as an agent in substantially all of the booking transactions. It targets primarily business and leisure travelers in China who do not travel in groups. These travelers form a traditionally under-served yet fast-growing segment of the China travel industry.

The company has experienced substantial growth since its inception in 1999 and has become one of the best-known travel brands in China. It is the largest consolidator of hotel accommodations in China in terms of the number of room nights booked. The company is also one of the leading consolidators of airline tickets in Beijing and Shanghai in terms of the number of airline tickets booked and sold. The company is the only airline ticket consolidator in China with a centralized reservation system and ticket fulfillment infrastructure covering all of the economically prosperous regions of China.

The company offers its services through an advanced transaction and service platform consisting of its centralized toll-free, 24-hour customer service center and bilingual Web sites.

The company's goal is to create long-term shareholder value by enhancing its position as a leading hotel and airline ticket consolidator in China. Going forward, the company intends to leverage the Ctrip brand to attract new travel suppliers and negotiate more favorable contractual terms with its existing suppliers; expand its hotel supplier network and room inventory; and expand air ticketing and other travel product offerings. The company also intends to pursue selective strategic acquisitions and expand into Hong Kong, Macau, and Taiwan.

The company is incorporated in the Cayman Islands and conducts substantially all of its operations in China. With its operational headquarters in Shanghai, it has branches in Beijing, Guangzhou, Shenzhen, and Hong Kong. The company also maintains a network of sales offices in about 30 cities in China.

The company went public on the Nasdaq under the symbol CTRP on December 9, 2003. It has experienced tremendous growth since then and its share price more than quadrupled. The success can be explained by the CSFs of m-commerce. Ctrip did not start with a technology strategy but a need-based strategy. As China's economy continues to expand, the disposable income of citizens grows as well. They will travel to more destinations than before. This creates a strong demand for a consolidator people can go to as a one-stop-shop and make all the travel arrangements.

The company understands that its customer base is mainly in the urban areas. Its marketing and advertising campaigns are targeted at customers in big cities. In addition to making reservations online, the company provides a national toll free number for both landline and mobile phones. It uses e-mail or short messages to remind customers of their reservations and destination weather information. When making a reservation, customers can elect to receive confirmation via e-mail or on cell phones. The advantage of having travel information on the mobile phone is that one does not have to get on the Internet to retrieve the information. Once a reservation is made, the company can deliver the ticket to a location selected by the customer in as little as two hours. Money is changes hands at this time. This ensures security and credibility to customers. It also avoids the following problem: most Chinese are not yet accustomed to using credit cards. Customers can pick up a reserved ticket at an airport, too. This is added convenience for people on-the-go. The company also provides very friendly customer service. The company leverages all the resources wisely. In addition, it has regular and VIP reward programs in which customers can earn points by purchasing air tickets and hotel rooms. The points allow customers to exchange various products ranging from free night stays to sneakers to Parker pens. All these allow the company to own a customer's total experience and deliver personalized services.

It is worth noting that Ctrip's model is not a big departure from other travel sites such as Expedia and Travelocity. What sets it apart from the rest is that the company realizes the different context, situation, and circumstances that people conduct their online activities. By modifying the existing e-commerce models according to the unique Chinese characteristics and adding mobile components, Ctrip is on the solid footing to create a successful business in China.

Now that we have assessed the importance of business models and the critical success factors in making a successful m-commerce company, let us look at some of the applications for mobility in the retail industry.

APPLICATIONS OF M-COMMERCE

A variety of consumer and business applications could be streamlined by integrating mobility. "Adding mobile devices as a choice of interface will create more easy online information access and data entry, extend the availability of key personnel for decision making and make purchasing more dynamic and real-time" (Muller-Veerse, 2001). The beginning of this section will explore consumer applications and later business applications will be revealed.

Consumer Applications

There are a number of consumer applications available relevant to finance, banking, security, information management, and entertainment, but in terms of the retail industry, the most pertinent aspects are mobile shopping, mobile advertising, and product location.

Mobile Shopping

Mobile extends your ability to make transactions across time and location and creates new transaction opportunities. (Muller-Veerse, 2001)

Mobile shopping offers customers to experience Internet e-commerce from one-button purchasing power. A number of the purchases that take place via m-commerce happen to be based on the customers behavior patterns, buying trends and other personalized data developed from digital databases. The following sections are subsets of mobile shopping styles.

Mobile Retail
There is a large space for e-retailers to become m-retailers when the personalization and location issues are well addressed. Books, CDs and groceries are often items, which the user knows well and where they need just a tool to make a purchase. *The purchase will be made when the user has spare time, independently of the shop opening hours and physical location.* (Muller-Veerse, 2001)

Mobile Ticketing
Mobile electronic purchase or reservations of tickets is one of the most compelling proposed services, because ticket reservation/purchase is hardly a pleasant experience. (Muller-Veerse, 2001)

In today's hectic world, it is more convenient for consumers looking forward to going to the movies or riding the train to purchase tickets with their mobile device while continuing to be mobile themselves.

Mobile Auctions
Mobile auctions are a perfect example of a traditional business model that adapted to the virtual world because bidders wanted to participate without the restriction and confinement of their PC. Wireless devices are ideal for auctions because users are not tied down for long periods of time in a stationary position and the user is able to be responsive in real time.

Mobile Reservations
Mobile reservations for restaurants and hotels has been one of the most featured applications in mobile commerce, since the prospect of easily finding a restaurant or hotel that suits personal taste and fits the relevant criteria at least is intuitively very appealing. (Muller- Veerse, 2001)

Mobile reservations are best for consumers that are constantly on the go and are too busy to locate restaurant directions, make reservations, or look at menus, because the mobile device will be able to track the user's location in relation to the desired destination and satisfy any of their requests.

Mobile Advertising

The conditions for one-to-one marketing are ideal using the mobile device. The mobile operator or service provider has not only all the demographic data of the subscriber, but also has been able to build a data profile with lots of information about that user's calling patterns. All of these factors combined would create the ultimate marketing tool. Since most business transactions are local and the mobile device is the only tool that enables location-dependant services so far, personalized advertising via mobile device seems to make sense. Vendors can reach their target customers when they are near the actual outlet (Muller-Veerse, 2001).

Product Location

Product location is an idyllic way for consumers to utilize mobile devices to find certain items in a particular area. Consumers clarify a specific good or service they are looking for and the mobile device will alleviate the need to visit several stores or comparison shop. It will provide a resulting list as well as the distance to the store from the user's location. Figure 3 is a visual aid representing product location.

Figure 4. Product location: A mobile user searches for a certain item by using wireless networks and a database. The user can specify the search range, or the database can assume the immediate neighborhood of the user's current location (Varshney & Vetter, 2002).

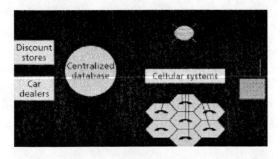

Business Applications

There are a number of business applications that would be more efficient by utilizing m-commerce as part of their business operation, such as distribution channels, job dispatching, supply chain management, and sales force automation, but in terms of the retail industry, the most prominent technological innovation is mobile inventory management.

Mobile Inventory Management

Mobile inventory management tracks the location of goods, services, and possibly even people so that providers can determine delivery times, thus improving customer service and enhancing a company's competitive edge. Mobile inventory management's success depends on cost, wireless infrastructure reliability, and users' level of comfort with new technology (Varshney & Vetter, 2002). Mobile inventory management could change the way retail companies operate by improving the theory of just-in-time service. By being able to locate a nearby truck carrying the desired inventory and delivering it to a particular store could eliminate inventory space and costs.

To summarize the previous applications of m-commerce in the retail industry, see Table 5.

FUTURE DIRECTION OF M-COMMERCE

Though it is impossible to predict the future of m-commerce in the retail industry, judging from the remarkable developments in the past and the current ever-changing technological advancements in wireless communication, it is an excellent indication that the future direction of m-commerce will be prosperous and full of new applications and uses.

Table 5. Adapted from Muller-Veerse (2001) and Varshney and Vetter (2002)

Consumer Application	Characteristics	Examples
Mobile shopping	The ability to make transactions across time and location from a mobile device	Amazon.com is an outlet for mobile shopping
Mobile retail	Using personalization and location as advantages to retail shopping	J.Crew.com is an outlet for mobile retail shopping
Mobile ticketing	The purchase of tickets or reservations via a mobile electronic device without having to wait in service lines	Purchase tickets for the local movie theater or play
Mobile auctions	Wireless devices are ideal for auctions because users are not tied down for long periods of time in a stationary position	Ebay.com is an outlet for mobile auctions
Mobile reservations	The ability to make restaurant reservations from a mobile device will be able to track the user's location in relation to the desired destination and satisfy any of their requests.	Make reservations to restaurants, such as Olive Garden, in a nearby location from a mobile device
Mobile advertising	Perfect for one-to-one marketing because it enables location-dependant services and personalized advertising via mobile device	SkyGo.com is a wireless advertiser targeting consumers on the move
Product location	Idyllic way for consumers to utilize mobile devices to find certain items in a particular area eliminating the need to visit several stores or comparison shop	A mobile user searches for a certain item by using wireless networks and a database.
Business Application	**Characteristics**	**Examples**
Mobile inventory management	Mobile inventory management tracks the location of goods and services so providers can determine delivery times, thus improving customer service and enhancing a company's competitive edge.	A business could track inventory status and location to provide just-in-time delivery, saving money and space.

First, it is important to review what we already know about m-commerce in the retail industry before we start to suspect what the future holds. Next, some of the main issues in m-commerce will be acknowledged as the predictions for the future of the retail industry. Finally, each of the issues will be discussed in detail. They are either in their infancy stages of design or are being developed in other countries of future introduction into the United States wireless retail arena.

Reflection of M-Commerce

Before we look into the future of m-commerce, it is helpful to summarize what is already understood about wireless technology in the retail industry. The chapter started by introducing that m-commerce means "the involvement of the delivery of products and services via wireless technologies to enable e-commerce activities at any time or location" and that the advantage of location is its main functionality over ordinary e-commerce.

M-commerce is exploding in the retail industry all over the world and this chapter has made clear what motives are driving the market growth, such as the mass market and the booming wire line Internet, and the expected sizing and forecast potential. The growth of m-commerce is made possible by the enabling network and service technologies like Global System for Mobile Communications (GSM) and short message service (SMS). Even though these technologies are remarkable in their applications, they are not flawless. The problems and concerns section outlined the obstacles, such as slow bandwidth and poor screen displays, of m-commerce in the retail industry.

This chapter covered the transformation process from a traditional brick-and-mortar retail company to a retail company operating in a digital economy. In addition, a framework was presented as a guideline in assisting retail companies in the jump to formulating e-commerce business models and strategies. Two different business models were investigated as well; e-commerce models, like e-shop, and m-commerce models, like mobile portals.

The CSFs section of the paper looked at the basic e-commerce success factors, for example, personalization and location that had been the cornerstone for developing the success factors crucial to m-commerce in the retail industry. This section mentioned the e-commerce value creation model, e-tailing competitive strategies, and real-life retail company case studies of companies such Amazon and Priceline. Understanding what contributes to the success of m-commerce is useful when implementing consumer and business applications, such as mobile shopping, mobile advertising, and mobile inventory management.

Now that we have reflected on some of the issues that we already know about m-commerce in the retail industry, it is time to concentrate on the main issues that are pertinent to the future direction of m-commerce.

Main Issues for the Future

This section is dedicated to giving an overview of the main issues significant to the future direction of m-commerce in the retail industry. There are a number of relevant issues that are prospects for the future of m-commerce, but in terms of issues specific to the retail industry, this chapter addresses technology developments, business application models, mobile content services, payment options, and dynamic information management.

Technology developments relates to the upcoming technological advancements, such as fourth generation (4G) language, that is utilized for increased bandwidth, greater storage, and advanced multimedia applications for the future development of mobile devices (PriceWaterhouseCoopers, 2001; Varshney & Vetter, 2001). Some of the upcoming *business application models* that

are projected for the future of mobile e-tailing are built on the concept of more personalized, location-based services such as location detectors and mobile grocery shopping (Eklund & Pessi, 2001; McDonough, 2002; PriceWaterhouseCoopers, 2001). In terms of *mobile content services,* the future of m-commerce in the retail industry holds a promising outlook for cell phones to be used as more than just a mobile conversation; instead it would be utilized for entertainment purposes (Eklund & Pessi, 2001; PriceWaterhouseCoopers, 2001). Another radical change in mobile e-tailing is the idea of new *payment options* such as using a mobile phone as a credit card or for vending machine transactions (PriceWaterhouseCoopers, 2001). *Dynamic information management* refers to the idea of using a mobile device as an e-wallet or to manage personal information such as credit cards, memberships, and frequent flyer miles (Muller-Veerse, 2001; Naik & Almar, 2002).

The following section will address these concepts significant to the future direction of m-commerce in the retail industry in further detail.

Description of the Main Issues for the Future

Technology Developments

In a perfect world, the greatest technological development would be to establish a global standard so that m-commerce could operate seamlessly across any boundary without complications or obstacles (Varshney & Vetter, 2001). Though this type of development is not feasible at this time, cellular companies and equipment suppliers are taking steps to improve the current state of mobile communication with a 4G language.

4G services are predicted to be launched by 2007. "4G services likely will be 50 times faster than 3G systems, with bandwidth approaching 100Mbps. That capacity will enable multimedia applications such as three-dimensional rendering and other virtual experiences. Features such as sophisticated knowledge management, speech recognition, and GPS will be standard, which implies that these mobile devices will have much greater storage and processing abilities than current devices without increased power consumption" (PriceWaterhouseCoopers, 2001).

Business Application Models

Business application models build upon location-based services to bring about more new personalized services. "Just as most people assume that wherever they go in the world, they will have access to the wired telephone network, in the not too long future, they will assume online, secure data connectivity. People no longer will need to wonder where a package, briefcase or even a pet or child is; rather they will be able to locate it from wherever they are quickly and easily" (PriceWaterhouseCoopers, 2001). These business applications could eventually save lives of people in danger.

There are a number of wireless shopping tools right around the corner that will be beneficial additions to mobile e-tailing. "In a short time, technology will let a business know when a mobile user is nearby, so the store can send a message advertising sales and offering special deals. For instance, when someone walks by the local grocery store, the store can immediately recognize the person as a mobile user and send a screen worth of special deals available that day" (McDonough, 2002).

Another shopping tool in the future will be to implement a location-based service called "A-GPS (assisted global positioning system) used for mobile phone "co-pilot" services. Instead of enabling stores to send advertisements to passersby, this type of wireless shopping tool helps mobile users find stores" (McDonough, 2002). This offers a navigation system implemented into mobile phones to assist users to find a destination with the aid of a digital map and directions.

An additional business application that could evolve in the near future is the ability to "send a

buying list of groceries to the local grocery store and collect them after work" (Eklund & Pessi, 2001). The future business functionality of m-commerce in the retail industry will be to harp on the concept of location-based services that are radically different from the way that consumers are used to shopping online.

Mobile Content Services

Mobile content services in the future will be able to "cope with movie clips and colorful displays" (Eklund & Pessi, 2001). Consumers would no longer treat a cell phone as just a tool for mobile conversation; instead it would be utilized for entertainment purposes. "Time spent on traveling and waiting could be converted into 'niche time,' a time for e-mailing, making online purchases and checking up information so that precious time will now be more fully used" (PriceWaterhouseCoopers, 2001).

Payment Options

One of the most radical changes in the future of m-commerce is the idea of different payment options using a wireless device. For instance, "technologies such as Bluetooth will be integrated into mobile data devices so that, perhaps when a consumer buys a beverage in the future, his or her mobile data device will work as a wallet, communicating via the public data network to get funds, store the funds on the handset and transfer the funds via Bluetooth to the vending machine" (PriceWaterhouseCoopers, 2001).

Another drastic payment option would be to utilize the mobile device as a credit card or debit card for transactions by allowing the billing be attached to the mobile phone bill.

Dynamic Information Management

The use of a mobile handset as a device to store extensive personal data will be enabled by the

Table 6.

Future Issues	Characteristics	Examples
Technology developments	Technological advancements that offer increased bandwidth, greater storage, and advanced multimedia applications	4G languages, knowledge management, speech recognition
Business application models	More personalized, location-based services	Location detectors and mobile grocery shopping
Mobile content services	Cell phones will be used as more than just a mobile conversation; instead it would be utilized for entertainment purposes	E-mailing, making online purchases, checking stocks
Payment options	Offers different payment options using a wireless device	Bluetooth, using a mobile phone as a credit card or for vending machine transactions
Dynamic information management	Idea of using a mobile device as an e-wallet or to manage personal information	Organizes credit cards, memberships, frequent flyer miles, personal information, passwords, and so forth all in one secure, consolidated location.

availability of multi-functional SIM cards. This will enable information such as club memberships, frequent flyer points, travel ticket and passes to be stored on the mobile device, alleviating 'fat wallet syndrome,' from which many people suffer today. (Muller-Veerse, 2001)

The idea of an e-wallet is not a new concept but for some reason has not been implemented in the United States. "The Europeans and Japanese use their mobile phones like electronic wallets, purchasing everything from newspapers, wine, parking space, soft drinks, bank transactions and rent payments. Thousands of Europeans and Japanese presently receive their sports scores and stock trading via mobile phones" (Naik & Almar, 2002, p. B1). In the future the U.S. will understand that it is redundant to carry both a wallet and a mobile handset, for the same personal information—credit card numbers, passwords, and so forth—could be stored in one secure, consolidated location.

To summarize the previous main issues for the future of m-commerce in the retail industry, see Table 6.

REFERENCES

Andreas, S., Andreou, A. S., Leonidou, C., Chrysostomou, C., Pitsillides, A., Samaras, G., et al. (2005). Key issues for the design and development of mobile commerce services and applications. *International Journal of Mobile Communications, 3*(3), 303-323.

Awan, I. (2006). Mobility management for m-commerce requests in wireless cellular networks *Information Systems Frontiers, 8*(4), 285-295.

Bibbo, L. (2002). *SkyGo study illustrates wireless advertising in an effective and direct response vehicle.* SkyGo, Inc. Retrieved October 23, 2002 from www.skygo.com

Brownlow, M. (2001, May 15). *M-Commerce.* Retrieved November 11, 2002, from www.ibizbasics.com

Carr, N. (1999). Redesigning business. *Harvard Business Review, 77*(6), 19.

Cellular Telecommunications Industry Association (CTIA). (1999, December). *CTIA semi-annual wireless industry survey.* Retrieved from Wow-com

Chang, S. E., Hsieh, Y. J., Chen, C. W., et al. (2006). Location-based services for tourism industry: An empirical study. *Lecture Notes in Computer Science, 4159,* 1144-1153.

Christensen, C., & Tedlow, R. (2000). Patterns of disruption in retailing. *Harvard Business Review, 78*(1), 42.

ClickZ Services.com (2000, February 25). *ClickZ Services.com unleashes a new Web portal for wireless Internet.* Retrieved from Wow-com

Davidson, P. (2002, July 9). Disinterest snags mobile commerce. *USA Today.* Retrieved September 12, 2002, from www.usatoday.com

E-Business Connection. (2002). *Critical success factors for e-business.* Retrieved November 12, 2002, from www.e-bc.ca

Eklund, S., & Pessi, K. (2001). *Exploring mobile e-commerce in geographical bound retailing.* Paper presented at the Hawaii International Conference on Systems Science (HICSS).

Fan, H. Y., & Poole, M. S. (2006). What is personalization? Perspectives on the design and implementation of personalization in information systems. *Journal Of Organizational Computing And Electronic Commerce, 16*(3-4), 179-202.

Hagel, J., & Singer, M. (1999). Unbundling the corporation. *Harvard Business Review, 77*(2), 133-141.

Haskin, D. (1999, November 3). *Analysts: Smart phones to lead e-commerce explosion.* allNet-Devices

Huang, C. J., Trappey, A. J. C., & Yao, Y. H. (2006). Developing an agent-based workflow management system for collaborative product design. *Industrial Management & Data Systems, 106*(5-6), 680-699.

Jutla, D., Bodorik, P., & Wang, Y. (1999). Developing Internet e-commerce benchmarks. *IEEE Computer, 24*(6), 475-493.

KPMG's Nolan Norton Institute. (2000). *Australia falling behind in e-commerce development.* Retrieved November 12, 2002, from www.cpaaustralia.com.au

Lee, C.-S. (2001). An analytical framework for evaluating ecommerce business models and strategies. *Internet Research—Electronic Networking Application and Policy, 11*(4), 349-359.

Lindstrom, M. (2001, May 17). *E-Tailing critical success factors.* Retrieved October 28, 2002, from www.clickz.com

Little, A. (2001). *Key success factors for m-commerce.* Retrieved November 12, 2002, from www.berlecon.de

Luarn, P., & Lin, H. H. (2005). Toward an understanding of the behavioral intention to use mobile banking. *Computers in Human Behavior, 21*(6), 873-891.

Mahadevan, B. (2000). Business models for Internet-based e-commerce: An anatomy. *California Management Review.*

Markides, C. (1999). A dynamic view of strategy. *Sloan Management Review, 40*(3), 55-63.

McDonough, D. (2002, June 24). *Wireless shopping tools of the future.* Retrieved November 11, 2002, from www.wirelessnewsfactor.com

M-Commerce Security. (2002). Retrieved September 12, 2002, from www.mli.hkkk.fi

Mennecke, B. E., & Strader, T. (2001). Where in the world does location matter? A framework for location based service in M-commerce. In *Proceedings of the International Conference on Information System (ICIS)* (pp. 450-455).

Mobility Magazine. (2002). *Feature—Content, 4*(1). Retrieved November 11, 2002, from www.mobility.com.au

Muller-Veerse, F. (2001). *Mobile commerce report.* Retrieved September 15, 2002, from www.durlacher.com

Mylonakis, J. (2005). Can mobile services facilitate commerce? Findings from the Greek telecommunications market. *International Journal of Mobile Communications, 2*(2), 188-198.

Naik, G., & Almar, L. (2002, August 18). M-Commerce: Mobile and multiplying. *Wall Street Journal*, p. B1.

Ondrus, J., & Pigneur, Y. (2006). Towards a holistic analysis of mobile payments: A multiple perspectives approach. *Electronic Commerce Research and Applications, 5*(3), 246-257.

PriceWaterhouseCoopers. (2001). *Mobile Internet: Unleashing the power of wireless. Technology Forecast 2001-2003* (pp. 40-41). Author.

Sackmann, S., Struker, J., & Accorsi, R. (2006). Personalization in privacy-aware highly dynamic systems. *Communications of the ACM, 49*(9), 32+.

Scharl, A., Dickinger, A., & Murphy, J. (2005). Diffusion and success factors of mobile marketing. *Electronic Commerce Research and Applications, 4*(2), 159-173,

Seybold, P. (2002). *E-Commerce success: Eight critical factors.* Retrieved November 12, 2002, from www.csref.org

Shim, J. P., Varshney, U., Dekleva, S., & Knoerzer, G. (2006). Mobile and wireless networks: Services, evolution and issues. *International Journal of Mobile Communications, 4*(4), 405-417.

Slade, K., Hale, & Dorr. (2002). *Success and failure of e-commerce in the US: Lessoned to be learned.* Retrieved October 23, 2002, from www.prac.org

Soroor, J. (2006). Models for financial services firms in developing countries based upon mobile commerce. *International Journal of Electronic Finance, 1*(2), 260-274.

Strategy Analytics. (2000, January 10). *Strategy analytics forecast $200 billion mobile commerce market by 2004.* Retrieved from Wow-com

Swatman, M. C., Krueger, C., & Van der Beek, K. (2006). The changing digital content landscape: An evaluation of e-business model development in European online news and music. *Internet Research, 16*(1), 53-80.

Thurm, S. (2000, December 11). *Don't hold your breath.* Retrieved November 11, 2002, from myphlip.pearsoncmg.com

Tsalgatidou, A., & Pitoura, E. (2001). Business models and transactions in mobile electronic commerce: Requirements and properties. *Computer Networks, 37,* 221-236.

Ung, K. (2001). *Critical success factors for the implementation of mobile commerce.* Unpublished thesis for the University of New South Wales, Australia.

Varshney, U., & Vetter, R. (2001). Emerging mobile and wireless networks. *Communications of the ACM, 43*(6), 73-81.

Varshney, U., & Vetter, R. (2001). *Mobile commerce: A new frontier.* Retrieved September 12, 2002, from www.computer.org

Varshney, U., & Vetter, R. (2001). A *framework for the emerging mobile commerce application.* Paper presented at the Hawaii International Conference of Systems Science (HICSS).

Wang, S., & Wang, H. (2005). A location-based business service model for mobile commerce. *International Journal of Mobile Communications, 3*(4), 339-349.

Wu, J. H., & Wang, S. C. (2005). What drives mobile commerce? An empirical evaluation of the revised technology acceptance model. *Source Information and Management, 42*(5), 719-729.

Yang, C. C. (2005). Exploring factors affecting the adoption of mobile commerce in Singapore. *Telematics and Informatics, 22*(3), 257-277.

APPENDIX A

Table A.1. Global M-Commerce Revenue Projections For 2009. Source: Juniper Research (http://www. juniperresearch.com/)

Category	Value (USD)
Global revenues	88 billion
Ticket purchases	39 billion
Phone-based retail POS sales	299 million

Table A.2. M-Commerce Revenues, 2001-2005. Source: Transaction Magazine (http://www.transactionmagazine.com/)

Research Entity (USD billion)	2001	2002	2003	2004	2005
Datamonitor (2000)	1.5	3.5	5.0	7.5	8.5
Forrester Research (2000)	1.0	2.5	7.5	14.0	22.0
Durlacher (realistic/interpreted)	3.0	3.5	5.1	10.0	19.0
Frost and Sullivan (1999)	8.0	10.0	15.0	19.0	24.0
Consult Hyperion (7 countries, 2001)	2.5	3.5	4.5	5.5	7.5
Jupiter Research (2000)	1.0	2.0	3.0	5.0	8.0

APPENDIX B: WORLDWIDE M-COMMERCE

Table B. 1. Prepaid Subscribers in World Regions, 2001 - 2004. Source: EMC (http://www.emc-database.com/)

Region	2001	2002	2003	2004
EMEA	258,1	320,9	375,6	427,6
Asia Pacific	27,7	40,7	55,4	71,3
Greater China	55,4	93,4	119,2	156,8
North America	12,5	15,7	18,4	20,3
South America	63,2	86,1	109,7	133
Worldwide	416,2	556,8	678,3	809

Table B. 2. Global Internet and Wireless Users, 2001, 2004, and 2007. Source: eMarketer (http://www. emarketer.com/)

Subscribers	2001	2004	2007
Internet users (millions)	533	945	1,460
Wireless Internet users as % of all Internet users	16	41.5	56.8

Table B.3. Percentage of Wireless Web Users by Region, 1998-2002. Source: Forbes Magazine (http://www.forbes.com/)

Region (millions)	1998	1999	2000	2001	2002
Europe	-	7	20	62	130
US	9	19	40	62	80
Japan	9	17	20	30	50

Table B.4. Worldwide Awareness, Usage, and Intent to Use Mobile Cash. Source: AT Kearney (http://www.atkearney.com/)

Region	Awareness	Current Usage	Intent To Use
Worldwide	40%	2%	44%
Japan	49%	2%	50%
Europe	44%	1%	46%
US	22%	0%	38%
Rest of Asia	38%	4%	43%

Table B. 5. US Mobile Commerce Revenues, 2001 - 2007

Year	Total (USD)
2001	127 million
2002	616 million
2003	2.1 billion
2004	5.7 billion
2005	13.1 billion
2006	29.0 billion
2007	58.4 billion

APPENDIX C: E-COMMERCE BUSINESS PROCESSES AND TRANSACTIONS

Business Process	Business Transaction	Description
Retail (External)	Buy	Customer clicks buy button on commerce server interface. The buy transaction is complex for goods that can be electronically delivered.
	Shopping Cart	Customer adds order line to temporary electronic order including quantity, item description etc. via a button click
	Payment	Customer selects a method of payment option from the commerce server interface. Some personal payment information may be required at this point such as credit card number
	Order Status	Customer tracks order through partner web sites. Most commonly, delivery sites such as Fedex and UPS are used to support this function
	Customer Registrat-ion	New customer provides personal information such as name and mailing address OR an existing customer is recalled from the customer database
Retail (Internal)	Credit check	A request is electronically transmitted to a third party finance company, e.g. a bank, and some authorization indicator is returned electronically
	E-broker contact	Access to the partnering Extranet e-broker's online databases is made. If the e-broker can supply our needs then procurement processing starts i.e. purchase order is generated and electronically transmitted
	Supplier contact	Access to the partnering Extranet suppliers' online databases for a sales district is made. Comparison of lowest prices, and delivery time windows may be optimized electronically thereby facilitating the determination of the order's suppliers
	Order Confirm	Sends order confirmation to the Customer either via web page or email
	Delivery	The supplier initiates delivery of goods directly to our customer. The supplier provides our business with a tracking number that is associated with our internal order number
	Customer History Update	Customer order is archived for future data mining purposes
Procurement	Issue Purchase Order (PO)	A Purchase order is automatically generated when a client buys and the e-business cannot supply out of its inventory (either because stock is not kept on hand, or for inventory replenishment)OR A PO is automatically generated if stock falls below a certain inventory threshold.
	Receipt confirm	Supplier issues electronic confirmation of PO receipt
	PO Status	Access supplier's web site to track PO status
	Item ships	Shipping note (tracking number) is electronically sent to the business
	Receipt of goods	If the e-business stocks goods, then goods received must be matched to the PO. Also triggers the creation of an accounts payable record
	Payment	Payment can be automatically generated within the credit conditions set out by the suppliers to optimize discounts

Chapter XIX
Perception of Mobile Technology Provision in Health Service

Astrid M. Oddershede
University of Santiago of Chile, Chile

Rolando A. Carrasco
University of Newcastle-upon-Tyne, UK

ABSTRACT

In this chapter the user interface perception and resources for mobile technology (MT) support in health care service activities is investigated. Most procedures oriented to provide better operation and quality of health service depend on the existing information and communication technology (ICT) system. However, the implementation of new technology competes with funding available for health institutions resources, hence introducing them is complex. The technical difficulties encountered in using ICT are: an inadequate physical infrastructure, quality of service (QoS) issues, and insufficient access by the user to the hardware/software communication infrastructure. A case study by multi-criteria approach was investigated involving three categories of hospitals in Chile and empirical data was collected comprising diverse health sector representatives. The main contribution is the proposed research decision-making model using the analytic hierarchy process (AHP) to evaluate and compare information and communications systems as fixed, wireless, or computer-assisted provisions for health-related activities and to identify the high priority dimensions in a health care service.

INTRODUCTION

A communications and IS provides an essential role for health-related activities. Most of the actions oriented to improve the operation and the quality of health service depend largely on the level of the information available and a communication system. The demand for health services increases each year by diverse demographic factors; (growth, immigration, ageing, etc.), cultural (greater information and expectations), technological (new therapeutic and diagnostic procedures), business (aggressive marketing of new procedures), professional (induced demand, preventive medicine), and organization (information deficiencies and management). The provision and management of services in the health sector implies processing enormous quantities of economic, welfare, clinical, and administrative data impossible to carry out by manual procedures (Oddershede, Carrasco, & Ontiveros, 2006). Nowadays, health centers are committed to putting into practice actions to facilitate clinical care activities, to satisfy professionals' aspirations, and citizen necessities.

The health communication system has changed from sending simple messages point by point, for example laboratory results, to the creation of virtual electronic records (Del Llano Señarís, 2003). The use of great data bases to collect health, social, and economic data, developed at a cost that is a fraction of the previous costs, means that files concerning the health of millions of people can be useful to predict future health requirements in a given population and to consequently assign and prioritize resources.

A demanding task of current innovation in health care processes is to improve the time to treatment in view of the fact that appropriate medical intervention immediately following an emergency or urgent situation significantly increases the chance of recovery for the patient.

The health sector has only recently had access to advanced ICT and there is confidence that modern ICT can progressively improve their performance, although a weak telecommunications infrastructure has shown in the past to be difficult to implement any plans, and therefore offer a good quality service to fulfil user expectations. (Suh, Suh, & Baek, 1994)

An emerging concept for health care provision is mobile health (m-health), which includes mobile computing, communications, and multimedia technologies in order to provide better access (Chan, 2000). This new evolutionary research area will provide new patterns for health care (Istepanian & Lacal, 2003). This will make available resources for both the health care professionals and patients with an efficient, secure, ubiquitous, and robust infrastructure coupled with tools for the assessment and management of patient health

status and the support of preventive programs. (Istepanian, Jovanov, & Zhang, 2004).

MT provides an easy information flow that has yet to be exploited to its full extent. Applications of mobile ICT and IS in health care can be recognized as both emerging and enabling technologies (Ammenwerth, Gräber, Herrmann, Bürkle, & König, 2003), which have been applied in several countries for either emergent care or general health care. For example, the variety of wireless technologies such as mobile computing, wireless networks and global positioning systems (GPS) have been applied to ambulance care in Sweden (Geier, 2003) and emergent trauma care in the Netherlands (Jan ten Duis, & Van der Werken, 2003). Relative information about the patient and the ambulance location can be transmitted to the hospital in real time. Then, the hospital can be well prepared for the arrival of the ambulance at any time. The challenge is to provide the appropriate treatment to the patient at the right time at the right hospital (Jan ten Duis, & Van der Werken, 2003). A system with secure mobile health care services has been tested in Finland, including health consulting, electronic prescription, and so forth. Authorized individuals can easily access the system via mobile devices such as mobile phones (Jelekäinen, 2004).

The recent expansion of mobile communications and computing technologies to support highly specialized health-related requirements has generated a substantial interest in understanding the factors related to accepting a suitable ICT and m-health system.

A number of researchers have studied user acceptance of MT and services including mobile Internet, text messaging, contact services, mobile payment, mobile gaming, and mobile parking services based on IS adoption models (e.g., Pedersen, 2002; Pedersen & Nysveen, 2003; Pedersen, Nysveen, & Thorbjørnsen, 2003). They found that usefulness and ease of use are very important factors to determine user acceptance of MT. Khalifa and Cheng (2002) found that exposure of an individual to mobile commerce (m-commerce) positively influences the individual's intention to adopt m-commerce.

However, at the present time, there are still some questions to be answered: How do contemporary health professionals accomplish their mission in highly mobile work settings? Does their distinct mode of mobility function characterize their work practices in relation to ICTs and MT? How will mobile communications change health care in the future? Will e-prescribing be adopted and accepted? How to integrate different mobile health care devices? What would be the areas of growth in the health care IT market?

Using as a reference frame other Latin American countries, the hospitals lack an appropriate methodology to measure the satisfaction of the patients. The used procedures are limited to fulfill the regulating minimum requirements. Nevertheless, the health subject has been a reason for controversy between the politicians, doctors, and other citizens of the countries (Alleyne, 1998). The mass media publish/broadcast innumerable articles that present the different opinions, impatience, and preoccupations of the population in relation to the health system (Colomer, 2002; Prados de Reyes & Peña Yánez, 2002). Doctors and health workers agree with these articles and suffer greater discontent, since they consider that the resources that are assigned to them are not sufficient to provide a good service. (Sosa, 2004).

The existing literature does not provide studies that reveal the derivations of MT value in health-related activities in terms of user satisfaction and user perception.

Nowadays, health systems are seen universally pressured to improve service as part of their activity. Therefore, the greatest challenge that health institutions face is to offer good service. However, measuring quality in health care systems involves competing goals to satisfy citizen necessities and to proportionate appropriate resources for health professionals aspirations (Oddershede &Carrasco, 2006). In order to provide a base for health service

it is necessary that health organizations recognize clearly their objectives; also, the activities and tasks that move toward the achievement of the stated objectives; the necessary resources and viability projects; the priorities, calendars, and responsibilities; and the mechanisms of control and evaluation of the fulfillment of the plan of its suitability. (Are we going well?)

Customer satisfaction is an important consideration of service quality in health care organizations. From a management perspective, customer/user (patient, doctors, clinical researchers, etc.) satisfaction with their health system is important for several reasons: satisfied users are more likely to keep a consistent relationship with a specific health service (Oddershede, Carrasco, & Ontiveros, 2006). Through detecting sources of users' dissatisfaction, an organization can deal with system weak points. User satisfaction dimension adds important information on system performance (Strasser & Davis, 1991).

Accordingly, developing a model that manages to capture the perception of satisfaction from the perspective of health-related representatives (patients, physicians, professionals, clinical researchers, etc.) towards the ICT system and MT services offered by the hospitals constitutes an important contribution (Weinstein, Toy, Sandbergea, et al., 2001).

Studies made by the Pan-American Organization of Health and 34 companies (Organización Panamericana de la salud, 2001) related to information on health in Latin America and the Caribbean show that the expectations in ITC, MT, and e-health is too high in many institutions.

In any health care system with limited resources, priorities for investment must be set on the basis of clear evidence of benefit to patients and good value for the money invested. The implementation of new technology competes for funding available to health services and simply introducing all of them is too expensive. This has encouraged the development of a case study that is being carried out in Chile to investigate user perception concerning ICT and MT in the health sector. The study is concerned with the quality of IT services and MT, as a means to evaluate service performance to assure customer satisfaction. The results will give information about user acceptance and will serve as a tool for medical decision makers in generating course of actions when facing critical and complex decisions, such as to create or change activities in budget allocations or for distributing resources according to user requirements.

The aim of this chapter is to provide a decision-making model to examine, compare, and evaluate user perception with regards to ICT and MT provision in health-related activities. The evaluation instrument will help health care users to identify the benefits of an adequate ICT network and to point out weaknesses in service. The information obtained will provide a starting point to analyze those ICT system parameters considered as more relevant for the QoS of ICT in a health care service. In addition, this pilot study will help the decision makers to decide on the courses of action required for resource distribution relative to user requirements.

This chapter describes the system in study and the methodology employed to reflect high priority dimensions concerning MT contributions to health-related activities. Empirical data was collected from three types of public and private hospitals in Chile that were categorized according to their ICT/MT system provision. The case study results will answer three important questions: Who are the main ICT/MT agents/users in health-related activities? What are the main activities they are involved in and now require ICT/MT support? Which is the more important ICT/MT system support for each activity?

A multi-criteria approach is applied for formulating a model by the use of the AHP (Alexander, Biggers, Forman, & Schleicher, 1990; Oddershede, Soto, & Carrasco, 2001; Saaty, 1990). The method developed by Saaty (1990) is used to state criteria and rank user preferences. The second section

describes the problem faced by the user in the case study. The third section introduces notions of the AHP approach to solve the problem. The fourth section presents a simplified hierarchical decision model based upon human expert's knowledge and experience. The results given in the fifth section generate information that is not currently available. In the final section, the conclusions are provided.

SYSTEM DESCRIPTION

This section outlines a framework for the development of a decision model regarding the MT and ICT system support for health-related activities.

Any health care requirement and service involves a wide range of participants, activities, resources, technologies, and others linked together within a complex environment.

The system under study is shown in Figure 1. Consider a user/consumer that has a health service requirement and there are many modus operandi that would, partially or totally, satisfy this demand. The user may desire many different features to improve the health care system. Moreover, the institutions will offer a variety of features showing differences in type, quality level, performance, cost, and so forth. These features rarely match with user requirements and depend on the user perspective. Many doubts need to be clarified such as, which features would be offered? Which feature would be more important for satisfying a particular service demanded? Which features are the users willing to ignore? How much are they willing to sacrifice? Hence, the goals surrounding a health care system are complex and conflicting since they are different in each subsystem. As a result, the user is faced with a decision-making process that is obliged to select a course of action within an uncertain environment.

Figure 1 illustrates the problems to be studied The set of criteria stated by the users to attain a specific goal, is denoted as $\vec{C} = \{c_1, c_2, ..., c_j, c_n\}$

Figure 1. The system model

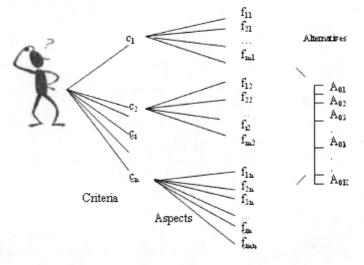

where c_j denotes the user perspective through criteria j and $j=1, 2\ldots n$ (i.e., cost, quality of service, etc.) .The system in study could be analyzed through n different criteria.

Taking into consideration that the actions surrounding health care requirements will rely to a greater extent on the ICT system provision, we can classify diverse users and an assortment of activities to be performed. Each activity, type of user, and necessity will have different requirements for ICT and MT provision.

For the implemented system in Figure 1 the criteria will be considered from the different MT and ICT system user perspectives. Also, for each criterion there are many features or aspects that could contribute to the achievement of the main goal stated according to the criteria considered. The set of elements related to each criteria is $\{(f_{11}, f_{21}, \ldots f_{ij}, \ldots f_{mn})\}$, for this case f_{ij} represents the element i that contributes to the achievement of the goal stated according to the criteria j and $i = 1,2\ldots\ldots\ldots m$.

The set of all the alternatives or course of action that will lead in some extent to the achievement to the goal expressed by the users is denoted by $\{(A_{01}, \ldots, A_{0K})\}$.

In Figure 1, if we consider physician perspective criteria, he/she will desire to have access to the best MT and ICT system to perform a particular assignment. Then the aspects could represent the activities related to meet the assignment. The alternatives would be the optional ICT and MT system that provides support to achieve a specific requirement. If we consider a patient's perspective their needs would be different, so we will have other criteria to take into consideration. An analogous assessment comprises the other system users.

In view of the fact that modern ICT and MT can support the operation and quality of health service, the participants want the system to offer attributes that make their commitment more efficient and satisfactory. Furthermore, the health center ICT system and MT system could rely on attributes that do not often agree with the user requirements (promptness, quality level, performance, cost, and others) for a specific assignment. At this point, the questions are related to the appropriate ICT and MT attributes for the execution of each activity. Do ICT and MT QoS have an effect on each activity? In what activity does the ICT support have more impact? Is MT important for health requirement and at what cost?

In general, from the ICT and MT QoS-user perspective, they expect fast, reliable, and easy access to online resources, applications, and Internet (databases, e-mails, voice, file transfer, browser, etc.). The QoS expectations will depend upon the area of use.

Having in mind that is not possible to satisfy the entire requirements simultaneously for all the participants, the omission of some characteristics in preference to others will occur (Oddershede, Carrasco, and Soto, 2005). Modeling under the existence of multiple conflicting objectives and subjective judgements becomes more complex (Birch & Gafni, 2003; Clemens, 1998). The multiple-objective decision method AHP is appropriate to help state criteria and rank user's preferences.

ANALYTIC HIERARCHY PROCESS APPROACH FOR MT SYSTEM PROVISION FOR HEALTH CARE

This section firstly reviews the AHP approach. Following the case study developed in the National Health Service in Chile the AHP process is applied to the collected data. It is initially structured to facilitate the empirical evaluation for obtaining results.

The Analytical Hierarchy Process Approach

The AHP engages decision makers in breaking down a decision into smaller parts, proceeding from the goal to criteria to sub-criteria down to the alternative courses of action. Decision makers then make simple pair-wise comparison judgements throughout the hierarchy to arrive at overall priorities for the alternatives. The decision problem may involve social, political, technical, and economic factors. This approach (Clemens, 1998; Saaty, 2001) provides the structure and the mathematics for helping decision makers make

Figure 2. A three level hierarchy

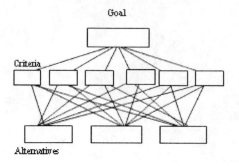

rational decisions. A rational decision is one which best achieves the multitude of objectives of the decision maker(s), (Claxton, Sculpher, & Drummond, 2002; Saaty, 1998). The three basic principles of AHP are:

1. **Hierarchy representation and decomposition:** A hierarchy is a representation of a complex problem in a multilevel structure whose first level is the goal followed successively by levels of factors, criteria, and sub criteria, and so on down to a bottom level of alternatives. Figure 2 shows an illustration of a simple three level hierarchy.

    The object of a hierarchy is to assess the impact of the elements of a higher level on those of a lower level or alternatively the contribution of elements in the lower level to the importance or fulfillment of the elements in the level above. This type of assessment is usually made by paired comparisons responding to an appropriately posed question eliciting the judgement. The mathematical definition of a hierarchy is given in Saaty's (2001) book.

2. **Priority discrimination and synthesis:** Setting priorities in a hierarchy requires that we perform measurements throughout the structure. We must then synthesize these measurements to obtain priorities for the bottom level alternatives. The AHP is based

Table 1. The fundamental scale

Importance Intensity	Definition
1	Equal importance
3	Moderate importance
5	Strong importance
7	Very strong or demonstrated importance
9	Extreme importance
Reciprocals of above	If activity i has one of the above nonzero numbers assigned to it when compared with activity j, then j has the reciprocal value when compared with i

on ranking activities in terms of relative ratio scales. In the paired comparison approach of the AHP, one estimates ratios by using a fundamental scale of absolute numbers in comparing two alternatives with respect to an attribute and one uses the smaller value as the unit for that attribute.

To estimate the larger one as a multiple of that unit, assign to it an absolute number from the fundamental scale. This process is done for every pair. Thus, instead of assigning two numbers w_i and w_j and forming the ratio w_i/w_j we assign a single number drawn from the fundamental 1-9 scale to represent the ratio $(w_i/w_j) : 1$. The absolute number from the scale is an approximation to the ratio w_i/w_j. The derived scale tells us what the w_i and w_j are. This is a central observation about the relative measurement approach of the AHP and the need of a fundamental scale. The scale of absolute values for judgments is shown in Table 1 (Saaty, 1998).

Let W be a matrix (1) whose row elements are ratios of the measurements w_i of each of n items with respect to all others.

$$W = \begin{bmatrix} w_1/w_1 & \dots & \dots & w_1/w_n \\ w_2/w_1 & & & w_2/w_n \\ \dots & & & \dots \\ w_n/w_1 & \dots & \dots & w_n/w_n \end{bmatrix} \quad (1)$$

A number in the matrix is a dominance judgment. A judgment of 1.0 means that two activities contribute equally to the objective or goal, a judgment of 3.0 means that experience and judgement slightly favor one activity over another or three times as much (if you are dealing with measurable), a judgment of 5.0 means that experience and judgement strongly favor one activity over another, a judgment of 7 means that activity is strongly favored over another; its dominance is demonstrated in practice and 9.0 means that the evidence favoring one activity over another is of the highest possible order of affirmation (nine times as much). The elements should be grouped into homogeneous clusters so that it is not necessary to use a number larger than 9. In this way, we can interpret all ratios as absolute numbers or dominance units.

3. **Logical consistency:** The AHP provides guidelines for a test of consistency of judgments to ensure that elements are grouped logically and ranked consistently according to a logical criterion. In order to achieve logical consistency it helps to make sure items are grouped into clusters of similar ideas or objects are grouped according to some form of homogeneity.

An inconsistency ratio is calculated for each set of judgments. Inconsistency follows the transitive property, for example, if you were to say that A > B, and B > C, then say that C > A, you would have been inconsistent. The Inconsistency Index, not ratio, is calculated for each node (and its cluster of children), and multiplied by the priority of the node, and summed over the entire model. A similar calculation is done for the Inconsistency Index for random judgments. The *overall inconsistency ratio* is the ratio of these two weighted sums. It has been shown that for any matrix small perturbations in the entries imply similar perturbations in the eigenvalues; thus the eigenvalue problem for the inconsistent case is:

$$Aw = \lambda_{max} w \qquad (2)$$

where the vector w is the eigenvector corresponding to the maximum eigenvalue, λ_{max} which will be close to n (actually greater than or equal to n) and the other values of λ will be close to zero. The estimates of the weights for the activities can be found by normalizing the eigenvector corresponding to the largest eigenvalue in the previous matrix equation.

The closer λ_{max} is to n, the more consistent the judgments. Thus the difference, $(\lambda_{max}-n)$, can be used as a measure of inconsistency (this difference will be zero for perfect consistency). Instead of using this difference directly, Saaty (2001) defined a consistency index (CI) as: $(\lambda_{max}-n)/(n-1)$ since it represents the average of the remaining eigenvalues. In order to derive an accurate interpretation of either the difference or the consistency index, Saaty simulated a very large number of random pairwise comparisons for different size matrices, calculating the consistency indices, and arriving at an average consistency index for random judgments for each size matrix (Saaty, 1990). He then defined the consistency ratio as the ratio of the consistency index for a particular set of judgments to the average consistency index for random comparisons for a matrix of the same size. Since a set of perfectly consistent judgments produces a consistency index of 0, the consistency ratio will also be zero. A consistency ratio of 1 indicates consistency akin to that which would be achieved if judgments were made at random rather than intelligently. This ratio is called the inconsistency ratio, since the larger the value, the more inconsistent the judgments.

The consistency of a hierarchy is obtained by first taking sums of products of each consistency index, with the composite priority of its criterion. Then the ratio is formed from this number with the sums of the products of the random consistency index for the order matrix with the composite priority of its criterion (Saaty, 2001).

In general, the ratio should be in the neighborhood of 0.10 in order not to cause concern for needed improvements in the judgments. Too great a departure from the perfectly consistent value indicates a need to improve the judgments or to restructure the hierarchy.

THE CASE STUDY

A preliminary case study considering a number of public and private hospitals was carried out in Chile.

Health Care Service in Chile

Chile is a unitary state with a democratic government. The population considered for 2000 is of 15,211,308 inhabitants, 85% of which live in urban areas. The Chilean Health Service is organized as a mixed system including public and private health care institutions. It combines a scheme of social security with a system of insurances of competitive character. Nevertheless, these two components share a source of financing that is the obligatory contribution of the wage-earning workers (7% of its taxable rent), with a fixed-limit amount. The public expenditure is around $220 per capita. The public sector offers 196 public hospitals where 20 are of high complexity. In the private sector there are 19 complex hospitals and 216 clinics or hospitals of low and intermediate complexity (Organización Panamericana de la Salud, 2002). If we refer to the quality perceived through surveys of opinion the public sector users show that the dissatisfaction areas are concentrated on the patient-service relationship, deficient environment, and shortness of technology, while the private sector is dissatisfied with high expectations of the system and long delays in waiting rooms. The greatest challenge in the future consists of facing the demographic and epidemic changes. ICT and MT system development offers a crucial function to increase efficiency in health.

The Process

The system of Figure 1 involved three stages. The first stage is concerned with the identification of decisive factors and attributes that user/client (patient, physician, administrative staff, etc.) consider important in evaluating the quality of ICT and MT provision in health-related operations. This task will need to recognize the concerned participants (patient, physician, administrative staff, medical researchers, others.). Individually each participant will have different expectations about the health care system and possibly will desire many different characteristics to provide a health care system. Empirical data were collected from different types of hospitals and as a result, a large number of factors arose. The critical impacts of undertaking certain activities are identified. This practice allowed us to specify the criterion and to structure the problem situation. Once criteria and elements involved are identified, the next stage is to prioritize the different attributes by implementing a multiple criteria method. A comparison process is then carried out.

The main participants or agents are: the *patients* who demand prompt medical assistance, without delay, with precise, safe, and confidential information on their state of health. Moreover, they request updated information on therapeutic or preventive options; benefits and risks; efficiency of the services; and so forth. The *professionals* require the information on their patients, including that elaborated on by other professionals and corresponding to complementary tests, instantaneously and at the place of the attendance. In addition, they need to use management tools to deal with the information in order to reduce paper work. Furthermore, they need information that allows them to evaluate its effectiveness and to practice the clinical management that the administrator requests, that is, tools of revision and data processing on its own results and costs. The *research professionals* demand better access to the specialized bibliography, guides of clinical practice, protocols, and the opinion of other colleagues and the opportunity to value and to discuss this information to optimize their individual and collective practice. Finally, *administrative personnel* demand equipment and means for making their work more efficient (updated software for billing, sending test results, etc.).

For this study, potential and current ICT/MT system users were organized into four groups: (1) a group constituted by the *patients* who would demand a health care service, (2) another group conformed by the *clinical care professionals* (physician, nurses, paramedics, etc.), who would make use of ICT to deliver a health care service, (3) a group represented by those users who develop *medical research*, collecting disease statistics and/or investigate new drugs and new devices; and (4) a group that is integrated by users who perform the *administrative* activities: billing, products distribution, and inventory control.

Data were collected from three categories of private and public health centers and hospitals which differ in resources, complexity, and infrastructure. The hospitals were classified according to their MT and ICT network infrastructure and resources availability. The three categories consisted of a group of hospitals with well provided ICT support, the other group constituted of hospitals that rely on scarce ICT support to perform its activities, and another group with intermediate ICT resources.

A team of experts consisted of representatives

from each of the three categories of health center and hospitals, six from a metropolitan region and three rural hospitals. The group of participants from each hospital includes users of the four groups indicated previously (patients, clinic care professionals, medical research, administrative personnel).The total number of participants adds up to 480 and their ages ranged from 20 to 70 years old.

When criteria, factors, and the main representatives or agents are stated, a hierarchical structure incorporating quantitative and qualitative variables and their relationships identifying critical categories at each level Guidance was obtained through the judgments issued by the opinion poll.

This allows the implementation of an evaluation method to rank the different factors and elements considered in the hierarchy based on the agent's judgements. A comparison process is carried out derived from criteria and user preferences to prioritize MT and ICT system support to health-related activities. The experts' judgment was based on their own expertise and knowledge.

The final step involves applying the weights to the measured attributes of each activity to derive a ranking about the value of ICT support for each activity that would bring about a service improvement.

Structuring the Problem Situation

A three level hierarchical structure model has been designed. Each level has multiple nodes against which the alternatives on the next level are compared.

The first level is concerned with the global objective that needs to be obtained. For the situation studied, it is to identify the level of significance MT and ICT support is used in health-related activities.

The other levels and nodes represent the decision factors that have contributed to attain the goal.

Figure 3. Hierarchic structure

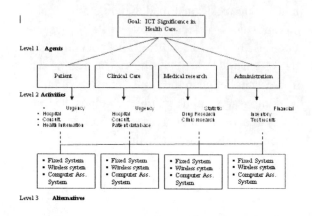

Table 2. The pairwise comparison process

Abbreviation	Definition
GOAL	ICT and MT system significance in health care.
Patient	Patient perspective criteria
Clinical care	Clinical perspective (physician, nurses, paramedics, etc.)
Medical research	Medical researcher group perspective
Administration	Administrative agent perspective
Urgency	Urgency-related activities to receive deliver health assistance
Hospitalization	Hospitalization and/or surgery requirement related activities
Consultant	Control and treatment related activities
Statistic	Statistic disease information and statistic records related activities
Drug research	Clinic and drug research and new devices investigation related activities
Financial	Administrative and financial activities
Inventory	Clinical needs distribution, supply, and inventory control actions related activities
Test results	Clinical and test result delivery, internal, and inter-institution communication activities
Fixed system	Includes fixed network communications (phones, fax, and office)
Wireless system	Wireless devices, mobile phones, radio communicationsdevices)
Computer-assisted system	Computer-assisted activities, Web, IP, browsing, and so forth

In this case the main agents are the users of the system and the main activities they perform.

The levels are represented as follows:

- Level 0 stand for the global objective indicated as, "ICT and MT system significance in Health care."
- Level 1 takes into consideration the implicated agents' perspective.
- Level 2 comprises the activities performed by the agents and would have an effect on each of them.
- Level 3 consists of the alternative ICT system that each activity depends on.

For this case, the alternative ICT systems were classified into four main groups labeled as: (1) fixed system (phone, fax, and office), (2) wireless system (wireless communications devices, mobile phones, radio communication devices), and (4) computer-assisted system (computer-assisted network communications).

Figure 3 shows the basic and initial structure, which is a realistic simplification of a larger developed hierarchy.

An expert panel consisted of representatives from each of the main agents involved within each type of hospital considered. The main agents involved with the ICT support in health-related services were the patient; the personnel and professionals implicated in giving clinic assistance; the clinical researchers; and the participants involved in administrative tasks within the hospital. The categorization for health institution was made according to the ICT resources each hospital could rely on.

In agreement with the described basic hierarchic structure, a pairwise comparison was made in such a way that all the elements of a same level are compared and weighed to each other. The expert panel went through the hierarchical structure and derived a priority matrix for each level. The numbers in the matrix of (1) express the intensity dominance of the criterion in the column heading over the criterion in the row heading. The ratio scale of the matrix is reciprocal, the numbers which are symmetric with respect to the diagonal are inverses of one another, $a_{ij} = 1 / a_{ji}$. In general, $n(n-1)/2$ comparisons are needed if n is the number of elements being compared in the triangle above the diagonal of ones.

The judgements are entered into the matrix in response to the question: How much more important is one criterion on the left side of the matrix when compared with another at the top of the matrix to justify a fair decision selection? When a criterion is compared with itself, it is of equal importance and is assigned the value 1. Once all the pairwise comparisons of the group are completed, a scale of relative priorities is derived from them.

The final step is a weighing process that uses these priorities to synthesize the overall importance of the criteria and alternatives. This

Table 3. Judgements and priorities of one of the members

Goal	Patient	Clinic Care	Administration	Medical research	**Priorities**
Patient	1	0.5	2	5	0.263
Clinic care		1	4	9	0.512
Administration			1	2	0.124
Medical research				1	0.101

procedure is repeated for all the elements of the structure, obtaining a ranking reflecting user perception. In addition, it was possible to detect inconsistencies when experts gave their judgments. Under such situations, it was necessary to review them until an acceptable index was obtained.

As an illustration, Table 3 shows the judgement and priorities that a single member of the expert team expressed with respect to ICT system importance from the perspective of the agents to develop their activity.

The numbers in Table 3 express the intensity dominance of the criterion in the column heading over the criterion in the row heading. From Table 3, the element in the second column and first row has an input of 0.5. It means that the expert considers that ICT is 2 times more important for a member of Clinic care group than for the patient. The value of 5 for the comparison of the ICT support for developing research activities versus the patient activities indicates that it is considered five times more important. The priorities are derived by applying the geometric mean and normalizing. The geometric average is the nth root of a product of n numbers.

To facilitate the calculations the method counts with the Expert choice (EC) software, which is a

Figure 4. Agents overall priority result and priorities for ICT alternatives

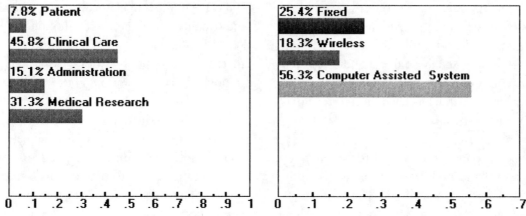

Figure 5. Fixed system vs. wireless system for each activity

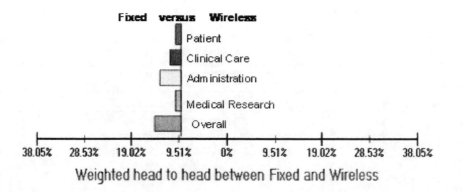

Figure 6. Priority results from the perspective of the patient

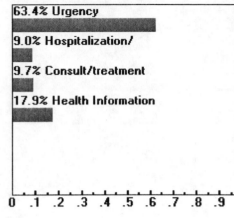

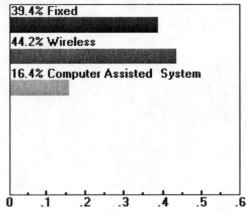

Figure 7. Fixed vs. wireless priority result for the patient's main activities

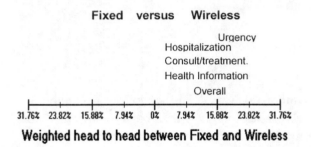

multi-objective decision support tool based on the AHP. This software is used to obtain the results (Saaty, 2003).

The Empirical Evaluation

Figure 4 shows it is possible to appreciate the overall prioritization results for the agents at level 1. It shows that globally, ICT support has a greater impact on supplying clinical care service. This service is concerned with the activities developed by the physician, nurses, and paramedics.

Taking into account that this is a global result for the present situation from Figure 4, it is possible to visualize that the support of the computer-assisted system (Internet, e-mails, Web, etc.) and the fixed network communications system have more significance for the participants, with a priority

of 56.3% and 25.4 % respectively.

The comparison in usage and importance for fixed and mobile is shown in Figure 5, where it can be seen that more importance is given to administrative activities, and a fixed system plays an essential role.

Patient Perspective

The results indicate that the importance of an ICT system for patient health-related activities are mainly concerned with an urgency service requirement as shown in Figure 6. Therefore, the importance of wireless and fixed network systems to satisfy its demand has the highest priority.

However if we observe the comparison of the fixed system vs. the wireless system it can be clearly seen that wireless system has greater relative importance from the perspective of the patient as seen in Figure 7.

Clinical Care Service Perspective

The overall result showed that the maximum importance regarding ICT and MT usage is to supply a clinical care service. The requirements related to urgency activities were the most relevant and there is a difference in the importance of the

Figure 8. Priority results for clinical care perspective

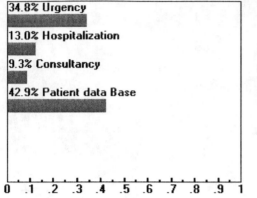

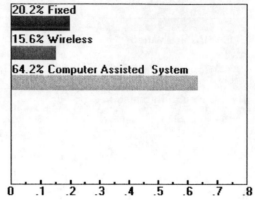

Figure 9. Fixed system vs. wireless from clinical care perspective

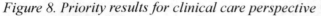

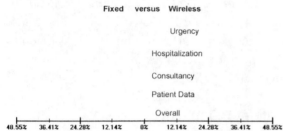

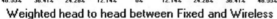

usage for providing service in hospitalization, control, and treatment activities. The different ICT systems are similar to the overall results as shown in Figure 8. The clinical care users found the computer-assisted system more useful for developing their tasks and did not consider the wireless system to be important.

Figure 10. Preferences for medical research agents

However, a comparison between fixed technology and wireless technology shown in Figure 9 shows that MT is more important when facing urgent situations.

Medical Research Perspective

The medical research requirement showed a strong interaction with database applications implying a preference to work with computer-assisted support as shown in Figure 10.

Administration Perspective

From this perspective, the clinical activities such as delivering tests and exams results within the institution or externally has the highest priority.

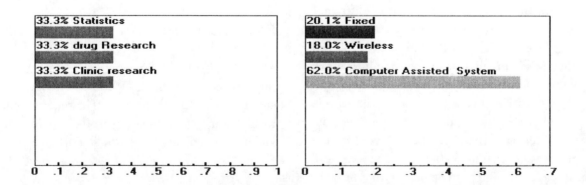

Table 4. Agents priority results

Agents	Activities	%	ICT system	%
Clinic care 45.8%	Urgency service	34.8	Fixed	20.2
		13.0	Wireless	15.6
	Hospital	9.3	Comp. assisted	64.2
	Consultant	42.9		
	Patient data base			
Medical research 31.3%	Statistics	33.3	Fixed	20.1
	Drug research	33.3	Wireless	18.0
	Clinic research	33.3	Comp. assisted	62.0
Administrative 15.1%	Financial	26.0	Fixed	45.1
	Test results	41.3	Wireless	13.8
	Inventory	32.7	Comp. assisted	41.2
Patient 7.8%	Urgency req.	63.4	Fixed	39.4
	Hospitalization	9.0	Wireless	44.2
	Consult, treatm.	9.7	Comp. assisted	16.4
	Health Inf	17.9		

Therefore, the use of a fixed network system (phone, fax, extensions, etc.) is of more importance.

The Overall Results

The process incorporated data from the agents to achieve an overall result as shown in Table 4. From the patient perspective the results indicated that patient priority is mainly concerned with urgency service requirement (63.4%). At the present time, the importance of having access to wireless technology was ranked in first place while fixed network systems were the second priority. Nevertheless, gradient sensitivity for patients with urgency requirement show that wireless technology tends to increase.

From a clinical care perspective, the priority is for the support from computer-related systems. However, gradient sensitivity indicated an increasing priority for wireless systems while fixed

Figure 11. Hierarchy sorted according to local and global priority results

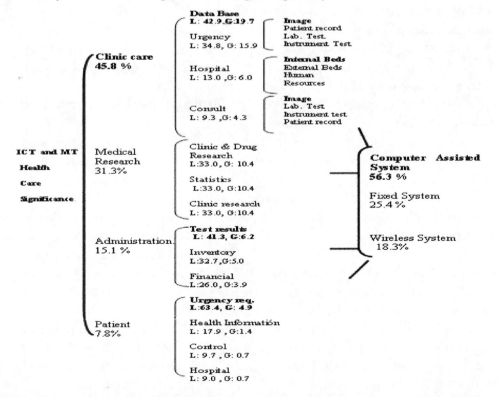

system priority declines. From an administration perspective, the activities such as delivering test and exams results within the institution or externally has the highest priority. A strong usage of fixed network systems (phone, fax, extensions, etc.) is observed. From a medical research perspective, there is a strong interaction with database applications implying an increasing demand for computer-assisted support.

Figure 11 shows the hierarchy structure already ranked with priorities sorted. The local (L) priority refers to the percentage of contribution of that aspect to attain the requirement of the decision factor considered in a superior level. The global (G) priority refers to the contribution of that decision factor to the formulated Goal.

Result Analysis and Observations

One of the goals of every nation should be to have a healthy population. This is fundamental to arrive at other national goals such as quality of life, prosperous economy, and national security. ICT and MT offer a crucial function to achieve these goals in an efficient and economical manner. Our goal was to empirically investigate the MT and ICT provision and acceptance by Chilean hospitals and to provide a methodology to analyze user preferences and its effect. Although the model is based on user preferences, it is perceived that the user looks for satisfaction rather than optimization, since there are so many goals to obtain and it is not possible to satisfy all of them simultaneously. The results obtained show it is possible to be aware of the level of importance of the ICT and MT system for each agent involved and their trends.

As mobile devices have become consumer products, and become available to increasing number of users of all ages, consideration to incorporate its use for the health care service has begun to gain importance in this country. In this context, the user expectations of the ICT and MT system are to assist in developing new sources of knowledge and research, to support health care management, and to help increase efficiency and QoS by improving the processes that rely on ICT and MT systems.

From Table 4 the importance of computer-assisted systems to develop their activities for all the participants can be seen. Fixed network systems are of the highest priority and even though the appeal for wireless systems is increasing there is still some apprehension about its use and further work needs to be carried out in this field. However, from the patients group, older participant's concerns were on obtaining information about their health status and urgency requirements (17.9% and 63.4% respectively). They also believed that the use of a wireless system was important (44.2%).

On the other hand, the results of the study indicated that mainly private hospitals are currently equipped with access to advanced networks and to develop e-business applications. From the physicians' point of view, they have a growing interest in adopting MT for customer applications and data records. Currently e-marketing applications in health care are low.

The application of AHP to the problem situation allows the integration of diverse judgements and preferences and therefore obtains an overall result.

Optional Actions Proposed

Based on the results, the next step is to propose optional actions and guidelines to follow with the purpose of managing efforts to obtain system improvement.

The options to follow are several and stick to the natural tendency to choose those factors that contribute with a greater relative weight to the objective. In this regard, three possible options for the result of the hierarchy are presented.

1. To consider each one of the decision factors of the first level with the same weight and the activities according to the ranking obtained. For the alternatives consider only the two high-priority ICT alternatives, concerning

Table 5. Optional path 1

User / Agent	Activities		ICT Alternatives
Clinical service	1 2 3	Urgency Hospital Control & treatment	• Computer-assisted system • Fix (phone, fax, etc.)
Medical research	1 2	Clinic & Drug Research Statistics	• Computer-assisted system • Fix (phone, fax, etc
Administration	1 2 3	Clinic activities (Test results) Inventory Financial	• Fix (phone, fax, etc.) • Computer-assisted system
Patient	1 2 3 4	Urgency Health information Control Hospital	• Wireless • Fix (phone, fax, etc.)

the particular agent to be developed as shown in Table 5.

2. Another option may be to develop all the agents proportional to the ranking and weights obtained and select two activities with higher priority. Then, choose the first rank alternative for each of the two activities considered.

3. Consider the whole structure and then pursue every activity in proportion and according to the ranking obtained.

These options could be related to the assignation of financial resources, governmental norms, technological resources, governmental support, and so forth.

CONCLUSION

The existence of competing goals in the health institution required a particular treatment, as the utilization of a scientific multi-criteria decision method. The AHP was beneficial for identifying the high-priority requirements of an ICT system in health-related activities, as well as, to be aware of MT acceptance and its importance in health care.

The process results identified the main ICT agents/users of health-related activities, the main activities they are involved in along with the ICT system support they require for each activity.

The AHP helped the experts and participants involved to identify the benefits of having an infrastructure of an adequate ICT network. From the results it can be seen that the user looks for satisfaction rather than optimization and they are willing to make a trade-off.

According to the resultant prioritization, efforts should be aimed at improving the QoS of the ICT system where they are most beneficial. It should be taken into account that the introduction of any new ICT could face problems not only in competing for financial support available but also possible interoperability problems. In this sense, the methodology helps to produce a distribution of the resources proportional to the users' requirement.

The attributes would be an improvement in clinical quality. The doctors, nurses, therapeutics, and other welfare personnel, provided with information to assist them, can offer a service of better quality in the clinical environment. Reduced costs: Health institutions can improve administrative efficiency and thus reduce medical costs. It can also achieve real savings in labor if the network is used for the execution of those manual tasks that are time consuming. This is particularly true in the traditional transactions among institutions such as derivations, claims, election, and even clinical data. Improved service to the client: The health institutions can use the ICT network system to provide faster ways for receiving/delivering health information through telephone aid links even between other organizations, to reduce the waiting period for hospital medical data and to avoid repetitive form filing.

This pilot study concludes that the combination of fixed and wireless networks can give the desired support to the patients when requiring information. The patients involved in the study gave a priority of 63.4% for urgency requirement and when selecting an alternative ICT system they revealed a 44.2% acceptance for wireless system, where a mobile device plays an important role for them. When comparing fixed vs. wireless systems they found it more important to use wireless technology for urgency requirements and for the rest of their activities they prefer a fixed system. For clinical care activities, computer-assisted technology support is preferable since professionals need relevant and timely information for better decisions. Comparing fixed vs. wireless systems for their normal activities they still preferred a reliable fixed system, however for urgency requirements the importance of having an efficient MT system is increasing.

When considering the factors for measuring quality in health care systems, the availability of the services and the need for ubiquitous access to integrated information are considered the most important.

The study revealed that mainly private hospitals have access to advanced network and Internet access; hence the technical basis for developing new applications is in position. Patient interest is online health information, e-health, and e-care services. Physicians would desire patients using MT and ICT applications where the support of MT is of increasing importance.

REFERENCES

Alexander, H. R., Biggers, J., Forman, E., & Schleicher, D. (1990). *Prioritization of civil tiltrotor technologies using the analytic hierarchy process.* Paper presented at the Third International Symposium on the Analytic Hierarchy Process, George Washington University, Washington, DC.

Alleyne, G. (1998). *Información en Salud para Todos.* En: Laerte PA, Castro E de. Biblioteca virtual en salud. Sao Paulo: OPS/OMS: pp 17-34.

Ammenwerth, E., Gräber, S., Herrmann, G., Bürkle, T., & König, J. (2003). Evaluation of health information systems problems and challenges. *International Journal of Medical Informatics, 71,* 125-135.

Birch, S., & Gafni, A. (2003). Inclusion of drugs in provincial drug benefit programs: Should *"reasonable decisions"* lead to uncontrolled growth in expenditures? *Canadian Medical Association Journal, 168,* 849-851.

Chan, A. T. S. (2000). WWW + smart card: Towards a mobile health care management system. *International Journal of Medical Informatics, 57,* 127-137.

Claxton, K., Sculpher, M., & Drummond, M. (2002). *A rational framework for decision making.* National Institute for Clinical Excellence (NICE). *Lancet, 360,* 711-715.

Clemens, R. T. (1998). *Making hard decisions: An introduction to decision analysis.* Duxbury Press Brooks/Cole publishing Company.

Colomer, M. J. (2002). El desafío es conseguir adaptar los hábitos y costumbres para afrontar la gestión clínica del presente Editorial. *Gestión Clínica y Sanitaria, 4,* 111-113.

Del Llano Señarís, J. E. (2003). Gestión Clínica y Sanitaria: ayudando a conciliar necesidad y escasez [Editorial]. *Gestión Clínica y Sanitaria,* 5(3-6), 2.

Geier, J. (2001, February 5). *Saving lives with roving LANs.* Retrieved from http://wireless.itworld. com/4246/NWW0205bgside/pfindex.html

Hikmet, N., & Chen, S. K. (2003). An investigation into low mail survey response rates of information technology users in health care organizations. *International Journal of Medical Informatics,* 72, 29-34.

Istepanian, R. S. H., Jovanov, E., & Zhang, Y. T. (2004). *M-Health: Beyond seamless mobility for global wireless healthcare connectivity* [Editorial]. *IEEE Transactions on Information Technology in Biomedicine,* 8(4), 405-412.

Istepanian, R. S. H., & Lacal, J. (2003, September 17-21). *Emerging mobile communication technologies for health: Some imperative notes on m-health.* In *Proceedings of the 25th. Annual International Conference of the IEEE Engineering in Medicine and Biology* (pp. 1414-1416). Cancun, Mexico.

Jan ten Duis, H., & Van der Werken, C. (2003). Trauma care systems in The Netherlands. *Injury—International Journal of the Care of the Injured,* 34(9), 722-727.

Jelekäinen, P. (2004). GSM–PKI solution enabling secure mobile communications. *International Journal of Medical Informatics,* 73, 317-320.

Khalifa, M., & Cheng, S. (2002). Adoption of Mobile Commerce: Role of Exposure, In *proceedings of the 35th Annual Hawaii International Conference on System Sciences* (HICSS'02)(Vol. 1, p. 46).

Mahmood, M. A., & Mann, G. J. (1993). Measuring the organizational impact of information technology investment: An exploratory study. *Journal of Management Information Systems,* 10, 1.

Oddershede, A., & Carrasco, R. A. (2006, November 5-8). *Analytic hierarchy process decision model for health institution selection: User perception.* Institute for Operations Research and the Management Sciences. Paper presented at the Informs Annual Meeting, Pittsburgh, PA.

Oddershede, A., Carrasco, R. A., & Ontiveros, B. (2006). Perception of wireless technology provision in health service using the analytic hierarchy process. *WSEAS Transactions on Communications,* 5(9), 1751-1757.

Oddershede, A., Carrasco, R. A., & Soto, I. (2005, October). Decision model for information and communications technology implications in health service: User perception. In *Proceedings of the SMDM 27th Annual Meeting, Society for Medical Decision Making Conference,* San Francisco, CA.

Oddershede, A., Soto I., & Carrasco, R. A. (2001, April). Analysis and prioritisation of Chilean mobile communication system. In *Proceedings of the International Conference on System Engineering, Communications and Information Technologies ICSECIT,* Punta Arenas, Chile.

Organización Panamericana de la salud. (2001). Marco general e institucional para el desarrollo de sistemas de información en servicios de Salud. Parte A. Organización Panamericana de la salud.

Organización Panamericana de la Salud, Programa de Organización y Gestión de Sistemas y Servicios de Salud, "Perfil del Sistema de Servicios de Salud, Chile",(1ra edición, marzo de (1999),(2da edición, enero de 2002)*,(Revisado, abril de 2002)

Pedersen, P., Nysveen, H., & Thorbjørnsen, H. (2003). *The adoption of mobile services: A cross service study. SNF-report no. 31/02.* Bergen, Norway: Foundation for Research in Economics and Business Administration.

Pederson, P. E. (2005). Adoption of mobile Internet services: An exploratory study of mobile commerce early adopters. *Journal of Organizational Computing and Electronic Commerce, 15*(3), 203-221.

Prados de Reyes, M., & Peña Yánez, M. C. (2002). *Sistemas de información hospitalarios: Organización y Gestión de Proyectos.* Ed.: Escuela Andaluza de Salud Pública, Granada.

Saaty, R. W. (2003). *Tutorial for building AHP hierarchical decision models.* Creative Decision Foundation.

Saaty, T. L. (1990). *Multicriteria decision making: The analytic hierarchy process, planning, priority setting, resource allocation.* RWS Publications.

Saaty, T. L. (2001). *Decision making for leaders.* Vol. II, AHP Series 315 pp., RWS Publications.

Saaty, T. L. (2006). *Fundamentals of decision making & priority theory* (2nd ed.). Vol. VI of the AHP series. RWS Publications.

Sonnenberg, F. A., & Beck, J. R. (1993). Markov models in medical decision making. *Medical Decision Making, 4,* 322-338.

Sosa, O El Nuevo Día, 10 de marzo de (2004), El País. *Boicot de aseguradoras a la contratación directa.*

Strasser, S., & Davis, R. M. (1991). *Measuring patients satisfaction for improved patient services.* Ann Arbor, MI: Health Care Administration Press.

Suh, C.-K., Suh, E.-H., & Baek, K. C. (1994). Prioritizing telecommunication for long range R&D planning. IEEE *Transactions on Engineering Management, 41*(3).

Weinstein, M. C. (2001). Toy E. L., Sandbergea, et al. Modelling for health care and other policy decisions: Uses, roles and validity. *Value Health, 4,* 348-361.

Chapter XX
The Implementation of Wi–Fi Technology in Higher Education in the United States

Xubin Cao
Southwestern University of Finance and Economics, China

Eric Y. Lu
Bloomsburg University of Pennsylvania, USA

Hongyan Ma
Salisbury University, USA

Istvan Molnar
Bloomsburg University of Pennsylvania, USA

ABSTRACT

This chapter discusses the implementation of Wireless Fidelity (Wi-Fi) technology in higher education in the United States. It includes Wi-Fi standards; security; the adoption of the technology; Wi-Fi to support teaching and learning; and challenges of Wi-Fi implementation. The last section is a case study of Wi-Fi at Ohio University. Although Wi-Fi technology has a great promise in higher education, institutions are still at the beginning stage of adoption. Institutions need to make a long-term sustainable plan to develop instructional strategies, successful practices, and technology supports to improve teaching and learning using Wi-Fi technology

INTRODUCTION

Wi-Fi technology uses a radio frequency that allows laptop or handheld computer users in the vicinity of a "hotspot" to access the Internet or corporate networks. It includes a set of product compatibility standards for wireless local area networks (WLAN) based on the IEEE 802.11 specifications

Wi-Fi technology can keep everyone connected all the time and is changing the way people work, play, travel, shop, and bank. Wi-Fi technology is also quickly gaining a foothold in many institutions as a means to achieve mobility and anywhere, anytime access. The Campus Computing Project 2003 (Green, 2003a, 2003b) conducted a national survey of IT in U.S. higher education (Figure 1). The survey data revealed that Wi-Fi technology became an increasingly important issue across all sectors of higher education and showed "dramatic gains over the past year regarding campus planning for the deployment of wireless networks" (Green, 2003a, p. 1). More than four-fifths (81%) of the campuses participating in the 2004 Campus Computing Survey reported having Wi-Fi technology, up from 77% in 2003, 68% in 2002 and 30% in 2000 (Table 1) (Green, 2002, 2003a, 2003b, 2004). "Higher education institutions feel the impact of computing freedom throughout their (Wi-Fi) operation" (Arabasz & Pirani, 2002).

Wi-Fi technology opens a new dimension of computer networking in higher education. Wi-Fi technology is affecting not just the classroom environment and technology access, but also the actual activities of learning and teaching. Students, faculty, and staff can open their laptops in classrooms, libraries, or outdoors to become connected. Wi-Fi technology "represents a user-centered shift, providing students and faculty with greater access than ever before" (EDUCAUSE Center for Applied Research [ECAR] Respondent Summary, 2002, p. 4).

In this chapter—the application of Wi-Fi technology in higher education in the United States—the authors first provide the general picture of Wi-Fi technology implementation in a global setting and in higher education in the

Figure 1. Percentage of wireless networks by sector, 2000-2003. From "Campus Computing, 2003," by K. C. Green, 2003b, p. 12. Retrieved September 6, 2004, from http://www.educause.edu/ir/library/pdf/EDU0324a.pdf

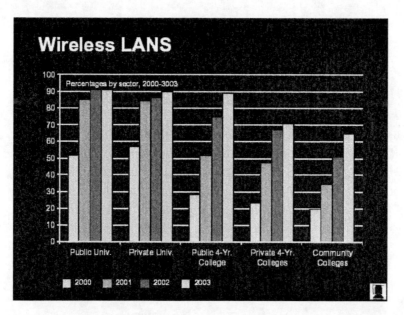

Table 1. Percentage of wireless networks on campus (Green, 2002, 2003a, 2003b, 2004)

Year	2004	2003	2002	2001	2000
Wireless LANs	81.1%	77.2%	67.9%	50.6%	29.6%
Full-campus wireless networks	19.8%	14.2%	10%	6.2%	3.8%

United States, and then the following aspects of Wi-Fi technology are examined: Wi-Fi standards, Wi-Fi security, the adoption of Wi-Fi, Wi-Fi to support teaching and learning, challenges of Wi-Fi implementation, and future trends and directions. The last section is a case study of Wi-Fi implementation at Ohio University.

THE GENERAL PICTURE OF Wi-Fi TECHNOLOGY

The General Picture of Wi-Fi Technology in a Global Setting

Wi-Fi technology can keep everyone connected all the time. It also makes obtaining information more convenient than ever. The wireless technology will change the way people work, play, and communicate. Wi-Fi technology is dramatically changing the degrees of interaction throughout the world, further creating a ubiquitous network society. According to JiWire (2006), a provider of hotspot information and services in South San Francisco, California, there are now more than 100,000 free and paid Wi-Fi hotspots in 128 countries. The number of hotspots worldwide has grown 87% between January 2005 and January 2006, up from 53,779 in 93 countries to 100,355 in 115 countries (Table 2).

The U.S. has more hotspots than any other country, 40,213 hotspots, as of July 31, 2006, followed by the UK, Germany, South Korea, and Japan. Seoul has the most hotspots of any city, with 2,056 as of July 31, 2006. The other top five hotspot cities are London, Tokyo, Taipei, and Paris (Table 2).

Businesses are realizing the value-added service by offering free or paid wireless services to attract customers. The consumers' embrace of Wi-Fi will push the worldwide market for Wi-Fi equipment to $3.4 billion in revenue in 2006, up from $2.5 billion in 2005, according to Dell'Oro's forecast (Lawson, 2006). By 2009, the overall Wi-Fi market, not including integrated routers, will reach $4.8 billion in revenue. Locations such as school campuses, airports, restaurants, hotels, general offices, and citywide deployment of Wi-Fi technology will benefit users.

Table 2. Wi-Fi hotspots, as of July 31, 2006 (JiWire, 2006)

Top 10 Countries		Top 10 Cities		Top 10 Location Types	
United States	40,213	Seoul	2,056	Hotel/Resort	31,217
United Kingdom	14,879	London	1,916	Restaurant	24,827
Germany	11,861	Tokyo	1,846	Cafe	15,596
South Korea	9,415	Taipei	1,785	Store/Shopping mall	14,816
Japan	6,249	Paris	1,140	Other	7,626
France	5,020	San Francisco	802	Pub	5,342
Taiwan	2,897	Berlin	796	Office Building	2,377
Australia	2,612	Daegu	787	Gas Station	1,927
Italy	2,539	Singapore	671	Airport	1,569
Netherlands	2,492	New York	660	Library	1,368

The General Picture of Wi-Fi Technology in Higher Education in the United States

Wi-Fi technology is also coming into prominence in higher education in the United States. There are a few studies on how higher education is implementing Wi-Fi technology. ECAR conducted quantitative and qualitative research for a comprehensive picture of wireless LAN activity (Arabasz & Pirani, 2002; Boggs, 2002; ECAR Respondent Summary, 2002). The research found that Wi-Fi technology "has moved from an interesting curiosity to an appealing technology alternative for potential users. Successful pilot projects are encouraging a growing number of institutions to move toward major wireless commitments" (ECAR Respondent Summary, 2002, p. 1). Many institutions began Wi-Fi as pilots for research and experimental purposes. They phased in their Wi-Fi projects, perhaps to test the technology in a controlled situation, handle a building's specific requirements, or to install it as funding allowed (Arabasz & Pirani, 2002).

For several years the Campus Computing Project (Green, 2002, 2003a, 2003b, 2004) has conducted annual national surveys of IT in U.S. higher education. The survey data revealed that Wi-Fi technology became an increasingly important issue across all sectors of higher education and showed "dramatic gains over the past year regarding campus planning for the deployment of wireless networks" (Green, 2003a). More than four-fifths (81.1%) of the institutions participating in the 2003 survey reported that they had Wi-Fi, compared to 77.2% in 2003, 67.9% in 2002, 50.6% in 2001, and 29.6% in 2000. One fifth (19.8%) of the institutions reported that full-campus Wi-Fi is running at their institutions as of fall 2004, compared to 14.2% in 2003, 10% in 2002, 6.2 % in 2001 and 3.8% in 2000 (Table 1). "Wireless is clearly exploding across college campuses, much as it is in the corporate and consumer sectors" (Green, 2003a).

Wi-Fi TECHNOLOGY STANDARDS

Before the description of the Wi-Fi technology standards, the method how Wi-Fi operates is described briefly. Wi-Fi uses electromagnetic waves to transmit and receive data without physical connection between an access point (AP) and end users. APs are the components that act as a bridge between the wired network and the Wi-Fi end users.

Wi-Fi transmits data radio waves at low gigahertz (GHz) range. The advantage of this is that the communication is tolerant of some noise and interference. It also allows many users to share a common frequency band and hence simultaneous transmission waves can travel on a single frequency (Bartel & DiLorenzo, 2003).

The range of the APs is directly proportional to Internet bandwidth speed. As distance between APs and users increases, the speed will decrease. Furthermore, the surrounding environment also matters. Building materials, floor plans, and types of interfering devices can significantly decrease availability and data rates.

Network interface cards (NICs), which are either inserted or already built into laptops, handheld devices, and other mobile devices are assigned a media access control (MAC) address that is recognized by the APs. The MAC controls the communication access between the user's device and the APs.

Wi-Fi technology is based on the IEEE 802.11 specifications. The most popular techniques are those defined by the b, a, and g amendments to the original standard; security was originally included and was later enhanced via the 802.11i amendment. Other standards in the family (c–f, h, j, n) are service enhancements and extensions or corrections to previous specifications. 802.11b was the first widely accepted wireless networking standard, followed (somewhat counter-intuitively) by 802.11a and 802.11g (Table 3).

802.11b Standard

Most of the Wi-Fi technology in place today is based on 802.11b standard, which became available on the market in 1999, providing a transmission rate up to 11 Mbps. Later, it has migrated to *direct sequence spread spectrum* (DSSS) modulation, providing security by "spreading" the signal over a range of frequencies. One drawback of 802.11b is that it lacks guaranteed quality of service (QoS[1]), a uniform performance standard. QoS will be an issue with applications such as voice and streaming audio/video (Gast, 2005).

802.11a Standard

802.11a is designed to replace 802.11b with improved performance. The 802.11a standard uses *orthogonal frequency division multiplex* (OFDM) modulation, which provides better performance in a multipath environment, such as a downtown business district, where buildings can reflect a signal and cause distortion. 802.11a promises improvements over 802.11b, including faster data rates (up to 54 Mbps) at the less congested 5 GHz frequency (Boggs et al., 2002).

However, the implementation of 802.11a has challenges. It is not backward-compatible with 802.11b. For the many institutions that have 802.11b in place, the replacement challenge could be significant. The end users who have already invested in 802.11b products will be required to replace their NICs and APs, resulting in costs to individuals and the institutions.

802.11g Standard

802.11g is an extension of 802.11b. Although it uses the same frequency band (2.4 GHz), it increases speed up to 22 Mbps (compared to 11 Mbps for 802.11b). The 802.11g has the advantage of being compatible with 802.11b. This advantage, however, will not be enough to overcome the timing, price, and performance of 802.11a (Boggs et al., 2002).

802.11b and 802.11g standards use the 2.4 GHz band. Because of this choice of frequency band, 802.11b and 802.11g equipment can incur interference from microwave ovens, cordless telephones, Bluetooth devices, and other appliances using this same band. The 802.11a standard uses the 5 GHz band and is therefore not affected by products operating on the 2.4 GHz band.

The solution for many institutions will be to use coexisting networks, at least for the short term. 802.11b and 802.11a can coexist with few

Table 3. Three versions of 802.11 standards (Boggs, Smolek, & Arabasz, 2002)

	802.11b	802.11a	802.11g
Frequency	2.4 GHz	5 GHz	2.4 GHz
Total bandwidth	11 Mbps (using DSSS)	54 Mbps (using OFDM)	22 Mbps (theoretically can reach 54 Mbps using OFDM)
Interference issues	2.4 GHz band increasingly congested (HomeRF, Bluetooth, microwaves, etc.)	Less congested band (5 GHz), so minimal interference	2.4 GHz band increasingly congested (same as 802.11b)
Power consumption	N/A	Double, but will decrease significantly	25% higher
QoS	Poor/undeveloped	Most flexible/potentially very good	Fair/untested
Cost	N/A	Double, but will decrease to about 25% higher	25%
Release data	1999	1999	2003

difficulties; there is no interference between them. The initially higher price of 802.11a equipment will also encourage a dual-solution approach. International Data Corporation (IDC), however, believes that ultimately 802.11a will become the dominant standard for the following reasons (Boggs et al., 2002):

- 802.11a has the higher bandwidth needed to support multi-site collaboration and videoconferencing as well as audio/video and streaming media. This is especially important as institutions look to support e-learning applications through Wi-Fi technology.
- Although power consumption is a short-term issue for 802.11a, IDC believes that developers will be able to reduce the power consumption of 802.11a products to levels approaching those for 802.11b products.
- 802.11g reached the market too late to be a serious contender.
- While 802.11a is costly today, the price of the technology should drop.

SECURITY OPTIONS FOR Wi-Fi TECHNOLOGY

Security is a critical part of Wi-Fi networks. According to ECAR's survey, security was the challenge most frequently mentioned by the respondents (69%). Wi-Fi security should address both the intruder who might have devious motives, as well as those who simply want free access. There are several options for Wi-Fi security.

Wired Equivalency Privacy (WEP) was the original encryption standard for wireless. As its name implies, this standard was intended to make wireless networks as secure as wired networks. Unfortunately, this never happened as flaws were quickly discovered and exploited. WEP comes in different key sizes. The common key lengths are currently 128- and 256-bit. The longer the better, as length increases the difficulty for "crackers."

While WEP can guard against simple unauthorized access, it is less effective against more determined security threats (Wi-Fi Alliance, 2003).

Wi-Fi Protected Access (WPA) is an early version of the 802.11i security standard that was developed by the Wi-Fi Alliance to replace WEP. The TKIP encryption algorithm was developed for WPA to provide improvements to WEP that could be fielded as firmware upgrades to existing 802.11 devices. The WPA profile also provides optional support for the AES-CCMP algorithm that is the preferred algorithm in 802.11i and WPA2 (Wi-Fi Alliance, 2003).

WPA2 is a Wi-Fi Alliance branded version of the final 802.11i standard. The primary enhancement over WPA is the inclusion of the AES-CCMP algorithm as a mandatory feature. Both WPA and WPA2 support EAP authentication methods using RADIUS servers and pre-shared key (PSK) based security (Wi-Fi Alliance, 2003).

802.1x provides user authentication and authorization using dynamic keys (versus static keys in WEP). This standard defines the extensible authentication protocol (EAP), which uses a central authentication server.

802.1x/EAP needs to have the supporting Remote Authentication Dial In User Service (RADIUS). This is a AAA (authentication, authorization, and accounting) protocol used for remote network access. The idea is to have an inside server act as a gatekeeper through the use of verifying identities through a username and password that is already predetermined by the user. A RADIUS server can also be configured to enforce user policies and restrictions as well as recording accounting information such as time connected for billing purposes (Wi-Fi Alliance, 2003).

Looking ahead, there are newer standards in the works, including temporal key integrity protocol (TKIP). The continuous strengthening of security by suppliers attests to the importance of ongoing review of security by institutions.

THE ADOPTION OF Wi-Fi TECHNOLOGY

Wi-Fi Access Devices

PCs are indeed at the heart of Wi-Fi technology today. According to the ECAR's 2001 survey (Table 4), although the device most commonly connected to a Wi-Fi network is the notebook PC, 46% of Wi-Fi networks also support desktop PCs. PDAs are most likely to be added to the mix of products supported by the Wi-Fi network: 27% of those with Wi-Fi networks plan to support PDAs in the future. Cell phones and other handheld devices can also provide Wi-Fi network access. Arabasz and Pirani (2002) suggested that the best device for those planning a Wi-Fi network is to think beyond PCs. "Many envision a future in which student will pull a PDA out of their pocket—not a laptop from their backpack—to access the network" (p. 49). It is easier for students and faculty to use a PDA than a laptop while strolling across campus. Wi-Fi networks and devices with portable form allow students and faculty to increase their mobility.

Reasons for Wi-Fi Technology Adoption

According to Arabasz and Pirani's (2002) research of Wi-Fi technology in higher education, the leading reason for Wi-Fi technology use was the desire to provide a greater degree of anywhere, anytime network access to students. Other reasons included meeting future computing needs and improving classroom and faculty access to networks. Overall, Arabasz and Pirani (2002) stated that "wireless is considered a success in higher education. The vast majority of institutions using wireless networks say they have met or exceeded their expectations" (p. 11).

Boerner (2002) listed some characteristics of Wi-Fi networking in higher education: mobility; installation speed and simplicity; installation flexibility; reduced cost of ownership; and scalability.

- **Mobility:** The Wi-Fi technology enables users to move from classroom to classroom, building to building, and still access the Internet, file servers, library resources, and so forth.
- **Installation speed and simplicity:** The use of Wi-Fi in older buildings can save

Table 4. Wi-Fi access devices, by Carnegie Classification (Arabasz & Pirani, 2002, p. 50)

Device	Total (N=299)		Doctoral (N=64)		Master's (N=75)		Bachelor's (N=62)		Associate's (N=28)	
	Now	Add in 24 Months	Now	Add in 24 Months	Now	Add in 24 Months	Now	Add in 24 Months	Now	Add in 24 Months
Laptop Computers	**94%**	10%	**98%**	11%	**96%**	9%	**95%**	11%	**93%**	14%
Desktop Computers	46%	14%	41%	9%	43%	19%	45%	18%	61%	11%
PDAs	39%	**27%**	53%	**38%**	40%	17%	24%	**32%**	21%	**25%**
Handheld Devices	9%	22%	16%	25%	8%	**24%**	5%	18%	4%	21%
Cellular Phones	4%	15%	5%	23%	3%	15%	2%	15%	4%	18%

* Current and planned use. Equipment type most often mentioned by respondents is highlighted.

considerable money and challenges posed by renovating to support networking.

- **Installation flexibility:** Flexibility is offered in both the networking of dedicated computer labs and the use of mobile computer labs. This can allow any classroom to become a computer lab, as needed, with the use of computer carts.

- **Reduced cost of ownership:** Although mid-to high-end APs are expensive, the overall investment in the Wi-Fi infrastructure is, in the long run, less expensive than retrofitting cables into old buildings. And by not having fixed positions, rooms can be adapted for different uses in the future without writing off the cost of the wiring.

- **Scalability:** The Wi-Fi LAN could start off small, perhaps with a mobile computer lab, and then grow in size and complexity as needed and when funds become available. Likewise, devices like APs can be upgraded when the instructional needs and infrastructure dictate. The current APs can be migrated to other locations when new equipment is purchased.

According to the ECAR Respondent Summary (2002) study, most institutions implemented the Wi-Fi technology as a complement to current wired network operations. Dartmouth College reported: "We wanted to provide network access literally anywhere, indoors or outdoors." Another reason for implementing Wi-Fi is to augment wired networks to provide comprehensive network access. As the University of Wisconsin Madison explained: "We had run out of space for additional computer labs. We were trying to find ways to reduce the long wait lines in our public computing labs. Since we knew 25% of the students who owned a computer had a laptop, we wondered if they would use a wireless area instead of a lab." Others felt Wi-Fi represented a means to meet future computing needs. Florida State University reported: "The college of Law and

MBA program in the College of Business wanted to deploy a laptop/wireless initiative. Both programs indicated this was becoming the norm for teaching in their respective disciplines to benefit students and faculty." Wake Forrest reported that they "wished not to be left behind."

Wi-Fi Technology Adopter Characteristics

Arabasz and Pirani's research (2002) found that students were the earliest adopters of Wi-Fi technology. Most institutions that implement Wi-Fi technology reported that students readily incorporate it into their daily activities: whether studying in the library, taking notes in class, checking e-mail, or browsing Web pages. Besides, Wi-Fi technology provided faculty better network to access and share information. A faculty member at the University of Pennsylvania stated, "It gives faculty more flexibility whenever they meet colleagues and students. They bring their laptops to the lab and have the information right there. They can download information and project it on a big screen; it's helpful when lecturing in large classes" (Arabasz & Pirani, 2002, p. 45). The research also found that fewer institutions reported administrative use (Table 5), primarily because staff worked from assigned workstations and used the wired network for access. Nevertheless, the research found that as full-time enrollment (FTE) increased, Wi-Fi networking extended to more constituents of the academic community (Table 6).

From "Wireless Networking in Higher Education," by P. Arabasz, and J. Pirani, p. 42, 2002. Retrieved August 9, 2004, from http://www.educause.edu/ir/library/pdf/ers0202/

From "Wireless Networking in Higher Education," by P. Arabasz, and J. Pirani, p. 42. 2002. Retrieved August 9, 2004, from http://www.educause.edu/ir/library/pdf/ers0202/

While all sections of higher education were increasing their Wi-Fi networks, the actual per-

Table 5. Percentage of institutions reporting types of users

Users	Total (N=299)	FTE: 1–4,999 (N=154)	FTE: 5,000–9,999 (N=50)	FTE: 10,000–19,999 (N=45)	FTE: 20,000+ (N=20)
Undergrads	77%	77%	78%	76%	75%
Faculty	73%	65%	80%	73%	90%
Administration	53%	45%	52%	69%	85%
Grad Students/Researchers	44%	27%	56%	53%	95%
Other	6%	6%	10%	2%	5%

Table 6. Students with access to wireless networks by Carnegie classification

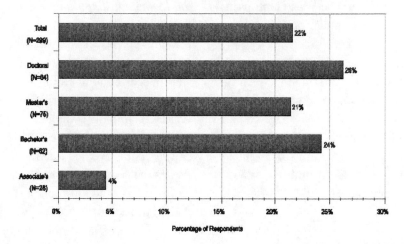

Table 7. Departments reported to have wireless access

Department	Total (N=299)	Doctoral (N=64)	Master's (N=75)	Bachelor's (N=62)	Associate's (N=28)
Computer Sciences	38%	47%	36%	32%	18%
Physical Sciences	33%	41%	32%	34%	36%
Business	32%	55%	33%	19%	14%
Languages/History	23%	23%	17%	27%	25%
Engineering	21%	47%	13%	5%	14%
Social Science	21%	23%	19%	31%	11%
Math	18%	27%	13%	21%	11%
Law	10%	31%	4%	2%	0%
Medical	10%	23%	4%	0%	0%
Other	39%	25%	57%	37%	43%

centage of students who had access to it varies by Carnegie classification (Table 6). Doctoral institutions had the highest percentage of users: 26%, while associate's institutions had the lowest percentage of users: 4%. Arabasz and Pirani (2002, p. 42) listed several factors that could affect student access to Wi-Fi technology at associate institutions:

- Less common student ownership of laptops
- Fewer institutional computer labs or laptop checkout programs to enable student access
- Fewer colleges or department programs with mandatory laptop requirements
- Fewer opportunities to use Wi-Fi laptops in the classroom and/or on campus

Arabasz and Pirani's research (2002) found that users of Wi-Fi technology were most frequently in the computer sciences, physical sciences, and business department (Table 7).

From "Wireless Networking in Higher Education," by P. Arabasz, and J. Pirani, p. 43, 2002. Retrieved August 9, 2004, from http://www.educause.edu/ir/library/pdf/ers0202/

TEACHING AND LEARNING IN USING Wi-Fi TECHNOLOGY

Wi-Fi Technology to Facilitate Student Learning

Since Wi-Fi technology is becoming mainstream, some articles in the literature are discussing Wi-Fi technology to facilitate student learning in higher education. As Arabasz and Pirani (2002) put it: "students have readily incorporated wireless access into their day-to-day social and academic activities, and usage is expanding" (p. 10).

According to Boggs (2002, p. 38), an administrator at the College of Mount St Joseph said that:

The main advantages though are related to the user. They don't have to go looking for a network port. They just turn on, log in and go. Or they can leave their machine on and just roam from place to place, connected and logged in all the time. Two of the most interesting aspects of wireless computing, coupled with a universal student computing requirement, have been the new workplaces students create and the forms of collaboration that take place. Now students can plop down just about anywhere and do some quick homework, or several of them can gather around a single laptop and work on something together.

Drexel University was one of the few universities to have Wi-Fi technology on the entire campus. It conducted a Wi-Fi survey (2001) to determine the characteristics of Wi-Fi users, how Wi-Fi technology was used and whether it was used to enhance the academic experience. The survey data revealed that most students used the Wi-Fi network for a combination of personal, coursework, and job-related work. Students used Wi-Fi most for the following activities: in class to access professor's notes; for group work or collaborative learning; to look up reference material in class; to access notes, assignments and homework in class; for controlling robots in the robotics lab; and for laptop-based experiments in the science lab.

Wi-Fi Technology and Teaching

Arabasz and Pirani (2002) stated that Wi-Fi networking was a "relatively inexpensive way to guarantee Internet access in any classroom, providing new locations for hands-on teaching" (p. 44). They listed some impacts of Wi-Fi technology on classroom teaching: greater collaboration and communication, greater access to resources, changes to pedagogy, and distraction in the classroom.

Greater Collaboration and Communication

Wi-Fi technology enables students to access databases on the Web for in-class manipulation, brainstorm in a foreign language via chat functions, and conduct real-time research with a class topic. Besides, students can modify the environment to facilitate their collaboration, for example, sitting together at a table or configuring their desks into a circle. One of the MBA students of the University of Tennessee explained, "We'll all be accessing different information, talking about it at the same time so we can share information. And we flip back and forth between screens" (Arabasz & Pirani, 2002, p. 44)

Greater Access to Resources

Wi-Fi technology enables faculty members to present relevant online material in class while lecturing. An instructor in geology used Wi-Fi technology to access Web pages in class to look at large images of rocks and dinosaur fossils. The instructor commented, "The speed of access and the exposure to a wider variety of information and material online enhances their learning," and "The experience is more life-like because they are not analyzing some diagrams in a book" (Arabasz & Pirani, 2002, p. 45).

More importantly, faculty members noticed that students used Wi-Fi technology proactively to access Web sites during class to enrich their knowledge of the subject under discussion. "You start to see students think differently," explained a professor of the University of Tennessee. "You start to see them automatically think when we're approaching a subject or a review of a concept in

class, 'let's go to company X's Web Site to see how they do it'" (Arabasz & Pirani, 2002, p. 45). While greater access to information resources is clearly an advantage for students, escaping the controlled and directed learning environment might be a disadvantage.

Changes to Pedagogy

Arabasz and Pirani (2002) commented that "wireless is just one aspect of the entire technological evolution impacting higher education pedagogy in general, but it can accelerate the process" (p. 45). Although it took a significant time investment to learn how to use Wi-Fi technology in the classroom, many faculty members thought the effort was worthwhile because it enhanced the learning environment and the quality of students' work. A director of elementary education at Middlebury College explained:

It became clear to me that I had to change, to make a huge leap forward in the way I dealt with my students. I had to accept multitasking among my students…Students were way ahead of me in terms of how to use the Wi-Fi laptop effectively. But I will never revert to the old way, because now they can accomplish twice as much in class in the same amount of time. It was an epiphany! (Arabasz & Pirani, 2002, p. 45-46)

Distraction in the Classroom

There is another growing debate about Wi-Fi access in the classroom: inappropriate use. Some faculty members insist that Wi-Fi technology provides a source of diversion. One faculty member described it as "fun and sexy ways to wander during class" (Arabasz & Pirani, 2002, p. 46). Yet many believe it was a new angle to an old problem: class management. A professor of Dartmouth College explained:

Students can check their e-mail during lectures, but because they are so engaged, they tend not to...When a class is well taught, wireless distraction is a non-issue. Wireless tends to amplify the climate of learning in that particular classroom, not change the direction. (Arabasz & Pirani, 2002, p. 46)

Almost 63% of respondents of the ECAR's online survey (Arabasz & Pirani, 2002) agreed that Wi-Fi technology did not encourage inappropriate classroom use. One big challenge for Wi-Fi technology in teaching "is for faculty to meaningfully incorporate Wi-Fi into the classroom curriculum" (Arabasz & Pirani, 2002, p. 10). Larry Levine, director of computing at Dartmouth College, one of the first institutions having a campus-wide network 15 years ago and one of the first campus-wide Wi-Fi networks now, reported that although students love Wi-Fi technology, the teaching has not changed. He said:

I don't think that it (Wi-Fi) has changed how faculty teach. For the typical faculty, teaching is still lecture- or classroom-style. They may say, 'Let's look this up...' but they don't, for the most part, say, 'Be sure to bring your laptop to class.' ("Campus-wide wireless," 2002, p. 15)

He continued, "There is not a lot of live teaching use with wireless. Where the use takes place, I think, is outside the classroom as people do their work and as they communicate with each other. It frees people up" (Campus-wide wireless, 2002, p. 16).

Bhave (2002) predicted Wi-Fi technology would be a challenge for teacher control and a revolution in learning. He said that when Wi-Fi technologies permeate classrooms in schools and colleges:

They (wireless technology) will raise issues of stewardship and control for the teacher. How can a teacher assert the necessary and traditional control over classroom proceedings to remain

effective? How can a teacher retain focus and discipline in the classroom when students multi-task with ease? Can the technologies be used for educational benefits, e.g., through augmenting subject matter with instant research or through greater participation? (p. 17)

Although Wi-Fi technology has the potential to enhance learning, it poses challenges to the teachers' classroom objectives, requires new etiquette, and protocols for control. Bhave (2002) proposed some possibilities: "No laptops allowed in the room." "Laptops allowed for taking notes, for local contents but no access to the Internet in the classroom." "Laptops allowed, access to enterprise LAN and the Internet permitted, and with the teacher's permission, can be used to augment learning" (p. 22). Bhave suggested a technical solution to the problem of regulating access to outside content during class: "a 'master' computer belonging to the teacher can control the access point (AP) that is feeding the classroom" (p. 22). At different times during the class, the AP may be "opened" in various ways by the teacher. For example, sometimes the teacher may allow the students to have full access to the Internet; sometimes the teacher may allow "one-to-many" access where only the instructor can send information to the class through the AP. Non-pertinent LAN access can be managed by the teacher but an appropriate behavioral change of students might be longer lasting and more positive.

THE CHALLENGES OF Wi-Fi TECHNOLOGY IMPLEMENTATION

Security is the biggest challenge of Wi-Fi technology implementation. The ECAR Respondent Summary (2002) study revealed that security was the most frequently faced challenge for Wi-Fi networks. The respondents from Wake Forest said: "Security has not yet been a problem. When it develops, it could be immense." According to

Project's 2002 Campus Computing Survey, the respondents across all sectors considered network security as a critical issue: score in 2002 was 6.5 on the 1 to 7 scale of importance, compared to 6.4 in 2001 and 6.2 in 1999. Additionally, the survey data suggested that network security might have improved slightly between 2001 and 2002, because the respondents rated their "network security against hackers and virus attacks" at 5.0 on the 1 to 7 scale from poor to excellent, compared to 4.9 in 2001.

Wi-Fi technology installation is a challenge. The installation and implementation is complex and time consuming because of the inexact nature of AP placement and channel allocation. It requires learning, or the support of experienced Wi-Fi technology contractors. Pilot implementations are valuable for Wi-Fi installation (Arabasz & Pirani, 2002).

Technology and end-user support is another key issue. Wi-Fi technology has increased the need for support, including technology trouble-shooting, end-user support, and teaching in classroom support.

Another issue is equal access for students and faculty to Wi-Fi technology. Mandatory laptops and Wi-Fi networking are in their first phase, usually limited to specific departments or colleges.

According to Arabasz and Pirani's (2002) study, there are problems with inappropriate student access. About one-fifth of institutions that have implemented Wi-Fi networks reported that there was a problem with students using Wi-Fi access during class/lecture time for non-pertinent content. One administrator at Florida State University said: "we see a significant exposure for abuse and misuse" (p. 61).

A CASE STUDY: Wi-Fi TECHNOLOGY AT OHIO UNIVERSITY

Ohio University is a major state university in southeast Ohio. Ohio University has one main campus and five regional campuses. Enrollment at the main campus (Athens) totaled 19,962 students (20,452 including Lifelong Learning) while 8,636 students were enrolled at regional campuses, for a total enrollment of 29,088 in fall 2003. Ohio University committed to provide the technology students need to succeed in today's educational environment. As evidence of that commitment, a computer with printer and Internet access was provided in every student's room in the residence halls (Office of Institutional Research, 2004).

In January 2002, Communication Network Services (CNS) of Ohio University started a wireless networking project (called "First Wave"), and free wireless Internet access for students, faculty, staff, and visitors was available in selected locations, including indoor and outdoor areas. In the summer of 2004, Ohio University approved a plan to expand wireless Internet coverage to the whole campus in a two-year implementation cycle, and to "create a ubiquitous and seamless wireless computing environment" (Wireless Deployment Sub-Committee, 2004; "Wireless Future," 2004). The university was more than halfway to becoming a completely wireless campus in September 2005. Wireless Internet will be available campus-wide by the summer 2006.

Through vendor interviews and hardware evaluation, Cisco access points (802.11b/g) and Bluesocket middle box (for authentication and authorization) were chosen and deployed on campus. A user needs to provide a university ID and password to login to the wireless network. A Bluesocket middle box checks the login information against the central database to verify the ID and password.

Wireless networks were deployed in stages. The library, engineering, and telecommunication buildings were the first few buildings to have wireless access. Then CNS received "excellent 'buy-in' from departments wanting to deploy wireless" (Communication Network Services, 2004a, p. 24). In the summer of 2004, the university approved the plan to expand wireless Internet coverage to the whole campus in a two-year implementation cycle and to "create a ubiquitous and seamless wireless computing environment" (Wireless Deployment Sub-Committee, 2004). Wireless coverage was expanded and new locations are being added constantly. By summer 2006, the Athens campus will have 100% wireless coverage. The project includes indoor and outdoor spaces at Athens campus. The cost to the university averaged $4.54 per student per academic month (Communication Network Services, 2004a).

CNS thought mobility and wireless access were critical to the current generation of students. It became one of the most frequent asked technology questions from parents and students at pre-college orientation. From CNS Wireless Report (Communication Network Services, 2004a), the number of unique wireless Internet users on track surpassed 2,000 and the number of log-in approached 10,000 in the month of February 2004 (Figure 2). The data also showed that the wireless use is clearly linked to students: the reason for the big dip in December 2003 was that students were on winter break.

In a CNS presentation of "Wireless Future" (Communication Network Services, 2004a), it was mentioned that "Wireless is the next wave," and some benefits for student multi-tasking (p. 4)

were listed as, "incredible profusion of communications, multiple conversational threads, several technologies used simultaneously, tremendous amount of social interaction, and great concentration required." According to the presentation, the future wireless profile should be:

* Single mobile computing platform for voice, data and video
* Multi-tasking integrated into the learning environment
* Robust network providing access to educational assets from anywhere, anytime
* Substantial, secure and reliable personal network storage
* High availability, easy to use communications application environment (p. 8)

In the fall of 2004, The Center for Innovations in Technology for Learning (CITL) hosted a wireless pilot group meeting of faculty members interested in incorporating wireless technology into classroom environments. The goal of the project was "to develop and test creative teaching strategies using wireless technology, documenting related pedagogical and ethical issues" (Ohio University Wireless Pilot Group, n.d.). More than 20 faculty members from different colleges and

Figure 2. Number of unique wireless users. From "Wireless Progress Report," 2004 (Retrieved April 4, 2004, from http://www.cns.ohiou.edu/hot_topics/wirelessprogress/frame)

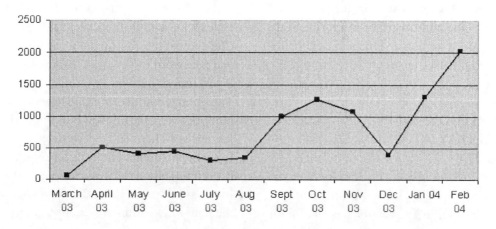

departments attended. After the meeting, they set near-term and long-term goals: "First, to develop several web-based case studies for your colleagues based on your practices and experiences…; second, to develop a proposal for designing an optimal learning space that supports wireless technologies."

A study about Wi-Fi technology at Ohio University found that students showed consistently positive attitudes reflecting their belief that Wi-Fi technology could help their study and learning. Wi-Fi technology can promote student-centered learning by providing a choice of location, better learning environment, flexibility of time, easy involvement in group projects, and improved communication with instructors and other learners (Lu, Ma, & Turner 2004; Lu, Ma, Turner, & Huang, in press).

There were a handful of faculty members starting to implement Wi-Fi technology in their classroom teaching. The courses they taught included: linguistics, English, instructional technology, principles of curriculum, statistics, communication systems, and software engineering. These faculty developed curriculum and methods of using wireless laptops as a pedagogical tool. Their teaching strategies and practices included: collaborative learning, contextual learning, flexible teaching practices, posting instructional material online, accessing online relevant sources or databases, speeding up learning acquisition, and on-going assessment and instant feedback. They understood that wireless technology could be used as a means to increase the quantity and quality of exchanges both between themselves and their students and among students. They encouraged their students to collaborate on data collection, hands-on experiments, and team work. They began to leave behind the "sage on the stage" to become the "guide by the side" (Lu, 2006).

As shown from the case study, students are ready to learn in a wireless classroom, and they are enthusiastic about the potential of Wi-Fi technology because it allows them to be active

learners where they can choose the location, time, and mode of communication for their learning. Although there are some successful teaching practices of Wi-Fi technology, there are only a few instructors using this technology in their classrooms. Some did not even know about it. Institutions need to make a long-term sustainable plan to develop Wi-Fi technology, instructional strategies, and technology support. Strategies are needed to promote more widespread dissemination of successful practices and models to improve teaching and learning using Wi-Fi technology (Lu, 2006). We are at the beginning of an era when students, faculty, and administrative staff must learn how to use advanced wireless technology in a heterogeneous network. Exploiting the teaching and learning opportunities of these technologies is certainly a future challenge.

FUTURE TRENDS AND DIRECTIONS

Wi-Fi technology opens a new dimension of computer networking in higher education. It is quickly gaining a foothold on many campuses as a means to achieve mobility and anywhere, anytime access. Here are the future trends and directions of Wi-Fi technology in higher education.

Most institutions plan to maintain both wired and wireless networks. Many want to continue expanding wireless networks throughout their campus as a way to provide ubiquitous computing. An administrator of Harvey Mudd College explained, "They (wired and wireless networks) are complementary. We use wireless as an additional way of accessing the networking, broadly defined. We have not used wireless for building-to-building connectivity" (Arabasz & Pirani, 2002, p. 69).

The pace of Wi-Fi technology development is rapid. The current leading Wi-Fi standard, 802.11b, is beginning to be replaced by newer standards, 802.11a and 802.11g. 802.11a is emerging as the future technology of choice. It provides faster data rates than 802.11b and runs in the less-congested 5 GHz frequency. Alternatively, if 802.11g will prevail, it will double the bandwidth of 802.11b and will not require replacement of the installed base.

Institutions plan to continue fostering Wi-Fi technology in the classroom to promote teaching and learning. PDAs and handheld devices intrigue IT administrators, faculty, and students. One IT manager of Middlebury College expected that "wireless will mimic the wired network environment, potentially serving a mix of laptop and PDA equipment" (Arabasz & Pirani, 2002, p. 69).

Wi-Fi technology, with a distance and penetration of approximately 50 feet, are physical addresses where people can connect to a public wireless network, such as a cafe, hotel, or airport. WiMAX is a metropolitan-scale wireless technology with speeds over 1Mbps and a longer range than Wi-Fi. The IEEE developed the 802.16 with the idea of creating a wireless networking technology suitable for coverage of large metropolitan areas. WiMAX has the potential to cover large geographic areas, up to 30 miles, which is suitable for some large university campuses.

SUMMARY

Wi-Fi technology has a great promise in higher education for classroom teaching and technology access. Although Wi-Fi access to the campus network is becoming more commonplace, institutions are still at the beginning stage of adoption in education. There are many possible applications of Wi-Fi technology for teaching and administration (Grush, 2002). Like Hammond and Salpeter (n.d.) said, "As with any use of technology in education, the key to successful implementation of Wi-Fi computing involves planning, staff development, partnerships, community-wide support and an emphasis on what is really important: empowering students to learn and grow" (p. 7).

REFERENCES

Arabasz, P., & Pirani, J. (2002). *Wireless networking in higher education*. Retrieved September 06, 2004, from http://www.educause.edu/ir/library/pdf/ers0202/

Bartel, C., & DiLorenzo, E. (2003). Network infrastructure, wireless technology. Retrieved July 4, 2006, from http://www.educause.edu/ir/library/pdf/DEC0304.pdf

Bhave, M. P. (2002). Classrooms with Wi-Fi: A challenge for teacher control and a revolution in learning. *T.H.E. Journal, 30*(4), 17-23.

Boerner, G. (2002). The brave new world of wireless technologies: A primer for educators. *Syllabus, 16*(3), 19-30.

Boggs, R. (2002). ECAR study: *Trends in wireless communications in higher education*. Retrieved January 29, 2003, from http://www.educause.edu/ir/library/pdf/EDU0218.pdf

Boggs, R., Smolek, J., & Arabasz, P. (2002). Choosing the right wireless network: A technology challenge for higher education. Retrieved September 6, 2004, from http://www.educause.edu/ir/library/pdf/ERB0212.pdf

Campus-wide wireless: Mobility and convergence: An interview with Lawrence M. Levine. (2002). *Syllabus, 16*(3), 14-18.

Carlson, S. (2001). Wireless technology is a double-edged sword, researchers conclude. *The Chronicle of Higher Education, 47*(32), A55.

ECAR Respondent Summary. (2002). *Wireless networking in higher education in the U.S. and Canada*. Retrieved January 19, 2003, from http://www.educause.edu/ir/library/pdf/ecar_so/ers/ers0202/EKF0202.pdf

Gast, M. S. (2005). *802.11 Wireless Networks: The Definitive Guide*. O'Reilly.

Green, K. C. (2002). Campus computing looks ahead: Tracking the digital puck. *Syllabus, 16*(5), 22-25.

Green, K. C. (2003a). *The 2003 national survey of information technology in U.S. higher education.* Retrieved September 6, 2004, from http://www.educause.edu/ir/library/pdf/EDU0324.pdf

Green, K. C. (2003b). *Campus computing, 2003.* Retrieved September 6, 2004, from http://www.educause.edu/ir/library/pdf/EDU0324a.pdf

Green, K. C. (2004). *The 2004 national survey of information technology in US higher education.* Retrieved May 14, 2005, from http://www.campuscomputing.net/

Grush, M. (2002). Editor's note. *Syllabus, 16*(3), 4.

Hammond, K., & Salpeter, J. (n.d.). *Cutting the cord: Wireless computing comes of age.* Retrieved January 20, 2003, from http://www.cosn.org/initiatives/compendium/3.pdf

JiWire. (2006). Retrieved August 05, 2006, from http://www.jiwire.com/search-hotspot-locations.htm

Lawson, S. (2006). Faster gear to drive Wi-Fi market. *PC Magazine.* Retrieved August 05, 2006, from http://www.pcworld.com/article/124478-1/article.html

Lu, Y. (2006). *The diffusion of wireless Internet technology among university faculty members.* Unpublished doctoral dissertation, Ohio University, Athens.

Lu, Y., Ma, H., & Turner, S. (2004). *How are college students using wireless Internet to support student-centered learning?* Paper presented at the National Educational Computing Conference, New Orleans, LA.

Lu, Y., Ma, H., Turner, S., & Huang, W. (in press). Wireless Internet and student-centered learning: A partial least squares model. *Computers & Education.*

Office of Institutional Research. (2004). *Ohio University fact book.* Retrieved October 17, 2004, from http://www.ohiou.edu/instres/index.html

Ohio University Wireless Pilot Group. (n.d.). Retrieved June 03, 2005, from http://teach.citl.ohiou.edu/wireless/index.htm

Patton, M. Q. (2002). *Qualitative research and evaluation methods.* Thousand Oaks, CA: Sage.

Wi-Fi Alliance. (2003). *Wi-Fi protected access: Strong, standards-based, interoperable security for today's Wi-Fi networks.* Retrieved July 4th, 2006 from http://main.wi-fi.org/membersonly/getfile.asp?f=Whitepaper_Wi-Fi_Security4-29-03.pdf

Wireless Deployment Sub-Committee. (2004). *Final report and recommendations from the wireless deployment sub-committee.* Retrieved September 10, 2004, from http://www.ohio.edu/itsc/loader.cfm?url=/commonspot/security/getfile.cfm&PageID=51965

Wireless future. (2004). Retrieved September 10, 2004, from http://www.cns.ohio.edu/hot_topics/wirelessfuture/frame.htm

Wireless progress report. (2004). Retrieved April 4, 2004, from http://www.cns.ohiou.edu/hot_topics/wirelessprogress/frame

ENDNOTE

[1] QoS refers to the performance attributes of an end-to-end mobile connection. The particular elements of a QoS definition depend on the information being transported. For example, QoS for voice commonly defines the acceptable limits on parameters such as delay, signal loss, and noise. In the case of data, it refers to attributes such as error rates, lost packet items, throughput, and delay. A commitment to QoS is becoming increasingly important as Wi-Fi solutions compete with each other.

Compilation of References

3GNewsroom.com. (2006, January 22). World Cup to promote 3G. *3GNewsroom.com*.

Aaker, D. A., Kumar, V., & Day, G. (1995*). Marketing research*. New York: Wiley.

Aarnio, A., Enkenberg, A., Heikkilä, J., & Hirvola, S. (2002). *Adoption and use of mobile services. Empirical evidence from a Finnish survey*. Paper presented at the 35th Annual Hawaii International Conference on System Sciences (HICSS-35'02), Big Island, HI.

Abowd, G. D., & Mynatt, E. D. (2000). Charting past, present, and future research in ubiquitous computing. *ACM Transactions on Computer-Human Interaction, 7*(1) 29-58.

Ahn, S. (2004). Mobile business strategy of SKT. SK-Telecom.

Ajzen, I. (1991). The theory of planned behaviour. *Organizational Behavior & Human Decision Processes, 50*(2), 179-211.

Ajzen, I., & Fishbein, M. (1980). *Understanding attitudes and predicting social behavior*. Englewood Cliffs, NJ: Prentice Hall.

Aksit, M., Tekinerdogan, B., Marcelloni, F., & Bergmans, L. (1999). Deriving frameworks from domain knowledge. In M. E. Fayad, D. C. Schmidt, & R. E. Johnson (Eds.), *Building application frameworks—Object-oriented foundations of framework design* (pp. 169-198). New York: John Wiley & Sons.

Akyldiz, I., Su, W., Sanakarasubramaniam, Y., & Cayirci, E. (2002). Wireless sensor networks: A survey. *Computer Networks Journal, 38*(4), 392-422.

Alanko, T., Kojo, M., Liljeberg, M., & Raatikainen, K. (1999). Mobile access to the Internet: A mediator-based solution. *Internet Research: Electronic Networking Applications and Policy, 9*(1), 58-65.

Alexander, H. R., Biggers, J., Forman, E., & Schleicher, D. (1990). *Prioritization of civil tiltrotor technologies using the analytic hierarchy process*. Paper presented at the Third International Symposium on the Analytic Hierarchy Process, George Washington University, Washington, DC.

Ali, S., Torabi, T., & Ali, H. (2006). A case for business process deployment for location aware applications. *International Journal of Computer Science and Network Security, 6*(8a), 118-127.

Alleyne, G. (1998). *Información en Salud para Todos*. En: Laerte PA, Castro E de. Biblioteca virtual en salud. Sao Paulo: OPS/OMS: pp 17-34.

Allison, R. B. (1998). Multiple personality disorder, dissociative identity disorder, and internalized imaginary companions. *Hypnos, 25*(3), 125-133.

Al-Muhtadi, J., Mickunas, D., & Campbell, R. (2002). A lightweight reconfigurable mechanism for 3G/4G mobile devices. *IEEE Wireless Communications*.

Alwitt, L. F., & Prabhaker, P. R. (1994). Identifying who dislikes television advertising: Not by demographics alone. *Journal of Advertising Research, 34*(6), 17-29.

Amberg, M., & Remus, U. (2003). Multi-channel commerce: Hybridstrategien und controlling. In W. Uhr, W. Esswein, & E. Schoop (Eds.), *Wirtschaftsinformatik 2003/Band II* (pp. 795-817). Heidelberg, Germany: Physica-Verlag.

Amberg, M., Figge, S., & Wehrmann, J. (2003). A cooperation model for personalised and situation dependent services in mobile networks. In A. Olivé, M. Yoshikawa, & E. S. Yu (Eds.), *Advanced conceptual modeling techniques* (2784 ed.). Berlin, Germany: Springer.

Aminuzzaman, S. (2005). Is mobile phone a socio-cultural change agent? A study of the pattern of usage of mobile phones among university students in Bangladesh. In *Proceedings of the International Conference on Mobile Communication and Asian Modernities II, Information, Communications Tools & Social Changes in Asia,* Beijing, China.

Ammenwerth, E., Gräber, S., Herrmann, G., Bürkle, T., & König, J. (2003). Evaluation of health information systems problems and challenges. *International Journal of Medical Informatics, 71,* 125-135.

Anckar, B., & D'Incau, D. (2002). Value creation in mobile commerce: Findings from a consumer survey. *Journal of Information Technology Theory & Application, 4*(1), 43-64.

Anckar, B., & D'Incau, D. (2002, January 7-10). *Value-added services in mobile commerce: An analytical framework and empirical findings from a national consumer survey.* Paper presented at the 35th Annual Hawaii International Conference on System Sciences, Big Island.

Anckar, B., & Eriksson, N. (2003). Mobility: The basis for value creation in mobile commerce? In *Proceedings of the SSGRR 2003s Conference,* L'Aquila, Italy.

Anckar, B., Carlsson, C., & Walden, P. (2003). Factors affecting consumer adoption decisions and intents in mobile commerce: Empirical insights. In *Proceedings of the 16th Bled eCommerce Conference* (pp. 886-902).

Andreas, S., Andreou, A. S., Leonidou, C., Chrysostomou, C., Pitsillides, A., Samaras, G., et al. (2005). Key issues for the design and development of mobile commerce services and applications. *International Journal of Mobile Communications, 3*(3), 303-323.

Andrews, K. (1969). Toward professionalism in business management. *Harvard Business Review, 47*(2), 49-60.

Angehrn, A. (1997). Designing mature Internet business strategies: The ICDT Model. *European Management Journal, 15*(4), 361-369.

Angeles, R. (2005). RFID technologies: Supply-chain applications and implementation issues. *Information Systems Management, 22*(1), 51-65.

Ansoff, I. (1965). *Corporate strategy: An analytical approach to business policy for growth and expansion.* New York: McGraw-Hill.

Ansoff, I. (Ed.). (1969). *Business strategy.* Harmondsworth, UK: Penguin.

Anthony, R. N. (1965). *Planning and control systems.* Boston: Harvard University Press.

Arabasz, P., & Pirani, J. (2002). *Wireless networking in higher education.* Retrieved September 06, 2004, from http://www.educause.edu/ir/library/pdf/ers0202/

Aswin, R. (2003). *From e-commerce to m-commerce: The wireless proposition, HSBC's guide to cash and treasury management in Asia.* Retrieved from www.infosys.com/industries/banking/white-papers/11_Wireless_RoongtaHSBC.pdf?page=bcmwphsbc

AT Kearney. (2003). *The new mobile mindset.*

Atlas Research. (2004). [Statistics] mobile contents market trend in Korea. *Mobile Contents & Application.*

Avital, M., Robey, D., Sawyer, S., & Sorensen, C. (2004). *Social and organizational issues in ubiquitous computing.* In K. J. Lyytinen, Y. Yoo, U. Varshney, M. Ackerman, G. Davis, M. Avital, D. Robey, S. Sawyer, & C. Sørensen (Eds.), (pp. 708-712).

Awan, I. (2006). Mobility management for m-commerce requests in wireless cellular networks *Information Systems Frontiers, 8*(4), 285-295.

Babin, B. J., Darden, W. R., & Griffin, M. (1994). Work and/or fun: Measuring hedonic and utilitarian shopping value. *Journal of Consumer Research, 20*(4), 644-656.

Bahl, P., & Padmanabhan, V. N. (2000). Radar: An in-building rf-based user location and tracking system. In *Proceedings of the IEEE Infocom,* Tel-Aviv, Israel.

Bai, L., Chou, D. C., Yen, D., & Lin, B. (2005). Mobile commerce: Its market analyses. *International Journal of Mobile Communications, 3*(1), 66-81.

Bakos, J. Y., & Treacy, M. E. (1986). Information technology and corporate strategy: A research perspective. *MIS Quarterly, 10*(2), 106-120.

Balasubramanian, S., Peterson, R. A., & Jarvenpaa, S. L. (2002). Exploring the implications of m-commerce for markets and marketing. *Journal of the Academy of Marketing Science, 30*(4), 348-362.

Ballon, P. (Ed.). (2005). *Best practice in business modelling for ICT services* (TNO-ICT Report No. 33561). Delft, The Netherlands: TNO-ICT.

Ballon, P., Pierson, J., & Delaere, S. (2005, September 4-6). *Open innovation platforms for broadband services: Benchmarking European practices.* Paper presented at ITS (International Telecommunications Society) 16th European Regional Conference, Porto, Portugal.

Bar, F. (2001). The construction of marketplace architecture. In The BRIE-IGCC E-conomy Project Task Force on the Internet (Eds.), *Tracking a transformation: E-Commerce and the terms of competition in industries* (pp. 27-49). Washington, DC: Brookings Institution Press.

Bardram, J., & Hansen, T. (2004, November 6-10). Paper presented at the CSCW'04, Chicago.

Barnes, S. (2004). Wireless support for mobile distributed work: A taxonomy and examples. In *Proceedings of the 37th Hawaii International Conference on System Sciences,* Big Island, HI.

Barnes, S. J. (2002). Unwired business: Wireless applications in the firm's value chain. In *Proceedings of the Sixth Pacific Asia Conference on Information Systems,* Tokyo, Japan.

Barnes, S. J. (2002). Wireless digital advertising: Nature and implications. *International Journal of Advertising, 21*(3), 399-421.

Barnes, S. J. (2003). Enterprise mobility: Concept and examples. *International Journal of Mobile Communications, 1*(4), 341-359.

Barnes, S. J. (2003). *M-Business: The strategic implications of wireless communications.* Oxford, UK: Elsevier/Butterworth-Heinemann.

Barnes, S. J., & Scornavacca, E. (2004). Mobile marketing: The role of permission and acceptance. *International Journal of Mobile Communications, 2*(2), 128-139.

Barnes, S. J., & Scornavacca, E. (2005). *The strategic impact of wireless applications in NZ business.* Paper presented at the Hong Kong Mobility Roundtable, Hong Kong.

Barney, J. B. (1991). Firm resources and sustained competitive advantage. *Journal of Management, 17*(1), 99-120.

Barney, J. B. (1997). *Gaining and sustaining competitive advantage.* Reading, MA: Addison-Wesley.

Barr, J., & Mata, R. (2000). OSGi: Spec basics, interface issues. *Electronic Engineering Times, 1144,* 112.

Bartel, C., & DiLorenzo, E. (2003). Network infrastructure, wireless technology. Retrieved July 4, 2006, from http://www.educause.edu/ir/library/pdf/DEC0304.pdf

Bartel, M., Boyer, J., Fox, B., LaMacchia, B., & Simon, E. (2002). *XML-signature syntax and processing.* W3C Recommendation. Retrieved from http://www.w3.org/TR/xmldsig-core/

Barthel, H. (2005). *EPCglobal—RFID standards & regulations.* Paper presented at the *Radio Frequency Identification (RFID) Applications and Public Policy Considerations, OECD Foresight Forum,* Paris.

Becker, S. (1996). *Panel discussion on introduction of intelligent vehicles into society: Technical, mental and legal aspects. Mental models, expectable consumer behaviour and consequences for system design and testing.* Paper presented at the IEEE Intelligent Vehicles Symposium.

Becker, S. (1999). Konzeptionelle und experimentelle Analyse von Nutzerbedürfnissen im Entwicklungsprozess. In Bundesanstalt für Straßenwesen (Ed.), *Informations- und Assistenzsysteme im Auto benutzergerecht gestalten. Methoden für den Entwicklungsprozess.*

(pp. 64-72). Bergisch Gladbach: Verlag für neue Wissenschaft.

Bellavista, P., Corradi, A., Montanari, R., & Stefanelli, C. (2003). Dynamic binding in mobile applications: A middleware approach. *IEEE Internet Computing, 7*(2) 34-42.

Benbasat, I., Goldstein, D. K., & Mead, M. (1987). The case research strategy in studies of information systems. *MIS Quarterly.*

Best, J. (2006, February 16). Is free the way forward for mobile TV? *Silicon.com.* Retrieved from http://networks.silicon.com/mobile/0,39024665,39156508,00.htm

Beulen, E., & Streng, R.-J. (2002). The impact of online mobile office applications on the effectiveness and efficiency of mobile workers behavior: A field experiment in the IT services sector. In *Proceedings from the International Conference on Information Systems,* Barcelona, Spain.

Bhave, M. P. (2002). Classrooms with Wi-Fi: A challenge for teacher control and a revolution in learning. *T.H.E. Journal, 30*(4), 17-23.

Bibbo, L. (2002). *SkyGo study illustrates wireless advertising in an effective and direct response vehicle.* SkyGo, Inc. Retrieved October 23, 2002 from www.skygo.com

Birch, S., & Gafni, A. (2003). Inclusion of drugs in provincial drug benefit programs: Should *"reasonable decisions"* lead to uncontrolled growth in expenditures? *Canadian Medical Association Journal, 168,* 849-851.

Blechar, J., Constantiou, I. D., & Damsgaard, J. (2006). Exploring the influence of reference situations and reference pricing on mobile service user behaviour. *European Journal of Information Systems, 15*(3), 285-291.

Blechar, J., Constantiou, I., & Damsgaard, J. (2006). Understanding behavioural patterns of advanced mobile service users. *Electronic Government: An International Journal, 3*(1), 93-104.

Boerner, G. (2002). The brave new world of wireless technologies: A primer for educators. *Syllabus, 16*(3),

19-30.

Boggs, R. (2002). ECAR study: *Trends in wireless communications in higher education.* Retrieved January 29, 2003, from http://www.educause.edu/ir/library/pdf/EDU0218.pdf

Boggs, R., Smolek, J., & Arabasz, P. (2002). Choosing the right wireless network: A technology challenge for higher education. Retrieved September 6, 2004, from http://www.educause.edu/ir/library/pdf/ERB0212.pdf

Bohn, J. (2006). Prototypical implementation of location-aware services based on super-distributed RFID tags. In W. Grass, B. Sick, & K. Waldschmidt (Eds.), *Proceedings of the 19th International Conference on Architecture of Computer Systems* (LNCS 3894, pp. 69-83).

Boone, J. (1999). Harvesting design. In M. E. Fayad, D. C. Schmidt, & R. E. Johnson (Eds.), *Building application frameworks—Object-oriented foundations of framework design* (pp. 199-210). New York: John Wiley & Sons.

Bose, I., & Pal, R. (2005). Auto-ID: Managing anything, anywhere, anytime in the supply chain. *Communications of the ACM, 48*(8), 100-106.

Botaschanjan, J., Kof, L., Kühnel, C., & Spichkova, M. (2005, May). *Towards verified automotive software.* Paper presented at the 2nd International ICSE workshop on Software Engineering for Automotive Systems.

Boyle, J. (1997). *Foucault in cyberspace: Surveillance, sovereignty, and hard-wired censors.* Retrieved January 18, 2005, from www.law.duke.edu/boylesite/foucl.html

Bradford, A. (2003). *Consumers need local reasons to pay by mobile.* http://www.gartner.com/resources/115600/115603/115603.pdf

Braet, O., Ballon, P., & Dreessen, K. (2006). *Cooperation models for DVB-H rollout.* Final Report for IBBT-project MADUF ("Maximize DVB-H Usage in Flanders").

Brenner, M. R., Grech, M. L. F., Torabi, M., & Unmehopa, M. R. (2005). The open mobile alliance and trends in supporting the mobile services industry. *Bell Labs Technical Journal, 10*(1), 59-75.

Brey, L. (in press). Theorizing the cultural quality of new media. *Téchne: Journal of the Society for Philosophy and Technology*.

Brodie, R. J., Coviello, N. E., Brookes, R. W., & Little, V. (1997). Towards a paradigm shift in marketing? An examination of current marketing practices. *Journal of Marketing Management, 13*(5), 383-406.

Brownlow, M. (2001, May 15). *M-Commerce*. Retrieved November 11, 2002, from www.ibizbasics.com

Brynjolfsson, E. (1993). The productivity paradox of information technology: Review and assessment. *Communication of the ACM, 12*(36), 66-77.

Brynjolfsson, E., & Hitt, L. M. (2000). Beyond computation: Information technology, organizational transformation and business performance. *Journal of Economic Perspectives, 14*(4), 23-48.

Budde, P. (2002). Asia and Australia telecommunications industry overview. *Annual Review of Communications, 55*, 243-250.

Buhan, D., Cheong, Y. C., & Tan, C. (2002). *Mobile payments in m-commerce*. Retrieved from http://www.capgemini.com/tme/pdf/ MobilePaymentsinMCommrce.pdf

Campus-wide wireless: Mobility and convergence: An interview with Lawrence M. Levine. (2002). *Syllabus, 16*(3), 14-18.

CapGemini Consulting Inc. (2005). *What European consumers think about radio frequency identification and the implications for business*. Author.

Carat, G. (2002). *E-Payment systems database: Trends and analysis*. Retrieved from http://epso.jrc.es/Docs/Background-9.pdf

Carlson, S. (2001). Wireless technology is a double-edged sword, researchers conclude. *The Chronicle of Higher Education, 47*(32), A55.

Carlsson, C., & Walden, P. (2002). Mobile commerce: Some extensions of core concepts and key issues. In *Proceedings of the SSGRR International Conference on Advances in Infrastructure for e-Business, e-Education, e-Science and e-Medicine on the Internet*, L'Aquila, Italy.

Carlsson, C., Carlsson, J., Hyvönen, K., Puhakainen, J., & Walden, P. (2006). *Adoption of mobile devices/services—Searching for answers with the UTAUT*. Paper presented at the 39th Annual Hawaii International Conference on System Sciences (HICSS-39'06), Big Island, HI.

Carlton, D. W., & Perloff, J. M. (2000). *Modern industrial organization* (3rd ed.). Reading, MA: Addison-Wesley.

Carr, N. (1999). Redesigning business. *Harvard Business Review, 77*(6), 19.

Carrascal, M. J., Pau, L. F., & Reiner, L. (1995). Knowledge and information transfer in agriculture using hypermedia: A system review. *Computers and Electronics in Agriculture, 12*(2), 83-119.

Carter, J. (1998). Why settle for early adopters? *Admap, 33*(3), 41-44.

Castells, M. (2001). *The Internet galaxy: Reflections on the Internet, business, and society*. UK: Oxford University Press.

Cellular Telecommunications Industry Association (CTIA). (1999, December). *CTIA semi-annual wireless industry survey*. Retrieved from Wow-com

Celuch, K., Goodwin, S., & Taylor, S. A. (2007). Understanding small scale industrial user Internet purchase and information management intentions: A test of two attitude models. *Industrial Marketing Management, 36*, 109-120.

Chan, A. T. S. (2000). WWW + smart card: Towards a mobile health care management system. *International Journal of Medical Informatics, 57*, 127-137.

Chandler, A. (1962). *Strategy and structure*. Boston: Harvard University Press.

Chandler, A. (1977). *The visible hand*. Boston: Harvard University Press.

Chang, S. E., Hsieh, Y. J., Chen, C. W., et al. (2006). Location-based services for tourism industry: An empirical study. *Lecture Notes in Computer Science, 4159,* 1144-1153.

Chaudhuri, A., & Holbrook, M. B. (2002). Product-class effects on brand commitment and brand outcomes: The role of brand trust and brand affect. *Brand Management, 10*(1), 33-58.

Chen, H. (2003). *An intelligent broker architecture for context-aware systems.* PhD dissertation proposal. Retrieved May 1, 2006, from http://umbc.edu/~hchen4/

Chen, M. (2005). A methodology for building mobile computing applications: Business strategy and technical architecture. *International Journal of Electronic Business, 2*(3), 229-243.

Chen, Y.-F. R., & Petrie, C. (2003). Ubiquitous mobile computing. *IEEE Internet Computing, 7*(2) 16-17.

Christensen, C. M. (1997). *The innovator's dilemma: When new technologies cause great firms to fail.* Boston: Harvard Business School Press.

Christensen, C., & Tedlow, R. (2000). Patterns of disruption in retailing. *Harvard Business Review, 78*(1), 42.

Churchill, G. A. J., & Iacobucci, D. (2002). *Marketing research; Methodological foundations.* South-Mason, OH: Western Publishing.

Clarke III, I. (2001). Emerging value propositions for m-commerce. *Journal of Business Strategies, 18*(2), 133-148.

Clarke, I., & Flaherty, T. (2003). Mobile portals: The development of m-commerce gateways. In B. E. Mennecke & T. J. Strader (Eds.), *Mobile commerce, technology, theory and applications* (pp. 185-201). Hershey, PA: Idea Group.

Claxton, K., Sculpher, M., & Drummond, M. (2002). *A rational framework for decision making.* National Institute for Clinical Excellence (NICE). *Lancet, 360,* 711-715.

Clemens, R. T. (1998). *Making hard decisions: An introduction to decision analysis.* Duxbury Press Brooks/Cole publishing Company.

ClickZ Services.com (2000, February 25). *ClickZ Services.com unleashes a new Web portal for wireless Internet.* Retrieved from Wow-com

Colgate, M. R., & Danaher, P. J. (2000). Implementing a customer relationship strategy: The asymmetric impact of poor versus excellent execution. *Journal of the Academy of Marketing Science, 28*(3), 375-387.

Colomer, M. J. (2002). El desafío es conseguir adaptar los hábitos y costumbres para afrontar la gestión clínica del presente Editorial. *Gestión Clínica y Sanitaria, 4,* 111-113.

Constantiou, I. D., Damsgaard, J., & Knutsen, L. (2004). *Strategic planning for mobile services adoption and diffusion: Empirical evidence from the Danish market.* Paper presented at the Mobile Information Systems (MOBIS), Oslo, Norway.

Constantiou, I. D., Damsgaard, J., & Knutsen, L. (2005). *Beware of Dane-geld: Even if paid, m-service adoption can be slow.* Paper presented at the European Conference on Information Systems (ECIS), Regensburg, Germany.

Constantiou, I. D., Damsgaard, J., & Knutsen, L. (in press). The four evolution steps to advanced mobile services' adoption. *Communications of the ACM.*

Constantiou, I., Damsgaard, J., & Knutsen, L. (2006). Exploring perceptions and use of mobile services: User differences in an advancing market. *International Journal of Mobile Communications, 4*(3), 231-247.

Consumer Protection Board (CPB). (2004). *Summary: A survey of teenagers' mobile phone and wireless Internet usage pattern.* Author.

Cotte, J., Tilottama, G. C., Ratneshwar, S., & Ricci, L. (2006). Pleasure or utility? Time planning style and Web usage behaviors. *Journal of Interactive Marketing, 20*(1), 45-57.

Coursaris, C., Hassanein, K., & Head, M. (2003). M-Commerce in Canada: An interaction framework for wireless privacy. *Canadian Journal of Administrative Sciences, 20*(1), 54-73.

Crawford, R., & Mathews, R. (2001). *The myth of excellence: Why great companies never try to be the best at everything.* New York: Crown Business.

Creswell, J. W. (2003). *Research design qualitative, quantitative and mixed methods approaches* (2nd ed.). Chennai, India: Sage.

Cronin, J., & Taylor, S. (1992). Measuring service quality: A reexamination and extension. *Journal of Marketing, 56*(3), 55-68.

Cronin, J., & Taylor, S. (1994). SERVREF vs. SERVQUAL: Reconciling performance-based and perceptions-minu-expectations measurement of service quality. *Journal of Marketing, 58*(1), 125-131.

Cummings, S., & Angwin, D. (2004). The future shape of strategy: Lemmings or chimeras? *Academy of Management Executive, 18*(2), 21-36.

Curwen, P. (2006). Mobile television. *Communications & Strategies, 62,* 183-195.

Cyr, D., & Trevor-Smith, H. (2004). Localization of Web design: An empirical comparison of German, Japanese, and United States Web site characteristics. *Journal of the American Society for Information Science and Technology, 55*(13), 1199-1208.

Cyr, D., Head, M., & Ivanov, A. (2006). Design aesthetics leading to m-loyalty in mobile commerce. *Information & Management, 43*(8), 950-963.

Dabholkar, P. A. (1996). Customer evaluations of new technology-based self-service options: An investigation of alternative models of service quality. *International Journal of Research in Marketing, 13,* 29-51.

Daemen, J., & Rijmen, V. (2001). Rijndael, the advanced encryption standard. *Dr Dobb's Journal.*

Daft, R., & Lengel, R. (1986). Organizational formation requirements, media richness and structural design. *Management Science, 32*(5), 555-571.

Dahlbom, B., & Ljungberg, F. (1998). Mobile informatics. *Scandinavian Journal of Information Systems, 10*(1&2), 227-234.

Daishin Security. (2005). *Daishin equity report (SK Telecom).* Author.

Damsgaard, J., & Marchegiani, L. (2004). Like Rome, a mobile operator's empire wasn't built in a day! A journey through the rise and fall of mobile network operators. In J. Marjin, et al. (Eds.), *ICEC '04, ACM Sixth International Conference on Electronic Commerce* (pp. 639-648).

Davidson, P. (2002, July 9). Disinterest snags mobile commerce. *USA Today.* Retrieved September 12, 2002, from www.usatoday.com

Davis, F. (1986). *Technology acceptance model for empirically testing new end-user information systems: Theory and results.* Boston.

Davis, F. D. (1989). Perceived usefulness, perceived ease of use, and user acceptance of information technology. *MIS Quarterly, 13*(3), 319-340.

Davis, F. D., & Venkatesh, V. (1996). A model of the antecedents of perceived ease of use: Development and test. *Decision Sciences, 27*(3), 451.

Davis, F. D., Bagozzi, R., & Warshaw, P. R. (1989). User acceptance of computer technology: A comparison of two theoretical models. *Management Science, 35*(8).

Davison, J., Brown, D., & Walsh, A. (2000). *Mobile e-commerce market strategy.* Ovum.

Dawkins, S., Montenegro, G., Kojo, M., & Magret V. (2001). End-to-end performance implications of slow links. *RFC3150.* Retrieved from http://www.faqs.org/rfcs/rfc3150.html

Del Galdo, E., & Neilson, J. (1996). *International user interfaces.* New York: Wiley.

Del Llano Señarís, J. E. (2003). Gestión Clínica y Sanitaria: ayudando a conciliar necesidad y escasez [Editorial]. *Gestión Clínica y Sanitaria, 5*(3-6), 2.

Dernbach, C. (2003). *UMTS-Start in Deutschland nicht in Sicht.* Retrieved April 20, 2006, from http://www.heise.de/newsticker/meldung/print/39973

DeZoysa, S. (2002, February). Mobile advertising needs to get personal. *Telecommunications International.*

Dickinger, A., Arami, M., & Meyer, D. (2006, January 4-7). *Reconsidering the adoption process: Enjoyment and social norms—Antecedents of Hedonic mobile technology use.* Paper presented at the 39th Hawaii International Conference on System Sciences, Kaua'i.

Dierks, T., & Allen, C. (1997). The TLS Protocol [Version 1.0]. Internet-Draft.

Ding, M. S., & Hampe, J. F. (2003, June 9-11). Reconsidering the challenges of mPayments: A roadmap to plotting the potential of the future M-Commerce Market. Paper presented at the *16ᵗʰ Bled eCommerce Conference eTransformation,* Bled, Slovenia.

Ding, M. S., & Unnithan, R. C. (2004). Mobile payments (m-payments)—An exploratory study of emerging issues and future trends. In P. C. Deans (Ed.), *E-commerce and m-commerce technologies.* Hershey, PA: Idea Group.

Dittrich, K., & Van den Ende, J. (2006, June 18-20). *Organizational forms for the development of new broadband services: A dynamic model for the degree of integration between collaborating firms.* Paper presented at the DRUID Summer Conference 2006, Copenhagen, Denmark.

Dix, A., Rodden, T., Davies, N., Trevor, J., Friday, A., & Palfreyman, K. (2000). Exploiting space and location as a design framework for interactive mobile systems. *ACM Transactions on Computer-Human Interaction, 7*(3), 281-321.

Dous, M., Salomann, H., Kolbe, L., & Brenner, W. (2004). *CRM—Status quo und zukünftige Entwicklungen.* Switzerland: Universität St. Gallen.

Downes, M., Hemmasi, M., Graf, L. A., Kelley, L., & Huff, L. (2002). The propensity to trust: A comparative study of United States and Japanese managers. *International Journal of Management, 19*(4), 614-621.

Ducoffe, R. H. (1995). How consumers assess the value of advertising. *Journal of Current Issues and Research in Advertising, 17*(1), 1-18.

Ducoffe, R. H. (1996). Advertising value and advertising on the Web. *Journal of Advertising Research, 36,* 21-36.

Duguid, P. (2005). "The art of knowing": Social and tacit dimensions of knowledge and the limits of the community of practice. *The Information Society, 21,* 109-118.

Durlacher. (1999). *Mobile commerce report.*

Dursch, A., & Yen, D. (2004). Bluetooth technology: An exploratory study of the analysis and implementation frameworks. *Computer Standards and Interfaces, 26*(4), 263-277.

Dursch, A., Yen, D., & Huang, S. (2005). Fourth generation wireless communications: An analysis of future potential and implementation. *Computer Standards and Interfaces, 28*(1), 13-25.

Dwyer, F. R., Schurr, P. H., & Oh, S. (1987). Developing buyer-seller relationships. *Journal of Marketing, 51*(2), 11-27.

E-Business Connection. (2002). *Critical success factors for e-business.* Retrieved November 12, 2002, from www.e-bc.ca

ECAR Respondent Summary. (2002). *Wireless networking in higher education in the U.S. and Canada.* Retrieved January 19, 2003, from http://www.educause.edu/ir/library/pdf/ecar_so/ers/ers0202/EKF0202.pdf

Ehmer, M. (2002). Mobile Dienste im Auto—Die Perspektive der Automobilhersteller. In R. Reichwald (Ed.), *Mobile Kommunikation: Wertschöpfung, Technologies, neue Dienste* (pp. 459-472). Wiesbaden, Germany: Gabler.

Eisenhardt, K. M. (1989). Building theories from case study research. *Academy of Management Review, 14*(4), 532-550.

Eklund, S., & Pessi, K. (2001). *Exploring mobile e-commerce in geographical bound retailing.* Paper presented at the Hawaii International Conference on Systems Science (HICSS).

Eom, M. (2006). T-DMB overview in Korea. In *Proceedings of 2006 Wireless Telecommunications Symposium,* Pomona, CA.

EPCglobal—The source—Global round-up. (2004, August). Retrieved May 9, 2006, from http://www.epc-globalinc.org/thesource/2004_08/html/global_roundup.html

EPCglobal—The source—Global round-up. (2005, January). Retrieved May 9, 2006, from http://www.epc-globalinc.org/thesource/2005_01/html/global_roundup.html

EPCglobal—The source—Global round-up. (2006, January). Retrieved May 9, 2006, from http://www.epc-globalinc.org/thesource/2006_01/html/global_roundup.html

Eppler, M., Seifried, P., & Röpnack, A. (1999, April 8). *Improving knowledge intensive processes through an enterprise knowledge medium.* Paper presented at the ACM SIGCPR conference on computer personnel research.

Ersala, N., & Yen, D. (2002). Bluetooth technology: A strategic analysis of its role in global 3G wireless communication era. *Computer Standards & Interfaces, 24*(3), 193-206.

ETRI. (2004). *Korea's mobile services gross revenue.* Author.

Eurobarometer. (2006). *Safer Internet.*

Faber, E., Ballon, P., Bouwman, H., Haaker, T., Rietkerk, O., & Steen, M. (2003, June 9-11). *Designing business models for mobile ICT services.* Positioning paper for workshop on concepts, metrics & visualization. In *Proceedings of the Bled E-commerce conference,* Bled, Slovenia.

Fagrell, H., Ljungberg, F., & Kristoffersen, S. (1999). Exploring support for knowledge management in mobile work. In *Proceedings of the 6th European Conference on Computer Supported Cooperative Work,* Copenhagen, Denmark.

Fan, H. Y., & Poole, M. S. (2006). What is personalization? Perspectives on the design and implementation of personalization in information systems. *Journal Of Organizational Computing And Electronic Commerce,*

16(3-4), 179-202.

Färber, B., & Färber, B. (1984). *Sprachausgaben im Fahrzeug. Handbuch für Anwender.* Frankfurt am Main: Forschungsvereinigung Automobiltechnik e.V.

Faria, G., Henriksson, J., Stare, E., & Talmola, P. (2006). DVB-H: Digital broadcast services to handheld devices. *Proceedings of the IEEE, 94*(1), 194-209.

Feagin, J. R., Orum, A. M., & Sjoberg, G. (1991). *A case for the case study.* Chapel Hill, NC: The University of North Carolina Press.

Fei, X. (1992). *From the soil: The foundations of Chinese society (A translation of Fei Xiatong's Xiangtu Zhongguo)* (G. Hamilton & W. Zheng, Trans.). Berkeley: University of California Press.

Feldman, S. (2000). Mobile commerce for the masses. *IEEE Internet Computing, 4*(6), 74-75.

Ferro, E., & Potorti, F. (2005). Bluetooth and Wi-Fi wireless protocols: A survey and a comparison. *Wireless Communications, IEEE, 12*(1), 12-26.

Fife, E., & Pereira, F. (2005). Global acceptance of technology (GAT) and demand for mobile data services. In *Proceedings of the Hong Kong Mobility Roundtable (CD).*

Figge, S. (2001, May 3). *Situation dependent m-commerce applications.* Paper presented at the Conference on Telecommunications and Information Markets—CO-TIM, Providence, RI.

Figge, S. (2002). Die open mobile architecture—Systemumgebung für mobile Dienste der nächsten Generation. *Wirtschaftsinformatik, 44*(4), 375-378.

Figge, S., Schrott, G., Muntermann, J., & Rannenberg, K. (2002, June 16). *EARNING M-ONEY—A situation based approach for mobile business models.* Paper presented at the European Conference on Information Systems, Neapel, Italy.

Flanagan, S., Fong, J., Horne, S., McIntyre, F., & Robert, P. (2003). *Mobile commerce: Regulatory and policy outlook,* Melbourne VIC 8010: Discussion Paper. Australian

Communications Authority.

Flanigan, M. (2006). *TIA's 2006 telecommunications market review and forecast.* Telecommunications Industry Association. Retrieved from www.tiaonline.org

Fleisch, E. (2001). *Business perspectives on ubiquitous computing.* St. Gallen, Switzerland.

Fleisch, E., & Bechmann, T. (2002). *Ubiquitous computing: Wie "intelligente Dinge" die Assekuranz verändern.* St. Gallen, Switzerland.

Fleisch, E., Mattern, F., & Österle, H. (2002). *Betriebliche anwendungen mobiler technologien: Ubiquitous commerce.* St. Gallen, Switerzland.

Floch, J., Hallsteinsen, S., Lie, A., & Myrhaug, H. I. (2001). *A reference model for context-aware mobile services.* Retrieved July 29, 2003, from www.nik.no/2001/06-floch.pdf

Flörkemeier, C., Anarkat, D., Osisnki, T., & Harrison, M. (2003). *PML core specification 1.0* (White Paper). Cambridge, MA: MIT, Auto-ID Center.

Floyd, C. (1983). *A systematic look at prototyping.* Paper presented at the Approaches to Prototyping, Namur, Belgium.

Fortunati, L. (2001). The mobile phone: An identity on the move. *Personal and Ubiquitous Computing, 5*(2), 85-98.

Four in ten users want to carry out mobile commerce. (2002). *Card Technology Today, 14*(5), 7-8.

Fournier, S., Dobscha, S., & Mick, D. G. (1998). Preventing the premature death of relationship marketing. *Harvard Business Review, 76*(11), 43-51.

Frattasi, S., Fathi, H., Fitzek, F. H. P., Prasad, R., & Katz, M. D. (2006). Defining 4G technology from the user's perspective. *Network, IEEE, 20*(1), 35-41.

Freier, A., Karlton, P., & Kocher, P. (1996). The SSL protocol [Version 3.0]. Internet-Draft.

Frichol, M. (2004). There's no business like e-business. *IIE Solutions, 33*(3), 38.

Fritsch, L., & Rossnagel, H. (2004). SIM-based mobile electronic signatures: Enabling m-business with certification on demand. *Card Forum International, 8*(1), 38-40.

Frost & Sullivan. (2003). *Customer attitudes and perceptions towards telematics in passenger vehicles market.*

Fuhr, A. (2001). *Die Telematik ist tot—es lebe die rollende Schnittstelle.* Paper presented at the Euroforum Jahrestagung "Telematik," Bonn.

Fullerton, G. (2005). How commitment both enables and undermines marketing relationships. *European Journal of Marketing, 39*(11/12), 1372-1388.

Funk, J. L. (2003). *Mobile disruption: The technologies and applications driving the obile Internet.* Hoboken, NJ: Jon Wiley & Sons.

Funk, J. L. (2004). Key technological trajectories and the expansion of mobile Internet applications. *Info—The Journal of Policy, Regulation and Strategy for Telecommunications, 6*(3), 208-215.

Garcia-Martin, M., Henrikson, E., & Mills, D. (2003). *Private header (P-Header) extensions to the session initiation protocol (SIP) for the 3rd-generation partnership project (3GPP)* (No. RFC 3455): The Internet Engineering Task Force.

Gardner, M. P. (1985) Does attitude toward the ad affect brand attitude under a brand evaluation set? *Journal of Marketing Research, 22,* 192-198.

Gast, M. S. (2005). *802.11 Wireless Networks: The Definitive Guide.* O'Reilly.

Gebauer, J. (2002, June 17). *Assessing the value of emerging technologies: The case of mobile technologies to enhance business to business applications.* Paper presented at the 15th Bled Electronic Commerce Conference, Bled, Slovenia.

Gebauer, J., & Shaw, M. J. (2004). Success factors and impacts of mobile business applications: Results from a mobile e-procurement study. *International Journal of Electronic Commerce, 8*(3), 19-41.

Gebert, H., Geib, M., Kolbe, L. M., & Brenner, W. (2003). Knowledge-enabled customer relationship management. *Journal of Knowledge Management, 7*(5), 107-123.

Geib, M., Reichold, A., Kolbe, L. M., & Brenner, W. (2005, January 3). *Architecture for customer relationship management approaches in financial services,* Big Island, HI.

Geier, J. (2001, February 5). *Saving lives with roving LANs.* Retrieved from http://wireless.itworld.com/4246/NWW0205bgside/pfindex.html

Geng, X., & Whinston, A. B. (2001). Profiting from value-added wireless services. *Computer, 34*(8), 87-89.

Get Process AG. (2006). *Income process designer.* Retrieved May 25, 2006, from http://www.get-process.de

Gharavi, H. P., Love, & Cheng, E. (2004). Information and communication technology in the stockbroking industry: An evolutionary approach to the diffusion of industry. *Industrial Management & Data Systems, 104*(9), 756-765.

Ghosh, A., Wolter, D. R., Andrews, J. G., & Chen, R. (2005). Broadband wireless access with WiMax/802.16: Current performance benchmarks and future potential. *IEEE Communications Magazine, 43,* 129-136.

Giaglis, G. M., Kourouthanassis, P., & Tsamakos, A. (2003). Towards a classification framework for mobile location services. In B. E. Mennecke & T. J. Strader (Eds.), *Mobile commerce: Technology, theory, and applications* (pp. 67-85). Hershey, PA: Idea Group.

Gibert, A. L., & Kendall, J. D. (2003, January). A marketing model of for mobile wireless services. In *Proceedings of 36th Hawaii International Conference on Systems Sciences,* Big Island, HI.

Gilbert, A. L., & Han, H. (2005). Understanding mobile data services adoption: Demography, attitudes or needs? *Technological Forecasting & Social Change, 72,* 327-337.

Gilbert, D., Lee-Kelley, L., & Barton, M. (2003). Technophobia, gender influence and consumer decision-making for technology-related products. *European Journal of Innovation Management, 6*(4), 253-263.

Gleason, D. H., & Friedman, L. (2005). Proposal for an accessible conception of cyberspace. *Journal of Information, Communication & Ethics in Society, 1,* 15-23.

Global Wireless Telecommunication Services. (2006). London: Datamonitor PLC. Retrieved April 12, 2007, from Business Source Premier database.

Goldin, D., & Wegner, P. (2004). *The origins of the Turing thesis myth* (Tech. Rep. No. CS-04-13). Providence, RI: Brown University.

Goldsmith, R. E., Lafferty, B. A., & Newell, S. J. (2000). The impact of corporate credibility and celebrity credibility on consumer reaction to advertisements and brands. *Journal of Advertising, 29*(3), 43-54.

Gordon, M. E., & De Lima-Turner, K. (1997). Consumer attitudes towards Internet advertising. *International Marketing Review, 14*(5), 352-375.

Goth, G. (2004). Wireless MAN standard signals next-gen opportunities. *IEEE Distributed Systems Online, 5*(8), 4.

Green, K. C. (2002). Campus computing looks ahead: Tracking the digital puck. *Syllabus, 16*(5), 22-25.

Green, K. C. (2003). *The 2003 national survey of information technology in U.S. higher education.* Retrieved September 6, 2004, from http://www.educause.edu/ir/library/pdf/EDU0324.pdf

Green, K. C. (2003). *Campus computing, 2003.* Retrieved September 6, 2004, from http://www.educause.edu/ir/library/pdf/EDU0324a.pdf

Green, K. C. (2004). *The 2004 national survey of information technology in US higher education.* Retrieved May 14, 2005, from http://www.campuscomputing.net/

Green, N., Harper, R. H. R., Murtagh, G., & Cooper, G. (2001) Configuring the mobile user: Sociological and industry views. *Personal and Ubiquitous Computing, 5*(2), 146-156.

Greiling, M., & Hofstetter, J. (2002). Patientenbehandlungspfade optimieren—Prozessmanagement im Krankenhaus. Baumann Fachverlag, Kulmbach (Germany).

Grob, L. (1999). *Einführung in die Investitionsrechnung* (3rd ed.). München, Germany: Vahlen.

Groenroos, C. (1994). From marketing mix to relationship marketing: Towards a paradigm shift in marketing. *Marketing Decision, 32*(2), 4-20.

Gross, S., Fleisch, E., Lampe, M., & Miller, R. (2004). *Requirements and technologies for ubiquitous payment.* Retrieved from http://www.vs.inf.ethz.ch/res/papers/MKWI_UPayment.pdf

Grush, M. (2002). Editor's note. *Syllabus, 16*(3), 4.

Gummesson, E. (1987). The new marketing. Developing long-term interactive relationships. *Long Range Planning, 20*(4), 10-20.

Gupta, V., & Gupta, S. (2001). Securing the wireless Internet. *IEEE Communication.*

Gutmann, A., & Sochatzky, C. (2003). *Mobile applications for teenagers.* Unpublished masters thesis, Vienna University of Economics and Business Administration, Austria.

Ha, L. (1996). Observations: Advertising clutter in consumer magazines: Dimensions and effects. *Journal of Advertising Research, 36*(4), 76-84.

Haaker, T., Bouwman, H., & Faber, E. (2004). Customer and network value of mobile services: Balancing requirements and strategic interests. In R. Agarwal, L. Kirsch, & J. I. DeGross (Eds.), *Proceedings of the 25th international conference on Information systems (ICIS 2004)* (pp. 1-14).

Hagel, J., & Singer, M. (1999). Unbundling the corporation. *Harvard Business Review, 77*(2), 133-141.

Haghirian, P., & Dickinger, A. (2004). *Identifying success factors of mobile marketing.* ACR Asia-Pacific 2004, Association of Consumer Research, 28-29.

Haghirian, P., Dickinger, A., & Kohlbacher, F. (2004, November). Adopting innovative technology—A qualitative study among Japanese mobile consumers. In *Proceedings of the 5th International Working with e-Business Conference (WeB-2004),* Perth, Australia.

Hair, J. F. (1998). *Multivariate data analysis.* Prentice Hall.

Hair, J. F. J., Bush, R. P., & Ortinau, D. J. (2000). *Marketing research: A practical approach for the new millennium*: McGraw-Hill International Editions.

Hall, E. T., & Hall, M. R. (1987). *Hidden differences; Doing business with the Japanese.* New York: Anchor Books, Doubleday.

Hämäläinen, M. (2006). Enabling innovation in mobile games—Going beyond the conventional. In *Proceedings of Mobility Round Table,* Finland: Helsinki School of Economics.

Hammond, K., & Salpeter, J. (n.d.). *Cutting the cord: Wireless computing comes of age.* Retrieved January 20, 2003, from http://www.cosn.org/initiatives/compendium/3.pdf

Han, S.-Y., Cho, M.-K., & Choi, M.-K. (2005, July 11). *Ubitem: A framework for interactive marketing in location-based gaming environment.* Paper presented at the Proceedings of the Fourth International Conference on Mobile Business (mBusiness), Sydney, Australia.

Haque, A. (2004). Mobile commerce: Customer perception and it's prospect on business operation. *Journal of American Academy of Business, 4*(1/2), 257.

Harrington, S., & Niehaus, G. R. (2003). *Risk management & insurance* (2nd ed.). Boston: McGraw-Hill.

Harter, A., Hopper, A., Steggles, P., Ward, A., & Webster, P. (1999). The anatomy of a context-aware application. In *Proceedings of the ACM/IEEE MobiCom.*

Hartline, M. D., Maxham, J. G., & McKee, D. O. (2000). Corridors of influence in the dissemination of customer-oriented strategy to customer contact service employees. *Journal of Marketing, 64*(2), 35-50.

Hartmann, J. (2004). Wo viel Licht ist, ist starker Schatten - Softwareentwicklung in der Automobilindustrie. *Automatisierungstechnik, 52*(8), 353-358.

Hartmann, S., & Dirksen, V. (2001). Effizienzsteigerungen von unternehmensinternen Prozessen durch die Integration von Komponenten des M-Business. *Information Management & Consulting, 16*(2), 16-19.

Haskin, D. (1999, November 3). *Analysts: Smart phones to lead e-commerce explosion.* allNetDevices

Hawick, K. A., & James, H. A. (2003). Middleware for context sensitive mobile applications. In C. Johnson, P. Montague, & C. Steketee (Eds.), *Workshop on Wearable, Invisible, Context-Aware, Ambient, Pervasive and Ubiquitous Computing* (Vol. 21). Adelaide, Australia. Conferences in Research and Practice in Information Technology.

Heidingsfelder, M., Kintz, E., Petry, R., Hensley, P., & Sedran, T. (2001). *Telematics: How to hit a moving target—A roadmap to success in the Telematics arena.* Detroit/Stuttgart/Tokyo: Roland Berger.

Heinonen, K. (2004). Reconceptualizing customer perceived value: The value of time and place. *Managing Service Quality, 14*(2/3), 205-215.

Heinonen, K. (2004). Time and location as customer perceived value drivers. Unpublished doctoral thesis, Hanken, Swedish School of Economics and Business Administration, Finland.

Heinonen, K. (2006). Temporal and spatial e-service value. *International Journal of Service Industry Management, 17*(4), 380-400.

Heinonen, K., & Andersson, P. (2003). Swedish mobile market: Consumer perceptions of mobile services. *Communications & Strategies, 49,* 151-171.

Heitmann, M., Prykop, C., & Aschmoneit, P. (2004). Using means-end chains to build mobile brand communities. In *Proceedings of the 37th Hawaii International Conference on System Sciences*, Big Island.

Hengst, M. den, & De Vreede, G. J. (2004). Collaborative business engineering: A decade of lessons from the field. *Journal of Management Information Systems, 20*(4), 87-115.

Henkal, J. (2001) *Mobile payment: The German and European perspective.* In G. Silberer (Ed.), Mobile commerce.

Retrieved from http://www.inno-tec.de/forschung/henkal/M-Payment%20e.pdf

Henten, A., Olesen, H., Saugstrup, D., & Tan, S.-E. (2004). Mobile communications: Europe, Japan and South Korea in a comparative perspective. *The Journal of Policy, Regulation, and Strategy for Telecommunications, Information and Media, 6*(3), 197-207.

Hevner, A. R., March, S. T., Park, J., & Ram, S. (2004). Design science in information systems research. *MIS Quarterly, 28*(1), 75-105.

Hightower, J., & Borriello, G. (2001). Location systems for ubiquitous computing. *IEEE Computer Magazine, 34*(8), 57-66.

Hikmet, N., & Chen, S. K. (2003). An investigation into low mail survey response rates of information technology users in health care organizations. *International Journal of Medical Informatics, 72,* 29-34.

Hitt, L., & Brynjolfsson, E. (1994, December). *Creating value and destroying profits? Three measures of information technology's contribution.*

Hjorth, L. (2005). Postal presence: A case study of mobile customisation and gender in Melbourne. In P. B. Glotz, S. & Locke, C (Eds.), *Thumb culture: The meaning of mobile phones for society.* Bielefeld, Germany: Transcript-Verlag.

Hofstede, G. H. (2001). *Culture's consequences: Comparing values, behaviors, institutions and organizations across nations* (2nd ed.). Thousand Oaks, CA: Sage.

Högler, T. (2006). Framework für eine holistische Wirtschaftlichkeitsanalyse mobiler Systeme. In *Proceedings of the MKWI Multikonferenz Wirtschaftsinformatik 2006*, Universität Passau, Germany.

Holma, H., & Toskala, A. (2000) *WCDMA for UMTS: Radio access for third generation mobile communications.* New York: Wiley.

Holmlund, M. (1997). Perceived quality in business relationships (Doctoral dissertation No. 66). Hanken, Swedish School of Economics and Business Administration, Finland.

Holtmann, C., Rashid, A., Weinhardt, C., Gräfe, A., & Griewing, B. (2006). Time is brain—Analyse der Rettungskette im Schlaganfall. In *Proceedings of the 5th Workshop of the GMDS Workgroup Mobiles Computing in der Medizin,* Frankfurt, Germany: Shaker Verlag.

Huang, C. J., Trappey, A. J. C., & Yao, Y. H. (2006). Developing an agent-based workflow management system for collaborative product design. *Industrial Management & Data Systems, 106*(5-6), 680-699.

Huh, W. (2006, May 10). The gap of data ARPU among mobile carriers. *Financial News.*

Humpert, F., & Habbel, F.-R. (2002). Mobile Dienste für die Öffentlichkeit. *HMD Praxis der Wirtschaftsinformatik, 226,* 37-43.

Hyvönen, K., & Repo, P. (2005). Mobiilipalvelut suomalaisten arjessa (Mobile Serives in the quotidienne of Finns). In Vox consumptoris—Kuluttajan ääni, Johanna Leskinen and Hannele Hallman and Merja Isoniemi and Liisa Perälä and Taina Pohjoisaho & Erja Pylvänäinen (Eds.). Kerava: Kuluttajatutkimuskeskus.

IBM & Microsoft (2002). *Security in a Web Services World: A Proposed Architecture and Roadmap.* Retrieved from, http://www-128.ibm.com/developerworks/library/specification/ws-secmap/

Imamura, T., Dillaway, B., & Simon, E. (2002). *XML. Encryption, syntax and processing.* W3C Recommendation. Retrieved from http://www.w3.org/TR/xmlenc-core/

Information Society Technologies (IST). (2000). *Global communication architecture and protocols for new QoS services over IPv6 networks (GCAP).* EU Framework 4 program. Author.

International Telecommunication Union (ITU). (2001). *ASN.1 encoding rules: XML encoding rules (XER). ITU-T Recommendation X.693.* Retrieved from http://www.itu.int/ITU-T/studygroups/com17/languages/X.680-X.693-0207w.zip

International Telecommunications Union (ITU). (2005). *ITU Internet reports 2005: The Internet of things.* Geneva, Switzerland: Author.

International Telecommunications Union (ITU). (2006). *World telecommunications indicators.* Author.

International Telecommunications Union. (2005). *Mobile cellular subscribers per 100 people.* Retrieved May 9, 2006, from http://www.itu.int/ITU-D/ict/statistics/at_glance/cellular04.pdf

Isoniemi, K., & Wolf, G. (2001). Three segments of mobile users. In *Proceedings of the Seamless Mobility Workshop,* Stockholm, Sweden.

Istepanian, R. S. H., & Lacal, J. (2003, September 17-21). *Emerging mobile communication technologies for health: Some imperative notes on m-health.* In *Proceedings of the 25th. Annual International Conference of the IEEE Engineering in Medicine and Biology* (pp. 1414-1416). Cancun, Mexico.

Istepanian, R. S. H., Jovanov, E., & Zhang, Y. T. (2004). *M-Health: Beyond seamless mobility for global wireless healthcare connectivity* [Editorial]. *IEEE Transactions on Information Technology in Biomedicine, 8*(4), 405-412.

Itani, W., & Kayssi, A. (2003). J2ME end-to-end security for m-commerce. In *Proceedings of the IEEE Wireless Communications and Networking Conference.* New Orleans, LA.

Itani, W., & Kayssi, A. (2004). SPECSA: A scalable, policy-driven, extensible, and customizable security architecture for wireless enterprise applications. In *Proceedings of the Workshop on Information Assurance (WIA04).* Phoenix, AZ.

Itani, W., Gaspard, C., Kayssi, A., & Chehab, A. (2006). PRIDE: Policy-driven Web security for handheld wireless devices. In *Proceedings of IEEE GLOBECOM 2006,* San Francisco.

Itani, W., Kayssi, A., & Chehab, A. (2005). PATRIOT—A policy-based, multi-level security protocol for safekeeping audit logs on wireless devices. In *Proceedings of IEEE/CreateNet First International Conference on Security and Privacy for Emerging Areas in Communication Networks (SecureComm).* Athens, Greece.

Itani, W., Kayssi, A., & Chehab, A. (2005). SPARTA: A secure, policy-driven architecture for content distribution and storage in centralized wireless networks. In *Proceedings of Fist International Workshop on Security, Privacy, and Trust in Pervasive and Ubiquitous Computing (SecPerU'05)*. Santorini, Greece.

Itani, W., Kayssi, A., & Chehab, A. (2006). An enterprise policy-based security protocol for protecting relational database network objects. In *Proceedings of the 2006 International Wireless Communications and Mobile Computing Conference (IWCMC 2006)*. Vancouver, Canada.

Itani, W., Kayssi, A., & Chehab, A. (2006). SECERN: A secure enterprise backup and recovery protocol for mission-critical relational database servers. In *Proceedings of the Innovation in Information Technology Conference (IIT 06)*, Dubai, UAE.

Jain, R. (2003). *Enterprise mobile services: Framework and industry-specific analysis*. Paper presented at the Americas Conference on Information Systems 2003, Tampa, FL.

Jan ten Duis, H., & Van der Werken, C. (2003). Trauma care systems in The Netherlands. *Injury—International Journal of the Care of the Injured, 34*(9), 722-727.

Järvenpää, S. L., & Lang, K. R. (2005). Managing the paradoxes of mobile technology. *Information Systems Management, 22*(4), 7-23.

Järvenpää, S. L., & Leidner, D. E. (1999). Communication and trust in global virtual teams. *Organization Science, 10*(6), 791-815.

Jelekäinen, P. (2004). GSM–PKI solution enabling secure mobile communications. *International Journal of Medical Informatics, 73*, 317-320.

JiWire. (2006). Retrieved August 05, 2006, from http://www.jiwire.com/search- hotspot-locations.htm

Johansson, J. K., & Nonaka, I. (1996). *Relentless—The Japanese way of marketing*. New York: Harper Business.

Jones, N. (2003, January 28). *Pay box retrenches, but its technology remains active*. Retrieved from http://gartner11.gartnerweb.com/resources/112800/112827/112827.pdf

Jutla, D., Bodorik, P., & Wang, Y. (1999). Developing Internet e-commerce benchmarks. *IEEE Computer, 24*(6), 475-493.

Kadyte, V. (2005, July 11). *Process visibility: How mobile technology can enhance business-customer care in the paper industry*. Paper presented at the Proceedings of the Fourth International Conference on Mobile Business (mBusiness), Sydney, Australia.

Kakihara, M., & Sørensen, C. (2001). Expanding the "mobility" concept. *ACM SIGGROUP Bulletin archive, 22*(3), 33-37.

Kakihara, M., & Sørensen, C. (2002). Mobility: An extended perspective. In *Proceedings of the Hawai'i International Conference on System Sciences*, Big Island.

Kallinikos, J. (2002, December 14-16). Re-opening the black box of technology: Artifacts and human agency. In *23rd ICIS* (pp. 287-294). Barcelona, Spain.

Kanter, T. G. (2003). Attaching context-aware services to moving locations. *IEEE Internet Computing, 7*(2), 43-51.

Karat, C.-M., Blom, J., & Karat, J. (2003). Designing personalized user experiences for E-Commerce: Theory, methods, and research. In *CHI 2003: New Horizons* (pp. 1040-1041).

Karnouskos, S., & Fraunhofer, F. (2004). Mobile payment: A journey through existing procedures and standardization initiatives. *IEEE Communications Surveys, 6*, 44-66.

Katz, M. L., & Shapiro, C. (1985). Network externalities, competition, and compatibility. *American Economic Review, 75*(3), 424-440.

Katz, M. L., & Shapiro, C. (1992). Product introduction with network externalities. *Journal of Industrial Economics, 40*(1), 55-83.

KBS. (2006). *Baseball boom in sports and marketing.* Retrieved May 11, 2006, from http://english.kbs.co.kr/life/trend/1388891_11857.html

Keen, P. G. W., & Mackintosh, R. (2001). *The freedom economy: Gaining the M-Commerce edge in the era of the wireless Internet.* New York: Osborne/McGraw-Hill.

Keil, D., & Goldin, D. (2003). Modelling indirect interaction in open computational systems. In *Proceedings of the Twelfth IEEE International Workshops on Enabling Technologies: Infrastructure for Collaborative Enterprises (WETICE'03)*, Linz, Austria.

Kenny, D., & Marshall, J. F. (2000). Contextual marketing—The real business of the Internet. *Harvard Business Review, 78*(6), 119-125.

Kharif, O. (2007, February 20). Coming up: Vonage wireless? *BusinessWeek.com.* Retrieved April 20, 2007, from http://businessweek.com/technology/content/feb2007/tc20070220_452876.htm

Kilie, K., & Klaus, C. (2006). *Neuvermessung der Logistik: Aktuelle Ergebnisse aus der Studie Die „Top 100 der Logistik" 2006.* Retrieved May 9, 2006, from www.logistik-inside.de/fm/2239/LDL_Top_00Exec_2006.pdf

Kim, H.-S., & Yoon, C.-H. (2004). Determinants of subscriber churn and customer loyalty in the Korean mobile telephony market. *Telecommunications Policy, 28*(9-10), 751-765.

Kim, H.-W., Chuan Chan, H., & Gupta, S. (2005). Value-based adoption of mobile Internet: An empirical investigation. *Decision Support Systems, In Press.*

Kim, J. (2004). Terrestrial DMB's effects on the electronics industry. In *Proceedings of 2004 Terrestrial DMB International Forum* (pp. 131-142).

Kim, J. K. (2005). *Mobile subscribers' willingness to churn under the mobile number portability (MNP).* Paper presented at the the Eleventh Americas Conference on Information Systems, Omaha, NE.

Kim, M.-K., Park, M.-C., & Jeong, D.-H. (2004). The effects of customer satisfaction and switching barrier on customer loyalty in Korean mobile telecommunication services. *Telecommunications Policy, 28*(2), 145-159.

Kim, W. C., & Mauborgne, R. (1999). Creating new market space. *Harvard Business Review, 77*(1), 83-93.

Kim, W. C., & Mauborgne, R. (2005). *Blue ocean strategy: How to create uncontested market space and make the competition irrelevant.* Boston: Harvard Business School Press.

Kinnear, T. C., & Taylor, J. R. (1996). *Marketing research: An applied approach* (5th ed.). McGraw-Hill.

Kivirinta, T., Ali-Vehmas, T., Mutanen, T., Tuominen, T., & Vuorinen, M. (2004). *Forecasting market demand for mobile broadcast services in Finland* (Rep. No. 51530C). Finland: Helsinki University of Technology.

Kivisaari, E., & Luukainen, S. (2005). Markets and strategies for mobile broadcast in Finland. In *Proceedings of Information Society Technologies 2005*, Shiraz, Iran. Retrieved from http://www.tml.tkk.fi/~ekivisaa/Markets_and_Strategies_for_Mobile_Broadcast.pdf

Kleijnen, M., De Ruyter, K., & Andreassen, T. W. (2005). Image congruence and the adoption of service innovations. *Journal of Service Research, 7*(4), 343-359.

Kleijnen, M., Wetzels, M., & De Ruyter, K. (2004). Consumer acceptance of wireless finance. *Journal of Financial Services Marketing, 8*(3), 206-217.

Kleijnen, M., Wetzels, M., & De Ruyter, K. (2004). Consumer acceptance of wireless finance. *Journal of Financial Services Marketing, 8*(3), 206-217.

Kleinrock, L. (1996). Nomadicity: Anytime, anywhere in a disconnected world. *Mobile Networks and Applications, 1,* 351-357.

Kleinrock, L. (2001). Breaking loose. *Communications of the ACM, 44*(9), 41-45.

Kluver, R., & Powers, J. H. (1999). *Civic discourse, civil society, and Chinese communities.* Ablex.

Knoblauch, H. (2005). Focused ethnography. *Qualitative Social Research, 6*(3). Retrieved May 24, 2006, from http://www.qualitative-research.net/fqs-texte/3-05/05-3-44-e.htm

Köhler, A., & Gruhn, V. (2004, February 2-3). Mobile process landscaping am Beispiel von Vertriebsprozessen in der Assekuranz. Mobile economy: Transaktionen, Prozesse, Anwendungen und Dienste. In *Proceedings of the 4th Workshop Mobile Commerce,* Universität Augsburg, Germany.

Kohli, R., & Devaraj, S. (2004). Realizing the business benefits of information technology investments: An organizational process. *Misqe, 3*(2), 53-68.

Koivumäki, T., Ristola, A., & Kesti, M. (2006). Predicting consumer acceptance in mobile services: Empirical evidence from an experimental end user environment. *International Journal of Mobile Communications, 4*(4), 418-435.

Kopf, W. (2005). *The European mobile industry—A case for consolidation?* T-Mobile International AG & Co. KG.

Kopomaa, T. (2000). *The city in your pocket. Birth of the mobile information society.* Helsinki, Finland: Gaudeamus.

KORA Research. (2004, May). *A market policy study on DMB* (Rep. No. 2003-10). Author.

Korea Electronics Technology Institute (KETI). (2004). *Mobile contents market of 2004 in Korea.* Seoul: Author.

Korea Information Society Development Institute (KISDI). (2005). *The statues of telecommunication industry in Korea* (Issue report). Seoul, Korea: Author.

Korea Radio Station Management Agency. (2004). *A market policy study on DMB.* Author.

Korea's free mobile broadcasting faces snag. (2005, January 18). *The Korea Times.*

Korean Society for Journalism and Communication Studies. (2003). *A study on satellite DMB.* Author.

Kotler, P. (2003). *Marketing management.* Upper Saddle River, NJ: Pearson Education.

Kotler, P., & Keller, K. L. (2005). *Marketing management* (12 ed.). Upper Saddle River, NJ: Prentice Hall.

Kountz, E. (2002). Mobile commerce: No cell, no sale? *Card Technology, 7*(9), 20-22.

KPMG's Nolan Norton Institute. (2000). *Australia falling behind in e-commerce development.* Retrieved November 12, 2002, from www.cpaaustralia.com.au

Kramer, J., Noronha, S., & Vergo, J. (2000). A user-centered design approach to personalization. *Communications of the ACM, 42*(8), 45-48.

Kreyer, N., Pousttchi, K., & Turowski, K. (2002). *Characteristics of mobile payment procedures.* M-Services 2002. ftp.informatik.rwth-aachen.de/ Publications/CEUR-WS/Vol-61/paper1.pdf

Krishnamurthy, S. (2001). A comprehensive analysis of permission marketing. *Journal of Computer Mediated Communication, 6*(2). Retrieved from http://www.ascusc.org/jcmc/vol6/7issue2/krishnamurthy.html

Krishnamurthy, S. (2003). *E-Commerce management.* Mason, OH: Thomson Publishing.

Kristensen, B. B. May, D. Jensen, L. K., Gersbo-Møller, C., & Maersk, P. N. (2003). *Reality-virtuality continuum systems empowered with pervasive and ubiquitous computing technology: Combination and integration of real world and model systems.* Retrieved June 5, 2006, from http://scholar.google.fi/scholar?hl=en&lr=&q=cache: hr5pv8eE-EMJ:www.mip.sdu.dk/~bbk/teaching/sw04/reality54.pdf+kristensen+2003+virtual

KTF. (2002, November 4). KTF launches the world's first mobile payment handset based on IC chip. *KTF News.*

KTF. (2005a, April 27). 3 mobile carriers partner for release of mobile t-money service. *KTF News.*

KTF. (2005b, July 25). KTF's music portal "Dosirak" finds strong foundation in the market. *KTF News.*

KTF. (2005c, May 25). KTF expands service in Indonesia. *KTF News.*

KTF. (2005d, May 24). KTF opens music portal service Dosirak. *KTF News.*

KTF. (2005e, August 17). Mobile SMS now on PC messengers! *KTF News.*

KTF. (2005f, June 14). Singing a song, making it my ringtone! *KTF News.*

Kuhn, T. (1962). *The structure of scientific revolutions.* IL: University of Chicago Press.

Kung, H.-Y., Hsu, C.-Y., Lin, M.-H., & Liu, C.-N. (2006). Mobile multimedia medical system: Design and implementation. *International Journal of Mobile Communications, 4*(5), 595-620.

Kunze, C. P., Zaplata, S., & Lamersdorf, W. (2006, June 13). *Mobile process description and execution.* Paper presented at the 6th IFIP WG 6.1 International Conference on Distributed Applications and Interoperable Systems, Bologna, Itlay.

Kvale, S. (1983). The qualitative research interview: A phenomenological and a hermeneutical mode of understanding. *Journal of Phenomenological Psychology, 14*(2), 171-196.

Lafferty, B. A., Goldsmith, R. E., & Newell, S. J. (2002). The dual credibility model: The influence of corporate and endorser credibility on attitudes and purchase intentions. *Journal of Marketing Theory and Practice, 10*(3), 1-12.

Langley, C. Jr., Van Dort, E., Ang, A., & Sykes, S. R. (2005). *2005 third-party logistics. Results and findings of the survey* (Research Report), CapGemini, Georgia Institute of Technology, SAP, DHL.

Larkin, E. F. (1979). Consumer perceptions of the media and their advertising content. *Journal of Advertising, 8*(2), 5-48.

Larsen, T., & Sorebo, O. (2005). Impact of personal innovativeness on the use of the Internet among employees at Work. *Journal of Organizational and End User Computing, 17*(2), 43-63.

Lastovicka, J. L. (1983). Convergent and discriminant validity of television commercial rating scales. *Journal of Advertising, 12*(2), 14-23.

Laukkanen, T. (2005, July 11). *Comparing consumer value creation in Internet and mobile banking.* Paper presented at the Proceedings of the Fourth International Conference on Mobile Business (mBusiness), Sydney, Australia.

Laukkanen, T., & Kantanen, T. (2006). Customer value segments in mobile bill paying. In *Proceedings of the 3rd International Conference on Information Technology: New Generations 2006 (ITNG 2006),* Las Vegas, NV: IEEE Computer Society Press.

Laukkanen, T., & Lauronen, J. (2005). Consumer value creation in mobile banking services. *International Journal of Mobile Communications, 3*(4), 325-338.

Lawrence, S. (2005, January). Wireless on wheels—The latest advances in telematics. *Technology Review.*

Lawson, S. (2006). Faster gear to drive Wi-Fi market. *PC Magazine.* Retrieved August 05, 2006, from http://www.pcworld.com/article/124478-1/article.html

Lawton, G. (2002). Moving java into mobile phones. *IEEE Computer.*

Lazarsfeld, P., Jahoda, M., & Zeisel, H. (1933). *Die Arbeitslosen von Marienthal. Ein soziographischer Versuch über die Wirkungen langdauernder Arbeitslosigkeit.* Germany: Suhrkamp Leipzig.

Leavitt, N. (2000). Will WAP deliver the wireless Internet? *Computer, 33*(5), 16-20.

Lee, C.-S. (2001). An analytical framework for evaluating ecommerce business models and strategies. *Internet Research—Electronic Networking Application and Policy, 11*(4), 349-359.

Lee, C-W., Kou, W., & Hu, W-C. (2005). Mobile commerce security and payment methods. In W-C. Hu, C-W Lee, & W. Kou (Eds.), *Advances in security and payment methods for mobile commerce.* Hershey, PA: Idea Group.

Lee, H., & Sawyer, S. (2002). Conceptualizing time and space: Information technology, work, and organization. In *Proceedings of the Twenty-Third International Conference on Information Systems* (pp. 279-286).

Lee, J., Lee, J., & Feick, L. (2001). The impact of switching costs on the customer satisfaction-loyalty link: Mobile phone service in France. *Journal of Services Marketing, 15*(1), 35-48.

Lee, K.-M. (2005, September 22). Mobile network operators, 2,354billion KWON revenue of CID and SMS. *ISSUE-1.*

Lee, S. M. (2003). South Korea: From the land of morning calm to ICT hotbed. *Academy of Management Executive, 17*(2), 7-18.

Lee, Y. E., & Benbasat, I. (2003). Interface design for mobile commerce. *Communications of the ACM, 46*(12), 49-52.

Lee, Y., Kim, J., Lee, I., & Kim, H. (2002). A cross-cultural study on the value structure of mobile Internet usage: Comparison between Korea and Japan. *Journal of Electronic Commerce Research, 3*(4), 227-239.

Lehmann, H., Kuhn, J., & Lehner, F. (2004). The future of mobile technology: Findings from a European Delphi study. In *Proceedings of the 37th Hawaii International Conference on System Sciences,* Big Island, HI.

Lehmkuhl, F. (2003, January 6). Küsse und machotests. *FOCUS.*

Lehner, F. (2003). *Mobile und drahtlose Informationssysteme: Technologien, Anwendungen, Märkte.* Berlin, Germany: Springer.

Lerner, T., & Frank, V. (2004). *Best practices mobile business* (2nd ed.). BusinessVillage.de.

Levitt, T. (1983). After the sale is over... Author(s): Source: ; Sep/Oct83, Vol. 61 Issue 5, p87, 7p. *Harvard Business Review, 61*(5), 87-94.

LGRI. (2005). *The propensity to consume to new generation: White book* (CEO Report).

Liang, T.-P., & Wei, C.-P. (2004). Introduction to the special issue: Mobile commerce applications. *International Journal of Electronic Commerce, 8*(3), 7-17.

Libai, B., & Nitzan, I. (2005). Customer profitability over time in the presence of switching costs. In *Proceedings of 14th Annual Frontiers in Services Conference,* Arizona: The Center for Service Leadership, W.B. Carey School

of Business, Arizona State University.

Lieber, R., & Bentz, B. A. (2004). *The year 2004 survey: CEO perspectives on the current status and future prospects of the European third party logistics industry* (Report). Boston: Northeastern University, College of Business Administration.

Lieber, R., & Bentz, B. A. (2005). *The year 2004 survey: CEO perspectives on the current status and future prospects of the third party logistics industry in the Asia-Pacific region* (Report). Boston: Northeastern University, College of Business Administration.

Lieber, R., & Bentz, B. A. (2005). *The year 2004 survey: CEO perspectives on the current status and future prospects of the third party logistics industry in North America* (Report). Boston: Northeastern University, College of Business Administration.

Liljedal, A. (2002). *Design implications for context aware mobile games.* Retrieved February 18, 2003, from www.interactiveinstitute.se/mobility/Files/Master%20Thesis.pdf

Lim, E.-P., Wang, Y., Ong, K.-L., & Hwang, S.-Y. (2003). In search of knowledge about mobile users. *ERCIM News, 54,* 10-11.

Lim, J. Y., & Nam, C. (2003). *An empirical study on the factors influencing the adoption of m-payments service in Korea.* Paper presented at the International Telecommunications Society Asia-Australasian Regional Conference, Perth, Australia.

Lin, H-H., & Wang, Y-S. (2006). An examination of the determinants of customer loyalty in mobile commerce contexts. *Information & Management, 43,* 271-282.

Lindstrom, M. (2001, May 17). *E-Tailing critical success factors.* Retrieved October 28, 2002, from www.clickz.com

Ling, R. (2004). *The mobile connection. The cell phone's impact on society* (3rd ed.) Morgan Kaufmann.

Little, A. (2001). *Key success factors for m-commerce.* Retrieved November 12, 2002, from www.berlecon.de

Little, A. D. (2004). *Making m-payments a reality.* Retrieved from http://www.adlittle.de/

Lloyd, E., Maclean, R., & Stirling, A. (2006). Mobile TV—Results from the BT Movio DAB pilot in London. *EBU Technical Review.* April 2006 1 / 12. Retrieved from http://www.ebu.ch/en/technical/trev/trev_306-movio.pdf

Lombardi, C. (2006, April 10). *Cell phone subscriptions surge in India.* Retrieved from http://news.com.com/Cell+phone+subscriptions+surge+in+India/2110-1037_3-6059482.html

Longford, G. (2005). Pedagogies of digital citizenship and the politics of code. *Téchne, 9*(1), 68-96.

Looney, C. A., Jessup, L. M., & Valacich, J. S. (2004). Emerging business models for mobile brokerage services. *Communications of the ACM, 47*(6), 71-77.

Lovelock, C. H. (1983). Classifying services to gain strategic marketing insights. *Journal of Marketing, 47,* 9-20.

Lu, J., Yao, J.-E., & Yu, C.-S. (2005). Personal innovativeness, social influences and adoption of wireless Internet services via mobile technology. *Journal of Strategic Information Systems, 14*(3), 245-268.

Lu, Y. (2006). *The diffusion of wireless Internet technology among university faculty members.* Unpublished doctoral dissertation, Ohio University, Athens.

Lu, Y., Ma, H., & Turner, S. (2004). *How are college students using wireless Internet to support student-centered learning?* Paper presented at the National Educational Computing Conference, New Orleans, LA.

Lu, Y., Ma, H., Turner, S., & Huang, W. (in press). Wireless Internet and student-centered learning: A partial least squares model. *Computers & Education.*

Luarn, P., & Lin, H. H. (2005). Toward an understanding of the behavioral intention to use mobile banking. *Computers in Human Behavior, 21*(6), 873-891.

Luck, M., McBurney, P., Preist, C., & AgentLink community. (2003). *Agent technology: Enabling next generation computing.* Retrieved May 9, 2006, from http://www.agentlink.org/roadmap/

Luff, P., & Heath, C. (1998). Mobility in collaboration. In *Proceedings of the 1998 ACM conference on Computer Supported Cooperative Work* (pp. 305-314).

Luo, H., Jiang, Z., Kim, B.-J., Shankaranarayanan, N. K, & Henry, P. (2003). Integrating wireless LAN and cellular data for the enterprise. *IEEE Internet Computing, 7*(2), 25-33.

Luo, X., & Seyedian, M. (2003). Contextual marketing and customer-orientation strategy for e-commerce: An empirical analysis. *International Journal of Electronic Commerce, 8*(2), 95-118.

Lutz, R. J. (1985). Affective and cognitive antecedents of attitude toward the ad: A conceptual framework. In L. F. Alwitt & A. A. Mitchell (Eds.), *Psychological processes and advertising effects: Theory, research and application* (pp. 54-63). Hillsdale, NJ: Lawrence Erlbaum Associates.

Lyytinen, K. J., Yoo, Y., Varshney, U., Ackerman, M., Davis, G., Avital, M., et al. (2004). Surfing the next wave: Design and implementation challenges of ubiquitous computing. *Communications of the AIS, 13*(40). Retrieved May 1, 2006, from http://cais.aisnet.org/

Lyytinen, K., & Yoo, Y. (2002). Issues and challenges in ubiquitous computing. *Communications of the ACM, 45*(12), 63-65.

Lyytinen, K., & Yoo, Y. (2002). Research commentary: The next wave of nomadic computing. *Information Systems Research, 13*(4), 377-388.

MacKenzie, S. B., & Lutz, R. L. (1989). An empirical examination of the structural antecedents of attitude toward the ad in an advertising pretesting context. *Journal of Marketing, 53,* 48-65.

Madlberger, M. (2004). *Electronic retailing.* Wiesbaden, Germany: Deutscher Universitätsverlag.

Mahadevan, B. (2000). Business models for Internet-based e-commerce: An anatomy. *California Management Review.*

Mahmood, M. A., & Mann, G. J. (1993). Measuring the organizational impact of information technology investment: An exploratory study. *Journal of Management Information Systems, 10*, 1.

Maier, M. (2005, March 1). *Song sharing for your cell phone.* Retrieved November 10, 2006, from http://money.cnn.com/magazines/business2/business2_archive/2005/03/01/8253120/index.htm

Maitland, C. F., Bauer, J. M., & Westerveld, R. (2002). The European market for mobile data: Evolving value chains and industry structures. *Telecommunications Policy, 26*(9/10), 485-504.

Maki, J. (2005). *Finnish mobile TV pilot: Results.* Retrieved from http://www.mobiletv.nokia.com/download_counter.php?file=/pilots/finland/files/RI_Press.pdf

Malhotra, Y., & Galletta, D. F. (1999). Extending the technology acceptance model to account for social influence: Theoretical bases and empirical validation. In *Proceedings of the Thirty-Second Annual Hawaii International Conference on System Sciences 1* (pp. 6-19).

Mallat, N., Rossi, M., & Tuunainen, V. K. (2004). Mobile banking services. *Communications of the ACM, 47*(5), 42-46.

Marcus, A., & Could, E. W. (2000). Cultural dimensions and global Web user-interface design. *Interactions, 7*(4), 33-46.

Markides, C. (1999). A dynamic view of strategy. *Sloan Management Review, 40*(3), 55-63.

Marshall, P., Signorini, E., & Entner, R. (2004). *An analysis of UMTS as a mobile data solution for the enterprise market.* Retrieved May 9, 2006, from http://www.attwireless.com/media/downloads/umts/umts-2004analysis.pdf

Massey, A. P., Khatri, V., & Ramesh, V. (2005). *From the Web to the wireless Web: Technology readiness and usability.* Paper presented at the 38th Annual Hawaii International Conference on System Sciences (HICSS-38'05), Big Island, HI.

McDonough, D. (2002, June 24). *Wireless shopping tools of the future.* Retrieved November 11, 2002, from www.wirelessnewsfactor.com

McKitterrick, D., & Dowling, J. (2003). *State of the art review of mobile payment technology.* Retrieved from http://www.cs.tcd.ie/publications/tech-reports/reports.03/TCD-CS-2003-24.pdf

M-Commerce Security. (2002). Retrieved September 12, 2002, from www.mli.hkkk.fi

McQuail, D. (1983). *Mass communication theory: An introduction.* London: Sage.

Meij, S., & Pau, L.-F. (2006). Auctioning bulk mobile messages. *Computational Economics, 27*, 395-430.

Meister, R. (2005, June 27). *The situation of M-Commerce after Simpay's retreat.* Retrieved from http://www.payboxsolutions.com/327_397.htm

Mennecke, B. E., & Strader, T. (2001). Where in the world does location matter? A framework for location based service in M-commerce. In *Proceedings of the International Conference on Information System (ICIS)* (pp. 450-455).

Mennecke, B., & Strader, T. (2003). *Mobile commerce: Technology, theory, and applications.* London: Idea Group.

Mercator Advisory Group. (2006). *Research report 1, Mobile payments in the United States: SMS and NFC implementations enter the market.* Retrieved from http://www.paymentsnews.com/mercator_advisory_gr/index.html

Mercator Advisory Group. (2006). *Research report 2, Predicting mobile payment success in Asia.* Retrieved from http://www.mercatoradvisorygroup.com/index.php?doc= emerging_technologies&action=view_item&id=137&catid=5

Merrill Lynch. (2002). *Wireless matrix—3Q02, quarterly update on global wireless industry metrics.* Author.

Messeter, J., Brandt, E., Halse, J., & Johansson, M. (2004). Contextualizing mobile IT. In *Proceedings of* the 2004 conference on Designing interactive systems: processes, practices, methods, and techniques (pp. 27-36). New York: ACM Press.

MeT. (2003). *MeT white paper on mobile transactions.* Retrieved from http:// www.mobiletransactions.org/pdf/R200/white_papers/MeT_White_paper_on_mobile_transactions_v1.pdf

Meuter, M. L., Ostrom, A. L., Roundtree, R. I., & Bitner, M. J. (2000). Self-service technologies: Understanding customer satisfaction with technology-based service encounters. *Journal of Marketing, 64*(3), 50-64.

Micheal, K., Rochford, L., & Wotruba, T. R. (2003). How new product introductions affect sales management strategy: The impact of type of "newness" of the new product. *Journal of Product Innovation Management, 20*(4), 270-283.

Microsoft Corporation. (2004). *Mobile business solutions case studies.* Author.

Microsoft. (n.d.). *The .Net compact framework.* Retrieved from http://msdn.microsoft.com/vstudio/device/compact.aspx

Middleton, C. A. (2002). *Exploring consumer demand for networked services: The importance of content, connectivity, and killer apps in the diffusion of broadband and mobile services.* Paper presented at the Twenty-Third International Conference on Information Systems (ICIS), Barcelona, Spain.

Milne, G., & Gordon, M. E. (1993). Direct mail privacy—Efficiency trade-offs within an implied social contract framework. *Journal of Public Policy & Marketing, 12*(2), 206-216.

Min, H., Zhou, F., Jui, S-l., Wang, T., & Chen, X. (2003). *RFID in China* (White Paper). Fudan, China: Fudan University, Department of Microelectronics, Auto-ID Center.

Ministry of Information and Communication (MIC). (2006). *Wireless telecommunication subscriber report.*

Ministry of Information and Communication. (2005). *IT 839 Strategy.* Republic of Korea.

Ministry of Information Industry of China. (2006). *Telecommunication industry development statistics 2005.* Beijing, China: Author.

Ministry of Public Management, Home Affairs, Post, and Telecommunications (MPHPT). (2003). *2003 white paper: Information and communications in Japan.* Retrieved September 29, 2003, from http://www.johotsusintokei.soumu.go.jp/whitepaper/eng/WP2003/2003-index.html

Mintzberg, H. (1980). Structure in 5's: A synthesis of the research on organization design. *Management Science, 26*(3), 322-341.

Mintzberg, H. (1987). The strategy concept II: Another look at why organizations need strategies. *California Management Review, 30*(3), 11-24.

Mitchell, K., & Whitmore, M. (2003). Location based services: Locating the money. In B. E. Mennecke & T. J. Strader (Eds.), *Mobile commerce, technology, theory and applications* (pp. 51-66). Hershey, PA: Idea Group.

Mobile game. (n.d.). Retrieved September 28, 2006, from http://en.wikipedia.org/wiki/Mobile_game

Mobility Magazine. (2002). *Feature—Content, 4*(1). Retrieved November 11, 2002, from www.mobility.com.au

Mohan, L. R. (2006). Driving down the fast lane: Increasing automotive opportunities the EMS provider way. *Frost & Sullivan Market Insight* Retrieved April 29, 2006, from http://www.frost.com/prod/servlet/market-insight-print.pag?docid=67150588

Möhlenbruch, D., & Schmieder, U.-M. (2001). Gestaltungsmöglichkeiten und Entwicklungspotenziale des Mobile Marketing. *HMD Praxis der Wirtschaftsinformatik, 220,* 15-26.

Moon, B. (2005, November 8). Mobile game addiction spreading. *Dong-a Ilbo.*

Moore, D. L., & Hutchinson, J. W. (1983). The effects of ad affect on advertising effectiveness. In R. P. Bagozzi & A. M. Tybout (Eds.), *Advances in consumer research* (Vol. 10, pp. 526-531). Ann Arbor, MI: Association for Consumer Research.

Moore, G. A. (1999). *Crossing the chasm* (2nd ed.). Oxford: Capstone.

Mort, G. S., & Drennan, J. (2005). Marketing m-services: Establishing a usage benefit typology related to mobile user characteristics. *Database Marketing & Customer Strategy Management, 12*(4), 327-341.

Muller-Veerse, F. (2001). *Mobile commerce report*. Retrieved September 15, 2002, from www.durlacher.com

Munnukka, J. (2005). Dynamics of price sensitivity among mobile service customers. *Journal of Product & Brand Management, 14*(1), 65-73.

Music Industry Association of Korea (MIAK). (2005). *Statistics of digital music market in Korea.* Author.

Mylonakis, J. (2005). Can mobile services facilitate commerce? Findings from the Greek telecommunications market. *International Journal of Mobile Communications, 2*(2), 188-198.

Mylonopoulos, N. A., & Doukidis, G. I. (2003). Mobile business: Technological pluralism, social assimilation, and growth [Special issue]. *Internation Journal of Electronic Commerce, 8*(1), 5-22.

Nah, F. F.-H., Siau, K., & Sheng, H. (2004). *Values of mobile technology in education.* Paper presented at the Tenth Americas Conference on Information Systems, New York.

Nah, F. F.-H., Siau, K., & Sheng, H. (2005). The value of mobile applications: A utility company study. *Communications of the ACM, 48*(2), 85-90.

Naik, G., & Almar, L. (2002, August 18). M-Commerce: Mobile and multiplying. *Wall Street Journal,* p. B1.

Nambiar, S., & Lu, C. (2005). M-payment solutions and m-commerce fraud management. Mobile Commerce Security and Payment methods. In W-C. Hu, C-W. Lee, & W.

Kou (Eds.), *Advances in security and payment methods for mobile commerce.* Hershey, PA: Idea Group.

National Bureau of Statistics of China. (2005). *Statistical communiqué on the 2005 national economic and social development.* Beijing, China: Author.

National Bureau of Statistics of China. (2006). *Monthly data (September): Post and telecommunication services.* Beijing, China: Author.

National Internet Development Agency of Korea (NIDA). (2005). *Summary: Mobile Internet consumer research 2005.* Author.

Neable, C. (2002). The .NET compact framework group. *IEEE Pervasive Computing, 1,* 84-87.

Neslin, S. A., Grewal, D., Leghorn, R., Shankar, V., Teerling, M. L., Thomas, J. S., et al. (2006). Challenges and opportunities in multichannel customer management. *Journal of Service Research, 9*(2), 95-112.

Nicholson, M., Clarke, I., & Blakemore, M. (2002). One brand, three ways to shop: Situational variables and multichannel consumer behaviour. *The International Review of Retail, Distribution and Consumer Research, 12*(2), 131-148.

Nieminen, S. (2005, November 8-9). Finnish mobile TV. *EBU Forecast.* Retrieved from www.hetky.fi/Finnish-MobileTV_05062004.pdf

Nikulainen, K. (2003). *Fishermen hooked in mobile in Oulu (Oulussa kalastajat iskivät mobiilikoukkuun).* Retrieved January 26, 2006, from http://www.digitoday.fi/page.php?page_id=11&news_id=20035391

Nokia. (2001). *Introducing mobile IPv6 in 2G and 3G mobile networks* (White Paper). Retrieved May 9, 2006, from http://www.nokia.com/BaseProject/Sites/NOKIA_MAIN_18022/CDA/Categories/Business/NetworkSecurity/Firewalls/IPv6/_Content/_Static_Files/mobileipv6in3gnetworks.pdf

Novak, T. P., Hoffman, D. L., & Duhachek, A. (2003). The influence of goal-directed and experiental activities on online flow experiences. *Journal of Consumer Psychology, 13*(1&2), 3-16.

NTT DoCoMo. (2001). *Docomo report current trends in mobile phone usage among adolescents* (Company Report). Author.

Nyberg, A. (2004). Positioning DAB in an increasingly competitive world. In *Proceedings of 2004 Terrestrial DMB International Forum* (pp. 131-142).

Nystedt, D. (2006, February 24). *China passes 400 million mobile phone user mark.* Retrieved from http://www.infoworld.com/article/06/02/24/75849_HNchinaphoneusers_1.html

Nysveen, H., Pedersen, P. E., & Thorbjornsen, H. (2005). Explaining intention to use mobile chat services: Moderating effects of gender. *Journal of Consumer Marketing, 22*(5), 247-256.

Nysveen, H., Pedersen, P. E., & Thorbjørnsen, H. (2005). Intentions to use mobile services: Antecedents and cross-service comparisons. *Journal of the Academy of Marketing Science, 33*(3), 330-346.

O'Hare, & Gregory, M. P. (2000). Agents, mobility and virtuality: A necessary synergy. *Proceedings of International ICSC Symposium on Multi-agents and Mobile Agents in Virtual Organisations and E-Commerce—MAMA 2000.*

Oddershede, A., & Carrasco, R. A. (2006, November 5-8). *Analytic hierarchy process decision model for health institution selection: User perception.* Institute for Operations Research and the Management Sciences. Paper presented at the Informs Annual Meeting, Pittsburgh, PA.

Oddershede, A., Carrasco, R. A., & Ontiveros, B. (2006). Perception of wireless technology provision in health service using the analytic hierarchy process. *WSEAS Transactions on Communications, 5*(9), 1751-1757.

Oddershede, A., Carrasco, R. A., & Soto, I. (2005, October). Decision model for information and communications technology implications in health service: User perception. In *Proceedings of the SMDM 27th Annual Meeting, Society for Medical Decision Making Conference,* San Francisco, CA.

Oddershede, A., Soto I., & Carrasco, R. A. (2001, April). Analysis and prioritisation of Chilean mobile communication system. In *Proceedings of the International Conference on System Engineering, Communications and Information Technologies ICSECIT,* Punta Arenas, Chile.

Odlyzko, A. M. (2001). Content is not king (Vol. 6): First Monday.

OECD. (2005, December). *Telecommunications and Internet policy: OECD broadband statistics.*

Office of Institutional Research. (2004). *Ohio University fact book.* Retrieved October 17, 2004, from http://www.ohiou.edu/instres/index.html

Ogilvy, D. (1963). *Confessions of an advertising man.* New York: Ballantine Books.

Ohio University Wireless Pilot Group. (n.d.). Retrieved June 03, 2005, from http://teach.citl.ohiou.edu/wireless/index.htm

Okazaki, S. (2004). How do Japanese consumers perceive wireless ads? A multivariate analysis. *International Journal of Advertising, 23*(4), 429-454.

Okazaki, S. (2005). New perspectives on m-commerce research. *Journal of Electronic Commerce Research, 6*(3), 160-64.

Okazaki, S. (2006). What do we know about mobile Internet adopters? A cluster analysis. *Information & Management, 43*(2), 127-141.

Olla, P., & Atkinson, C. (2004). Developing a wireless reference model for interpreting complexity in wireless projects. *Industrial Management & Data Systems, 104*(3), 262-272.

Omojokun, O., & Isbell, C. L. (2003). User modeling for personalized universal appliance interaction. In *Proceedings of the 2003 Conference on Diversity in Computing* (pp. 65-68).

Ondrus, J. (2003). *Mobile payments: A tool kit for a better understanding of the market.* Retrieved from http://www.hec.unil.ch/jondrus/files/papers/mpayment.pdf

Ondrus, J., & Pigneur, Y. (2006). A multi-stakeholder multi-criteria assessment framework of mobile payments: An illustration with the Swiss public transportation industry. In *Proceedings of the 39ᵗʰ Hawaii IEEE International Conference on System Sciences* (pp. 1-10).

Ondrus, J., & Pigneur, Y. (2006). Towards a holistic analysis of mobile payments: A multiple perspectives approach. *Electronic Commerce Research and Applications, 5*(3), 246-257.

Organisation for Economic Co-operation and Development (OECD). (2006). *OECD fact book: Total and public expenditures in health.* Retrieved May 25, 2006, from http://thesius.sourceoecd.org/vl=5439459/cl=16/nw=1/rpsv/factbook/data/10-01-04-t01.xls

Organización Panamericana de la Salud, Programa de Organización y Gestión de Sistemas y Servicios de Salud, "Perfil del Sistema de Servicios de Salud, Chile",(1ra edición, marzo de (1999),(2da edición, enero de 2002)*,(Revisado, abril de 2002)

Organización Panamericana de la salud. (2001). Marco general e institucional para el desarrollo de sistemas de información en servicios de Salud. Parte A. Organización Panamericana de la salud.

Organization for the Advancement of Structured Information Standards (OASIS). (2002). *SAML 1.0 Specification.* Retrieved from http://www.oasisopen.org/committees/download.php/1383/oasis-sstc-saml-1.0-pdf.zip

Organization for the Advancement of Structured Information Standards (OASIS). (2006). Web services security: SOAP message security 1.1 (WS-Security 2004).

Orlikowski, W. J., & Iacono, C. S. (2001). Desperately seeking the "IT" in IT research: A call to theorizing the IT artifact. *Information Systems Research, 12*(2), 121-134.

OSGi Alliance. (2005). *About the OSGi service platform.* Technical Whitepaper. San Ramon, CA: Author.

Paavilainen, J. (2002). *Mobile business strategies: Understanding the technologies and opportunities.* London: Addison-Wesley.

Pagani, M. (2004). Determinants of adoption of third generation mobile multimedia services. *Journal of Interactive Marketing, 18*(3), 46-59.

Page, M., Watt, M., & Menon, N. (2005). *Mobinet 2005—Raising the stakes.* Retrieved from http://www.atkearney.com/main.taf?p=5,3,1,121,1

Palenchar, J. (2002). OSGi networks ready to roll. *TWICE.*

Parasuraman, A., & Grewal, D. (2000). The impact of technology on quality-value-loyalty chain: A research agenda. *Academy of Marketing Science, 28*(1), 168.

Park, C. (2006). Hedonic and utilitarian values of mobile Internet in Korea. *International Journal of Mobile Communications, 4*(5), 497-508.

Parnell, K. (2002). Telematics drives the new automotive business model. *Xcell Journal.*

Parvatiyar, A., & Sheth, J. N. (2000). The domain and conceptual foundations of relationship marketing. In J. N. Sheth & A. Parvatiyar (Eds.), *Handbook of relationship marketing* (pp. 3-38). Thousand Oaks: Sage.

Patokorpi, E. (2006). Low knowledge in cyberspace: Abduction, tacit knowledge, aura and the mobility of knowledge. *Journal of Human Systems Management, 25*(3), 211-220.

Patokorpi, E., Tétard, F., Qiao, F., & Sjövall, N. (2007). Mobile learning objects to support constructivist learning. In K. Harman & A. Koohang (Eds.), *Learning objects: Applications, implications and future directions.* Informing Science Press.

Patton, M. Q. (2002). *Qualitative research and evaluation methods.* Thousand Oaks, CA: Sage.

Pau, L.-F. (2001). *Note on proposal to IETF as to use of IPv6 flow label for tariffing and encoding thereof.* Ericsson Utvecklings AB.

Pau, L.-F. (2002). The communications and information economy: Issues, tariffs and economics research areas. *Journal of Economic Dynamics and Control, 26*(9-10), 1651-1675.

Pedersen, P. E., & Ling, R. (2003). *Modifying adoption research for mobile Internet service adoption: Cross-disciplinary interactions.* Paper presented at the 36th Hawaii International Conference on System Sciences (HICSS'03), Big Island, HI.

Pedersen, P., Nysveen, H., & Thorbjørnsen, H. (2003). *The adoption of mobile serves: A cross service study.* Retrieved from http://ikt.hia.no/perep/publications.htm

Pederson, P. E. (2002). *Adoption of mobile Internet services: An exploratory study of mobile commerce early adopters.* Retrieved from http://ikt.hia.no/perep/publications.htm

Perry, M., O'Hara, K., Sellen, A., Brown, B., & Harper, R. (2001). Dealing with mobility: Understanding access anytime, anywhere. *ACM Transactions on Computer-Human Interaction, 8*(4), 323-347.

Petty, R. D. (2003). Wireless advertising messaging: Legal analysis and public policy issues. *Journal of Public Policy & Marketing, 22*(1), 71-82.

Pica, D., & Kakihara, M. (2003). The duality of mobility: Designing fluid organizations through stable interaction. Paper presented at the *11th European Conference on Information Systems (ECIS 2003)*, Naples, Italy.

Pica, D., Sørensen, C., & Allen, D. (2004). *On mobility and context of work: Exploring mobile police work.* Paper presented at the 37th Hawaii International Conference on System Sciences, Big Island, HI.

Pieck, R. (2005, September 14). *DVB-H broadcast to mobile devices.* Retrieved from http://www.newtec.be/fileadmin/webfolder/whitepaper/DVB-H_White_Paper.pdf

Pilz, K. (2005). *TV goes mobile with DVB-H—Swisscom's approach developing a market entry scenario with DVB-H based products.* Retrieved from http://www.ipdc-forum.org/resources/documents/6-Swisscom.pdf

Pirc, M. (2006). Mobile service and phone as consumption system—The impact on customer switching. In *Proceedings of the Helsinki Mobility Round Table.* Helsinki: Helsingin kauppakorkeakoulu.

Porter, M. E. (1979). *How competitive forces shape strategy.* Boston: Harvard Business School Press.

Porter, M. E. (1996). What is strategy? *Harvard Business Review, 74*(6), 61-78.

Porter, M. E. (1998). *Competitive advantage: Creating and sustaining superior performance.* New York: Free Press.

Pousttchi, K., Turowski, K., & Weizmann, M. (2003). *Added value-based approach to analyze electronic commerce and mobile commerce business models.* Paper presented at the International Conference of Management and Technology in the New Enterprise, La Habana, Cuba.

Prados de Reyes, M., & Peña Yánez, M. C. (2002). *Sistemas de información hospitalarios: Organización y Gestión de Proyectos.* Ed.: Escuela Andaluza de Salud Pública, Granada.

Prasopoulou, E., Panteli, N., & Pouloudi, N. (2004). Social accessibility and the mobile phone: A temporal perspective. In T. W. Bynum, N. Pouloudi, S. Rogerson, & T. Spyrou (Eds.), *Proceedings of the seventh international conference Ethicomp 2004: Challenges for the Citizen of the Information Society* (Vol. II, pp. 773-784). Mytilene, Greece: University of the Aegean.

Prasse, M., & Rittgen, P. (1998). Why Church's thesis still holds. Some notes on Peter Wegner's tracts on interaction and computability. *The Computer Journal, 41*(6), 357-362.

PriceWaterhouseCoopers. (2001). *Mobile Internet: Unleashing the power of wireless. Technology Forecast 2001-2003* (pp. 40-41). Author.

Priyantha, N. B., Miu, A. K. L., Balakrishnan, H., & Teller, S. (2001). *The cricket compass for context-aware mobile applications.* Retrieved February 18, 2003, from http://nms.lcs.mit.edu/papers/CricketCompass.pdf

Punie, Y. (2003). *What bends the trend? Technological foresight and the socialization of ubiquitous computing.* EMTEL2, KEY DELIVERABLE Work Package 2.

Punie, Y., Bogdanowicz, M., Berg, A.-J., Pauwels, C., & Burgelman, J.-C. (2003, September). *Living and working in the information society: Quality of life in a digital world.* A Final Deliverable of the European Media Technology and Everyday Life Network (EMTEL).

Pura, M. (2003). Case study: The role of mobile advertising in building a brand. In B. Mennecke & T. Strader (Eds.), *Mobile commerce: Technology, theory, and applications* (pp. 291-308). London: Idea Group.

Pura, M. (2003). Linking perceived value and loyalty to mobile services. In *Proceedings of the ANZMAC 2003,* Adelaide, Australia.

Pura, M. (2003). Measuring loyalty to mobile services. In *Proceedings of the Third International Conference on Electronic Business (ICEB),* National University of Singapore.

Pura, M. (2005). Linking perceived value and loyalty in location-based mobile services. *Managing Service Quality, 15*(6), 509-538.

Pura, M., & Brush, G. (2005). Hedonic and utilitarian motivations for mobile service use. In *Proceedings of SERVSIG,* National University of Singapore.

Pura, M., Viitanen, J., & Liljander, V. (2003). Customer perceived value of mobile services. In *Proceedings of the 32th EMAC Conference,* Glasgow: University of Strathclyde.

Purao, S., & Krogstie, J. (2004). *Impact of ubiquitous computing.* In K. J. Lyytinen, Y. Yoo, U. Varshney, M. Ackerman, G. Davis, M. Avital, D. Robey, S. Sawyer, & C. Sørensen (Eds.), (pp. 705-707).

QUALCOMM Incorp. (2004). *Starting with BREW.* Retrieved from http://brew.qualcomm.com/brew_bnry/pdf/developer/resources/gs/starting_brew.pdf

QUALCOMM Incorporated. (2005). *MediaFLO: FLO technology brief.* Retrieved from www.qualcomm.com/mediaflo

Raisinghani, M. (2002). Mobile commerce: Transforming the vision into reality. *Information Resources Management Journal, 15*(2), 3-4.

Rannenberg, K. (2004). Identity management in mobile cellular networks and related applications. *Information Security Technical Report, 9*(1), 77-85.

Rao, B., & Minakakis, L. (2003). Evolution of mobile location-based services. *Communications of the ACM, 46*(12), 61-65.

Rao, B., & Parikh, M. A. (2003). Wireless broadband networks: The U.S. experience. *International Journal of Electronic Commerce, 8*(1), 37.

Rappa, M. (2004). The utility business model and the future of computing services. *IBM Systems Journal, 43*(1), 32-42.

Reichold, A., Schierholz, R., Kolbe, L. M., & Brenner, W. (2003, September 1). *M-Commerce at Helsana health insurance: Mobile premium calculator.* Paper presented at the Dexa '03, Prag.

Reichold, A., Schierholz, R., Kolbe, L., & Brenner, W. (2004). Mobile-commerce bei der Helsana: Mobile Prämienerstellung. In K. Wilde & H. Hippner (Eds.), *Management von CRM-Projekten*: Gabler.

Reichwald, R. (2002). *Mobile Kommunikation: Wertschöpfung, Technologien, neue Dienste.* Wiesbaden: Gabler.

Reichwald, R., & Meier, R. (2002). Generierung von Kundenwert mit mobilen Diensten. In R. Reichwald (Ed.), *Mobile Kommunikation—Wertschöpfung, Technologien, neue Dienste* (pp. 207-230). Wiesbaden, Germany: Gabler.

Reschovsky, C. (2004). *Journey to work: 2000.*

Rettie, R. (2003). *Connectedness, awareness and social presence.* Paper presented at the 6th Annual International Workshop on Presence.

Roberts, K. G., & Pick, J. B. (2004). Technology factors in corporate adoption of mobile cell phones: A case study analysis. In *Proceedings of the 37th Hawaii International Conference on Systems Sciences,* Big Island, HI.

Robins, F. (2003). The marketing of 3G. *Marketing Intelligence & Planning, 21*(6), 370-378.

Rodgers, S., & Sheldon, K. (2002). An improved way to characterize Internet users. *Journal of Advertising Research, 42(*5), 82-94.

Rogers, E. M. (1983). *Diffusion of innovation* (3rd ed.). New York: The Free Press.

Rogers, E. M. (1995). *Diffusion of innovations* (4th ed.). New York: The Free Press.

Rogers, E. M. (2003). *Diffusion of innovations* (5th ed.). New York: Free Press.

Romano, N. C., & Fjermestad, J. (2002). Electronic commerce customer relationship management: An assessment of research. *International Journal of Electronic Commerce, 6*(2), 61-113.

Romano, N. C., & Fjermestad, J. (2003). Electronic commerce customer relationship management: A research agenda. *Information Technology and Management, 4*(2-3), 233-258.

Royce, W. W. (1970). *Managing the development of large software systems.* Paper presented at the International Conference on Software Engineering, Monterey, CA.

Rust, R. T., Inman, J. J., Jia, J., & Zahorik, A. (1999). What you don't know about customer-perceived quality: The role of customer expectation distributions. *Marketing Science, 18*(1), 77-92.

Rust, R. T., Kannan, P. K., & Peng, N. (2002). The customer economics of Internet privacy. *Journal of the Academy of Marketing Science, 30*(4), 455-464.

Rust, R. T., Lemon, K. N., & Zeithaml, V. A. (2004). Return on marketing: Using customer equity to focus marketing strategy. *Journal of Marketing, 68*(1), 109-127.

Rust, R. T., Zeithaml, V. A., & Lemon, K. N. (2000). *Driving customer equity: How customer lifetime value is reshaping customer strategy.* New York: The Free Press.

Saaty, R. W. (2003). *Tutorial for building AHP hierarchical decision models.* Creative Decision Foundation.

Saaty, T. L. (1990). *Multicriteria decision making: The analytic hierarchy process, planning, priority setting, resource allocation.* RWS Publications.

Saaty, T. L. (2001). *Decision making for leaders.* Vol. II, AHP Series 315 pp., RWS Publications.

Saaty, T. L. (2006). *Fundamentals of decision making & priority theory* (2nd ed.). Vol. VI of the AHP series. RWS Publications.

Sabat, H. K. (2002). The evolving mobile wireless value chain and market structure. *Telecommunications Policy, 26*(9/10), 505-535.

Sackmann, S., Struker, J., & Accorsi, R. (2006). Personalization in privacy-aware highly dynamic systems. *Communications of the ACM, 49*(9), 32+.

Sadeh, N. (2002). *M-Commerce: Technologies, services, and business models.* New York: John Wiley & Sons.

Saha, S., Jamtgaard, M., & Villasenor, J. (2001). Bringing the wireless Internet to mobile devices. *Computer, 34*(6), 54-58.

Sandell, L. (2005). *Finnish MobileTV: Analysis on logfile data, April-June 2005.* Retrieved from www.mobiletv.nokia.com/download_counter.php?file=/pilots/finland/files/Finnpanel_press_all_channels.pdf

Sattler, C. (2005, November 8). *BMCO newsletter.* Retrieved from http://www.bmco-forum.org/

Scharl, A., Dickinger, A., & Murphy, J. (2005). Diffusion and success factors of mobile marketing. *Electronic Commerce Research and Applications, 4*(2), 159-173,

Schierholz, R., Glissmann, S., Kolbe, L. M., & Brenner, W. (2006, July 6). *Mobile systems for customer service differentiation—The case of Lufthansa.* Paper presented at the 10th Pacific Asia Conference on Information Systems, Kuala Lumpur, Malaysia.

Schierholz, R., Kolbe, L. M., & Brenner, W. (in press). Mobile customer relationship management: Foundations, challenges and solutions. *Business Process Management Journal.*

Schilit, B., Adams, N., & Want, R. (1994). Context-aware computing applications. Paper presented at the *IEEE*

Workshop on Mobile Computing Systems and Applications, Santa Cruz, CA.

Schneidewind, D. (1998). *Markt und Marketing in Japan—Shin Hatsubai.* Munich, Germany: Verlag C. H. Beck.

Schnell, R., Hill, P.-B., & Esser, E. (1995). Methoden der empirischen Sozialforschung (5th ed.). München, Germany: R. Oldenbourg Verlag.

Schulze, J., Thiesse, F., Bach, V., & Österle, H. (2000). Knowledge enabled customer relationship management. In H. Österle, E. Fleisch, & R. Alt (Eds.), *Business networking: Shaping enterprise relationships on the Internet* (pp. 143-160). Berlin, Germany: Springer.

Schwiderski-Grosche, S., & Knospe, H. (2002). Secure mobile commerce. In C. Mitchell (Ed.), *Special issue of the IEE Electronics and Communication Engineering Journal on Security for Mobility, 14*(5), 228-238. Retrieved from http://www.isg.rhul.ac.uk/~scarlet/ documents/Secure%20m-commerce%20ECEJ.pdf

Scornavacca, E., & Barnes, S. J. (2003). M-Banking services in Japan: A strategic perspective. *International Journal of Mobile Communications, 2*(1), 51-66.

Scornavacca, E., Barnes, S. J., & Huff, S. L. (2005). Mobile business research, 2000-2004: Emergence, current status, and future opportunities. In *Proceedings of the 13th European Conference on Information Systems (CD).*

Scornavacca, E., Barnes, S., & Huff, S. (2006). Mobile business research published in 2000-2004: Emergence, current status, and future opportunities. *Communications of the Association for Information Systems, 17*(28), 20.

Seah, W., Pilakkat, S., Shankar, P., Tan, S. K., Roy, A. G., & Ng, E. (2001). *The future mobile payments infrastructure: A common platform for secure m-payments.* Retrieved from http://www.itu.int/ITU-D/pdf/4597-13.3bis-en.pdf

Segerstrale, K. (2006). *Enabling innovation in mobile games—Going beyond the conventional.* Helsinki: Helsinki.

Seybold, P. (2002). *E-Commerce success: Eight critical factors.* Retrieved November 12, 2002, from www.csref.org

Shani, D., & Chalasani, S. (1992). Exploiting niches using relationship marketing. *The Journal of Consumer Marketing, 9*(3), 33-42.

Shapiro, C., & Varian, H. (1999). *Information rules: A strategic guide to the network economy.*

Sharma, S., & Deng, X. (2002). *An empirical investigation of factors affecting the acceptance of personal digital assistants by individuals.* Paper presented at the Americas Conference on Information Systems, Dallas, TX.

Shavitt, S., Lowrey, P., & Haefner, J. (1998). Public attitudes towards advertising: More favourable than you might think. *Journal of Advertising Research, 38*(4), 7-22.

Sheng, H., Nah, F. F.-H., & Siau, K. (2005). Strategic implications of mobile technology: A case study using value-focused thinking. *The Journal of Strategic Information Systems, 14*(3), 262-190.

Sheth, J., Newman, B., & Gross, B. (1991). *Consumption values and market choices, theory and applications.* South-Western.

Shiffman, et al. (2004, August). Pen-based, mobile decision support in healthcare. *SIGBIO Newsl, 19*(2), 5-7.

Shim, J. P. (2005). Korea's lead in mobile cellular and DMB phone services. *Communications of the Association for Information Systems, 15,* 555-566.

Shim, J. P. (2005). Why Japan and Korea are leading in the mobile business industry. *Decision Line, 36*(3), 8-12.

Shim, J. P., Ahn, K. M., & Shim, J. (2006). Empirical findings on the perceived use of digital multimedia broadcasting mobile phone service. *Industrial Management & Data Systems, 106*(2), 155-171.

Shim, J. P., Bekkering, E., & Hall, L. (2002). *Empirical findings on perceived value of mobile commerce as a distribution channel.* Paper presented at the Americas Conference on Information Systems, Dallas, TX.

Shim, J. P., Shin, Y. B., & Nottingham, L. (2002). Retailer Web site influence on customer shopping: An exploratory study on key factors of customer satisfaction. *Journal of the Association for Information Systems, 3*, 53-75.

Shim, J. P., Varshney, U., & Dekleva, S. (2006). Wireless evolution 2006: Cellular TV, wearable computing, and RFID. *Communications of the Association for Information Systems, 18*, 497-518.

Shim, J. P., Varshney, U., Dekleva, S., & Knoerzer, G. (2006). Mobile and wireless networks: Services, evolution and issues. *International Journal of Mobile Communications, 4*, 405-417.

Shim, J. P., Varshney, U., Dekleva, S., & Knoerzer, G. (2006). Mobile and wireless networks: Services, evolution & issues. *International Journal of Mobile Communications, 4*(4), 405-417.

Shin, D. H. (2006). Prospectus of mobile TV: Another bubble or killer application? *Telematics and Informatics, 23*, 253-270.

Siau, K., & Shen, Z. (2003). Building customer trust in mobile commerce. *Communications of the ACM, 46*(4), 91-94.

Siau, K., & Shen, Z. (2003). Mobile communications and mobile services. *International Journal of Mobile Communications, 1*(1/2), 3-14.

Siau, K., Lim, E.-P., & Shen, Z. (2001). Mobile commerce: Promises, challenges, and research agenda. *Journal of Database Management, 12*(3), 4-13.

Siau, K., Sheng, H., & Nah, F. F.-H. (2004). *Value of mobile commerce to customers.* Paper presented at the Tenth Americas Conference on Information Systems, New York.

Silberer, G., Wohlfahrt, J., & Wilhelm, T. (Eds.). (2001). *Mobile commerce. Grundlagen, Geschäftsmodelle, Erfolgsfaktoren.* Wiesbaden, Germany: Gabler Verlag.

Skelton, G. W., & Chen, L.-d. (2005). Introduction to m-business applications: Value proposition, applications, technologies and challenges. In G. W. Skelton & L.-d. Chen (Eds.), *Mobile commerce application development*

(pp. 1-21). Hershey, PA: Idea Group Inc.

Skiöld, D. (2006). An economic analysis of DAB and DVB-H. *EBU Technical Review.* Retrieved from http://www.ebu.ch/en/technical/trev/trev_305-skiold.pdf

SK Telecom. (2003, December 9). *SK Telecom establishes the national standard for mobile banking services* [Press release]. Seoul, Korea: Author.

SK Telecom. (2003, October 27). SK Telecom launches "MONETA Membership Pack Service" for teenagers [Press release]. Seoul, Korea: Author.

SK Telecom. (2003, December 22). SK Telecom launches "Liquid Screen Small Payment" service [Press release]. Seoul, Korea: Author.

SK Telecom. (2003, August 12). SK Telecom starts "Moneta Online Payment Service" [Press release]. Seoul, Korea: Author.

SK Telecom. (2004, July 27). SK Telecom exceeds ten millions US dollars in export sales of call ring (so called Coloring) service solution [Press release]. Seoul, Korea: Author.

SK Telecom. (2004, August 18). SK Telecom forms strategic alliance with Samsung Card for mobile payment service [Press release]. Seoul, Korea: Author.

SK Telecom. (2004, November 15). SK Telecom presents a new paradigm for promoting the digital music market [Press release]. Seoul, Korea: Author.

SK Telecom. (2004, September 30). SK Telecom starts "M-Bank Service" in a joint effort with KB [Press release]. Seoul, Korea: Author.

SK Telecom. (2004, March 16). SK Telecom starts M-Bank international roaming service [Press release]. Seoul, Korea: Author.

SK Telecom. (2004, October 18). Stock trading chip service launched as part of a succession of mobile banking service advances [Press release]. Seoul, Korea: Author.

SK Telecom. (2005, December 15). Melon subscribers hit four million mark [Press release]. Seoul, Korea:

Author.

SKTelecom. (2005, October 14). Satellite DMB customers reach over 200,000 [Press release]. Seoul, Korea: Author.

SKTelecom. (2005, April 19). SK Telecom introduces mobile multi-use financial chip [Press release]. Seoul, Korea: Author.

SKTelecom. (2005, October 31). SK Telecom releases the world's first PMP phone [Press release]. Seoul, Korea: Author.

SKTelecom. (2006, February 16). SK Telecom executes an agreement for jointly developing a music file CODEC technology with Germany's CT company [Press release]. Seoul, Korea: Author.

Slade, K., Hale, & Dorr. (2002). *Success and failure of e-commerce in the US: Lessoned to be learned.* Retrieved October 23, 2002, from www.prac.org

Smagt, T. (2000). Enhancing virtual teams: Social relations v. communication technology. *Industrial Management & Data Systems, 100*(4), 148-156.

Smith, A. (2006). Exploring m-commerce in terms of viability, growth and challenges. *International Journal of Mobile Communications, 4,* 682-703.

Smyth, B. (2003). The missing link—User-experience and incremental revenue generation on the mobile Internet. *ERCIM News, 54.*

Södergard, C. (Ed.). (2003). *Mobile television: Technology and user experiences: Report on the Mobile TV project* (VTT publications 506).

Song, M. (2005). *KT's media business and content strategy.* Retrieved May 3, 2006, from http://ct.kaist.ac.kr/file/seminar/20051025_Song.pdf

Sonnenberg, F. A., & Beck, J. R. (1993). Markov models in medical decision making. *Medical Decision Making, 4,* 322-338.

Sørensen, C. (2002). Digital nomads and mobile service. *Receiver. Vodafone.* Retrieved December 11, 2004, from www.receiver.vodafone.com

Sørensen, C. (2003). *Research issues in mobile informatics: Classical concerns, pragmatic issues and emerging discourses.* Retrieved January 5, 2005, from is.lse.ac.uk/staff/sorensen/downloads/Sorensen2003.pdf

Sørensen, C., & Pica, D. (2005, April 1). Tales from the police: Rhythms of interaction with mobile technologies. *Information and Organization, 15*(2), 125-146.

Soriano, M., & Ponce, D. (2002). A security and usability proposal for mobile electronic commerce. *IEEE Communication.*

Soroor, J. (2006). Models for financial services firms in developing countries based upon mobile commerce. *International Journal of Electronic Finance, 1*(2), 260-274.

Sosa, O El Nuevo Día, 10 de marzo de (2004), El País. *Boicot de aseguradoras a la contratación directa.*

Spriestersbach, A., & Vogler, H. (2002). *Location-awareness for improving the usability of mobile enterprise applications.* Retrieved February 18, 2003, from http://www.sapdesignguild.org/community/readers/reader_mobile.asp

Srivastava, L. (2004). Japan's ubiquitous mobile information society. *The Journal of Policy, Regulation, and Strategy for Telecommunications, Information and Media, 14*(4), 234-251.

Stafford, T. F., & Gillenson, M. L. (2003). Mobile commerce: What it is and what it could be. *Communications of the ACM, 46*(12), 33-34.

Stake, R. E. (1995). *The art of case study research.* London: Sage.

Stallings, W. (2000). *Network security essentials: Applications and standards.* Pearson Education.

State Council of the People's Republic of China. (2000). *Regulations of the People's Republic of China on telecommunications.* Beijing, China: Author.

Statistisches Bundesamt Deutschland. (2005). *Leben und Arbeiten in Deutschland - Ergebnisse des Mikrozensus 2004.* Wiesbaden, Germany: Author.

Statistisches Bundesamt. (2003). *Im Jahr 2050 wird jeder Dritte in Deutschland 60 Jahre oder älter sein.* Retrieved May 25, 2006, from http://www.destatis.de/presse/deutsch/pm2003/p2300022.htm

Steinbock, D. (2003). Globalization of wireless value system: From geographic to strategic advantages. *Telecommunications Policy, 27*(3/4), 207-235.

Stender, M., & Ritz, T. (2006). Modeling of B2B mobile commerce processes. *International Journal of Production Economics, 101*(1), 128-139.

Stewart, D. W., & Pavlou, P. A. (2002). From consumer response to active consumer: Measuring the effectiveness of interactive media. *Journal of the Academy of Marketing Science, 30*(4), 376-396.

Stone, A. (1996). *The war of desire and technology at the close of the mechanical age.* The MIT Press.

Strasser, S., & Davis, R. M. (1991). *Measuring patients satisfaction for improved patient services.* Ann Arbor, MI: Health Care Administration Press.

Strategy Analytics. (2000, January 10). *Strategy analytics forecast $200 billion mobile commerce market by 2004.* Retrieved from Wow-com

Suh, C.-K., Suh, E.-H., & Baek, K. C. (1994). Prioritizing telecommunication for long range R&D planning. IEEE *Transactions on Engineering Management, 41*(3).

Suh, Y. (2005). *Current overview of S-DMB.* TU Media.

Sullivan Mort, Gillian & Judy Drennan. (2005). Marketing m-services: Establishing a usage benefit typology related to mobile user characteristics. *Database Marketing & Customer Strategy Management, 12*(4), 327-41.

Swatman, M. C., Krueger, C., & Van der Beek, K. (2006). The changing digital content landscape: An evaluation of e-business model development in European online news and music. *Internet Research, 16*(1), 53-80.

Tarasewich, P. (2003). Designing mobile commerce applications. *Communications of the ACM, 46*(12), 57-60.

Telekom Austria. (2004, March 29). [Press release].

Mobilkom Austria Group.

TeliaSonera. (2006, January 30). [Press release]. Retrieved April 25, 2006, from http://wpy.observer.se/wpyfs/00/00/00/00/00/06/D7/7B/wkr0007.pdf

Tellis, G. J. (1997). Effective frequency: One exposure or three factors? *Journal of Advertising Research, 37*(4), 75-80.

Teltarif. (2006). *UMTS: Wo sind die neuen Netze schon verfügbar?* Retrieved April 30, 2006, from http://www.teltarif.de/i/umts-coverage.html

Teng, R. (2005, January). Digital multimedia broadcasting in Korea. *In-Stat.*

Tétard, F., Shengnan, H., Harkke, V., & Collan, M. (2006). Smart phone as a medium to access medical information: A field study of military physicians. In *Proceedings of Helsinki Mobility Roundtable.*

Teuteberg, F., & Weberbauer, M. (2006). *Mobile supply chain event management: Eine empirische Studie zum aktuellen Stand in deutschen Unternehmen* (Research Report).

Thaler, R. H. (1985). Mental accounting and consumer choice. *Marketing Science, 4,* 199-214.

Thomas, B. (2000). *A model of the diffusion of technology into SMEs.* WEI Working Paper Series 4. Garmogan, University of Carmogan, Welsh Enterprise Institute.

Thompson, C. J., Locander, W. B., & Pollio, H. R. (1989). Putting consumer experience back into consumer research: The philosophy and method of existential-phenomenology. *Journal of Consumer Research, 16,* 133-146.

Thurm, S. (2000, December 11). *Don't hold your breath.* Retrieved November 11, 2002, from myphlip.pearson-cmg.com

Tijerina, L. (2000, May). *Issues in the evaluation of drive distraction associated with in-vehicle information and telecommunication systems.* Retrieved May 5, 2006, from http://www-nrd.nhtsa.dot.gov/departments/nrd-13/driver-distraction/PDF/3.PDF

Tijerina, L., Parmer, E. B., & Goodman, M. J. (2000). *Individual differences and in-vehicle distraction while driving: A test track study and psychometric evaluation.* Retrieved April 5, 2006, from http://www-nrd.nhtsa.dot.gov/departments/nrd-13/driver-distraction/PDF/4.PDF

Tirole, J. (2002). *The theory of industrial organization.* Cambridge, MA: The MIT Press.

Titkov, L., Poslad, S., & Tan, J. J. (2006). An integrated approach to user-centered privacy for mobile information services. *Applied Artificial Intelligence, 20*(2-4), 159-178.

Trappey, A., Trappey, C., Hou, J., & Chen, B. (2004). Mobile agent technology and application for online global logistic services. *Industrial Management & Data Systems, 104(*2), 169-183.

Treacy, M., & Wiersema, F. (1994). *The discipline of market leaders.* Reading: Addison-Wesley.

Tsaih, R., Chang, H., & Huang, C. (2005). The business concept of utilizing the interactive TV. *Industrial Management & Data Systems, 105*(5), 613-622.

Tsalgatidou, A., & Pitoura, E. (2001). Business models and transactions in mobile electronic commerce: Requirements and properties. *Computer Networks, 37,* 221-236.

Turowski, K., & Pousttchi, K. (2003). *Mobile commerce: Grundlagen und Techniken.* Berlin, Germany: Springer.

Twist, D. C. (2005). The impact of radio frequency identification on supply chain facilities. *Journal of Facilities Management, 3*(3), 226-239.

Ung, K. (2001). *Critical success factors for the implementation of mobile commerce.* Unpublished thesis for the University of New South Wales, Australia.

United States Census Bureau. (2003). *2003 American community survey.* Washington DC: Author.

Urbaczewski, A., Valacich, J. S., & Jessup, L. M. (2003). Mobile commerce—Opportunities and challenges. *Communications of the ACM, 46*(12), 31-32.

Van Akkeren, J., & Harker, D. (2003). Mobile data technologies and small business adoption and diffusion: An empirical study of barriers and facilitators. In B. Mennecke & T. Strader (Eds.), *Mobile commerce: Technology, theory and applications* (pp. 218-244). Hershey, PA: Idea Group.

Van Camp, S. (2005, May 1). 15 minutes with Derek Pollock on markets for tablet PC. *Adweek Magazines' Technology Marketing.*

Van der Heijden, H. (2004). User acceptance of hedonic information systems. *MIS Quarterly, 28*(4), 695-704.

Van der Heijden, H., & Valiente, P. (2002, June 6-8). *The value of mobility for business process performance: Evidence from Sweden and The Netherlands.* Paper presented at the European Conference on Information Systems, Gdansk, Poland.

Van der Heijden, H., Ogertschnig, M., & Van der Gaast, L. (2005). Effects of context relevance and perceived risk on user acceptance of mobile information services. In *Proceedings of 13th European Conference on Information Systems.* Regensburg, Germany: Institute for Management of Information Systems at the University of Regensburg.

Van House, N., Davis, M., Ames, M., Finn, M., & Viswanathan, V. (2005, April 2-7). *The uses of personal networked digital imaging: An empirical study of cameraphone photos and sharing.* Paper presented at the CHI 2005, Portland, OR.

Vandenwauver, M., Govaerts, R., & Vandewalle, J. (1997). Overview of authentication protocols: Kerberos and SESAME. In *Proceedings 31ˢᵗ Annual IEEE Carnahan Conference on Security Technology.*

Varoutas, D., Katsianis, D., Sphicopoulos, T., Stordahl, K., & Welling, I. (2006). On the economics of 3G mobile virtual network operators (MVNOs). *Wireless Personal Communications, 36*(2), 129-142.

Varshney, U. (2003). Location management for mobile commerce applications in wireless Internet environment. *ACM Transactions on Internet Technology, 3*(3), 236-255.

Varshney, U. (2004). *Technology issues in ubiquitous computing.* In K. J. Lyytinen, Y. Yoo, U. Varshney, M. Ackerman, G. Davis, M. Avital, D. Robey, S. Sawyer, & C. Sørensen (Eds.), (pp. 699-702).

Varshney, U., & Vetter, R. (2001). A *framework for the emerging mobile commerce application.* Paper presented at the Hawaii International Conference of Systems Science (HICSS).

Varshney, U., & Vetter, R. (2001). Emerging mobile and wireless networks. *Communications of the ACM, 43*(6), 73-81.

Varshney, U., & Vetter, R. (2001). *Mobile commerce: A new frontier.* Retrieved September 12, 2002, from www.computer.org

Varshney, U., & Vetter, R. (2002). Mobile commerce: Framework, applications and networking support. *Mobile Networks and Applications, 7,* 185-198.

Venkatesh, V., Morris, M., Davis, G. B., & Davis, F. D. (2003). User acceptance of information technology: Towards a unified view. *MIS Quarterly, 27*(3), 425-478.

Venkatesh, V., Ramesh, V., & Massey, A. P. (2003). Understanding usability in mobile marketing. *Communications of the ACM, 46*(12), 53-56.

Ventatesh, W. (2000). Age differences in technology adoption decisions: Implications for a changing work force. *Personnel Psychology, 53,* 375-403.

Vrechopoulos, A. P., Constantiou, I. D., Mylonopoulos, N., & Sideris, I. (2002). *Critical success factors for accelerating mobile commerce diffusion in Europe.* Paper presented at the 15th Bled E-commerce Conference, e-Reality: Constructing the e-Economy, Bled, Slovenia.

Vrechopoulos, A. P., Constantiou, I. D., Sideris, I., Doukidis, G. I., & Mylonopoulos, N. (2003). The critical role of consumer behavior research in mobile commerce. *International Journal of Mobile Communications, 1*(3), 329-340.

Walker, B., & Barnes, S. J. (2005). Wireless sales force automation: Concept and cases. *International Journal of Mobile Communications, 3,* 411-427.

Wamser, C. (2003). Die wetbbwerbsstrategischen Stoßrichtungen des Mobile Commerce. In J. Link (Ed.), *Mobile commerce* (pp. 65-93). Berlin, Germany: Springer.

Wamser, C., & Buschmann, D. (2006). *Erfolgsfaktoren des Mobile Business.* Rheinbach: Deutsche Gesellschaft für Management Forschung (DMGF).

Wang, S., & Wang, H. (2005). A location-based business service model for mobile commerce. *International Journal of Mobile Communications, 3*(4), 339-349.

Wang, T.-Y. (2006). Clan's function and its historical changes. *Journal of Shangrao Normal College, 25*(2), 50-53.

Wang, Y., Van de Kar, E., & Meijer, G. (2005). Designing mobile solutions for mobile workers: Lessons learned from a case study. In *Proceedings of the 7th international conference on Electronic commerce ICEC'05.*

WAP Forum. (2000). *Wireless application protocol architecture specification.* Retrieved from http://www.wapforum.org/what/technical_1_2_1.htm

WAP Forum. (2002). *WAP 2.0 technical white paper.* Retrieved from http://www.wapforum.org/what/WAP-White_Paper1.pdf

Watson, R. T., Pitt, L. F., Berthon, P. R., & Zinkhan, G. M. (2002). U-commerce: Expanding the universe of marketing. *Journal of the Academy of Marketing Science, 30*(4), 333-47.

Weck, C., & Wilson, E. (2006, January). Broadcasting to handhelds: An overview of systems and services. *EBU Technological Review.* Retrieved from http://www.ebu.ch/en/technical/trev/trev_305-wilson.pdf

Wee, J., & Gutierrez, J. A. (2005). A framework for effective quality of service over wireless networks. *International Journal of Mobile Communications, 3,* 138-149.

Weerawarana, S., Curbera, F., Leymann, F., Storey, T., & Ferguson, D. F. (Eds.). (2005). *Web services platform architecture: SOAP, WSDL, WS-policy, WS-addressing, WS-BPEL, WS-reliable messaging, and more.* Prentice Hall.

Wegner, P. (1997). Why interaction is more powerful than algorithms? *Communications of the ACM, 40*(5), 81-91.

Wegner, P., & Goldin, D. (1999). *Interaction, computability, and Church's thesis*. [Draft]. Retrieved October 29, 2004, from http://www.cse.uconn.edu/~dqg/papers/

Weill, P. (1992). The relationship between investment in information technology and firm performance: A study of the valve manufacturing sector. *Information Systems Research, 3*(4), 307-333.

Weill, P., & Broadbent, M. (1998). *Leveraging the new infrastructure—How market leaders capitalize on information technology*. Boston: Harvard Business School Press.

Weill, P., & Vitale, M. (2002). What IT infrastructure capabilities are needed to implement e-business models. *MIS Quarterly Executive, 1*(1), 17-34.

Weill, P., Subramani, M., & Broadbent, M. (2002). Building IT infrastructure for strategic agility. *MIT Sloan Management Review, 44*(1), 57-65.

Weinstein, M. C. (2001). Toy E. L., Sandbergea, et al. Modelling for health care and other policy decisions: Uses, roles and validity. *Value Health, 4*, 348-361.

Weiser, M. (1991). The computer for the twenty-first century. *Scientific American*, 94-104.

Wellman, B. (2001). Physical place and cyberplace: The rise of personalized networking. *International Journal of Urban and Regional Research, 25*(2), 227-252.

Werder, H. (2005). *Verkehrstelematik als Element der Verkehrspolitik*. Paper presented at the its-ch, Olten, Switzerland.

Wernerfelt, B. (1984). A resource based view of the firm. *Strategic Management Journal, 5*(2), 171-180.

Westelius, A., & Valiente, P. (2004, June 14-16). *Bringing the enterprise system to the fronline—Intertwinig computerised and conventional communication at BI Europe*. Paper presented at the 12th European Conference on Information Systems, Turku, Finland.

Whitaker, L. (2001). Ads unplugged. *American Demographics, 23*(6), 30-34.

Wiberg, M., & Ljungberg, F. (2001). Exploring the vision of "anytime, anywhere" in the context of mobile work. In Y. Malhotra (Ed.), *Knowledge management and virtual organizations* (pp. 157-169). Hershey, PA: Idea Group.

Wi-Fi Alliance. (2003). *Wi-Fi protected access: Strong, standards-based, interoperable security for today's Wi-Fi networks*. Retrieved July 4th, 2006 from http://main.wi-fi.org/membersonly/getfile.asp?f=Whitepaper_Wi-Fi_Security4-29-03.pdf

Wikipedia. (2006). *Mobile payment*. Retrieved from http://en.wikipedia.org/wiki/Mobile_payment

Wikipedia. (2006). *Ringback*. Retrieved from http://en.wikipedia.org/wiki/Ringback

Wikman, A.-S., Nieminen, T., & Summala, H. (1998). Driving experience and time-sharing during in-car tasks on roads of different width. *Ergonomics, 41*(3), 358-372.

Winner, L. (1986). *The whale and the reactor: A search for limits in an age of high technology*. IL: University of Chicago Press.

Wireless Deployment Sub-Committee. (2004). *Final report and recommendations from the wireless deployment sub-committee*. Retrieved September 10, 2004, from http://www.ohio.edu/itsc/loader.cfm?url=/commonspot/security/getfile.cfm&PageID=51965

Wireless future. (2004). Retrieved September 10, 2004, from http://www.cns.ohio.edu/hot_topics/wirelessfuture/frame.htm

Wireless progress report. (2004). Retrieved April 4, 2004, from http://www.cns.ohiou.edu/hot_topics/wirelessprogress/frame

Wohlfahrt, J. (2001). One-to-one marketing in mobile commerce. *Information Management & Consulting, 16*(2), 49-54.

Wolf, H., & Wang, M. (2005, July 11-13). *A framework with a peer fostering mechanism for mobile P2P game*.

Paper presented at the Proceedings of the Fourth International Conference on Mobile Business (mBusiness), Sydney, Australia.

Wolfe, R. A. (1994). Organizational innovation: Review, critique and suggested research directions. *Journal of Management Studies, 31*(3), 405-432.

Wong, C. C., & Hiew, P. L. (2005, July 11-13). *Mobile entertainment: Review and refine.* Paper presented at the Proceedings of the Fourth International Conference on Mobile Business (mBusiness), Sydney, Australia.

Wong, W. (2001). Open services gateway initiative: OSGi links devices and clients. *Electronic Design*, 86.

Wu, J. H., & Wang, S. C. (2005). What drives mobile commerce? An empirical evaluation of the revised technology acceptance model. *Source Information and Management, 42*(5), 719-729.

Wu, J.-H., & Wang, S.-C. (2003). *An empirical study of consumers adopting mobile commerce in Taiwan: Analyzed by structural equation modelling.* Paper presented at the Seventh Pacific Asia Conference on Information Systems, Adelaide, Australia.

Xia, W., & Lee, G. (2000). The influence of persuasion, training and experience on user perceptions and acceptance of IT innovation. In *Proceedings from the International Conference on Information* Systems, Brisbane, Queensland, Australia.

Xu, Y., Gong, M., & Thong, J. Y. L. (2006). Two tales of one service: User acceptance of short message service (SMS) in Hong Kong and China. *Info-The journal of policy, regulation and strategy for telecommunications, 8*(1), 16-28.

Yang, C. C. (2005). Exploring factors affecting the adoption of mobile commerce in Singapore. *Telematics and Informatics, 22*(3), 257-277.

Yen, D., & Chou, D. C. (2000). Wireless communications: Applications and managerial issues. *Industrial Management & Data Systems, 100*(9), 436-443.

Yin, R. K. (2002). *Case study research. Design and methods* (Vol. 5, 3rd ed.). London: Sage.

Yoo, Y., & Lyytinen, K. (2005). Social impacts of ubiquitous computing: Exploring critical interactions between mobility, context and technology. *Information and Organization, 15*, 91-94.

Yoshida, J. (2006, March 2). Protocol spat threatens to fragment DVB-H market. *EE Times.* Retrieved from http://www.eetimes.com/news/latest/business/show-Article.jhtml?articleID=181500546

Yrjänäinen, J., & Neuvo, Y. (2002). Wireless meets multimedia. *Wireless Communications and Mobile Computing, 2*(6), 553-562.

Yuan, Y., & Zhang, J. J. (2003). Towards an appropriate business model for m-commerce. *International Journal of Mobile Communications, 1*(1/2), 35-56.

Yufei, Y., & Detlor, B. (2005). Intelligent mobile crisis response systems. *Communications of the ACM, 48*(2), 95-98.

Zeng, E. Y., Yen, D., & Hwang, H. (2003). Mobile commerce: The convergence of e-commerce and wireless technology. *International Journal of Services Technology and Management, 4*(3), 302-322.

Zhang, J. J., & Yuan, Y. (2002). *M-commerce versus Internet-based e-commerce: The key differences.* Paper presented at the Americas Conference on Information Systems, Dallas, TX.

Zilliox, D. (2002). *The get-started guide to m-commerce and mobile technology.* AMACOM.

Zmijewska, A., Lawrence, E., & Steele, R. (2004, July 12-13). Classifying m-payments—A user-centric model. In *Proceedings of the International Conference on Mobile Business 04,* New York.

Zobel, J. (2001). *Mobile business und m-commerce—Die Märkte der Zukunft erobern.* München, Germany: Hanser.

About the Contributors

Kyungmo Ahn is an assistant professor of the Graduate School of Tourism at Kyung Hee University in Seoul. He is the president of the Korean Convention Sciences Society and director of International Tourism Strategy Research Institute. Ahn has written 10 books including *Festival and Special Event Management* and has published a number of journal articles. He is a member of the Convention Improvement Committee of the Ministry of Culture & Tourism in Korea. He has received grants and awards, including the Best Researcher from the Korea Convention Council and the Best Teach Award from Kyung Hee University.

Seung Baek is an assistant professor with the College of Business Administration, Hanyang University, Seoul, Korea. He earned an MBA and a PhD from the College of Business Administration, The George Washington University. Before joining Hanyang University, he was an assistant professor at Georgia State University and Saint Joseph's University. His main research interests include business intelligence and e-service in the telecommunication industry.

Pieter Ballon is the program manager at IBBT-SMIT (Centre for Studies on Media, Information and Telecommunication) at the Vrije Universiteit Brussel in Belgium. He is also a senior consultant at TNO, the Netherlands Organisation for Applied Scientific Research. He specializes in innovations in broadband services, new business models, and the mobile telecommunications industry, on which topics he has published extensively. Clients of his consultancy work include the European Commission, the World Bank, the Netherlands Ministry of Economic Affairs, and several telecommunications firms. Ballon is currently coordinating the cross issue on future mobile business models for all European Sixth Framework Program projects of the Wireless World Initiative.

Maria Bina is a PhD candidate at the Department of Management Science and Technology at the Athens University of Economics and Business and a member of the ELTRUN Wireless Research Center. She holds a degree in electrical engineering and computer science from the National Technical University of Athens and an MSc in decision sciences (e-commerce specialization) from the Athens University of Economics and Business. Her research interests lie in the area of wireless and mobile networks, focusing on business and service models.

Olivier Braet is a researcher at IBBT-SMIT (Centre for Studies on Media, Information and Tele-communication) at the Vrije Universiteit Brussel. He focuses on the business aspects of information and communication technologies (ICT) and is involved with a wide variety of research projects. Before this function he was a research assistant at the Faculty of Economics and Business Administration of Ghent University (Belgium). Before that he worked as an ICT advisor at the Ministry of Interior Affairs, as IT'er at Electrabel, and as scientific collaborator in the Flemish administration.

Walter Brenner is a professor of IS at the University of St. Gallen and managing director of the Institute of Information Management. After earning his graduate, his doctorate degree, and his venia legendi from the University of St. Gallen, he worked for several years for the Alusuisse-Lonza AG based in Basel, Switzerland, among other positions as the head of application development. He was professor for business administration and information management at the TU Bergakademie Freiberg, Germany (1993 to 1999) and subsequently professor for information management and business administration at the University of Essen, Germany. His research focus is on integrated information management, customer relationship management, and innovative technologies.

Xubin Cao is the director of the Research & Education Center at Southwestern University of Finance and Economics in China. His research interests include knowledge management, e-learning, and e-business.

Rolando A. Carrasco (BSc, Hons., CEng, FIEE: University of Santiago of Chile, PhD, University of Newcastle-upon-Tyne, for work on implementing digital filters using several processors, followed by research into underwater data communications). He was awarded the IEE Heaviside Premium for his work in multi-processor systems (1982). He was employed by Alfred Peters Limited, Sheffield (now Meditech) and carried out research and development in signal processing associated with cochlear stimulation and response (1982 to 1984). He has been with Staffordshire University (since 1984) and is now professor of mobile communications at the University of Newcastle-upon-Tyne. His principle research interests are digital signal processing algorithm for data communication systems; mobile and network communication systems; and speech recognition and processing. Carrasco has over a hundred scientific publications, five chapters in telecommunications reference texts, and a patent to his name. He has previously supervised 37 successful PhDs (31 as the primary supervisor and a further six as a secondary supervisor) and is currently supervising a further eight. He has previously supervised several EPSRC projects, BT research project, and teaching company schemes. He has twice been the local chairman on international conference organizing committees. He is a member of several organizing committees, a member of the EPSRC College, as well as a member of the EPSRC assessment panel. He is an external examiner for the MSc in Mobile Communications at Lancaster, Cranfield and Sussex University. He also has international collaboration with Chilean and Spanish Universities.

Ali Chehab received his bachelor degree in electrical engineering (EE) from the American University of Beirut (AUB) (1987), a master's degree in EE from Syracuse University, and a PhD degree in electrical and computer engineering (ECE) from the University of North Carolina at Charlotte, (2002). He was a lecturer in the ECE Department at AUB (1989 to 1998). He rejoined the ECE Department at AUB as an assistant professor (2002). His research interests are VLSI design and test, and information security.

Hong Chen is a PhD candidate (2004-Present) at Rotterdam School of Management. He received an MSc degree (*cum laude*) in computer science from the University of Twente, the Netherlands (2003). He studied telecommunications engineering at Beijing University of Posts and Telecommunications (1995 to 1999). He worked in Huawei Technologies as an engineer (1999-2001). Hong Chen's PhD research is about individual tariffs and service personalization. His research framework and interim research results have been presented at IEEE Service Computing Conference, IEEE International Conference on E-business, International Conference on Mobile Business, and the Conference of the International Telecommunication Society.

Heasun Chun is a PhD student of the Department of Communication at the University at Buffalo, SUNY. She has an MA and a BA from Ewha Womans University in Seoul in Korea. She worked at the Media & Future Institute as a senior researcher and Korea Information Strategy Development Institute (KISDI) as a research associate. She was involved in research projects on media policy and regulations. Her research has appeared in the following conferences: International Sunbelt Social Network Conference (Sunbelt XX VI), Telecommunications Policy Research Conference (TPRC), and Korean Academic Society for Public Relations (KASPR). Her current research interests include media policy, digital convergence, transnational media, and international information flow.

Ioanna D. Constantiou is an assistant professor in the Department of Informatics, Copenhagen Business School, Denmark. Her research is focused on the economics of IS and in particular on consumer behavior in IT markets. She holds a PhD from the Department of Management and Technology at Athens University of Economics and Business.

M. Ehlers is an MIS major student doing research in m-commerce, MIS Department, College of Business, Ohio University, USA.

Jochen Friedemann graduated in business administration from the University of Osnabrueck (2006). He has been working as a student assistant for the chair of e-business and information systems, University of Osnabrueck (since August 2004). His main focuses of study and research are E-Logistics, executive IS, and Web engineering. He has participated in several academic and commercial projects concerning these topics. He has been employed at an international auditing firm (since January 2007).

Raymond D. Frost is professor and chair of the Management Information Systems Department, Ohio University, USA. He is also the director of studies for the College of Business students in the Honors Tutorial College (HTC). Frost joined the College of Business (in 1999). His primary research areas are instructional pedagogy, information design, and database design. He has received multiple teaching awards at both the college and university level. Frost earned a doctorate in business administration and an MS in computer science at the University of Miami (Florida), and received his BA in philosophy at Swarthmore College. He lives in Athens with his wife, Tere, and two boys, Raymond and Luke.

Parissa Haghirian is an assistant professor in international management at the Faculty of Liberal Arts at Sophia University in Tokyo, Japan. She obtained her masters in Japanese Studies from Vienna University and was awarded a masters degree and PhD in international management from Vienna University of Economics and Business Administration. She is currently holding visiting professorships at

Groupe HEC in Paris, Helsinki School of Economics, and Vienna University of Economics and Business Administration. Her research and consulting interests include knowledge management within Euro-Japanese multinational corporations, market entries of Western corporations into the Japanese market, and Japanese consumer behavior.

Kristina Heinonen holds a PhD in marketing and is a Hanken Foundation assistant professor in marketing (tenure track) at HANKEN Swedish School of Economics and Business Administration in Helsinki, Finland. Heinonen is currently involved in research projects concerning service value, e-services, and mobile services; dynamics of customer relationships; and digital marketing communication. Her work has been published and/or is forthcoming in the *International Journal of Mobile Communications, International Journal of Service Industry Management, Managing Service Quality, Journal of Financial Services Marketing, Management Decision*, and *Communications & Strategies*.

Dieter Hertweck works as a full professor in the Business Faculty, Heilbronn University with a focus on electronic business. He holds a PhD degree in IS. IS has emerged as an academic discipline that integrates many different disciplines such as computer science, management, and social sciences. Dieter himself is the product of such multiple disciplines and he has been awarded degrees in social science, business/management, and IS. He has industrial work experience in software project management as well as long-term research experience in different universities and research centers. His current research interests are in electronic business, business process management, relationship management, knowledge management systems, and software project management.

Holger Hoffmann has been a researcher and lecturer at the Chair for Information Systems at Technische Universität München (Munich University of Technology [TUM]), Germany, (since September 2004). Prior to that he studied computer science with business sciences as his minor subject at TUM, gaining work experience in the banking sector. He currently works on publicly funded as well as industry-driven research projects. His teaching and research areas include mobile computing and automotive service engineering.

Wayne Wei Huang is a professor in the MIS Department at the College of Business, Ohio University, USA. He has worked as faculty in universities in Australia, Singapore, China, and Hong Kong and received research awards from universities in Australia and the USA. Huang has had more than 18 years of full-time teaching experience in universities as well as a few years of IT industrial working experience (as a system analyst/programmer). His research combines both quantitative and qualitative research methodologies. He published more than 10 books and/or book chapters on IS internationally. He has published more than 100 refereed research papers in international journals and conference proceedings, including some leading international MIS/IS journals such as *IEEE Transactions on Systems, Man, and Cybernetics; Journal of Management Information Systems (JMIS); Communications of ACM (CACM); IEEE Transactions on Professional Communication; Information & Management (I&M); Decision Support Systems (DSS); Communications of AIS (CAIS); and European Journal of Information Systems (EJIS)*. He has presented his research papers in most leading and prestigious international conferences on IS, such as ICIS (the top MIS/IS annual conference in the world, USA), HICSS (USA), DSI (USA), AMCIS (USA), IFIP (Europe), PACIS (Asia), and ECIS (Europe). Huang is currently a senior editor for the *International Journal of Data Base: Advanced in Information Systems*, an ACM publication, USA;

and on the editorial boards of *Information & Management (I & M), International Journal of Global Information Management (JGIM),* and *Journal of Database Management (JDM),* USA. Huang is the founding chair of AIS SIG-ISAP (IS in Asia Pacific), which is an academic association for IS/MIS researchers/scholars in the world who are interested in IS issues in Asia Pacific, being officially approved by the Association for Information Systems (AIS).

Wassim Itani was born in Beirut, Lebanon (1978). He holds a masters degree in computer and communications engineering from the American University of Beirut (AUB). Since his graduation from AUB (June 2003), he worked as a part-time research assistant in the Department of Electrical and Computer Engineering. He currently fills a systems engineer position at KATech, a storage solution provider in the Gulf region. Wassim's current research interests include policy-based networking, mobile computing, and cryptographic protocols performance.

Ayman Kayssi was born in Lebanon (1967). He received his BE with distinction from the American University of Beirut, Lebanon and an MSE and PhD from the University of Michigan, Ann Arbor, USA, all in electrical engineering (1987, 1989, and 1993, respectively). He is currently professor and chairman of electrical and computer engineering at the American University of Beirut, where he has been working since 1993. His research and teaching interests are in the areas of information security and trust, and digital system testing.

Bong Jun Kim is doctoral student with the College of Business Administration, Hanyang University, Seoul, Korea. He received a BA and an MA from Hanyang University, Seoul, Korea. Before joining Hanyang University, he worked as a researcher at Korea Telecom (KT) and Korea Information Strategy Development Institute (KISDI). His main research interests include telecommunication policy and market strategy.

Jin Ki Kim is a PhD candidate in the Department of Management Science and Systems at the University at Buffalo, SUNY. He has an MS and a BS from Hanyang University in Seoul in Korea. He worked at the Korea Information Strategy Development Institute (KISDI) as a research fellow. He was involved in research projects on telecom policy and management. His research has appeared in the following conferences: Telecommunications Policy Research Conference (TPRC), Hawaii International Conference on System Sciences (HICSS), Americas Conference on Information Systems (AMCIS), and International Telecommunications Society (ITS) conference. His current research interests include telecom policy and management, digital convergence, diffusion of new telecom services, and emergency management system.

Lutz M. Kolbe heads the Competence Center Customer Management (CC CM) and teaches at the University of St. Gallen, Switzerland. His research interests are customer relationship management and security management as well as advanced technologies. After having worked as financial consultant Lutz studied information management at Brunswick Technical University, Germany, where he received a masters degree. He went on working on his dissertation at Freiberg Technical University, Germany, and the University of Rhode Island, USA. He received his PhD (1997). After that he worked at Deutsche Bank in Frankfurt and New York where he became managing director (2001).

Helmut Krcmar holds the chair for IS, Facutly of Informatics at Technische Universität München (Munich University of Technology), Germany. He worked as a researcher and consultant at the Institute for Information Systems at Saarbrücken University (1978 until 1984). After that he worked as post doctoral fellow at the IBM Los Angeles Scientific Center, as assistant professor of information systems at the Leonard Stern School of Business, NYU, and at Baruch College, CUNY. He was Chair for Information Systems, Hohenheim University in Stuttgart, (1987 to 2002). He served as Dean, Faculty of Business, Economics and Social Sciences (2000-2002). His teaching and research interests include information and knowledge management, IT service management and computer supported cooperative work.

Sean Lancaster is a lecturer with the Department of Decision Sciences and Management Information Systems at Miami University. He teaches undergraduate courses on IS and business strategy, Web design, Visual Basic, .NET, database design, and e-commerce. Lancaster earned his MBA from Miami University (2002).

Hans Lehmann is an associate professor at the School of Information Management at Victoria University of Wellington, New Zealand. He has more than 25 years of business experience with management and IT. His present research involves the application of wireless and mobile technology in the field of business-to-business (B2B) applications.

Jan Marco Leimeister is a senior researcher and assistant professor at the Chair for Information Systems at Technische Universität München (Munich University of Technology), Germany. He runs research groups on e-health and ubiquitous/mobile computing and manages several publicly funded research projects. Leimeister received a PhD from Hohenheim University, Stuttgart, Germany and worked on different occasions for companies such as DaimlerChrysler, IBM, Debis Systemhaus, and Siemens Business Services. His teaching and research areas include e-health, online communities, IT innovation management, e-commerce, ubiquitous and mobile computing, computer supported cooperative work, and information management.

Yong (Eric) Lu is teaching in the Department of Computer & Information at Bloomsburg University of Pennsylvania. He received his PhD from Ohio University. His current research interests focus on wireless technology; computer security and forensics; and technology diffusion and adoption.

Hongyan Ma is an instructional designer at Salisbury University, Maryland. She received her PhD in instructional technology from Ohio University. Her research interests include instructional design; faculty training and development; and young people's experience using the Internet

Maria Madlberger is an assistant professor at the Institute for Management Information Systems at the Vienna University of Economics and Business Administration. She received her PhD from the Department of Retailing and Marketing at this university. In her PhD thesis, published in the book "Electronic Retailing," she elaborated Internet-based marketing and market research instruments for e-commerce. Madlberger's research interests refer to e-commerce and interorganizational IS and their application. She is focusing on antecedents of B2B information sharing, direct and indirect electronic data interchange (EDI) benefits in retailing, and radio frequency identification (RFID) application. Further research activities are dealing with IT-supported collaboration in supply chain management and multi-channel retailing.

Sean T. McGann is an assistant professor of IS and the associate director of the Integrated MBA Program at Ohio University. His research interests include IS pedagogy and curriculum, IS user improvisation, inter-organizational systems, and supply chain systems. He teaches systems development; systems analysis and design; and database courses. He also serves as faculty advisor to Ohio University's chapter of the Association for Information Technology Professionals and Phi Gamma Nu Business Fraternity. He has received teaching awards such as MIS Professor of the Year and the Senior Student Recognition Award. McGann earned a PhD in IS from Case Western Reserve University, an MBA from Ohio University, and a BS in electronics engineering from Bowling Green State University. He spent 5 years in Andersen's Business Consulting Practice, 2 years as CEO of Pogonet Internet Solutions, Inc., and continues to operate an independent systems consulting company.

Istvan Molnar was educated at the Corvinus University, in Budapest, Hungary, where he received his MSc and PhD. He has completed his postdoctoral studies in Darmstadt, Germany and took part in different research projects in Germany as guest scientist in the 1980s and 1990s. He received his CSs degree from the Hungarian Academy of Sciences (1996). Currently, he is an associate professor at the Bloomsburg University of Pennsylvania. His main fields of interest are simulation and education. Molnar is a senior member of SCS International, member of the editorial board of SCS-European Publishing House and *International Journal of Mobile Learning and Organization.*

Ravi Mukkamala received a PhD from the University of Iowa (1987) and an MBA from Old Dominion University (1993). Since 1987, he has been with the Department of Computer Science at Old Dominion University, Norfolk, Virginia (USA), where he is currently a professor. His research interests include distributed systems, data security, performance analysis, and PKI. His research has been sponsored by NRL, DARPA, NASA, and CISC. For more information, visit the URL: www.cs.odu.edu/~mukka.

Astrid M. Oddershede obtained an industrial engineer degree from the University of Santiago of Chile, Chile. Diploma (Hons) in operations research, Woodsworth College, University of Toronto, Canada. Master of industrial engineering, University of Toronto, Toronto, Canada. Currently, Oddershede is an associate lecturer in the Department of Industrial Engineering of the University of Santiago, Chile. Her research activities and interests are on decision analysis modeling and operations research. She is a PhD student at the University of Newcastle-upon-Tyne. Her PhD research project involves investigating implications of ICT and quality of service (QoS) for health. Oddershede has scientific publications and participated on local and international conference organizing committees. She is a member of the Operations Research Chilean Institute and a member of the Society of Medical Decision Making (SMDM) Philadelphia, USA.

Erkki Patokorpi is currently working as a researcher at the Institute for Advanced Management Systems Research (IAMSR), at the Åbo Akademi University, Finland. His main research interests include human-computer interaction; the epistemology of advanced ICT; and mobile learning. He has also worked as a science studies researcher, focusing on the sociology and rhetoric of science. He received his PhD degree from the University of Oulu (1996), majoring in the history of science and ideas. Presently, he is completing his second doctoral dissertation on digital interaction for the Department of Information Technologies, the Faculty of Technology at the Åbo Akademi University, Finland.

L F Pau has been a professor of mobile business, Rotterdam School of Management (part-time, since 2001), besides being an adjunct professor at Copenhagen Business School (since 2004). He has been CTO in Ericsson's new Infrastructure Division (since 1995). Previously he was the Technical Director Europe for Digital Equipment (now part of HP) (1990-1995). He has been on tenure faculty at the Danish Technical University (Lyngby), E.N.S. Télécommunications (Paris), MIT (Cambridge, Mass), and University of Tokyo. He is a Fellow of IEEE (USA), BCS (UK), and JSPS (Japan). He is on government or research advisory boards in Japan, Singapore, China, and Taiwan. He is or has been on several standardization boards, including IEEE Standards Board, OMG, RapidIO, and Java Consortium. He is associate editor of six academic journals and has published over 350 articles, nine books, and edited 12 volumes.

Mishul Prasad is currently working at Medialab Ltd. He has completed his BCA with honors in IS and recently a masters in IS at the School of Information Management at Victoria University of Wellington, New Zealand. Prasad has been the recipient of a Technology Industry Funding (TIF) scholarship from TechNZ.

Minna Pura holds a degree in business economics from HANKEN, the Swedish School of Economics and Business Administration, Helsinki, Finland and is a doctoral candidate at the Centre for Relationship Marketing and Service Management (CERS), Department of Marketing and Corporate Geography at HANKEN. Her research focuses on perceived value of and customer loyalty to mobile and Internet services. Her work has been published and/or is forthcoming in *Managing Service Quality*, *Journal of Information Technology, Theory and Applications*, *Yearbook on Services Management 2002—E-Services*, and *Mobile Commerce: Technology, Theory, and Applications*.

Jing "Jim" Quan is an assistant professor in the Department of Information and Decision Sciences at Perdue School of Business, Salisbury University. He holds a PhD from the University of Florida and is an MCT/MCSE and CNI/CNE. His research interests include IT and organizations, knowledge management, project management, and IT human resource management. His work has appeared in such journals as the *Journal of Management Information Systems, the Communications of the ACM, the Communications of the AIS, Information Resources Management Journal, Journal of Global Information Management, International Journal of Information Management, Journal of Information Technology and Information Management,* and *Journal of Computer Information Systems.* He presented papers at the national and international conferences on IS and technology.

Asarnusch Rashid studied computer science at the University of Karlsruhe with a focus on human-computer interaction and robotics. He currently works as a senior researcher at the Research Centre for Information Technology (FZI) Karlsruhe. His main research interests are on case studies about the applicability of modern IT in enterprises. At the moment, Rashid works on two different research projects with the name CollaBaWue and PerCoMed. CollaBaWue aims to improve collaborative software development processes by using Web 2.0 methods and social software. PerCoMed analyzes chances and risk of future pervasive computing applications for the German health care system.

Ragnar Schierholz works as a researcher at the Institute of Information Management of the University of St. Gallen, Switzerland. He is a member of the Competence Center Customer Management (CC CM), in which large European companies do joint research on customer relationship management

(CRM) and knowledge management. His research focus is on the application of mobile business technology in the field of CRM. Prior to his work in St. Gallen he has worked as an IT consultant for IBM Germany, Lotus Professional Services Germany, and as an IT service engineer for ONEstone GmbH Germany. He earned an MS in computer science from the Western Michigan University, Kalamazoo, USA and as Diplom.

Eusebio Scornavacca is a senior lecturer of e-commerce at the School of Information Management, Victoria University of Wellington, New Zealand. Scornavacca has published and presented more than 50 papers in conferences and academic journals. He is the founder of M-lit—the mobile business literature online database (www.m-lit.org). He recently received an award in the ICT category at the prestigious MacDiarmid Young Scientist of the Year Awards. His research interests include mobile business, electronic business, electronic surveys, and IS teaching methods.

J. P. Shim is professor and doctoral program coordinator of Management Information Systems and the director of International Business Strategy Program at Mississippi State University (MSU). He received his PhD from the University of Nebraska-Lincoln and completed the Harvard Business School's Executive Education Program. He was the winner of MSU's prestigious Ralph E. Powe Research Excellence Award (2006). He is a past winner of the university's John Grisham Faculty Excellence Award, as well as an eight-time recipient of the outstanding faculty award. Shim has written over 150 research papers. He served as the principal investigator for more than $1.1M in funded grants from various sources (NSF, Microsoft, Mississippi IHL, Booz-Allen & Hamilton, and private funding agencies). Shim serves as a senior editor, associate editor, and a member of editorial boards of numerous journals. He has contributed to the field as a fellow, fellow chair, program chair, and keynote speaker. He has lectured frequently in the USA, UK, France, Korea, Kuwait, Hong Kong, Taiwan, Japan, Jamaica, and others. Shim served as a chair for several university research and awards committees at MSU. He currently serves on Chair for University Research Initiation Program Review Committee and serves on University Task Force Committee on Research, Graduate Education, and International.

Julie M. Shim is a project manager for SoldierDesign in Cambridge, MA. She received her BA in international relations and business from Boston University. She has extensive working experience in the ICT field from Boston University Information Technology Help Desk, FedEx, Booz-Allen & Hamilton, Salomon Smith Barney, and Bite Communications. She was the undergraduate representative at the U.S.-Japan Joint Seminar in E-Business and M-Commerce sponsored by NSF. Her research publications appeared in *Industrial Management & Data Systems* and *Decision Line*.

Franck Tétard is currently working as a researcher at the Institute for Advanced Management Systems Research (IAMSR), and as an assistant professor in the Department of Information Technologies, Faculty of Technology at the Åbo Akademi University, Finland. His main research interests include usability, user-centered design, and mobile ICT. He received his PhD degree from the Åbo Akademi University (2002), majoring in IS.

Frank Teuteberg is junior professor of e-business and IS at the University of Osnabrueck. He was awarded his Diplom in business administration/IS by the University of Goettingen and his PhD from the European University Viadrina Frankfurt (Oder) (1996 and 2001, respectively). His research interests include mobile business and innovation networks. He is currently involved in a research project supported by the German Federal Ministry of Education and Research to identify and assess the opportunities presented by mobile applications to support business processes in supply chain management. He has published two books and more than 55 scientific papers, which have appeared in numerous international conference proceedings, books and scientific journals, including the *Journal of Electronic Markets* and the *Journal of Computer Systems Science & Engineering*.

Valli Kumari Vatsavayi is a professor of computer science and systems engineering of Andhra University College of Engineering in Visakhapatnam, India. She holds a BE in electronics and communications engineering, an M. Tech in computer science and technology, and a PhD in computer science and systems engineering all from Andhra University. Her research interests include security, mobile commerce, Web technologies, mobile agents, and software testing.

David C. Yen is a Raymond E. Glos Professor in Business and a professor of MIS in the Department of Decision Sciences and Management Information Systems at Miami University. He received a PhD in MIS and a MS in computer science from the University of Nebraska. Yen is active in research, he has published three books and many articles which have appeared in *Communications of the ACM, Decision Support Systems, Information & Management, International Journal of Information Management, Information Sciences, Journal of Computer Information Systems, Interfaces, Telematics and Informatics, Computer Standards and Interfaces, Information Society, Omega, International Journal of Organizational Computing and Electronic Commerce, Communications of AIS*, and *Internet Research* among others.

Jinglong Zhang is professor and dean of the Management School of Huazhong University of Science & Technology, China. His main research areas are in IS, strategic issues of IS, IT/IS outsourcing, and e-commerce. He has published numerous research papers in domestic and international journals and conference proceedings.

Index

W